Read SAP PRESS online also

With booksonline we offer you online access to leading SAP experts'
knowledge. Whether you use it as a beneficial supplement or as an
alternative to the printed book – with booksonline you can:

• Access any book at any time
• Quickly look up and find what you need
• Compile your own SAP library

Your advantage as the reader of this book

Register your book on our website and obtain an exclusive and free test
access to its online version. You're convinced you like the online book?
Then you can purchase it at a preferential price!

And here's how to make use of your advantage

1. Visit www.sap-press.com
2. Click on the link for SAP PRESS booksonline
3. Enter your free trial license key
4. Test-drive your online book with full access for a limited time!

Your personal **license key** for your test
access including the preferential offer

tdjk-cgy8-4xr5-iw6u

SAP® NetWeaver Business Warehouse: Administration and Monitoring

 **PRESS**

SAP PRESS is a joint initiative of SAP and Galileo Press. The know-how offered by SAP specialists combined with the expertise of the Galileo Press publishing house offers the reader expert books in the field. SAP PRESS features first-hand information and expert advice, and provides useful skills for professional decision-making.

SAP PRESS offers a variety of books on technical and business related topics for the SAP user. For further information, please visit our website: *www.sap-press.com*.

Ingo Hilgefort
Integrating SAP BusinessObjects XI 3.1 Tools with SAP NetWeaver
2009, 260 pp.
978-1-59229-274-5

Larry Sackett
MDX Reporting and Analytics with SAP NetWeaver BW
2009, 380 pp.
978-1-59229-249-3

Muke Abdelnaby, Subhendu Roy, Hisham Ismail, Vu Pham, and Joseph Chica
Mastering Information Broadcasting with SAP NetWeaver BW 7.0
2009, 220 pp.
978-1-59229-276-9

Daniel Knapp
SAP NetWeaver BI 7.0 Migration Guide
2008, 180 pp.
978-1-59229-228-8

Olaf Klostermann and Milco Österholm

SAP® NetWeaver Business Warehouse: Administration and Monitoring

Galileo Press

Bonn • Boston

Galileo Press is named after the Italian physicist, mathematician and philosopher Galileo Galilei (1564–1642). He is known as one of the founders of modern science and an advocate of our contemporary, heliocentric worldview. His words *Eppur se muove* (And yet it moves) have become legendary. The Galileo Press logo depicts Jupiter orbited by the four Galilean moons, which were discovered by Galileo in 1610.

Editors Florian Zimniak, Maike Lübbers
English Edition Editor Erik Herman
Translation Lemoine International, Inc., Salt Lake City, UT
Copyeditor Julie McNamee
Cover Design Jill Winitzer
Photo Credit Masterfile/RF
Layout Design Vera Brauner
Production Editor Kelly O'Callaghan
Assistant Production Editor Graham Geary
Typesetting Publishers' Design and Production Services, Inc.
Printed and bound in Canada

ISBN 978-1-59229-330-8

© 2010 by Galileo Press Inc., Boston (MA)
1st Edition 2010
1st German edition published 2009 by Galileo Press, Bonn, Germany

Library of Congress Cataloging-in-Publication Data
Klostermann, Olaf.
   SAP NetWeaver BW : administration and monitoring / Olaf Klostermann. — 1st ed.
      p. cm.
   Includes bibliographical references.
   ISBN-13: 978-1-59229-330-8 (alk. paper)
   ISBN-10: 1-59229-330-1 (alk. paper)
   1. SAP NetWeaver BW.   2. Data warehousing.   3. Database management.
4. Business intelligence — Data processing.   I. Title.
   QA76.9.D37K575 2010
   005.74'5 — dc22   2009047737

Contents at a Glance

PART I Basic Principles

1 SAP Implementation Concept 25

2 Overview of AS ABAP and AS Java 31

3 Database Management 75

4 System Connections and Access 103

5 Monitoring and Analysis Tools 123

6 Basic Principles of Processes and Objects 185

PART II SAP NetWeaver BW Administration

7 User Administration and Authorization
   Management 207

8 Archiving and Data Maintenance 249

9 Maintenance 291

10 Technical Content and BI Administration Cockpit 333

11 Process Chains 361

12 Administration of SAP NetWeaver BW Processes
    in Detail 377

13 Reporting Monitoring and Administration 443

PART III Management and Support

14 SAP Support 531

15 Organizing SAP NetWeaver BW Administration
    Teams 565

Appendices

A Transactions, Reports, and Function Modules 577

B Glossary 583

C Bibliography 591

D The Authors 593

Contents

Preface 19

PART I Basic Principles

1 SAP Implementation Concept 25

1.1 IT Practices and Scenarios 25
    1.1.1 Enterprise Data Warehousing 27
    1.1.2 Enterprise Reporting, Query, and Analysis 28
    1.1.3 Business Planning and Analytical Services 28
1.2 Usage Types 30

2 Overview of AS ABAP and AS Java 31

2.1 SAP NetWeaver Application Server ABAP 31
2.2 SAP NetWeaver Application Server Java 33
2.3 Cooperation of Both Platforms 34
2.4 SAP NetWeaver Portal 37
    2.4.1 Portal Platform 37
    2.4.2 SAP NetWeaver BW Software Components 39
2.5 Basis Parameters 41
    2.5.1 Determining Parameters 42
    2.5.2 Recommendations 44
    2.5.3 Recommendations for BI Java 47
    2.5.4 Recommendations for Parameters in the
            Source System 48
2.6 RSADMIN Parameters 50
    2.6.1 Parameters 51
    2.6.2 Obsolete Parameters 65
2.7 Lock Management 67
2.8 Number Range Buffer 70
    2.8.1 Number Ranges in an SAP NetWeaver
            BW System 71
    2.8.2 Analysis and Repair 73

3	Database Management		75
3.1	Indexes		75
	3.1.1	Primary Index and Secondary Index	76
	3.1.2	Clustered Index	76
	3.1.3	Main Index Types	77
	3.1.4	Indexes for InfoCubes	80
	3.1.5	Indexes for Master Data	83
	3.1.6	Indexes for DataStore Objects	84
	3.1.7	Index Management in an SAP NetWeaver BW System	85
	3.1.8	Temporarily Deleting Indexes	88
	3.1.9	DB Statistics	89
3.2	Database Memory Parameters for BW Objects		90
3.3	Buffering InfoObject Tables		92
3.4	DBA Cockpit		93
	3.4.1	Database Monitoring and Administration	94
	3.4.2	New Functions	94
	3.4.3	Restrictions	95
	3.4.4	Postprocessing	95
3.5	Provider-Specific Information		96
	3.5.1	Database Management Systems DB2, DB4, and DB6	96
	3.5.2	IBM DB2 RUNSTATS	96
	3.5.3	RSADMIN Parameter for IBM DB2	97
	3.5.4	Statistics in Microsoft SQL Server	99
3.6	Backup and Recovery Strategies		100

4	System Connections and Access		103
4.1	SAP NetWeaver BW Source Systems		103
	4.1.1	Creating Source Systems	104
	4.1.2	Logical System Name	106
	4.1.3	Maintaining Source System IDs	107
4.2	IDoc, ALE, RFC, and Similar Technology		107
	4.2.1	RFC and tRFC	107
	4.2.2	IDoc Interface	108
	4.2.3	Application Link Enabling	111
	4.2.4	IDoc Communication During Data Extraction	112
4.3	Web Services, SOAP, and Similar Technology		116

	4.3.1	SOA Manager	116
	4.3.2	Data Transfer Using Web Services	117
4.4		BAPI, MDX, and Similar Technology	118
	4.4.1	MDX	119
	4.4.2	OLE DB for OLAP	120
	4.4.3	OLAP BAPI	120
	4.4.4	XML for Analysis	121

5	**Monitoring and Analysis Tools**	**123**

5.1		General Tools (SAP Basis)	125
	5.1.1	SAP Central Process Scheduling	125
	5.1.2	Runtime Analysis (Transaction SE30)	125
	5.1.3	Application Log (Transaction SLG1)	128
	5.1.4	System Log (Transaction SM21)	132
	5.1.5	Job Overview (Transaction SM37)	135
	5.1.6	Process Overview (Transaction SM50)	137
	5.1.7	System Trace (Transaction ST01)	139
	5.1.8	Tune Summary (Transaction ST02)	142
	5.1.9	Workload Monitor (Transaction ST03N)	146
	5.1.10	Database Performance Analysis (Transaction ST04)	147
	5.1.11	Performance Analysis (Transaction ST05)	149
	5.1.12	OS Monitor (Transaction ST06N)	150
	5.1.13	Application Monitor (Transaction ST07)	150
	5.1.14	ABAP Runtime Error (Transaction ST22)	151
5.2		Special SAP NetWeaver BW System Tools	154
	5.2.1	BI Monitor (Transaction BWCCMS)	154
	5.2.2	BI Background Management (Transaction RSBATCH)	155
	5.2.3	Displaying SAP NetWeaver BW Jobs (Transaction RSM37)	159
	5.2.4	Monitoring Process Chains (Transaction RSPCM)	160
	5.2.5	Extraction Monitor (Transaction RSMO)	161
	5.2.6	Query Monitor (Transaction RSRT)	163
	5.2.7	Trace Tool (Transaction RSRTRACE)	165
	5.2.8	Analyzing BW Objects (Transaction RSRV)	166
	5.2.9	RS Trace Tool (Transaction RSTT)	183
	5.2.10	Reporting Function Modules (Transaction RSZT)	184

6 Basic Principles of Processes and Objects 185

6.1	DataStore Object 185
6.2	InfoCubes 188
	6.2.1 Real-Time InfoCubes 188
	6.2.2 Further Processing of InfoCube Data 188
6.3	Aggregates 189
6.4	SAP NetWeaver BW Accelerator 190
	6.4.1 How to Achieve High Performance 191
	6.4.2 SAP NetWeaver BW Accelerator Architecture 192
6.5	Open Hub Destinations and InfoSpokes 194
	6.5.1 Extraction Mode and Delta Administration 194
	6.5.2 Open Hub Monitor 196
6.6	Reporting 196
	6.6.1 OLAP Server 196
	6.6.2 Internet Communication Framework 199
	6.6.3 Documents 202
	6.6.4 Internet Graphics Service 203

PART II SAP NetWeaver BW Administration

7 User Administration and Authorization Management 207

7.1	Basic Principles 207
	7.1.1 AS ABAP Authorization Concept 207
	7.1.2 User Administration 208
	7.1.3 Central User Administration 209
	7.1.4 User Information System 210
	7.1.5 Identity Management 214
	7.1.6 SAP GRC 215
	7.1.7 AS Java Authorization Concept 216
7.2	Basic Principles of Authorizations in the SAP NetWeaver BW System 219
7.3	Role Maintenance in Transaction PFCG 220
7.4	Analysis Authorizations 226
	7.4.1 New Concept with SAP NetWeaver 7.0 227
	7.4.2 Authorization Dimensions 228
	7.4.3 Management of Analysis Authorizations 230
	7.4.4 Example of Creating Analysis Authorizations 232

7.4.5 Defining Authorizations 234
7.4.6 Troubleshooting 243
7.4.7 Migration 247

8 Archiving and Data Maintenance 249

8.1 Archiving Concepts 249
8.2 Data Archiving Process 252
8.3 Archive Development Kit 255
    8.3.1 Tasks 256
    8.3.2 Archiving Data and Monitoring Activities 259
    8.3.3 Accessing Archived Data 262
    8.3.4 Other Archiving Functions 264
    8.3.5 Special Characteristics of Write-Optimized
          DataStore Object 265
8.4 Nearline Storage 266
    8.4.1 Basic Principles 266
    8.4.2 Creating a Nearline Storage Connection 268
    8.4.3 Changes to Archived InfoProviders 269
8.5 Archiving Request Management Data 270
8.6 Archiving PSA Data 272
8.7 Scheduling Archiving Using Process Chains 273
8.8 Decision-Making Support for Archiving Concept 275
8.9 Partitioning and Clustering 276
    8.9.1 Partitioning 277
    8.9.2 Repartitioning 281
    8.9.3 Clustering 285
    8.9.4 Reclustering 287
8.10 Master Data Cleansing 288
    8.10.1 Deleting Individual Master Data Records 289
    8.10.2 Deleting All Master Data and Texts 289

9 Maintenance 291

9.1 Support Package Stacks, Support Packages, and Patches ... 292
9.2 ABAP Support Packages 294
    9.2.1 Functions 294
    9.2.2 Adjusting Modifications 296
9.3 Java Support Packages 300
9.4 Transport System 303
    9.4.1 Transport Landscape 304

	9.4.2	Change and Transport System	306
	9.4.3	Transporting Roles	308
	9.4.4	Special Feature When Transporting BW Objects	309
	9.4.5	SAP Solution Manager	320
	9.4.6	Organization	324
9.5	Maintenance Optimizer		326
9.6	SAP NetWeaver BW Accelerator Revisions		329
9.7	System Copies		329
	9.7.1	Deleting Source System Assignments in the Target SAP NetWeaver BW System after Copying	330
	9.7.2	Renaming the Target SAP NetWeaver BW System and Conversion of Logical System Names	331
	9.7.3	Executing SAP NetWeaver BW–Specific Adjustments	332

10 Technical Content and BI Administration Cockpit 333

10.1	Updating Statistics Data		334
10.2	Installing the Technical Content		335
	10.2.1	Scheduling Process Chains	336
	10.2.2	Activating the Direct Access for Virtual Providers	337
	10.2.3	BI Administration Business Package	338
	10.2.4	Optional Definition of Importance	338
10.3	Runtimes of Queries		340
	10.3.1	Technical Content for Query Runtime Statistics	340
	10.3.2	Query Execution	341
	10.3.3	Details of Statistics Information	343
10.4	Data Load Status		345
10.5	Data Load Statistics		348
10.6	Evaluation of CPH Data		354
10.7	Workload Monitor (Transaction ST03)		356
10.8	Loading and Deleting Statistics Data		357
10.9	Enhancements		358
	10.9.1	Example: BI Administration Cockpit with SAP NetWeaver BW 7.0 Objects	358
	10.9.2	Example: Proactive Alerts	359

11 Process Chains 361

11.1	Processes Relevant for the Operation	362
	11.1.1 Interrupt Process	363
	11.1.2 Start Process	363
	11.1.3 AND (Last), OR (Every), and EXOR (First)	364
	11.1.4 ABAP Program	365
	11.1.5 Operating System Command	366
	11.1.6 Local Process Chain and Remote Process Chain ...	366
	11.1.7 Deciding Between Multiple Alternatives	367
11.2	Administration of Process Chains	368
	11.2.1 User for Execution	368
	11.2.2 Starting Terminated Processes	368
	11.2.3 Process Status Valuation	369
	11.2.4 Executing Process Chains Synchronously	370
	11.2.5 Alerting	370
	11.2.6 Batch Process Requirements	371
	11.2.7 Monitoring Process Chains	372
11.3	Jobs in Process Chains	375

12 Administration of SAP NetWeaver BW Processes in Detail 377

12.1	Extraction and Load Processes	377
	12.1.1 Delta Queue	378
	12.1.2 Number of Packages and Request Size	382
	12.1.3 Common Loading Processes	383
	12.1.4 InfoPackage in Process Chains	385
	12.1.5 Number of Dialog Processes	385
	12.1.6 Defining the Server or Host and User	388
	12.1.7 Direct Loading of Master Data	391
	12.1.8 Extractor Checker	392
	12.1.9 IDoc Errors	395
	12.1.10 Real-Time Data Acquisition	396
	12.1.11 Replication of DataSources	399
12.2	Change Run	404
	12.2.1 Detailed Flow	405
	12.2.2 Important Notes	409
12.3	Administration of InfoCubes	412
	12.3.1 InfoCube Content	412
	12.3.2 Selective Deletion	415

12.3.3 Requests in InfoCubes 415
12.3.4 Automatic Further Processing 418
12.3.5 Rebuilding InfoCubes 419
12.4 Performance Settings for InfoCubes 420
12.4.1 Indexes 421
12.4.2 Database Statistics 421
12.5 Compressing InfoCubes 422
12.5.1 Compression After a Change Run 424
12.5.2 Compressing All Aggregates 425
12.5.3 Noncumulative InfoCubes 425
12.6 Further Processing of Data in a DSO 426
12.6.1 Activating Data 426
12.6.2 Analysis of Unexpected Data 427
12.6.3 Troubleshooting 430
12.6.4 Simulating and Debugging a DTP Request 432
12.7 Deleting Data from a DSO 433
12.7.1 Delete by Request 434
12.7.2 Selective Deletion 435
12.7.3 Deleting from the Change Log 437
12.7.4 Deleting Already Updated Data 437
12.8 Monitoring Analysis Processes 438
12.8.1 Exceeding the Maximum Allowed Runtime 438
12.8.2 Memory Overflow During Executions and
       Simulations 439
12.8.3 Using Queries 441

13 Reporting Monitoring and Administration 443

13.1 Administration of the BEx Analyzer 443
13.1.1 SAP NetWeaver Check Workstation Wizard 443
13.1.2 SAP BEx Installation Check 444
13.1.3 Statistics Workbook 445
13.1.4 BEx Analyzer Trace 447
13.2 Query Administration 448
13.2.1 Processing Queries 448
13.2.2 Query Read Mode 449
13.2.3 Cache Mode 450
13.2.4 Delta Caching 453
13.2.5 Caching for Virtual Characteristics and Key
       Figures 454
13.2.6 Backup Versions 455
13.3 Internet Communication Frameworks Administration 455

13.3.1 ICF Services 456
13.3.2 Internet Communication Manager 457
13.4 OLAP Caching 460
13.5 Aggregates 465
13.5.1 Displaying Aggregates and Their Components 468
13.5.2 Further Processing Functions for Aggregates 471
13.5.3 Activating Aggregates and Providing Them
with Data 472
13.5.4 Checking Aggregates 476
13.6 SAP NetWeaver BW Accelerator 482
13.6.1 Connection to SAP NetWeaver BW Accelerator ... 483
13.6.2 Which InfoCubes Should Be Indexed? 485
13.6.3 SAP NetWeaver BW Accelerator Index
Maintenance Wizard 487
13.6.4 Effects of Data Changes 490
13.6.5 SAP NetWeaver BW Accelerator Delta Indexes ... 492
13.6.6 Information about Existing Indexes 493
13.6.7 Analysis and Repair of Indexes 495
13.6.8 Analysis of SAP NetWeaver BW Accelerator
Data 502
13.6.9 Tracing of SAP NetWeaver BW Accelerator 504
13.7 Information Broadcasting 506
13.7.1 Sending Email 507
13.7.2 Reorganization 508
13.8 Results in Reporting 509
13.8.1 Size Restrictions for Result Sets 510
13.8.2 Analysis of Report Results 511
13.8.3 Query Execution in Safe Mode 512
13.8.4 Different Data in ABAP and Java 513
13.8.5 Incorrect Data When Using Aggregates 514
13.9 Integrating SAP NetWeaver BW Contents into SAP
NetWeaver Portal 515
13.10 Analysis and Monitoring in the Portal 517
13.10.1 Availability Checks 517
13.10.2 Monitoring of Log Files 518
13.10.3 Usage of the Portal Cache (BW iViews) 519
13.11 Communication Problems with BEx Web Java 520
13.11.1 Usage of RFC 521
13.11.2 Usage of HTTP(S) 524
13.12 Performance of Web Applications 525
13.12.1 Runtime Measurements in BI Java 525
13.12.2 Guidelines for Performance Improvements 525

PART III Management and Support

14 SAP Support 531

14.1 Tools for the Support 531
14.2 SAP Solution Manager 533
14.3 SAP Active Global Support 534
  14.3.1 SAP Enterprise Support 535
  14.3.2 Run SAP 536
  14.3.3 SAP MaxAttention 537
14.4 SAP Service Marketplace 538
14.5 Service Connections 541
  14.5.1 Basic Setup 541
  14.5.2 BW RFC and BW GUI Service Types 545
  14.5.3 HTTPconnect Service Type 545
  14.5.4 Connection to SAP NetWeaver BW Accelerator ... 546
14.6 Customer Messages 547
  14.6.1 Procedure for SAP NetWeaver BW-Specific
         Messages 548
  14.6.2 Priority 551
  14.6.3 Secure Area for Access Data 551
  14.6.4 Faster Processing 553
  14.6.5 Message Escalation 554
14.7 Additional Functions in the SAP Service Marketplace 555
  14.7.1 SAP Notes Search 555
  14.7.2 SAP Software Change Registration 557
  14.7.3 Namespaces 557
  14.7.4 Product Availability Matrix 559
14.8 BI Diagnostics & Support Desktop Tool 559
14.9 SAP EarlyWatch Alert and other Solutions 561
  14.9.1 SAP EarlyWatch Alert in SAP Solution
         Manager 563
  14.9.2 SAP EarlyWatch Alert Processed at SAP 563
  14.9.3 Additional Services 564

15 Organizing SAP NetWeaver BW Administration
      Teams 565

15.1 Teams and Responsibilities 565
15.2 Best Practices (ITIL) 566
  15.2.1 Service Desk 567

15.2.2 Technical Management 568
15.2.3 Application Management 568
15.2.4 Operations Management 569
15.3 Operating Documentation 569
15.4 Regular Tasks 571

Appendices **575**

A   Transactions, Reports, and Function Modules 575
B   Glossary 581
C   Bibliography 589
D   The Authors 591

Index 593

Preface

Modern concepts and technologies, such as SOA (service-oriented architecture) and SAP NetWeaver improve the service quality and transparency of business processes considerably. At the same time, however, they are also more complex. The new tools, processes, and methods have to be integrated with existing landscapes and function as smoothly as possible. For SAP customers, it becomes more and more critical to pay special attention to the administration of these complex systems and landscapes for reasons of operating safety, availability, and overall costs of the system and, for example, to centrally monitor operations so they can interfere if problems occur. This particularly applies to complex systems such as SAP NetWeaver Business Warehouse (BW).

Administration of a BW system

Why are the administration tasks in a BW system so comprehensive and complex? On the one hand, SAP NetWeaver Business Warehouse is closely linked to the source systems, but also to SAP NetWeaver Application Server ABAP (AS ABAP), SAP NetWeaver Application Server Java (AS Java), and SAP NetWeaver Portal so that you need to have an overview of all of these areas and provide the corresponding technical basis, such as interface technologies. Often, good knowledge exists in the AS ABAP area owing to many years of experience, but an upgrade to SAP NetWeaver BW 7.0 also involves the additional operation of a *Java 2 Enterprise Edition* (J2EE)–based application server without having the necessary administration knowledge. On the other hand, business information solutions based on SAP NetWeaver BW are unfortunately still rather technology-driven and less process-driven. In implementation projects and consequently in subsequent operation, that is, in administration and monitoring, you frequently face major technology challenges, for example, typical flexibility and performance requirements despite mass data and high user load.

Regardless of their many years of experience in the administration of *SAP Enterprise Resource Planning* (ERP) systems, the administrator teams of numerous customers do not have the knowledge that is required for smooth operation of a BW system. One of the reasons for this is that there are too many differences and special aspects compared to an SAP ERP system. Even though there is a common technical basis, the user behavior and requirements and thus the technical options in a BW system are specific, so you cannot expect that an administration team can maintain a new SAP NetWeaver BW system landscape in addition to the existing SAP ERP systems without further training.

Administrators versus BW administrators

If you consider how to set up the administration of a BW system landscape in the best possible way, you have to define the activity profiles of individual roles, such as administrators, BW administrators, BW experts, basic employees, database specialists, and so on, or responsibilities of various competence centers. Of course, the employees in the different teams must know which responsibilities and requirements they will face and what knowledge and experience are required.

Structure of the book

This book tries to close the gap between basic and BW experts. On the one hand, it introduces experienced administrators to the special administration and monitoring aspects of a BW system; on the other hand, it describes the relevant basic principles. The book primarily consists of two topics: basic principles and BW administration. The basic principles deal with different basic topics, such as system connections and database administration, and with the available administration and monitoring tools. In the next part, the book discusses the topics that are critical for administration, such as archiving, authorization management, and particularly, monitoring and analysis of BW processes.

Basic principle chapters

When describing the implementation concept, **Chapter 1**, SAP Implementation Concept, details the relevant IT scenarios, namely, enterprise data warehousing, enterprise reporting, query and analysis, and business planning and analytical services. In addition to analyzing the BI platform with BI ABAP and BI Java, **Chapter 2**, Overview of AS ABAP and AS Java, explains the basic parameters, lock management, and number range buffering. **Chapter 3**, Database Management, discusses database concepts that are of interest to BW administrators, such as indexes for InfoCubes and DataStore objects and the DBA Cockpit. **Chapter 4**, System Connections and Access, describes system connections and accesses, such as source system connections, the IDoc interface, and Web services. **Chapter 5**, Monitoring and Analysis Tools, provides a complete overview of all tools that are critical for BW administration. In addition to general basic transactions, such as ST03N and SLG1, the chapter discusses BW-specific transactions, for example, RSBATCH, RSRV, and RSM37, in detail. **Chapter 6**, Basic Principles of Processes and Objects, provides important information on processes and objects, such as the DataStore object and BW Accelerator. (You can find further information that is particularly interesting for administrators in the administration part of the book.)

Administration chapters

Chapter 7, User Administration and Authorization Management, addresses the concept of analysis authorizations and their administration and problem analysis. Information Lifecycle Management in SAP NetWeaver BW consists of strategies and methods for optimal data maintenance and history management and is detailed in **Chapter 8**, Archiving and Data Maintenance. **Chapter 9**, Maintenance, discusses topics such as support packages, transport systems, and system copies. **Chapter 10**, Technical Content and BI Administration Cockpit, covers the usage of the technical content and the BI Administration Cockpit for monitoring and analysis of reporting objects and data-loading processes. **Chapter 11**, Process Chains, provides information on how to use process chains and some selected processes. **Chapter 12**, Administration of BW Processes in Detail, deals with the administration of processes, such as during an extraction or when deleting data from InfoProviders. **Chapter 13**, Reporting Monitoring and Administration, covers all reporting aspects, for example, the administration of queries and BW Accelerator. In this context, the analysis of results in reporting and the options for problems with the communication between BI ABAP and BI Java also play a major role.

Management and support

Information on support by SAP and the functions of the SAP Service Marketplace can be found in **Chapter 14**, SAP Support. **Chapter 15**, Organizing BW Administration Teams, describes the organization of administration teams according to best practices (ITIL).

Acknowledgements

When writing this book, we counted on the support and inspiration of numerous persons. A huge thank you for their great support goes to our families and especially our wives, Tina and Marielle: Thank you for your understanding. Although we were physically present at home, you still spent many weekends alone while we were, yet again, busy working on this book.

We would also like to thank Maike Lübbers and Florian Zimniak from Galileo Press for their great and friendly collaboration.

Likewise, we want to say thank you to our numerous colleagues and friends who — despite their busy schedules — have supported us in many ways, for example, with general remarks and tips or by providing information on typical issues related to current customer projects and information from daily administration operations. A particular thank you goes to our colleagues at K-42 eG in Rosenheim and at E1NS SE in Stockholm, whose good proposals, constructive criticism, and honest responses contributed to the quality of the book: Robert Klein, Thilo Zelmer, Siegfried Köberle, and Johan Weckström.

Thank you also to Roger Jalsing and Per-Olof Johansson for their expert support and inspiring discussions and for all the time they spent to read individual chapters and parts of this book.

Olaf Klostermann and **Milco Österholm**
Vechta/Stockholm
olaf.klostermann@k-42.com
milco.osterholm@eins.se

Part I
Basic Principles

Before discussing the technical SAP NetWeaver BW platform and technical topics regarding the administration and monitoring in detail, this chapter briefly introduces the relevant software components and how they can be categorized from the IT process perspective without considering the technical aspects.

1 SAP Implementation Concept

IT practices, IT scenarios, and usage types represent the process-oriented view of SAP NetWeaver and, at this level, facilitate an implementation in phases (see Table 1.1).

Hierarchical View	Example
IT practices	Business Information Management
▶ IT scenarios	▶ Enterprise Data Warehousing (EDW)
▶ Variants	
▶ Processes	▶ EDW operation
	▶ User administration

Table 1.1 Example of a Process-Oriented View

If you consider not the processes, but the necessary software installation, an implementation of an IT scenario requires specific usage types (for example, BI Java), standalone engines (for example, SAP NetWeaver BW Accelerator), and clients (for example, BEx analyzer).

1.1 IT Practices and Scenarios

The defined IT practices and IT scenarios (key activities) structure solutions for the implementation of processes that the individual SAP NetWeaver components support. Table 1.2 provides an overview of the integrated and predefined IT scenarios that are based on the SAP NetWeaver components and split up into one or multiple IT scenarios.

An IT scenario contains a set of clearly structured IT processes used to attain a defined business objective.

IT Practices	IT Scenarios
User productivity enablement	Enterprise portals
	Enterprise knowledge management
	Enabling user collaboration
Data unification	Master data consolidation
	Master data harmonization
	Centralized master data management
	Product information management
	Global data synchronization
Business information management	Enterprise reporting, query, and analysis
	Business planning and analytical services
	Enterprise data warehousing (EDW)
End-to-end process integration	B2B processes (*business to business*)
	Cross-application business processes
	Business process management
	Auto ID infrastructure
	Global data synchronization
Custom development	Developing, configuring, and adapting applications
	Platform interoperability
Unified lifecycle management	Software lifecycle management
	SAP NetWeaver–based system landscape
Application governance	User administration and access management
	Authentication and single sign-on
	Identity management
Consolidation	Consolidation of user interfaces
	Consolidation of information
	Consolidation of processes
	Adaptive computing
Business event management	Business task management
Service-oriented architecture (SOA)	Web services–based applications

Table 1.2 IT Practices and Scenarios

Business information management, which is of interest to us in this context, is one of the SAP NetWeaver platform's IT practices and includes the following key activities, which can be implemented using SAP NetWeaver Business Warehouse (BW), SAP NetWeaver Process Integration (PI), and SAP NetWeaver Portal: enterprise reporting, query and analyses, business planning and analytical services, and enterprise data warehousing.

1.1.1 Enterprise Data Warehousing

Enterprise data warehousing (EDW) enables you to set up and use a data warehouse in an enterprise-wide environment. EDW combines strategic analyses with operational reporting. In addition, it enables the enterprise to run reports in real time, integrate various systems, and improve the design time and runtime of BW models and processes. EDW consists of all steps that the system administration needs to perform to configure a very flexible, reliable, stable, and scalable BW solution and ensure smooth administration.

This variant enables you to implement and model an enterprise data warehouse. It covers data modeling (modeling of InfoProviders), data provision (definition of the sources and transfer mechanisms), data transformation, and data distribution and allows for metadata and document management.

Modeling

The EDW variant allows for integration of different source systems with an enterprise data warehouse. You can unite various technical platforms and consolidate diverse master data and transaction data semantics.

EDW also enables you to manage and monitor your enterprise data warehouse. It consists of binding control, administration and monitoring of the loading with processing processes, performance optimization measures (using the SAP NetWeaver BW Accelerator concept), and information lifecycle management (for example, archiving). Furthermore, it also provides for flexible user administration. This variant allows you to facilitate the administration and monitoring of all processes in the enterprise data warehouse and to support possible performance problem handling. Consequently, this book mainly focuses on this variant.

Operation

1.1.2 Enterprise Reporting, Query, and Analysis

Enterprise reporting, query, and analysis consists of all reporting and analysis tool and functions in SAP NetWeaver BW that you can use to create customized reports, cockpits, dashboards, and so on using the available BW information for the various user types.

The BW applications are created via the numerous SAP Business Explorer (BEx) tools or the SAP NetWeaver Visual Composer tool and can be published in SAP NetWeaver Portal. The BEx Query Designer creates queries, which you can then use for Microsoft Excel–based analyses in the Excel analyzer tool or for web-based analyses in the Web analyzer tool. BEx also provides the Web application designer tool for the creation of web-based applications, the report designer tool for the creation of formatted reports, and the Web analyzer tool for web-based ad-hoc analyses. BEx Information broadcasting additionally enables you to send the generated BW content via email or publish it in the portal. Integrating SAP NetWeaver BW with SAP NetWeaver Visual Composer allows you to integrate BW data with composite applications that users can access in the portal.

1.1.3 Business Planning and Analytical Services

Business planning and analytical services consists of processes that collect data from InfoProviders, queries, or other BW objects, convert it in various ways, and write back the new information to the BW objects (such as InfoObjects or DataStore objects).

Business Planning | You use the *business planning* variant if you want to implement planning scenarios. For this purpose, the SAP NetWeaver BW system provides BW business planning and simulation (BW-BPS) as of SAP NetWeaver 2004 and *BW integrated planning* (SAP BW-IP) as of SAP NetWeaver 7.0. Both solutions work with similar concepts and can run in parallel in the system. In contrast to BW-BPS, however, the new solution is completely integrated into the SAP NetWeaver BW system. This enables you to build integrated analytical applications that include planning and analysis functions. You should therefore use the integrated planning infrastructure when implementing new scenarios.

The *analytical services* variant allows for easy exploration and identification of hidden or complex relationships between data. SAP NetWeaver BW collects, consolidates, manages, and provides data for evaluation purposes from the different databases of the systems that are used in an enterprise. This data usually contains another valuable potential. It contains entirely new information that is represented in the form of meaningful relationships between the data but that is too complex is or concealed so that it cannot be revealed by intuition or simply viewing it.

Analysis Process Designer

The analysis process designer (APD) enables you to explore and identify these hidden or complex relationships between data easily. For this purpose, several data transformation methods are provided, such as statistical and mathematical calculations, data cleansing or structuring processes, and so on (see Figure 1.1). This tool is also well suited to calculate status values, which can be stored as characteristic attributes and then easily made available in reporting.

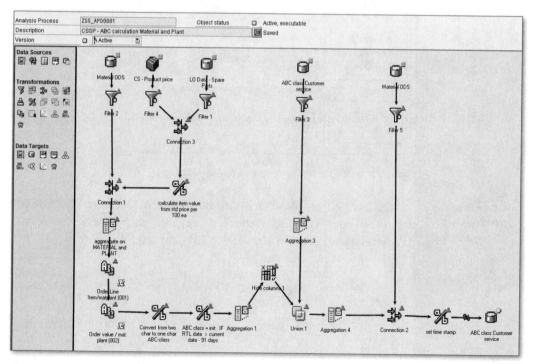

Figure 1.1 Calculations in the APD

1.2   Usage Types

Usage types map the structuring of SAP software at a technical level and represent all of the functions of a software component group. All of the three IT scenarios within business information management — business planning and analytical services, enterprise reporting, and query and analysis — as well as enterprise data warehousing require an installation of the usage types that are illustrated in Figure 1.2.

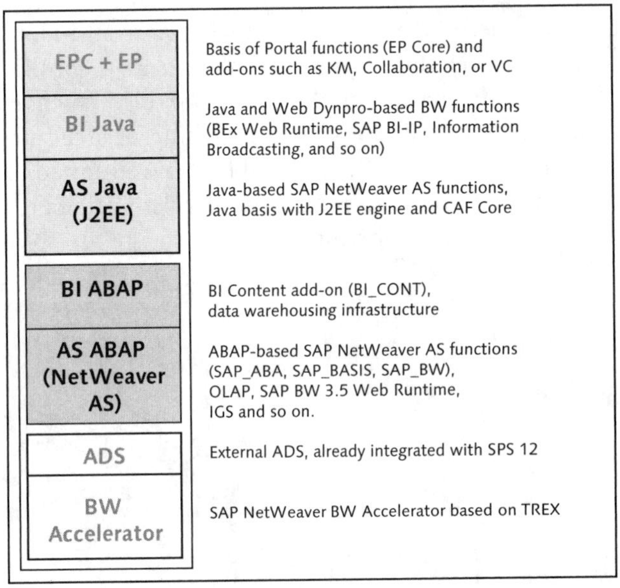

EPC + EP	Basis of Portal functions (EP Core) and add-ons such as KM, Collaboration, or VC
BI Java	Java and Web Dynpro-based BW functions (BEx Web Runtime, SAP BI-IP, Information Broadcasting, and so on)
AS Java (J2EE)	Java-based SAP NetWeaver AS functions, Java basis with J2EE engine and CAF Core
BI ABAP	BI Content add-on (BI_CONT), data warehousing infrastructure
AS ABAP (NetWeaver AS)	ABAP-based SAP NetWeaver AS functions (SAP_ABA, SAP_BASIS, SAP_BW), OLAP, SAP BW 3.5 Web Runtime, IGS and so on.
ADS	External ADS, already integrated with SPS 12
BW Accelerator	SAP NetWeaver BW Accelerator based on TREX

Figure 1.2   Software Components in a BW Installation

Complete SAP NetWeaver BW installation   A complete SAP NetWeaver BW implementation refers to the individual usage types including standalone engines, such as SAP NetWeaver BW Accelerator, and clients, such as BW frontend software.

In this chapter, we describe important base parameters, lock management and number range buffering for SAP NetWeaver BW, and the BI platform with BI ABAP and BI Java.

2 Overview of AS ABAP and AS Java

The SAP NetWeaver Application Server (previously known as SAP Web Application Server) is part of SAP NetWeaver and represents the basis of a SAP NetWeaver BW. It consists of an ABAP application server (formerly known as SAP R/3 Basis) and a Java application server. These two stacks are normally each installed as standalone instances on SAP NetWeaver BW 7.0, but up to Enhancement Package 1 (EhP 1) a double-stack installation was also supported. SAP NetWeaver AS ABAP and SAP NetWeaver AS Java have long proved their worth as high-performance platforms for ABAP-based and J2EE-based (Java 2 Enterprise Edition) applications and are a complete infrastructure for SAP NetWeaver BW.

2.1 SAP NetWeaver Application Server ABAP

SAP NetWeaver Application Server ABAP (AS ABAP) is the actual SAP NetWeaver BW platform and forms the uniform platform for the majority of SAP software products. As for previous SAP BW 3.x versions, all data warehouse functions of SAP NetWeaver BW are based on AS ABAP, and this is why it must be installed for operation purposes, whereas AS Java is an optional component.

AS ABAP provides a complete development and runtime environment for ABAP-based applications. The ABAP development and runtime environment enables you to develop complex applications without explicitly having to take into account technical details such as process or memory management, multiuser capabilities, database connections, or similar issues. These are provided by basic services or integrated directly into the ABAP runtime. You can also develop the applications irrespective of the platform in question. In this case, the application server decouples the application development completely from the operating system and database (DB) that are used.

AS ABAP process concept An SAP application server must process SAP requests from many frontends. It does this using the SAP Web dispatcher, which compiles the requests and transfers them for processing to corresponding work processes; these work processes then execute the required requests (for example, an ABAP program).

Table 2.1 describes the different work processes.

Work Process Type	Usage
Dialog (DIA)	Executes dialog programs (ABAP)
Update (UPD or UP2)	Asynchronous database changes (activated by a `COMMIT WORK` statement in a dialog work process)
Background (BTC)	Executes time-dependent or event-driven background jobs
Enqueue (ENQ)	Executes lock operations (if SAP transactions have to synchronize)
Spool (SPO)	Print formatting (for printer, file, or database)

Table 2.1 Work Process Types

Dispatcher The SAP Web dispatcher is the central process of the application server that generates work processes after it is started. You can configure how many work processes of different types run on an application server. In brief, the dispatcher fulfills the following main tasks:

▶ Initializes, reads profile parameters, starts work processes, and logs on to the message server

▶ Distributes the transaction load evenly onto each available work process

▶ Connects to the GUI level

▶ Organizes communication processes

Message server The message server is used to transfer requests between ABAP application servers when several instances are being used.

2.2   SAP NetWeaver Application Server Java

As a Java technology in the SAP NetWeaver Application Server, the J2EE Engine follows the J2EE standard that the Java community defined according to the rules of the Java community process, and is copyright protected by Sun Microsystems. Adhering to this standard ensures conformity to Java Management Extensions (JMX) 1.3; as a result, you can implement Enterprise JavaBeans, servlets, Java Server Pages (JSPs), Java Naming and Directory Interface (JNDI), Java Message Service (JMS), and so on. SAP enhanced this standard using, to name a few, SAP Java Connector (SAP JCo), which links the ABAP and Java worlds, using Java Persistence for implementing a persistence layer that is independent of the database and using Web Dynpro, which as a frontend technology exceeds JSP and servlet options. Because SAP NetWeaver BW 7.0 provided numerous applications based on Java (hereafter referred to as BI Java) and because Java technology is new territory for most BW administrators, in the following pages we will discuss in more detail what exactly BI Java actually is and the relevance and effects the J2EE Engine and portal have for administration and monitoring.

An AS Java instance normally consists of at least one server process and a dispatcher. Server processes run the actual application. Because every server process is multithreaded, meaning they can run several parts of program code in parallel, many processes can be processed simultaneously. The dispatcher assigns the different requests to individual server processes. It receives the relevant client requests and forwards them to the server process with the lowest current utilization. If a server process that is processing a request for the same client already exists, this process receives the request.

AS Java process concept

A Java cluster needs a special instance (central service) consisting of the message server and enqueue server to manage locks and synchronize communication when transferring messages and data. The message server keeps a list of all dispatchers and all server processes in the Java cluster and represents the entire infrastructure for exchanging data between the relevant nodes. The message server also makes information about the load balancing of many Java instances available to a SAP Web dispatcher. The enqueue server manages logical database locks set in the server processes by the executed application programs and supports synchronizing data in the cluster.

Message server and enqueue server

Request Process on AS Java

When a request (for example, the execution of a BW iView) reaches the dispatcher for the first time, it is received by a *connection request handler* (see Figure 2.1). This connection request handler then creates a connection object, which is assigned to this special update from that point onward. This means that the client will also have a fixed connection for future requests. The dispatcher also checks with the load balancer to see which server can execute the process for this client.

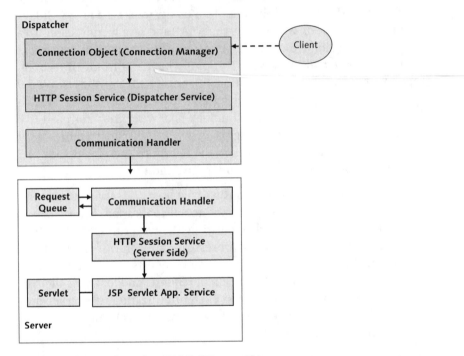

Figure 2.1 Request Process on SAP NetWeaver AS Java

2.3 Cooperation of Both Platforms

A complete SAP NetWeaver BW system with installed AS ABAP and AS Java with one or more instances offers a combination of the following functions:

Functions in an SAP NetWeaver BW system

▶ **Executes operations in SAP GUI**
Users are logged on through the dispatcher, and work processes perform the individual tasks.

▶ **Executes web-based requests**

The *Internet Communication Manager* (ICM) received requests. These HTTP(S) requests either address the *Internet Communication Framework* (ICF) for execution in ABAP work processes (SAP NetWeaver BW 3.5 Web templates or BSP applications), or they are J2EE requests for execution on the J2EE Engine. Based on the URL information, the ICM decides whether the request has to be forwarded to the ABAP engine or Java engine.

Figure 2.2 shows the architecture of a BW system with one instance.

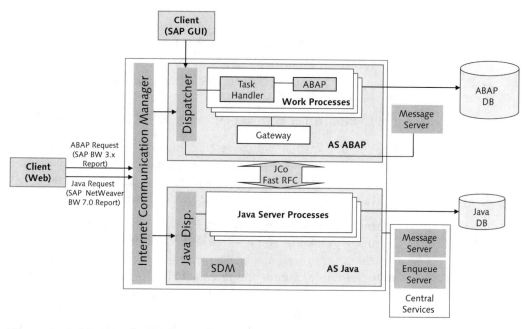

Figure 2.2   Architecture of an Instance with AS ABAP and AS Java

If your BW system has several instances, an ICM is run in every instance to receive web requests because the system must provide ABAP and Java. | **Several instances**

Each SAP NetWeaver AS instance also contains an ABAP dispatcher and corresponding work processes for processing ABAP programs and a Java dispatcher with Java server processes, to which incoming J2EE requests are assigned.

One of the instances must be installed to provide the enqueue service as a central ABAP instance (*central instance*), unless a dedicated stand-alone enqueue server is set up.

Communication between ICM and Java Dispatcher A separate protocol that the ICM and J2EE Engine have agreed on is used for communication between the ICM and the Java dispatcher. If the ICM forwards an HTTP(S) request to the J2EE Engine, the procedure is as follows:

1. If there is secure socket layer encryption (HTTPS), the ICM decodes the data. This changes the request to an HTTP request.

2. The ICM determines the Java dispatcher ports on which HTTP and HTTPS requests are received. This information is transferred from the Java dispatcher to the ICM via the ABAP dispatcher.

3. The ICM adds other information to the request (such as the length of the request and an HTTP/HTTPS ID) and then sends it to the Java dispatcher.

4. The Java dispatcher distributes the request to a local server process.

A reply request, in other words, sending information from a Java server process to a client, is processed in the same way. The Java dispatcher adds relevant information to this request and transfers it to the ICM, which takes over sending the request to the client.

Technological separation As already described, access to data contents is encapsulated on both platforms — AS ABAP and AS Java — by a persistence layer. Because there is no overall lock management for the platforms and individual memory formats are used, no shared data basis is used. These separate database schemas mean that separation between AS ABAP and AS Java is technologically integrated. Therefore, on close examination, there are still actually separate systems that, strictly speaking, do not have much to do with each other; different programming languages and separate databases are used. This factor affects individual functions within SAP NetWeaver BW. The actual data warehouse functions, like future developments, are still based on AS ABAP, whereas new functions run more and more on AS Java. SAP NetWeaver Portal and SAP NetWeaver PI are examples of J2EE-based applications within SAP NetWeaver.

2.4   SAP NetWeaver Portal

SAP NetWeaver Portal in relation to monitoring and managing BW systems should be regarded as the BW portal here (in other words, the portal that provides individual portal functions within BI Java), not the enterprise portal.

Technically, of course, there is no difference because it is SAP NetWeaver Portal, but this is meant to illustrate that you do not have to set up a portal project for BI Java, and administration remains manageable because of restricted use. This generally also reflects customer's system landscapes because of several advantages: The portal within BI Java is integrated into the enterprise portal as a dedicated BW portal using a *federated portal network* (FPN), and BW iViews are made available to users in this portal via *remote delta links* (RDLs) or *remote role assignments* (RRAs).

The portal framework provides components and services for managing and executing applications in SAP NetWeaver Portal. It therefore represents the core of the portal and is the basis for all actions executed on the portal. The framework consists of the runtime environment, portal runtime, portal components, a range of services (portal services), and the connector framework, which all run within AS Java. To begin with, we will briefly describe how SAP NetWeaver Portal is set up before explaining what BI Java actually is.

Portal framework

2.4.1   Portal Platform

The portal platform, the basis of the portal, is divided into two usage types, *EP Core* (EPC) and *Enterprise Portal* (EP).

EP Core only provides the core functions of the portal and consequently offers significantly more flexibility, mainly when the functions that exist in the SAP NetWeaver Portal are not required. This is why the collaboration function in a BW application has only seldom been used so far. EP Core includes portal functions for three subareas:

EP Core

▸ **Portal**
The portal subarea is a standard user interface you can use to access SAP and non-SAP systems and additional sources of information centrally beyond organizational enterprise and system boundaries.

▶ **Guided procedures**
Guided procedures are a framework you can use to create reusable components and develop user-related business processes (workflow modeling). They enable you to trigger a process from a process template at runtime and monitor it and its execution until completion. Different views of this process are available, which can help you better understand and follow the overall context of your tasks.

▶ **Universal worklist**
The universal worklist offers portal users standard and central access to their work and all of the important and necessary information for it. It collects the tasks and messages of the business workflow, collaboration tasks, alert framework, and knowledge management notifications and displays them in a standard list. For example, you can access alerts triggered by failed load processes by jumping to the relevant process chain.

Enterprise Portal The SAP NetWeaver Portal subarea includes the following functions:

▶ **Knowledge management (KM)**
Knowledge management enables portal users to access, distribute, and manage unstructured information beyond a heterogeneous repository landscape. For example, this includes creating and publishing documents or version management for documents. You can integrate BW documents into KM through the repository manager for BW documents, the repository manager for BW metadata, and through migration, so that the portal document store on the Java server rather than the server document store on the ABAP server is used as the storage area for these documents.

▶ **Collaboration**
The collaboration area covers everything that enables users to cooperate efficiently beyond spatial boundaries. This includes email and calendar integration as well as collaboration rooms, instant messaging, and application sharing. In BW solutions, collaboration, unfortunately, is so far only rarely used, even though scenarios such as reconciling planned figures would be entirely possible.

▶ **SAP NetWeaver Visual Composer**

You can create content for SAP NetWeaver Portal on the basis of SAP NetWeaver Visual Composer. The application in this case is developed on a model-driven basis, and this development is carried out using a visual user interface, not programming. The integration potential of SAP NetWeaver Visual Composer makes it a particularly powerful tool you can use to integrate a query from SAP NetWeaver BW, for example, with data from SAP ERP. So, unlike the BEx Web application designer tool, you do not have to work in a purely BW context.

▶ **Portal Development Kit for Microsoft's .Net Platform (PDK for .Net)**

PDK for .Net provides numerous tools you can use to develop portal content based on .Net (for example, in C# or Visual Basic programming languages).

The EP Core and Enterprise Portal usage types are synchronized and make SAP NetWeaver and applications running in it available to users in a uniform way.

2.4.2 SAP NetWeaver BW Software Components

From a technical point of view, in addition to SAP NetWeaver Portal components and AS Java (J2EE Engine), BI Java is made up of certain software component archives (SCAs) that provide Java-based functions in SAP NetWeaver BW. Table 2.2 lists the relevant software components for SAP NetWeaver Business Warehouse.

SCA	Description
BIBASES	BI basic services
BIWEBAPP	BI Web runtime for BI web applications
BIIBC	BI information broadcasting
BIREPPLAN	BI reporting and planning
BIUDI	BI UDI, for example, for UDI access in SAP NetWeaver Visual Composer

Table 2.2 SAP NetWeaver BW Software Components

The BIMMR (metamodel repository) and BIWDALV (BI Web Dynpro ALV) components are used in a broader environment, without SAP NetWeaver BW functions necessarily being involved.

Example You can see from the example in Figure 2.3 which versions of individual components (BI-BASE-S and so on) are installed. For instance, the BIWEPAPP component is in Version 1000.7.01.3.4.20090507x, and therefore in SAP NetWeaver 7.0 EHP 1, Support Package 3 (SP 3) and Patch Level 4, and was installed on 05/07/2009 (see Section 9.1, Support Package Stacks, Support Packages, and Patches, in Chapter 9).

Software Components Vendor	Name	Version	Provider	Location	Applied
sap.com	ADSSAP	7.01 SP3 (1000.7.01.3.0.20081208163600)	SAP AG	SAP AG	20090408145634
sap.com	BASETABLES	7.01 SP3 (1000.7.01.3.0.20081208163400)	SAP AG	SAP AG	20090408142452
sap.com	BI-BASE-S	7.01 SP3 (1000.7.01.3.4.20090507074209)	SAP AG	SAP AG	20090520113644
sap.com	BI-IBC	7.01 SP3 (1000.7.01.3.1.20090327151950)	SAP AG	SAP AG	20090520113653
sap.com	BI-REPPLAN	7.01 SP3 (1000.7.01.3.0.20081210084849)	SAP AG	MAIN_NW701P03_C	20090519125500
sap.com	BI-WDALV	7.01 SP3 (1000.7.01.3.0.20081210084901)	SAP AG	MAIN_NW701P03_C	20090519125317
sap.com	BI_MMR	7.01 SP3 (1000.7.01.3.0.20081207153200)	SAP AG	SAP AG	20090408142850
sap.com	BI_UDI	7.01 SP3 (1000.7.01.3.0.20081207154100)	SAP AG	SAP AG	20090408143344
sap.com	BIWEBAPP	7.01 SP3 (1000.7.01.3.4.20090507074244)	SAP AG	SAP AG	20090520113057
sap.com	CAF	7.01 SP3 (1000.7.01.3.0.20081210084856)	SAP AG	MAIN_NW701P03_C	20090408145944
sap.com	CAF-KM	7.01 SP3 (1000.7.01.3.0.20081210084850)	SAP AG	MAIN_NW701P03_C	20090519124143
sap.com	CAF-UM	7.01 SP3 (1000.7.01.3.0.20081210084907)	SAP AG	MAIN_NW701P03_C	20090408150013
sap.com	CORE-TOOLS	7.01 SP3 (1000.7.01.3.0.20081208163400)	SAP AG	SAP AG	20090408142451
sap.com	EP-PSERV	7.01 SP3 (1000.7.01.3.2.20090327152404)	SAP AG	SAP AG	20090520113757
sap.com	EP-WDC	7.01 SP3 (1000.7.01.3.0.20081211162000)	SAP AG	SAP AG	20090519120142
sap.com	EPBC	7.01 SP3 (1000.7.01.3.1.20090327152248)	SAP AG	SAP AG	20090520112749
sap.com	EPBC2	7.01 SP3 (1000.7.01.3.0.20081211160800)	SAP AG	SAP AG	20090519120147
sap.com	JLOGVIEW	7.01 SP3 (1000.7.01.3.0.20081208163500)	SAP AG	SAP AG	20090408142452
sap.com	JSPM	7.01 SP3 (1000.7.01.3.0.20081208163500)	SAP AG	SAP AG	20090408145459

Figure 2.3 Installed Components

One of the places where this overview is available is in the System Information area of AS Java, which you can access via the URL *http://<server>: <port>/index.html* (see Figure 2.4).

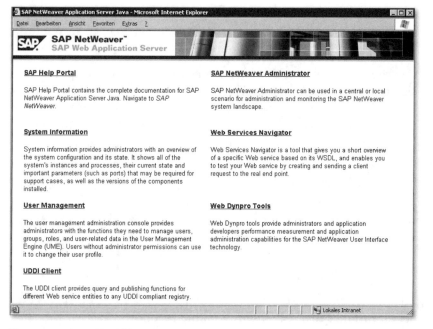

Figure 2.4 Access to AS Java

2.5 Basis Parameters

Only by optimally setting the BW basis parameters can you guarantee that the BW system will work without any errors and perform well. In particular, we would like to point out that recommendations for BW systems differ greatly in places from recommendations for ERP systems. In terms of parameterization, we follow SAP NetWeaver BW 7.0 and do not necessarily comply with recommendations for earlier releases.

Each SAP instance (central instance, dialog instance, standalone gateway, SAP Central Services (SCS) instance, Java application server) normally uses an instance profile for its configuration and a start profile containing the start framework configuration. As of SAP Kernel Release 7.10, SAP instances only have an instance profile that simultaneously contains the start framework configuration. Every SAP profile parameter has a hard-coded default value and can be changed in different phases using the general *default.pfl* profile and instance-specific values defined in the instance profile. You can override some of these param-

Basic details

eters by command line parameters when the process starts; therefore, to determine the profile parameters, it is not enough to search for a specific entry in the specified profile.

Saving old profiles You should save your old profile before you make any changes in case the instance with the new parameters does not start, in which case you can still use the old profile. It is essential that you check all parameter settings before you use them. The SAPPFPAR program is suitable for this purpose, or you can perform a check in a test system.

Pay attention to the architectural constraints of the operating systems (for example, shared memory constraints). Not heeding these constraints may result in errors and terminations. Note that specific recommendations on parameter settings can only be given by SAP Active Global Support within the context of service sessions.

2.5.1 Determining Parameters

You determine an instance profile parameter for an ABAP application server instance that is currently running as follows:

1. Log on to the application server instance.
2. Execute the RSPARAM report or preferably the more user-friendly RSPFPAR report in Transaction SA38.
3. Search for the parameter name.
4. Use the user-defined value.

The RSPFPAR report, which you can call using the transaction of the same name, RSPFPAR, contains documentation on the individual parameters (see Figure 2.5); you can access these parameters by placing the cursor on the relevant parameter and pressing the F1 key.

Determining instance profile parameters You determine an instance profile parameter of a Java instance, SCS instance, or stopped ABAP server instance or define the start profile parameter of an instance as follows:

1. Log on as the <SAPSID>adm user to the Windows server where you want the instance to run according to its configuration.
2. Call the profile name of the instance for which you want to receive the parameter value. The instance profile and start profile can be read in a very user-friendly way with the SAP Microsoft Management Console (SAP MMC). To do this, right-click the instance in SAP MMC and select ALL TASKS • VIEW TRACE FILE or VIEW START PROFILE.

Display Profile Parameter

Parameter Name	User-Defined Value	System Default Value
rdisp/max_cmdrun_time		0
rdisp/max_comm_entries	4000	500
rdisp/max_cs_delays		
rdisp/max_debug_lazy_time		
rdisp/max_file_entries		
rdisp/max_gateways		
rdisp/max_hold_time		
rdisp/max_jvm		
rdisp/max_listener		
rdisp/max_priv_time		
rdisp/max_sleep		
rdisp/max_slock_entries		
rdisp/max_snc_hold_time		
rdisp/max_vb_server		
rdisp/max_vm_debug_attach_time		
rdisp/max_vm_forced_sgc_time		
rdisp/max_vm_sgc_lazy_time		
rdisp/max_wprun_time		
rdisp/min_jvm		
rdisp/ms_keepalive		
rdisp/ms_keepalive_timeout		
rdisp/mshost		
rdisp/msserv		
rdisp/msserv_internal		

Display Profile Parameter

Parameter

Parameter Name	disp/max_comm_entries
Short Description	Maximum number of communication entries

Value

1.1 C kernel	500
2.1 Default Profile	500
\\p26sap31\sapmnt\P26\SYS\profile\DEFAULT.PFL	
3.1 Instance Profile	4000
\\p26sap31\sapmnt\P26\SYS\profile\P26_D11_debosap41	
3.2 program parameters	4000
3.3 Replace $$ and $(..)	4000
3.4 Generate file name	4000
4.4 Current Value	4000

Figure 2.5 Displaying Profile Parameters in Transaction RSPFPAR

3. Call the profile parameter value using the following command:

```
sappfpar.exe pf=<complete path> <name of profile parameter>.
```

The profile parameter value is returned in the command line. If the profile parameter does not exist, the program returns an empty line.

SAP MMC forms a generally usable infrastructure for managing systems. You can use it to integrate previously separately implemented tools into a common user interface, thereby enabling systems to be managed centrally. Although SAP MMC itself does not provide any management functions, it is an environment for integrating and accessing such tools. Tools are integrated into SAP MMC in the form of snap-ins for standardized access to functions. SAP has developed SAP Systems Manager (also a snap-in), which you can use to monitor, start, and stop SAP systems centrally from SAP MMC. SAP recommends that you use SAP MMC because it simplifies system management and provides many new functions.

2.5.2 Recommendations

Below we discuss recommendations for some parameters, on the basis of which you can set your own parameters, taking into consideration the relevant technical environment.

▶ **Export/import buffer**
This buffer is intensely used in BW systems and should therefore be at least 40 MB. When working with large hierarchies, you may have to increase this buffer considerably. You should be able to store at least 5,000 objects in the buffer. We recommend the following parameterization:

  ▶ `rsdb/obj/buffersize` M 10,000 (corresponds to 10 MB)

  ▶ `rsdb/obj/max_objects` M 5,000 (entries)

  ▶ `rsdb/obj/large_object_size` = 10,000 (corresponds to 10 MB)

▶ **Export/import SHM buffer**
The size of the shared memory should be at least 200 MB. If this memory is too small, long query execution times will occur, whereby high database times will be listed in the statistics. If the system is being heavily utilized, the following message may appear: RS_EXCEPTION000: No space left in shared memory. We recommend that you set the following values:

  ▶ `rsdb/esm/buffersize_kb` M 200,000
    (size of exp/imp SHM buffer in KB)

  ▶ `rsdb/esm/max_objects` = 10,000
    (maximum number of objects in buffer)

▶ **Program buffer (abap/buffersize)**
Depending on the available main memory, the program buffer should be between 200 and 400 MB. Also, unlike in transactional SAP systems, a higher number of program buffer swaps in BW systems are less critical and often difficult to avoid because the reusability of information stored in the program buffer is significantly lower. Whereas the response times of ERP transactions only move in the range of several hundred milliseconds, the response times of BW queries are in the range of seconds. You can only achieve an increase in performance in milliseconds by tuning the program buffer.

If not much main memory is available, if anything, you should increase the *extended memory*. However, you should not set the program buffer to lower than 200 MB. If there is sufficient main memory, you should set the program buffer in SAP NetWeaver BW to at least 300 MB.

▶ **Extended memory**
The extended memory needed by a BW user is significantly higher than that required by an ERP user. The size of the extended memory depends on the available main memory but should not be less than 512 MB.

▶ **Table buffer**
The table buffer buffers the content of tables that are characterized as completely or generically buffered in the ABAP Dictionary.

The size in the shared memory is determined by the `zcsa/table_buffer_area` parameter. There are a maximum of 2,147,480,000 bytes for kernel releases up to 6.20 with a patch number lower than 1129. For higher releases, there are no more relevant size restrictions in 64-bit systems. If you make the size of the table buffer bigger than 2 GB, you still have to set the following profile parameters: `ipc/shm_psize_19 = 0`. This parameter ensures that the table buffer is taken from the pool.

The number of bufferable tables or generic areas (*directories*) is determined by `zcsa/db_max_buftab`. The default value for this parameter is 5,000.

You must adjust the number of directories to the overall buffer size: Each directory requires approximately 300 bytes of management information in the buffer. All directories together should no longer need more than 10% of the buffer space to leave enough memory space for the objects to be buffered.

▶ **Single-record buffer**
The single-record buffer buffers records of tables identified as single-record buffered in the ABAP Dictionary. For the single-record buffer in particular, binding guideline values cannot be specified for optimum buffer sizes. The sizes are determined by the hardware, release version, dataset in the system, and applications used. Your system must have sufficient main memory. Main memory is particularly limited on 32-bit platforms, and increasing the buffer must be in line with existing memory management.

▶ **Recommendations specifically for the 64-bit ERP kernel**
In addition to general parameter recommendations for a 64-bit kernel

(which is explained in more detail in SAP Note 146289), you should set the `em/blocksize_KB` parameter to 4096 specifically for SAP NetWeaver BW.

▶ **Maximum runtime for a work process**
The runtime selected should generally be considerably greater than is the usual case in SAP ERP. Set the `rdisp/max_wprun_time` parameter to at least 3600.

▶ **Connecting to the frontends**
To avoid connection terminations, you should ensure the `gw/cpic_timeout` parameter is set big enough, for example, 60.

▶ **Other CPI-C-/RFC settings**
The following parameters in the CPI-C (Common Programming Interface for Communication) and RFC (remote function call) areas are crucial for system communication:

  ▶ **rdisp/rfc_max_wait_time**
  Maximum number of seconds a work process goes into idle mode if it does not receive any resources.

  ▶ **rdisp/rfc_check**
  This parameter controls the check to verify whether enough dialog work processes are free for processing asynchronous RFC calls.
  The number of dialog work processes available depends on the number of free dialog work processes and the number of work processes to be kept free for the dialog application. If a free work process is not currently available, the request is placed in the queue and processed later.

  ▶ **rdisp/rfc_max_comm_entries**
  Quota for the number of communication entries used. If the number of entries used exceeds this quota, no resources are returned to the caller. The default value is 90 (percent).
  The number of communication entries is set by the `rdisp/max_comm_entries` profile parameter, for which we recommend a value of 2,000.

  ▶ **rdisp/rfc_use_quotas**
  Switch that activates (value 1) or deactivates (value 0) resource allocation. You should never change the default value. If the value of the parameter is 0, no more work can be done with the parallel

RFC because a server cannot be determined for the next RFC. If you do change this value to 0, the RESOURCE_FAILURE exception condition will always be issued when asynchronous RFCs are called.

► **gw/max_conn**
This parameter specifies the number of parallel RFC connections that can be opened. We recommend that you set this parameter to 2,000.

► **gw/max_overflow_size**
This parameter defines the maximum swap space for CPI-C requests in the gateway and should be set to 25,000,000.

2.5.3 Recommendations for BI Java

The recommendations for systems with the BI Java usage type also differ in places from the general recommendations for Java Virtual Machine:

► **Permanent space**
The size should be 512 MB. If additional applications are installed, you may need to increase the permanent space. Note that you will need more permanent space if additional applications are installed or if the complexity of the applications (simply put, the number of classes) increases.

An increase in the heap size or permanent space in 64-bit systems is not a problem (provided there is enough physical memory); in 32-bit systems (particularly in Windows), you must take the limitations of virtual address space into account.

► **Heap size**
BI Java applications generally require more memory than other Java applications. We recommend configuring a heap size of 2.5 GB on 64-bit systems. This is a standard recommendation for initially configuring the system; an even bigger heap may also be useful and necessary in the BW environment. Bear in mind that the duration of an individual *garbage collection* (automatic memory cleanup) increases if the heap increases. The heap must be held in the physical main memory to avoid runtime problems caused by paging. In double-stack installations, note that ABAP and Java components compete for CPU

and memory resources. The maximum heap size for a 32-bit system is limited to 1.3 GB.

▶ **New generation**
We recommend that you set the `NewSize` and `MaxNewSize` parameters to approximately 1/6 of the heap.

You should regard the recommendations described here as initial settings before a system goes live. After a system goes live, you may have to correct and optimize individual parameters.

2.5.4 Recommendations for Parameters in the Source System

If performance bottlenecks occur sporadically or always in a source system, or if you notice that dialog users do not get any free work processes (all dialogs are occupied in Transaction SM50), or if terminations occur in the source system gateway, you should check the parameters for RFCs or the gateway and the *application link enabling* (ALE) customizing).

RFC Parameters

Set the `rdisp/rfc_min_wait_dia_wp` parameter in the instance profile of the instance where the background job for supplying BW is running to the number of configured dialogs if online users are working simultaneously on this instance. You should also set the `rdisp/rfc_max_own_used_wp` parameter to 50 in this case. You should set the value for the parameter to 2 if you only want to use this instance for supplying BW (and perhaps for other interfaces). You should also set the value for the `rdisp/rfc_max_own_used_wp` parameter to 75 in this case.

Gateway Parameters

Parameters for a very high interface load | Set the value of the `rdisp/max_comm_entries` parameter to 2,000 and the `/max_conn` parameter to 2,000. If the interface load is high, you can further adjust the instance profile parameters. First, carefully examine whether you have the described status in your system and whether you really need to increase the parameter values. The default values have been tried and tested for many years and are generally completely sufficient for standard scenarios. Setting the parameters to high values may require additional memory of approximately 100 MB, which you will otherwise sometimes need.

Adjusting values is especially critical in cases where lowest values have already been set for the operating system. When you increase parameters, this simultaneously causes the address space available for transactions to be reduced. Therefore, on 32-bit systems in particular, it is absolutely essential that you first determine the status of the system and only then, if necessary, increase the parameter values. We recommend the following parameter values if you have a high interface load:

▶ **rdisp/tm_max_no = 6,000 (no maximum limit)**
You use this parameter to set the number of connections to an instance; this includes dialog users and interfaces.

▶ **rdisp/max_comm_entries = 6,000 (no maximum limit)**
With this parameter, you set the number of communications from and to an instance (without dialog users).

▶ **rdisp/max_arq = 6,000 (= rdisp/max_comm_entries, no maximum limit)**
This parameter limits the maximum number of asynchronous messages used for internal communication, to make information known throughout the system. If a very high RFC load accumulates on an application server and you increased the `rdisp/max_comm_entries` parameter for this reason, we would advise you to set `rdisp/max_arq` to the same value.

▶ **gw/max_conn = 6,000 (no maximum limit)**
This parameter corresponds to the number of logical connections to a gateway, in other words, the number of connected gateways and external programs.

▶ **gw/max_sys = 2,000**
This is the maximum number of gateway clients. Note here that an ERP server is only a single client for the gateway.

▶ **gw/max_overflow_size = 100,000,000 (1 MB)**
You use this parameter to set the maximum swap space for CPI-C requests in the gateway. If many clients send their data quicker than recipients can accept them, you can increase this parameter. Because the gateway allocates process-local memory, you only need more swap. You need approximately 200 KB for each client that sends data quickly.

▸ **rdisp/appc_ca_blk_no = 2,000**
This parameter defines the buffer for TCP/IP communications). Note that this parameter occupies memory in the shared memory, and you must take into account operating-system-dependent requirements for some 32-bit operating systems in terms of the sizes of pools and shared memory segments and/or the size of the entire shared memory area.

▸ **rdisp/wp_ca_blk_no = 2,000**
This parameter defines the buffer for DIAG communications. Here too, you need to bear in mind that memory is occupied in the shared memory.

ALE Customizing   In ALE Customizing in Transaction WE20, you should set the dispatch mode to Transfer IDocs Immediately for the RSSEND and RSRQST message types.

2.6   RSADMIN Parameters

The parameters of the RSADMIN BW control table naturally play a large role in many chapters of this book, and whenever possible we discuss the parameters you need to be aware of. Also, although the intention is not to discuss all parameters, we do briefly describe a large portion of the most important parameters centrally. Exceptions here are explicitly database-relevant parameters, which are discussed in Chapter 3, Database Management.

You can insert, update, or delete RSADMIN entries using the SAP_RSADMIN_MAINTAIN program (called via Transaction SA38) (see Figure 2.6).

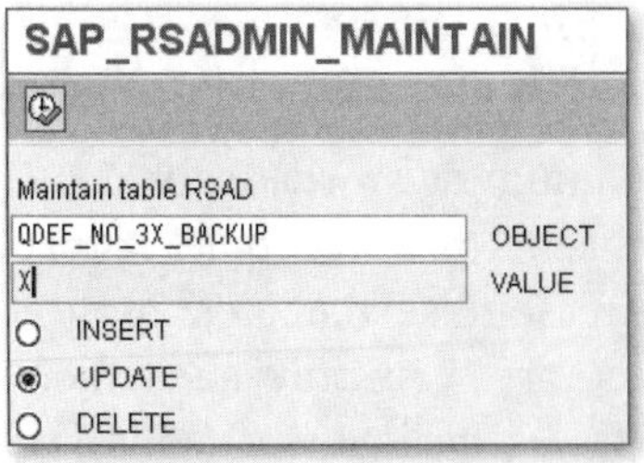

SAP_RSADMIN_MAINTAIN

Maintain table RSAD

| QDEF_NO_3X_BACKUP | OBJECT |
| X | VALUE |

○ INSERT
◉ UPDATE
○ DELETE

Figure 2.6   SAP_RSADMIN_MAINTAIN Program

Note that the RSADMIN table is buffered. You should execute a /$tab RSADMIN (invalidate buffer for RSADMIN) or /$sync command (invalidate all table buffers) after any parameter updates.

2.6.1 Parameters

In this section we describe the most important RSADMIN parameters.

AGGRCHECKADR

The aggregate check sends an email to a specified address if a check reports that an aggregate is incorrect. The status of the affected aggregate may also be set to Inactive. The following parameters are relevant:

▶ **AGGRCHECKADR, value: <e-mail address>**
If the email address is longer than 30 characters, enter the first 30 characters in the AGGRCHECKADR parameter.

▶ **AGGRCHECKADR_PLUS, value: <all other characters>**
These are characters of an email address that exceed the first 30 characters.

▶ **AGGRCHECK_SETINA, value: X**
You must set this parameter if you want to set an aggregate to Inactive if it was marked as incorrect in the check.

An email is sent for every incorrect aggregate. The email is sent regardless of whether you execute the check as a program, within the context of an aggregate process, or online.

AUTH_ODSO_DEL_REQUESTS

To delete requests from a DataStore object (known as Operational Data Store [ODS] in earlier releases), the user now needs authorization for the *Delete* (ACTVT = "06") activity for the DATA (RSODSPART = "DATA") subobject of the Data Store Object in question. The corresponding authorization object is S_RS_ODSO (Administrator Workbench – ODS object). This is the same authorization required for deleting the entire data content of a DataStore object, for example, using the Delete Data function in the context menu for an object in Transaction RSA1. The separate authorization check is only carried out if you maintain the AUTH_ODSO_DEL_ REQUESTS RSADMIN parameter with the VALUE = X value.

BICS_DA_RESULT_SET_LIMIT_MAX

The maximum number (BICS_DA_RESULT_SET_LIMIT_MAX parameter) defines the maximum number of cells a user can manually enter for a specific query view in the properties of an InfoProvider as a size restriction of result sets.

BICS_DA_RESULT_SET_LIMIT_DEF

The standard number for restricting the size of result sets (BICS_DA_ RESULT_SET_LIMIT_DEF) contains the number of cells used for all queries (and query views) without a customized number. If the allowed number is exceeded, instead of the system displaying a table with values, it issues a message indicating that the result set is too big, and data retrieval is restricted by the configuration.

BW_AGGRFILL_INTRABLOCK_COMMIT

The first time a database aggregate is filled, resources may sometimes run out or a different database problem may occur. This may happen in rare cases if the relevant InfoCubes are very large. The problem occurs if the F or E fact table of the higher-level aggregate (this can also be the basic InfoCube) contains more entries than defined by the BLOCKSIZE RSADMIN parameter. The first time the aggregate is filled (under the characteristics of the higher-level element), the system then searches for a lock characteristic it can use to create data blocks with a few rows as specified in the BLOCKSIZE parameter. The assumption in this case is that the data is distributed evenly for the characteristic in question. If this is not the case, some blocks may contain significantly more entries than indicated in the BLOCKSIZE parameter. Because a COMMIT follows every block, the database problem can still occur.

Non-flat aggregates The solution using this parameter works for aggregates containing more than 13 characteristics (non-flat aggregates) and performs additional COMMIT operations within a block. These additional COMMITs are performed after every 500,000 entries, which represents the internal packet size when aggregates are being filled.

For flat aggregates (fewer than 14 characteristics), only a single SQL statement is used on the database, so there is no way of retrieving this control (for additional COMMITs) until this statement has been executed successfully. Because you will — albeit it very rarely — need these additional COMMITs, you must activate them by setting the BW_AGGRFILL_INTRABLOCK_COMMIT parameter to X (any value; it is crucial that the parameter is available).

Flat aggregates

BW_AGGREGATE_DELTA_PAKETSIZE

If the change run terminates with dump entries that specify the TSV_TNEW_PAGE_ALLOC_FAILED exception, and the RSDDK_CHANGE_DELTA function is executed in the call stack, a delta request is presumably written into an aggregate that is based on an InfoCube with a very high number of key figures. In such cases, the internal tables used become very wide, and the default value of 500,000 records, which are read all at once, may lead to memory shortage.

If absolutely all of these requirements apply, you can use the BW_AGGREGATE_DELTA_PAKETSIZE parameter to set a smaller size. We recommend that you go from 500,000 down to 50,000 in steps until the problem no longer occurs. It is essential in this case to bear in mind that overextended parallelization of the change run may cause memory bottlenecks, which could have a similar effect.

BW_USER

You must use this parameter to maintain the user for ALE, which you will need if you have to connect a source system in the Workbench.

BW_SELDEL_PERC_THRES

You can use this parameter to control the method for deleting data (direct deletion or copying). Deleting data from a table is one of the most expensive operations (in terms of time and resource consumption for a rollback) because if you delete data using a delete statement, the database must also be able to restore the previous version of the table through a rollback if the last record fails to be deleted.

Deleting data

For example, if you want to delete data from the F table of an InfoCube, it might be better in some cases to copy the data not for deletion in a temporary table, delete the original table, and then rename the temporary table accordingly. This copying of data not for deletion into a temporary table can be performed much more efficiently using statements such as Create Table ... As Select ..., which are optimized for the relevant database, than by deleting data using the delete statement.

Default threshold

In tests, a threshold of 10% turned out to be reasonable, so if more than 10% of data is deleted in a BW InfoCube or ODS table, use the copy/rename procedure. You may have situations where the default value of 10% is not very suitable, or there may even be cases where you should not use the copy/rename procedure at all. This may be because you want to keep certain manually implemented changes to the fact tables, which cannot be changed using BW resources.

The BW_SELDEL_PERC_THRES parameter specifies the percentage rate (in whole numbers) as of which data is no longer deleted using DELETE, but using COPY/RENAME instead. The ratio [number of records to be deleted]/[number of all records in the table] is compared with the value of the BW_SELDEL_PERC_THRES parameter, divided by 100 (in other words, numbers ranging from 0 to 1). If the parameter is not set, the default value is 10. If the parameter is set to 50, and 5 out of 100 records are deleted from the F table, they are deleted using DELETE. If, say, 110 out of 200 existing records are then deleted from the E table, they are deleted using COPY/RENAME.

COMPOUNDED_KEY_WEB_F4_DISPLAY

The input help F4 in the standard system does not display any compounded keys in Web reporting. You can change this using the COMPOUNDED_KEY_WEB_F4_DISPLAY parameter, so that you can switch to the display of compounded keys in dialogs. The important thing to remember here is that this only applies to the display, not to the further processing of the characteristic based on the compounded value. The system always takes into account noncompounded keys for further processing data, for example, in the variable screen.

DEL_UNUSED_DIMS

Deleting master data

You can use this parameter to speed up the deletion of master data if the InfoCubes used by the relevant InfoObject contain lots of unused dimensions. The deletion generally removes all unused dimensions, which adversely affects the runtime if the InfoObject is used in too many InfoCubes and there are many unused dimensions. If the DEL_

UNUSED_DIMS entry is in the RSADMIN table, but a value is not set, the unused dimensions are not deleted while the master data is being deleted.

EXCEL_DOWNLOAD_NO_HIERICONS

When you download data from BW Web reporting to Excel, icons are also exported (for example, in the display of hierarchies), and this (possibly unnecessarily) slows down the download. To stop icons from being exported, you can set the value of the EXCEL_DOWNLOAD_NO_HIERICONS parameter to X.

IPAK_WARNINGS_AT_ACCESS_OFF

If data targets are not displayed when you call the scheduler (for instance, because they are not active), corresponding information indicating the reasons for this is displayed. If you do not want these warnings to be displayed at the beginning when you call the InfoPackage, you can set the IPAK_WARNINGS_AT_ACCESS_OFF parameter to X. However, the warning will continue to be displayed when you save, start, and schedule the InfoPackage.

MD_LOOKUP_PREFETCH_LOGIC and MD_LOOKUP_MAX_BUFFER_SIZE

By setting the value of this parameter to X, you specify that transformation programs switch to the new master data lookup mode. This is activated by default in SAP NetWeaver 7.0 BW SP 16. Remember here that this is a system-wide setting, which means that all transformations containing a master data lookup will use the new mode when you maintain this parameter. However, you can switch back to the old master data lookup mode by removing the value for this parameter or deleting the parameter itself from the RSADMIN table.

A master data lookup in the new mode involves masses of data being selected from the master data table to overcome the communication overhead between the database server and application server. This means that the master data lookup for all unique key values within a single data package performs a prefetch of the required master data attributes in the memory. Individual attribute values are then read for each record from this internal table in the transformation program during the record processing phase.

Memory
management

When you perform a master data lookup for several attributes of several characteristics in a transformation, this may lead to an overflow of memory if you carry out a prefetch in the memory for the corresponding master data. Therefore, a second parameter, MD_LOOKUP_MAX_BUF-FER_SIZE, is also evaluated in such a way that the management of the memory provided for the prefetch data is activated. This parameter defines the maximum size of the memory area available for the prefetch data of a data package. The size is defined in terms of the number of rows. For example, a value of 100,000 means that a prefetch will be performed in the memory for a maximum of 100,000 rows. The master data lookup will carry out a data prefetch in the memory for each data package until the maximum buffer size has been reached. When the limit has been reached, all other reads for master data will be performed by being selected directly from the database. After the data package has been processed, the corresponding memory for the prefetch data will be released.

MPRO_MAX_RESULT

The parallel processing of a MultiProvider query is cancelled by default as soon as the interim result contains more than 30,000 rows. The MultiProvider query is then restarted automatically and processed sequentially. Superficially, this leads to the impression that sequential processing is quicker than parallel processing.

Interim result
in KB

You can use the MPRO_MAX_RESULT parameter to set the parameters of a system in such a way that the described effect occurs as of an interim result of more than X kilobytes (KB), rather than when an interim result of more than 30,000 rows has been reached. This may be worthwhile if the effect described above occurs with critical queries and the performance has to be improved and if you have application servers with sufficient main memory. The default setting of a maximum of 30,000 results rows corresponds to a main memory consumption of about 3.5 to 4.5 megabytes (3.584 to 4.608 KB) in typical queries.

MULTICUBE_WP_LIMIT

You can use this parameter to define the maximum number of work processes when making your selection using a MultiProvider, to prevent too many processes from being assigned in this application case.

NO_DIFFERENT_FILENAMES_FOR_DL

When you download data to Microsoft Excel or into a *comma-separated values* (CSVs) file from a Web application, a dialog box normally appears in which the user is asked whether he wants to open the downloaded file directly or save it. This also happens if the local settings for the corresponding file type do not immediately provide for such a window. You can use the NO_DIFFERENT_FILENAMES_FOR_DL parameter to achieve the following, depending on the value field:

- ▶ **INLINE**
  This causes the created file rather than the dialog box to always open in the web browser with the inplace application for MS Excel (or the application associated with the file type).

- ▶ **ATTACHMENT or " " (blank spaces)**
  Each time you download data, this default value causes a dialog box to appear, asking you what you want to do with the created file.

- ▶ **X**
  This means that the dialog box for asking about the next action will not appear if not otherwise defined on the relevant client (for example, the Confirm Open after Download option is set on Windows XP under TOOLS • FOLDER OPTIONS • FILE TYPES • ADVANCED for the relevant file ending.

ODS_SORTED_FULL_EXTRACTION

If you set this parameter to X, the data for a DataStore object will be sorted according to the primary key if this data is extracted in full mode.

ODS_STATISTICS_LEVEL_IN_PERC

Statistics for the active table of a DataStore object are calculated again if they do not yet exist or if more than 10% of the data has changed. You can use the ODS_STATISTICS_LEVEL_IN_PERC RSADMIN parameter to change the 10% mark. The value field for the parameter specifies a percentage value that determines the percentage of necessary data changes before the statistics in the table are recalculated.

OLAP_CURRENCY_ERROR

The ERROR currency is displayed by default if the currency of all data records selected for the cell is initial. You therefore have to check the currencies and correct the corresponding data records in the InfoProvider. You can use the OLAP_CURRENCY_ERROR parameter to store your own text for ERROR. This will then be shown instead of the default value and can also be initial.

OLAP_UNIT_ERROR

The ERR unit is displayed by default if the unit of all data records selected for the cell is initial. You must therefore check the units and correct the corresponding data records in the InfoProvider. You can use the OLAP_UNIT_ERROR parameter to store your own text for ERR. This will then be shown instead of the default value and can also be initial.

QDEF_NO_3X_BACKUP

If the value for this parameter is set to X, this deactivates the creation of backup versions of query elements. The backup process minimizes any possible risk of data loss during the occasional migration of queries and query components from Version 3.x into Version 7.x. Deactivating the function makes sense if users are only using BEx Query Designer 7.0.

QUERY_MAX_WP_DIAG

By default, the maximum number of parallel work processes for each query is limited to six work processes for each user and decreases further depending on the load on the system. You can use the QUERY_MAX_WP_DIAG RSADMIN parameter to change the maximum number of work processes for each user, but the value will still decrease depending on the system load. The allowed value range is between 1 and 50.

RRT_GET_DIM_CARDINALITY

BAPI_MDPROVIDER_GET_DIMENSIONS requires a great deal of runtime after master or transaction data is loaded. You can use the RRT_GET_DIM_CARDI-NALITY parameter to optimize the function for determining the number of characteristic values. Three values are available for this purpose:

▶ **EXACT (default)**
Determines the number as before, but with optimization for InfoProviders that are not InfoCubes.

▶ **FAST**
Determines the number faster without restriction by the InfoCube.

▶ **CONST**
The number of characteristic values is not determined, but is instead set to a constant value.

RRMX_VERSION_CUST

You use Transaction RRMX or Transaction RRMXP to call the BEx Analyzer in the SAP GUI. You can use the RRMX_VERSION_CUST parameter to define which version you want to start (see Figure 2.7).

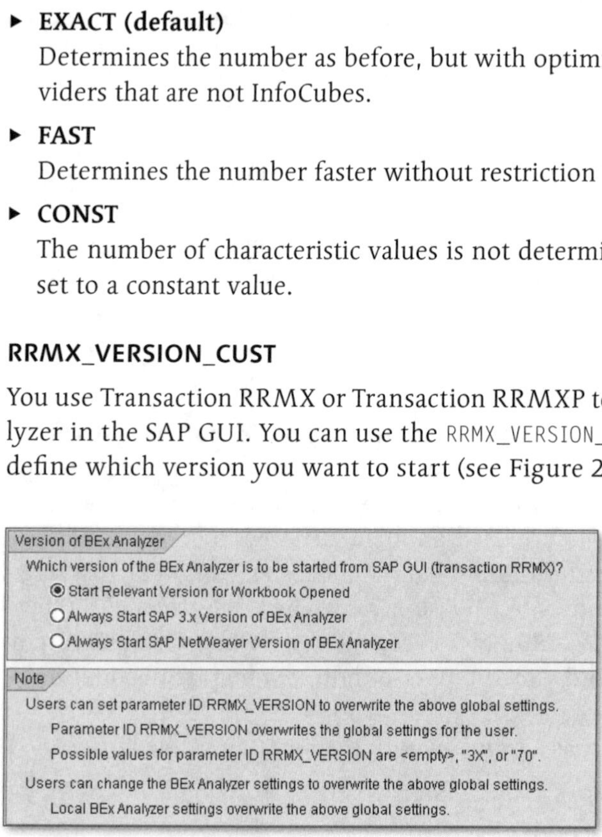

Figure 2.7 contents:

Version of BEx Analyzer

Which version of the BEx Analyzer is to be started from SAP GUI (transaction RRMX)?
- ⦿ Start Relevant Version for Workbook Opened
- ○ Always Start SAP 3.x Version of BEx Analyzer
- ○ Always Start SAP NetWeaver Version of BEx Analyzer

Note

Users can set parameter ID RRMX_VERSION to overwrite the above global settings.
Parameter ID RRMX_VERSION overwrites the global settings for the user.
Possible values for parameter ID RRMX_VERSION are <empty>, "3X", or "70".
Users can change the BEx Analyzer settings to overwrite the above global settings.
Local BEx Analyzer settings overwrite the above global settings.

Figure 2.7 Setting the BEx Analyzer Version

You can also implement the setting in the SAP Customizing Implementation Guide (Transaction SPRO) by selecting the menu path SAP Reference IMG • SAP Customizing Implementation guide • SAP NetWeaver • Business Intelligence • Settings for Reporting and Analysis • General Settings for Reporting and Analysis • Set BEx Analyzer Version (or directly in Transaction RRMX_CUST).

Customizing

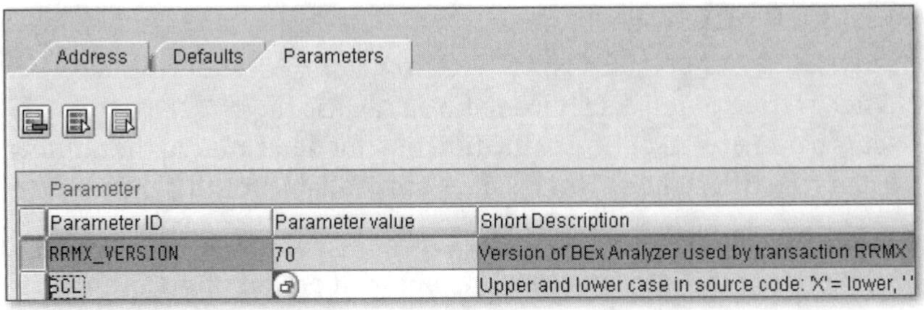

Figure 2.8 User-Specific BEx Analyzer Version

The RRMX_VERSION parameter ID (SYSTEM • USER PROFILE • OWN DATA • PARAMETERS) enables you to implement a user-specific setting (see Figure 2.8). This setting applies for a user on all computers across the system. You can use the global settings on the BEx Analyzer to set a local setting for a computer.

RSDRH_BUFFER_SIZE

Hierarchy table buffer

The hierarchy table buffer buffers hierarchy node calculations that have already been calculated. A separate table managed by an entry in the RSDRHLRUBUFFER buffer table is created for each hierarchy node. If queries in a system are used on many different hierarchies or very large hierarchies with different nodes, entries may often be displaced in the hierarchy buffer. In this case, hierarchy nodes frequently have to be recalculated accordingly. You can change the size of the hierarchy buffer (in other words, the number of buffered hierarchy node calculations) using the RSDRH_BUFFER_SIZE parameter. Proceed as follows to check whether there is a problem with the hierarchy table buffer:

1. In Transaction SE16, look at the RSDRHLRUBUFFER table without limiting the number of hits.

2. Sort the entries according to the Timestamp field.

3. If more than 90% of tables show a timestamp with a current date or a date from the day before and if the table has more than 170 entries, it may be beneficial to increase the buffer.

The default buffer size is 200 entries. The parameter value is only taken into account if it exceeds 200. Between 200 and 1,000 is a reasonable value range.

RSRCACHE_ACCESS_STATS

When you execute queries, in particular when the access load is high, entries may disappear in the OLAP cache. When you execute such an affected query again, the data must be read from the database again. The information about the data in the OLAP cache is saved in a directory located in a cache entry. When an entry is written in the cache, the entry is locked, read, changed, rewritten, and unlocked again with the directory. When an entry is read, the directory entry is read without a lock being set. If the read statistics for an entry are modified (the cache statistical values are held in the cache directory), the cache rewrites the directory into the storage medium. Because a lock was not set, another process may have started a write process at the same time, modified the directory, and rewrote it again.

To prevent the problem, you can explicitly deactivate the writing of read statistics by setting the value of the RSRCACHE_ACCESS_STATS parameter to NO_READ_STATS.

RSRCACHE_ENQUEUE_DUMP_FAILED and RSRCACHE_ENQUEUE_LOOP_COUNT

To avoid losing data when working with cache entries, you must ensure that you always set a lock (enqueue) for processing a cache entry. Only one process at a time can ever set the enqueue. All subsequent processes repeatedly try to set the enqueue themselves through a loop, whereby there is always a wait of approximately one second between two attempts. As soon as the earlier process that set the enqueue releases it, another process can set and continue working with the enqueue. Previously, the number of attempts for setting the enqueue was set to 3,000. If a process has not received the enqueue after 3,000 attempts, it terminates with an X message because the assumption is that an error has occurred.

▶ **RSRCACHE_ENQUEUE_DUMP_FAILED**
Set the value to X if you want the process to terminate with an X message.

▶ **RSRCACHE_ENQUEUE_LOOP_COUNT**
Specify the required number of attempts here (for example, 10).

You can use both the RSRCACHE_ENQUEUE_DUMP_FAILED and RSRCACHE_ENQUEUE_LOOP_COUNT parameters to set the number of attempts yourself for setting enqueues and consequently also reduce this number. Because a lower number, of perhaps 10 attempts, also progresses quickly without a positive result (enqueue not set), you can also specify whether you want a process to terminate with an X message or not.

RSRCACHE_LOGGING

To be able to analyze some cache problems better, SAP Support needs a mechanism for logging some important data about the OLAP cache and about storage media. This parameter is entered in the RSADMINA table for this purpose, and its value is set to LOGGING_ON. The logging results are written into the RSENQSTACK table but are very difficult to read and are only utilized by SAP Support for internal use.

Communication between processor and cache

The data is used to detect problems in the communication between the OLAP processor and the OLAP cache. For example, the information cannot be used to find out why the OLAP processor cannot read cache entries but reads data from the InfoProvider again, even though the user expects that the processor reads the data from the cache.

RSDRI_READ_WITH_GROUP_BY

When data is extracted from a standard DataStore object, it is normally read by the database in aggregated form and forwarded to the transformation. However, owing to database limitations, aggregation cannot be performed for all data transfer processes. If you want to deactivate aggregation across the system, set the value of the RSDRI_READ_WITH_GROUP_BY parameter in the system to NONE.

RSR_CACHE_ACTIVATE_NEW

New "BLOB/cluster enhanced" cache mode

The new cache mode, *BLOB/cluster enhanced,* was provided in SP 16 for SAP NetWeaver BW 7.0 and has a different architecture from previous cache modes, so it should not have the problems that these modes encounter (for example, entries disappearing, enqueue deadlocks). The new cache mode saves its data in database tables, exactly like the BLOB and cluster table persistence modes. To activate the new mode, you must insert the RSR_CACHE_ACTIVATE_NEW parameter into the RSADMIN table and set its value to X.

Activating the new cache mode makes it available for selection in the query properties of Transactions RSRT and RSDIPROP, and it can be assigned to a query. Like the other cache modes, you can also display saved cache entries in the cache monitor (Transaction RSRCACHE).

RSSM_PROT_SETTINGS

You can adapt the authorization log of the old concept on SAP NetWeaver BW 3.x (RSSM log) to meet specific needs, so that this can be interpreted more easily. You specify a 12-digit key as a value for this parameter, with which you set different switches for logging purposes. Refer to SAP Note 943139 for more information.

SAVE_HISTORY_OF_IPAK_ON

If you set the value of this parameter to X, you activate the change history for InfoPackages. The values of the RSLDPSEL and RSSDBATCH tables are stored in the following backup tables before and after you save an InfoPackage:

▶ RSLDPSELHIST

▶ RSSDBATCHHIST

▶ RSLDPSTACK (caller stack)

▶ RSLDPUSEDHIST (use in process chains)

SPLIT_SX_TABL_THRES

When characteristics are being activated, all SID tables of time-dependent or time-independent navigation attributes must be joined to the master data table of the characteristic to create the X/Y tables with the *Surrogate IDs* (SIDs) of all time-dependent or time-independent navigation attributes of a characteristic. A large number of navigation attributes for a single characteristic may increase the complexity of a SQL statement for creating these tables to such an extent that database optimizers can no longer find a suitable access plan.

A new function splits these unusually complex SQL statements into several less complex SQL statements, so that partial results are stored in temporary database tables during processing. You can control this function using a threshold entry for the SPLIT_SX_TABL_THRES parameter. The value specifies the number of tables in an SQL statement as of which the statement is split into less complex statements. If the new function causes errors, you can deactivate it by setting the threshold value very high (500 tables or more).

Splitting SQL statements

STANDARD_TRFC and STANDARD_TRFC_3x

With BW Service API 7.0 (*Application Programming Interface*), data transfer was changed over to the default tRFC scheduler (see Figure 2.9). This changeover is active by default as of BW Service API 7.0 in combination with a BW system as of SAP NetWeaver 7.0.

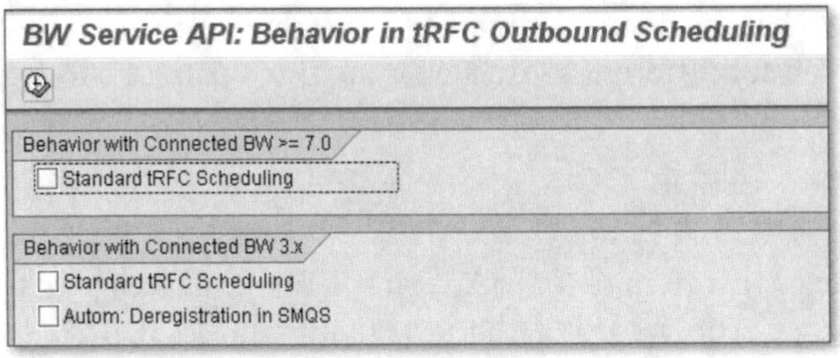

BW Service API: Behavior in tRFC Outbound Scheduling

Behavior with Connected BW >= 7.0
☐ Standard tRFC Scheduling

Behavior with Connected BW 3.x
☐ Standard tRFC Scheduling
☐ Autom: Deregistration in SMQS

Figure 2.9 tRFC Setting for Service API

You must set the number of dialog processes in Transaction SMQS. You can use the RSA1_TRFC_OPTION_SET report (maintains both RSADMIN parameters) to activate and deactivate this default SAP NetWeaver BW 7.0 scheduling.

TCT_KEEP_OLAP_DM_DATA_N_DAYS

The 0TCT_DS01, 0TCT_DS02 and 0TCT_DS03 DataSources, which with SAP NetWeaver BW 7.0 are part of the BI Administration Cockpit, are used for extracting statistical data at query runtime.

If the data is extracted in delta mode, source data no longer required is deleted from the tables of the RSDDSTAT_OLAP and RSDDSTAT_DM views during extraction. You cannot stop source data from being deleted for a specific period of time, for example, to enable you to perform further analyses with the data. However, you can now use the TCT_KEEP_OLAP_DM_DATA_N_DAYS parameter to specify a minimum retention period for data relating to views.

For instance, if you set this parameter to 30, only data older than 30 days will be deleted. The STARTTIME time stamp stored in the RSDDSTATINFO table is used here as a reference time. If the parameter is not found in the parameter table, a minimum retention period of 14 days is used by default.

USE_FACTVIEW

Every InfoCube in SAP NetWeaver BW systems on iSeries has a fact-view that displays the union of F and E fact tables, through the use of the UNION ALL operator. This view is not in BEx queries, but it is used for access purposes for data marts, SAP Strategic Enterprise Management (SEM), SAP Advanced Planner and Optimizer (APO), or InfoSets containing InfoCubes. An InfoCube view is used by default for the access purposes mentioned, but you can implement the following value settings of the USE_FACTVIEW parameter to control usage of the view:

▶ **FALSE**
Deactivates usage in all cases except data mart or open hub access

▶ **TRUE**
Activates usage

▶ **NEVER**
Basic deactivation setting, which you should only use temporarily for bypassing database problems or similar issues

VAR_SCREEN_SAPGUI_TECHNM

You can use this parameter to specify whether you want the technical name in the variable screen for a BW 3.x query to be displayed in the header. Set the value to X if you want the technical name displayed.

WEBPROTOCOL

HTTP is used as the protocol by default when you go from an SAP NetWeaver BW web application to a transaction or program. In most cases, both protocols are set up in the target system, and you can therefore define the default protocol using the WEBPROTOCOL RSADMIN parameter.

2.6.2 Obsolete Parameters

Some parameters in the RSADMIN table have become obsolete with SAP NetWeaver BW 7.0 because they were copied into Customizing or the technical concept changed (through the new parallelization concept). The parameters listed in Table 2.3 are no longer valid in SAP NetWeaver BW 7.0.

Parameter	Application Area
<MultiProvider name>	DBIF
ADA_OUTER_WITH_ROWNUM	SDB
AGGRFILLMODE	AGGR
CDS_INACT_<XXX>	SDB
CR_MAXWAIT	AGGR
CR_MAXWPC	AGGR
CR_RFCGROUP	AGGR
DB_STATISTICS	DBIF
DB2_HIERARCHY_NTE_LIMIT	DB2
DB2_MAPDEVT	DB2
DB2_MAPDSN	DB2
DB2_MAPSPACE	DB2
DB2_NO_BLOCKSIZE_UPPER_LIMIT	DB2
DB2_PSA_NUM_PARTITIONS	DB2
DB2_SHOW_RUNSTATS_PROTOCOL	DB2
DB2_STATS_ON_TMP_TABLES	DB2
DB2_SUBSTITUTE_JOINTAB	DB2
DB2_USE_NTE	DB2
DB2_USE_NTE_FOR_XY_FILL	DB2
DB2_WORKDEVT...	DB2
DB2_WORKDSN...	DB2
DB2_WORKSPACE...	DB2
DBIF_EQSID_THRES	DBIF
DBMS_STATS	ORA
DONT_DROP_INDEX	AGGR
LEAVE_VIEWS	DBIF
MPRO_MAX_RESULT	DBIF
MULTICUBE_WP_LIMIT	OLAP
NEVER_EVER_DROP_INDEX	WHM
ORA_DBMS_STATS (DBMS_STATS)	ORA
ORA_ENABLE_NTE	ORA
ORA_PARALLEL_DEGREE	ORA
ORA_TABTRUNCATE_MINIMUM	ORA

Table 2.3 Obsolete RSADMIN Parameters

Parameter	Application Area
QUERY_MODE	DB2
RS_STAGING_BAPI_TRACE	WHM
RSA8XP01	SAPI
RSAR_LONG_FIELDNAME	WHM
RSDRD_ADA_MAX_DEL	SDB
RSDRS_EXECUTE_GC	DBIF
RSFO_COMPILER_OFF	WHM
SAPI_SYNC	WHM
SPLIT_DATAMART_TABL_THRES	OLAP
SPLIT_QUERY_TABL_THRES	OLAP
SWITCH_OFF_OPENSQL	DBIF
USE_HIERATTR	OLAP
VCUBE_<CUBENAME_SEL>	OLAP

Table 2.3 Obsolete RSADMIN Parameters (Cont.)

2.7 Lock Management

SAP NetWeaver AS ABAP has an independent lock mechanism that is used to synchronize access to databases and at the same time ensure that two transactions can change the same data in the database simultaneously. It is important for the administrator to understand lock management to the extent that redundant lock entries may have to be deleted; the period for creating or deleting a lock entry cannot be manipulated.

Different types of locks can be created from ABAP programs. The programmer determines which of the possible kinds of locks will be used. The following list provides an overview:

Types of locks

▶ **Shared lock (S, Shared)**
Several users (transactions) can access locked data at the same time in display mode. Requests from other shared locks are accepted, even if they come from other users. An exclusive lock on an object that already has a shared lock is will be rejected.

▶ **Exclusive lock (E, Exclusive)**
An exclusive lock protects the locked object against all types of locks

from other transactions. Only the same lock owner can reset (accumulate) the lock.

- **Exclusive but not cumulative (X, eXclusive noncumulative)**
  Whereas exclusive locks can be requested several times by the same transaction and released again successively, an exclusive noncumulative lock can only be requested once. Every other lock request, even from the same transaction, will be rejected.

- **Optimistic lock (O, Optimistic)**
  Optimistic locks initially behave like shared locks but can be changed into exclusive locks.

Lock owners

A lock entry can have one or two owners. Two owners, the dialog owner and the update owner, are created when a transaction is begun. Both may require locks. When a lock is required, the programmer can define the lock owner.

Enqueue server and lock table

The enqueue server (also called a lock server) is the instance of an SAP NetWeaver installation that manages the lock table. If an installation consists of several instances (distributed installation), an enqueue work process (ENQ) is required for managing the locks centrally. Lock requests from programs of different instances are forwarded by the dispatcher there to the message server. This in turn forwards the lock request via the lock server dispatcher to the enqueue work process, which checks the lock table for any potential lock collisions.

The lock table is a table in the main memory of the lock server, where the current lock time is specified. When a lock request reaches the lock server, this server initially checks the lock table to see whether the requested lock might collide with an existing lock entry. If this is not the case, the requested lock will be written into the lock table as a lock entry. Table 2.4 describes the lock table fields.

The important thing to remember here is that locks in the lock table are not set at the database level.

Managing lock entries

Lock management (Transaction SM12) is available as a tool for monitoring the lock logic in the system (see Figure 2.10). You can get the list of lock entries after you have limited the entries to be displayed to a certain user on the selection screen. The lock mode, table, and lock argument are included in the list (in other words, the information about the table fields).

Field	Description
Owner 1	Owner ID and cumulation counter of owner 1: The ID contains the computer name, work process, and a time stamp and is also used to identify the SAP logical unit of work (LUW). The cumulation counter specifies how often the owner has already set this elementary lock.
Owner 2	Same as owner 1.
Backup ID	Backup ID (index used to save the lock entry in the backup file) and backup flag (0 indicates no backup or 1 indicates a backup). If you set the backup indicator, the system saves the lock on the hard disk when the lock server is restarted.
Lock mode	S (shared lock) O (optimistic lock) E (exclusive) X (eXclusive noncumulative lock)
Name	Name of database table where you want fields to be locked.
Argument	Locked fields in the database table (linked key fields; can also contain wildcards).

Table 2.4   Lock Table Fields

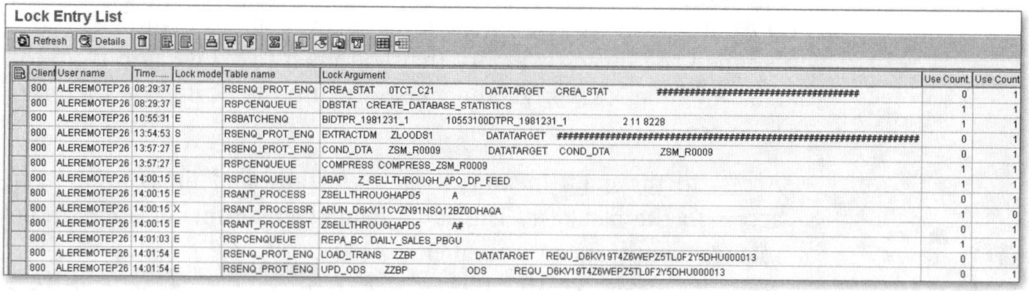

Figure 2.10   Lock Management in Transaction SM12

In the example, the lock information when a process chain is being processed is displayed. This is an exclusive lock for the RSPCCHAINATTR table (attributes for a process chain) with the 0TCT_C2_DELTA_P01 lock argument, which in this case is the unique technical name of a process chain for the key field in the database table. The option to delete lock entries is directly available in lock management. However, this should only be done in exceptional cases because database inconsistencies may occur if lock entries are deleted carelessly. You can display lock statistics in the menu by selecting the EXTRAS • DISPLAY STATISTICS menu options. The fill level of the lock table is important for monitoring the lock mechanism. Under no circumstances should this "overflow," though this will hardly be the case in an SAP NetWeaver BW system because, unlike transactional systems, data and objects are predominantly accessed in read-only mode, and as a result very few locks have to be set.

2.8 Number Range Buffer

You use number ranges to assign numbers to individual database records for business or technical objects (purchasing documents, addresses, and so on, but also dimension or surrogate IDs). To be able to use number ranges, you must have defined a number range object for the corresponding business object. You can then specify number ranges for the number range object. The numbers to be assigned from the number range are used to create a unique key for individual database records in the system.

The number range buffer increases performance when numbers are being assigned. Instead of retrieving the numbers from the database every time, access to the buffer in the main memory is sufficient. It is only when the buffer is empty that you need to fill it again from the database (Table NRIV). The benefits of using the buffer are therefore as follows:

▶ Access to the main memory is about a thousand times faster than access to the database. This is particularly relevant for applications that frequently assign a number.

▶ Access to the database is always subject to the transaction mechanism of the database. After an application has assigned a number for a user, a second user can only assign a new number if the first user has executed a commit operation on the database. The application blocks access for this duration, and the second user has to wait.

▶ The number range buffer also prevents deadlock situations that might occur from different numbers being assigned in a different sequence.

No changes to NRIV table Because the kernel for filling the number range buffer accesses the NRIV table directly, you must never change the table structure. This also applies for adding fields.

2.8.1   Number Ranges in an SAP NetWeaver BW System

Number ranges, and consequently their buffering, for load processes in an SAP NetWeaver BW system are important for transaction data (dimension ID, DIMID) and surrogate IDs (SIDs) and for master data (hierarchies [HIEID] and SIDs). If you load data with value combinations that are not yet contained in the corresponding dimension and SID tables, you must create a new entry in these tables. To do this, you must assign a new DIMID or SID value from the NRIV number range table. If the corresponding number ranges are not buffered, this results in a COMMIT for every assigned value. A high number of new entries in DIMID or SID tables results in a very high number of COMMITs on the NRIV table, which may lead to a high number of "log file sync" waits. Therefore, you should ensure that number ranges are buffered for DIM-IDs and SIDs.

In number range object maintenance (Transaction SNRO), you can activate main memory buffering for a number range object by selecting the menu path EDIT • SET BUFFERING • MAIN MEMORY. You can also specify how many numbers you want to have held in the buffer in each case. This value depends on the extent of the numbers required by an application and is generally between 10 and 1,000 but can also be set to 10,000 in certain situations.

Transaction Data

You should buffer the number range object for a dimension table in the following cases:

▶ Per request, the dimension table always grows in size by a high number of data records.

▶ Although the size of the dimension table levels off, a very sharp increase is expected at the beginning.

▶ Many access actions to the NRIV table relating to the number range object of the dimension table are monitored.

▶ The InfoCube or dimension table is deleted regularly, and the dimension table periodically increases sharply as a result.

If you want to change the buffer for a dimension, you can use the RSD_CUBE_GET function module to determine the object name of the   Changing buffers dimension with the expected high number of tuples. Settings in the function module are:

- I_INFOCUBE is the InfoCube name
- I_OBJVERS is set to A
- I_BYPASS_BUFFER is set to X

The numbers for the dimensions (for example, 0007165) then appear in the NUMBRANR column in the E_T_DIME table. You must place "BID" in front of this number, which will give you the required number range (for instance, BID0007165). Entering "BID*" in Transaction SNRO enables you to see all of the number ranges for dimensions used in the SAP NetWeaver BW system. You can find the number range you are looking for by using the object name you previously determined.

Amount of
numbers

The amount of numbers is determined in the buffer in number range maintenance (Figure 2.11). Set this value to 500, for example. The sizes depend on the expected volume of data of the initial and future (delta) upload. Ensure that the number range for the package dimension is never buffered.

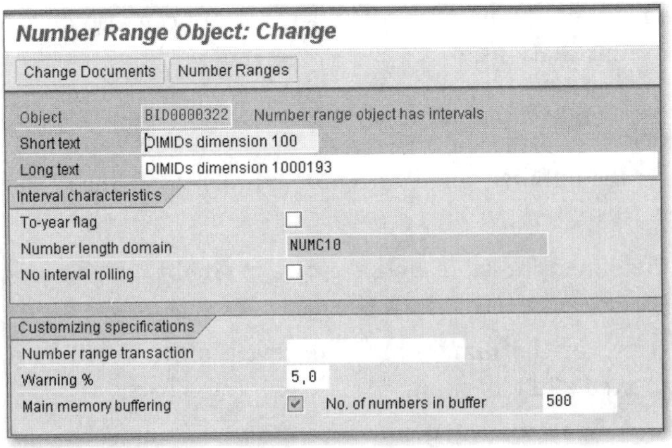

Figure 2.11 Number Range Maintenance

Master Data

As is the case when loading transaction data, when the volume of data is high, the number range buffer for InfoObjects should also be increased with an expectedly high number of tuples. You can use the

RSD_IOBJ_GET function module to find the number range name of the InfoObject with the expected number of tuples. The settings in the function module are as follows:

- ► I_IOBJNM is the InfoObject name
- ► I_OBJVERS is set to A
- ► I_BYPASS_BUFFER is set to X

The number for the InfoObject then appears in the NUMBRANR column in the E_S_VIOBJ table. You must place "BIM" in front of this number, which will give you the required number range (for instance, BIM0000053). Depending on the volume of data to be expected, also set the amount of numbers in the buffer to 500 here, for example. To view the current status, you can also display the relevant number range object for an InfoObject under the menu path EXTRAS • NUMBER RANGE OBJECT in characteristics maintenance (Transaction RSD1). Make absolutely sure that the number range object for the 0REQUEST characteristic is never buffered. The reason for this is that you must ensure that the sequence of SID values for the characteristic corresponds exactly to the sequence of load processes, although this cannot be guaranteed when several application servers are being buffered and used.

2.8.2 Analysis and Repair

There is one inconsistency if an SID table already contains higher values than the current version of the number range interval. In such a case, if the system tries to insert this SID with a different characteristic value, this will result in a BRAIN071 error message.

The problem may be caused by the fact that, despite the number range being buffered, a new number is taken directly from the NRIV table and updates cannot be undone consistently if a termination occurs. You must ensure that the numbers are taken from the buffer and never from the NRIV table. However, if all dialog work processes are occupied, buffer management cannot store a new interval in the buffer and switches from the buffer to the database after a short waiting time. This is usually the case with load processes if data is loaded in PSA and Data Targets in Parallel mode.

Analysis and Repair Using Transaction RSRV

You can check and repair BW-relevant number ranges using the analysis and repair tool (Transaction RSRV or by branching directly from InfoProvider administration). You can adjust number ranges for Info-Cube dimensions using the maximum dimension ID and repair incorrect statuses of number range objects in repair mode. In this case, you check whether there is actually a number range object for the Info-Cube dimension and, if so, whether the most widely used dimension ID (DIMID) of the dimension is lower than or the same as the status of the number range object. If the number range object is missing, you can also reactivate the InfoCube.

Adjusting number ranges for characteristics
You can adjust number ranges for characteristics using the maximum SID. This test checks whether there is a number range object for the SIDs of the characteristic and, if so, whether the most widely used SID is lower than or the same as the status of the number range object. You can correct the status of the number range object in repair mode. You can also create a number range object if it is missing. You can activate the characteristic again to create a missing number range object.

If number range inconsistencies frequently occur for an object, you should limit the degree of parallelism during the update process. You can do this by using the PSA and Data Target in Series loading mode to load the data. You can now control the parallelism of the update and consequently avoid the problem. If several load processes are running, you must ensure that one dialog process is always free.

This chapter focuses on two main topics. First, it describes some DB-specific parameters that are important for SAP NetWeaver BW systems and the administrator's main activities in this area. Second, this chapter aims to give you a thorough understanding of indexes and statistics and how to administrate them, because this is a central issue in SAP NetWeaver BW systems.

3 Database Management

The major differences between online transaction processing (OLTP) and a data warehouse in terms of their requirements of the database (DB) and DB administration give rise to some points that an SAP NetWeaver BW administrator needs to take into account. One thing that is particularly important in an SAP NetWeaver BW system with mass data is indexes. These play a central role both in data loading processes and in reporting.

In this chapter, we deal with the various DB management systems, but it is not possible to address every aspect of DB administration. As in many other chapters of this book, we concentrate on the points that are relevant to SAP NetWeaver BW.

3.1 Indexes

Indexes are indispensable in relational DBs for a number of reasons. First, if properly constructed, they help optimize DB access, and second, unique indexes can guarantee unique value sets.

All DB administration systems (such as Oracle) contain a range of index types. Besides the classic B trees, there can also be bitmap indexes, reverse key indexes, and functional indexes. In SAP NetWeaver BW systems in particular, it is important to have detailed knowledge of these individual index types and of how to administrate indexes, because optimal access to mass data is a central consideration in these systems. The DB optimizer makes the decisions regarding the use of indexes

Index types

for specific SQL statements, taking into account the syntax of the relevant SQL command, the available statistics, and the specific statements (hints) themselves.

Indexes can be created as unique or nonunique. The most important thing when constructing composite indexes is the order of columns, because it is this order that determines how the optimizer uses indexes. An index table can be regarded as a copy in sorted form of the actual DB table, reduced to specific fields. Besides the data itself, an index also contains pointers to the corresponding data records so you can gain access to fields that are not contained in the index.

Example: indexes for an InfoCube Let's take an InfoCube as an example. Indexes are created for each individual dimension so that the data can be searched and selected easily. However, the benefits always have to be weighed against the additional effort required for existing indexes. If data is loaded into an InfoCube, the indexes also have to be updated, and this has a negative effect on the performance of data changes. Therefore, when it comes to loading, you may have to decide whether to completely delete an index.

3.1.1 Primary Index and Secondary Index

A primary index contains the key field of a DB table and a pointer to the nonkey fields in the table. It is always unique, because the key fields identify one specific data record. All SAP tables have a primary index that is created along with the table. You can create as many additional indexes (*secondary indexes*) as you like, depending on requirements. This may be necessary if, for example, the table is regularly accessed in such a way that the sorted primary index offers no particular advantage.

3.1.2 Clustered Index

Many DB administration systems also allow you to define clustered indexes. Clustered indexes are different from nonclustered indexes in the following ways: Not only is the list of pointers to the data records available in sorted form in clustered indexes, but also, the DB management system (DBMS) tries to store newly added data records that are located near each other in a clustered index in such a way that they are physically close to each other in the memory as well, thus further speeding up value searching in this column.

As a rule, only one cluster index is permitted per DB table. In SAP DBs, this index is usually the primary key. In an SAP NetWeaver BW system, you can use Transaction ST04 to determine the quality of a cluster index in relation to a specific index.

You can help the DB optimizer select the cluster index more often by sorting the dimensions of an InfoCube in accordance with the data and queries. We recommend that you first define dimensions with a high cardinality. If the query execution process frequently reads dimensions with a low cardinality, these dimensions should be positioned as high up in the sequence as possible.

3.1.3   Main Index Types

As we mentioned at the start of this chapter, some index types are particularly important in SAP NetWeaver BW systems.

Binary Search and B tree Index

One important index type arises from the binary search) concept in sorted lists: the binary tree. The new B tree concept was developed to deal with the fact that indexes of the binary tree type have some disadvantages, such as high administrative overhead.

First, in a binary search, the value of the middle component in a sorted list is calculated (❶ in Figure 3.1). If this value is too low (lower than the searched value), the focus switches to the middle of the upper half, and the value found there is compared with the searched value (❷). This process of dividing the remainder is repeated until the value is found (❸ and ❹). In the example in Figure 3.1, a sequential read process would require 13 accesses, whereas a binary search would require a maximum of 4.

Dividing the remainder

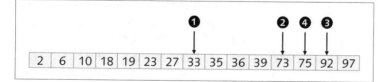

Figure 3.1   Binary Search in a Sorted List

Binary searches are supported by binary trees, in which each node has two successor nodes or end nodes. The depth of the tree hierarchy is what determines the number of accesses.

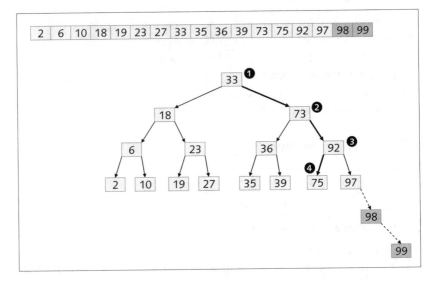

Figure 3.2 Search in a Binary Tree

When new values are added, it is always possible that the tree may then no longer be balanced, which makes access more difficult. In the example in Figure 3.2, the values 98 and 99 were retroactively added to the balanced binary tree.

B-tree Binary trees are used primarily when the data can be stored in full in working memory. Unlike in binary trees, a node in a B tree can have more than two child nodes. This enables us to reduce the number of nodes read in a data search when there is a variable number of keys (or data values) per node. B trees are used to process very large data volumes, of which only a fraction can fit in the main memory of a computer at any one time. With B trees, data is stored persistently on the hard disk and can be read block by block (Figure 3.3). A binary tree node can then be either read or stored as a block. The high degree of branching in B trees means that the size of the tree and, thus, the number of (slow) write and read accesses is reduced. Also, the variable key quantity per node means that there is no need to frequently balance the tree.

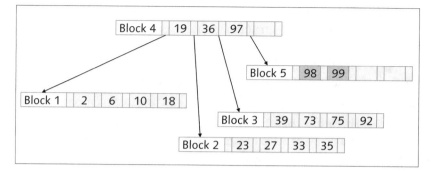

Figure 3.3 Dividing a B tree into Blocks

If new values are added, they are inserted into the right block, in accordance with the sorting rules. If there is not enough space in the block in question, it is divided into two blocks. Figure 3.4 shows how when a new value is added (here, 24), block 2 from Figure 3.3 becomes block 2 and a new block 6.

Division into new blocks

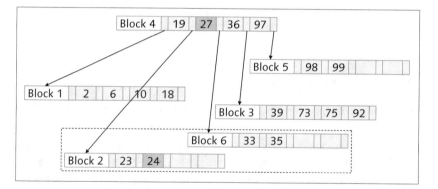

Figure 3.4 New Value in a B Tree

The origin of the name B tree is unclear, although we do know that it does not stand for binary tree. It seems probable that it comes from *balanced*.

Bitmap Indexes

A bitmap index is used to index multidimensional data efficiently. The properties of the bitmap index mean that it is used primarily in data warehouses, such as SAP NetWeaver BW. Its name comes from the fact that the bitmap index stores one or more attributes in the form of a bitmap. It is most useful for indexing table columns with a low cardinality, in other words, a column with a low number of different values. This is precisely the kind of situation where a conventional index, implemented using a B tree, cannot improve access performance.

In a bitmap index, a bit is used for every data record or value combination, with the result that the size of the index depends directly on the number of values. Each bit has the value 1 if the combination exists and 0 if the combination does not exist (see Table 3.1). As with all DB indexes, there is a reference from each of these entries to an (external) DB entry.

Employee	Male	Female	Single	Married
Anne	0	1	0	1
Hank	1	0	1	0
Charlie	1	0	1	0
Marcus	1	0	0	1
Peter	1	0	1	0
Steven	1	0	0	1
Tina	0	1	0	1

Table 3.1 Example of Bitmap Indexes

Simple binary operations

Simple binary operations are used to search the index table (preferably one that is stored internally). In our example, this is done using the AND operator in a search screen. If, in our example, you search for people who are male and single, the search screen is 1010 (the references from the hits point to Hank and Peter). Thus, you can see that using binary operations on the processor level speeds up comparison operations. This means that computing resources are replaced by extra space in the memory.

3.1.4 Indexes for InfoCubes

An InfoCube consists of a set of DB tables that are structured in accordance with a star schema. Transaction LISTSCHEMA provides a good overview of all of the tables in an InfoCube (fact tables, dimension tables, and so on) (see Figure 3.5).

```
┌─────────────────────────────────────────────────────────────────┐
│  Call up schema viewer for InfoCubes                              │
│  ┌──┬──┬──┬──────────┬──────────┬────┐                            │
│  │🔍│⊞ │▤ │▥ Row     │▥ Subtree │▦ ✍ │                           │
│  └──┴──┴──┴──────────┴──────────┴────┘                            │
│                                                                   │
│  ZZPRCUST                                                         │
│    └─▣ /BIC/FZZPRCUST           Product/Customer Inf             │
│        ├─▣ /BIC/DZZPRCUSTP       Data Package                    │
│        ├─▣ /BIC/DZZPRCUSTT       Time                            │
│        ├─▣ /BIC/DZZPRCUSTU       Unit                            │
│        ├─▣ /BIC/DZZPRCUST1       Company code                    │
│        │      ├─── /BI0/YCOMP_CODE    Company code               │
│        │      ├─── /BI0/XCOMP_CODE    Company code               │
│        │      └─▣ /BI0/SCOMP_CODE     Company code               │
│        │             ├─── /BI0/QCOMP_CODE     Company code       │
│        │             ├─── /BI0/PCOMP_CODE     Company code       │
│        │             └─── /BI0/MCOMP_CODE     Company code       │
│        ├─▣ /BIC/DZZPRCUST2       Currency                        │
│        ├─▣ /BIC/DZZPRCUST3       Plan version/value t            │
│        ├─▣ /BIC/DZZPRCUST4       Product                         │
│        ├─▣ /BIC/DZZPRCUST5       BU/PU                           │
│        ├─▣ /BIC/DZZPRCUST6       Final destination               │
│        ├─▣ /BIC/DZZPRCUST7       Ship to party                   │
│        ├─▣ /BIC/DZZPRCUST8       Sales organisation              │
│        │      ├─── /BI0/YSALES_OFF    Market Unit                │
│        │      ├─── /BI0/XSALES_OFF    Market Unit                │
│        │      ├─▣ /BI0/SSALES_OFF     Market Unit                │
│        │      ├─── /BI0/YSALES_GRP    Market                     │
│        │      ├─── /BI0/XSALES_GRP    Market                     │
│        │      ├─▣ /BI0/SSALES_GRP     Market                     │
│        │      ├─── /BI0/YSALES_DIST   Sales Region               │
│        │      ├─── /BI0/XSALES_DIST   Sales Region               │
│        │      ├─▣ /BI0/SSALES_DIST    Sales Region               │
│        │      ├─── /BI0/YCUST_GROUP   Market region              │
│        │      ├─── /BI0/XCUST_GROUP   Market region              │
│        │      └─▣ /BI0/SCUST_GROUP    Market region              │
│        ├─▣ /BIC/DZZPRCUST9       Buying dimension                │
│        ├─▣ /BIC/DZZPRCUSTA       Customer dimension              │
│        └─▣ /BIC/DZZPRCUSTB       Accounting dimension            │
└─────────────────────────────────────────────────────────────────┘
```

Figure 3.5 LISTSCHEMA View of an InfoCube

Figure 3.6 shows how a fact table with a dimension table is linked to a master data table in a subsequent step. The F fact table /BI0/F0RPA_C01 stores dimension IDs (DIMIDs) for the dimension 0RPA_C011. In the example shown here, this dimension contains the material characteristic or, to put it more accurately, the surrogate ID (SID) value of the material characteristic. The associated SID is linked to the characteristic value in the S table of the characteristic.

The SAP standard contains a fact table that contains nonunique B tree indexes for each individual dimension column. Dimension tables have a primary index (in general, this is a unique B tree index) for the DIMID column and a composite, nonunique index for the SID columns of the individual characteristics.

► The order of SID columns in the index is based on the order contained in the InfoCube definition.

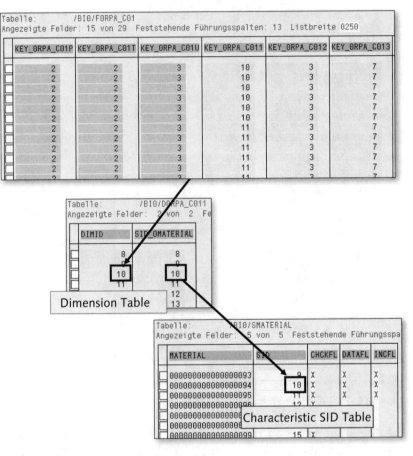

Figure 3.6 Star Schema of an InfoCube

► The composite index is used mainly during the load process to determine whether a specific combination of values (or SID values) already exists in the InfoCube.

Only one primary index is available in X and Y tables. Unique indexes for each SID column are created for S tables (SID tables for characteristics).

P Index for Fact Tables

In standard InfoCubes, indexes that are known as P indexes are created for the E and F fact tables (for example, /BIO/FORPA_C01~P). P indexes contain all of the dimension columns in a specified order (time, dim 1, dim 2 ... dim n, units, package). A P index is different from a primary index in terms of order and uniqueness and is of central importance for index clustering, among other things. Uniqueness is not mandatory in F tables but is in E tables. The purpose of these indexes is to support InfoCube compressions in which the E fact table is checked for existing dimension IDs to decide whether the processed data record has to be newly added or whether an existing data record can be used in modified form. The P index is therefore crucially important for the performance of compression processes.

However, since SAP NetWeaver BW 7.0, a new implementation of the compression function no longer requires the P index of the F fact table while increasing compression performance. Thus, whereas the unique P index of the E fact table is still required for the uniqueness check, the P index of the F fact table is no longer required for any InfoCubes or aggregates in an SAP NetWeaver BW 7.0 system. It makes sense to delete these nonrequired indexes to reduce the storage space taken up in the index table space and to leverage the reduced index maintenance to improve the performance of load and delete processes in the InfoCube.

Existing P indexes on F fact tables are retained even after an upgrade but can be deleted using program SAP_RSDB6_PINDEX_ON_FTABLE. This program enables you to select an individual InfoCube or all active InfoCubes. All active aggregates in the selected InfoCubes are also adapted. During execution, the P indexes on the F fact tables are deleted, and the time index or package index is re-created in the form of a clustering index.

Delete and create P indexes

3.1.5 Indexes for Master Data

Two unique B tree indexes are created for SID characteristics tables. These can be used to support the conversion of an SID to the associated characteristic value or vice versa:

▶ A primary index of the characteristic values
(for example, /BIO/SCUSTOMER~0)

▶ An index of the SID values (for example, /BIO/SCUSTOMER~001)

The unique index of the SID values column also ensures that no duplicate SID values are created (duplicate values have a very detrimental effect on the OLAP engine).

Indexes on other master data tables, such as the P table (non-time-specific master data) and the Q table (time-specific master data), are useful when these tables are accessed in load processes, for example. The procedure for doing this is explained in more detail in Section 3.1.7, Index Management in an SAP NetWeaver BW System.

3.1.6 Indexes for DataStore Objects

Because the optimal access paths to a DataStore object (DSO) cannot be made known to the system, and standard indexes would lead the DB optimizer to adopt poor access strategies, no indexes are created for DSOs as standard. Nonetheless, there are good reasons to create secondary indexes on DSOs either if the DSOs are used for reporting purposes or if they are used for rereading in load processes.

Data Warehousing Workbench
You use the Data Warehousing Workbench (Transaction RSA1) to define indexes for DSOs and then to transport them (see Figure 3.7).

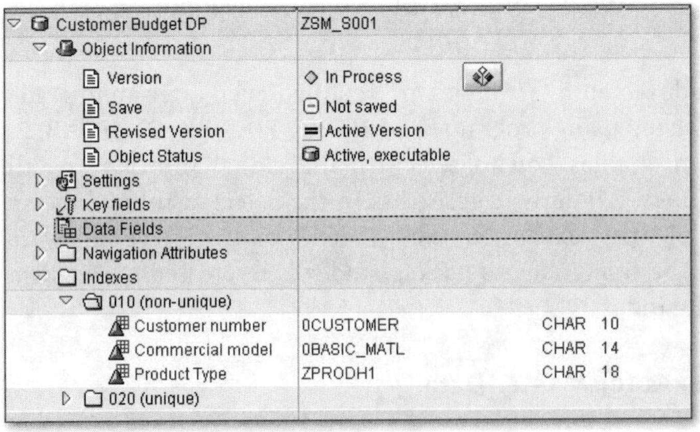

Figure 3.7 Indexes for a DataStore Object

Please also note the following points in relation to these indexes:

▶ You can transport secondary indexes for DSOs only if they are defined in the DSO administration function (Transaction RSA1 or RSDODSD).

▸ If you want to create indexes with the SE11 DB tool, you have to do so in the target system. However, this procedure is not advisable.

▸ By defining indexes, you are not changing any structures or data in the DSO, and you therefore do not need to activate the object or implement any data.

▸ Because many DSOs contain a large number of data records, it takes a long time to create an index.

▸ In the DSO administration function, defined indexes are filled automatically, so you do not need to do this manually in Transaction SE14.

The tables RSDODSOINDX (directory of DSO indexes) and RSDOD-SOIOBJIND (directory of InfoObjects contained in the indexes) contain details on the defined indexes.

3.1.7   Index Management in an SAP NetWeaver BW System

SAP NetWeaver BW systems contain various tools and functionalities for administrating and monitoring indexes, especially indexes on InfoCubes.

In later chapters, we will go into more detail on activities such as administrating indexes in InfoCube administration and monitoring indexes in Transaction RSRV.

Creating Indexes in Transaction SE11

You can use the ABAP Dictionary (Transaction SE11) to create and edit indexes, such as indexes on master data tables (Figure 3.8).

Either open the table in question directly in Transaction SE11, or display the characteristic (in Transaction RSD1, for example) and from there use forward navigation (double-click the table name) to go to the ABAP Dictionary. Because the SAP NetWeaver BW master data tables are usually generated tables in package $TMP, and the package of these objects cannot be changed, you cannot transport these indexes and therefore you have to create them directly in the system. Consequently, production systems have to be explicitly enabled to allow creation of indexes for changes.

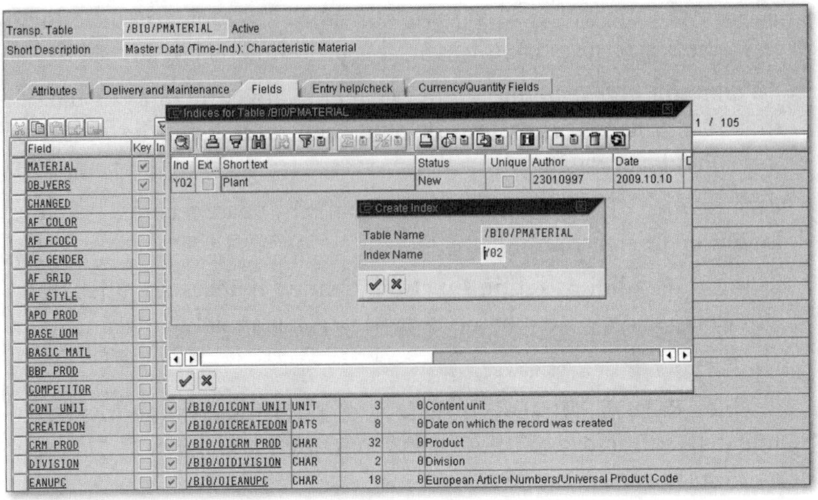

Figure 3.8 Maintaining Indexes in Transaction SE11

Control tables

There are two issues concerning control tables: a production system has to be explicitly enabled for these activities, and indexes on master data tables in SAP NetWeaver BW system landscapes have to be defined in a consistent manner. To tackle these issues, in many customer systems, these indexes are defined in control tables and created, changed, or deleted by customer programs in the individual systems.

Missing Indexes in the DB

As explained above, indexes are very important both for reporting and for data load processes. Therefore, as well as analyzing the required indexes, it is also necessary to monitor existing indexes. One thing that the latter point involves is carrying out regular checks to establish whether any indexes defined in the ABAP Dictionary are missing from the DB and whether any DB indexes are not defined in the ABAP Dictionary. To check for inconsistencies in index definitions, see Transaction DB02 under DIAGNOSTICS • MISSING TABLES AND INDEXES (see Figure 3.9).

Sources of error

For customer-specific objects in particular, inconsistencies can arise if, for example, the object was deliberately deleted from the DB during development or if a DB error occurred when the object was created. Likewise, incomplete or incorrect transports and canceled implementations can make it impossible to find the object in the DB. If there are no problems with incomplete transports or canceled implementations, usually the object can be simply stored in the DB using Transaction DB02.

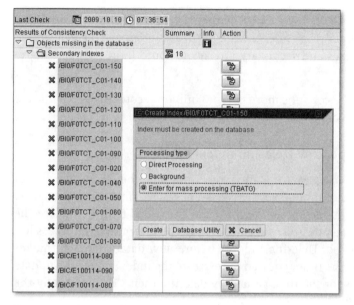

Figure 3.9 Missing Indexes in Transaction DB02

The processing type Enter for Mass Processing (TBATG) enters the object in table TBATG. This marks the object for DB modification. The TBATG entries can then be processed by means of a job (overnight, for example). To access the list of mass processing requests, go to the initial screen of Transaction SE14 and select DB REQUESTS • MASS PROCESSING. You should select this option if you want to modify a large number of objects.

If missing primary and secondary indexes are displayed for several fact tables, you should consider using programs SAP_UPDATE_DBDIFF and SAP_INFOCUBE_INDEXES_REPAIR, as specified in SAP Note 157918.

► **SAP_UPDATE_DBDIFF**
You can use this program to update table DBDIFF, which lists tables and tablespaces that do not conform to the ABAP Dictionary standards. For the SAP NetWeaver BW systems, these are fact tables with-

out primary indexes and temporary objects such as tables and views. Table DBDIFF is used to ensure that the DB management system takes these differences into account and therefore does not identify them as errors.

▶ **SAP_INFOCUBE_INDEXES_REPAIR**
This program repairs degenerated primary indexes and creates missing P indexes and secondary indexes for both InfoCubes and aggregates.

If the InfoCube contains more than 50 million records, as a general rule you should avoid deleting and re-creating indexes.

3.1.8 Temporarily Deleting Indexes

When write accesses are made to an InfoCube, the DB system has to modify the relevant indexes. This has a negative effect on performance. Therefore, it is recommended in some situations that you delete the indexes in question and re-create them in full after the write access has been completed. Deleting indexes before new data is updated makes sense only if the time required to re-create the indexes after the update compensates for the time gained by deleting them. This is usually the case in the following scenarios:

▶ InfoCubes are initially populated with a large volume of legacy data.

▶ A delta upload takes place that writes more than 15% new data to the uncompressed fact table.

You can delete indexes in the InfoCube administration function, among other places. However, this causes all of the indexes of an InfoCube and the associated aggregates, except the primary key of the compressed fact table, to be deleted. This option should be used in exceptional cases only because it usually results in serious disadvantages. For example, deleting all indexes is not necessary for most processes that would benefit from missing indexes, such as rollup or compression, because these processes can delete the relevant indexes themselves if required.

Delete index process type

A much more suitable way of deleting indexes in process chains is the process type Delete index. The delete action in this process type comprises the indexes of the uncompressed fact table of an InfoCube only. However, you must always be aware that deleting indexes can have such a negative impact on performance that running reports becomes almost impossible. The general rule is that you should not delete indexes too early; in other words, you should delete them only immediately before the data is updated.

3.1.9   DB Statistics

All DB management systems on which an SAP NetWeaver BW system is run use the cost-based optimizer to determine the best possible access paths. To calculate the costs of an access strategy, the optimizer needs statistical information on the tables and indexes in the DB. Other important information includes the number of table and index data records, the number of blocks in use, and the cardinality of all table columns. Out-of-date table statistics can lead to incorrect optimizer decisions and, consequently, inefficient data accesses. To ensure that indexes are used in the most efficient way and to optimize the performance of an SAP NetWeaver BW system, it is therefore very important to update all DB statistics. The following sections go into more detail on the statistics-related activities of an administrator.

Cost-based
optimizer

Switching Off Statistics

Up to SAP NetWeaver SPS 8, it was possible to switch off the DB statistics activated by the SAP NetWeaver BW system by setting the entry DB_STATISTICS in table RSADMIN to OFF. This could also be done in Customizing under SAP NETWEAVER • BUSINESS INTELLIGENCE • PERFORMANCE SETTINGS. We would like to emphasize at this point that this step is recommended only if the user fully understands its implications. Switching off the SAP NetWeaver BW–activated DB statistics when there is no genuine need can cause serious performance problems.

It makes sense to switch off DB statistics if, for example, extensive rollup or change run processes are running in a time period during which no queries, or very few queries, are executed. In such a case, the DB statistics can be collectively re-created at the end of the process. However, the parameter for switching off DB statistics is not used from SAP NetWeaver BW 7.0 SP 8 on; the creation of DB statistics is initiated from within the SAP NetWeaver BW system, independently of this parameter. The database or the database porting itself decide whether or not the statistics are then actually created or changed.

Rollup and change
run processes

3.2 Database Memory Parameters for BW Objects

The DB memory parameters can be maintained for persistent staging area (PSA) tables, master data tables, fact and dimension tables of the InfoCube, DSO tables, and error stack tables of the data transfer process.

Data type You use the data type to determine the physical area of the database (tablespace) in which the table is to be created. Every data type (master data, transaction data, organizational and Customizing data, customer data) corresponds to a physical area of the database in which all tables assigned to this data type are stored. Once you have made the correct selection, your table is automatically assigned to the right area of the database after the table is created. The following are the available data types:

▸ APPL0: master data, transparent tables

▸ APPL1: transaction data, transparent tables

▸ APPL2: organization and Customizing

▸ DDIM: dimension tables in SAP NetWeaver BW

▸ DFACT: fact tables in SAP NetWeaver BW

▸ DODS: operational data store (ODS) tables in SAP NetWeaver BW

▸ USER: customer data type

▸ USER1: customer data type

If you use separate tablespaces for the sake of database organization or performance, for example, a new data type can be introduced to ensure that the new table is stored in the new memory area. See SAP Note 46272 for a detailed description of how to do this in each DB management system.

Size category The size category determines the expected database space required by a table. A number of categories are available for this purpose in the input help, as listed below with details of the data record number. When you create the table, an initial memory space is reserved for it in the database. If the table requires more memory space later on, this is added in accordance with the size category. Selecting the correct size category prevents too many small extents (memory areas) of a table from being created and prevents memory space from being wasted by overly large extents.

- ► Table size < 500 K
- ► Table size < 1.5 MB
- ► Table size < 6.5 MB
- ► Table size < 25 MB
- ► Table size < 160 MB

Maintaining Parameters in the SAP NetWeaver BW System

You can maintain parameters for various tables in several locations in the SAP NetWeaver BW system:

- ► **PSA table**
  You can maintain the DB memory parameters for PSA tables in the DataSource maintenance function under GOTO • TECHNICAL ATTRIBUTES. In the data flow in SAP NetWeaver BW 3.x, this setting is located under EXTRAS • Maintain DB MEMORY PARAMETERS in the transfer rule maintenance menu.
  You can also assign memory parameters for an existing PSA table. However, this has no effect on the existing table. If changes to the DataSource cause the system to generate a new version of the PSA — that is, a new PSA table — this table is created in the data area of the current memory parameters.

- ► **InfoObject tables**
  You can maintain the database memory parameters for InfoObject tables under EXTRAS • MAINTAIN DB MEMORY PARAMETERS in the InfoObject maintenance menu.

- ► **Fact tables and dimension tables**
  You can maintain the database memory parameters for fact and dimension tables of InfoCubes or aggregates under EXTRAS • DB PERFORMANCE • MAINTAIN DB MEMORY PARAMETERS in the InfoCube maintenance menu.

- ► **DSO tables**
  You can maintain the database memory parameters for tables of the DSO object (activation queue and table for active data) under EXTRAS • DB PERFORMANCE • MAINTAIN DB MEMORY PARAMETERS in the DSO maintenance menu.

- ► **DTP error stack tables**
  You can maintain the database memory parameters for error stack tables under EXTRAS • ERROR STACK SETTINGS in the DTP maintenance menu.

You can view the memory parameters of any table — such as the fact tables of an InfoCube or PSA table — in the ABAP Dictionary (Transaction SE11) via the menu commend GOTO • TECHNICAL SETTINGS.

3.3 Buffering InfoObject Tables

InfoObjects with high cardinalities

As standard, the SID and master data tables in all InfoObjects have the technical settings Single Record Buffering and Buffering Active when they are created. These settings do not make sense for InfoObjects with very high cardinalities, because the individual tables of such InfoObjects occupy very large areas of the single record buffer in load processes, and the buffer is not designed to cope with such loads. Also, transferring in new records and reading records from the buffer become much slower if the number of full frames in the buffer increases. Another problem is the high number of synchronization records that have to be written when new entries are made in these tables. Therefore, it is necessary to switch off buffering for SID and master data tables (from 100,000 records) in the SAP Data Dictionary (DDIC).

Nonpermitted settings

It is crucial to note that you are not permitted to change the Single Record To Generic and Fully Buffered buffer settings, because this could lead to incorrect query results. Numeric columns in the generic buffer are the problem here. The binary search does not work if there are such columns in the buffer. The technical properties of the InfoObject tables are transferred from what are known as template tables when the tables are first created. You can change the technical settings of the tables of a specific characteristic directly in the Data Dictionary. Such changes are retained when the characteristic is reactivated. Alternatively, you can change the technical settings of the template table. These settings are then valid for all characteristics that are re-created from this point on. However, you still have to adapt the old tables individually.

You have to do this in all systems, because, with the exception of the data type and the size category, the technical settings of the InfoObject tables are not transported (the tables themselves are not transported either because they are created as local objects). The following template tables are used for characteristics.

Template tables

▸ RSDMSIDTAB for SID tables (/BIO/S<characteristic>)

▸ Text table /BIO/T<characteristic>: RSDMTXTTAB

- RSDMCHNTAB for non-time-specific master data tables (/BI0/P<characteristic>)

- RSDMCHTTAB for time-specific master data tables (/BI0/Q<characteristic>)

- RSDMCHKTAB for the views of master data tables (/BI0/M<characteristic>)

- RSDMASITAB for non-time-specific attribute SID tables (/BI0/X<characteristic>)

- RSDMASTTAB for time-specific attribute SID tables (/BI0/Y<characteristic>)

- RSDMSIDVIEW for the views of SIDs (/BI0/R<characteristic>)

- RSDMHIETAB for hierarchy tables (/BI0/H<characteristic>)

- RSDMHSITAB for hierarchy SID tables (/BI0/K<characteristic>)

- RSDMINCTAB for SID tables of the hierarchical structures (/BI0/I<characteristic>)

- RSDMHINTAB for hierarchy interval tables (/BI0/J<characteristic>)

- RSDMHSIVIEW for the views of hierarchy SIDs (/BI0/Z<characteristic>)

You can view the buffering data of the InfoObject tables in the ABAP Dictionary (Transaction SE11) via the menu path GOTO • TECHNICAL SETTINGS. If you are uncertain about the technical names of the tables of an InfoObject, you can check these easily in Transaction RSD1 and then go directly to the ABAP Dictionary by double-clicking the relevant table name (forward navigation).

3.4   DBA Cockpit

In SAP_BASIS SP 12, SAP provides the new DB monitor Transaction DBACOCKPIT, which combines the functions of the older Transactions ST04, DB02, DB12, and DB13 and other things, including the ABAP program MSSPROCS. The main benefits of the new transaction are improved functions, a more consistent user interface, and the option to remotely monitor multiple SAP and third-party databases from a central system (such as the SAP Solution Manager).

Database monitor

3.4.1 Database Monitoring and Administration

The DBA Cockpit provides a central point of entry that enables you to monitor and administrate DBs for all supported DB platforms. Start the DBA Cockpit by calling Transaction DBACOCKPIT or any of the DB administration transactions, such as ST04, DB02, or DB13. If you use a DB administration transaction to call the DBA Cockpit, this transaction determines the initial screen. In the navigation frame of the DBA Cockpit, you can navigate between the main areas of database administration:

- Performance (Transaction ST04)
- Space (Transaction DB02)
    - Backup and recovery (Transaction DB12))
    - Jobs (Transactions DB13, DB13C, DB24)
- Configuration
- Alerts
- Diagnosis

To monitor remote DBs via DB connections, you have to install the relevant DB client software and the DB-specific part of the SAP DBSL libraries (DB shared *library*). For up-to-date information on the DBA Cockpit and the requirements for monitoring remote systems, see SAP Note 1027146.

3.4.2 New Functions

The new Transaction DBACOCKPIT also contains some new functions:

- **DB monitoring** for all platforms
  You can configure all SAP-supported DBs using the remote DB connection in the DBA Cockpit. You can access this remote DB connection independently of the application that is running on your DB.

- **Integration with the System Landscape Directory (SLD)**
  You can configure the monitored systems and keep them up to date using the SLD instead of doing the configuration manually.

- **Integrated centralized scheduling calendar**
  The DBA Cockpit contains a new, centralized scheduling calendar (see Section 3.4.4, Postprocessing).

For the latest information on your DB platforms, see SAP Notes 1027336 (DB2 for Linux, UNIX, and Windows), 1028173 (DB2 for i5/OS), 1027452 (DB2 for z/OS), 1027512 (Microsoft SQL Server), and 1028624 (Oracle).

3.4.3 Restrictions

If you are using the new DBA Cockpit transactions without installing the associated program files and the relevant kernel, the following problems may arise:

▶ Some completely new actions may not run smoothly, because they are based on new functions that are provided by the underlying monitoring programs or kernel APIs.

▶ Some actions that replaced old functions may have no results, or faulty results, owing to incompatible changes to the underlying monitoring programs.

Potential problems

It is strongly recommended that you use the last available kernel patch.

3.4.4 Postprocessing

Usually, you have to adapt the new central scheduling calendar. This calendar is based on a completely new configuration and uses the system configuration in the DBA Cockpit. Proceed as follows to migrate the system configuration from the old, central calendar to the new calendar.

1. Start the DBA Cockpit and select Jobs • Central Calendar.

Adapt the calendar

2. Select Administration • Migrate DB13C Configuration in the central scheduling calendar. System configuration entries are created automatically. If the entries from Transaction DB13C are migrated on the basis of RFC destinations, you have to manually check whether the system configuration was created in full or whether you need to add or edit the relevant DB connection to complete it.

Other postprocessing is required to monitor remote databases by means of additional DB connections. In such as case, you have to install the relevant DB client software and the DB-specific part of the SAP DBSL libraries.

3.5 Provider-Specific Information

Special features of
the database
platforms
Detailed information on all of the activities and technical background of the different DB platforms is outside the scope of this book. However, we would like to make you aware of some special features that are of interest in the context of administrating BW systems.

3.5.1 Database Management Systems DB2, DB4, and DB6

IBM sells the database management system DB2 for various platforms:

- There is the product line for IBM mainframes, on which the operating system VSE (Virtual Storage Extended) led to the development of MVS (Multiple Virtual Storage), and OS/390 ultimately led to the development of the system for z/OS.

- Another product line was originally designed for the OS/2 operating system. This software is written in C and was the basis for the variants of the operating systems Linux, Unix, and Windows.

In the SAP environment, DB2 for OS/390 is referred to as *DB2*, DB2 for AS/400 or iSeries as *DB4,* and DB2 for Windows/UNIX as *DB6*.

3.5.2 IBM DB2 RUNSTATS

RUNSTATS is the DB2 tool for creating statistical data on the content of tables and their indexes. For example, it calculates the minimum and maximum values of a column and the cardinality of the columns and the table. This data is stored in the DB2 system catalog. This catalog is a collection of tables in which DB2 information on all objects, such as tables, indexes, columns, and so on, is stored.

Optimal access
path
This statistical data is used to determine the optimal access path for the table accesses (for example, it does not usually make sense to use index accesses if the entire table contains only a few rows). Besides the access path information that is important for the database optimizer, administration data is also compiled, such as the quota of used memory pages or the compression level. You should always use RUNSTATS when table content undergoes significant changes or when new indexes are created.

Additional entries
In some cases, you have to make additional entries in the DB2 catalog to guarantee that the optimal access path is calculated. However, these additional entries are usually overwritten when RUNSTATS, which is

controlled by the SAP NetWeaver BW system, is run. There is a solution to this problem that is supported by the following index-specific RSADMIN parameters:

▶ Modify the cluster ratio of an index.

- ▶ Syntax: `DB2_<index name> = CLUSTERRATIO x`
- ▶ Example: `DB2_/BIC/FMYCUBE~030 = CLUSTERRATIO 100`

▶ Modify the NLEVELS of an index.

- ▶ Syntax: `DB2_<index name> = NLEVELS x`
- ▶ Example: `DB2_/BIC/FMYCUBE~030 = NLEVELS 4`

▶ Collect additional frequencies for an index.

- ▶ Syntax: `DB2_<index name> = FREQVAL NUMCOLS n COUNT c`
- ▶ Example: `DB2_/BIC/DMYDIMT~0 = FREQVAL NUMCOLS 5 COUNT 30`

▶ Collect additional frequencies for all indexes of a table.

- ▶ Syntax: `DB2_<table name>~ALL = FREQVAL NUMCOLS n COUNT c`
- ▶ Example: `DB2_/BIC/DMYDIMT~ALL = FREQVAL NUMCOLS 5 COUNT 30`

▶ Modify the frequency of a value.

- ▶ Syntax: `DB2_<table name> = DIST <column> <value> <frequency>`
- ▶ Example: `DB2_/BIC/SMYSID = DIST SID 42 0.10`

When the above-mentioned parameters are set, either the DB2 tool for the associated object is executed with the required option, or the DB2 catalog is updated accordingly after RUNSTATS is run.

Likewise, the relevant `UPDATE` statements in the DB2 statistics table with the function module `RSDU_ANALYZE_TABLE_DB2` and the associated `I_SHOW_RUNSTATS_PROTOCOL = X` parameter are tested and displayed.

3.5.3 RSADMIN Parameter for IBM DB2

Some IBM-specific parameters are explained in detail below.

DB6_DELETE_PIECEWISE and DBMS_MAX_DELETE

In the standard configuration, InfoCube data requests are deleted by a single `SQL DELETE` statement. Now, InfoCube data requests can be deleted one by one using multiple `SQL DELETE` statements (piecewise deletion). This ensures that the database space required for the deletion log does not get too big.

The RSADMIN parameter DB6_DELETE_PIECEWISE enables you to select the piecewise deletion method. If you set the value to YES, the InfoCube data request is deleted by means of multiple statements, and every statement deletes a maximum of 100,000 records. You can overwrite this standard value by setting the RSADMIN parameter DBMS_MAX_DELETE to a different value. Use this deletion method when InfoPackages are to be deleted and there is not enough log space.

Standard delete method

If you set the value to NO, the InfoCube data request is deleted using an SQL delete statement. This is also the standard delete method when the parameter DB6_DELETE_PIECEWISE is not defined in table RSADMIN.

DB6_COMPRESS_PARALLEL

Database performance can be improved if you use intrapartition parallelism for compressing requests. If parameter DB6_COMPRESS_PARALLEL is active, the DB2 register current degree is set to "any" before a request is compressed. This means that the DB2 optimizer can processes the SQL statements in parallel. A prerequisite of parallel processing, however, is that parameter INTRA_PARALLEL is set in the DB manager.

Usually, performance will improve only if the number of CPUs is greater than the number of database partitions across which the fact table is distributed.

DB6_PINDEX_ON_FTABLE

From release SAP NetWeaver BW 7.0, the P index of the F fact table is by default not created when new InfoCubes are activated. If you still want the P index of the F fact table to be created, set parameter DB6_PINDEX_ON_FTABLE to YES.

DB6_SAMPLED_INDEX_STATS

Index statistics: samples

You use this parameter to determine whether the index statistics that were used as samples should be entered. The default value of this parameter is NO, which means that the full version of the index statistics are entered. If you do want to enter index statistics that were used as samples, set this parameter value to YES.

Statistics that are used as samples are a DB2 function that has been available since version 8.2 of DB2 Universal DB (DB2 UDB).

DB6_SAMPLED_TABLE_STATS

You use this parameter to determine the sample rate for the table data statistics. The default value of this parameter is 100, which means that no data samples are used. If you do want to use data samples, set the parameter to a value between 1 and 99. This parameter is used as the lower limit for data samples when the fact table statistics are entered during SAP NetWeaver BW operations, such as loading data, deleting data, and compression.

Data samples

3.5.4 Statistics in Microsoft SQL Server

Microsoft SQL Server automatically updates the table statistics when you set the database options auto create statistics and auto update statistics. However, an exception to this is very small tables (a few hundred rows) in which no new statistics are created automatically and no existing statistics are updated. This behavior on the part of Microsoft SQL Server is deliberate and does not normally cause any problems, because a small table requires only a small number of pages, and all possible access paths are therefore short. In reality, the lack of statistics on small tables means that no performance problems have occurred with OLTP systems.

For star joins in SAP NetWeaver BW systems (and, correspondingly, in systems that are based on SAP NetWeaver BW, such as SAP APO), however, the SQL Server Query Optimizer requires statistical information on the dimension tables to be able to select the appropriate index for accessing the fact table and the best join method. Joining very small tables with very large ones is a typical scenario in SAP NetWeaver BW systems when processing star joins, and this is where the standard system behavior often runs into problems.

Star joins

There is a standard SAP NetWeaver BW functionality for SQL Server to deal with these problems. You can use this functionality to schedule statistics update jobs, for both large and small dimension tables. For older releases, a correction is available; see SAP Note 783750.

The Create Statistics (batch) and Refresh Statistics buttons on the Performance tab page in the InfoCube administration function are used to update statistics.

The required buttons are hidden in the standard installation on Microsoft SQL Server; simply run the ABAP report RSDD_MSSQL_PROG_01 to show them.

3.6 Backup and Recovery Strategies

In every production system, regular backup copies of the operating system and the database have to be made to ensure that the SAP system can be restored, if necessary. One of the most important tasks of the system and database administrator is to implement a suitable backup and recovery concept. There is no general recommendation on what concept to use, because the issue depends on a variety of factors, including the following:

Factors
- Disaster recovery concept
- Maximum permitted downtime during recovery
- Maximum permitted data loss
- Available budget

But what effects does a backup and recovery concept have in a system landscape that is connected to an SAP NetWeaver BW system? In other words, what effects does it have on the SAP NetWeaver BW system, on the source systems, and on data consistency across all of the systems involved?

As a general rule, you should consider importing a backup with an incomplete recovery into an SAP NetWeaver BW system or a connected source system only if there is no way to fully restore the system or switch to an identically run system. In doing so, you have to differentiate between hardware problems and logical errors. For hardware problems, you have no other choice but to import the kind of incomplete backup referred to above, but with logical errors (for example, incorrectly deleted data in the application), this step is not recommended. Importing a backup into an SAP NetWeaver BW system or a connected source system can lead to serious inconsistencies in the delta process, and the likelihood of the occurrence of such inconsistencies increases in line with the amount of time that has elapsed since the time of the recovery.

We would now like to introduce you to application-based solutions. These are an alternative to backups on the one hand and the data import procedure, should you decide to use it, on the other. You should analyze these solutions separately for consistency and required resources, in accordance with the individual problem.

Alternatives to Importing the Backup

If, for example, you want to restore the data of a table, it may be sufficient to copy the data of this table from a backup. Ideally, you will have what is known as a standby database that you can use to restore the system status from multiple days. To use this functionality for troubleshooting, you probably need in-depth knowledge of the relevant application. Also, the checking process can involve a llot of manual work.

Standby databases are not a standalone concept; they simply make this manual work faster, simpler, and more flexible. However, all other things being equal, you could also do this using tape backups. The main thing here is that in production systems, only individual tables (and sometimes only some of these) are reset to the status they had before the error occurred and that you are absolutely sure which tables and transactions are affected by the error. Each customer is strongly advised to consult SAP in this matter.

Backups in the SAP NetWeaver BW System

If you import a backup from a specific point in the past (backup time) into the SAP NetWeaver BW system, requests that were loaded since this point in time will no longer exist in the system. However, in the delta queue of the source system, the data from the last load process was deleted with every new data request. In the delta queue of the source system, it is not possible to restore the status that existed at the backup time of the SAP NetWeaver BW system.

Therefore, you usually have to reinitialize all DataSources to which delta data has been added since the backup time. The option of reloading the data by repeating the delta data request and thus restoring a consistent data state is available, but only in cases where delta data has been loaded just once since backup time. To do this, you have to set the last executed data request to the status "red" in the monitor and then repeat the request. When doing this, remember that this procedure is not transparent in the monitoring function. To be sure about which load process is the second-last one, you should make a careful note of the times of the last and second-last requests before running a backup recovery process. If you can uniquely identify the missing data, it is sometimes possible to use a full data extraction that is independent of the delta download with the relevant selection to synchronize the dataset in the SAP NetWeaver BW system with the source system.

Repeat the delta data request

It is also possible in certain cases to ensure that the delta data request is consistent in relation to the backup time by adapting the internal data administration (usually time stamps) of special extractors. However, note that this is a useful solution only when a single SAP NetWeaver BW system is used, because the time stamp administration function is independent of the SAP NetWeaver BW system.

Reinitialization

If you have to carry out a reinitialization, we recommend that you restrict this to the dataset that cannot be described as static. (An example of static data is data from the previous year, in other words, data that can no longer be changed in the delta queue of the source system.) It is possible to carry out a reinitialization process if the DataSource has a suitable selection. Proceed as follows:

1. Delete the dataset to be reinitialized from all data rows.

2. Carry out a full or selective reinitialization.

3. For time-based selections, set the upper interval in the InfoPackage to "infinite."

In some cases, it may be necessary to stop all updates in the source system. The static data should also be transferred to the SAP NetWeaver BW system by means of a full data extraction.

Source System Backups

A source system backup resets the delta queue in the source system to its previous state. Data that was already transferred to the SAP NetWeaver BW system no longer exists in the source system after the backup. It is often possible in the case of a correction to locate the requests that have been loaded into the SAP NetWeaver BW system since backup time and to delete these in all data rows. Any subsequent delta data request would then create a consistent dataset in the SAP NetWeaver BW system, and the data problem would therefore be solved. However, this step involves a lot of manual effort and requires great care. If you decide against this step, you will have to reinitialize the delta download as described above.

A basic understanding of the technologies that are relevant for system connections (for example, IDocs) is indispensable to an SAP NetWeaver BW administrator, in particular when it comes to managing and monitoring loading processes at the required quality level. This chapter is devoted to describing key aspects of these technologies.

4   System Connections and Access

As a data warehouse, SAP NetWeaver BW is highly interconnected with other systems. It is usually connected to several source systems while also acting as a source system for data marts. Because changes to one system within a source system–SAP NetWeaver BW group also affect all connected systems, they cannot be examined in isolation. A connection between a source system and SAP NetWeaver BW consists of a series of individual connections and settings made in both systems:

Data marts

▸ RFC connections

▸ ALE settings

  ▸ Partner agreements

  ▸ Port

  ▸ IDoc types

  ▸ IDoc segments

▸ BW settings

This chapter discusses these connections and the corresponding settings.

4.1   SAP NetWeaver BW Source Systems

You can make general Customizing settings that are relevant for the connections between source systems and the SAP NetWeaver BW system in the SAP NetWeaver BW Customizing Implementation Guide

under BUSINESS INFORMATION WAREHOUSE • CONNECTIONS TO OTHER
SYSTEMS.

4.1.1   Creating Source Systems

Once you have made the required configurations the SAP NetWeaver
BW system and in the source system, you can create the source system
in the Data Warehousing Workbench (Transaction RSA1) (Figure 4.1).

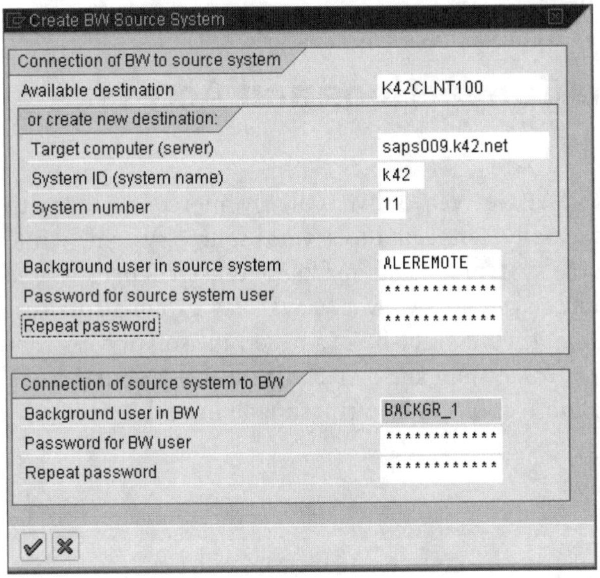

Figure 4.1   Creating a Source System

Creating a
source system

Select Create from the context menu of the BI or SAP folder in the
source system tree of the Data Warehousing Workbench. Select the destination for the SAP source system if it has already been created. Otherwise, enter the details of the application server (Target Host (Server))
after you check these in the source system, as well as the system ID and
the system number.

Assign a password for the Background User in The Source System and
confirm this password in the second input line. If the user already
exists in the source system, enter the valid password. For the Background User in BW, enter and confirm the password you defined in

the Implementation Guide under SAP NETWEAVER • BUSINESS INTEL-LIGENCE • CONNECTIONS TO OTHER SYSTEMS • CONNECTION BETWEEN SAP SYSTEMS AND BW • MAINTAIN PROPOSAL FOR USERS IN THE SOURCE SYSTEM (ALE COMMUNICATION).

Once you have maintained and confirmed this data, the RFC destination for the SAP NetWeaver BW system and the background user are created automatically, and you can then log on to the source system directly. It is very important that you test the RFC destination — in particular if it already existed, and you did not create it as a new destination.

The destination created here is ultimately used for the background creation of the ALE settings required for an SAP NetWeaver BW system to communicate with an SAP source system. These settings are stored in both SAP NetWeaver BW and the source system.

Once you have created the new SAP source system, the metadata is requested automatically from the source system. The metadata for DataSources in the D version is also replicated to the SAP NetWeaver BW system.

Source System Administration

If you have made the basic settings and you want, for example, to check the connections to all source systems, but it would take to much time to do this in the Data Warehousing Workbench owing to the large number of systems involved, you can select the menu option TOOLS • SOURCE SYSTEM ADMINISTRATION to check the connections centrally (Figure 4.2).

In addition to checking source system connections, you can perform activations and replications here. A traffic light icon indicates whether the last tasks you executed were completed successfully or failed. More detailed information about each operation is written to an SLG1 log, which you can display under EDIT • LOG.

Activations and replications

Before you can activate source systems in this transaction, an RFC connection must already be set up. Source systems can be reactivated in this transaction. When you activate source systems, the source system connections are first checked automatically.

Check Source Systems

Source system	Type	Description	Activation Sta	Check	Activate	Replicate	Task Status	Date of La	Time of La
D46CLNT100		D46 Client 100	▢	☐	☐	☐	∞	2009.10.10	13:34:52
D47CLNT100		D47 Client 100	▢	☐	☐	☐	∞		
DX1CLNT100		DX1 client 100 CRM	▢	☐	☐	☐	∞		
S37CLNT100		S37 Client 100	▢	☐	☐	☐	∞		
BRUDFILE		Files from BRUD	▢	☐	☐	▢	∞		
PC_FILE		PC Files	▢	☐	☐	▢	∞		
PC_FILETT		Flat Files	▢	☐	☐	▢	∞		
PSI_FILE		PSI files from vendo	▢	☐	☐	▢	∞		
QUOTATION		Quotation data file	▢	☐	☐	▢	∞		

Figure 4.2 Administration of Source Systems

It is also possible to replicate the DataSources of the selected source systems here. Note, however, that you cannot replicate DataSources for database source systems or file source systems. You can check and activate all source systems and replicate their DataSources (if replication is permitted for the source system type) provided that you have set all of the indicators under EDIT • SELECT ALL.

4.1.2 Logical System Name

Owing to the distribution of data between systems, each system within a network must be uniquely identifiable. The logical system name is used for this purpose. A logical system is an application system within which applications interact on a shared data basis. In an SAP context, a logical system corresponds to a client.

Because the logical system name uniquely identifies a system within a system group, no two systems can have the same name if they are connected or are to be connected with each other either directly or indirectly as SAP NetWeaver BW or source systems. However, because it is recommended that you do not create a connection between test systems and production systems, a test system can have the same name as a production system. This greatly simplifies the process of copying production systems to test systems. Changes to the logical system name are only permitted if the system is not connected to other systems because a name change would mean that none of these connections could be used.

Maintaining the logical system name
You can make settings for the logical system name in the SAP NetWeaver BW Customizing Implementation Guide under BUSINESS INFORMATION WAREHOUSE • CONNECTIONS TO OTHER SYSTEMS • GENERAL CONNECTION

SETTINGS. In the source system, you will find the settings for the logical system in the IMG under CROSS-APPLICATION COMPONENTS • DISTRIBUTION (ALE) • BASIC SETTINGS.

4.1.3 Maintaining Source System IDs

The source system ID (characteristic 0SOURSYSTEM) is a two-digit ID for an individual source system or a group of source systems, and can be maintained in the Data Warehousing Workbench (Transaction RSA1) under TOOLS • ASSIGNMENT OF SOURCE SYSTEM TO SOURCE SYSTEM ID.

For example, the master data that is stored in the SAP NetWeaver BW system and is unique to a source system can be compounded with the source system ID characteristic. In this way, you can keep identical characteristic values that refer to different objects in various systems separate from one another. The characteristic is updated with the ID of the relevant source system in each case. If you use this characteristic, it is therefore essential that you assign an ID to the source system in question. Otherwise, errors occur when master data is loaded for the characteristics that use 0SOURSYSTEM as an attribute or in compounding.

You can only delete an existing source system ID assignment if it is no longer used in the master or transaction data. Use the Release IDs that are not in use function to check this. Note, however, that this is a time-consuming process, so this check may take a long time to complete.

Deleting existing assignments

4.2 IDoc, ALE, RFC, and Similar Technology

An understanding of the middleware and interface technology is absolutely essential to the analysis of processes during data extraction from an SAP source system.

4.2.1 RFC and tRFC

Communication between applications from different systems in the SAP environment may involve a connection between SAP systems and other SAP systems or non-SAP systems. The remote function call (RFC) is the SAP standard interface for implementing this communication. The RFC calls a function that is to be executed in a remote system.

Transactional RFC

Unlike asynchronous RFC (aRFC), transactional RFC (tRFC, originally also referred to as asynchronous RFC) is a truly asynchronous method of communication, which executes the function module called in the RFC server exactly once. Despite its name, aRFC is not a truly asynchronous type of communication, because it does not fulfill all of the conditions for this. For example, the system that is called must be available when the call is executed, as is also the case with synchronous RFC (sRFC). The remote system does not need to be available when the RFC client program executes a tRFC. The tRFC component stores the RFC function that is called, together with the corresponding data, in the SAP database with a unique transaction ID (TID). If the remote system is unavailable when the call is executed, the call remains in the local queue. The calling dialog program can then proceed without waiting to see whether the remote call has been successful. If the remote system is not activated within a certain period of time, the call is scheduled as a background job. A tRFC is always used if a function is to be executed as a logical unit of work (LUW). Within an LUW, all calls are then executed in the sequence in which they are called within a single transaction. It is therefore useful to use tRFC whenever you want to preserve the transactional sequence of the calls.

Queued RFC

Queued RFC (qRFC) is an enhancement of tRFC, which ensures that LUWs are also processed in the order specified by the application.

4.2.2 IDoc Interface

The *IDoc* (intermediate document) interface is used for the exchange of business data with a third-party system. The IDoc interface consists of the definition of a data structure (the IDoc) and the processing logic for this structure. It therefore represents the exchange format agreed upon between the systems that are in communication with one another. Content, structure, sender, recipient, and status are defined in the IDoc header data.

SAP Business
Workflow

With IDocs, you can use SAP Business Workflow to define exception handling within the SAP system without the data having to exist in the form of an SAP application document. You can use IDoc interfaces in the following scenarios:

▸ Electronic data interchange (EDI)

- The coupling of any other business application systems (for example, PC applications or external workflow tools) with IDocs
- Application Link Enabling (ALE)

In this way, an IDoc serves as a vehicle for data transfer, for example, in an ALE system. The status values for outbound IDocs are numbered 01 to 49, whereas those for inbound IDocs start at 50. All possible status values are listed in Table 4.1.

IDoc status	Meaning
1	Not used, only R/2
2	Error passing data to port
3	Data passed to port OK
4	Error within control information of EDI subsystem
5	Error during translation
6	Translation OK
7	Error during syntax check
8	Syntax check OK
9	Error during interchange handling
10	Interchange handling OK
11	Error during dispatch
12	Dispatch OK
13	Retransmission OK
14	Interchange acknowledgment positive
15	Interchange acknowledgment negative
16	Functional acknowledgment positive
17	Functional acknowledgment negative
18	Triggering EDI subsystem OK
19	Data transfer for test OK
20	Error triggering EDI subsystem
21	Error passing data for test
22	Dispatch OK, acknowledgment still due
23	Error during retransmission
24	Control information of EDI subsystem OK
25	Processing despite syntax error (outbound)

Table 4.1 Statuses of Inbound and Outbound IDocs

IDoc status	Meaning
26	Error during syntax check of IDoc (outbound)
27	Error in dispatch level (ALE service)
28	IDoc sent to ALE distribution unit retroactively
29	Error in ALE service
30	IDoc ready for dispatch (ALE service)
31	Error, no further processing
32	IDoc was edited
33	Original of an IDoc that was edited
34	Error in control record of IDoc
35	IDoc reloaded from archive
36	Electronic signature not performed (timeout)
37	IDoc added incorrectly
38	IDoc archived
39	IDoc is in the target system (ALE service)
40	Application document not created in target system
41	Application document created in target system
42	IDoc was created by test transaction
50	IDoc added
51	Application document not posted
52	Application document not fully posted
53	Application document posted
54	Error during formal application check
55	Formal application check OK
56	IDoc with errors added
57	Test IDoc: error during application check
58	IDoc copy from R/2 connection
59	Not used
60	Error during syntax check of IDoc (inbound)
61	Processing despite syntax error (inbound)
62	IDoc passed to application
63	Error passing IDoc to application
64	IDoc ready to be transferred to application
65	Error in ALE service

Table 4.1 Statuses of Inbound and Outbound IDocs (Cont.)

IDoc status	Meaning
66	IDoc is waiting for predecessor IDoc (serialization)
67	Not used
68	Error, no further processing
69	IDoc was edited
70	Original of an IDoc that was edited
71	IDoc reloaded from archive
72	Not used, only R/2
73	IDoc archived
74	IDoc was created by test transaction
75	IDoc is in inbound queue

Table 4.1 Statuses of Inbound and Outbound IDocs (Cont.)

4.2.3 Application Link Enabling

ALE (ALE) is a means of creating and operating distributed applications. The basic purpose of ALE is to ensure a distributed yet integrated SAP system installation. This involves business-controlled message exchange with consistent data storage across loosely linked SAP applications. This is possible because the applications are integrated not through a central database, but through synchronous and asynchronous communication. Local databases are used, with the result that data storage is redundant. ALE enables the distribution and synchronization of master data, control data, and transaction data through asynchronous communication. ALE offers a host of benefits:

- Distribution of application data between SAP systems with different release versions
- Data exchange after a release upgrade without subsequent maintenance
- Customer-specific enhancements
- Connection of non-SAP systems using communication interfaces

Benefits of using ALE

The IDoc provides a basis for message distribution. IDocs are generated and sent when you use distribution based on method types or based on SAP business object methods (Business Application Programming Interfaces [BAPIs]). When you define a new source system and the corresponding RFC connection in a SAP NetWeaver BW system, the ALE settings required for the SAP NetWeaver BW system to communicate with an SAP source system are created in the background. These settings are stored in both the SAP NetWeaver BW system and the source system.

Basic process flow

An IDoc containing the data to be transferred is generated in the source system, formatted for transfer and, finally, sent to the target system. In the target system, the IDoc triggers inbound processing. Specifically, the data is processed either automatically or with manual interim steps (depending on the settings) until it is updated in the application. IDocs can be processed in inbound or outbound processing either individually or as a package. With mass processing, several IDocs are processed together as a package in a single step.

Delta for master data

Delta management with ALE change pointers is also of interest in the SAP NetWeaver BW environment. For some types of master data, changes to master data objects are logged using change pointers. If a master data record is relevant for distribution, the application writes a change document, and the contents of this document are transferred to the shared master data (SMD)) tool. Whenever a change is made that is relevant for a DataSource, a change pointer of a specific message type is written to the BDCPV2 table.

4.2.4 IDoc Communication During Data Extraction

Data extraction from an SAP source system is usually a pull mechanism; in other words, Sap NetWeaver BW requests the data for extraction. In terms of communication between SAP NetWeaver BW and the source system, this means that a request IDoc is initially sent from the SAP NetWeaver BW system to the source system. The data is then extracted in the source system and transferred to the SAP NetWeaver BW system. During this transfer, additional information is constantly exchanged in the form of info IDocs. For example, these info IDocs convey information about the extracted data, details of the DataSource, package numbers, and the number of data records involved. Table 4.2 shows the various statuses an info IDoc can have (request statuses).

Info IDoc Status	Meaning
0	Data request received
1	Data selection started
2	Data selection running
5	Error in data selection
6	Obsolete transfer structure
8	No data available, data selection ended
9	Data selection ended

Table 4.2 Status of an Info IDoc (Request Status)

To display the individual IDocs relating to an extraction in the data load monitor, select Goto • ALE Administration • In the Data Warehouse or In the Source System. The specific steps involved in the communication that takes place during data extraction are as follows: When an InfoPackage is executed, the request IDoc is sent to ALE inbound processing in the source system (Figure 4.3). This IDoc contains various pieces of information, including the request ID (REQUEST), the request date (REQDATE), the request time (REQTIME), the InfoSource (ISOURCE), and the update mode (UPDMODE). The source system confirms to the SAP NetWeaver BW system that the request IDoc has been received using an info IDoc (RSINFO) with the status 0 (data request received) or 5 (error during data extraction).

Communication during data extraction

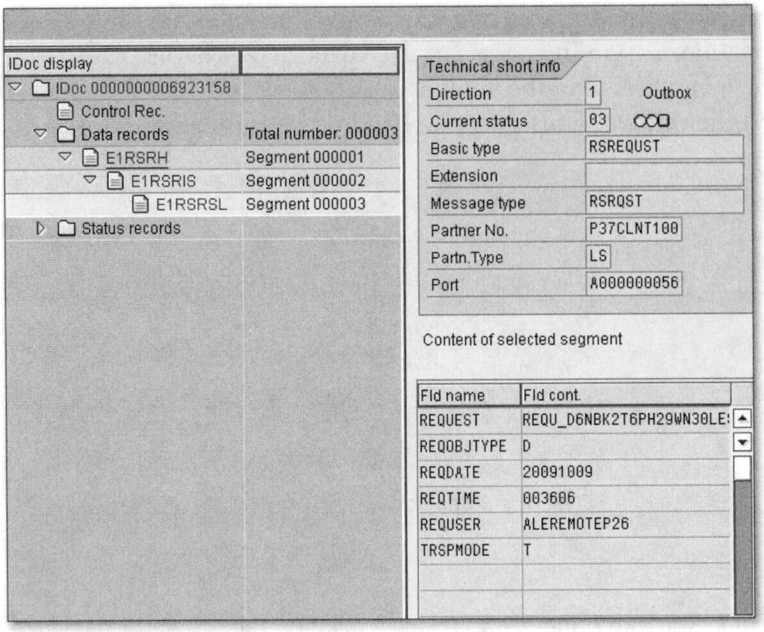

Figure 4.3 Request IDoc in the Source System

Start of the extraction process

As soon as the source system has successfully received the request IDoc, the process of extracting the data in accordance with the information specified in the IDoc can begin. Usually, a single batch job, following the naming convention BIREQ*, is started (Figure 4.4). The request IDoc is assigned the status 53 (application document posted) to ensure that this IDoc is not processed any further. Another IDoc with request status 1 confirms to the SAP NetWeaver BW system that the extraction process has begun.

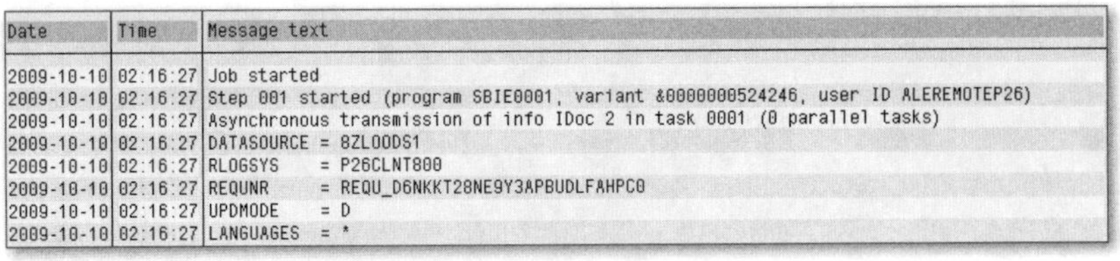

Figure 4.4 Request Batch Job in the Source System

Data package

The extracted data is finally sent to the SAP NetWeaver BW system in data packages using tRFCs. Information about the request number and the corresponding number of data records is transferred using an info IDoc with request status 2 (data selection running) (Figure 4.5).

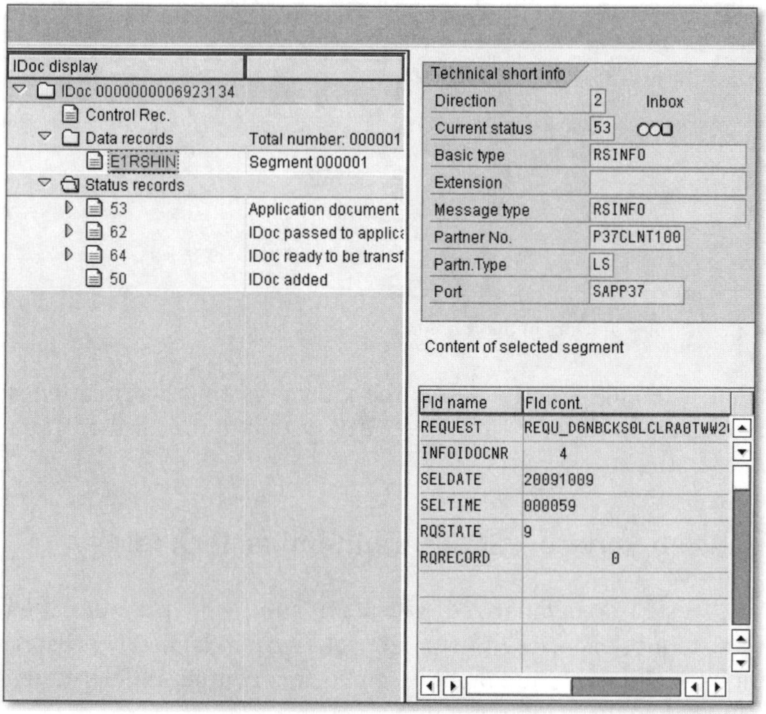

IDoc display	
▽ ☐ IDoc 000000006923134	
📄 Control Rec.	
▽ ☐ Data records	Total number: 000001
📄 E1RSHIN	Segment 000001
▽ ☐ Status records	
▷ 📄 53	Application document
▷ 📄 62	IDoc passed to applic:
▷ 📄 64	IDoc ready to be transf
📄 50	IDoc added

Technical short info

Direction	2	Inbox
Current status	53	∞
Basic type	RSINFO	
Extension		
Message type	RSINFO	
Partner No.	P37CLNT100	
Partn.Type	LS	
Port	SAPP37	

Content of selected segment

Fld name	Fld cont.
REQUEST	REQU_D6NBCKS0LCLRA0TWW2
INFOIDOCNR	4
SELDATE	20091009
SELTIME	000059
RQSTATE	9
RQRECORD	0

Figure 4.5   Info IDoc Indicating the Number of Data Records

When the extraction process is completed — in other words, when all of the requested data has been extracted and transferred to the SAP NetWeaver BW system — one last info IDoc is sent. This IDoc has request status 9 and confirms a successful loading process.

You can also trace the individual IDocs in the data load monitor directly (Figure 4.6). In our example, info IDoc number 2007015 with info status 2 first confirms that 1,466 data records have been sent (see above). Info IDoc 2007016 with info status 9 then confirms that the loading process has been completed.

Data load monitor

Monitor - Administrator Workbench

2009-10-06	Header	Status	Details
2009-10-07		
2009-10-08	Overall status: Everything OK
2009-10-09	Requests (messages): Everything OK
P37CLNT100 (P37 Client 100)	Extraction (messages): Everything OK
00:00:02 (1130 From 1130 Records)	Transfer (IDocs and TRFC): Everything OK
00:00:17 (533 From 533 Records)	Request IDoc : Application document posted
00:00:32 (837 From 837 Records)	Info IDoc 1 : Application document posted
00:00:55 (17 From 17 Records)	Info IDoc 4 : Application document posted
00:01:28 (864 From 864 Records)	Info IDoc 3 : Application document posted
00:01:47 (1036 From 1036 Records)	Info IDoc 2 : Application document posted
00:02:53 (1138 From 1138 Records)	Data IDoc 1 : (1130 Records) Application document posted
00:05:10 (827 From 827 Records)	Processing (data packet): Everything OK
23:46:32 (13 From 13 Records)	Subseq. processing (messages) : No errors
23:47:26 (9 From 9 Records)	Process Chains : Everything OK
23:48:45 (994 From 994 Records)	

Figure 4.6 Display of IDocs in the Monitor

If no data is found for extraction in the source system, this situation is communicated to the SAP NetWeaver BW system in the form of IDocs with the status 8.

4.3 Web Services, SOAP, and Similar Technology

A Web service is a modularized, executable unit, which can be called across system boundaries in heterogeneous system landscapes. Based on a number of transferred input parameters, an output is determined and returned to the calling program.

SAP NetWeaver implements the basic standards for Web services, namely, Extensible Markup Language (XML), SOAP, Web Service Definition Language (WSDL) and Universal Description, Discovery, and Integration (UDDI).

Communication with other providers

SOAP defines the lightweight protocol for XML-based information exchanged between partners in a distributed environment. SOAP Version 1.2 supports essential functions for communicating with other providers of Web services.

4.3.1 SOA Manager

As of SAP NetWeaver 7.0 Support Package 14, new service definitions that are created in the ABAP development environment are managed in the SOA Manager (Transaction SOAMANAGER), rather than in Transactions WSADMIN and WSCONFIG, as was previously the case. Transactions WSADMIN and WSCONFIG will remain active until the migration of old Web service configurations is completed and will enable the continued configuration of Web services from old versions. These transactions will also allow you to continue using runtime configurations of old service definitions. However, service definitions that are newly created in the ABAP development environment are hidden in these transactions. Web services and Web service clients are configured and monitored in the new SOA Manager (Figure 4.7).

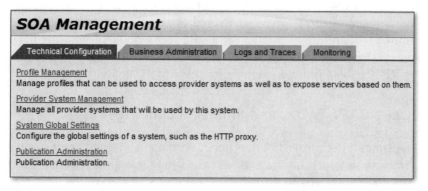

Figure 4.7 SOA Manager

4.3.2 Data Transfer Using Web Services

Data is normally transferred to the SAP NetWeaver BW system using a data request sent from SAP NetWeaver BW to the source system (pull from the scheduler). However, you can also use Web services for externally controlled sending of data to the inbound layer of the SAP NetWeaver BW system, the Persistent Staging Area (PSA). In this case, we refer to a data push into the SAP NetWeaver BW system.

If you use Web services to transfer data into the SAP NetWeaver BW system, you can use real-time data acquisition (RDA; for information about monitoring, refer to Section 12.1.10, Real-Time Data Acquisition, in Chapter 12) for further updating of the data in the SAP NetWeaver BW system. Alternatively, you can update the data using a standard data transfer process.

Push-Package   In SAP NetWeaver 7.0 you create Web services for data loading by activating a DataSource defined in the SAP NetWeaver BW system. When you activate this DataSource, the system generates a PSA table and a transfer program. Before data for the DataSource can be loaded into the SAP NetWeaver BW system using Web services, you must create a corresponding InfoPackage (referred to as a push package). If an InfoPackage exists for the DataSource, you can test the Web service push in Web service administration.

SOAP-based data transfers are still supported in data models with SAP NetWeaver BW 3.x objects, but RDA cannot be used. In this case, the delta queue of the service API is used as an inbound queue. A DataSource is therefore generated for a data transfer based on a file data source that has an interface with the delta queue. The system generates an RFC-enabled function module for this XML DataSource.

4.4   BAPI, MDX, and Similar Technology

Implementation projects often begin with a certain degree of uncertainty as to which interface is best used to access an SAP NetWeaver BW system externally. In the early days of SAP NetWeaver BW 1.x, this was still a simple question to answer because the only interface available was the Object Linking and Embedding Database for Online Analytical Processing (OLE DB for OLAP). However, as early as BW SAP NetWeaver 2.x, SAP added the OLAP-BAPI interface, which many developers preferred. Finally, XML for Analysis (XMLA) was added in SAP NetWeaver BW 3.x, and uncertainty began to grow.

MDX processor   Whereas each of these interfaces is very different, for example, in terms of the platforms they support, they all use Multidimensional Expressions (MDX) as a command language to access the SAP NetWeaver BW system data, and all therefore use the MDX processor in the SAP NetWeaver BW system. In this way, monitoring of MDX statements provides a basis for performance analyses by an administrator, for example. As a result, when it comes analyzing the performance of third-party tools or customer-developed frontends, the execution of the MDX statement is identical in all cases, and the tools differ only in the way they generate the statement (is it geared as far as possible to meet the requirements of the SAP NetWeaver BW system and BW objects?) and process the data.

The only exceptions among the various access options are the SAP BEx tools, which do not use any of the interfaces specified above and do not use the MDX processor. Table 4.3 lists the transactions that are relevant for MDX and for these interfaces.

Exception: BEx tools

Transaction/Tool	Description
SICF	Service administration
MDXTEST	Direct execution of MDX statements
BAPI	BAPI interface administration
RSBB_URL_PREFIX_GET	This function module provides details of the generated URL, including protocol, server and port.

Table 4.3 Key Tools and Transactions for MDX

4.4.1 MDX

MDX is a query language developed by Microsoft for retrieving multidimensional data (see Listing 4.1). An MDX expression returns a multidimensional dataset consisting of axis data and cell data. The syntax for MDXs is defined in the Microsoft "OLE DB for OLAP" specification.

```
SELECT
  { [Measures].[0D_DOCUMENT],
    [Measures].[0D_OORVALSC]
  } ON COLUMNS,
NON EMPTY
  [0D_PLANT].MEMBERS
ON ROWS
FROM [$0D_SD_C03]
WHERE
  ( [0CALMONTH].[200101],
  [0D_COUNTRY].[US] )
```

Listing 4.1 Listing 4.1 Example of an MDX Statement

Direct access
In an SAP NetWeaver BW system, you can use MDX statements to access InfoCubes and MultiProviders directly. However, it is generally recommended that you use queries for this purpose instead.

4.4.2 OLE DB for OLAP

OLE DB for OLAP (OLE DB for Online Analytical Processing) is an interface specification for database-independent access to relational and multidimensional data. In this standard defined by Microsoft (and therefore only available on Windows platforms), OLE DB and ADO (ActiveX Data Objects) represent the core of universal data access for accessing data in various formats using the same technology. An example of how this applies in practice is OLE DB for Microsoft Excel 2007, which allows Excel to access an SAP NetWeaver BW system directly to analyze the data in a pivot table in that system. In this case, users work in Excel and require no prior knowledge of SAP Business Explorer frontend components.

4.4.3 OLAP BAPI

Standard for third-party providers
OLAP BAPI is a standard that SAP provides for third-party providers and customers to allow their own frontend tools to access the data in an SAP NetWeaver BW system. Among others, Microstrategy uses this standard. The OLAP BAPIs are defined as methods of SAP business object types in the Business Object Repository (BOR) and are implemented as RFC-enabled function modules. In the system, the BAPI Explorer (Transaction BAPI; or select the menu option TOOLS • ABAP WORKBENCH • OVERVIEW • BAPI EXPLORER) provides an overview of all BAPIs in the BOR in the form of a hierarchical or alphabetical listing of all SAP business object types and interface types (Figure 4.8).

The OLAP BAPIs available comprise MDDataProviderBW (methods for browsing the SAP NetWeaver BW metadata and master data) and MDDataSetBW (methods for executing multidimensional datasets and fetch data).

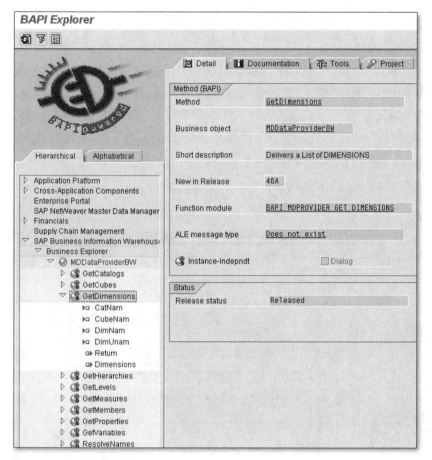

Figure 4.8 BAPI Explorer

4.4.4 XML for Analysis

XMLA is a protocol for exchanging analytical data between client applications and servers using HTTP and SOAP and is available as a service on the Web (Figure 4.9). The URL of the Web service must follow the convention *<Protocol>://<Server>:<Port>/sap/bw/xml/soap/xmla*.

In contrast to OLE DB, XMLA ensures universal data access to any source on the Internet, without any requirement for a specific component to be set up on the client. It is optimized for the Internet in terms of the effort involved in sending queries to the server and stateless

Web optimization

client requests (the connection to the Web server is severed once the client has received the requested data).

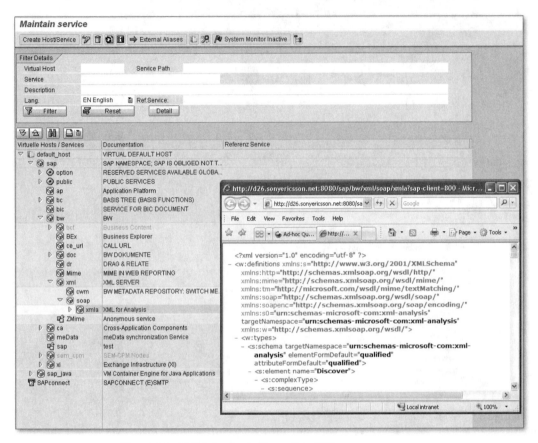

Figure 4.9 XMLA Service in Transaction SICF

Owing to the vast number of monitoring and analysis options available, it is sometimes difficult to have a proper overview of all of these options and to know when to use each one. This chapter will present the most important tools for an SAP NetWeaver BW administrator.

5 Monitoring and Analysis Tools

An administrator can deploy a wide range of tools in his daily work. These include analysis tools for analyzing performance problems, for example, and tools for proactive system monitoring (for example, various monitors, alerting functions and, for BI ABAP and BI Java, the browser-based SAP NetWeaver Administrator tool (Figure 5.1)).

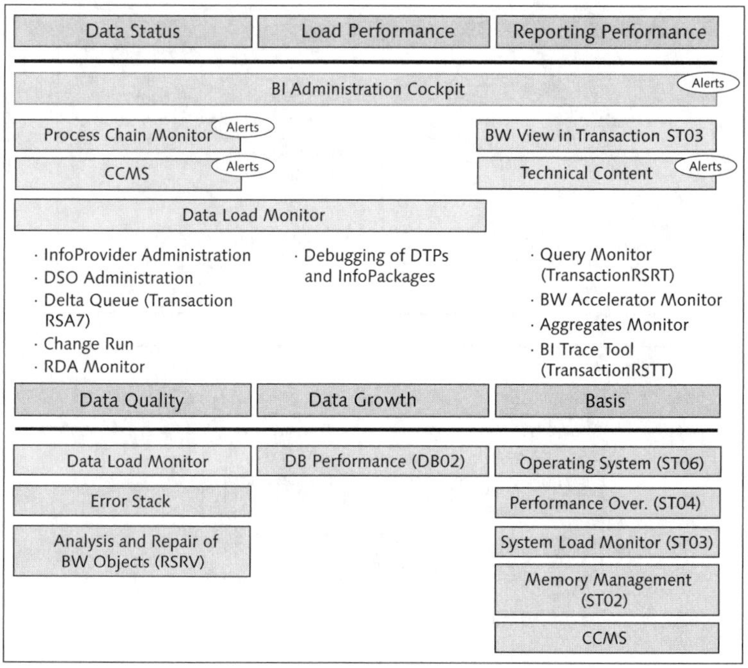

Figure 5.1 Overview of Monitors in the SAP NetWeaver BW System

SAP NetWeaver
Administrator SAP NetWeaver Administrator combines the most important administration and monitoring tools for ABAP-based and Java-based systems
into a new browser-based overview (see Figure 5.2), the goal of which
is to replace Computing Center Management System (CCMS) alert monitors and Visual Administrator monitoring. The advantages of this integrated tool include:

▶ Avoiding, to a large extent, the need to switch between the various
tools used for administration, problem-solving, and analysis purposes
in the SAP NetWeaver system landscape.

▶ SAP NetWeaver Administrator has a central tool for starting and stop-
ping instances, checking configurations and logs, and monitoring all
components for ABAP and Java systems.

▶ The user interface follows the latest concepts in interface design and
is both user-friendly and task-oriented. Execution within the browser
of the Web Dynpro application avoids installations or technical dependencies.

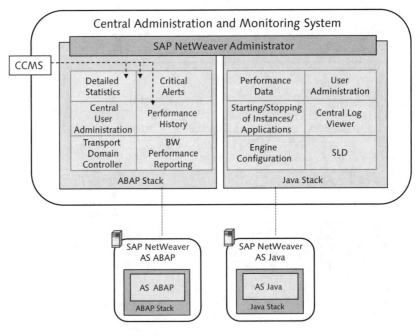

Figure 5.2 SAP NetWeaver Administrator

5.1 General Tools (SAP Basis)

In the sections below, we will present the SAP Basis tools available to you for monitoring and analysis purposes.

5.1.1 SAP Central Process Scheduling

Specifically designed to integrate process automation for SAP and non-SAP environments across platforms, the SAP Central Process Scheduling (CPS) application by Redwood provides a central point of control for all processes. The use of SAP Central Process Scheduling to centrally control the load on all systems in your IT landscape provides the basis for greater flexibility and a tailored hardware configuration. Event-driven, automated load balancing enables you to adopt a dynamic approach when managing unpredictable peak loads, both in SAP and non-SAP environments. When required, the central processing unit (CPU) load is automatically balanced and the load on existing system resources is optimized. You can use this application to:

▸ Reduce the administrative overhead for applications that considerably influence the workload

▸ Integrate processes not only from SAP enterprise applications, but also from third-party applications

▸ Optimize resource usage and reduce the need for additional hardware

▸ Lower the risk of outages and errors by automatically balancing the CPU load and make the server landscape more efficient

▸ Ensure high availability and improve response times by reconciling event-driven tasks with external activities such as data transfers or other system events

SAP Central Process Scheduling provides a dynamic control environment and central infrastructure for jobs, facilitating an IT environment, in the form of a service-oriented architecture (SOA) that is compatible with enterprise-wide automation.

5.1.2 Runtime Analysis (Transaction SE30)

You can use runtime analysis (Transaction SE30) to analyze recordings from a transaction, program, or function module. ICF services and Web

Dynpro ABAP applications or Business Server Page (BSP) applications can also be analyzed in this way. In an SAP NetWeaver BW system, you generally use this transaction to analyze your own ABAP routines in transformations or customer exits to improve the performance of load runs. This transaction is available in the ABAP Editor under the menu path UTILITIES • MORE UTILITIES • RUNTIME ANALYSIS or, in general, from any transaction under the menu path SYSTEM • UTILITIES • RUNTIME ANALYSIS (Figure 5.3).

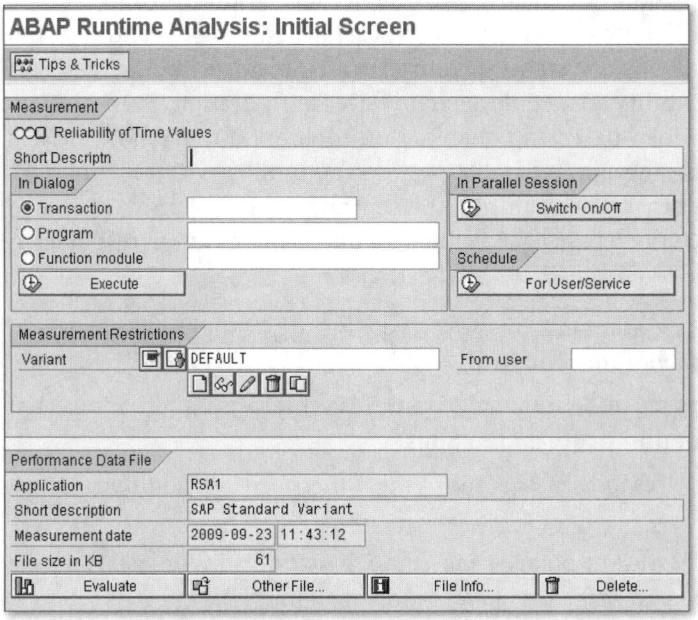

ABAP Runtime Analysis: Initial Screen

Tips & Tricks

Measurement

Reliability of Time Values

Short Descriptn

In Dialog
- Transaction
- Program
- Function module

Execute

In Parallel Session
Switch On/Off

Schedule
For User/Service

Measurement Restrictions

Variant   DEFAULT   From user

Performance Data File

Application	RSA1
Short description	SAP Standard Variant
Measurement date	2009-09-23 11:43:12
File size in KB	61

Evaluate   Other File...   File Info...   Delete...

Figure 5.3 Starting a Runtime Analysis

Setting the level of precision

In runtime analysis, you can set the level of precision in the menu under Settings. When you select HIGH, the system uses one microsecond as the level of precision. However, if the level of precision is high, this can result in incorrect time values for multiprocessors because the clocks of the individual processors are not always regularly synchronized on all platforms. The high level of precision on the following platforms always returns correct values: AIX, SINIX, SUN-OS, Linux, OS/400, and Windows NT.

To avoid incorrect time values on other platforms, you can select LOW to specify a low level of precision whose resolution depends on each platform. For a simple analysis in the current mode, you specify a short description and the object to be analyzed (transaction, program, or function module).

You can then use measurement restrictions to define specific restrictions for runtime analysis. For example, it may make sense to analyze certain statements only or to perform an analysis within a specific time interval only. The performance files of past runtime measurements continue to be available for further analyses.

To perform a runtime analysis for another process (for example, to analyze the performance of ABAP code in a transformation), you can activate logging of individual processes (Figure 5.4). To select a process, first place the cursor on the number in the first column and follow the menu path EDIT • MEASUREMENT • START or select Activate to start logging.

Logging individual processes

Start/end measurement in selected WP

Number	On	Type	Status	Reason	Time	User Names	Report	Action	Table
0		DIA	Running			23010997	SAPLTHFB		
1		BTC	Running		862	ALEREMOTEP26	GP100JVWM0JROI3DOWCAGW80DA0	Sequential Read	/BIC/DZOPPORT7
2		DIA	Waiting						
3		DIA	Waiting						
4		DIA	Waiting						
5		DIA	Running		1	23057443	SAPLRRK0		
6		DIA	Waiting						
7		DIA	Waiting						
8		DIA	Waiting						
9		BTC	Running		26	ALEREMOTEP26	GPA2EDCT170SD9AMPP6CSMLYCD4	Direct Read	/BIC/AZLOODS100
10		BTC	Running		20	ALEREMOTEP26	CL_RSSM_STATMAN===============CP	Direct Read	RSSTATMANSTATUS
11		BTC	Running		18	ALEREMOTEP26	SAPLRSSM_LOAD	Direct Read	RSREQDONE
12		BTC	Waiting						
13		BTC	Running		20	ALEREMOTEP26	CL_RSDD_DTA==================CP	Sequential Read	RSSTATMANREQMAP
14		DIA	Waiting						
15		DIA	Waiting						
16		DIA	Running		7	23057443	CL_SQL_RESULT_SET=============CP	Sequential Read	/BIC/AZSM_R00100
17		DIA	Waiting						
18		DIA	Running		1	XP000293	SAPLRSSM_LOAD	Direct Read	RSHASHTYP
19		DIA	Waiting						
20		UPD	Waiting						
21		UPD	Waiting						
22		UPD	Waiting						
23		UPD	Waiting						
24		DIA	Waiting						
25		DIA	Waiting						
26		DIA	Waiting						
27		DIA	Waiting						
28		DIA	Waiting						
29		DIA	Waiting						
30		SPO	Waiting						
31		SPO	Waiting						
32		UP2	Waiting						
33		UP2	Waiting						

Figure 5.4 Selecting Processes in Parallel Mode

The analysis results overview contains general performance information. Execution times are specified in microseconds, and the distribution of the time required for ABAP (time required on the application server), database, and system is executed on a percentage basis. These are the first indications of whether the performance load is on the database or application server.

Hit list For ABAP and System, the performance is green if the relevant statements correspond to less than 50% of the total runtime. For database statements, this limit is set to 25%. A hit list of all statements measured in the relevant transaction or program is available under the menu path GOTO • HIT LIST • STANDARD (Figure 5.5).

Runtime Analysis Evaluation: Hit List

No.	Gross	=	Net	Gross (%)	Net (%)	Call	Program Name
1	4.061.383		0	100,0	0,0	Runtime analysis	
1	4.061.323		6.081	100,0	0,1	Call Transaction RSA1	SAPMS38T
1	4.053.893		607	99,8	0,0	Program RSAWBN_START	
1	4.051.010		71	99,7	0,0	Call M. CL_RSAWBN_AWB=>START	RSAWBN_START
1	2.812.904		22	69,3	0,0	Call M. CL_RSAWBN_AWB=>CALL_TOOL	CL_RSAWBN_AWB=============CP
1	2.812.201		4	69,2	0,0	Call M. CL_RSAWBN_TOOLREQ=>EXECUTE	CL_RSAWBN_AWB=============CP
1	2.812.197		27	69,2	0,0	Call M. CL_RSAWBN_DWB_MODELLING_TOOL=>HANDLE_REQUEST	CL_RSAWBN_TOOLREQ=========CP
1	2.812.093		87	69,2	0,0	Call Func. RSAWBN_MAIN_DYNPRO	CL_RSAWBN_DWB_MODELLING_TOOL==CP
1	2.811.192		5.287	69,2	0,1	Call Screen 1000	SAPLRSAWBN_MAIN
3	2.805.905		248	69,1	0,0	Dynpro Entry	SAPLRSAWBN_MAIN
5	1.894.672		376	46,7	0,0	Call M. CL_RSAWBN_TREE_VIEW=>EXPAND_NODE	CL_RSAWBN_TREE_VIEW=======CP
5	1.891.980		1.244	46,6	0,0	Call M. CL_RSAWBN_TREE_MODEL=>GET_CHILDREN	CL_RSAWBN_TREE_VIEW=======CP
1	1.817.766		6.445	44,8	0,2	Call M. CL_TREE_MODEL=>HANDLE_EXPAND_NO_CHILDREN	CL_TREE_CONTROL_BASE======CP
1	1.810.542		12	44,6	0,0	Raise E. CL_COLUMN_TREE_MODEL=>EXPAND_NO_CHILDREN	CL_TREE_MODEL=============
1	1.810.530		4	44,6	0,0	Call M. CL_RSAWBN_TREE_VIEW=>HANDLE_EXPAND_NO_CHILDREN	CL_TREE_MODEL=============CP
1	1.810.526		5	44,6	0,0	Call M. CL_RSAWBN_TREE_VIEW=>EXPAND_NODE_BOTH	CL_RSAWBN_TREE_VIEW=======CP
1	1.809.950		80	44,6	0,0	Call M. CL_RSAWBN_TREE_MODEL=>EXPAND_CHILDREN	CL_RSAWBN_TREE_MODEL======CP

Figure 5.5 Analysis Result in Transaction SE30

All of the ABAP statements are listed in descending order according to gross runtime. If the net time is the same as the gross time, only the net time is displayed. The number in the first column tells you how many times each statement was executed. The type specifies one of the following areas: ABAP (» «), database (»DB«), and system (»Syst«). The hit list provides a lot of additional information about the individual statements and the option to navigate directly to the source code or the database tables that have been read.

5.1.3 Application Log (Transaction SLG1)

Logging events The application log enables you to log events on an application or object basis. You enter each log for an object and, if required, a subobject that belongs to this object (see Figure 5.6). The logs are also analyzed on an object basis (if necessary, also for subobjects). The object follows the following naming conventions:

▸ First and second position: application abbreviation (for example, RS)

▸ Third and fourth position: any

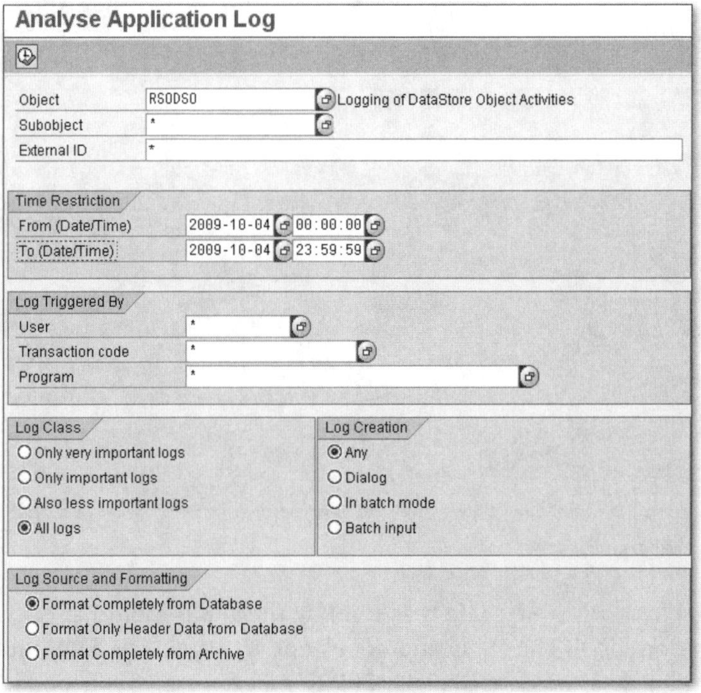

Figure 5.6 Selecting Application Logs

The example in Figure 5.7 shows, for the selected date, the activity logs for a DataStore object (object RSODSO) and contains all of the details concerning the loading and activation processes.

Example

Note that the logs are written to the database (to tables BALHDR, BAL-DAT, and BAL_INDX), but they are not automatically deleted. In addition, there is no general procedure for deactivating the application log, even if some applications provide this option or the option for reducing the number of entries created.

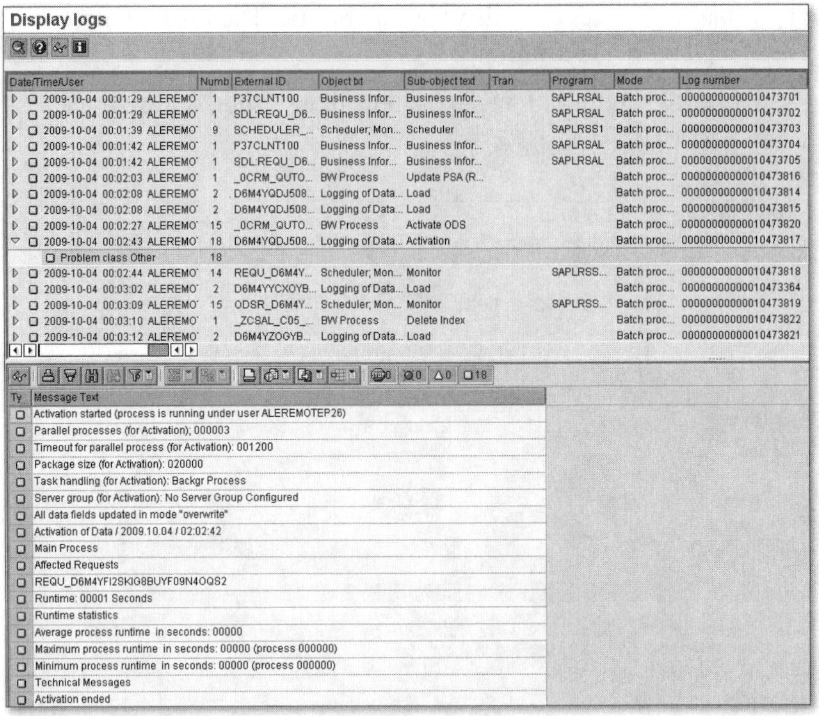

Figure 5.7 Analyzing Logs

Expiry date
A log usually has an expiry date that is set by the application that calls the application log. If the application does not set an expiry date, the application log sets the date Dec. 31, 2098 or Dec. 31, 9999, depending on the release level, to ensure that these logs remain in the system for as long as possible. The expiry date does not mean that logs are automatically deleted when this date is reached. Instead, it is used to control the deletion of logs when calling deletion reports. The DEL_ BEFORE flag in the table BALHDR determines whether or not the log must also be deleted before the expiry date is reached:

▸ DEL_BEFORE = SPACE means that the log must be deleted before the expiry date is reached (default value).

▸ DEL_BEFORE = "X" means that the log can only be deleted after the expiry date has been reached.

The logs of the application log are deleted in Transaction SLG2 (Figure 5.8).

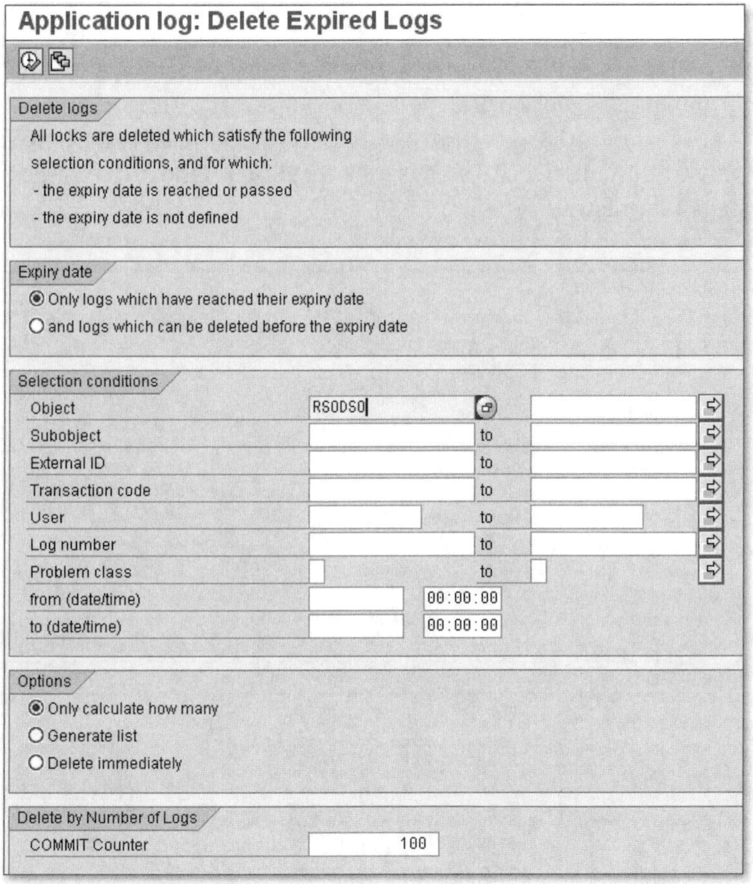

Application log: Delete Expired Logs

Delete logs

All locks are deleted which satisfy the following
selection conditions, and for which:
- the expiry date is reached or passed
- the expiry date is not defined

Expiry date

◉ Only logs which have reached their expiry date
○ and logs which can be deleted before the expiry date

Selection conditions

Object	RSODSO			⇨
Subobject		to		⇨
External ID		to		⇨
Transaction code		to		⇨
User		to		⇨
Log number		to		⇨
Problem class		to		⇨
from (date/time)		00:00:00		
to (date/time)		00:00:00		

Options

◉ Only calculate how many
○ Generate list
○ Delete immediately

Delete by Number of Logs

COMMIT Counter   100

Figure 5.8 Deleting Logs

The corresponding report for Transaction SLG2 is SBAL_DELETE, which can also be scheduled as a background job at regular intervals. Since Release 6.20, it is possible to archive logs. You use the archiving object BC_SBAL to archive logs in Archive Administration (Transaction SARA).

The specifications for writing entries to the application log are defined as objects and associated subobjects in Transaction SLG0. For example, the two subobjects REALTIME (logs for SAPI Close to Realtime) and RSAP_INFO (error handling during the data transfer in OLTP) exist for the object RSAP (BW data transfer from the OLTP system).

Customizing

5.1.4   System Log (Transaction SM21)

You can use the system log to detect and solve errors in your system and its environment. To work with the system log, select TOOLS • ADMINISTRATION on the initial screen of the SAP system or call Transaction SM21 directly. Then select MONITOR • SYSTEM LOG on the initial screen for system administration (Figure 5.9).

```
System Log: Analysis for all Remote Instances

[Q][B Sys log doc.] [C Section] [C Section] [B Contents]

                System Log: Analysis for all Remote Instances            1

From date/time............ 2009-10-04 / 09:00:00
To date/time..............

User......................
Transaction code..........
Terminal..................
Task / Number.............
Problem class.............
Further restrictions......
Sorted ? ................ SOFI
Pages with single entries 00000150
With statistics...........


                System Log: Analysis for all Remote Instances            2

Date : 2009-10-04
```

Time	SAP instance	Type	Nr	Clt	User	TCode	Priority	Grp	N	Text
09:00:13	debosap170_P26_11	WRK	000				☐	Q0	Q	Start Workproc 0, Pid 5064
09:00:18	debosap170_P26_11	BTC	000	000	SAPSYS		☐	A1	0	Initialization complete
09:01:12	debosap171_P26_11	WRK	000				☐	Q0	Q	Start Workproc 4, Pid 10004
09:01:12	debosap171_P26_11	WRK	000				☐	Q0	Q	Start Workproc12, Pid 9548
09:03:52	debosap171_P26_11	WRK	000				☐	Q0	Q	Start Workproc 8, Pid 3892
09:05:15	debosap41_P26_11	WRK	000				☐	Q0	Q	Start Workproc30, Pid 5136
09:06:41	debosap40_P26_11	WRK	000				☐	Q0	Q	Start Workproc26, Pid 9484
09:07:33	debosap170_P26_11	WRK	000				☐	Q0	Q	Start Workproc 2, Pid 5948
09:08:13	debosap170_P26_11	WRK	000				☐	Q0	Q	Start Workproc 4, Pid 2244
09:08:53	debosap170_P26_11	WRK	000				☐	Q0	Q	Start Workproc 3, Pid 5764
09:09:52	debosap171_P26_11	WRK	000				☐	Q0	Q	Start Workproc 9, Pid 6628
09:10:17	debosap170_P26_11	BTC	004	800	ALEREMOTEP26		◙	BY	2	Database error 7719 at EXE
09:10:17	debosap170_P26_11	BTC	004	800	ALEREMOTEP26		○	BY	0	> CREATE/ALTER partition function failed as only a maximum of
09:10:17	debosap170_P26_11	BTC	004	800	ALEREMOTEP26		○	BY	0	> 1000 partitions can be created

Figure 5.9 System Log

SAP servers record events and problems in system logs. If your SAP system runs on a UNIX host, there are two logging options: local logging and central logging. Each SAP application server has a local log that contains the messages issued by this server. You can also work with central logging, whereby each application server copies its local log to a central log.

Local logs   On Windows NT and AS/400 hosts, only local logs are generated (one for each application server). They are not combined into a central log. Select SYSLOG • SELECT to select a log. Here, you can display the following log categories:

▶ **Local system log**
Messages issued by the application server to which you are currently logged on (this is the default).

▶ **Remote system log**
Log from an application server other than the one to which you are logged on. Use the Instance name option to display a particular remote system.

▶ **All remote system logs**
The logs from the system to which you are logged on and from all other application servers in this SAP system.

▶ **Central system log**
To use this option, you must have previously configured each application server to forward the messages from its local log to a central log. The information contained in the central system log may differ from the data in the individual logs.

Figure 5.10 shows a sample log entry whose detailed information can be displayed under the menu path EDIT • DETAILS or by double-clicking the relevant entry.

System activities irrespective of the user

System Log: Analysis for all Remote Instances

| Sys log doc. | Previous entry | Next entry |

Details Page 1 Line 36 System Log: Analysis for all Remote Instances   1

Time	SAP instance	Type	Nr	Clt	User	TCode	Grp	N	Text
09:10:17	debosap170_P26_11	BTC	004	800	ALEREMOTEP26		BY	2	Database error 7719 at EXE

Database error 7719 at EXE

Details
Recording at local and central time....................... 2009-10-04 09:10:17

Task	Process	User	Terminal	Session	TCode	Program	Cl	Problem cl	Package
02244	Background Processor No. 004	ALEREMOTEP26		1		RSBATCH_EXECUTE_PROZESS	K	SAP Web AS Problem	SBAC

Module nam	Line	Table Name	Field Name
dbds	691	7719	EXE

Documentation for system log message BY 2 :
After the attempt to call a database operation, the database system has returned the error code specified in the message, which indicates that the operation concerned could not be executed successfully.

Technical details

File	Offset	RecFm	System log type	Grp	N	variable message data		
16542	18000	h	Database Error (Non-SQL)	BY	2	7719 EXE	dbds	691

Figure 5.10 Details in the System Log

If the User field in a log is empty, this means that the system has issued the message irrespective of a user (for example, while starting or shutting down the SAP system). There are other system activities that are not assigned to an individual user. The Environment menu provides the following functions:

▶ **Display SAPPARAM**
Displays the settings for system log parameters in the system profile.

▶ **Display authorizations**
Display the authorizations required for the system log.

▶ **Clocks**
Displays the system clocks used for message time stamps. It may be useful to check the system clocks if you need to clarify time discrepancies between messages from different application servers. The display shows you whether the system clocks of your SAP systems are set to the same time.

▶ **Process status**
Displays the current status of the system log's send processes.

Log accuracy A local log is always up to date. However, this is not always true for a central log. There may be brief delays between recording a message in a local log and writing it to the central log because the send processes in local systems are not always active. The period in which a send process is inactive varies with the logging intensity on a particular system.

Delays A central log file may take longer to build when a message is sent from a system that normally has little log activity. Longer delays and lost messages in local systems can occur as a result of major network disruptions or a failed collection process on the machine containing the central log.

Switching On/Off Status Traces

You can use the report RSSM_TRACE_SWITCH (which you execute in Transaction SE38) to maintain some RSADMIN parameters for the system log. This makes it possible to control whether, or the extent to which, various processes are logged in an SAP NetWeaver BW system.

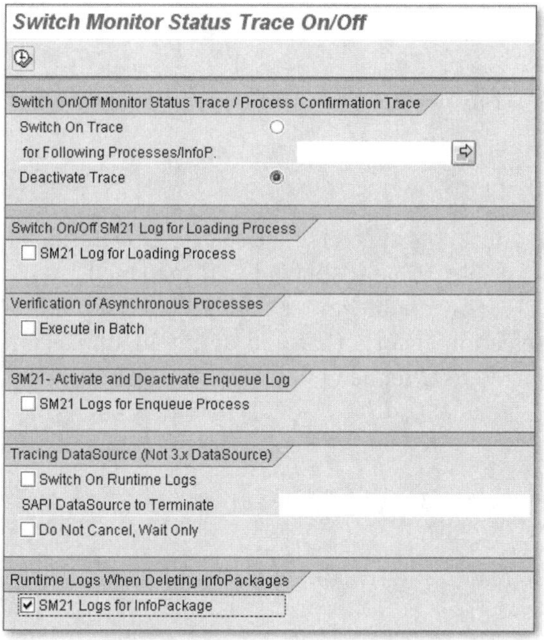

Figure 5.11 Switching On/Off SM21 Traces

As you can see in Figure 5.11, you can switch on runtime measurement for loading processes, among other things. This indicator corresponds to the RSADMIN parameter RSDSRUNTIMETRACE, and when it is switched on, selected loadings steps such as FETCH, PARSE, or CONVERT are logged in table RSDSRUNTIMETRACE when loading data into the PSA object (not for DataSources 3.x) and can be analyzed using the function module RSDS_RUNTIME_RESULT.

Logging load steps

5.1.5 Job Overview (Transaction SM37)

The job overview (Transaction SM37) is used to manage jobs and is a central area for executing a wide range of tasks relating to job monitoring and job management. These include:

▶ Defining, scheduling, repeating, canceling, and deleting jobs

▶ Debugging an active job

▶ Displaying information about a job

▶ Canceling a job's release status

▶ Comparing the specifications of several jobs

- ▶ Checking the status of a job
- ▶ Displaying job logs
- ▶ Releasing a job so that it can run
- ▶ Rescheduling and copying existing jobs
- ▶ Rescheduling and editing jobs and job steps

Simple job selection

In simple job selection, you enter the relevant selection criteria for restricting the selection of jobs to be displayed and managed. Additional job selection criteria are available under the Extended Job Selection option. All of the selection criteria that you define in simple job selection are then transferred to extended job selection. The individual selection fields are:

- ▶ **Job name**
  Name for identification purposes.

- ▶ **User name**
  Name of the user who created and scheduled the job.

- ▶ **Job start condition**
  The start condition for a job can be a time frame or an event that must occur before the job will start. If you specify both, the system displays jobs whose start condition is one of these two conditions.

- ▶ **Job step**
  Name of an ABAP program that acts as a step within a job.

- ▶ **Job status**
  The current job status; the Planned option is not selected by default. If you want to display scheduled jobs, you must explicitly select this option. The status of a background job can represent six different conditions, each of which is explained in Table 5.1.

Job Status	Explanation
Planned	The steps that comprise a job have already been defined, but the start condition has not been defined yet.
Released	The job has been fully defined, including a start condition. A job cannot be released without a start condition.
	Only an administrator or a user with the relevant authorizations for background processing can release a job, preventing unauthorized users from running jobs without prior approval.

Table 5.1 Status of Background Jobs

Job Status	Explanation
Ready	The start condition of a released job has been fulfilled. A job scheduler has placed the job in a queue to wait for an available background work process.
Active	The job is currently running and can no longer be changed or deleted.
Completed	All of the steps that comprise this job have been successfully completed.
Canceled	The job has been canceled. This can happen in two ways:
	An administrator intentionally cancels a job in Transaction SM37 (JOB • CANCEL ACTIVE JOB).
	A job step contains a program that produces an error (for example, an error message or termination message in an ABAP program or a failure return code from an external SAPXPG program)

Table 5.1 Status of Background Jobs (Cont.)

Once the jobs in the database have been defined, they are stored in the following important tables in the background processing system:

Technical background

▶ **TBTCO**
Job header table (job management data)

▶ **TBTCP**
Job step table (individual processing steps)

▶ **TBTCS**
Control table for the time-based job scheduler

▶ **BTCEVTJOB**
Jobs that are waiting for an event

Job logs are stored as files in the TemSe (Temporary Sequential Objects) database.

5.1.6   Process Overview (Transaction SM50)

The work process overview (Transaction SM50) shows a snapshot of the status of the work processes on the application server to which you are logged on or on a server selected in the SAP Application Server Overview (Transaction SM51) (Figure 5.12). You must refresh the display to obtain the latest information. The primary purpose of the process overview (Figure 5.13) is to collate information. For example, you can monitor processes to determine whether the number of work processes in your system is adequate and to assess if the instance is working to full capacity or to gather information for troubleshooting or tuning purposes.

SAP Servers

Server Name	Host Name	Message Types	Server Status
debosap170_P26_11	debosap170	Dialog Batch Update Upd2 Spool ICM	Active
debosap171_P26_11	debosap171	Dialog Batch Update Upd2 Spool ICM	Active
debosap30_P26_11	debosap30	Dialog Batch Update Spool ICM	Active
debosap31_P26_11	debosap31	Dialog Batch Update Spool ICM	Active
debosap40_P26_11	debosap40	Dialog Batch Update Upd2 Spool ICM	Active
debosap41_P26_11	debosap41	Dialog Batch Update Upd2 Spool ICM	Active

Figure 5.12 Selecting a Server in Transaction SM51

Process Overview

No.	Type	PID	Status	Reason	Start	Err	Se	CPU	Time	Report	Cl.	User Names	Action	Table
0	BGD	6488	Waiting		Yes									
1	DIA	7504	Waiting		Yes	2								
2	BGD	8736	Running		Yes				114	CL_RSMD_A	800	ALEREMOTEP2		
3	BGD	5304	Running		Yes	2			308	SAPLRSS1	800	ALEREMOTEP2	Sequential Read	RSSTATMANI
4	DIA	10064	Waiting		Yes									
5	DIA	9952	Waiting		Yes	1								
6	BGD	5744	Running		Yes	1			275	CL_RSODSC	800	ALEREMOTEP2	Sequential Read	/BIC/B000148
7	DIA	7628	Waiting		Yes									
8	DIA	8024	Waiting		Yes	1								
9	DIA	5572	Waiting		Yes									
10	DIA	1684	Waiting		Yes									
11	BGD	8228	Running		Yes				11720	GPD3HUG3v	800	ALEREMOTEP2	Sequential Read	/BIO/AFIAR_O

Figure 5.13 Overview of Processes in a Selected Server

If a transaction is running, you can cancel it with or without core, that is, with or without creating a core file. If you "cancel with core," the system writes a core file that can be viewed in Transaction ST11 for further analysis.

Managing users

You should use the User Overview (Display and Manage User Sessions) function to manage users. In the process overview, you cannot know with certainty whether the user mode that you want to cancel or delete is still active in the work process that you select. You could therefore unintentionally disrupt another user mode.

In addition to the work process types, the following information in the process overview is of particular interest:

▶ **Status**

The current work process status.

▶ **Cause**

The reason a process has the status Hold. Typical reasons include debugging, CPI-C activities, locks, updates, and GUI (system waits for a response from the SAP GUI frontend program, for example, in the case of an RFC). You can use the (F1) help to obtain a detailed list of possible reasons.

The entry PRIV (private use) may also be displayed in this column. PRIV indicates that a work process is reserved for a single user for memory management purposes. The work process has exceeded the limit for shared SAP memory. The process is held as long as the current user requires the local memory space. For more information, refer to the documentation on memory management (private memory). If a certain percentage of work processes have the status PRIV, the PRIV transactions are automatically ended if the user does not perform any actions within the time span specified in the system profile.

▶ **Report**

The report currently being executed (ABAP program).

▶ **Time**

The time already required by a work process for the dialog step currently being processed.

▶ **Table**

The table currently being accessed.

For example, the option to navigate directly to debugging mode for a program that is currently running can be very helpful when analyzing transformations. This function is available under the menu path Program/Mode • Program • Debugging.

5.1.7 System Trace (Transaction ST01)

The system trace is primarily used when an authorization trace is to be used. The system log (Transaction SM21) or the developer trace (available, for example, via the process overview in Transaction SM50) are recommended for system monitoring and problem analysis.

The SAP system trace can be used to monitor the following components: authorization checks, kernel functions, kernel modules, database accesses (SQL trace), table buffers, RFC calls, and lock operations (client side). Some of these components can also be monitored, for example, using performance analysis (Transaction ST05).

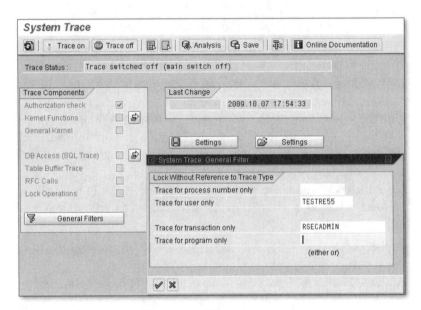

Figure 5.14 System Trace (Transaction ST01)

Recording and
analyzing a trace

To record and analyze a trace, proceed as follows:

1. Switch on the trace in Transaction ST01 and select the components you require (Figure 5.14). Use the general filter (Lock Without Reference to Trace Type) to restrict, for example, the recording to a particular user or transaction.

2. Perform the operations that produce the error or cause the problem. For an authorization check, you may have to ask the relevant user to execute the individual steps that cause the authorization problem to occur.

3. Switch off the trace again.

4. Analyze the trace.

Once you have created a trace, you can evaluate it to analyze system behavior while the steps are being executed. You can set various analysis options on the Options for Trace Analysis screen. In addition to the trace components, you can restrict the analysis to particular users, work processes, transactions, and times.

For performance analysis, you can use the Duration field to analyze only records for which the duration of a trace record exceeds a specific period of time. This applies only to trace components that also have a duration. This setting does not make sense for the authorization trace, for example. You can also set a restriction whereby only specific tables are included in the trace analysis (this applies only to the SQL trace and table buffer trace). You can enter two table names directly on the screen. If you want to add more tables, select More Tables.

In the File Selection group box, you can specify a separate file to protect a trace from being automatically overwritten. If you specify a separate file here, the system ignore the default trace files and reads only the file specified. The display screen for SAP trace analysis contains the following elements:

▶ **Time**
Double-click to see the time to the microsecond.

▶ **Type of trace entry**
The component selected when the trace was switched on or when the analysis settings were made:

▶ **Authorization check (AUTH)**
Authorization object used

▶ **Kernel functions (CMOD)**
Corresponding C function in the kernel

▶ **General kernel (USER)**
C module in the kernel in which the trace is written

▶ **Database access (SQL)**
Database table being accessed

▶ **Table buffer trace (BUFF)**
Database table whose buffer is being accessed

▶ **RFC calls (RFC)**
The function module called

> ▶ **Lock operations (ENQUE)**
> The lock object used

▶ **Duration of the trace**
Specified if this is useful information: A duration is not useful in the case of an authorization trace, a user trace (free text that can be written by a kernel module), and the beginning of a C function in a customer exit trace.

▶ **Object**
The object differs depending on the trace component and can be obtained from the table above. For an authorization trace, for example, the relevant authorization object is specified as an object.

▶ **Trace message text**
The message text depends on the trace component. It generally contains detailed information about the object specified. For an authorization trace, the text contains the authorization fields and their authorization values.

Saving and profile parameters

The data is stored in several files, which are written sequentially. You can use system profile parameters to restrict the size of SQL files and system trace files and specify their relevant paths. All trace parameter names begin with the string `rstr/`. The parameter `rstr/filename` defines the base name of these files. There is always one file with this exact name. If the file is full (parameter `rstr/max_filesize_MB`), the file is renamed and a new file is created with the base name. When the file is renamed, a number between 00 and 99 is added to the file name. The parameter `rstr/max_files` defines the maximum number of files. If this value is exceeded, the files are overwritten. For performance reasons, the files are not written directly. Instead, a buffer within the process is used for this purpose. The profile parameter `rstr/buffer_size_kB` determines the size of this buffer in kilobytes.

5.1.8 Tune Summary (Transaction ST02)

The tune summary (see Figure 5.15) displays buffer information and, as part of memory management, the current status and the memory resource usage for a specific application server.

Buffer	HitRatio %	Alloc. KB	Freesp. KB	% Free Sp.	Dir. Size	FreeDirEnt	% Free Dir	Swaps	DB Accs
Tune Summary (DEBOSAP67_S26_11)									
System:	DEBOSAP67_S26_1			Tune summary					
Date + Time of Snapshot: 2009.10.08			12:50:32	Startup:	2009.10.07 16:54:35				
Nametab (NTAB)								0	
Table definition	94,60	11.897	7.986	80,02	35.000	28.004	80,01	0	7.628
Field definition	96,40	32.734	21.372	71,24	35.000	31.512	90,03	0	3.809
Short NTAB	97,05	4.094	2.949	98,30	8.750	8.569	97,93	0	181
Initial records	5,53	11.094	8.371	83,71	8.750	6.056	69,21	0	2.694
								0	
program	99,39	500.000	252.080	54,16	125.000	119.835	95,87	0	15.519
CUA	99,15	3.000	662	26,93	1.500	1.381	92,07	0	134
Screen	99,51	19.531	16.572	89,51	10.000	9.862	98,62	0	143
Calendar	100,00	488	478	100,00	200	200	100,00	0	201
OTR	100,00	4.096	3.375	100,00	2.000	2.000	100,00	0	
								0	
Tables								0	
Generic Key	99,79	136.719	6.887	5,15	10.000	5.973	59,73	1	4.235
Single record	94,77	40.000	34.791	87,71	1.000	922	92,20	0	7.483
								0	
Export/import	58,56	26.000	16.615	88,33	20.000	19.181	95,91	0	
Exp./ Imp. SHM		40.000	39.279	100,00	2.000	2.000	100,00	0	

SAP Memory	Curr.Use %	CurUse[KB]	MaxUse[KB]	In Mem[KB]	OnDisk[KB]	SAPCurCach	HitRatio %
Roll area	0,24	629	1.552	262.144	0	IDs	100,00
Page area	0,05	128	680	131.072	131.072	Statement	100,00
Extended memory	12,51	524.288	606.208	4.190.208	0		0,00
Heap memory		0	0	0	0		0,00

Figure 5.15 Tune Summary

The buffer monitor displays information about the buffer and memory
load for the instance on which the user is logged on. Statistical information about the repository, program, and CUA (for GUI elements such
as menus and buttons) buffers and the table buffers is compiled since
the time when the server was started. The hit ratio, among other items,
is displayed. A hit is when an object (for example, a table, screen, or
program) in the buffer is successfully accessed. If the object has to be
read from a database, the buffer access fails. As already shown in Figure
5.15, there are numerous types of buffer. Table 5.2 describes each buffer and provides detailed information such as the corresponding profile
parameter for the buffer types shown in Transaction ST02.

Buffer

Buffer	Description
Table definition	With the TTAB buffer, you cannot set the size of the areas for management and user data separately. Both are managed using the parameter `rsdb/ntab/entrycount`, which defines the number of directory entries in the buffer. Each entry is approximately 0.1 KB in size. The parameter also determines the number of directory entries for the other three repository buffers.
Field definition	The number of directory entries is twice as high as the number specified with the parameter `rsdb/ntab/entrycount`. Each entry requires approximately 0.026 KB in the management part of the buffer. The size of the data section in KB is defined by the parameter `rsdb/ntab/ftabsize`.
Short NTAB	The number of directory entries is twice as high as the number specified with the parameter `rsdb/ntab/entrycount`. Each entry requires approximately 0.026 KB in the management part of the buffer. The size of the data section in KB is defined by the parameter `rsdb/ntab/sntabsize`.
Initial records	The number of directory entries is twice as high as the number specified with the parameter `rsdb/ntab/entrycount`. Each entry requires approximately 0.026 KB in the management part of the buffer. The size of the data section in KB is defined by the parameter `rsdb/ntab/irbdsize`.
Program	Only one parameter, `abap/buffersize`, can be used to define the size of the program buffer. The size is defined in KB. The number of directory entries is calculated from this parameter. You can use the parameter `ipc/shm_psize_06` to control where the buffer is positioned. This parameter is generally set to 0; that is, the buffer is not located in a pool.
CUA	The parameter `rsdb/cua/buffersize` defines the total size of the buffer in KB. The number of directory entries is calculated as total size/2KB. You can use the parameter `ipc/shm_psize_47` to control where the buffer is positioned. This parameter is generally set to -40; that is, the buffer is located in pool 40.

Table 5.2 Buffer Types

Buffer	Description
Screen	You can use the parameter `zcsa/bufdir_entries` to define the size of the directory, that is, the maximum number of screens (dynpros). You define the total size of the buffer in KB using the parameter `zcsa/presentation_buffer_area`. The storage space for the directory is included here.
Calendar	You can use the profile parameter `zcsa/calendar_area` to define the size of the calendar buffer in bytes.
Tables, generic key	You define the number of directory entries (one for each resident table or each generic area) is defined using the parameter `zcsa/db_max_buftab`. Use the parameter `zcsa/table_buffer_area` to define the size of the data area in bytes. You can use the parameter `ipc/shm_psize_19` to control where the buffer is positioned. This parameter is generally set to 10 (pool 10). You should not change the parameter `zcsa/exchange_mode`. Keep the default value Off.
Tables, single record	To define the number of directory entries (one for each table), use the parameter `rtbb/max_tables`. Define the size of the data area in KB using the parameter `rtbb/buffer_length`. You can use the parameter `ipc/shm_psize_33` to control where the buffer is positioned. This parameter is generally set to 0; that is, the buffer is not located in a pool. The parameter `rtbb/frame_length` defines the length of a frame in KB and should always be set to the default value 4.

Table 5.2 Buffer Types (Cont.)

SAP Memory provides a snapshot of current usage (a percentage of total usage in KB) and maximum memory usage for various memory types. It also specifies whether and to what extent the main memory or hard disk satisfies the demand for memory.

SAP Memory

The roll area is a memory area with a fixed (configurable) size and belongs to a work process. It is located in the heap of the virtual address space of the work process.

SAP Paging allocates memory for the current internal mode by moving memory pages, similar to operating system paging. It enables you to extend the roll area at ABAP runtime if a large amount of data is being processed (for example, large internal tables). The SAP memory management concept intends SAP Paging to be used only if the ABAP commands EXTRACT and EXPORT... TO MEMORY... are used.

SAP Extended Memory is at the core of the SAP Memory Management system. Each work process has a part for extended memory reserved in its virtual address space. You can set the size using the profile parameter em/initial_size_MB (size of extended memory).

Other processes cannot use private (heap) memory. Even after releasing the allocated memory, the operating system still considers the (virtual) memory as continuing to be occupied by the allocating process. If a dialog work process has used up all of the roll area and extended memory assigned to it, the system allocates it some private memory; that is, it runs in PRIV mode.

5.1.9   Workload Monitor (Transaction ST03N)

You use the workload monitor to analyze statistical data from the kernel. When you analyze the performance of a system, you should generally start by analyzing the workload statistics. For example, you can display the total values for all instances and compare the performances of individual instances over specific periods of time, or you can analyze workload statistics for the individual task types (for example, background processing, dialog processing, updates, ALE, and RFC) for the application servers in your system. You can use the workload monitor to display:

Information in the workload monitor

- ▶ Number of configured instances for each SAP system
- ▶ Data for all application instances, not only those to which you are logged on
- ▶ Transactions used and their users
- ▶ Number of users who work in the various instances
- ▶ Performance history over certain periods of time for all instances
- ▶ Distribution of response times and resource usage for all application servers
- ▶ Workload on the application server for the current day or for another period of time

In administrator mode, the system displays the workload for the current day only. In expert mode, it displays weekly and monthly cumulated statistics for the workload and the daily, weekly, and monthly statistics for each instance. In service engineer mode, it displays information about the workload for the current day and the previous week. Because all SAP NetWeaver BW statistics have been fully revised with SAP NetWeaver BW 7.0 and information is now written to several database tables on an event basis rather than to table RSDDSTAT only, the workload monitor now accesses the statistical data of the technical content.

The global workload monitor (Transaction ST03G) displays statistics records for entire landscapes and is therefore used to analyze statistical data from ABAP and non-ABAP systems. You can use this data to analyze the workload of monitored components in detail. Whereas statistics records for an ABAP system can only trace actions that are processed by ABAP components, you can use distributed statistics records (DSRs) to trace actions that are processed using, for example, the J2EE Engine, Internet Transaction Server (ITS), and TREX (SAP NetWeaver Search and Classification). This also works across component boundaries.

Global workload monitor

5.1.10 Database Performance Analysis (Transaction ST04)

The database monitor (Transaction ST04) checks important performance indicators in the database system such as the database size, the quality of the database buffer, and the database indexes. The monitor uses statistics that are provided by the database system that you are using. Even though the database monitor accesses and analyzes database-specific statistics tables, it always has the same appearance irrespective of which database system you are using (Figure 5.16).

You can use the monitor to check the database while a production SAP system is running, analyze various problems, and obtain the information required for the database system settings.

The database buffer cache (also known as the data buffer) is the area within the System Global Area (SGA) used to temporarily store copies of data blocks read from the hard disk. Oracle user processes cannot read data directly from data files, which is why all data must be read into this buffer cache first.

Data buffer size and quality

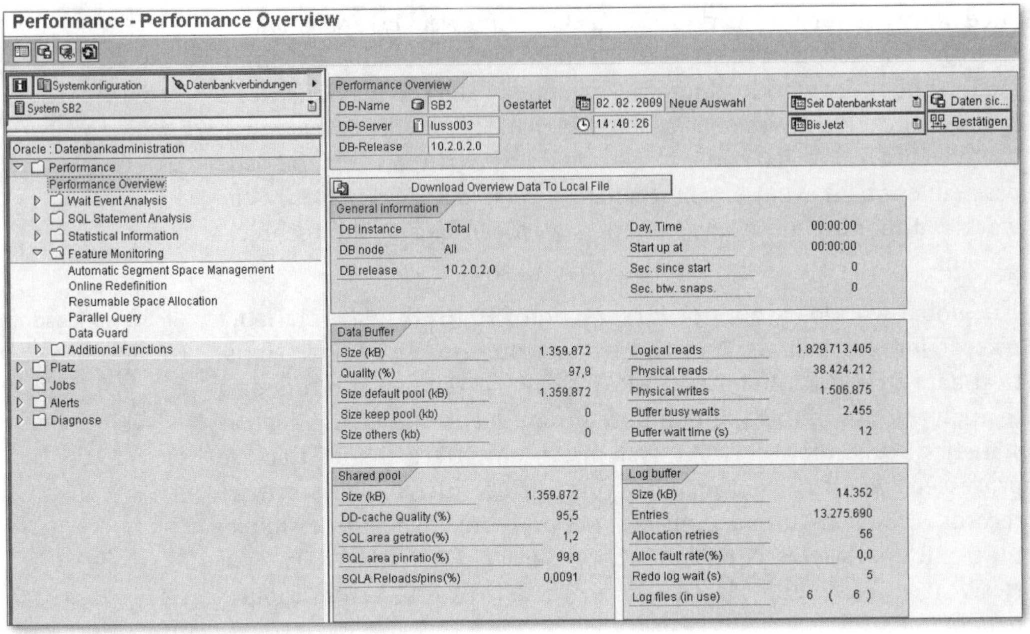

Figure 5.16 Performance Analysis in Transaction ST04

When a user process requests a data block that is already in the data buffer, it can be read without having to access the hard disk again (if the block has not been changed since the last time it was read into the buffer). It goes without saying that this saves considerable processing time. In this scenario, the user process requests a data block that is in the data buffer; this is known as a *hit*. When a user process requests a data block that is not in the data buffer, this is called a *miss*. The relationship between hits and misses is known as the *hit ratio*, which can also be regarded as the quality of the database buffer cache. SAP recommends a minimum data buffer quality of 97% in a production SAP system.

Read and write operations

The statistics for read and write operations help you quickly determine the level of database activity since the last time an instance was started. If the number of physical write operations is on the same scale as the number of physical read operations, you should also monitor the activities of the database writer, the rollback activities, and the redo log activity. In particular, this situation may occur in online transaction environments when individual table lines are updated many times.

A wait situation in a buffer occurs when an Oracle process attempts to access a block that still has an inconsistent status. The number of wait situations displayed on the main screen is the average number for all Oracle block classes. Numerous Oracle block classes may cause wait situations to occur. In general, however, only the following four are found when monitoring the SAP system: data block, segment header, undo header, and undo block. If the total number of wait situations exceeds 5% of the total number of read operations, you should analyze the situation more closely.

Wait situations

5.1.11 Performance Analysis (Transaction ST05)

The performance trace enables you to record database calls, lock management calls, and remote calls concerning reports, transactions, and the SAP system itself in a trace file and to display the logged measurement results as a list. The performance trace also provides extensive support when you are analyzing individual trace records in detail.

The SQL trace part of the performance trace enables you to trace how the OPEN SQL statements used in reports and transactions are converted into standard SQL statements and the parameters used to transfer the embedded SQL statements to the database system used. When the trace is switched on, it records all database activities by a particular user or group of users. The SAP NetWeaver BW system first converts OPEN SQL statements into embedded SQL statements. It then transfers them to the database used and makes the results available. The embedded SQL statement transferred to the database is logged together with its associated parameters. The results of the SQL statement (for example, the return code and the number of records retrieved, inserted, or deleted by the database) are written to the SQL trace file. A log file containing the execution time of the statement and the place in the application program or application transaction from which it was called enables you to perform extensive analyses, which are supported by the SQL trace function. The SQL trace recording can provide the following information:

SQL trace analysis

- The SQL statements executed in your application
- The values the system uses for particular database accesses and changes

- How the system converts ABAP OPEN SQL statements (such as SELECT) into standard SQL statements

- Where your application repeats the same database access

Developers often use this transaction to directly test and analyze SQL statements by using the Enter SQL Statement function and the Explain function available on the subsequent screen.

5.1.12 OS Monitor (Transaction ST06N)

You use the *operating system monitor* (Transaction ST06N) to monitor the system resources provided by the operating system.

An SAP NetWeaver BW instance runs within an operating system, which provides the instance with resources such as virtual memory, physical memory, CPU), file system management, and a physical hard disk or network. Bottlenecks in these areas can have a noticeable effect on SAP system performance. You can use the operating system monitor to monitor these resources.

You can also use it to identify the cause of a performance problem. If the root of the problem is in the operating system, it can be analyzed further and resolved using external tools or other external resources. Typical performance indicators include, for example, CPU average load and utilization, memory utilization, and information about hard disk utilization or the local area network (LAN) activity.

Swap space   In particular, the relevant swap space requirement can be monitored here. SAP NetWeaver BW application servers are important users of swap space. If the swap space in a host system is used up, serious system problems occur. Therefore, it is important to monitor swap space usage.

The operating system collector (OS collector) collects data concerning operating system resources. This is a standalone program called SAPOS-COL that runs independently of the SAP NetWeaver BW instances in the operating system background.

5.1.13 Application Monitor (Transaction ST07)

The application monitor (Transaction ST07) breaks down user information for each module. Examples include the load per application (response time) and the buffer usage per application (SAP buffer).

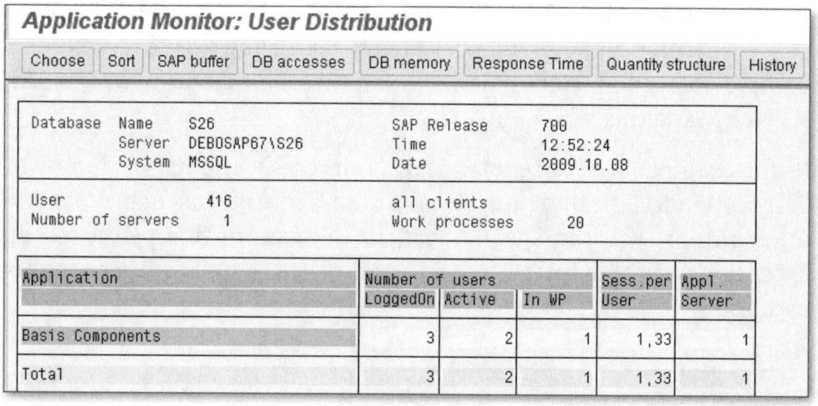

Application Monitor: User Distribution

| Choose | Sort | SAP buffer | DB accesses | DB memory | Response Time | Quantity structure | History |

Database	Name	S26		SAP Release	700	
	Server	DEBOSAP67\S26		Time	12:52:24	
	System	MSSQL		Date	2009.10.08	
User		416		all clients		
Number of servers		1		Work processes	20	

Application	Number of users			Sess.per	Appl.
	LoggedOn	Active	In WP	User	Server
Basis Components	3	2	1	1,33	1
Total	3	2	1	1,33	1

Figure 5.17   User Distribution in Transaction ST07

As you can see, for Transaction ST07 in Figure 5.17, the applications have a hierarchical structure, for example, BASIS • CCMS • ST07. Transaction ST07 is particularly helpful because it provides detailed monitoring data for the SAP buffer, database accesses, and the database memory. The data analyzed for the application monitor is the same data analyzed for Transaction DB02. Consequently, the actions RUNSTATS and REORGCHK for all tables (see SAP Note 434495) and the standard job SAP_COLLECTOR_FOR_PERFMONITOR (see SAP Note 16083) must be scheduled as a prerequisite.

In principle, all table data is available. However, the application monitor shows only a subset of these tables. Transaction DB21 controls the selection here. The application monitor records all tables with usage type A (SAP delivers approximately 300–400 tables with this setting).

5.1.14   ABAP Runtime Error (Transaction ST22)

If an ABAP program terminates, the system usually generates an ABAP dump that contains a description of the exact cause of the error. If an error occurs in an ABAP program that is running in the background, it generally causes the background job to terminate immediately. The only exception to this rule is if the error is output by a function module called in the program, and the program was instructed to catch the error as an exception. In this case, control is returned to the ABAP program, which then tries to resolve the error and continue to run.

Calling an analysis
method
To call an analysis method, follow the menu path TOOLS • ABAP WORK-
BENCH • TEST • DUMP ANALYSIS. Figure 5.18 shows an example of a
dump displayed in Transaction ST22 and troubleshooting in the SAP
Service Marketplace.

If, for example, a user reports a program crash, the list of dumps in
Transaction ST22 can be restricted to the relevant user name. Among
other things, you can specify that, in the case of dumps caused by
exceptions, the dump text contains all of the data required for this
exception.

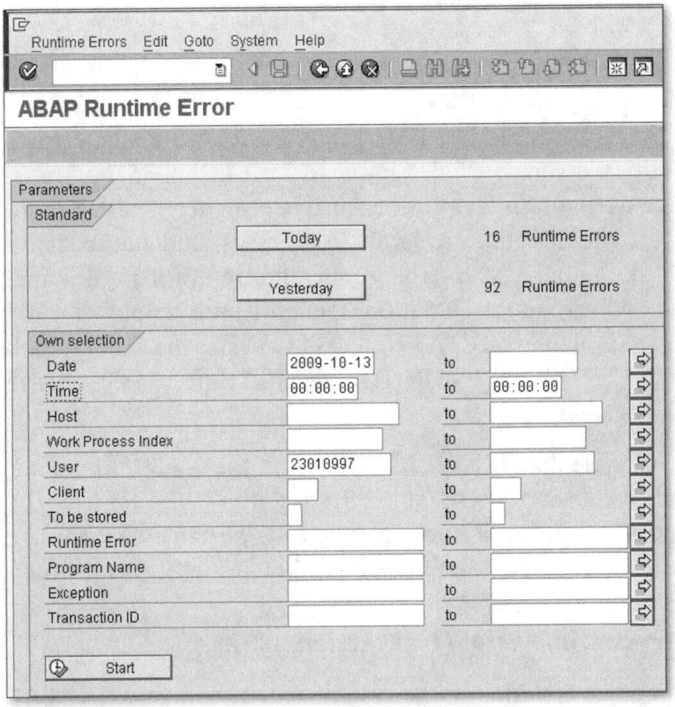

Figure 5.18 Finding Runtime Errors in Transaction ST22

This includes the name and triggering point of the exception and various other attributes.

Sample
troubleshooting
The content of a dump is structured in such a way that you can easily
analyze the cause of the dump. In the example shown in Figure 5.19,
the How to Correct the Error area recommends that you search the SAP

Notes system for the keyword LOOK_UP_STAR_VARIABLES, among others.

Runtime Error Long Text

ABAP Editor

- Runtime Error
  - System environment
    - System environment
    - User and Transaction
  - User view
    - What happened?
    - What can you do?
  - ABAP developer view
    - Short text
    - Error analysis
    - How to correct the error
    - Information on where te
    - Source Code Extract
    - Contents of system fiel(
    - Chosen variables
    - Active Calls/Events
    - List of ABAP programs :
  - BASIS developer view
    - Internal notes
    - Active Calls in SAP Kern
    - Directory of Application
    - ABAP Control Blocks (C

```
Runtime Errors       TIME_OUT
Date and Time        2009-09-28 03:04:56

How to correct the error
    Programs with long runtime should generally be started as background
    jobs. If this is not possible, you can increase the system profile
    parameter "rdisp/max_wprun_time".

    Depending on the cause of the error, you may have to take one of the
    following measures:
    - Endless loop: Correct program;
    - Dataset resulting from database access is too large:
        Instead of "SELECT * ... ENDSELECT", use "SELECT * INTO internal table
        (for example);
    - Database has unsuitable index: Check index generation.

    If the error occures in a non-modified SAP program, you may be able to
    find an interim solution in an SAP Note.
    If you have access to SAP Notes, carry out a search with the following
    keywords:

    "TIME_OUT" " "
    "GP8IHRVH1UX64C4VFXMJTLBDC72" or "GP8IHRVH1UX64C4VFXMJTLBDC72"
    "VALUE_TO_SID_CONVERT_DB"
```

Figure 5.19 Detailed Information about Runtime Errors in Transaction ST22

Search options		
Used Template	no template used	Load Template
Language	German · English	
Search Term	LOOK_UP_STAR_VARIABLES	Search
Search Method	All Terms (AND)	
Search Range	All	
Search behavior	· Linguistic search Exact search	
Application Area	BW*	Select
Restrictions	No Restriction	Select
Additional Criteria	Default selection	Select
Search result		
Results Per Page	10	View / Sorting Configure

Figure 5.20 SAP Notes Search on the SAP Service Marketplace

As described in Chapter 14, SAP Support, SAP Notes are available on the SAP Service Marketplace. In our example, the SAP Notes search (Figure 5.20) proposes SAP Note 1244842, which is valid for this particular release and must be implemented to resolve the error (Figure 5.21).

3 SAP Notes found					Page 1 of 1
Ranking	Application Area	Number	Short text		Released On
☐ 1. 0.620	BW-BEX-OT-OLAP-AUT	1244842	Termination LOOK_UP_STAR_VARIABLES-01-		15.09.2008
☐ 2. 0.280	BW-BEX-OT-OLAP-AUT	1179181	Display attributes not displayed		05.09.2008
☐ 3. 0.240	BW	1136884	SAPBINews NW7.00 BI ABAP Support Package 19		28.08.2009

Figure 5.21 Corrections Available for the Keyword Searched

5.2   Special SAP NetWeaver BW System Tools

The following sections describe the tools provided by the SAP NetWeaver BW system for monitoring and analysis purposes.

5.2.1   BI Monitor (Transaction BWCCMS)

The CCMS monitor sets of the alert monitor, together with the BI monitor, contain a selection of SAP NetWeaver BW–relevant standard SAP monitoring trees and monitoring trees for process chains and consistency checks in the analysis and repair environment. You can access the alert monitor under the menu path TOOLS • CCMS • CONTROL DATA/ MONITORING • CCMS MONITOR SETS or in Transaction RZ20. The BI monitor is available under the node SAP BI Monitors in the overview tree of the CCMS monitor sets. You can also start the BI monitor directly in Transaction BWCCMS.

Monitoring objects and attributes
The monitoring trees for which the monitoring objects are displayed are located under the node for your SAP NetWeaver BW system. In other words, a monitoring tree combines a group of logically related monitoring objects. Monitoring objects are specific components in your SAP system or its environment that you can monitor.

The monitoring attributes are displayed for a monitoring object, and they describe data types that can be reported for a specific monitoring object. Alerts can be triggered on the basis of values reported for an attribute.

Process chains
In the Process Chains monitoring tree, process chains that have run since the last time the system was started are displayed as monitoring objects, along with those process chains that were defined in Transac-

tion RZ21. The nodes show the technical name of the process chain. You can double-click a process chain to navigate to the maintenance screen for the chain. In the RSRV Checks monitoring tree, you can display messages in relation to the consistency checks that you performed in the analysis and repair environment (Transaction RSRV).

5.2.2 BI Background Management (Transaction RSBATCH)

All of the functions for managing background processes in the SAP NetWeaver BW system are available in Transaction RSBATCH (BI background management), which can also be called, among others, in the Data Warehousing Workbench (in the Administration functional area under Batch Manager). This transaction has been extended to include various system management reports and troubleshooting functions in the SAP NetWeaver BW system.

Background and parallel processes

The central function of Transaction RSBATCH is to manage background processes and therefore display jobs and processes and maintain the relevant settings.

Select a list of batch manager jobs. Here, you can display and delete messages concerning individual jobs and delete the internal parameters of the background process. Select Display Batch Process. The overview contains various pieces of background process information, such as the number of jobs in a work process, the number of jobs with errors in a work process, and the work process load over a period of time (Figure 5.22).

Displaying background processes

Select the process type for which you want to make settings. The system displays detailed information about the process chain variants for which settings have already been made. Select Parallel Settings. On the next screen, select the process whose settings you want to change. Specify whether you want serial or parallel processing in the background. For the latter, specify how many processes can be split in parallel. Define the server or server group on which the processes are to be executed. If you do not define a server or server group, the system selects an available server and balances the load evenly across all servers that have free background work processes.

Settings for parallel processing

You can change the settings for process variants here. The settings are initially made on the variant maintenance screen for the relevant process. The settings are globally valid for all processes that are not executed using process chains.

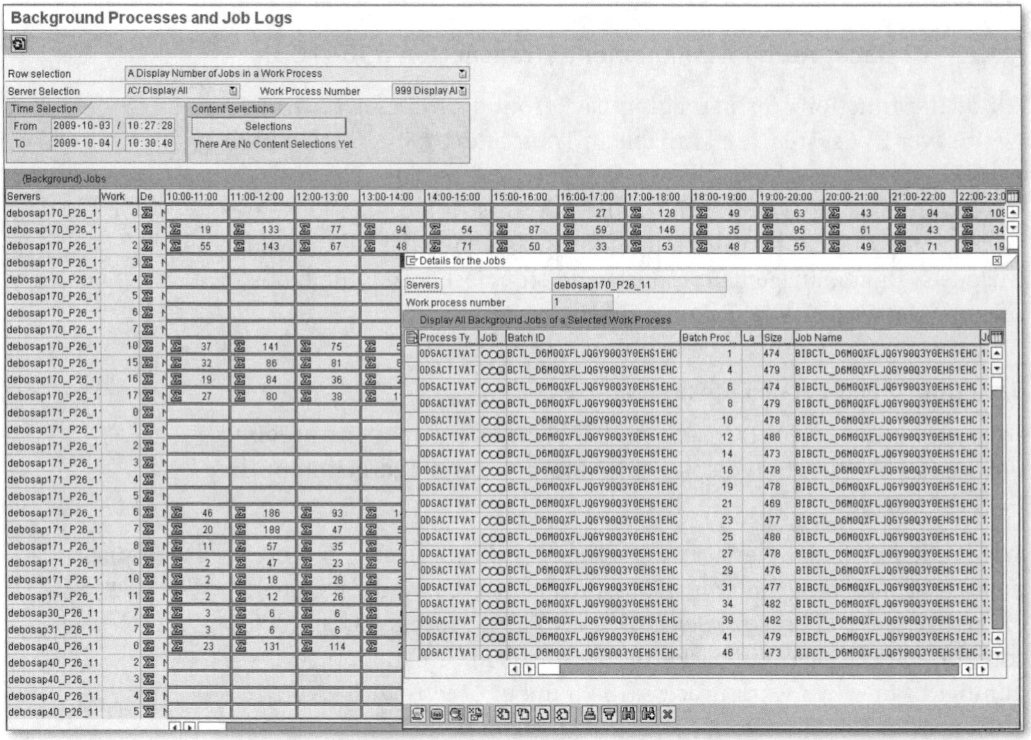

Figure 5.22 Background Processes

Specifying the delete selections

Select Delete Selections. Define the number of days after which the system deletes internal messages in BI background management and the internal parameters of background processes that are executed in background management. We recommend that you delete messages and parameters that are older than 30 days. Generally, this setting should prevent table RSBATCHDATA from becoming overcrowded. When defining the delete selections, note that you must store the data as long as required to conduct investigations if a problem occurs. Select Schedule to define the start conditions. We recommend that you run the job daily. Save the start conditions. On the next screen, specify the server on which you want the job to run and select Transfer to schedule the delete job. You can display delete jobs and stop a scheduled delete job.

Check and conversion programs for request information

To obtain better performance when displaying requests (for example, on the administration screen of the InfoProvider) and when loading data, the administrative information for requests is stored in special tables (RSSTATMANPART and RSSTATMANPARTT for InfoProviders and RSSTATMANPSA and RSSTATMANPSAT for PSA tables) as of SAP NetWeaver 7.0 to facilitate faster access.

After an upgrade to SAP NetWeaver 7.0, execute the reports RSSTAT-MAN_CHECK_CONVERT_DTA and RSSTATMAN_CHECK_CONVERT_PSA for all objects (InfoProviders and PSA tables) at least once in the background. In this way, the request information for existing objects is written to the new tables for faster access, and the new status management is filled with existing data. The request information for objects that you create after the upgrade and for newly loaded requests is automatically written to the new tables. Therefore, these functions and reports are primarily used to transfer existing data to the new administration tables. We recommend that you execute the reports again if there are inconsistencies between the contents of the table RSSTAT-MANPART or RSSTATMANPSA and the correct status or information for the request.

Request information after an upgrade

When you execute check and conversion programs, the system checks the status of all requests for the selected objects, changes or includes entries where necessary, and deletes entries for deleted requests.

Select Edit Loadable InfoProviders to execute the report RSSTATMAN_CHECK_CONVERT_DTA and Edit PSA Tables to execute the report RSSTATMAN_CHECK_CONVERT_PSA. Select the objects for which you want to execute the reports. Specify whether you want the system to check status management when you execute a report. This check only makes sense if you have already executed the reports once or if inconsistencies concerning status management for the requests become apparent later, for example, if deleted requests or the incorrect request status is displayed on the administration screen of the InfoProviders after you run the reports. Make the settings for parallel processing (see above) and execute the reports in the background.

Executing reports

Logs

An extensive log search provides support when required (Figure 5.23). You can specify various search criteria for logs and messages. The following searches are supported: search logs for ABAP runtime errors (Transaction ST22), system logs (Transaction SM21), application logs (Transaction SLG1), monitoring logs, job logs (Transaction SM37), traces for Transaction SM50, logs for BI background processing, and transport logs and activation search results.

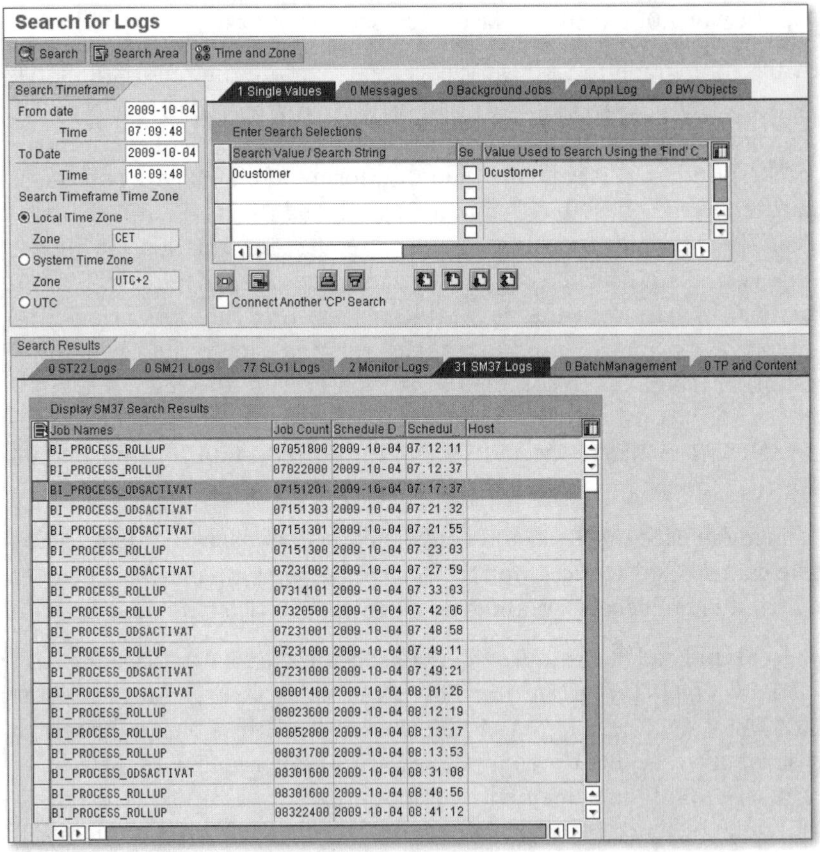

Figure 5.23 Log Overview

Debugging processes in BI background management

A function that debugs processes in BI background management is also available. You can specify selections for debugging a process that is managed in BI background management (Debug Selections) and then debug this BI process directly (Execute Debugging). This function is primarily used by the SAP support to detect errors.

5.2.3 Displaying SAP NetWeaver BW Jobs (Transaction RSM37)

You can use the background processing (Transaction RSM37) delivered with ABAP Support Package 13 (contained in SAP NetWeaver Support Package Stack 12) to schedule and manage background jobs for process chains and other SAP NetWeaver BW processes. Like the general background processing in Transaction SM37, this tool is used to automate routine tasks and to optimize the use of SAP computing resources. Background jobs run in a special type of work process known as the background work process, which differs from the dialog work process in two ways:

▶ A dialog work process has a runtime limit that prevents users from running especially long reports interactively. By default, the system terminates any dialog work process in a transaction that exceeds 300 seconds. Even though you can change the value of the limit (in the system profile parameter `rdisp/max_wprun_time`), this limit is always in effect for dialog work processes. No such limit applies to background work processes.

Dialog vs. background process

▶ Background work processes allocate memory in a different way than dialog work processes. Consequently, background work processes can use as much allocated memory as required to process large volumes of data in the background.

The use of special work processes for background processing provides an additional dimension for separating background processing from interactive work. In general, the time of day is used to separate background processing from interactive work. For example, interactive users use the system during the day, and background processing uses the system at night. In the case of background work processes, you can also use servers to separate background processing from interactive work because background jobs can only be executed on servers that provide background work processes.

Transaction RSM37

Transaction RSM37 is tailored to the BW objects involved in each case and displays the background jobs in an SAP NetWeaver BW context: process chains and variants, DataTransfer process/InfoPackage, InfoSource/DataSource, and so on. The selection of relevant background jobs corresponds to the standard Transaction SM37 (Figure 5.24).

Display Jobs with Program Parameters

Standard View

Background Job Name	Job no.	User	ID	Status	Start date	Start time	Duration	Del	Selection	Selection value
BI_PROCESS_PC_ACTIVE	00322700	SAPSYS		Cancelled	2009-10-06	01:02:49	28	0	CHAIN	ZMETA_SM_1007
BI_PROCESS_PC_ACTIVE	00335000	SAPSYS		Cancelled	2009-10-06	01:05:09	1	0	CHAIN	ZMETA_SM_1010
BI_PROCESS_PC_ACTIVE	01024900	SAPSYS		Cancelled	2009-10-06	01:32:42	29	0	CHAIN	ZMETA_SM_1007
BI_PROCESS_PC_ACTIVE	01321600	SAPSYS		Cancelled	2009-10-06	02:03:06	1	0	CHAIN	ZMETA_SM_1010
BI_PROCESS_PC_ACTIVE	01324200	SAPSYS		Cancelled	2009-10-06	02:04:31	55	0	CHAIN	ZMETA_SM_1007
BI_PROCESS_PC_ACTIVE	02043100	SAPSYS		Cancelled	2009-10-06	02:32:11	44	0	CHAIN	ZMETA_SM_1007
BI_PROCESS_PC_ACTIVE	02321100	SAPSYS		Cancelled	2009-10-06	03:02:11	46	1	CHAIN	ZMETA_SM_1007
BI_PROCESS_PC_ACTIVE	02330700	SAPSYS		Cancelled	2009-10-06	03:05:06	2	0	CHAIN	ZMETA_SM_1010
BI_PROCESS_REMOTE	01320701	ALEREMOTEP26		Cancelled	2009-10-06	01:40:18	0	0	CHAIN	ZATOM_SM_1502
BI_PROCESS_REMOTE	01322100	ALEREMOTEP26		Cancelled	2009-10-06	01:40:34	1	0	CHAIN	ZATOM_SM_1504
/BDL/TASK_PROCESSOR	00180308	SAPSYS		Finished	2009-10-06	01:18:03	0	0		
/BDL/TASK_PROCESSOR	0118036W	SAPSYS		Finished	2009-10-06	02:18:14	0	11		
/BDL/TASK_PROCESSOR	02181400	SAPSYS		Finished	2009-10-06	03:18:03	1	0		
0000000006905207	03312900	ALEREMOTEP26		Finished	2009-10-06	03:31:30	6	1	CRETIM	00:00:00
0000000006905208	03312900	ALEREMOTEP26		Finished	2009-10-06	03:31:30	3	1	CRETIM	00:00:00

Figure 5.24 Displaying Selected BW Jobs

5.2.4 Monitoring Process Chains (Transaction RSPCM)

The process chain monitor (Transaction RSPCM) provides an overview of the (daily) process chains with the goal of monitoring the status of loading processes, for example, and quickly responding to errors as they occur (Figure 5.25). This transaction displays the status of the last process chain in each case and facilitates easy navigation to the process chain log in Transaction RSPC. Only process chains that have been assigned to the monitor once are noted here.

Displaying process chains

You can use Transaction RSPC1 to display a particular process chain directly, enabling you to edit the associated processes or select a special log. This transaction also enables you to easily search process chains by technical name.

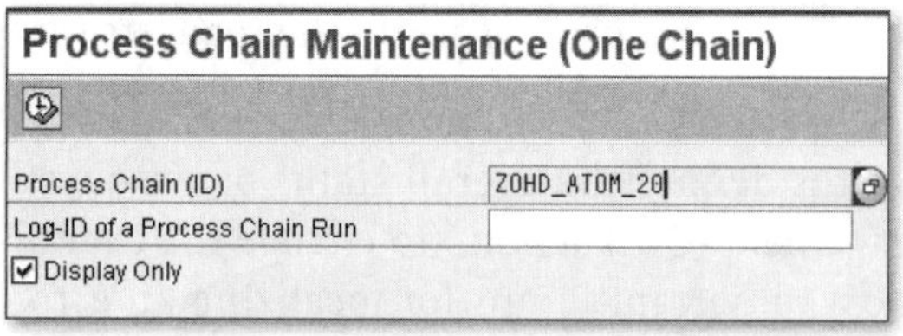

Process Chain Maintenance (One Chain)

Process Chain (ID)	ZOHD_ATOM_20
Log-ID of a Process Chain Run	
☑ Display Only	

Figure 5.25 Process Chain Monitoring

5.2.5 Extraction Monitor (Transaction RSMO)

You can use the extraction monitor to monitor and process data requests in the SAP NetWeaver BW system. To access the monitor, select Monitors in the Administration functional area of the Data Warehousing Workbench. The system displays the requests for the selected period. If you are in an object tree of the Data Warehousing Workbench in the Modeling functional area, you access the relevant monitor by selecting the required object and selecting Call Monitor from the toolbar for the object tree.

On the selection screen of the monitor (MONITOR • NEW SELECTIONS), you can select the display type of the request overview (Figure 5.26).

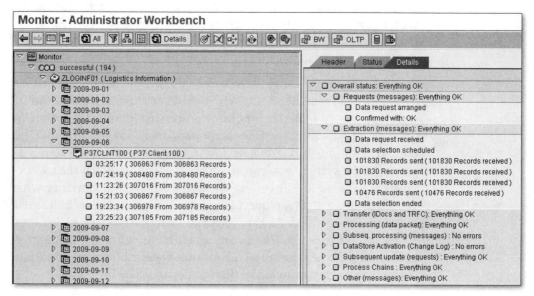

Figure 5.26 Extraction Monitor

You can also use various restriction options to specify the requests that you want to check.

QM action By default, the technical status defines the overall status of a request. You can use a quality management (QM) action) to change the overall status of a request. The most important jumps for localizing an error that has not been logged in an error message are available under the Environment menu option on the detailed screen for the monitor. A wizard supports you in localizing an error. If you schedule the wizard periodically, all of the requests that have not yet been assessed can be analyzed on a regular basis and, if necessary, the relevant person can be notified by email.

The monitor displays all of the information concerning all of the actions performed using the request in an overview tree in the detail view. You can use the context menu to display information and, if necessary, messages about a node. The request, extraction, transfer, processing, and postprocessing are all part of the loading process.

Customizing for traffic light times and colors

In Customizing (Transaction SPRO), you can specify the settings for traffic light times and colors for the extraction monitor. Here, you can set the period of time that can elapse before a system sets a request to terminated. The wait time is the time that has passed since the system received the last data record.

You can set the traffic light colors to be used in the monitor when no data is loaded from the source system or when warnings are issued. If warnings, but no errors, occur during processing, the request is usually yellow. Consequently, postprocessing steps are not performed, and the request is not finished. You have to manually set the request to red or green. In the system, you can automate the way in which such warnings are handled for all system requests so that, in accordance with your settings, a yellow request is automatically set to a technical red or green. For each InfoPackage, you can select SCHEDULER • WARNING HANDLING OR TIMEOUT TIME in the scheduler to define which status is to be assigned to a request and the maximum permitted wait time, thus overriding the system-wide settings for a particular InfoPackage.

5.2.6 Query Monitor (Transaction RSRT)

You use the query monitor (Transaction RSRT) to test, check, and manage BW queries. You can use the monitor to test or regenerate queries or query views and to check and change query properties. You can also display technical information about queries and access the cache monitor. Table 5.3 provides an overview of the functions of the query monitor.

Function	Description
Execute	Executes the query or query view.
	You access a screen where the query is displayed in an HTML control. You can test the display functions, with certain restrictions, as you would on the Web.
	In the upper part of the entry screen, the URL is displayed with all of its parameter settings.
Generate Report	Regenerates the query code.
	For a regeneration, the agreement is always given with the query definition.
Properties	The dialog box for query properties is displayed.
Messages	You access the Suppress Messages dialog box.
	Here, you can determine which messages for the chosen query are not to be shown to the user in the frontend.
	In the left-hand screen area, you can choose the message category (for example, Generation, Hierarchy, Variables, Key Figures, and Calculate As). In the right-hand screen area, you see messages that you can choose to suppress. When you double-click the message short text, the system displays the associated long text in the lower screen area.
	Set the indicator next to messages that you want to suppress and then go back. The system automatically saves your entries.
Generation Log	You access the screen in which you analyze the application log. If the Generation Log option has been activated for the query, you can display the corresponding generation log after you regenerate the query.

Functions of the query monitor

Table 5.3 Overview of Query Monitor Functions

Function	Description
Performance Info	The system displays performance-relevant information about the query that does not correspond to the system recommendations.
	The information refers to the following areas: query definition (use of aggregates and a cache, read mode, noncumulative values) and InfoProviders (statistics, indexes).
Technical Info	You access the Technical Information screen (see below).
Cache Monitor	You access the Cache Monitor screen.
Query Variants	If the query contains variables that are ready for input, the subsequent screen displays the query variants. You can change these variants and create new ones.
Test IGS	You use SAP Internet Graphics Service (IGS) to create the charts and maps for Web-based reporting in the SAP NetWeaver BW system.
	If you select Test IGS, the system checks whether the Internet Graphics Server can be accessed. If the system displays a graphic with two sets of three bars, you have a connection. You can also analyze performance here.

Table 5.3 Overview of Query Monitor Functions (Cont.)

Technical
information
The Technical Information screen provides an overview of important, technical reference numbers for a query. The technical information for the selected query is grouped by category. In addition, the query definition determines whether all or only part of the categories is displayed. The first line of the HTML control contains links to the categories listed in table form in the lower page area. For some categories, values are specified in the first column:

▶ A green traffic light means that the value of the technical reference number corresponds exactly to the system recommendation.

▶ A yellow traffic light means that the value of the technical reference number may not correspond to the system recommendation.

▶ A red traffic light means that the value of the technical reference number does not correspond to the system recommendation. It may make sense to change the value. However, this does not necessarily mean that there is an error.

The cache monitor provides information about the global cache parameters, the amount of memory used by query runtime objects, and the current underlying cache structure. Global cache parameter settings are made in Customizing (see Global Cache Parameters). The cache-relevant settings that have been defined for an InfoProvider or query can override the global cache parameters. You can set the standard cache mode for an InfoProvider in Customizing. If you change these settings later, the changes do not affect existing queries for this InfoProvider, but only affect future queries created for this InfoProvider. You can change the cache mode for a query in the query properties area in Transaction RSRT. You can obtain an overview of the cache-relevant data for a query (for example, important time stamps) in the Technical Info area.

Cache monitor

The query monitor facilitates the execution of individual queries with various debugging options. After you select a query, you can select EXECUTE • DEBUG to execute the query (with a selection of various debugging options). The debugging options provide different variants for a detailed examination of the query. For example, you can use the Display SQL Query debugging option to display the SQL statement for the query.

Debugging

5.2.7 Trace Tool (Transaction RSRTRACE)

If you use Transaction RSRTRACE to activate the query trace, you can configure the trace for a specific topic (Figure 5.27). For the trace, you must use the Plus button to add individual users and the Minus button to remove them. You can select Configure User to configure the trace for specific users.

Irrespective of whether you use the trace option in BEx Analyzer or the trace tool RSRTRACE to switch on the trace, the trace is only effective when the user logs on again after having switched on the trace.

The query trace provides the option of logging individual query steps when you execute a query. You must switch the trace on for each user for whom you want to record a trace. You can activate the trace in Transaction RSRTRACE or by using the Trace option in BEx Analyzer. You should switch on the trace only for specific analyses because the log recordings related to the trace can have a negative effect on performance. After you execute the query steps that you want to analyze, you should turn off the trace because continuous trace recordings can place an unnecessary strain on the system. The log recordings are stored in a trace log, and you can call them at any time. You can select DB Debugging to go through the individual steps of a trace at a later time.

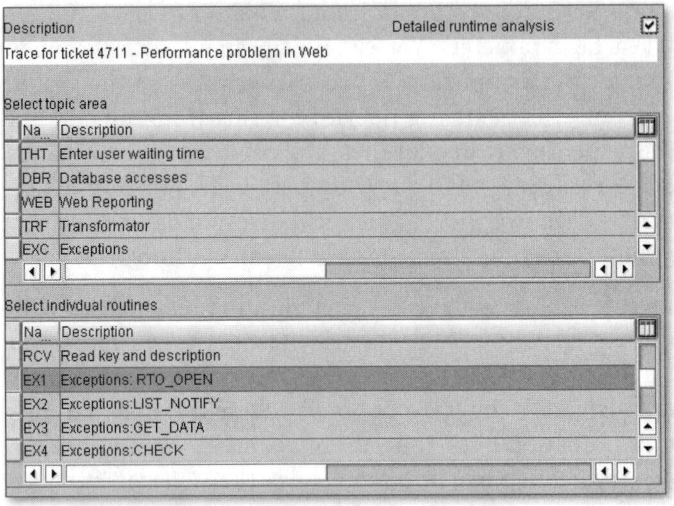

Figure 5.27 Trace Configuration for Individual Users

Analyzing trace logs

You can select All Logs to list the recorded trace logs. Double-click one of the trace logs in the list to display the recorded trace.

5.2.8 Analyzing BW Objects (Transaction RSRV)

Transaction RSRV is used to perform consistency checks on the data stored in the SAP NetWeaver BW system. These checks mainly investigate foreign key relationships between the individual tables in the enhanced star schema of the SAP NetWeaver BW system. You can access the test and repair environment by calling Transaction RSRV or selecting SAP MENU • ADMINISTRATION • ANALYSIS TOOL.

Executing tests

Use drag and drop or double-click to select one or more tests. In your test package view, each test that you have selected is displayed as a closed folder. (An exception to this is elementary tests without parameters. These tests appear not as folders, but as simple entries.) You can also drag an entire test folder from the list of tests to the right-hand screen area. All of the tests in the hierarchical structure of this folder are then added to the test package.

You then have to provide parameters for the tests. You do not have to provide parameters for tests that do not have them. Note the message issued by the system after you make your selection. To provide parameters, double-click a test (test package) or expand the relevant test folder.

Entering parameters

Enter the required parameter values in the dialog box displayed. In many cases, an input help is available. Once you have entered the parameters, a Parameter folder is inserted below the test. This folder contains the parameter values. The name of the test may also change so that you can see, at a glance, the parameter values for which the test is to be performed. It is possible and often helpful to select the same test several times and assign it different parameters. If you have provided parameters for a combined test, an Elementary Tests folder is inserted too. This folder contains the elementary tests that comprise the combined test. You can use drag and drop to delete individual elementary tests from the list of tests.

Once you have provided parameters for all tests, you can start the test run. While the test is running, the test icons change from grey diamonds to a green, yellow, or red icons, depending on whether the test produces no errors, warnings only, or actual errors.

Repairs

Some tests can repair any error or inconsistency. In general, however, automatic corrections are not possible. If, for example, entries are missing from the SID table for a characteristic, but the lost SIDs are still being used in a dimension table of an InfoCube (and the corresponding dimension key is still in the fact table), you can only correct this by reloading the transaction data for the InfoCube. You must also remember to perform repairs in the correct sequence. Before you perform any repair, you should read the test documentation and get a clear idea of where the error lies.

Once you have executed a test run, exit the application log and return to the start view for the test environment so you can perform the necessary repairs. If you want to start a repair run, select Solve Error. Because the dataset may change between the test run and repair run,

Starting a repair run

the required tests are performed again before the actual repair is performed. Once again, the output is provided in the application log.

Once you have performed a repair, you should execute the test package again to examine which errors the system was able to solve.

Execution in process chains

In process chain maintenance (Transaction RSPC), add the ABAP program RSRV_JOB_RUNNER to your process chain by using drag and drop to select the process type ABAP Program under General Services in the process type view.

When you maintain a process variant, you have to enter a program name and program variant. Here, enter the program name "RSRV_ JOB_RUNNER." Select a program variant name and then select Change. On the next screen, you can change or display a variant that already exists, or you can create a new variant. When creating a new variant, you have to enter a package name (an input help is available), the level of detail for the log in Transaction RSRV, which is to be integrated into the process chain, and a message type that signifies that process chain processing is to be terminated.

Log
The log for the RSRV process in the process chain consists of the following:

► A summary that specifies whether errors, warnings, or no errors at all were output for each elementary test

► A view of the log for the RSRV test package, in the level of detail specified

Sample level of detail
If you choose the value 3 as the level of detail, only messages up to level 3 are included in the log of process chain processes. Therefore, any messages that have been output at a lower test level in the test package are not displayed in this log. Note that (unlike the application log) errors in the process log are not propagated from low levels of detail to lower levels of detail. If, for example, a single error was output at level 4, the summary would state that the associated test had returned an error, but this error would not be recorded in the second part of the log.

A complete log is always written, irrespective of the log for the RSRV process in the process chain. You can view this log under the menu path APPLICATION LOG • DISPLAY LOG • FROM BACKGROUND PROCESSING.

Note that, at present, there is no transport object for test packages. Consequently, they cannot be transported. Process chains that execute RSRV test packages have to be reworked manually after they are transported to another system: In addition, the corresponding test packages have to be created.

Transport

Complete Characteristics Check

If you want to perform a detailed test on a particular characteristic or if you want to correct inconsistencies associated with this InfoObject, and if you want to schedule this as a regular job in the background, you can call the report RSDMD_CHECKPRG_ALL in Transaction SE38 (Figure 5.28).

```
┌─────────────────────────────────────────────────────────┐
│ RSDMD_CHECKPRG_ALL                                        │
├─────────────────────────────────────────────────────────┤
│ ⊕                                                         │
│                                                           │
│ Name of Basic Characteristic    [0MATERIAL|        ] [⌕]  │
│ ☐ Repair                                                  │
│ ☐ Force X message if error                                │
│ ☑ Display log                                             │
│ ☐ Check Mode                                              │
│                                                           │
│ ☑ Invalid object versions                                 │
│ ☑ Version A/D without M record                            │
│ ☑ Versions A and M - no D flag                            │
│ ☑ Time Interval Q, Text Table                             │
│                                                           │
│ ☑ Check initial entries                                   │
│ ☑ Specifications in SID,T                                 │
│ ☑ Versions in SID,P,Q                                     │
│                                                           │
│ ☑ Initial values of attributes                            │
│ ☑ Navigation attribute values                             │
│ ☑ Consistency of P,X,Q,Y tables                           │
│ ☑ SID Values in X and Y Tables                            │
└─────────────────────────────────────────────────────────┘
```

Figure 5.28 Report RSDMD_CHECKPRG_ALL

The sequence of the single tests provided by this program plays a central role in eliminating inconsistencies in the master data tables of a characteristic. The correction provided by a special single test may be influenced by successful corrections in other single tests.

Sequence for single tests

For example, the X or Y table is only successfully rebuilt using the single test "Consistency of P, X, Q, Y tables" if the single test "Navigation attribute values" has already been performed to ensure that a corresponding entry for each navigation attribute value exists in the SID table. If this condition it not fulfilled, it is not possible to fully build the X or Y table because characteristics that have navigation attribute values but no SID value are excluded from the rebuild. You should therefore always perform the single test "Navigation attribute values" in repair mode before the test "Consistency of P, X, Q, Y tables."

Incorrect initial values

If the initial values for attributes are incorrect, you may not be able to fully build an X or Y table. Therefore, you should implement the correction in the single test "Initial values of attributes" before you build a new X or Y table. This is why the single tests listed on the selection screen have been sorted from top to bottom in a logically correct sequence, making it possible to resolve inconsistencies by selecting all available single tests in a single correction run.

Selected Tests for Master Data

You can use master data tests to check and, if necessary, correct data for characteristics. For example, you can check the consistency of conversion functions and tables that have been generated:

▸ **Value in active version flagged for deletion, no M version exists**
This elementary test checks whether the active (A) version has characteristic values that are flagged for deletion (the D flag is set) without a modified (M) version. Such characteristic values would be lost during activation.

▸ **A and M versions of a value exist, no D flag set**
This test checks whether characteristic values exist in an active (A) and modified (M) version, but the active version is not flagged for deletion (the D flag is not set). This would result in a termination during activation.

▸ **Check time intervals in the Q table of a characteristic with time-dependent master data**
The Q table of a characteristic contains values for the time-dependent attributes of the characteristic. This test checks whether the system covers the entire period between Jan. 01, 1000 and Dec. 31, 9999 without any gaps or overlaps. The active version and changed (most recent) values are checked. If no time-dependent attributes are assigned to a characteristic, no such table exists, and the test is not performed.

In many cases, you can correct data records that may be incorrect. For example, an inconsistency whereby the deletion indicator (changed) is set incorrectly (D instead of a blank space or vice versa) can often be eliminated.

Note that after you repair characteristics that have navigation attributes, you must rebuild the associated Y table, which means you must also rebuild all relevant aggregates.

▶ **Existence of navigation attribute values**

This test checks whether the values for the navigation attributes of a characteristic (in master data table P or Q, depending on the time dependency) also exist in the SID table for the navigation attribute. First, the system compares the number of entries in the master data table (P or Q table) for the characteristic with the number of entries in the X table whose navigation attribute SID is listed in the SID table for the navigation attribute. If these numbers differ, the surplus entries are identified and the first 50 are output. This procedure results in the system performing this test very quickly.

▶ **Check flags in the SID table for an InfoObject**

This elementary test checks the following properties or objects:

  ▶ Does the specified (basic) characteristic have master data? If so, the With Master Data indicator is set on the Master Data tab on the InfoObject maintenance screen (Transaction RSD1).

  ▶ Are there any master data tables?

  ▶ If so, does the SID table contain records for which the data flag (DATAFL) is set, but the check flag (CHCKFL) is not?

The listed constellations are not supposed to occur and therefore result in error messages.

▶ **Existence of initial records in the SID and master data tables for a characteristic**

Once the SID and master data tables for a characteristic are created on the database, an initial record (also known as an initial entry) is written to these tables. This test checks whether the SID and master data tables contain valid initial records. The layout of an initial record changes depending on the master data table:

  ▶ The structure of an initial record in an SID table is as follows: The value of the characteristic and, if the characteristic is a compound characteristic, the values of the higher-level characteristics are initial. The SID field is also initial (= 0). The three indicators CHCKFL, DATAFL, and INCFL have the value X.

▶ If a P table contains an initial record, all of the fields are initial (apart from the field OBJVERS, which has the value A).

▶ The initial record in a Q table consists of initial fields (apart from OBJVERS = A, DATEFROM = 01.01.1000, and DATETO = 31.12.9999).

▶ In an X table, all of the fields are initial (apart from the field OBJVERS, which has the value A).

▶ In a Y table, all of the fields are initial (apart from OBJVERS = A, DATEFROM = 01.01.1000, and DATETO = 31.12.9999).

▶ **Type-related initial values of attributes**
The system searches the master data tables P (time-independent) and Q (time-dependent) for records in which SPACE is used as an initial value even though the type-related initial value is another value. This situation only arises if characteristics have the data type NUMC, DATS, or TIMS.

▶ **Invalid object version for characteristic values**
Only the following value combinations are valid for the version and the Delete(D)/Insert(I) flag of a characteristic value:

▶ A and D

▶ A and SPACE

▶ M and I

Other combinations of these two properties are not permitted and therefore are output as errors.

▶ **Non-permitted characters in characteristic values**
The following checks are performed on the characteristic values in SID tables:

▶ Only permitted characters and additional characters can be used.

▶ The characteristic values must correspond to the data type of the characteristic (for example, ABC would not be valid for a numerical characteristic).

▶ The values for characteristics with conversion routines must have an internal format.

▸ The values for time characteristics must represent valid values (for example, only the values 01 to 12 are used for the calendar month).

▸ Initial values correspond to the data type of the characteristic (for example, blank characters are only valid for characteristics of the type CHAR).

In technical terms, the check is performed using the function module `RRSV_VALUE_CHECK_PLAUSIBILITY`, which is also used to check characteristic values in loading processes.

▸ **Compare size of P or Q table with X or Y table**
The number of entries in the P or Q table is compared with the number of entries in the X or Y table, respectively. At any time, they should contain the same number of entries. X and Y tables contain the master data information of the characteristic with internal keys instead of characteristic values. They are used during reporting. An inconsistency gives rise to incorrect figures during reporting: Missing entries are like (hidden) filters. A scenario whereby the X table contains more entries than the P table or the Y table contains more entries than the Q table should not arise. If it does, there are serious inconsistencies in the system, possibly owing to a system error when deleting master data.

▸ **Compare characteristic values in S, P, and Q tables**
This test checks whether the master data tables S (SID), P (time-independent master data), and Q (time-dependent master data) contain the same characteristic values. More specifically, it checks whether the following three characteristic value quantities are the same:

▸ Characteristic values that occur in the SID table of the characteristic in data records with the check flag (CHCKFL field) = X

▸ Characteristic values that occur in the P table of the characteristic in data records with the object version (OBJVERS field) = A

▸ Characteristic values that occur in the Q table of the characteristic in data records with the object version (OBJVERS field) = A

▸ **SID values in X and Y table**
This test checks the values in the X and Y tables. These tables store the relationship between the characteristic values and the time-independent or time-dependent navigation attributes of the characteristics at SID level.

▶ **Reconcile the number range and maximum SID**

This elementary test checks whether a number range object exists for the SIDs of the characteristic, and if so, whether the largest SID used is smaller than or equal to the status of the number range object. If this is not the case, there is an error.

▶ **Check characteristic values against the conversion exit**

This test checks whether a conversion routine is used for the characteristic to be examined (see the General tab in Transaction RSD1). A conversion routine converts characteristic values between an external format (in which the user enters and views data) and an internal format (in which the data is stored in the database). In particular, the characteristic values in the master data tables must have an internal format.

The most important example is the conversion exit ALPHA. When converting an external display into an internal display, this ALPHA exit changes numerical values only. These are right-aligned in the target field. When converting an internal display into an external display, leading zeros are removed from numerical values. The following function modules are used for conversion exit ALPHA:

▶ Conversion of external display into an internal display: CONVERSION_EXIT_ALPHA_INPUT

▶ Conversion of internal display into an external display: CONVERSION_EXIT_ALPHA_OUTPUT

If the characteristic uses a conversion routine, the test checks whether all of the values in the SID table for the characteristic are valid internal values. By definition, the values of the function module that converts an external display into an internal display are valid internal values. In this test, the values to be checked are initially converted from an internal format into an external format and then from an external format into an internal format. If the value obtained no longer corresponds to the original value, it is not valid.

Invalid internal values may cause problems during reporting. If the master data tables contain several values, which are converted into just one value following the conversion from an internal format to an external format, the user can no longer differentiate between these values. Consequently, some lines may appear to be duplicated in reports. It is also possible that, for example, the user selects a filter value that seems to be in the result but does not find any data.

▶ **Check whether characteristic values in the text table also exist in the SID table**

The text table for a characteristic has the characteristic value as a key field. Any characteristic values in this column of the text table must also be contained in the SID table for the characteristic. Characteristic values that the test finds in the text table, but not in the SID table, do not affect normal SAP NetWeaver BW system operation. However, when characteristic values have an incorrect format (in terms of the conversion routine that you are using), a short dump may occur in the conversion program (the use of Transaction RSMDCNVEXIT to convert inconsistent internal characteristic values is no longer supported in newer releases).

▶ **SID conversion for InfoObject 0UNIT**

This test checks whether the entries in the SID table for the InfoObject 0UNIT are within the valid internal limits defined by the number range object BIM9999996. If the SID values are below the interval limits, you can repair the entries in the SID table for the InfoObject 0UNIT as follows:

  ▶ Convert the entries in the SID table for the InfoObject 0UNIT.

  ▶ Adjust the SID entries in the unit dimension of *all* InfoCubes.

  ▶ Possibly rebuild the tables for the hierarchies defined for the InfoObject 0UNIT.

If the SID values lie within the interval limits, a conversion is not required. The system nevertheless starts a simulation run that describes or checks a possible conversion. If the SID values lie outside the interval limits, this test does not have a repair option. In such cases, please contact the SAP support.

Simulation run

To resolve incorrect SAP NetWeaver BW system behavior, avoid executing SAP NetWeaver BW functions (in particular, staging and reporting) during the repair. If an error occurs during a repair, the SAP NetWeaver BW system may become inconsistent. Check the error messages in the log and, if necessary, eliminate the cause of the error.

▶ **Multibyte analysis for master data text tables**
This test checks the descriptive texts (short, medium, and long) for a characteristic in the T table.

Selected Tests for Transaction Data

You can use the tests in the Transaction Data folder to check and, if necessary, repair the data and structures of InfoCubes only. The tests for DataStore objects are summarized in a separate folder called ODS Objects.

▶ **Consistency of the time dimension of an InfoCube**
This test checks whether the time characteristics used in the time dimension of an InfoCube are consistent. It is extremely important that the time characteristics for noncumulative InfoCubes and partitioned InfoCubes are consistent because inconsistent values in the time dimension may produce incorrect results in these InfoCubes. If InfoCubes are partitioned according to time characteristics, the conditions for the partitioning characteristic are derived from the restrictions to the time characteristics. If an error occurs, the InfoCube is selected as an InfoCube with an inconsistent time dimension. This selection has the following effects:

▶ The derivation of conditions for partitioning criteria is deactivated because the time characteristics are inconsistent. Performance usually deteriorates as a result.

▶ If the InfoCube contains noncumulatives, the system issues a warning for each query, indicating that the data displayed is potentially incorrect.

▶ **Foreign key relationship between the dimension table and the SID table**
This test checks the referential integrity between the dimension tables of the InfoCube dimensions and the SID tables of the characteristics. All of the SIDs in the dimension tables must be contained in the relevant SID tables.

▶ **Fact table and dimension table of an InfoCube**
This elementary test checks the foreign key relationship between a fact table and a dimension table: It checks whether the column for the specified dimension in the fact table contains only those dimension keys that are also contained in the dimension table as a key field.

Note that it does not make sense to apply this test to the compressed fact table for an InfoCube and its package dimension because, during compression, all of the keys in the package dimension in the (compressed) fact table are set to the initial value (0).

▶ **Database parameters for tables in the *schema for InfoCubes**
This test checks whether the database parameters are set correctly for all tables that belong to the star schema of the InfoCube. The database determines how this test is implemented. Consequently, the test may not examine or repair the database that you are using. In this case, the system issues a corresponding message in the log.

▶ **Reconcile the number range of a dimension and the maximum dimension key**
This elementary test checks whether a number range object exists for the InfoCube dimension and, if so, whether the largest dimension key used (DIMID) for the dimension is smaller than or equal to the status of the number range object. If this is not the case, there is an error, which can be corrected in repair mode. If the number range object is missing, you have to reactivate the InfoCube.

▶ **Multiple entries in the dimensions of a (basic) InfoCube**
This elementary test recognizes whether a selected dimension table of the specified InfoCube contains several lines that have different DIM-IDs but the same SIDs. This situation can arise with parallel loading jobs, not because of an inconsistency, but because the storage space on the database has been filled unnecessarily.

▶ **Units of key figures in fact tables are initial**
The system searches the fact tables (E and F tables) of an InfoCube for records that contain unit-related key figures whose units are not filled. Because the value of the unit must correspond to the value of the key figure, you know an error has occurred during data loading if the system finds such records.

▶ **Status of InfoCube data**
This test checks whether the status information concerning the data in basic InfoCubes is consistent. This test has an optional InfoCube parameter, which can be assigned the name of a basic InfoCube. If this parameter remains empty, the test checks the following:

▸ Do all of the basic InfoCubes have an entry in table RSMDAT-ASTATE?

▸ Do all of the basic InfoCubes in table RSMDATASTATE exist?

▸ Are all of the basic InfoCubes for which the TECHOK field is not set in the table RSMDATASTATE empty?

▸ Is the information in the TECHOK, QUALOK, ROLLUP_RSVD_DUAL, ROLLUP, DMEXIST, DMALL, COMPR, and COMPR_DUAL fields consistent for basic InfoCubes?

If you specify a basic InfoCube, this test checks whether this basic InfoCube has an entry in table RSMDATASTATE, whether the Info-Cube is empty (if the TECHOK field is not set), and whether the information in the above fields is consistent. Note that in SAP NetWeaver BW 3.x, table RSMDATASTATE also contains entries for objects other than basic InfoCubes (for example, for DataStore objects and characteristics that act as InfoProviders).

▸ **Foreign key relationship of a reporting-relevant ODS object with characteristics in SID tables**
This test checks whether each characteristic value in the table with active records for a DataStore object also exists in the SID table for the corresponding characteristic.

Selected Tests for Hierarchies

The Hierarchy folder contains several tests for checking one or more hierarchies:

▸ **Check individual hierarchies**
This test checks the hierarchy using the name of the characteristic in the hierarchy version. Specifically, it checks whether the parent-child relationships in the hierarchy tables are consistent and whether certain artificial (hidden) hierarchy nodes, which are required for reporting, exist and have been sorted correctly in the hierarchy.

▸ **Text references for nodes in hierarchies associated with a characteristic**
The relationship between the node name and the (negative) SIDs for the hierarchy nodes of all hierarchies associated with a characteristic is coded in the K table of a characteristic. In the case of characteristic nodes, that is, hierarchy nodes whose node name is a characteristic value of another characteristic, the SID of the characteristic value is

also stored in the field OSID. The K table is used if the texts for hierarchy nodes need to be displayed. If entries are missing from the K table or if the field OSID contains SIDs that do not exist, terminations may occur when you execute a query.

Selected Tests for the Database

You can perform general tests (for example, for indexes or statistics) and tests for particular databases in the database test area:

▶ **Database indexes of an InfoCube and its aggregates**
This test checks the secondary indexes of an InfoCube and all of its aggregates. The optimum type of secondary indexes is strongly dependent on the database system used and the data saved there.

▶ **Check database parameters**
This test checks the extent to which general database parameters affect the performance of the BW system.

▶ **Database statistics for an InfoCube and its aggregates**
This test checks whether there are up-to-date database statistics for the tables of an InfoCube and its aggregates or whether these need to be created.

▶ **Database information about the tables of an InfoProvider**
This test checks the extent to which the general database parameters affect the performance of the Business Information Warehouse.

▶ **Space used by MDC InfoProviders in DB2 for Linux, UNIX, and Windows**
This test determines the free storage space allocated (as a percentage) to InfoProviders that use multidimensional clustering (MDC) on DB2 for Linux, UNIX, and Windows. If the free space is more than 33%, a new clustering should be considered.

An MDC table is structured in such a way that data rows that contain the same values as contained in the MDC dimension columns are grouped into separate blocks. Each unique value combination in the MDC dimension tables form a logical cell to which one or more page blocks can be assigned. The number of pages in a block corresponds to the extent size of the tablespace in which the table lies.

The test shows the following detailed information about the MDC space usage for the F and E fact tables of InfoCubes:

- Number of rows in the MDC table
- Number of logical cells in the MDC table to which blocks are assigned
- Cardinality of MDC dimensions
- Number of assigned pages in the MDC table
- Number of blank pages in the MDC table
- Space assigned to the MDC table (KB)
- Empty space assigned to the MDC table (KB)

If MDC is used for an aggregate, the test provides the free space assigned (as a percentage) to each aggregate. If the free space is more than 33%, you should consider deactivating MDC for the aggregate. For DataStore objects, the system provides detailed information about the MDC space usage for the table that contains the active data. Note that the test evaluates the information from the results of the last statistics collection. If the database statistics are not up to date, the results may be inaccurate.

- **Row suppression of InfoProvider tables in DB2 for Linux, UNIX, and Windows**
  This test checks whether data row suppression in DB2 for Linux, UNIX, and Windows is active for the fact tables of InfoCubes and aggregates as well as for DataStore object tables. Data row suppression is available in Version 9 of DB2 for Linux, UNIX, and Windows (DB2 LUW). It uses a static ABAP Dictionary–based suppression algorithm to suppress data according to rows. This makes it possible to replace patterns that repeat themselves and are spread across several column values within a row with short symbol characters. You can use data row suppression to save storage space and reduce hard disk output/input and data access times.

  The test checks the following information, which concerns DB2 LUW data row suppression for each fact table in an InfoCube and its aggregates or for DataStore object tables:

  - Activation of row suppression
  - Size of data object in the table
  - Availability of a suppression dictionary in the table
  - Size of suppression dictionary in the table in KB or bytes (if a suppression dictionary is available)

The test returns the status Red if tables have the following functions: **Red status**

▶ Row suppression is active.

▶ The size of the data object exceeds 1 MB on every database table partition in which the table is available.

▶ The table does not have a suppression dictionary.

Otherwise, the test returns the status Green.

▶ **Data row suppression in PSA database tables in DB2 for Linux, UNIX, and Windows**
This test checks whether data row suppression in DB2 for Linux, UNIX, and Windows is active for PSA tables. Both the procedure and functional capability correspond to the above description of row suppression for InfoProvider tables.

Selected Tests for Aggregates

An M version test and a list of aggregates without associated InfoCubes are available for aggregate checks.

▶ **Check M version of an aggregate**
This test checks the consistency of the M version of aggregate definitions. Either the technical name or the unique internal number (Unique Identifier [UID]) of an aggregate is specified as a parameter. Both parameters are optional. If you do not specify a value, the system checks all aggregates. Inconsistencies may arise due to problems when activating or transporting business content. In general, these situations concern characteristics or navigation attributes that are not added when the business content is activated and therefore can only be available in the active version (A), and not in the modified version (M). Examples include:

▶ Characteristics of unit dimensions and data package dimensions (for example, request ID or change ID)

▶ Navigation attributes of aggregates

In aggregate maintenance (Transaction RSDDV), the aggregate is generally displayed in the M version, enabling the system to check whether the aforementioned technical characteristics inadvertently exist.

▶ **Find aggregates for InfoCubes that do not exist**
This test checks whether the system contains aggregates for which the

InfoCube no longer exists. This inconsistency does not directly affect normal operation. However, it unnecessarily occupies space on the database.

Other Selected Tests

The following are some other important tests that are available in Transaction RSRV:

▶ **Consistency between PSA partitions and SAP administrative information**
For SAP NetWeaver BW systems with an ORACLE database, this test checks whether the physical partitions on the database correspond with the information contained in the administration tables RSTSODS and RSTSODSPART.

▶ **Check the technical properties of a query**
This check is the same as the check performed in Transaction RSRT when you select Technical Info.

▶ **Generate and execute queries**
The specified queries are generated and, if possible, executed. If you use patterns in the parameter field, you can select any number of queries. Once you have executed the selection, the system displays a log informing you which of these queries you can and cannot process.

▶ **Check the selection type of authorization variables**
Here, the system checks all query variables of the type Processed According to Authorization. Use this check if users with limited analysis authorizations obtain unusual results for a query with variables of this type.

▶ **Check authorization generation**
These checks search an internal "authorization generation" table for unused entries. If the table contains a few yellow entries, this is not problematic. However, if the number increases, you must take a closer look at authorization generation.

▶ **Delete HIESID values in the K table that do not exist in RSRHIEDIR_OLAP**
This is a check program for determining invalid hierarchy SID values (field HIESID) in the K table of the characteristic. If the K table contains an invalid HIESID entry without a corresponding entry in table RSRHIEDIR_OLAP (OLAP Relevant Information for the Hierarchies),

the system issues a warning. There is a condition that states that any entries with this field must be deleted. This check ensures that the internal hierarchy tables remain consistent.

These RSRV tests are described in detail in Section 13.6, SAP NetWeaver BW Accelerator.

5.2.9 RS Trace Tool (Transaction RSTT)

The trace environment contains special tools for recording and reproducing traces (RS Trace Tool) and for processing automatic regression tests (Computer Aided Test Tool, CATT). If an error situation occurs in reporting (owing to runtime errors when you execute a query or web template or owing to some unexpected result values), you use the RS Trace Tool (Transaction RSTT) to record traces (Figure 5.29).

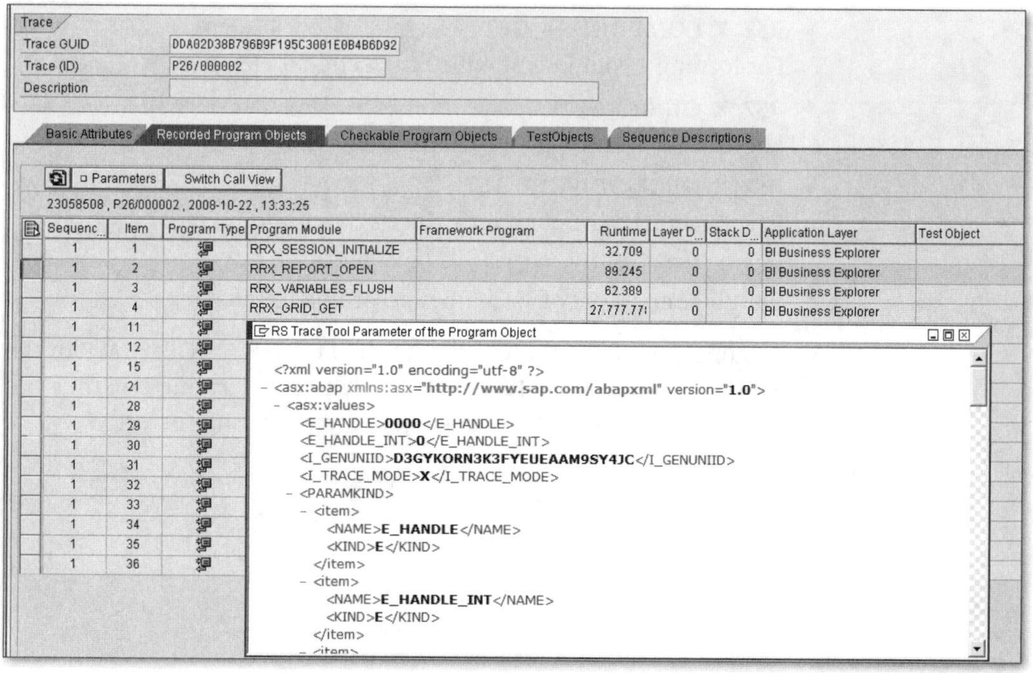

Figure 5.29 Analyzing a Trace ID in Transaction RSTT

To activate a user for a trace recording, you must define a user name in the User Activation area in the trace tool. You must then select the environment you require for executing, for example, the query (that is,

Activating users

execution in the query monitor, BEx Analyzer, web browser, planning modeler, and so on) and perform all actions until the error occurs.

After you deactivate the trace in Transaction RSTT, a list of traces is available in the Trace Collection area. This list is sorted by date in descending order, which means that it should be easy to find the most recent trace ID. An administrator or the SAP support can then run the recorded trace to analyze and reproduce the error. You can accurately control the position on the Recorded Program Objects tab, for example, by double-clicking the call position you require.

5.2.10   Reporting Function Modules (Transaction RSZT)

Transaction RSZT tests the function modules used in reporting and is therefore used, in particular, by the SAP support to analyze InfoProviders and reporting elements. The relevant function modules are:

▸ **RSZ_X_COMPONENT_GET**
For loading a component with all dependent elements

▸ **RSZ_X_QUERY_GET**
For loading a query via transformation tables

▸ **RSZ_X_INFO_OBJECTS_GET**
For obtaining a list of all InfoObjects in an InfoCube

▸ **RSZ_X_INFOCUBES_GET**
For obtaining a list of InfoCubes according to InfoArea

For example, you can analyze the internal table E_T_IOBJ_CMP in the function module RSZ_X_INFO_OBJECTS_GET to determine whether the system reads and processes InfoObject compounding correctly.

Because SAP NetWeaver BW system users need to be familiar with some basic technical principles concerning the system's numerous special objects, we want to provide this information here before discussing administration and monitoring in detail.

6 Basic Principles of Processes and Objects

It is not possible for this book to address every detail concerning special processes and objects in SAP NetWeaver BW systems. However, in preparation for our discussion of administration and monitoring in Chapter 12, Administration of SAP NetWeaver BW Processes in Detail, users need to have a general understanding of these special processes and objects. Nevertheless, we do not need to explain, for example, the various types of InfoObjects (characteristics, key figures, time characteristics, and units) here, nor do we need to define or explain how MultiProviders are used.

In the next chapter, we will limit our description to some technical details that are of interest to administrators. Such details are not usually explained in basic manuals but are nonetheless extremely important from an administration perspective.

6.1 DataStore Object

DataStore objects (DSOs) are generally used to store consolidated and cleansed transaction data or master data at the document level (at an atomic level). They are used, for example, in the data warehouse layers of modern layer architectures or for building a corporate memory. We make a distinction between the following DSO types:

▶ **Standard DataStore object**

This type consists of an activation queue, a table for active data, and a change log.

DSO types

▶ **Write-optimized DataStore objects**
This type consists of a table for active data and is used to save unique data records at the document level. You can define a semantic key for this object, but its uniqueness is ensured by a technical key generated by the system.

▶ **DataStore object for direct update**
This type consists of a table for active data, which is filled by application programming interfaces (APIs), and not by data loading processes. This type is often used, for example, as a data target for analysis processes.

In a standard DataStore object, the data reaches the change log via the activation queue and is written to the table for active data upon activation. During activation, the requests are sorted according to their logical keys. This ensures that the data is updated to the table for active data in the correct request sequence.

The table for active data is built in accordance with the DataStore object definition; that is, key fields and data fields are specified when the DataStore object is defined. The activation queue and change log have an almost identical structure: The activation queue has an SID, package ID, and record number as its key, whereas the change log has a request ID, package ID, and record number as its key.

Runtime measurements and logs
The following transactions, which were introduced and extended with SAP NetWeaver BW 7.0, are interesting from the perspective of managing and troubleshooting DataStore objects:

▶ **Transaction RSODSO_SETTINGS (formerly RSCUSTA2)**
You use this transaction to set runtime parameters for DataStore objects. You also have the option of setting object-specific parameters. If they do not exist, default values are used instead.

▶ **Transaction RSODSO_SHOWLOG**
You use this log transaction to display a log that contains all of the information you require about a request processed in a DataStore object (for example, information about the runtime parameters, the main process, the data package, and so on).

▶ **Transaction RSODSO_BRKPNT**
You can use this transaction to set breakpoints in DSO programs (Fig-

ure 6.1). Individual processing takes place in a maintenance view in Transaction SM30.

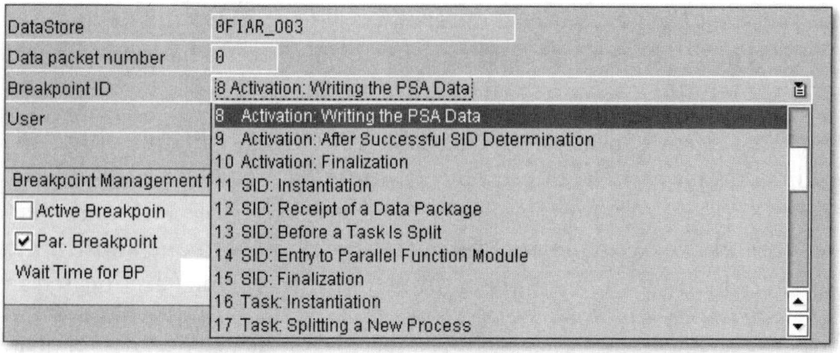

DataStore	0FIAR_003
Data packet number	0
Breakpoint ID	8 Activation: Writing the PSA Data
User	8 Activation: Writing the PSA Data
	9 Activation: After Successful SID Determination
	10 Activation: Finalization
Breakpoint Management f	11 SID: Instantiation
☐ Active Breakpoin	12 SID: Receipt of a Data Package
☑ Par. Breakpoint	13 SID: Before a Task Is Split
Wait Time for BP	14 SID: Entry to Parallel Function Module
	15 SID: Finalization
	16 Task: Instantiation
	17 Task: Splitting a New Process

Figure 6.1 Breakpoints for DSOs

Processes stopped at a breakpoint are displayed in the process overview in Transaction SM51. For example, the ID "6" can be assigned to a breakpoint to analyze the runtime behavior of the database statements in more detail. Table 6.1 lists the available parameters.

Parameter	Explanation
DataStore	Stopped for the specified DSO only
Data package	Stopped for the specified data package only
Breakpoint	Breakpoint ID, for example, 1 = start activation, 6 = fill internal tables, 22 = save package during loading
User	Stopped for the specified user only
Wait time	Time spent waiting for debugging

Table 6.1 Table 6.1 DSO-Specific Breakpoint Parameters

▶ **Transaction RSODSO_RUNTIME**
You can use Transaction RSODSO_RUNTIME to specify runtime measurements for activating DataStore data or for generating an SID within the context of a DataStore. Measurement results are saved in table RSODSO_RUNTIME.

To ensure that the activation processes perform well in DataStore objects, you should pay special attention to the need to generate SIDs, along with the multidimensional clustering options associated with the table for active data.

6.2   InfoCubes

An InfoCube consists of several InfoObjects and is structured according to the star schema; that is, a (large) fact table contains the key figures for the InfoCube, and several (smaller) dimension tables surround it and contain the characteristics of the InfoCube.

The data part of an InfoCube fact table contains key figures only. This is in contrast to a DataStore object, whose data part can also contain characteristics. An InfoCube's characteristics are stored in its dimensions, and the fact table and dimensions are linked to one another via abstract identification numbers (dimension IDs), which are located in the key part of the relevant database table. Consequently, the key figures of the InfoCube relate to the dimension's characteristics, which, in turn, determine the granularity (the degree of refinement) in which the key figures are managed in the InfoCube.

6.2.1   Real-Time InfoCubes

Real-time InfoCubes differ from standard InfoCubes in terms of their ability to support parallel write accesses and because they are used in connection with entering planning data. Standard InfoCubes are technically optimized for read accesses to the detriment of write accesses.

Entering planning data

When you enter planning data, the data is written to a data request for the real-time InfoCube. As soon as the number of records in this data request exceeds a threshold value, the request is closed and "rolled up" into defined aggregates (asynchronously). You can still roll up and define aggregates, collapse InfoCubes, and so on, as before.

Depending on the underlying database, real-time InfoCubes differ from standard InfoCubes in the way in which they are indexed and partitioned. For an Oracle database management system, this means, for example, no bitmap indexes for the fact table and no partitioning of the fact table (which would be initiated by the SAP NetWeaver BW system) in accordance with the package dimension.

6.2.2   Further Processing of InfoCube Data

If you have loaded data into an InfoCube, you can execute certain follow-up actions. On the one hand, there are various options for deleting data from the InfoCube, and on the other hand, you can schedule various follow-up actions for more efficient data processing when using process chains.

You can either delete the entire InfoCube, that is, its structure and its data, or you can delete the InfoCube data only and retain its structure. This function deletes the entire InfoCube (its structure and all of its data). You also have the option of deleting dependent objects such as queries and transformation rules. Please note that all InfoCube data and definitions are permanently lost if you use this function.

Deleting InfoCubes

To delete the InfoCube, select Delete from the context menu for your InfoCube in the InfoProvider tree. This function deletes all of the data contained in the InfoCube but retains the structure of the InfoCube. You can choose whether to delete the data from the fact table only or also the data from the dimension tables. To delete the InfoCube content, select Delete Data from the context menu for your InfoCube in the InfoProvider tree.

6.3   Aggregates

In relational aggregates, the InfoCube data is saved in aggregated form, making it possible to improve the read performance of BW queries on an InfoCube. Relational aggregates are useful if you want to specifically improve the performance of one or more particular BW queries or if you want to improve reporting with characteristic hierarchies. In all other cases, we recommend that you use SAP NetWeaver BW Accelerator (for example, if system performance with relational aggregates is insufficient, their definition and loading processes are too laborious, or they have other disadvantages).

You can use relational aggregates and an SAP NetWeaver BW Accelerator index for the same InfoCube. A query always tries to use performance-optimized sources by checking the sources from which it can draw the requested data. It checks the sources in the following order:

1. OLAP cache

2. SAP NetWeaver BW Accelerator index

3. Relational aggregates from the database

4. InfoCubes from the database

If an active SAP NetWeaver BW Accelerator index exists, the system always accesses this index and not the relational aggregates that may exist. From a modeling perspective, we therefore recommend that you create relational aggregates or an SAP NetWeaver BW Accelerator index for an InfoCube. When the query is executed, it is of no concern to the user whether the data is read from an aggregate, an SAP NetWeaver BW Accelerator index, or an InfoCube.

Testing aggregates In the maintenance transaction, you can temporarily deactivate one or more aggregates so that you can test the use of a particular aggregate, for example, for performance measurements or data consistency analyses. You can also use a corresponding debug option to execute the relevant query in the query monitor (Transaction RSRT). Here, select EXECUTE • DEBUG and in the next dialog box select Do Not Use Aggregates to execute the query with an InfoCube if there is no SAP NetWeaver BW Accelerator index.

6.4   SAP NetWeaver BW Accelerator

SAP NetWeaver BW Accelerator (formerly BI Accelerator, which was the name of the engine until early 2009) is a new approach to improving SAP NetWeaver BW system performance. It is based on the SAP search and classification engine (TREX) and is installed on hardware preconfigured by SAP's hardware partners. It is a preinstalled, preconfigured, and immediately usable packaged solution, which can be used together with an SAP NetWeaver BW system and offers improved performance for OLAP processes, especially for data manager runtimes (that is, the portion of the total query execution runtime used to read data).

Improving read performance SAP NetWeaver BW Accelerator uses a TREX Aggregation Engine to improve the read performance of the queries on an InfoCube. The accelerator is particularly suited to situations in which relational aggregates or other means of improving performance (such as database indexes) do not suffice, are too laborious, or have other disadvantages. If, for example, you have to maintain numerous aggregates for a particular InfoCube, this involves a great deal of maintenance effort, which you can avoid by using the SAP NetWeaver BW Accelerator. In contrast to using aggregates to improve performance, there is only ever one SAP NetWeaver BW Accelerator index for each InfoCube. Furthermore, no modeling decisions need to be made with the index, as is the case with aggregates.

You can also use relational aggregates and an SAP NetWeaver BW Accelerator index for the same InfoCube (see Section 6.3, Aggregates). The use of SAP NetWeaver BW Accelerator affects not only aspects of SAP NetWeaver BW operation (for example, administration), but also the relevant modeling and development strategy. Because SAP NetWeaver BW Accelerator can index a large number of data records in a comparably short time, the number of existing data records in an InfoProvider is no longer as relevant for modeling as it was previously. For example, in many cases, information at the document level can be stored in an InfoCube instead of in additional DataStore objects, or modeling of logical partitions such as yearly InfoCubes can be avoided. This not only simplifies the loading process (complexity of transformations, avoiding having to create SIDs, fewer InfoProviders, and so on), but also has other advantages in terms of reporting, namely, avoiding jumps and being able to perform analyses at a higher level of granularity and at document level on the same InfoProvider.

Effects on modeling

6.4.1 How to Achieve High Performance

After you create an accelerator index, the data is initially located on the file server of the accelerator server. When you first execute a query or start a special uploading program, the system uploads the data to the main memory, where it remains until it is displaced or removed from the main memory as a result of starting a special delete program. Such targeted deletion may be necessary, for example, if the SAP NetWeaver BW Accelerator server does not have sufficient main memory for all of the accelerator indexes or at special times when the data of a particular InfoCube needs to be loaded into the main memory but other InfoCubes are not required (at this time).

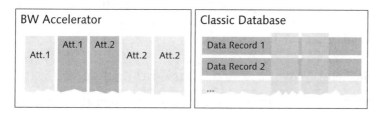

Figure 6.2 Vertical Breakdown

Column-based storage

The table data is stored in columns in the main memory (Figure 6.2). This vertical breakdown of data tables is more efficient than row-based storage, which traditional relational databases use. In a traditional database, the system must search all of the data contained in a table if there is no predefined aggregate for responding to a query. The SAP NetWeaver BW Accelerator engine, on the other hand, specifically accesses the relevant data columns only. It sorts the columns individually and then places the most important entries at the start, thus improving performance considerably (because the data flows are smaller) and significantly reducing the input and output load and main memory consumption.

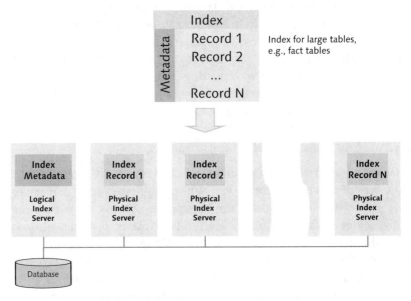

Figure 6.3 Horizontal Partitioning

Horizontal partitioning

You can also improve performance by partitioning index data horizontally (Figure 6.3). The data in large index tables is partitioned, and the individual parts are evenly distributed across the physical servers so that they can be accessed in parallel.

6.4.2 SAP NetWeaver BW Accelerator Architecture

An SAP NetWeaver BW Accelerator index contains all of an InfoCube's data in compressed, nonaggregated form. It stores the data at the same level of granularity as the InfoCube. Furthermore, it consists of several (possibly distributed) indexes that correspond to the tables in the enhanced star schema of the InfoCube and a logical index that, depending on the definition of the star schema, contains the metadata of the accelerator index. Figure 6.4 shows the architecture of SAP NetWeaver BW Accelerator and its relationship with the SAP NetWeaver BW system.

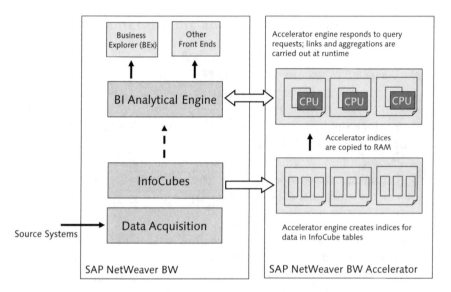

Figure 6.4 BW Accelerator System Landscape

SAP NetWeaver BW Accelerator is installed on a preconfigured blade system, which consists of hosts in the form of plug-in cards (known as server blades), which are connected to central mass storage (file server).

Blade system

The special feature of an SAP NetWeaver BW Accelerator installation on a blade system is that not only the accelerator data, but also that its software can be stored centrally. This means that the software is installed only once on the file server. Consequently, system maintenance is comparably efficient because you have to implement software updates once only (centrally). All server blades on which the accelerator runs access the same program files. However, each server blade has its own configuration files (copied from a master file). Because SAP NetWeaver BW Accelerator is delivered to the customer as an SAP

NetWeaver BW Accelerator box, that is, a preinstalled and preconfigured system on dedicated hardware, a hardware partner has already taken care of the installation and initial configuration. Consequently, the customer has to complete just a few administrative tasks before he can use SAP NetWeaver BW Accelerator for the first time. Section 13.6, SAP NetWeaver BW Accelerator, in Chapter 13 will discuss accelerator installations from an administration and monitoring perspective.

6.5   Open Hub Destinations and InfoSpokes

The open hub service enables you to distribute data from an SAP NetWeaver BW system into non-SAP data marts, analytical applications, and other applications, ensuring controlled distribution across multiple systems while the InfoSpoke can be used to define the object from which the data is retrieved and the destination to which it is forwarded. The open hub service enables the SAP NetWeaver BW system to become a hub for an enterprise data warehouse, and data distribution remains manageable through central monitoring of the distribution status in the SAP NetWeaver BW system.

Data source and destination

▸ BW objects such as InfoCubes, DataStore objects, and InfoObjects (attributes or texts) can act as open hub data sources. Note that you cannot use DataSources as a source.

▸ You can select database tables or flat files as an open hub destination. Here, you can use full mode and delta mode as extraction modes.

As of SAP NetWeaver 7.0 SPS 6, the new open hub destination object replaces the InfoSpoke previously used for the open hub service. Even though you can continue to use existing InfoSpokes, we recommend that you do not create any new InfoSpokes and instead use the new concept of open hub destinations.

6.5.1   Extraction Mode and Delta Administration

An InfoSpoke can extract data in two ways:

▸ **Full mode (F)**
Here, all of the data that corresponds to the selection criteria for the InfoSpoke is transferred from the data source to the relevant destination.

▶ **Delta mode (D)**

In this mode, only the new records added since the last extraction are transferred. This is only possible for InfoCubes and DataStore objects.

You can switch the extraction mode from full mode to delta mode at any time. However, you can only switch from delta mode to full mode if you have not loaded any deltas. Note that you should set the Technical Key indicator when extracting deltas from DataStore objects or InfoCubes into database tables.

Delta administration displays the requests available in the open hub data source, along with information about whether the requests have already been read or whether the open hub destination has not been delivered yet. In the latter scenario, the requests are available under the category Requests Not Yet Read. Delta administration provides the following functions:

Delta administration

▶ You can deactivate delta administration. Afterward, you cannot have another delta request. At the same time, the status of all source requests that have already been read is reset to Not Yet Read. Delta administration is also deactivated if one of the following events occur:

▶ A request that has already been extracted is deleted from the open hub data source.

▶ A request that has not been extracted yet is compressed in the open hub data source (InfoCube).

▶ You can reactivate delta administration. Afterward, you can have another delta request.

▶ If you select Delete Requests from the context menu, the system deletes the request from delta administration where it can be requested again (repeat). This may be necessary if a request has not properly reached the destination system.

You can use the data transfer process to update the data into the open hub destination. The data undergoes a transformation, but not all rule types are available to you; that is, you do not have the option of reading master data or converting times, currencies, or quantities.

6.5.2 Open Hub Monitor

If you activate and execute an InfoSpoke, the system creates a request that is displayed in the open hub monitor and whose status can be checked. Here, you select Monitor to call the open hub monitor from the InfoSpoke maintenance screen. The system then displays all of the requests for the relevant InfoSpoke, along with information about the logical destination system, the destination, the name, and the date and time when the data was delivered. The traffic light status for each request is shown under the date when the data was delivered, so you can easily tell whether or not the request was successful. You can use the filter function to restrict the time period for which requests are displayed.

Detail monitor On the right-hand side of the screen is the following information about each request: the request ID, the update mode, the technical name for the logical destination system, and the InfoSpoke or open hub data source. If you double-click any of the requests listed, the system displays the detail monitor in which you can, among other things, display runtime errors or evaluate job logs and view the InfoSpoke version at the time when the selected data was extracted.

6.6 Reporting

It goes without saying that the area of reporting is particularly concerned with executable reporting objects such as queries or Web templates. However, the supporting processes and functions in the backend (for example, the OLAP server or the Internet Communication Framework (ICF)) also belong to this area.

6.6.1 OLAP Server

On the one hand, an administrator does not usually need to understand the structure of the OLAP server because SAP Support should analyze any errors that occur in this area. On the other hand, however, it is helpful to understand the process associated with executing queries if, for example, you need to debug a query in Transaction RSRT owing to performance problems or incorrect data and therefore need to understand the various breakpoints. Figure 6.5 shows the structure of the analytical engine, also known as the OLAP server.

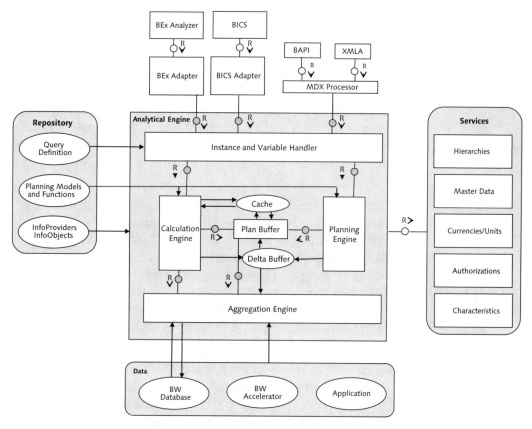

Figure 6.5 Analytical Engine

The sequence of the process steps for the OLAP server is extremely important, especially in terms of understanding a query result. **Process steps**

1. Data is received from the database.

2. The "drilled-down" InfoObject is aggregated. If you use exception aggregation (see below), the system also performs aggregation using the (hidden, drilled-down) reference characteristic.

3. Formulas or calculated key figures are calculated. When you use exception aggregation for formulas, the system performs the calculation, followed by aggregation using a reference characteristic.

4. List calculations such as Calculate Result As... are performed.

Java-based BI Consumer Services (BICS) are used to procure data, and they represent a new technology that all tools will use in the future.

For example, SAP Visual Composer (Version VC 7.1), which is used to access SAP NetWeaver BW data, has also been converted to this new BI Consumer Service technology.

The analysis of query statistical data based on technical content provides a good introduction to the analytical engine (shown in Figure 6.5). If detailed statistics are recorded while a query is being executed, the system writes a large amount of information, for example, for BICS-relevant statistic events such as 13003 (BICS – master data access for F4 help) or 13057 (BICS – reading hierarchy data).

Aggregation and Calculation Sequence

Aggregations and calculations take place at various times. By default, the system initially aggregates the data at the display level (specified by the characteristics in the drilldown) and then calculates the formula. The setting for exception aggregation with a relevant reference characteristic enables a formula to be calculated before the data is aggregated. The remaining aggregation is then executed using the defined exception aggregation (for example, Average or Last Value).

Calculation before
aggregation

Note that the function for calculating a formula before aggregating data is obsolete and should no longer be used. Calculating a formula before aggregating data impairs performance because the database reads the data at the most detailed level, and the system then calculates the formula for each data record. This also means that a key figure may provide different results before and after compression. Frequently, when you calculate formulas, the single record information is required for only one or two particular characteristics while the remaining InfoProvider data can be aggregated. We therefore recommend that you use an exception aggregation (for formulas) with the relevant reference characteristic to control the calculation level. If you require several exception aggregations or reference characteristics, you can nest formulas or calculated key figures within each other and specify an exception aggregation for each formula or calculated key figure.

List Calculations

List calculations are all functions that you can activate in BEx Query Designer for key figures on the Calculation tab (for example, Calculate Results As…). RESULTS and not TOTALS are usually displayed in the results row. This is true if, among other things, conditions are active (in the case of conditions, no figures are changed; they are hidden instead), exception aggregations are used (for example, first value, minimum or average value), or the result relates to a formula (calculated key figure), because calculations are always performed on a row-by-row basis.

To obtain totals in the results rows, you can use local calculations, which only use figures in the calculation if they are displayed in the current query view. This function changes the display only. For subsequent calculations in other formulas, the system uses the original value determined by the OLAP processor.

Exception Aggregation

You can define an exception aggregation for a basic key figure (Transaction RSD1) and for calculated key figures and formulas in BEx Query Designer. An exception aggregation determines how the key figure in the query is determined with regard to the exception characteristic (reference characteristic). Only one reference characteristic ever exists for a particular exception aggregation. If you use exception aggregation, you must note the following points:

▶ The reference characteristic is added to the drill-down characteristics, and the OLAP processor (not the database) performs aggregation (unseen by the user) for these drill-down characteristics.

▶ The system always performs exception aggregation last (that is, after all other required aggregations). If you have any doubts about the figures displayed, it is useful to add the reference characteristic as a free characteristic so it can be drilled down later for test purposes.

A typical example that involves the use of exception aggregations is a key figure for the number of employees: The number of employees would, for example, be totaled using the Cost Center characteristic, and not a time characteristic. Here, you would determine a time characteristic as an exception characteristic with, for example, aggregation as the last value.

6.6.2 Internet Communication Framework

The Internet Communication Framework (ICF) enables you to use standard Internet protocols to communicate with the SAP system. The Internet Communication Manager (ICM) is part of SAP NetWeaver Application Server, which represents the interface between the Internet and the SAP application server and ensures communication between the SAP system (SAP NetWeaver Application Server) and the outside world via the HTTP , HTTPS (secure HTTP), and SMTP (Simple Mail Transfer Protocol) protocols.

SAP NetWeaver Application Server can play both the role of a (Web) server and a client. In the case of a server, the ICM accepts the incoming HTTP requests and forwards them to the ICF (AS ABAP) or AS Java (J2EE engine) for further processing. In the case of a client, requests (for example, emails with SMTP) are sent from the SAP server via the ICM to any Internet server.

Internet Communication Manager

The ICM is implemented as a separate process, which is started and monitored by the SAP Web dispatcher, which in turn performs load balancing and forwards requests to the ICMs of the connected servers. The ICM process uses threads to process the accumulating load in parallel. A thread known as *thread control* accepts the incoming TCP/IP requests and creates (or "wakes") a worker thread from the thread pool to process the request. Worker threads handle connection requests and responses.

Processing Requests

One example of a typical request that needs to be processed in the SAP NetWeaver BW environment is that of executing a Web report. An ICM receives Web requests. These HTTP(S) requests can be designated for the ICF, that is, processed in an ABAP work process (for example, a Web template based on SAP NetWeaver SAP BW 3.x), or they can be J2EE requests that are designated for the J2EE engine (for example, a Web template based on SAP NetWeaver BW 7.0). The ICM uses the URL to decide where to forward the request. Because the system provides ABAP and Java, every instance must contain an ICM that accepts the Web request. Each of these integrated SAP NetWeaver AS instances contains the (ABAP) dispatcher and its work processes, which can work from the ABAP program, and the Java dispatcher with its server processes to which it distributes the relevant incoming J2EE requests.

SAP Web dispatcher

The SAP Web dispatcher is the central access point from the Internet into the SAP system, and it must choose the application server to which it will send each incoming request. The ICM must then decide whether to forward each incoming HTTP request for processing to the ABAP engine (that is, the ICF) or the J2EE engine. This decision is made using the URL prefix. The J2EE engine will not work unless the following services are activated in service maintenance:

► **/sap/public/icma**
For forwarding requests to the J2EE engine

► **/sap/public/icf_info**
For information about logon groups, server load, or SAP Web dispatcher queries

In principle, you can use other (software or hardware) load balancers to distribute HTTP(S) requests. However, SAP recommends that you use the SAP Web dispatcher because it is tailored to the SAP environment and ensures optimum distribution of the requests to the system without too much configuration effort.

ICM Monitor

The ICM monitor has the task of monitoring and managing the ICM (Figure 6.6). Typical administrator tasks include monitoring the ICM status and server cache to detect errors, for example.

To start the ICM monitor, follow the menu path ADMINISTRATION • SYSTEM ADMINISTRATION • MONITOR • SYSTEM MONITORING • INTERNET COMMUNICATION MANAGER or Transaction SMICM.

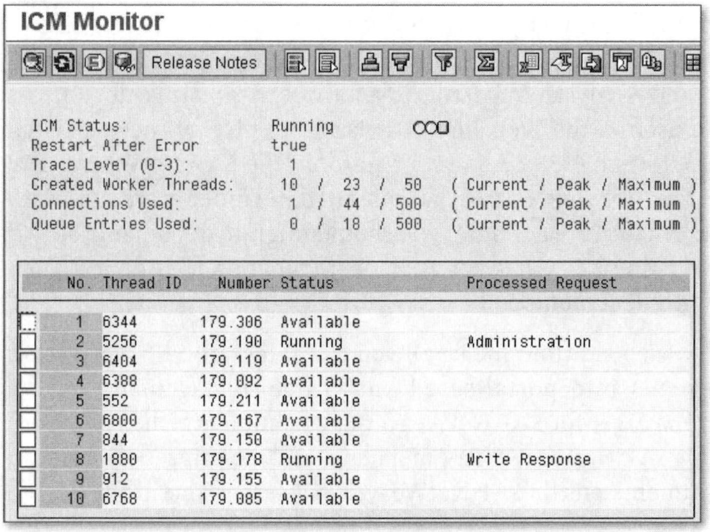

Figure 6.6 Figure 6.6 ICM Monitor (Transaction SMICM)

The ICM server cache or Internet server cache is part of the ICM and saves HTTP(S) objects such as Multipurpose Internet Mail Extensions (MIME) repository objects () before they are sent to the client. The next time this object is requested (via a request), the system can send the content directly from the cache to the client. The ICM server cache improves performance considerably through its use of a highly parallel, multithreaded architecture that supports simultaneous read and write accesses. Furthermore, a patented indexing algorithm is used to access the cache directory quickly. This is particularly suited to long Web URLs as cache keys, for example.

6.6.3 Documents

You can use BW objects to add, link to, and search one or more documents in various formats, versions, and languages. You can add documents to metadata, master data, and InfoProvider data.

In addition to storing documents on the SAP NetWeaver BW server, you can store documents in a special configuration management (CM) repository configured for the SAP NetWeaver BW system. This type of storage improves performance and makes it possible to assign documents for master data and InfoProvider data at the hierarchy node level (in addition to characteristic values). Existing backend documents can be migrated to the CM repository.

In Web applications, you can access documents on the SAP NetWeaver BW server and in the portal. You can use the Single Document, Document List, and Analysis Web items to add context-sensitive documents to the data used in the Web applications and to display the associated properties. Note that BEx Analyzer uses only the SAP NetWeaver BW server to store documents and that migrated documents are not available in BEx Analyzer. Therefore, you should migrate documents only if you are not using BEx Analyzer at all or if you are not using it in conjunction with documents.

Knowledge management In SAP BEx Web runtime (BI Java), you can integrate SAP NetWeaver BW documents into portal-based knowledge management via the repository manager for SAP NetWeaver BW documents, the repository manager for SAP NetWeaver BW metadata, and via migration. You can access documents on the SAP NetWeaver BW server and in the portal.

All knowledge management services are available to you when working with SAP NetWeaver BW documents.

You can maintain documents for BW objects in Customizing under SAP NETWEAVER • BUSINESS INTELLIGENCE • BI DOCUMENTS or directly in Transaction RSDODADMIN_DOC. The SAP NetWeaver BW system uses the knowledge provider content model to manage these documents. You can check the extent to which the characteristics that are to be available as properties for transaction data documents have already been used to generate document properties at a specific time. You only require the settings for document indexing if you use the document search instead of the recommended SAP NetWeaver BW metadata search. As a prerequisite, you must create a search server relation.

In the Documents functional area of the Data Warehousing Workbench, you can (within administration) specify the storage category as a physical storage medium for the document to be created, place documents (including the online documentation for metadata objects) in a queue for indexing, and schedule processing of this queue as a regular job, so that the documents can be incorporated into the search. You can also check whether these properties were generated from the characteristics used to generate the properties for the documents for the InfoProvider data.

Figure 6.7 shows the relevant architecture for document management. As you can see, you can store documents in knowledge management (more specifically in its portal document store) or in the server document store of the SAP NetWeaver BW server.

6.6.4   Internet Graphics Service

The Internet Graphics Service (IGS) is an infrastructure that application developers can use to display graphics in an Internet browser. The IGS has been integrated into various SAP UI technologies, ranging from HTML GUI to Web Dynpro ABAP/Java, and it provides a server architecture whereby data from an SAP system or another source can be used to create graphical and nongraphical output.

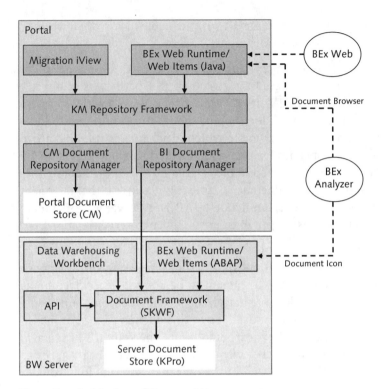

Figure 6.7 Architecture of Document Usage

As of SAP NetWeaver 7.0, you should use the integrated IGS version only (formerly, standalone engines were available on Windows). The integrated IGS is available on the SAP NetWeaver AS host and is started and stopped together with SAP NetWeaver AS. However, the IGS does not belong to the kernel, which means it must be patched separately.

To manage the IGS, you can use either the ABAP report GRAPHICS_IGS_ADMIN or Transaction SIGS, which encapsulates the report. For Java, access is via the URL *http://<hostname>:<port>*. You can use the report GRAPHICS_IGS_ADMIN to fetch dump files, which the IGS creates if a termination occurs and which can assist SAP Support in their analyses. The initial administration screen shows one graphic with the number of calls to the IGS and one graphic with the minimum, average, and maximum response times, and the status page provides additional information about connected listeners, registered port watchers, registered interpreters, and available servers.

Part II
SAP NetWeaver BW Administration

Before we turn our attention to SAP NetWeaver BW-specific analysis authorizations, we will discuss the concepts of authorization management for AS ABAP and AS Java. In addition to these concepts, we will outline the monitoring and troubleshooting options available to you, which are also extremely important.

7 User Administration and Authorization Management

It goes without saying that one of the tasks of SAP NetWeaver BW administration is to manage users and their authorizations. However, because the system platform consists of both AS ABAP and AS Java and because SAP NetWeaver BW systems also have some special features, user administration and authorization management is not restricted to defining and managing ABAP authorization roles. It also involves some portal activities and the concepts of analysis authorizations.

7.1 Basic Principles

Both the number and structure of objects and user types in SAP NetWeaver BW place special demands on user administration and authorization management. Such demands differ greatly from those placed on classic transactional systems. The concepts and maintenance of analysis authorizations are also special features here.

7.1.1 AS ABAP Authorization Concept

The ABAP authorization concept protects transactions, programs, and services in SAP systems against unauthorized access. On the basis of the authorization concept, the administrator assigns authorizations that determine which actions a user can execute in the SAP system after he has logged on to the system and authenticated himself.

If a user wants to access business objects or execute SAP transactions, he requires the corresponding authorizations because business objects or transactions are protected by authorization objects. The authorizations represent instances of generic authorization objects and are defined depending on the activity and responsibilities of the employee. They are combined into an authorization profile that belongs to a role. The user administrators then use the user master record to assign the corresponding roles to the employee so that he can use the appropriate transactions for his tasks within the enterprise.

7.1.2 User Administration

Flexible organization

The authorization system allows great flexibility in terms of organizing the way in which you manage user master records and roles. If your enterprise is small and centralized, all of the tasks associated with managing user master records and authorization components can be executed by a single user known as the superuser. Depending on the size and organization of your enterprise, however, you should distribute the task of managing user master records and authorizations among multiple administrators, each with limited areas of responsibility. This applies particularly to a decentralized environment that may have several valid time zones. It also helps achieve maximum system security. Each administrator should be able to perform only certain tasks. By separating these tasks, you ensure that no single superuser has total control over your user authorizations and that more than one person approves all authorizations and profiles. You also define standard procedures for creating and assigning your authorizations.

Role administration

We recommend that you use role administration tools and functions (Transaction PFCG) to manage your roles, authorization, and profiles. These functions make your job easier by automating various processes and providing greater flexibility in your authorization plan. You can also use the Central User Administration (CUA) functions to centrally edit the roles delivered by SAP or your own new roles and to assign any number of users.

Administrator types

If you are using the role administration tool (the profile generator), you can distribute the administration tasks within an area (such as a department, cost center, or other organizational unit) to the following administrator types:

▶ **Authorization data administrator**

This administrator type creates roles (transaction selection and authorization data), selects transactions, and edits authorization data. However, the authorization data administrator can only save data in the role administration tool because he is not authorized to generate the profile.

▶ **Authorization profile administrator**

This administrator type checks and approves the data and generates the authorization profile. To do this, he selects All Roles in Transaction SUPC and then specifies the abbreviation of the role to be edited. On the next screen, he uses Display Profile to check the data.

▶ **User administrator**

This administrator type uses user administration (Transaction SU01) to edit the user data and assigns roles to the users. The approved profiles are then entered in the user master records.

Administrators of one or more areas are managed by superusers who set up their user master records, profiles, and authorizations. We recommend that you assign the SUPER group to the user and authorization administrators. When you use the predefined user administration authorizations, this group assignment ensures that user administrators cannot modify their own user master records or those of other administrators. Only administrators with the predefined profile S_A.SYSTEM can edit users in the SUPER group.

7.1.3   Central User Administration

You can use Central User Administration (CUA) to centrally maintain user master records in one system. Changes are then automatically distributed to child systems, enabling you to have an overview in the central system of all user data in the entire system landscape.

Data distribution is based on a functional Application Link Enabling (ALE) landscape. This allows data to be exchanged in a controlled manner and remain consistent. Central User Administration uses an ALE system group to distribute user data between a central system and child systems linked by ALE. Central User Administration data is distributed asynchronously between the application systems in an ALE environment. This ensures that the data still reaches the receiving system even if it could not be reached when the data was sent. One system

ALE system group

209

in the ALE environment for Central User Administration is defined as the central system and linked with every child system in both directions. The child systems are not linked to each other, with the exception of the central system, which itself is a child system from the point of view of Central User Administration.

7.1.4 User Information System

You can use the User Information System (Transaction SUIM) to obtain an overview of the authorizations and users in your SAP system at any time by using search criteria that you define (Figures 7.1 and 7.2). In particular, you can display lists of users to whom critical authorizations are assigned. You can also use the User Information System to:

▶ Compare roles and users

▶ Display change documents for a user's authorization profile

▶ Display the transactions contained in a role

▶ Create where-used lists

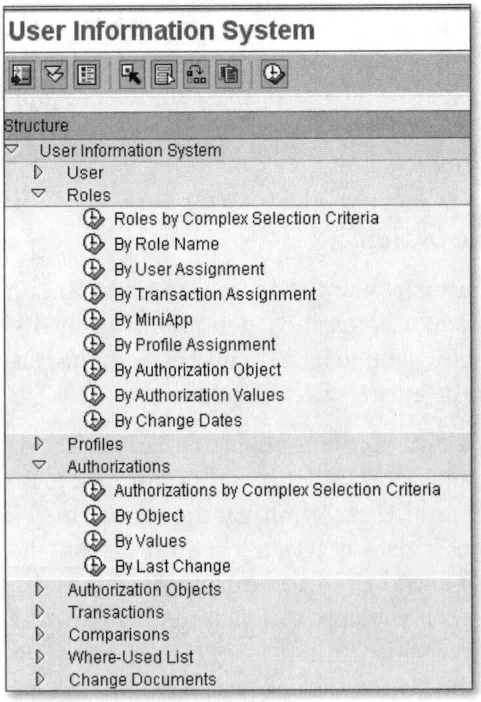

Figure 7.1 User Information System (Transaction SUIM)

We recommend that you regularly check the various lists that are important for you. Define a monitoring procedure and corresponding checklists to ensure that you continuously review your authorization plan. We especially recommend that you determine which authorizations you consider critical and regularly review which users have these authorizations in their profiles.

Monitoring procedure

Users by Complex Selection Criteria

Roles Profiles Change documents File...

Number of Users Selected:86

User	Complete name	Locked	Reason	Valid from	Valid through	User Type	Ref. User
23010997	Milco Österholm			2002-09-23	2010-05-23	A Dialog	
XP000133	Chengjie 2 Liu			2009-03-25	2009-12-31	A Dialog	
XP000134	Qian 5 Wang			2009-03-25	2009-12-31	A Dialog	
XP000135	Yingni Wang			2009-03-25	2009-12-31	A Dialog	
XP000142	Shanmugasundaram Balakrishnan			2009-03-30	9999-12-31	A Dialog	
XP000143	Rajesh Chopperla				2009-12-31	A Dialog	
XP000144	Sudhakarreddy Bheemireddy				2012-03-01	A Dialog	
XP000145	Subba R Paturu			2009-03-25	2009-12-31	A Dialog	
XP000146	Prakash Robinson Mathinini Dhanaraj			2009-04-01	2009-12-31	A Dialog	
XP000152	Nithya Rajagopal				2009-12-31	A Dialog	
XP000156	Sreekar S Tetali			2009-04-15	2009-12-31	A Dialog	
XP000158	Subrahmanien Uma			2009-06-10	2009-12-31	A Dialog	
XP000160	Pushkaran Deepa					A Dialog	
XP000170	Narayanan Venkatesan				2009-12-31	A Dialog	
XP000171	Niladri B Pradhan			2009-06-08	2009-12-31	A Dialog	
XP000174	Makesh Sukumaaran			2009-03-30	2009-12-31	A Dialog	
XP000183	Rajesh Annathurai				2009-12-31	A Dialog	
XP000184	Saravanan Ramalingamrani				2009-12-31	A Dialog	
XP000189	Shao Ning			2009-04-22	2009-12-31	A Dialog	
XP000191	XP000191			2009-04-01	2009-12-31	A Dialog	
XP000192	Anil Lambu				2009-12-31	A Dialog	
XP000196	Dhanesh Dayalan				2009-12-31	A Dialog	
XP000197	Jaimon Kanichai			2009-04-24	2009-12-31	A Dialog	
XP000198	Rajyam Kalpana	🔒	USR	2009-05-15	2009-12-31	A Dialog	

Figure 7.2 Sample Result in Transaction SUIM

The possible evaluations are described in the following sections.

User

The User node provides the following evaluation options:

▶ Cross-system information (if you are using CUA)

▶ Users by address data (RSUSR002_ADDRESS)
You use generic input options (placeholder, asterisk, and multiple

selection) for this evaluation. To obtain a result, you must maintain the corresponding criteria (for example, room) in the user data.

▶ Users by complex selection criteria (RSUSR002); see also the example provided in Figure 7.2

▶ Users by critical combinations of authorizations at transaction start (RSUSR008)

▶ Users with incorrect logon attempts (RSUSR006)
This evaluation is started immediately (without any additional selection criteria) when you select Execute in the User Information System. The result list provides the following information:

  ▶ Number of incorrect logon attempts (users who are not locked)

  ▶ Users locked owing to incorrect logon attempts

  ▶ List of users locked by administrators

  ▶ List of users locked globally in the central system (if you are using CUA)

▶ Users by logon date and password change (RSUSR200)

▶ Users with critical authorizations (RSUSR009)

▶ Users with critical authorizations (new version) (RSUSR008_009_NEW)

You can also execute the individual reports (for example, RSUSR200) in Transaction SE38.

Roles, Profiles, Authorizations, and Authorization Objects

Reports RSUSR070 (roles), RSUSR020 (profiles), RSUSR030 (authorizations), and RSUSR040 (authorization objects) are constructed in the same way: The first report for evaluations by complex selection criteria represents a combination of the subsequent reports in each case. For example, you can find all roles that contain the authorization for posting documents (F_BKPF_BUK, activity 01).

Transactions

You use this report (RSUSR010) to determine which transactions a user can start. A user can only start a transaction if he has the authorization S_TCODE and, if required, the authorization object entered in Transaction SE93 for this transaction. The report also determines transactions that can be executed with a certain profile (generated authorizations of a role), a particular single or composite role, or a particular authorization for an authorization object.

Cross-System Users, Authorizations, Roles, and Profiles

You use this report (RSUSR050) to compare two user master records, roles (including composite roles), profiles, or authorizations in the same system or different systems in the User Information System. You define the name of the RFC destination in Transaction SM59.

When you compare composite roles, you receive (as the result) a list of single roles and then, below this list, a comparison of the authorization objects. Note that this display allows you to perform a quick comparison. However, the interaction of the fields within an authorization is of vital importance, particularly in the case of the objects listed under Same Values, where two users may have the same values for an object, but they do not have the same authorizations because the field values are combined differently in different authorizations. You should therefore regard this comparison function merely as a way to determine differences but not to document equality.

Comparing composite roles

Where-Used Lists for Profiles

You use this report (RSUSR002) to create where-used lists for profiles, authorization objects, authorizations, and authorization values. For example, you may be looking for all users to which a certain profile (such as SAP_ALL) is assigned.

Where-Used Lists for Authorization Objects

With this report you can create where-used lists for profiles, authorization objects, authorizations, and authorization values. The result list displays the where-used list for the authorization object in the specified search area. Additional functions are available in the result list, for example, displaying the properties of a program or displaying a where-used list of all of the programs, classes, and so on that use the selected program.

Where-Used Lists for Authorizations

You use this report (RSUSR002) to create where-used lists for profiles, authorization objects, authorizations, and authorization values.

Where-Used Lists for Authorization Values

This report allows you to search for certain authorization values, for example, all users who have authorization to post a goods receipt.

Change Documents

You use this report to determine all changes to the following objects:

▶ User (RSUSR100)

▶ Profile (RSUSR101)

▶ Authorization (RSUSR102)

▶ Role assignment (RSSCD100_PFCG)

▶ Role (RSSCD100_PFCG)

Change areas
Note that changes to users, profiles, and authorizations are divided into two areas:

▶ **Changes to authorizations**
Creating the user; changing, adding, or removing profiles

▶ **Changes to header data**
Password changes, validity, user type, user group, account number, and lock status

You can select both fields to obtain all information. In this case, the left column shows the status before the change, and the right column shows the changed entry.

7.1.5 Identity Management

Identity management is defined as the secure and central management of user accounts, along with the related processes for authorization assignment and the consistent provision of all data. The purpose of identity management is to optimize productivity and security while lowering costs. Efficiently managed user identities, with all of their associated attributes and access data, play a key role here. Ultimately, the goal is to ensure secure access in accordance with the principle of *least privilege* (a basic principle whereby users should be granted as few authorizations as possible) and to increase productivity and efficiency within the identity lifecycle and the corresponding process, thus lowering the administration costs associated with user administration and authorization management.

When SAP acquired the Norwegian company MaxWare in May 2007, it also acquired its identity management technology (previously, SAP could only offer these functions via third-party products). At the heart of SAP NetWeaver Identity Management is the identity center, where all business roles are defined. These roles are subsequently converted into technical roles for the relevant system. In addition to SAP NetWeaver Identity Management's primary focus, namely, integrated user administration in all SAP systems (SAP ERP and SAP NetWeaver), adapters can be used to link various other connected systems (for example, Microsoft Active Directory or IBM Lotus Notes) to Central User Administration.

SAP plans to gradually embed SAP NetWeaver Identity Management into all of its products. For example, in the future, users will be able to replace the existing CUA with SAP NetWeaver Identity Management. However, SAP wants to provide continued support for CUA and not deactivate it. In fact, it plans to incorporate it into the new version of SAP NetWeaver Identity Management. SAP NetWeaver Identity Management is one of several modifications within SAP NetWeaver whose goal is to expand the platform in the direction of business process management. For example, the platform intends to harmonize user administration between SAP ERP and SAP NetWeaver Portal because, up to now, it has only been possible to synchronize the user data of both software products.

7.1.6   SAP GRC

A strategy for the area of governance, risk, and compliance (GRC) should be considered in conjunction with SAP NetWeaver Identity Management. One of the greatest challenges facing an enterprise is the harmonization of business activities with existing and future norms. Global guidelines, standards, and laws demand transparency from an enterprise in terms of data. This requires stringent monitoring, accurate traceability, and in particular, end-to-end documentation for business processes.

215

The task of IT is to protect enterprises against data misuse and to operate effective risk management to avert the danger of potential losses. Higher expectations on the part of shareholders and mounting pressure on the financial markets are forcing modern enterprises to introduce and establish solutions for the area of governance, risk, and compliance (GRC). This SAP solution provides you with an integrated approach that fulfills the demands of governance, risk, and compliance:

► SAP GRC Access Control

► SAP GRC Repository – Governance

► SAP GRC Risk Management – Risk Management

► SAP GRC Process Control – Business Process Control

► SAP GRC Global Trade Services – Global Trade

In addition to its GRC solution, the SAP product SAP ERP Financials also supports enterprises in adjusting their business processes to legal regulations and governance guidelines. In this context, for example, the Sarbanes–Oxley Act (the way enterprises control and monitor their activities and organize their financial reporting), Basel II (important implications for enterprise borrowings), IFRS (obligation to create and publish consolidated financial statements in accordance with International Financial Reporting Standards), and human resource management (national labor law, payroll, tax returns, and so on) play an important role.

7.1.7 AS Java Authorization Concept

On AS Java or in SAP NetWeaver Portal, you also control user access to applications and resources by assigning authorizations to user accounts (Figure 7.3). You assign these authorizations using J2EE standard methods or extended methods provided by SAP. AS Java supports the following types of authorization:

► **Roles**
Roles are used to assign activities to users either directly or indirectly through the use of groups.

► **Access control lists (ACLs)**
Access control lists are used to control the use of objects.

User Management Engine

The *User Management Engine* (UME) represents the Central User Administration for all Java applications. It is integrated into SAP NetWeaver AS so that administration can take place on an AS Java basis, for example.

You can configure the UME to read user-specific data from various data sources or to write such data to various data sources (Figure 7.4). LDAP directories (Lightweight Directory Access Protocol), AS ABAP user administration, and the AS Java databases are examples of such data sources. The use of the Java database is defined by default. However, the user administration for the ABAP system is generally used in the SAP NetWeaver BW environment (that is, for an SAP NetWeaver BW system consisting of both BI ABAP and BI Java).

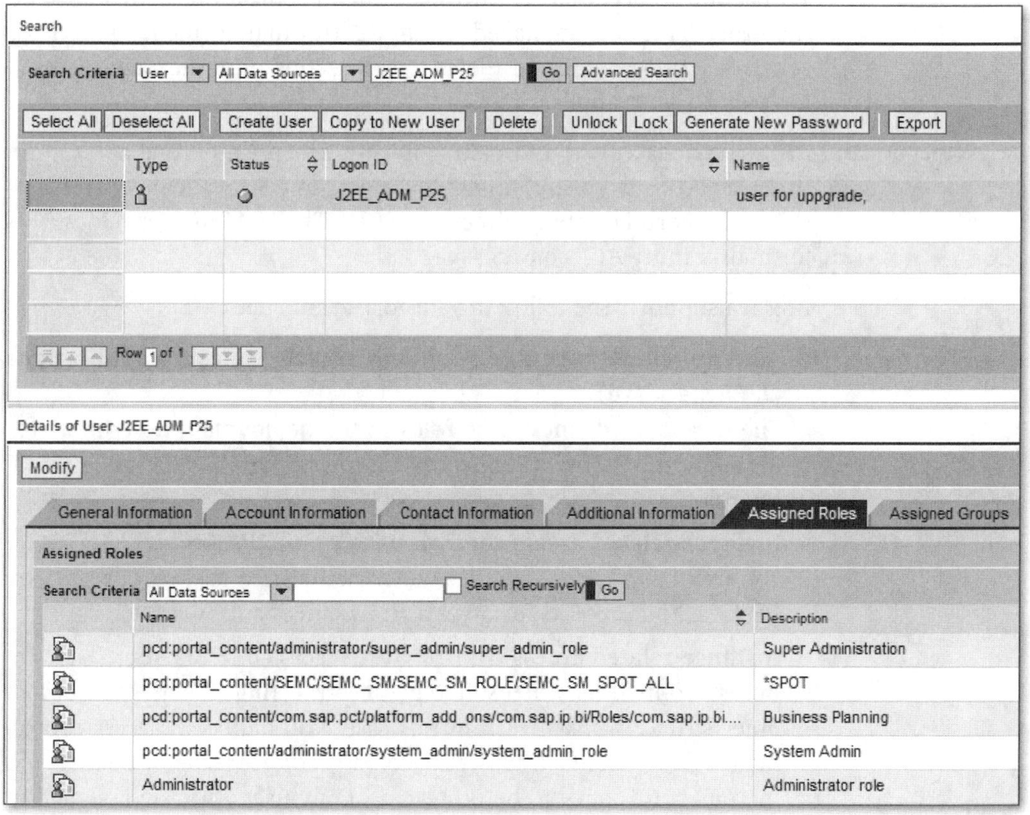

Figure 7.3 Role Assignment in AS Java

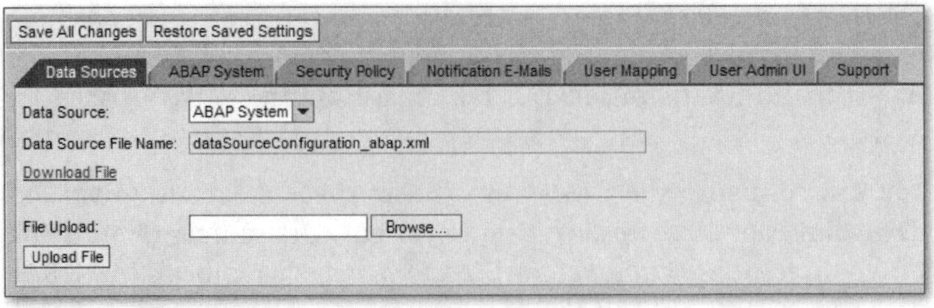

Figure 7.4 UME Data Sources

Roles AS Java uses J2EE security roles and UME roles. Security roles are managed using the Visual Administrator. If a new application is developed, the developer activates the security roles together with the J2EE application in accordance with the J2EE specification. UME roles, on the other hand, are managed using identity management tools. They consists actions, which in turn are collections of authorizations used for Web Dynpro applications.

Access control lists ACLs restrict access to individual objects. The portal is one application that uses ACLs to control access to objects in AS Java. One example of this is the Portal Content Directory (PCD). The UME also provides APIs for maintaining ACLs on AS Java.

AS Java supports the following authorization checks:

▶ **Activity-related access control with security roles for applications (J2EE standard)**
The developer defines these roles in the deployment descriptors for his application. The administrator assigns the users to the corresponding roles.

▶ **Instance-related access controls with roles (UME roles)**
You use these roles to specify which activities a user can execute on AS Java. You can also specify which instances a user can access.

▶ **Instance-related access control with access control lists**
Access control lists are suitable for protecting a large number of objects (that is, instances). In this case, you define an access control matrix that contains a subject (role), a predicate (type of access), and the object (instance to be protected). Only users that are assigned to at least one of these roles can access this resource. There are two ways to use access control lists:

▶ **J2EE server roles**
The developer or administrator defines the role using the corresponding API. The administrator uses the Security Roles tab in the Visual Administrator to assign users to the role. The administrator also manages the authorizations for accessing resources. To do this, he assigns roles in the corresponding access control lists (in resource management).

▶ **UME access control lists (UME ACLs)**
You can only manage these ACLs in the application context.

7.2 Basic Principles of Authorizations in the SAP NetWeaver BW System

In authorization management, you have to distinguish between two concepts. When accessing the Data Warehousing Workbench, user administration, or the BEx Query Designer, for example, users require standard authorizations, which are assigned to them (via roles) in the form of authorization profiles. Standard authorizations are based on the SAP authorization concept, and each authorization refers to an object and defines one or more values for each field contained in this authorization object. Individual authorizations are grouped into roles.

Standard authorizations

Any user who wants to display transaction data from authorization-relevant characteristics requires analysis authorizations for these characteristics. Analysis authorizations use a separate concept that takes account of the special features of reporting and analysis in SAP NetWeaver BW. For example, you can specify that employees can only view the transaction data associated with their cost center. You can include any number of characteristics in an analysis authorization, and you can authorize single values, intervals, simple patterns, variables, and hierarchy nodes. In addition, you can use special characteristics to restrict the authorizations to certain activities (for example, reading or changing), individual InfoProviders, and/or a certain period of time. You can then assign the authorization to one or more users either directly or via roles and profiles. When you execute a query, the system checks all of the characteristics that belong to the underlying InfoProvider and are flagged as authorization-relevant. You can therefore use the special SAP NetWeaver BW authorization concept for displaying query data to protect especially critical data.

Analysis authorizations

7.3 Role Maintenance in Transaction PFCG

The documentation on standard authorization objects is available via the menu path TOOLS • ADMINISTRATION • USER MAINTENANCE • INFORMATION SYSTEM • AUTHORIZATION OBJECTS • AUTHORIZATION OBJECTS BY COMPLEX SELECTION CRITERIA • BY OBJECT CLASS. For the object class, enter "RS" (for all BW objects apart from data mining) or "RSAN" (for data mining objects) and select Execute. Select the authorization object and then select Documentation. You obtain a description of the fields defined in the authorization object. The tables below list the most important authorization objects for data warehousing (Table 7.1), planning (Table 7.2), and reporting (Table 7.3).

Object	Description
S_RS_ADMWB	Objects in the Data Warehousing Workbench Authorizations for working in the Data Warehousing Workbench and its objects These include source system, InfoObject, monitor, application component, InfoArea, Data Warehousing Workbench, settings, metadata, InfoPackage, InfoPackage group, reporting agent setting, reporting agent package, documents (for metadata, master data, hierarchies, transaction data), document storage administration, administration (customer) content system, and broadcast settings.
S_RS_IOBJ	InfoObject Authorizations for working with individual InfoObjects and their subobjects Up to Release 3.0A, only general authorization protection was possible with the authorization object S_RS_ADMWB. The general authorization protection for InfoObjects continues to work as before. The special protection with the object S_RS_IOBJ is only used if there is no authorization for the object S_RS_ADMWB-IOBJ.
S_RS_DS	DataSource (release > SAP NetWeaver BW 3.x) Authorizations for working with the DataSource (release > SAP NetWeaver BW 3.x) or its subobjects
S_RS_DTP	Data transfer process (DTP) Authorizations for working with the data transfer process and its subobjects The authorizations for the DTP object have a higher priority than the authorizations for the underlying objects. Users who have a DTP authorization for a source or target combination do not require read authorization for the source object or write authorization for the target object to execute the DTP.
S_RS_ISNEW	InfoSource (release > SAP NetWeaver BW 3.x) Authorizations for working with InfoSources (release > SAP NetWeaver BW 3.x)

Table 7.1 SAP NetWeaver BW Authorization Objects

Object	Description
S_RS_ISOUR	InfoSource (flexible updating)
	Authorizations for working with InfoSources with flexible updating and their subobjects
S_RS_ISRCM	InfoSource (direct updating)
	Authorizations for working with InfoSources with direct updating and their subobjects
S_RS_TR	Transformation rules
	Authorizations for working with transformation rules and their subobjects
S_RS_ICUBE	InfoCube
	Authorizations for working with InfoCubes and their subobjects
S_RS_MPRO	MultiProvider
	Authorizations for working with MultiProviders and their subobjects
S_RS_ODSO	DataStore object
	Authorizations for working with DataStore objects and their subobjects
S_RS_ISET	InfoSet
	Authorizations for working with InfoSets
S_RS_HIER	Hierarchy
	Authorizations for working with hierarchies
S_RS_IOMAD	Maintain master data
	Authorizations for processing master data in the Data Warehousing Workbench
S_RS_PC	Process chains
	Authorizations for working with process chains
S_RS_OHDST	Open hub destination
	Authorizations for working with open hub destinations
S_RS_CTT	Currency translation type
	Authorizations for working with currency translation types
S_RS_UOM	Quantity conversion type
	Authorizations for working with quantity conversion types
S_RS_THJT	Key date derivation type
	Authorizations for working with key date derivation types
S_RS_RST	RS Trace Tool
	Authorizations for the RS Trace Tool
RSANPR	Analysis process
	Authorizations for working with analysis processes

Table 7.1 SAP NetWeaver BW Authorization Objects (Cont.)

Object	Description
S_RS_ALVL	Planning: aggregation level Authorization for working with aggregation levels
S_RS_PLSE	Planning function Authorization for working with planning functions
S_RS_PLSQ	Planning sequence Authorization for working with planning sequences
S_RS_PLST	Planning service type Authorization for working with planning function types
S_RS_PLENQ	Lock settings Authorizations for maintaining or displaying lock settings

Table 7.2 Planning Authorization Objects

Object	Description
S_RS_COMP	SAP BEx – components Authorizations for using different components for the query definition
S_RS_COMP1	SAP BEx – components SAP Authorization for queries from specific owners
S_RS_FOLD	SAP BEx – components Display authorization for folders
S_RS_TOOLS	SAP BEx – individual tools Authorizations for individual SAP Business Explorer tools
S_RS_ERPT	SAP BEx – enterprise reports Authorizations for BEx enterprise reports
S_RS_EREL	SAP BEx – enterprise report reusable elements Authorization for reusable elements of an SAP BEx enterprise report
S_RS_DAS	SAP BEx – data access services Authorizations for working with data access services
S_RS_BTMP	SAP BEx –Web templates (NW 7.0+) Authorizations for working with SAP BEx Web templates
S_RS_BITM	SAP BEx–reusable Web items (NW 7.0+) Authorizations for working with SAP BEx Web items
S_RS_BCS	SAP BEx – broadcasting authorization for scheduling Authorizations for registering broadcasting settings for execution
S_RS_BEXTX	SAP BEx –texts (maintenance) Authorizations for maintaining SAP BEx texts

Table 7.3 Reporting Authorization Objects

To create simple roles, proceed as follows:

1. Enter a name for the role and select Create Role. Note that all roles delivered by SAP begin with the prefix SAP_. Use the customer namespace when you create your own user roles.

2. On the next screen, describe the function the role will have.

3. On the Menu tab, assign transactions to the role, either directly or by assigning menu paths from the SAP menu. The menu options that you select in this step are displayed as a user menu in the Session Manager and on the SAP Easy Access logon screen for all users assigned to the role.

4. On the Authorizations tab, select Change Authorization Data. Depending on which transactions you have selected, a dialog box is displayed. You are prompted to maintain the organizational levels. These are authorization fields that occur in many authorizations and can be maintained collectively in this way. The concept of organizational levels will be explained in greater detail below. The system displays a tree that contains all of the authorizations the SAP proposes for the selected transactions. Some authorizations already have values.

   ▶ Yellow traffic lights in the tree display indicate that you have to manually edit the authorization values. You enter these values by clicking the white row next to the name of the authorization field. When you have maintained the values, the authorizations are regarded as having been manually modified and are not overwritten when you add more transactions and edit the authorizations again. You can click the traffic lights to assign the complete authorization for the relevant hierarchy level for all nonmaintained fields.

   ▶ Red traffic lights indicate that there are organizational levels with no values.

To display other functions in the tree display, for example, copying or compiling authorizations, select UTILITIES • SETTINGS and select the relevant option. Then select Generate to generate an authorization profile for the authorizations. In the next dialog box, enter a name for the authorization profile or use the valid name proposed in the customer namespace. Exit the tree display after the profile has been generated.

If you change the menu selection and call the authorization tree display again, the system tries to add the authorizations for the new transactions to the existing authorizations. Traffic lights may become yellow again because new, incomplete authorizations appear in the tree display. You must assign values manually or delete them. To delete an authorization, deactivate it first and then delete it. General authorizations (for example, spool display or print) are usually not defined for the transactions. To do this, you can add authorization templates to the existing data. Follow the menu path EDIT • INSERT AUTHORIZATIONS • FROM TEMPLATE..., and select one of the templates, for example, SAP_USER_B (basis authorization for application users) or SAP_PRINT (print authorization). Alternatively, you can create a separate role for these general authorizations, thus improving clarity.

Assigning users

5. On the User tab, assign users to the role. For the assigned users, the menu options for the role are displayed as a user menu in the Session Manager.

In addition, the generated authorization profiles are automatically entered in the user master record for these users if you perform the user master comparison. To do this, select User Comparison and the Complete Comparison option. If you do not want to restrict the assignment validity period and therefore transfer the proposed period (current date until Dec. 31, 9999), no further action is required. If you want to restrict the validity period, you must schedule the report PFCG_TIME_DEPENDENCY daily. This report updates user master records automatically. It must also be scheduled when you use organizational management.

Never enter generated authorization profiles directly into user master records, which you would do for authorization profiles that you create manually. You can only assign generated profiles to users by assigning the users to the corresponding roles and then comparing the users. During a user master comparison, the role profiles are entered for all users or the role.

6. If you want to transport the role to another system, you must enter the role in a transport request. To do this, select ROLE • TRANSPORT. You can specify whether the user assignment is to be transported too. The authorization profiles are transported unless you have explicitly specified that they are not to be transported.

Once the roles have been imported into a target system, you must perform a complete user master comparison for the imported roles. You can start this comparison manually, or you can start it automatically by using the report PFCG_TIME_DEPENDENCY if the report is scheduled periodically in the target system.

You can considerably simplify the task of role maintenance by deriving roles and using organizational levels. This is particularly useful for concepts with InfoProvider-specific roles. You can use organizational levels to maintain numerous authorization fields at once, considerably simplifying manual postprocessing (Figure 7.5).

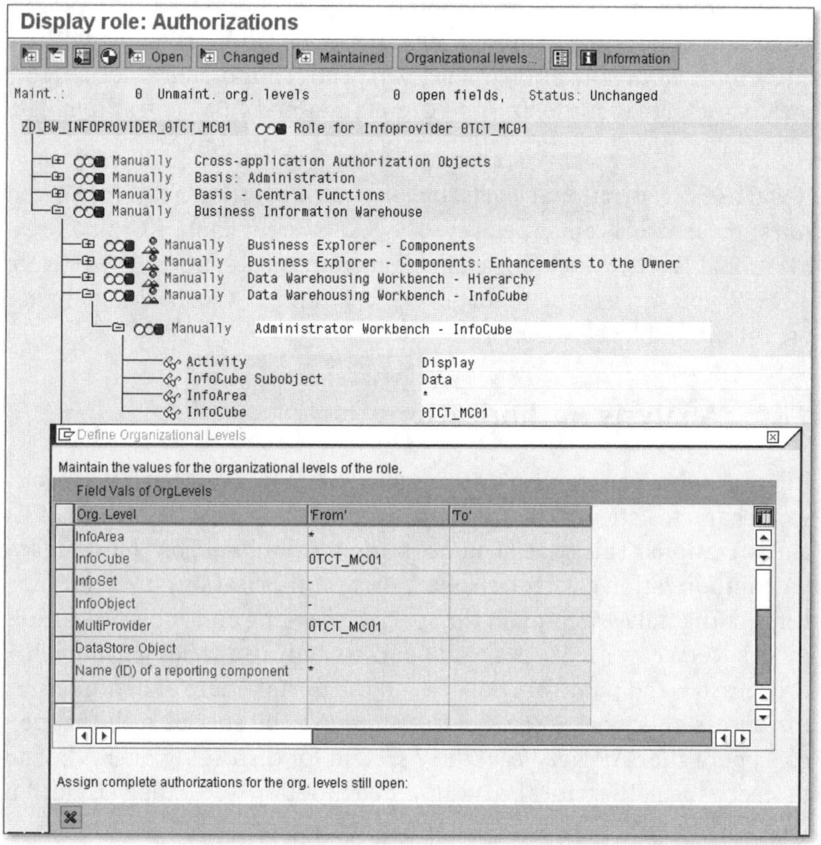

Organizational levels

Figure 7.5 Using Organizational Levels

Derived roles

Derived roles are based on existing roles. They inherit the menu structure and integrated functions (transactions, reports, Web links, and so on) of the referenced role.

However, this type of inheritance is only possible if the inheriting role has not previously assigned any transaction codes.

The authorizations for the bequeathing role are transferred to the derived role as default values that you can subsequently change. Organizational level definitions, on the other hand, are not passed on. Instead, they must be fully maintained as new definitions in the inheriting role. User assignments are not passed on either.

Derived roles enable you to maintain very elegant roles that have the same functions (same menus, same transactions) but are defined differently from an organizational-level perspective. In practical terms, this means the actual authorizations are maintained in a central template role and are therefore used uniformly in all derived roles.

If you use organizational levels to define authorization fields in derived roles, these fields remain empty. The SAP system contains some organizational levels, which are available to you. As described in SAP Note 323817, you can use the report PFCG_ORGFIELD_CREATE to enhance organizational levels at any time.

7.4   Analysis Authorizations

All users who want to display transaction data from authorization-relevant characteristics or navigation attributes in a query require analysis authorizations. This type of authorization is not based on the standard SAP authorization concept. Instead, these authorizations use their own concept that takes account of the special reporting and analysis features in SAP NetWeaver BW. As a result of distributing queries with the BEx Broadcaster and publishing queries to the portal, more and more users can access query data. You can therefore use the special authorization concept of the SAP NetWeaver BW system for displaying query data to protect especially critical data in a much better way. Analysis authorizations are not based on authorization objects. Instead, you create authorizations that contain a group of characteristics, and you restrict the values for these characteristics.

The authorizations can include any authorization-relevant character- istics, and they treat single values, intervals, and hierarchy authoriza- tions equally. Navigation attributes can also be flagged as authorization- relevant on the attribute maintenance screen for characteristics and added to authorizations as separate characteristics. You can then assign this authorization to one or more users. All characteristics flagged as authorization-relevant are checked when a query is executed. A query always selects a set of data from the database. If authorization-relevant characteristics are part of this data, you have to make sure that the user who is executing the query has sufficient authorization for the complete selection. Otherwise, a message is displayed indicating that the authorization is insufficient. In principle, the authorizations do not work as filters. Very restricted exceptions to this rule are hierarchies in the drilldown and variables that are filled from authorizations. Hierar- chies are, to a large extent, restricted to the authorized nodes. In addi- tion, variables that are filled from authorizations act like filters for the authorized values for the relevant characteristic.

Authorization- relevant characteristics

7.4.1 New Concept with SAP NetWeaver 7.0

After you have upgraded to SAP NetWeaver 7.0, you must decide whether you want to continue using the old reporting authorization concept or switch to the new, more user-friendly concept of analysis authorizations.

The new concept is a significant improvement because technical restric- tions no longer exist, (endless) other functions are available, and it has been consistently integrated into both reporting and the role concept. Some differences (improvements) from the old concept include:

▶ Objects can be edited later despite being used.

▶ The number of objects is no longer limited to 10.

▶ Hierarchy authorizations no longer have a different concept and defi- nition from value authorizations.

▶ Only InfoObjects are authorization-relevant now (not InfoObjects and InfoProviders, as was the case in the old concept).

▶ You can now define authorizations for navigation attributes individually (no longer only globally).

▶ Extensive logging functions are available.

The program RSEC_MIGRATION (which you execute in Transaction SE38) can support you in migrating from the old reporting authorization concept to the new analysis authorization concept. However, a manual adjustment is always necessary here because, for example, variables cannot be converted into hierarchy authorizations. Even if a migration requires some time and effort, we recommend that you switch over to analysis authorizations. Thanks to its many advantages over older reporting authorizations (in terms of maintenance effort and functions), migrations are performed in almost all customer systems.

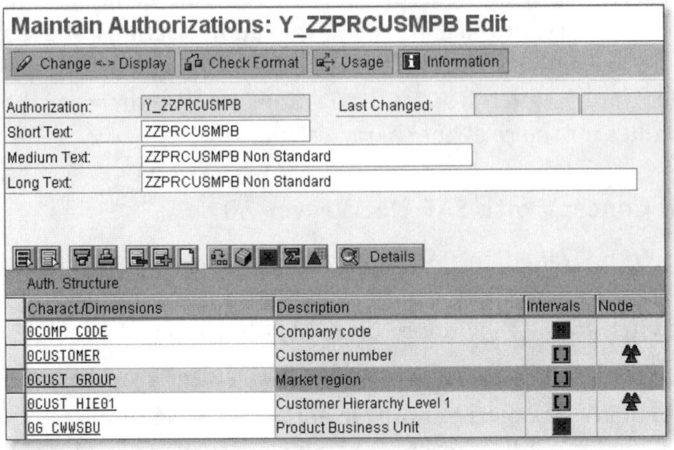

Figure 7.6 Dimensions in Authorizations

7.4.2 Authorization Dimensions

Authorizations can consist of any number of dimensions, and such authorization dimensions are characteristics or navigation attributes (Figure 7.6). You can use a set of single values, intervals, and hierarchy authorizations to authorize characteristics and navigation attributes independently of one another. The special characteristics Activity, Info-

Provider, and Validity can be inserted automatically and preassigned default values.

On the detail maintenance screen for a dimension, you use values or available hierarchies to maintain the authorizations (Figure 7.7). Here, you can also use, for example, reporting variables to determine authorization values dynamically.

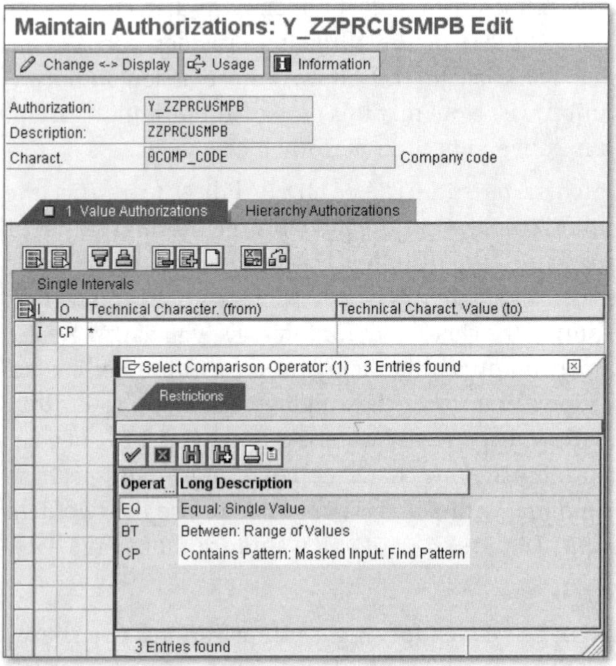

Maintain Authorizations: Y_ZZPRCUSMPB Edit

| Change <-> Display | Usage | Information |

Authorization:	Y_ZZPRCUSMPB
Description:	ZZPRCUSMPB
Charact.	0COMP_CODE	Company code

■ 1 Value Authorizations   Hierarchy Authorizations

Single Intervals

I	O	Technical Character. (from)	Technical Charact. Value (to)
I	CP	*	

Select Comparison Operator: (1)   3 Entries found   ⊠

Restrictions

Operat	Long Description
EQ	Equal: Single Value
BT	Between: Range of Values
CP	Contains Pattern: Masked Input: Find Pattern

3 Entries found

Figure 7.7 Maintaining Authorization Values

In addition to generic dimensions, an authorization also contains special dimensions that consists of the characteristics 0TCAACTVT (activity), 0TCAIPROV (InfoProvider), and 0TCAVALID (validity). You must include these special characteristics in at least one authorization for a user. Otherwise, the user is not authorized to execute a query. The special characteristics are delivered with the SAP NetWeaver BW content and are activated automatically. However, they are not yet flagged as authorization-relevant. Instead, you have to set this indicator in InfoObject maintenance before you use them in the authorizations.

Special dimensions

▸ You can use the characteristic 0TCAACTVT (activity) to restrict the authorization to different activities. Read (03) is set as the default activity. You must also assign the Change (02) activity for integrated planning.

▸ You can use the characteristic 0TCAIPROV (InfoProvider) to restrict the authorization to individual InfoProviders. The default setting is that all of the InfoProviders are authorized with an asterisk (*). The master data of the characteristic and the hierarchy characteristic for the InfoArea represent the structure of the InfoProvider stored in the Data Warehousing Workbench. This allows you to assign authorizations for entire InfoAreas. Note that this type of authorization assignment can have a negative impact on performance.

▸ You can use the characteristic 0TCAVALID (validity) to restrict the validity of an authorization. Always valid (*) is the default setting for validity. You can restrict this validity, by specifying either a single value or an interval. For single values, the comparison operator is set to EQ (equal to) during the check and, for intervals, you have a greater selection of comparison operators than you have with other characteristics, which allows you to set the validity accurately. To do this, you can use the following pattern: * (asterisk) for any number of characters or + (plus) for exactly one character. For a single-digit specification for days or months with patterns, continue to use the two-digit format, for example, Dec. 0+, 2005 if you want to authorize the dates Dec. 1 – 9, 2005.

To access the maintenance screen for single authorizations, you simply double-click the relevant characteristic. If you have defined intervals there, an interval icon appears on the maintenance screen for characteristics. If you have defined hierarchy authorizations, the system displays an icon with small triangles. If you have defined full authorization (*) as an interval, the system displays a special icon on the maintenance screen for characteristics, which tell you, at a glance, that full authorization has been defined.

7.4.3 Management of Analysis Authorizations

SAP NetWeaver BW 7.0 has a new, better-integrated maintenance transaction that provides all of the functions for managing analysis authorizations. All of the activities for managing the components of the analysis authorization system are maintained with authorizations for the new authorization object S_RSEC, which covers all relevant objects with namespace authorizations for certain activities.

The maintenance transactions have been completely redesigned, made accessible, and tailored to typical users. Closer integration enables faster administration and better control of the relevant objects than was previously possible. The management of analysis authorizations (Transaction RSECADMIN) provides a central entry point for all functions that you need to manage analysis authorizations.

On the Authorizations tab page, you can find all of the functions for creating, changing, generating, and transporting authorizations:

Authorizations tab page

▶ **Maintenance**
You access the transaction for creating and changing analysis authorizations.

▶ **Generation**
You access the transaction for generating analysis authorizations.

▶ **Transport**
You use this to write previously created authorizations to a transport request.

On the User tab page, you can find all of the functions that you need to assign analysis authorizations to a user:

User tab page

▶ **Assignment**
You access the transaction for assigning analysis authorizations to a user.

▶ **Transport**
You can transport authorizations that have been created and assigned.

▶ **User Maintenance**
You access the general user maintenance of SAP NetWeaver.

▶ **Role Maintenance**
You access the general role maintenance of SAP NetWeaver. You can use the authorization object S_RS_AUTH to include analysis authorizations in roles. You enter the authorizations (that you previously created) as fields for the authorization object S_RS_AUTH.

On the Analysis tab page, you can find all of the functions that you need to check and monitor analysis authorizations:

Analysis tab page

▶ **Execute as…**
You can execute various transactions as other users as a test to check their authorizations. This is password-protected.

▶ **Error logs**
You obtain a log for the authorization check.

▶ **Generation logs**
You obtain a log of all generation runs for authorizations.

The system automatically creates an authorization for all values of all authorization-relevant characteristics. This authorization is called 0BI_ALL, and it can be viewed but not changed. Each user who receives this authorization can access all data at all times. Each time you activate an InfoObject and change the property Authorization-Relevant for the characteristic or a navigation attribute, the authorization 0BI_ALL is adjusted. A user who has a profile with the authorization object S_RS_AUTH and has entered 0BI_ALL there (or has included it, for example, with the pattern *) is authorized to access all data.

7.4.4 Example of Creating Analysis Authorizations

We will now explain a sample procedure for creating authorizations:

1. Call the administration transaction RSECADMIN.

2. Enter a technical name for the authorization and select Create. You then access the Maintain Authorizations screen.

3. Provide a description for the authorization.

4. Use Insert Special Characteristics to insert the characteristics 0TCAACT-VT (activity), 0TCAIPROV (InfoProvider), and 0TCAVALID (validity).

Recommendation

In the interest of clarity and to reduce the maintenance and analysis effort, we recommend that you include these special characteristics in every authorization. Each user has to have authorizations for these three special characteristics.

By default, the special characteristics are preassigned standard values in the intervals: Read (03) is set as the default activity, Always Valid (*) is set as the validity, and All (*) is set for the InfoProvider. You also need to assign the Change (02) activity for changes to data in integrated planning.

5. Select Insert Row. You can use the input help to select characteristics and navigation attributes that were previously flagged as authorization-relevant.

If you want to create an authorization for a particular InfoProvider, you can choose InfoCube authorizations instead and select an Info-Provider. This makes it easier to select characteristics. The system then determines those characteristics contained in this InfoProvider that have been flagged as authorization-relevant. You can select the required characteristics and specify whether aggregation authorization (:) or full authorization (*) is to be assigned.

You can use Detail maintenance of Characteristic/Dimension to access the maintenance screen for value and hierarchy authorizations for the characteristic.

6. On the Value Authorizations tab page, you can specify an interval or a single value. You have the following options:

   ▶ You can use the information in the Including/Excluding column to control whether this value or value interval is included or excluded. You can only exclude values for the characteristic 0TCAVALID.

   ▶ You can still specify this information in the Operator column.

   ▶ You can select Insert Exit Variable to insert a customer exit variable.

   ▶ You can then select Check to check whether your specifications are useful. For a more detailed explanation, refer to the message long texts, which are displayed when you click the messages.

7. On the Hierarchy Authorizations tab page, you can specify one or more hierarchies. You can use the Maintenance Dialog for Hierarchy Authorizations to specify one or more hierarchy nodes and settings for the type of hierarchy authorization, hierarchy level, and area of validity.

8. Save the authorization. While saving the data, the system checks whether the format of the value authorizations is correct and issues a warning if necessary. The system corrects apparent errors and records them in a log.

The next section will show you how to define various types of authorizations.

7.4.5   Defining Authorizations

When you maintain authorizations, you can distinguish between assigning value authorizations and special authorizations (for example, aggregation and hierarchy authorizations).

Value Authorizations

The following input options are available when you define value authorizations:

- **Single value**
  For example, EQ 1000

- **Interval**
  For example, between A01 and A99

- **Pattern**
  You can use an asterisk (*) as a placeholder for any number of characteristics and a plus (+) for exactly one random character, for example, A* for all values beginning with the letter A or A+ for a two-digit value beginning with the letter A.

Thanks to a high level of transparency, the assignment of value authorizations simplifies administration. On the other hand, however, such an approach is often impractical owing to the large number of users and assigned values. Therefore, it generally makes sense to use the variables and hierarchies described below and the options for generating authorization values.

Aggregated Values

A special feature here is the authorization for aggregated values, assigned by a colon. This authorization will be explained in greater detail below. You must have authorization for aggregated values to display the values of an authorization-relevant characteristic in aggregated form in the query.

Example   The characteristic 0COUNTRY is authorization-relevant and is contained in the InfoProvider being used. The characteristic is contained in the free characteristics (not in the drilldown) without any selections. Alternatively, it is not used in the query. In both cases, no 0COUNTRY values are displayed in the query, and no restrictions are applied to 0COUNTRY values. The authorization for aggregated values is required during the authorization check. In these cases, the system displays the information "Check for : added" in the authorization log.

The following situation is often overlooked: An authorization check is also performed if the authorization-relevant characteristic is contained not in the query, but in the InfoProvider. The displayed key figures are implicitly aggregated over all of the characteristic values, and this display form must also be authorized. In a query, a selection can be made locally in a restricted key figure or in a structure. However, if the query contains other key figures for which this local selection is not valid (and for which no other selection is valid), the authorization for aggregated values is also required in the authorization.

Special features

If you want queries to display values without restrictions, you must assign the authorization for aggregated values to the user. If you do not want to assign this authorization to the user, you must restrict the characteristic in the query to a certain selection (single value, interval, hierarchy nodes, and so on) and explicitly authorize this selection.

You must implement one or another of these measures if the characteristic is authorization-relevant. The asterisk (*) authorization authorizes everything. Consequently, it also authorizes queries that require authorization for aggregated values. If you use a variable of the type Fill from Authorization, the system ignores the authorization for aggregated values because, when the variable is processed, it does not know if the characteristic in question is contained in the drilldown.

Hierarchy Authorizations

There are different ways to define authorizations that are based on a node in a hierarchy:

- Authorization for a node
- Authorization for the subtree below a node
- Authorization for the subtree below a node up to and including a level (absolute):

  You must specify a level for this type. A typical example of when you need to specify an absolute level is data protection with regard to the level of detail (according to the works council, reports cannot be at the employee level, only at more summarized levels).

- Authorization for the entire hierarchy

▶ Authorization for the subtree below a node up to and including a level (relative):

For this type, you must specify a level that is determined relative to the node. It is useful to specify a relative distance if an employee can only expand the hierarchy to a certain depth below his initial node, but this node moves to another level when the hierarchy is restructured.

Validity area You use the validity area to specify the exact extent to which a hierarchy authorization must match a selected display hierarchy so that it can be used in the authorization check:

▶ **Type 0 (very strict check)**
The name and version of the hierarchy on which the hierarchy authorization is based must agree with the display hierarchy selected. Your key date (the upper validity limit) must be later than or on the same day as the key date (the upper validity limit) for the display hierarchy selected.

▶ **Type 1**
The name and version of the hierarchy on which the hierarchy authorization is based must agree with the display hierarchy selected.

▶ **Type 2**
The name of the hierarchy on which the hierarchy authorization is based must agree with the display hierarchy selected.

▶ **Type 3 (the least strict check)**
None of these three properties have to match.

Note that setting a check level that is too low may result in more nodes being selected (using hierarchy node variables filled from authorizations) than actually exist in the display hierarchy for the query. This may cause the system to issue an error message. Also note the following: Even though hierarchy authorizations can authorize single values, which are the end nodes (leaves) of a hierarchy that is not displayed, the strictest check type (0) is always valid in this case.

Variables

Instead of using a single value or interval, you can also use variables of the customer exit type in authorizations (Figure 7.8). For these variables, the customer exit is called in the execution step 0 (I_STEP = 0) during the authorization check. The intervals of characteristic values or hierarchies for which the user is authorized can be returned in this step, considerably reducing the maintenance effort for authorizations and profiles in some circumstances.

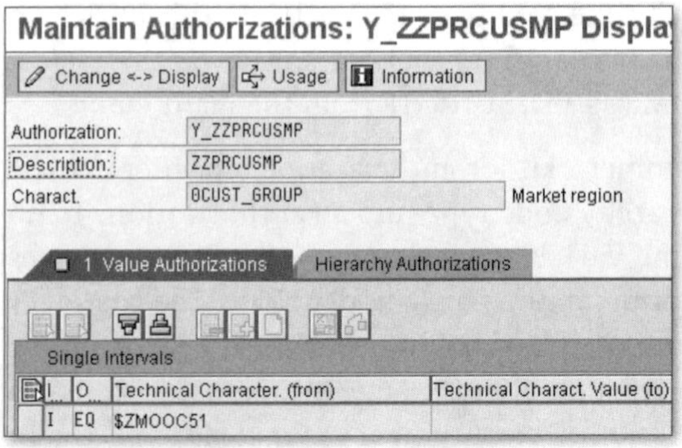

Figure 7.8 Using Variables

The type of variable (customer exit) shown in Figure 7.9 should not be confused with characteristic variables that are filled from authorizations.

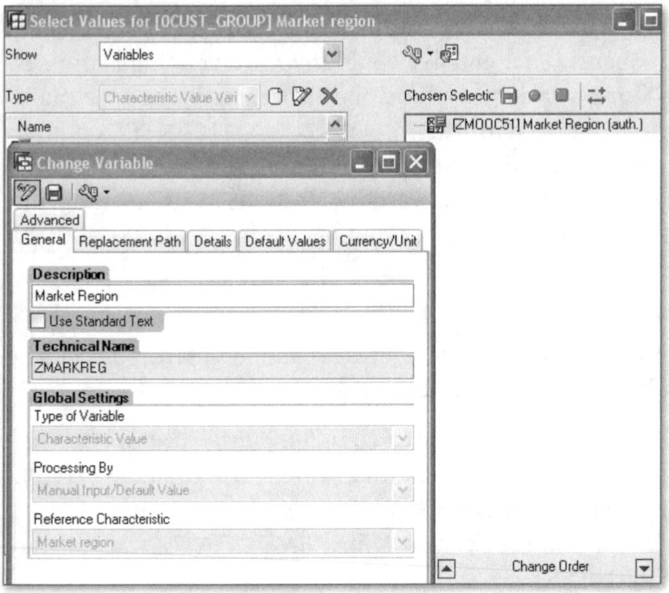

Customer exit type

Figure 7.9 Variable of the Customer Exit Type

One-time call
Note that there is a buffer for these variables. If you activate this buffer, the customer exit is only called once for a variable (during the authorization check). Consequently, you avoid repeatedly calling the customer exit for variables and decreasing performance. If you want to call the customer exit each time, you have to deactivate this buffer on the administration screen for analysis authorizations. To do this, select EXTRAS • BUFFERING VARIABLES • DEACTIVATE from the main menu.

You can also call the customer exit for authorizations for hierarchies. Enter variables of the hierarchy node type into an authorization. To do this, select a corresponding variable by selecting Select Exit Variables in the hierarchy authorization maintenance under Node. The customer exit is then called during the authorization check. In the return table E_T_RANGE, the technical name of one or more nodes is expected in the LOW field, whereas the InfoObject type of the node is expected in the HIGH field.

Example
Each cost center manager should only be allowed to evaluate the data for his cost center. Within the SAP authorization standard, a role or profile with authorization for the InfoObject 0COSTCENTER equal to XXXX (where XXXX stands for the particular cost center) would have to be made for every cost center manager X. This has to be entered in the user master record for the cost center manager. In organizations where cost centers frequently change, this would involve a very high administrative effort. Using a variable reduces the effort associated with maintaining an authorization with the InfoObject 0COSTCENTER equal to $VARCOST and with defining the role or profile maintained for all cost center managers. The value of the variable VARCOST is then set at runtime during the authorization check by the customer exit RSR00001.

Display Attributes

Authorization-relevant display attributes are hidden in the query if the user does not have sufficient authorization.

Characteristics
For characteristics, the user requires complete authorization (*)to see the display attribute in the query. If, for example, the attribute 0EMPL-STATUS of the characteristic 0EMPLOYEE is authorization-relevant, only users who have authorization * for 0EMPLSTATUS can display this attribute in the query.

Key figures cannot be flagged as authorization-relevant. If you nevertheless want to use this function for key figure attributes, you can perform a check against the meta object 0TCAKYFNM. The user then requires the field 0TCAKYFNM in an authorization. If, for example, the characteristic 0EMPLOYEE contains the key figure attribute 0ANSALARY, and a user has the field 0TCAKYFNM in his authorization, along with the authorization *, he can display all of the key figure attributes. If the user has the field 0TCAKYFNM in his authorization and the key figure 0ANSALARY as a value (that is, instead of *), he can see only this key figure attribute. If you do not want some users to see this key figure attribute, you should not assign the authorization * but only explicitly assign, as a value, those key figures for authorization that are to be displayed.

Key figures

Navigation Attributes

In authorizations, navigation attributes are treated like ordinary characteristics. You can flag navigation attributes as authorization-relevant irrespective of the basic characteristics assigned. To flag a navigation attribute as authorization-relevant, set the relevant indicator on the Attributes tab on the maintenance screen for InfoObjects.

Generation

Authorization generation is intended for scenarios that generate new authorizations periodically (in other words, scenarios that are constantly changing). In these cases, it does not necessarily make sense to assign these authorizations (in roles or profiles) to the users. This is also not possible for names that are automatically generated because they keep changing. Consequently, the generated authorizations are assigned directly to the SAP NetWeaver BW system (which is considerably faster than generating profiles). If a fixed name is assigned, you can do this manually in role maintenance. However, you should give this some thought because there is a danger of these constant names being overwritten.

Authorization generation is a dynamic authorization assignment concept, which is an alternative to the role concept. You can generate a large number of authorizations and assign them to a small number of users or you can generate a small number of (constantly changing) authorizations and assign them to a large number of users. If you create a technical name with eight digits (RSR_nnnnnnnn) for an authorization and then regenerate it, the existing names are deleted, and new technical names are generated. As a result, the previous authorization is deleted and replaced with the new authorization (which possibly has the same content). You can use a number range to prevent unwanted overwriting. An overflow occurs after 100,000,000 generated authorizations. Numbering then starts with 1 again.

Concept
The following five DataStore objects (DSOs) are available as templates for generating analysis authorizations: 0TCA_DS01, 0TCA_DS02, 0TCA_DS03, 0TCA_DS04, and 0TCA_DS05. The actual data to be used in the generated authorizations is contained in the two template DSOs 0TCA_DS01 and 0TCA_DS02, which must be copied for each application. Here, you have to adhere to the naming convention of digits 1 to 5 at the end.

Flat authorizations
The DataStore object for generating flat authorizations (single values, intervals, and selection options), "intervals" for short, has the following structure:

▶ You use the column 0TCTUSERNM to assign an authorization row in a DSO to users.

▶ You can use the column 0TCTAUTH to assign authorization names, and it has a special role.

▶ The fields 0TCTADFROM and 0TCTADTO specify the period during which you can use the associated DSO rows to generate authorizations. If these columns are empty, the associated rows are ignored.

▶ You use the fields 0TCTIOBJNM, 0TCTSIGN, 0TCTOPTION, 0TCTLOW, and 0TCTHIGH to generate intervals for the InfoObject in 0TCTIOBJNM. The permitted intervals can only use "including" selections (enter "I" in 0TCTSIGN for *Including*).

▶ You must always enter "A" for *active* in the field 0TCTOBJVERS.

▶ You can leave the field 0TCTSYSID empty or enter the system name here.

Hierarchy node authorizations
The DataStore object for generating hierarchy node authorizations has the following structure:

▶ You use the column 0TCTUSERNM to assign an authorization row in a DSO to users.

- You can use the column 0TCTAUTH to assign authorization names, and it has a special role.

- The fields TCTADFROM and 0TCATADTO specify the period during which you can use the associated DSO rows to generate authorizations.

- You use the fields 0TCTIOBJNM, 0TCTHIENM, 0TCTHIEVERS, 0TCTHIEDATE, 0TCTNODE, 0TCTNIOBJNM, 0TCTATYPE, 0TCTLEVEL, and 0TCTACOMPM to define the hierarchy node authorizations for the hierarchy whose name is in the column 0TCTHIENM and whose version is in the column 0TCTHIEVERS for the InfoObject in the column 0TCTIOBJNM. The hierarchy date is in the column 0TCTHIEDATE and is, for example, 99991231.

- Enter the authorized, technical node name in the field 0TCTNODE and the node type in the field 0TCTNIOBJNM (text node = 0HIER_NODE, chargeable characteristic node = characteristic name, leaf = empty/no entry).

- Define the details for the authorized node in the remaining fields, 0TCTATYPE (type of authorization), 0TCTLEVEL (level, if required), and 0TCTCOMPM (validity range of node authorization).

- Always enter "A" for *active* in the field 0TCTOBJVERS.

- You can leave the field 0TCTSYSID empty.

First, you must load the data into the DSOs. You can do this using CSV files or extractors. Automatic generation requires correctly filled DSOs. However, the system tries to detect incorrect intervals and some other errors and correct them if possible. It also records this information in a log.

Application

The DataStore objects are then used to generate the authorizations. For CSV files, the User and Authorization columns do not necessarily have to be filled with values. In general, however, you can fill these fields with names and numbers, which may provide different results when you assign authorizations. For the DataStore objects 0TCA_D01 and 0TCA_DS02, the following applies:

1. The field TCTUSERNM contains the name of the user who is to be assigned the authorizations. If you leave the field empty, authorizations are generated but not assigned. They are available as authorizations in a pool and can be assigned at a later time.

2. The field 0TCTAUTH can contain authorization names. If you leave this field empty, technical names are generated. You can enter numbers or real names, for example, to maintain different areas of similar characteristic combinations.

Examples of use

If you want to maintain user-specific authorizations, you can maintain the user in the DataStore object 0TCA_DS01. During authorization generation, the authorizations entered are assigned to the user. You can generate mass authorizations by leaving the User key field blank in the DataStore object 0TCA_DS01 so that user-independent authorizations can be generated. You can then assign these authorizations to any number of users. You can enter descriptive texts for the authorizations in the DataStore object 0TCA_DS03 and can then use the DataStore object 0TCA_DS04 to assign the authorizations to the users.

During the generation process, you can generate users by entering them in the DataStore object 0TCA_DS05. In each case, you must specify an existing reference user. Newly created users are assigned nontransparent, randomly generated initial passwords. Users can only log on after they have manually changed the password assigned in each case. You can load texts for the authorizations generated. Such texts are stored in the language-dependent short, medium, and long texts in the object 0TCA_DS03.

You can use the DataStore object 0TCA_DS01 to delete authorizations by entering the dummy user D_E_L_E_T_E in the user field for the authorization to be deleted. Please note that the authorization is not only deleted, but also withdrawn from all users in the SAP NetWeaver BW system.

Shorter runtimes

Authorization generation also processes thousands of data records. However, the runtimes are not comparable with the read performance of transaction data from a DSO. Consequently, authorization generation may take several hours. Therefore, you can use the program RSEC_GENERATE_AUTHORIZATIONS to perform a generation run in the background. When compared with SAP NetWeaver BW 3.x, however, the runtime is always considerably shorter. During the generation process, all of the authorizations generated are initially deleted, which means that all affected users do not have any authorizations during a generation run until the newly generated authorizations have been assigned. This applies even if the contents of the authorization structure have not changed at all. If the generation process takes several hours, this may also result in long downtimes.

In general, you should only generate authorizations that have actually changed. You can check this in the corresponding extraction program before the DSOs are filled. Because the number of changed authorizations is usually considerably lower than the total number of users, this procedure can shorten runtimes considerably. You can use the user D_E_L_E_T_E for occasional cleanup tasks, for example, for a complete, updated generation run once a month. You can also perform this cleanup task by adding a row to the DataStore object for the values, so that, for example, obsolete user authorizations that have already been locked or deleted and never regenerated are fully deleted. Otherwise, their generated authorizations are not automatically deleted.

7.4.6 Troubleshooting

To improve revision capabilities, a complete change recording of authorizations and assignments to users has been created. These changes can be analyzed using queries on remote InfoProviders and restricted using analysis authorizations.

In addition, a new troubleshooting tool (integrated into Transaction RSECADMIN) replaced the old authorization log. It uses the HTML format, can be saved and printed, and is persistently stored in the database. The readability of the messages contained in the log for authorization generation has improved significantly. For test purposes, it is now possible, among other things, to execute certain actions relating to the analysis as another user (you can also do this directly in Transaction RSUDO). Please note that in Transaction RSUDO, the user is only changed locally in the context of analysis authorizations and that the value of the system variable for the current user (sy-uname) continues to correspond to the user executing the action (in other words, the administrator). However, if database selections for sy-uname are used in the relevant transaction, the system may provide an incorrect result. An example here would be the management of authorized values in DataStore objects and the use of customer exit variables to read these values dynamically.

New troubleshooting tool

To correct this behavior, you can use the function module RSEC_GET_ USERNAME in customer exits. Usually, this module provides the user name, which is also in sy-uname. When you execute Transaction RSUDO, it correctly returns the name of the restricted user.

Example In the example below (Figure 7.10), the system executes the query from the perspective of the user TEST002 and records a detailed log for subsequent analysis. In most cases, the query monitor for the test user is called here, but other tests, for example, in the reporting agent monitor (Transaction RSRAM) or the execution of MDX queries directly in Transaction MDX_TEST are possible.

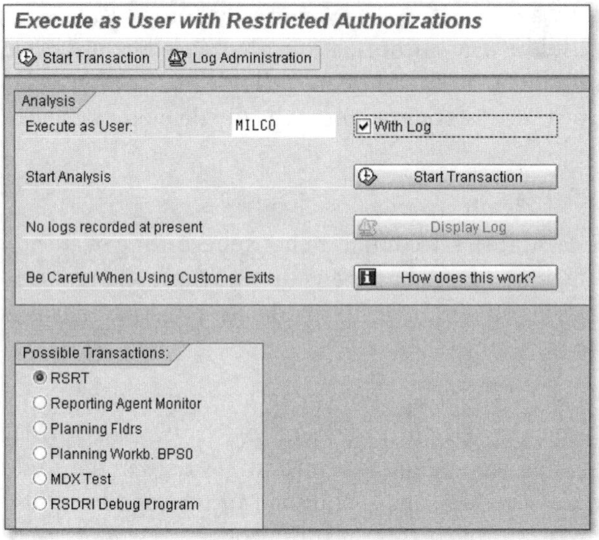

Figure 7.10 Starting the Logging Procedure

In the transaction that you call, the relevant action is performed without any additional settings. In the example shown in Figure 7.11, a query is executed in Transaction RSRT to better understand the behavior reported by a user.

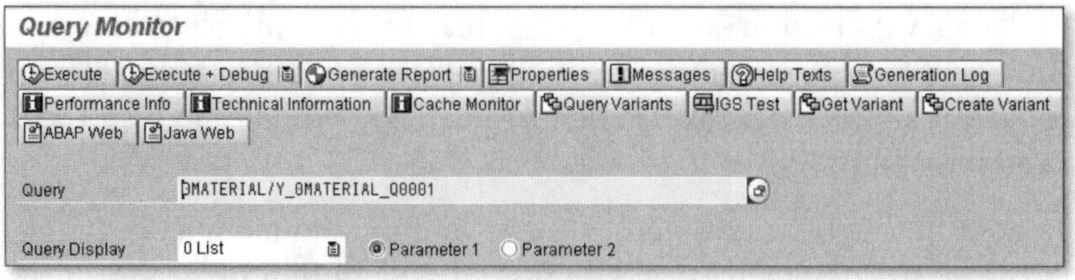

Figure 7.11 Executing the Query in Transaction RSRT

Because the log can be very long and unmanageable, you should take every opportunity to simplify it. If possible, remove all authorization variables from the relevant query and use a fixed filter with the relevant values instead. During execution, you should not use the input help (F4) or navigation steps, if possible. The bookmark function in Transaction RSRT is often useful here because executing a previously saved bookmark produces the shortest possible log.

Simplifying the log

In our example, the system issues a warning in relation to the missing authorizations (Figure 7.12). In the log, you can analyze this warning in greater detail to determine which data is not authorized for the user (Figure 7.13).

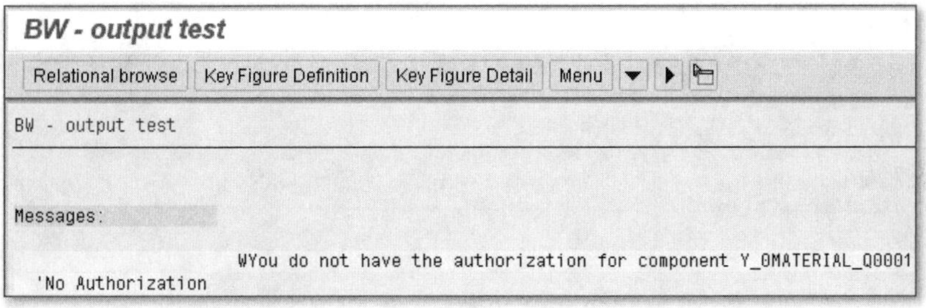

Log analysis

BW - output test

| Relational browse | Key Figure Definition | Key Figure Detail | Menu | ▼ | ▶ | 🗎 |

BW - output test

Messages:

WYou do not have the authorization for component Y_0MATERIAL_Q0001
'No Authorization

Figure 7.12 Query Result

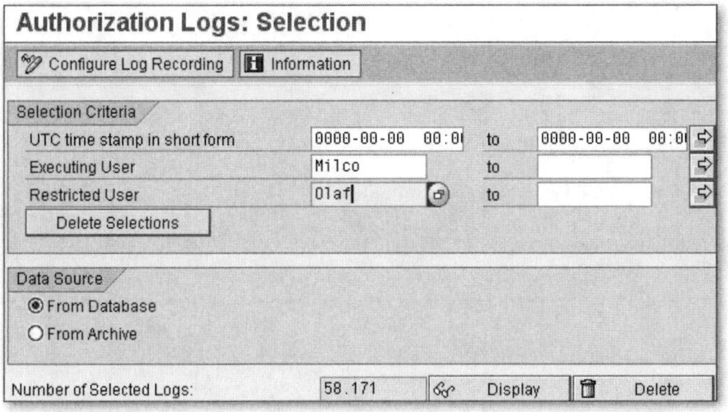

Authorization Logs: Selection

| 📝 Configure Log Recording | ℹ Information |

Selection Criteria

UTC time stamp in short form	0000-00-00 00:0(	to	0000-00-00 00:0(	⇨
Executing User	Milco	to		⇨
Restricted User	01af|	to		⇨
Delete Selections				

Data Source
◉ From Database
○ From Archive

| Number of Selected Logs: | 58.171 | &ₚ | Display | 🗑 | Delete |

Figure 7.13 Log Analysis in Transaction RSECPROT

For detailed information and explanations about the authorization log, read SAP Note 1234567. For detailed information about some of the subareas, read SAP Note 1233793, and for information about the check for colon authorization, read SAP Note 1140831.

In the upper part of the log, you can activate and deactivate various blocks. However, after you make such changes, you must select Update Display. The system then recreates the HTML page. As you can see in Figure 7.14, the header data contains some key data about the query that you have executed, for example, the date and time when the log was created, along with the name of the query executed (here ZFI_R0019/Y_ZFI_R0019_Q0001). The relevant user names are also specified here: the logon user (here 23053300) and the authorization-relevant user (here TEST002).

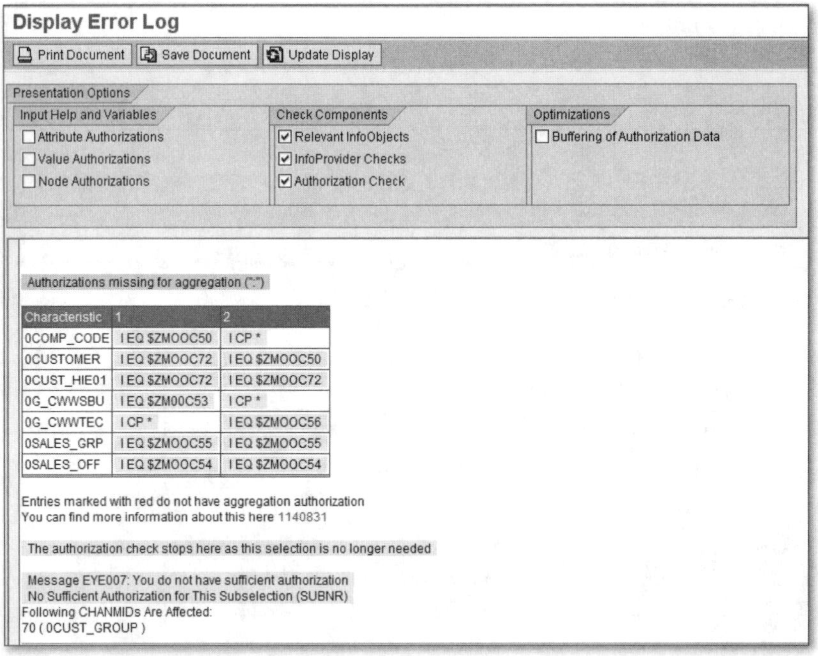

Display Error Log

Print Document | Save Document | Update Display

Presentation Options

Input Help and Variables	Check Components	Optimizations
☐ Attribute Authorizations	☑ Relevant InfoObjects	☐ Buffering of Authorization Data
☐ Value Authorizations	☑ InfoProvider Checks	
☐ Node Authorizations	☑ Authorization Check	

Authorizations missing for aggregation ("")

Characteristic	1	2
0COMP_CODE	I EQ $ZMOOC50	I CP *
0CUSTOMER	I EQ $ZMOOC72	I EQ $ZMOOC50
0CUST_HIE01	I EQ $ZMOOC72	I EQ $ZMOOC72
0G_CWWSBU	I EQ $ZM00C53	I CP *
0G_CWWTEC	I CP *	I EQ $ZMOOC56
0SALES_GRP	I EQ $ZMOOC55	I EQ $ZMOOC55
0SALES_OFF	I EQ $ZMOOC54	I EQ $ZMOOC54

Entries marked with red do not have aggregation authorization
You can find more information about this here 1140831

The authorization check stops here as this selection is no longer needed

Message EYE007: You do not have sufficient authorization
No Sufficient Authorization for This Subselection (SUBNR)
Following CHANMIDs Are Affected:
70 (0CUST_GROUP)

Figure 7.14 Error Log

The headers for the check results of the individual parts are colored light orange in the log (Figure 7.14). Depending on the query structure, the entire query selection is initially broken down into parts (SUB numbers, SUBNR). In most cases, a SUB number corresponds to a structure element in the query (for example, a column). The SUB numbers are checked individually and independently of one another, so that some of the many SUB numbers can be authorized and some are not.

If a subselection (SUB number) is authorized, this is colored green. However, if a subselection is not authorized, the subsequent rows are colored yellow (as shown in Figure 7.14): "Message EYE007: You do not have sufficient authorization. No Sufficient Authorization for this Subselection (SUBNR)." Note that each selected characteristic can be fully authorized on its own. However, the combination of all selected characteristic values is always relevant.

If you want the system to not only record logs when you use the Execute as function, but to also automatically record them for all actions by certain users, you can use Transaction RSECPROT to define a list of users for whom you want the system to automatically create a log.

Automatic logs

Such users are then listed in the table with their alias names (Figure 7.15), and you can click the Add User and Delete User buttons to edit this list.

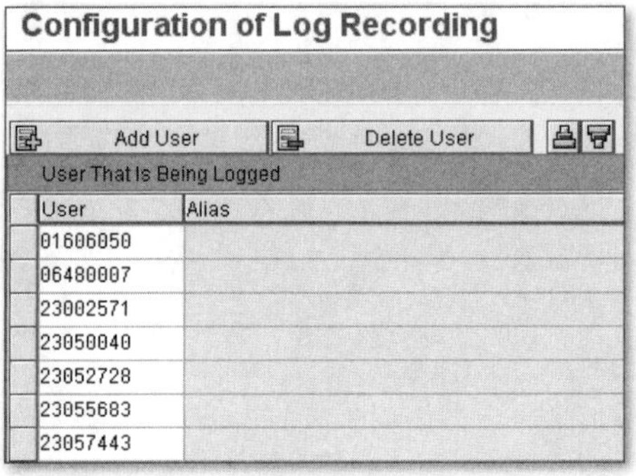

Configuration of Log Recording

Add User		Delete User		
User That Is Being Logged				
User	Alias			
01606050				
06480007				
23002571				
23050040				
23052728				
23055683				
23057443				

Figure 7.15 Log Recording in Transaction RSECPROT

7.4.7 Migration

For compatibility reasons, the old authorization system in SAP NetWeaver BW 3.x has been retained in SAP NetWeaver 7.0, but it will be fully removed in the next release. Consequently, any features due to expire should no longer be used in new implementations. SAP urgently recommends that you switch over to the new concept, which is also the default setting.

Transition during
the upgrade To make the transition easier when upgrading to SAP NetWeaver 7.0, SAP has retained and integrated the old source code as far as possible, so that the old authorization system should continue to work largely unchanged. To this end, there is a Customizing switch (Transaction RSCUSTV23), which enables the authorization system to revert to the old procedure in an emergency.

Because the new concept is not fully compatible with the old concept, which was based on authorization objects, there is a migration help that can semiautomate many of the steps. However, this involves some initial effort. For example, features that did not exist with SAP NetWeaver BW 3.x and do not work or only partly work with the old authorization system cannot be supported. A good example of this is integrated planning, which is not designed for the old authorization concept and can demonstrate inconsistent or unexpected behavior in some parts of the system.

Information lifecycle management in SAP NetWeaver BW con-
sists of strategies and methods for optimal data retention and
history management such as archiving processes. In this chapter
we describe the option to classify data based on its relevance in
terms of how up to date it is and either to archive it or store it in
nearline storage. We also discuss the controlled deletion of infor-
mation and the repartitioning and reclustering of InfoProvider
tables.

8 Archiving and Data Maintenance

Owing to the often very large volumes of data in SAP NetWeaver BW systems, we must not forget data management and influences on performance and stability in a complete administration concept. Besides classic archiving concepts and the specific nearline storage options in an SAP NetWeaver BW system (see Section 8.4, Nearline Storage), also included is the controlled deletion of data and partitioning and clustering strategies.

8.1 Archiving Concepts

When you run a live business application, large volumes of data generally accumulate in the database, which is often reflected in decreased system performance and increased resource consumption. A large volume of data also negatively affects costs because expenses for database administration steadily rise. For reasons of finance, performance, and system availability, you should therefore remove from the database data for completed business transactions that is no longer relevant for day-to-day activities. Simply deleting this data is often not an option, because you must retain it to fulfill legal requirements. You therefore have to remove the data from the database and store it in such a way that it can be accessed for reading at any time, as required.

You do this using SAP data archiving or, to put it more generally, the strategy for information lifecycle management (ILM). The objective is to enable you to remove application data from the database consistently and securely without any loss of data. This involves storing archived data in a file system, from where you can transfer it to other, more cost-efficient storage media.

SAP NetWeaver BW systems with more than 5 terabytes are no longer a rarity, and feasibility studies are already examining the possibilities of managing systems with more than 80 terabytes. In view of the growth of data in recent years, it is easy to suspect that demand will continue to increase. The particular challenge here, in addition to basic technical feasibility in terms of SAP NetWeaver BW processes (such as loading data), but also in terms of administrative activities (backing up or restoring databases) is to achieve a balance between requirements for accessing data and for total costs (total cost of ownership (TCO). According to Gartner, data administration costs amount to five to seven times the costs of actual storage media. An information lifecycle management strategy should pursue the following goals:

Goals ► **Better performance due to lower volumes of data**
Improved data loading process times and query executions

► **Reduced costs**
Data storage costs and administration costs

► **Better availability**
Improvements in the area of change runs, database backups, and upgrades

The diagram in Figure 8.1 illustrates that the size of the database grows rapidly annually, and this naturally means that costs for required hardware and administration expenses also increase.

We recommend scheduling the monitoring of the database size and in particular the growth of the largest tables in the SAP NetWeaver BW system as an administration task (performed weekly, for example). The basis for a suitable ILM strategy for the relevant system must be the use of data. In many cases you can assume that the ratio of data that is accessed frequently and regularly and therefore must be available online and the data that has to be accessed less often or only in exceptional cases and therefore can be archived is one to six. This means that in a system with 2.100 GB of analyzable data, only 300 GB is regularly used for reporting, and the vast majority is only required in exceptional cases.

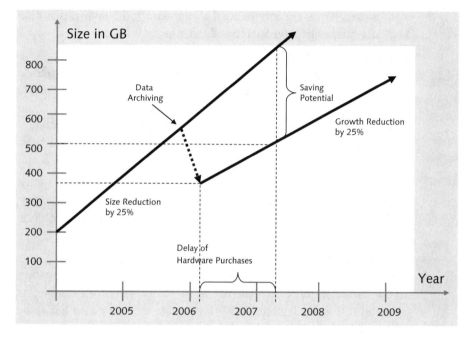

Figure 8.1 Data Growth

The relevant strategy for data archiving in a system is not generally universal because the data in an SAP NetWeaver BW system places very different requirements on data availability owing to the deliberately high redundancy and very different objectives of applications and data containers (InfoProviders, master data, technical tables, and so on). For example, the requirement of data availability for a corporate memory or propagation layer objects in a modern architecture based on a scalable layer model is entirely different from the requirements for Info-Cubes in the reporting layer.

Individual strategy

In addition to the requirements of archiving from the point of view of an SAP NetWeaver BW administrator (for example, which data can I archive and how?), there are a number of basic, technical requirements that we will only discuss briefly. Data archiving involves more than purely backing up table contents. Some of the requirements that must be taken into account with data archiving include the following:

Requirements of data archiving

▶ **Hardware independence**
Because the encoding of numeric fields such as integers is hardware-dependent, archiving must ensure that information about the currently used hardware is appended to the data to be archived so that the data can be displayed later with changed hardware.

▶ **Release dependence**
Because the data structure may depend on the SAP NetWeaver release being used, but also on customized versions (for example, future enhancements of DSOs), information about record structures and field definitions also needs to be archived in the archiving process.

▶ **Dependencies between data**
Many data objects can only be used in connection with other data objects or depend on them. This is why, when archiving, you must check whether archiving a certain data object will require you to archive other objects or whether you will have to archive other objects in parallel.

▶ **Enterprise and business structure**
Some data can only be interpreted in conjunction with information about the organizational structure of the enterprise, for example, its division into sales regions. This master data therefore also has to be archived in the archiving process.

The important thing to understand is that archiving may only be one (albeit very important) part of a complete ILM strategy. Also important are strategies for data prevention (writing only statistical information that is actually required), data aggregation (if summarized information is sufficient, this should be used and information at detailed level avoided), and data deletion (typical housekeeping activities such as deleting old statistical and log data).

8.2   Data Archiving Process

You can use Archive Development Kit (ADK)-based archiving and removal to nearline storage for InfoCubes and DataStore objects. The central object in this case is the data archiving process (DAP). When defining the data archiving process, you can choose between classic ADK archiving, removal to nearline storage, or a combination of both solutions.

ADK-based archiving uses the Archive Development Kit (ADK). ADK is an SAP NetWeaver tool for developing archiving solutions and provides the runtime environment for archiving (see also Section 8.3, Archive Development Kit). You mainly use it to read and write data to and from archive files. Which of the three options you choose depends on your application case:

Archive Development Kit

▶ **Archive data using ADK.**
We recommend this type of archiving for data that is no longer relevant for current analytical processes but that you still have to keep archived because of legal retention periods and even to provide for analysis in an emergency.

▶ **Remove data to nearline storage.**
We recommend nearline storage for data that may still be required. Removing historical data to nearline storage reduces the volume of data of InfoProviders, whereas the data is nevertheless available for BEx queries. You can also access archived data in nearline storage from the query monitor. You do not need to reload it into the SAP NetWeaver BW system. Database partitions and nearline storage partitions for an InfoProvider collectively reflect the entire dataset consistently.

▶ **Combine ADK-based archiving with removing data to nearline storage.**
We recommend this type of archiving if you want a backup of data in addition to storing it in nearline storage. Some third-party tools for nearline storage require you to connect to ADK to remove the data for storage. In this case, when creating a data archiving process, you must always remove the data to nearline storage and ADK-based archiving.

You can use the data archiving process to archive or remove transaction data from InfoCubes and DataStore objects (Figure 8.2). The data archiving process runs in three steps:

Data archiving process in detail

1. Create the archive file or nearline object.

2. Store the archive file in an archiving object (ADK-based) or in nearline storage.

3. Delete the archived data from the database.

A data archiving process is always assigned to exactly one InfoProvider and gets the same name as this InfoProvider. You can retrospectively create a data archiving process for an existing InfoProvider already filled with data.

Archiving and nearline objects

ADK archiving generates a separate archiving object for each InfoProvider. Like the archiving object role in ADK archiving, in the nearline storage process the nearline object is responsible for addressing the connected nearline storage solution. The data archiving process also generates this nearline object specifically for an InfoProvider. Nearline objects consist of different nearline segments that reflect different views of relevant InfoProviders and can also mirror different versions of an InfoProvider.

Depending on the modeling, an archiving object and/or a link to nearline storage is generated. For ADK-based archiving, an archiving object is generated locally on a system.

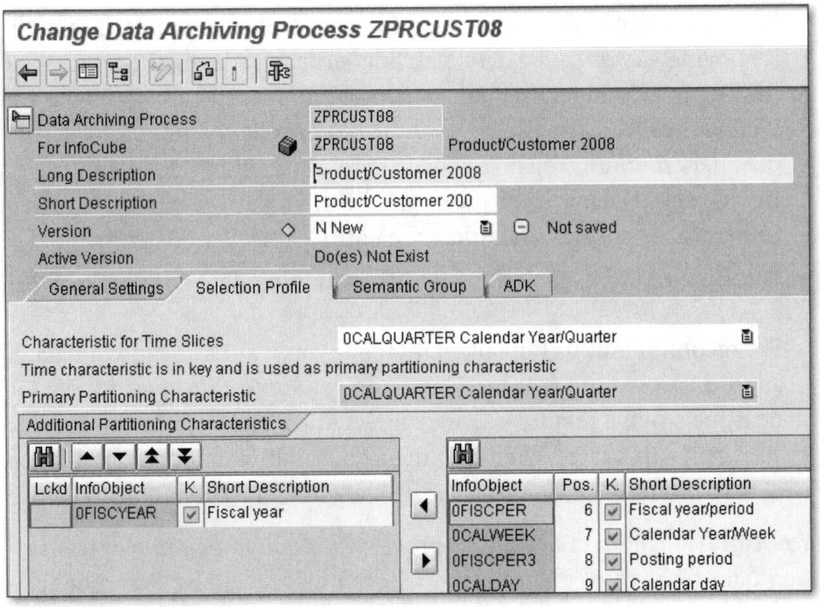

Figure 8.2 Data Archiving Process

The namespace for archiving objects is made up of BW as the prefix, followed by a letter for the object type (C = InfoCube, O = DataStore object) and then the object name shortened to seven characters because only ten characters in total are available for the name. In the next step you can schedule the data archiving process. We will discuss the details of scheduling for nearline and ADK-based processes in more detail in the following sections.

8.3   Archive Development Kit

With SAP NetWeaver BW 3.0, SAP introduced for the SAP NetWeaver BW system the ADK-based archiving that was successful in SAP ERP systems. The archiving based on the Archive Development Kit (ADK) supports archiving InfoProviders but restricts reporting because you cannot access archived data with queries. You can create archiving objects for InfoCubes and DataStore objects. We will discuss the options for archiving PSA data in Section 8.6, Archiving PSA Data.

You can create ADK files for existing archiving objects and store them on an application server. After the archiving session, you can use SAP ArchiveLink to transfer the files you have created to any external storage media. Following this procedure, archived data understandably cannot be accessed for queries, and the data will have to be loaded from the archive into the SAP NetWeaver BW system again for any corresponding requests. The archived data is read sequentially, and this makes the process somewhat slow. ADK-based archiving is available in Transaction SARA.

ArchiveLink

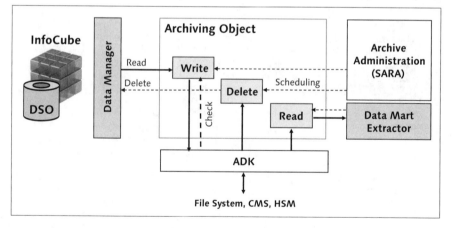

Figure 8.3 Archiving Process (ADK)

Figure 8.3 shows that archiving objects are used to write data into archiving files. The archiving object is relevant for accessing the Data Manager responsible for reading InfoProvider data when a query is executed and for the extraction process for data marts.

8.3.1 Tasks

The process of archiving application data is divided into phases of analyzing the data, actually archiving it, and finally accessing the archived data. The *access to archived data* phase is not part of the actual archiving process, but in terms of using the archived data later, it is very important, which is why we will discuss it here. The *data archiving administrator* role (its technical name is SAP_BC_CCM_DATA_ARCHIVING) is available in the SAP system to help you when performing data archiving. The role provides the system or data archiving administrator with direct access to all important information, tools, and systems required for carrying out data archiving.

Analysis   In the analysis phase, you identify the largest and fastest-growing database tables and the archiving objects for archiving table contents. The objective is to identify which data or tables should be archived. Based on the result of the analysis, you select the archiving object that can be used to archive data from critical tables. The analysis is supported by different tools, which we will explain in more detail below.

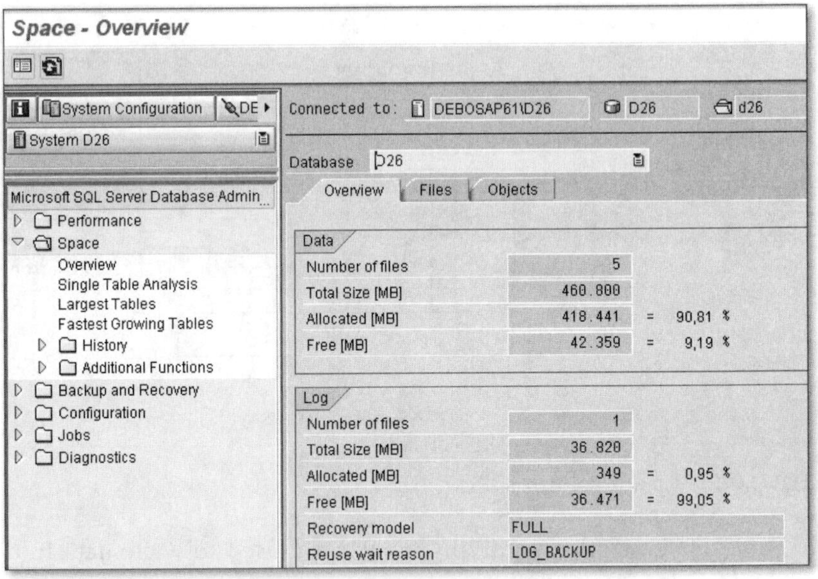

Figure 8.4 Database Size in Transaction DB02

You can use the database monitor (Transaction DB02) to determine table sizes and display how they have grown in the past (Figure 8.4). This transaction provides important database-specific key figures. The database monitor display depends on the database system used; on an Oracle database system, for example, it displays the number of free tablespaces or size and growth of individual tables and indexes.

Database monitor

Besides the database monitor, you can also use the SAPDBA tool and system load monitor (Transaction ST03) to determine other indicators relating to data archiving. Transaction DB15 (tables and archiving objects) also provides information about storage space statistics via its Space (Statistics) option.

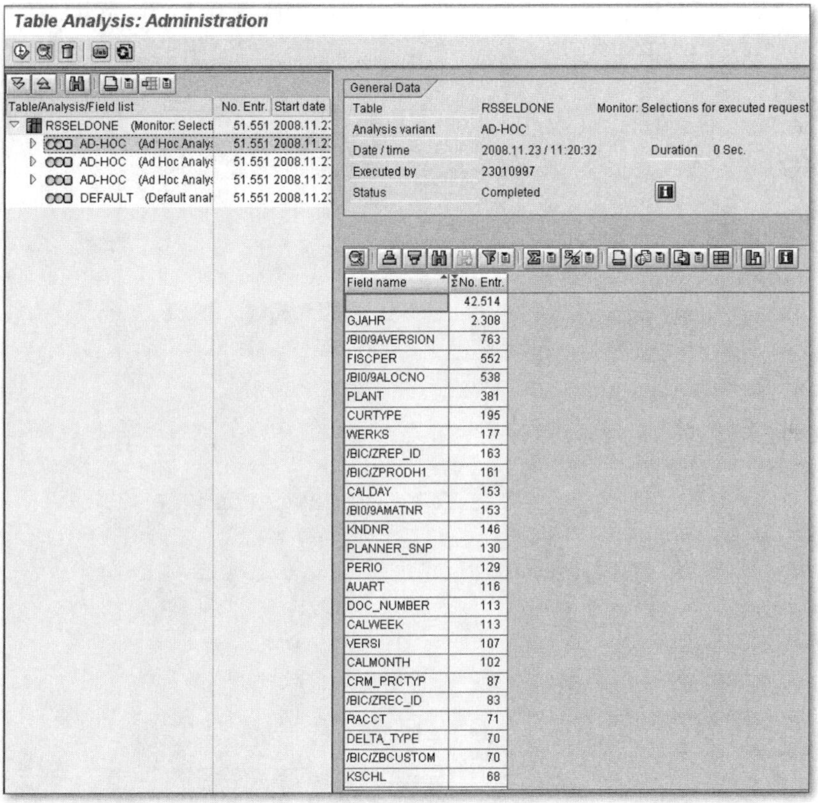

Figure 8.5 Transaction TAANA

You can use table analysis (Transaction TAANA) to analyze database tables and examine corresponding table contents (Figure 8.5). The

Table analysis

number of associated entries is assigned to specific field value combinations during this analysis. Analysis variants containing corresponding field lists are provided for this purpose. The generated analyses help in determining the required archiving objects and give information about which selection criteria might be most effective for the archiving process. This means you can avoid checking archiving objects that contribute little to the volume of data.

Tables and archiving objects

After you have identified the critical tables, you must determine the archiving objects to which these tables are assigned. You can do this using Transaction DB15 (Figure 8.6). This function enables you to determine the assignment of tables to archiving objects and archiving objects to tables. This consequently means you can assign the tables determined in the first analysis phase to a specific archiving object for archiving contents.

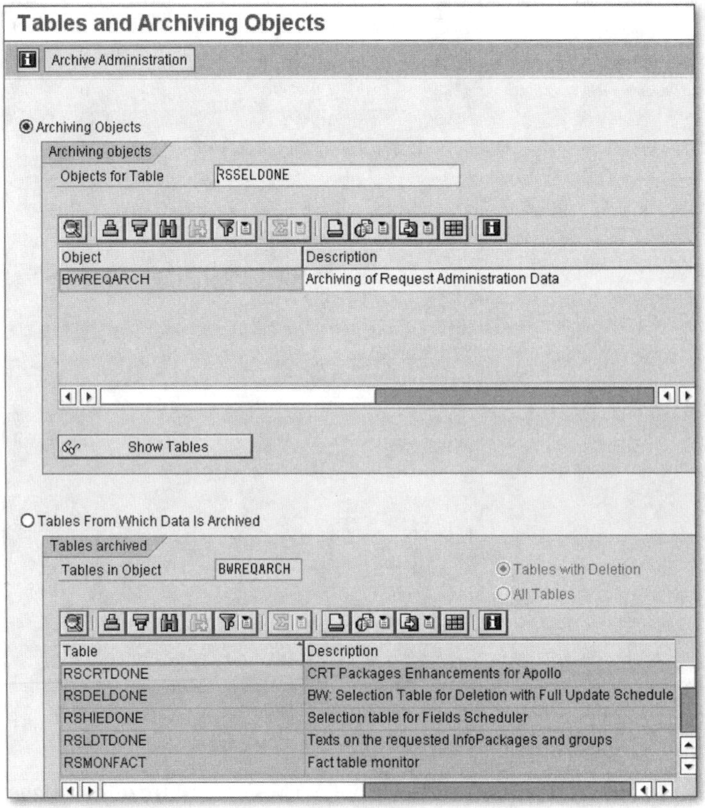

Figure 8.6 Table and Archiving Objects in Transaction DB15

The function is integrated into data archiving and is therefore also alternatively available in archive administration (Transaction SARA) via the DB Tables command.

8.3.2   Archiving Data and Monitoring Activities

In the following section, we will introduce tools you can use for scheduling, controlling, and monitoring archiving jobs.

You schedule archiving jobs (writing, deleting, and so on) in archive administration (Transaction SARA, as shown in Figure 8.7). This transaction also gives you access to the majority of other user activities in data archiving, such as storing and providing archive files or archiving customizing (Figure 8.8).

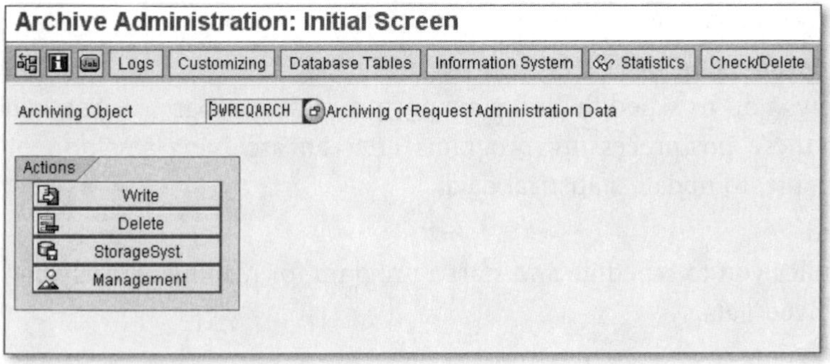

Archive administration

Figure 8.7   Archive Administration (Initial Screen)

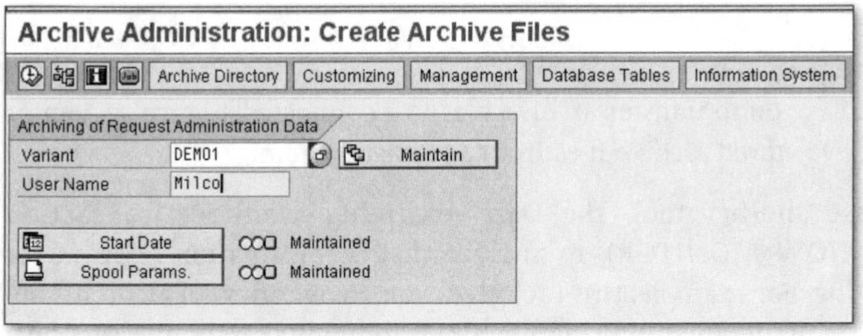

Figure 8.8   Archive Administration (Maintenance)

The definition of an archiving object specifies which actions are possible for this archiving object. Therefore, not all of the following archiving

Archiving actions

actions are always provided in archive administration. The list below represents a section of the range of functions:

▶ **Preprocessing**
Enables you to schedule and start preprocessing programs. This means you can prepare the data objects to be archived for the archiving session, for example, by setting a deletion indicator.

▶ **Write**
Allows you to schedule and start a write program to create archive files. The program copies the relevant data objects sequentially into the previously created archive files.

▶ **Delete**
Enables you to schedule and start a delete program. As a result, the data objects that were successfully read beforehand in the created archive file are deleted from the database.

▶ **Postprocessing**
Allows you to schedule and start postprocessing programs. You can use these postprocessing programs after an archiving session, for example, to update statistical data.

▶ **Read**
Enables you to schedule and start a program for reading or analyzing archived data.

▶ **Index**
Allows you retrospectively to build or remove an index for existing archive files. You need the index to display individual documents of some archiving objects.

▶ **Storage system**
Enables you to transfer archive files to a connected storage system or retrieve stored archive files from a storage system.

Data Archiving Monitor
You use another tool, the Data Archiving Monitor (Transaction SAR_SHOW_MONITOR), to analyze that is information relevant for archiving. For example, this tool gives you an overview of all archiving objects run, detailed information about individual archiving sessions, and a progress bar when you are processing archive files. To ensure that the relevant information is updated, you need to activate the Data Archiving Monitor in cross-archiving-object Customizing. The Data Archiving Monitor is part of the CCMS monitor set (Transaction RZ20)

and can be found here under SAP CCMS MONITOR TEMPLATES • DATA-
BASE • DATA ARCHIVING (Figure 8.9).

Figure 8.9 CCMS Archiving Monitor

The Data Archiving Monitor provides the following functions:

Functions of Data Archiving Monitor

▶ Complete overview of all executed archiving sessions

▶ Detailed information about all write and delete phases of archiving sessions such as the start time, runtime, size of archive files, and number of archived data objects

▶ Progress bar relating to processed archive files

▶ Identification of the need for action (for example, still outstanding or incomplete delete jobs) and error situations (I/O errors)

▶ Analysis of open alerts in the form of a jump to the triggering job and its logs

The first time each write and delete program based on the ADK (Archive Development Kit) runs, it generates a monitor node (according to the name of the archiving object) and Checkpoints and Statistics monitor attributes.

Important status messages and error messages (alerts) are compiled in the Checkpoints monitor attribute. If all alerts have been dealt with and, according to archive administration, there are no incorrect or incomplete sessions for this archiving object, the Checkpoints monitor attribute is automatically deleted with all messages and alerts. Statistical information about the last successfully ended write and delete phases are compiled in the Statistics monitor attribute. Unlike Checkpoints, the Statistics monitor attribute is not deleted.

The log function, which you can call from archive administration by clicking the Logs button, provides central access to the most important logs created during data archiving. These include the job overview, job log, spool list, and application log. These logs give you information about the archiving process and processing of objects to be archived.

Logs

After you call the log function, the existing logs are displayed in the left part of the screen and are sorted according to archiving object, action (preprocessing, writing, deleting), date, and time. The most recent log is selected in this case. You can see in the Process Control column whether the program was started in test or live mode. The field remains empty if the process control could not be determined. The Session column contains the number of the archiving session that was created in the corresponding program (for write programs) or processed (for delete programs). The field stays empty if the session number could not be determined (for preprocessing programs). Where reload programs are concerned, the number of the reloaded session is given in the Original Session column.

8.3.3 Accessing Archived Data

You can access data that you archived using SAP data archiving. Different tools are relevant for accessing archives.

Archive
Information
System

The Archive Information System (Transaction SARI) enables you to configure your own archive information structures (archive indexes), fill them with data from the archive, and search for archived data (Figure 8.10). To access archived data retrospectively, you need to build a corresponding infostructure. You can either allow this to be done automatically during the delete phase or do it manually at a later stage.

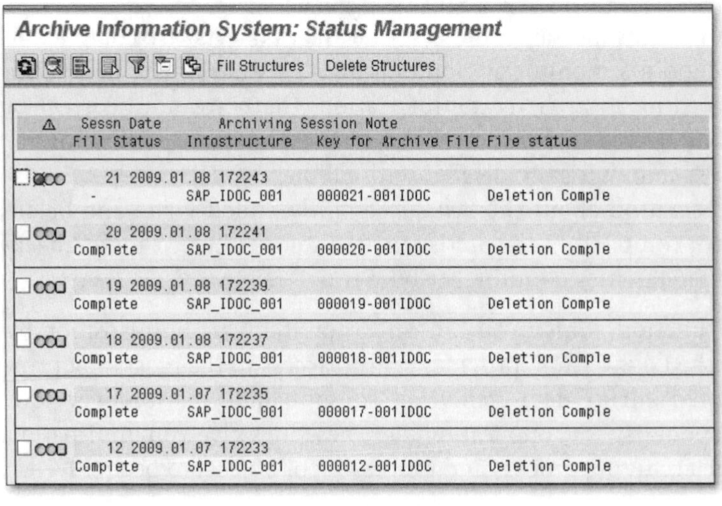

Figure 8.10 Status Management in Transaction SARI

In addition to the Archive Explorer, which enables you to find archived data quickly using archive information structures, the Archive Information System also includes the *Archive Retrieval Configurator* (ARC). You can use ARC to create archive information structures based on field catalogs and fill them with data from the archive (Figure 8.11). The archive information structure, which is a type of archive index, forms the basis for evaluating archive data.

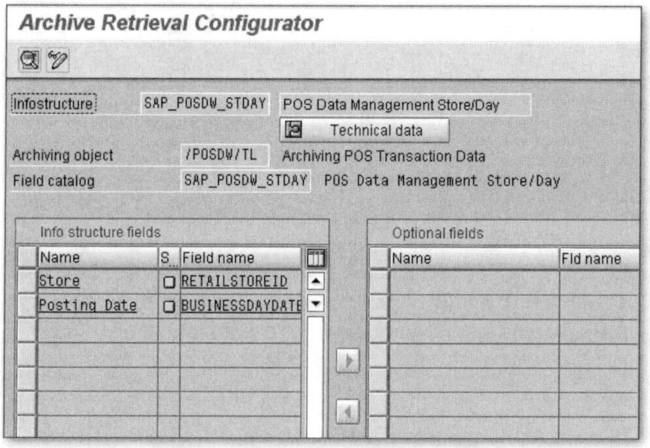

Figure 8.11 Archive Retrieval Configurator

You use the *Document Relationship Browser* (DRB) to display relationships between business objects. These are usually documents that were created during a shared business transaction or that belong to a common process. DRB can display archived data and data that is still contained in the database. IDocs and work items are connected to DRB in the SAP NetWeaver Application Server.

Document Relationship Browser

The *Archive File Browser* (Transaction AS_AFB) provides functions for displaying the content of archive files (Figure 8.12). It offers a technical view of the archived tables similar to the one shown by the Data Browser (Transaction SE16) for data from the database. The Archive File Browser (AFB) is specifically intended for administrators of data archiving and people looking for problems with data archiving and in archived data; it is not aimed at end users.

Archive File Browser

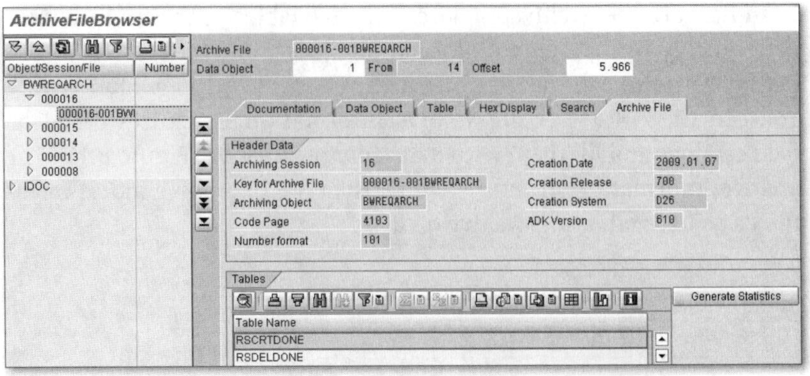

Figure 8.12 Archive File Browser

Limitation of archive information system for AFB

Table 8.1 compares the Archive Information System with the AFB.

Archive Information System	Archive File Browser
The primary focus is to create an index on archive files. You can use this index to find archived data quickly.	When searching for contents of archive files, AFB sequentially reads the area to be searched.
A search can only be performed based on specific criteria (fields in infostructures).	A search can be carried out using any fields.
The index can also be used by applications (for example, Document Relationship Browser or line item reports from cost accounting) to access archived data.	No comparable interface.
To access archived data, you must first create and activate an infostructure. This usually involves time and effort in the live system.	Archived data can be accessed immediately.
Contains business-related views, so it is also of interest to end users.	Contains a technical display of data, so it is only of interest to administrators.

Table 8.1 Archive Information System Compared with Archive File Browser

8.3.4 Other Archiving Functions

Data security

The archiving process consists of two steps to ensure that no data is lost owing to errors in the archiving session. The first step involves writing data into archive files. In the second step, the data is removed from the database — but only if the data was written completely and can subsequently be read successfully. This process can find errors that occur when data is transferred from the database to the archive files through the network. If an error occurs, you can start a new archiving session because the data is either in the database or in an archive file.

You can carry out an archiving session (consisting of several write and read jobs) while the system is available for users. The system is therefore fully available, even if data is archived. Nevertheless, performance bottlenecks can occur if data is being deleted from tables while other data is being read in these tables. Therefore, we recommend that you perform archiving when the system load is low.

Online archiving

Data is compressed up to a factor of 5 during the archiving process. However, data saved in a cluster table cannot be further compressed. Compression ensures that archive files occupy as little space as possible in storage systems.

Data compression

In addition to the actual application data, ADK also saves metadata in the archives to ensure that archived data can continue to be read successfully after a longer period. This metadata contains information about the relevant data runtime environment.

Release and platform independence

8.3.5 Special Characteristics of Write-Optimized DataStore Object

Owing to the specific structure of the write-optimized DataStore object, some special characteristics are involved with creating a data archiving process for this object. For example, request-based archiving is preset and cannot be changed. The reasons for this are as follows:

▶ The content of a write-optimized DataStore object is managed using requests.

Request-based archiving

▶ The request ID also forms the leading technical key characteristic of this DataStore object type.

Request-based archiving is a specific form of time slot archiving: A condition (high-water mark) for a chronologically monotonously growing partitioning characteristic is derived from a time characteristic (this may also be a technical attribute of the load request, such as the request creation date or request load date) that is not part of the technical key. The partitioning is actually done based on the SID of the request ID.

8.4 Nearline Storage

Classic data archiving prevents daily, high-performance access to data and must therefore remain the last possible solution in the SAP NetWeaver BW environment. However, the analysis in particular of current data in relation to historical data represents great added value of a data warehouse system.

Older data is still required, although typically less often and with unpredictable access models. This is where nearline storage (NLS) comes into play as a central concept of an ILM strategy: Older, less frequently used data is stored in an external system but continues to remain available "near-online" (with considerably reduced TCO) for read access. If you want older data to be included in analyses, you will doubtless have to accept that this will generally impair the execution performance. However, there will normally be problems if a process to be planned in advance (reloading data from archives) is required here.

8.4.1 Basic Principles

The solution for Information Lifecycle Management was extended with SAP NetWeaver 7.0 SPS 07. Besides ADK-based archiving, you can also use data storage in nearline storage with the data archiving process. A nearline storage strategy in SAP NetWeaver 7.0 is based on the notion that access frequency decreases over time; the older the data, the less often it must be accessed for analyses.

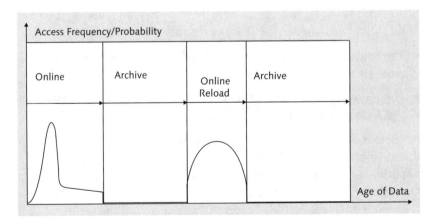

Figure 8.13 ILM Strategy in SAP NetWeaver BW 3.x Without NLS

As shown in the example in Figure 8.13, access frequency (and there- **Access frequency** fore also the general likelihood of accessing data) increases very sharply at the beginning and then decreases after a relatively short period of time. When you use ADK-based archives, you will decide at some point to archive this data according to the relevant ILM strategy. For sporadic (in other words, unscheduled) access, in the future you will need to reload the data, which will impair flexibility accordingly.

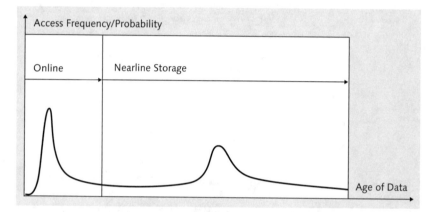

Figure 8.14 ILM Strategy in SAP NetWeaver BW 7.0.x with NLS

Compared to ADK-based archiving, an NLS strategy stores older data in nearline storage. This means that this data is available for analysis at any time, and the highest flexibility is guaranteed (Figure 8.14). To give you a quick overview, we have listed the basic features of nearline storage below:

- NLS data is directly available in loading processes and in reporting.
- NLS is available for InfoCubes and DataStore objects and is processed using data archiving processes (DAPs).
- NLS data retention together with online data retention forms a consistent InfoProvider dataset.
- NLS data can only be accessed in read-only mode.
- An open interface is available for certified partners.

Nearline storage fills the gap between data retention on the database **Advantages of NLS** (that is, *online*) and ADK-based archiving (that is, *offline*) and consequently facilitates a more flexible ILM strategy. The major advantage of

NLS is that you can access a query in the data stored in nearline storage, for example, and thereby rarely need data directly available without additional effort (Figure 8.15). If you want the NLS data in a query to be available, all you need to do is set the Also Read Nearline Storage indicator in the query properties of Transaction RSRT.

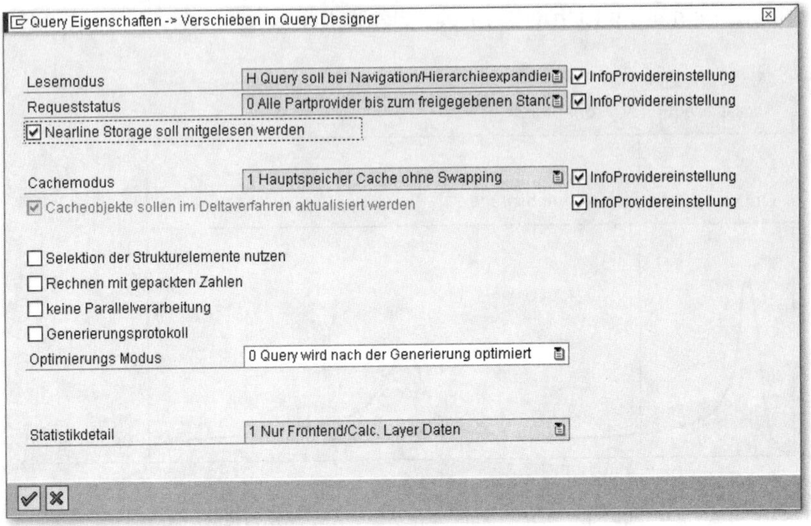

Figure 8.15   Reading NLS Data in a Query (Transaction RSRT)

A data archiving process splits the InfoProvider content into two parts. If a query is now executed on this InfoProvider, the Data Manager must decide whether the requested data is directly in the InfoProvider (in other words, on the SAP NetWeaver BW system database) or in nearline storage.

8.4.2   Creating a Nearline Storage Connection

If you want to create a data archiving process with nearline storage, you must first create a connection to your nearline storage. Note that you should not change a nearline storage connection if it is being used in an active data archiving process. Above all, you should no longer subsequently change the implementing class. Proceed as follows to create a connection:

Transaction
RSDANLCON

1. You can access Transaction RSDANLCON for processing nearline storage connections either in Customizing under SAP CUSTOMIZING

IMPLEMENTATION GUIDE • SAP NETWEAVER • BUSINESS INTELLIGENCE • GENERAL BI SETTINGS • PROCESS NEARLINE STORAGE CONNECTION or in the Data Warehousing Workbench under ADMINISTRATION • CURRENT SETTINGS • NEARLINE STORAGE CONNECTIONS.

2. Select New Entries.

3. Specify a name for the nearline storage connection. This name will be offered to you for selection when you create a data archiving process.

4. Specify the name of the class that implements the connection of the nearline storage solution.

5. Your nearline storage solution determines the specifications for the Destination and Connection Parameters fields.

6. Save your entries.

When you save, the connection for the nearline storage solution opens and closes again. In addition to system information, the nearline storage solution in this case returns a status indicating whether the connection works. The connection with its status and system information is displayed in the upper part of the screen. The log is displayed in the lower part of the screen.

8.4.3 Changes to Archived InfoProviders

If you have created a data archiving process for an InfoProvider, you may only make limited changes to this InfoProvider, so that you can still archive data or access archived data. All type or structural changes not listed below are not allowed if data is already stored in nearline storage. You can only make incompatible structural changes if data is not yet stored or if the stored data has been reloaded completely.

Changes not allowed

The following type and structural changes are allowed in an InfoCube or DataStore object when you are using nearline storage:

Allowed changes

▶ You may add new characteristics and key figures.

▶ You may extend characteristics of the CHAR data type.

▶ You may change characteristics from DATS, NUMC, and TIMS data types to the CHAR data type, as long as the character length is not shortened.

- You may change characteristics from DATS and TIMS data types to the NUMC data type, as long as the character length is not changed.

- You may change key figures from the INT4 data type to the DEC, CURR, or QUAN data type if the value range (number of places before the decimal point) does not decrease.

- For key figures of the CURR, DEC, and QUAN data types, you may increase the value range (number of places before the decimal point) or accuracy (number of places after the decimal point).

- You may change key figures from the CURR, DEC, and QUAN data types to the INT4 data type if the value range is increased.

- You can assign a characteristic to another dimension in an InfoCube.

- When you delete an InfoProvider and build it again later, the new InfoProvider must have the same structure as the previous one so you can access archived data through it.

Also note that the connection to already archived data will be lost if you delete a data archiving process.

8.5   Archiving Request Management Data

The archiving process for request management data archives management and log information about requests, so the performance will increase for any actions on requests. However, the proviso here is that you currently cannot archive request management data for data transfer processes.

Checking for completeness

When you display a request in the extraction monitor or management area of an InfoProvider, the system performs a check for completeness of the management tables for the scheduler and log tables for the extraction monitor (Tables RS*DONE and RSMON*). If entries for a request are incomplete or missing in the tables, the system displays a red status for this request. The management data for the request is required because the system uses it to calculate the request status dynamically. If the request becomes red because management and log information is not found, the system resets the technical and QM status in all lines that were provided by this request. You may have to expect a termination as a possible reaction or anticipate that the queries that were defined on the affected InfoProviders will display obsolete data or not display any data anymore.

Therefore, you also cannot delete entries in these tables. However, the scheduler management tables and the log tables of the extraction monitor increase with each new request made by the SAP NetWeaver BW system. This in turn affects performance.

When you now store the management and log information for requests in an archive, totals records are kept in the relevant tables in the SAP NetWeaver BW system. This prevents the status of the request being changed to red if information is missing and enables you limit the table size for the RS*DONE and RSMON* management and log tables. This means you improve the performance of the system for actions on a request and in the affected InfoProviders, and you save storage space on the database without disrupting the system status calculation.

Archiving request management data is based on the SAP NetWeaver data archiving concept. The BWREQARCH archiving object specifies which database tables are used for archiving and which programs (write, delete, reload programs) can be run. You execute the programs from Transaction SARA (archive administration for an archiving object). In archive administration for requests in the Administration functional area of the Data Warehousing Workbench, you can also manage archiving sessions for requests and execute different functions for the archiving sessions.

Integration

As you will see in Transaction DB15 (tables and archiving objects), the relevant tables are already assigned to the BWREQARCH archiving object (Figure 8.16).

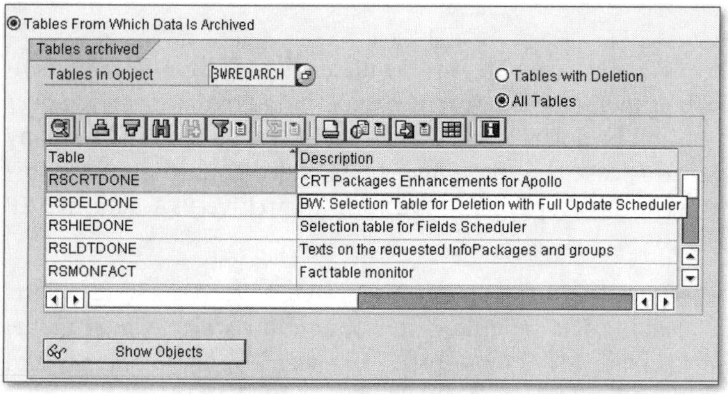

Archived tables

Figure 8.16 BWREQARCH Archiving Object

In Table 8.2 we have summarized once more the relevant request tables for the BWREQARCH archiving object.

Table	Description
RSCRTDONE	RDA packages (real-time data acquisition)
RSDELDONE	Selection table for deleting when a full update occurs
RSHIEDONE	Selection table for hierarchies
RSLDTDONE	Texts for the requested InfoPackages
RSMONFACT	Information about requests in monitor
RSMONICTAB	Information about InfoProvider in monitor
RSMONIPTAB	Information about InfoPackages in monitor
RSMONMESS	Messages used in monitor
RSMONRQTAB	Details about request IDocs in monitor
RSREQDONE	Information about QM details of requests
RSRULEDONE	ABAP selections in scheduler
RSSELDONE	Selections of executed requests
RSTCPDONE	Selections by third-party provider tools
RSUICDONE	InfoProviders to be updated

Table 8.2 Tables for the BWREQARCH Archiving Object

8.6   Archiving PSA Data

To date, you can only archive data from InfoCubes and DataStore objects, but another option is to archive persistent staging area data (PSA).

This requirement is based on arguments similar to those already mentioned in the general topic on archiving: Volumes of data increase over time but cannot be deleted because they will still be required in many cases (or in this case, can no longer be reloaded from the source system). You have three options if you want to archive PSA data in SAP NetWeaver BW:

Archiving options

▶ A (further) persistent staging area is created where DataStore objects will be used for data retention. This option in a scalable layer model is used in many EDW (enterprise data warehousing) concepts and enables you to archive DSOs using ADK or nearline storage.

▶ There are also some solutions from third-party software providers. Information about these solutions is available in the SAP Partner Information Center (see SAP EcoHub at *https://www.sdn.sap.com/irj/ecohub*).

▶ The third solution is explained in a how-to document, available in the SDN since the middle of 2008: "How To... Archive PSA Data in SAP NetWeaver BI."

This how-to document describes how, on the basis of additional programs provided with SAP Note 1178734, you can archive all requests up to a specific date. You can use the standard Transaction SARA for scheduling, controlling, and monitoring the archiving.

8.7   Scheduling Archiving Using Process Chains

You can use the Archive Data from an InfoProvider process type to schedule existing data archiving processes in process chains (Figure 8.17).

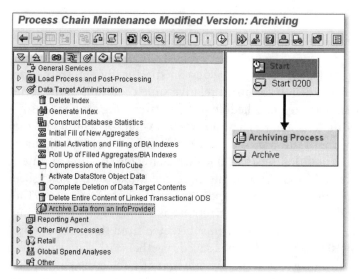

Figure 8.17   Process Chain for Archiving

Under Process Flow Control you can either continue open archiving processes or specify whether you want the archiving process to continue only up to a certain status (Figure 8.18).

Functions

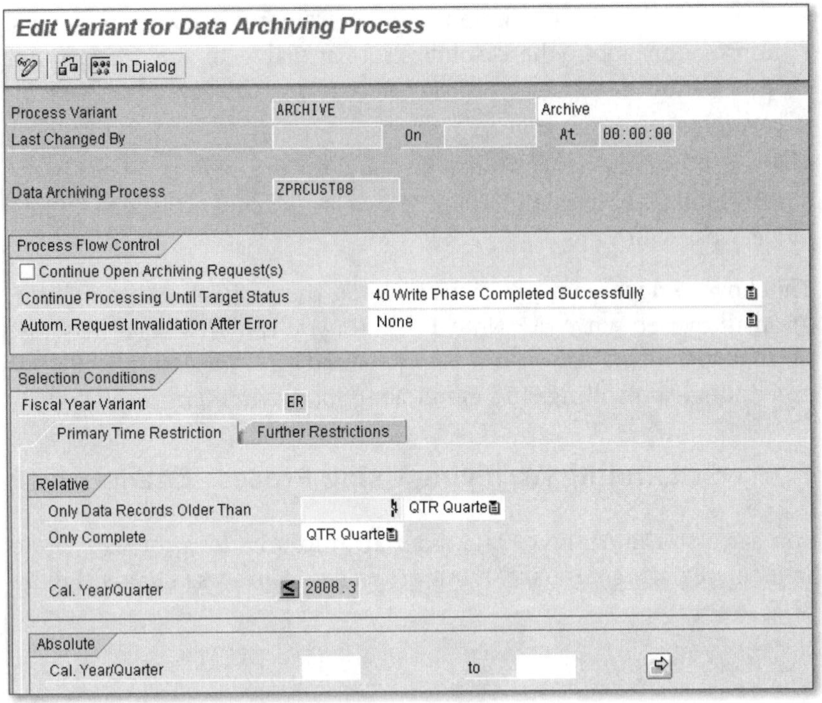

Figure 8.18 Details About the Data Archiving Process

Under Relative Time Restrictions you can specifically determine the area to be archived. You can use a relative time condition in the form of a minimum data age to schedule periodic archiving sessions easily, without having to adapt a variant for each session. Depending on the start time of the write process, the relative time restriction changes to a selection condition for the time slice characteristic, and an intersection is created from the absolute time conditions of the time slice characteristic and the selection conditions of other characteristics. The section already archived and the selection conditions of other archiving requests that are still open are then subtracted from this intersection. The resulting selection condition is saved together with the newly created archiving request and used for subsequently selecting data in the write phase and later in the delete phase.

Under Further Restrictions you can select values for your partitioning characteristics.

The InfoProvider to be archived is not locked throughout the entire process flow for loading data. This lock is only necessary for a short period before the copying process begins. After it begins, only the already archived data areas and the area currently being archived are locked.

Lock

8.8   Decision-Making Support for Archiving Concept

You can use ADK-based archiving and removal to nearline storage for InfoCubes and DataStore objects. When defining the data archiving process, you can choose between classic ADK archiving, removal to nearline storage, and a combination of both solutions. Which of the three options you choose depends on your application case (see Section 8.2, Data Archiving Process).

Table 8.3 lists the advantages and disadvantages of ADK-based archiving and nearline storage.

Advantages and disadvantages

Option	Advantages	Disadvantages
ADK	Standard process in SAP NetWeaver BW	Complex administration
	Platform-independent	You need to reload InfoCubes/DSOs
	Easy-to-use tool for writing, deleting, and storing data	May not satisfy requirements for quick availability of data
	You can use many different, cost-efficient media	You cannot access queries directly
	Structural changes to SAP NetWeaver BW objects are supported	You cannot adapt future structural changes such as InfoCube enhancements
NLS	Standard process in SAP NetWeaver BW	New procedure, so training and expertise required
	Platform-independent	Definition of interface between SAP NetWeaver BW and NLS currently not yet automated
	You can access queries directly	Only available in SAP NetWeaver BW 7.0
	You do not need to reload InfoCubes and DSOs	

Table 8.3   Comparison of ADK-Based Archiving and NLS

Option	Advantages	Disadvantages
	Removes potential SAP NetWeaver BW system or database restrictions in terms of volume of data	
	Easy-to-use tool for writing, deleting, and storing data	
	You can use many different, cost-efficient media	

Table 8.3 Comparison of ADK-Based Archiving and NLS (Cont.)

Particularly when using NLS technologies, you must take into account the costs of required hardware. Archiving (ADK-based or NLS-based) naturally also implies purchasing and operating costs. Nonetheless, these expenses will certainly not correspond with those for large volumes of data without archiving. It could be argued that the disk space costs consistently decrease while their performance increases. You could therefore acquire more memory to solve this problem and maintain the usual level of service for users in the Data Warehouse. However, data volumes increase even more quickly than improvements in the price to performance ratio of memory technology. It is also estimated that every dollar invested in disk space results in five to ten dollars for operating costs during runtime, so expanding storage capacity is a very expensive alternative. Even more obvious is the problem of a lack of system availability resulting from large volumes of data: This cannot be solved by more storage capacity because operational bottlenecks (for example, drawn-out backup recovery times) increasingly cause problems if the volumes of data increase further. In the meantime there are a number of providers of NLS solutions, such as Sybase with its PBS CBW NLS nearline solution on Sybase IQ and SAND Technology with its SAND/DANN solution.

8.9 Partitioning and Clustering

In the following sections we will deal with different options for organizing datasets.

8.9.1 Partitioning

By partitioning you can divide the entire dataset for an InfoProvider into several small, physically independent and redundancy-free units. This separation can improve performance for data analysis or also for deleting data from the InfoProvider. Partitioning is supported by all database providers, expect DB2 for Linux, UNIX, and Windows. You can use clustering to improve the performance of DB2 for Linux, UNIX, and Windows (see Section 8.9.3, Clustering).

If you use IBM DB2 for i5/OS as a DB platform, you need a database version of at least V5R3M0 and must install the DB2 Multi Systems component. Note that SAP NetWeaver BW systems with active partitioning under this system configuration can only be copied to other IBM iSeries using the SAVLIB/RSTLIB procedure (homogeneous system copy). You can also partition PSA tables when using this database. You must first activate this function using the DB4_PSA_PARTITIONING = "X" RSADMIN parameter. SAP Note 815186 includes additional information about this.

The F fact table on Oracle and Microsoft SQL servers is always partitioned dynamically using the package dimension. The partitioning of the E fact table is static and can be set in the maintenance interface before you activate the InfoCube. As described in more detail below, you can select the calendar month or fiscal period as partitioning conditions. The SIDs of these two partitioning characteristics are included as an additional column in both fact tables, which is filled according to the entries in the time dimension when new data requests are loaded.

You can only perform partitioning using the partitioning condition calendar month (0CALMONTH) or fiscal year/period (0FISCPER) (Figure 8.19). One of the two InfoObjects must therefore at least be contained in the InfoProvider. When you activate the InfoProvider, the table is created on the database with a number of partitions corresponding to a value range. Select EXTRAS • DB PERFORMANCE • PARTITIONING in the InfoProvider maintenance area and define the value range. Also limit the maximum number of partitions, if necessary.

Procedure

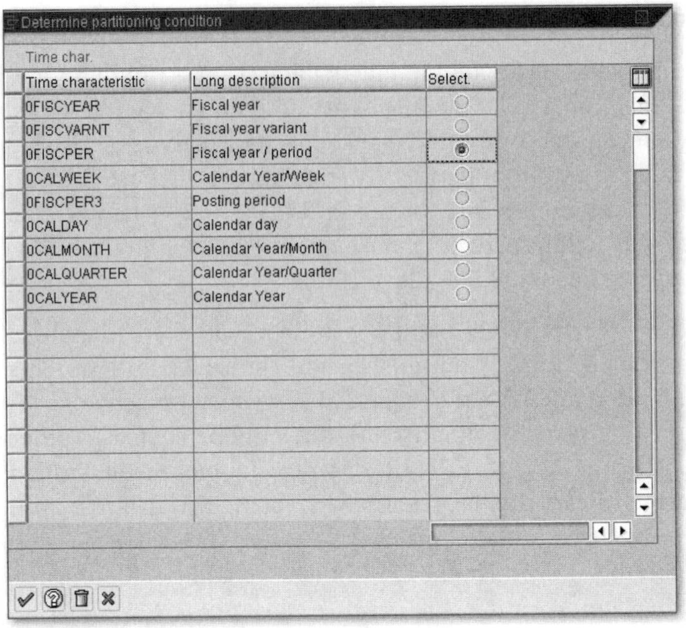

Figure 8.19 Partitioning Conditions

Example   If as shown in Figure 8.20 you choose a value range of 01.1998 to 12.2003 and a maximum number of 30 partitions for the 0CALMONTH partitioning indicator, this will result in 74 partitions (6 years × 12 calendar months + 2 marginal partitions, whereby the marginal partitions correspond to the value ranges <01.1998 or >12.2003).

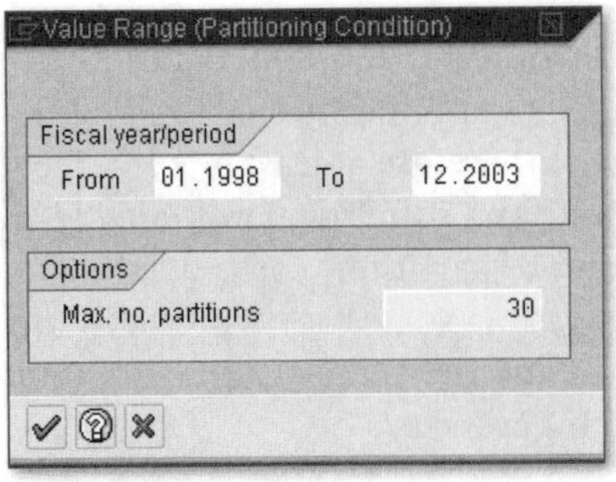

Figure 8.20 Value Range for Partitioning

Maximum number   You can also define the maximum number of partitions you want to be
of partitions   created for this table on the database. If you choose a maximum num-

ber of 30 partitions, with the above example the system will merge every 3 months together in a partition (in other words, a partition corresponds to exactly one quarter); this means that 6 years × 4 partitions/year + 2 marginal partitions = 26 partitions created on the database.

To improve performance with partitioned InfoProviders, it is absolutely imperative that the time characteristics be consistent. For a partitioning using 0CALMONTH, for example, this means that all values of CAL* characteristics for a data record must match.

If you want to partition an InfoCube using the fiscal year/period characteristic (0FISCPER), you must first set the fiscal year variant characteristic (0FISCVARNT) to Constant (Figure 8.21).

You can access the displayed dialog box in the InfoProvider maintenance area from the context menu of the 0FISCVARNT characteristic (in the time dimension) under InfoProvider-Specific Properties.

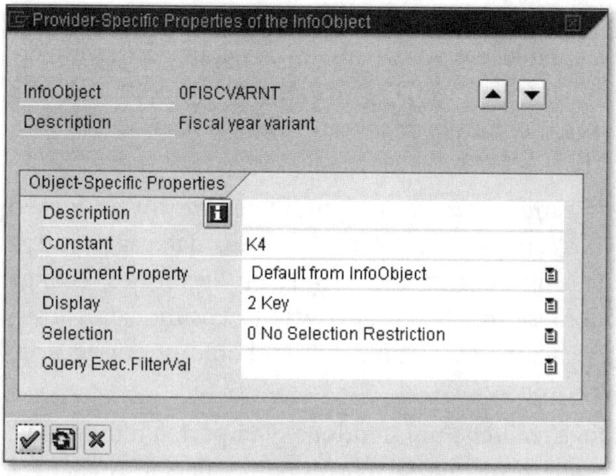

Figure 8.21 Setting a Constant for the Fiscal Year Variant

What you essentially have to remember is that you can only change the value range if the InfoProvider does not contain any data. If data has already been loaded into the InfoProvider, you must perform a repartitioning. We recommend a *partition on demand,* which means you should not make the partitions too small or too big. If the time period you select is too small, the partitions will be too big. If the time period extends too far into the future, the number of partitions will be too

Partition on demand

high. We therefore generally recommend that you create a partition for one year and repartition the InfoProvider after this time has expired.

Transporting Partitioning Properties

Partitioning InfoCubes is a property on a local system and cannot be transported for the following reasons:

▶ You may often want to use different partitioning in a live system with lots of data than in a development system with a little data because partitioning may be counterproductive if there is not much data.

▶ Changing partitioning generally means reorganizing fact tables; in other words, you have to copy every data record. Because the runtime on the database is in linear relation to the size of the InfoCube in the target system and can last several hours, you should schedule these types of operations and carry them out when the system load is low (for example, on the weekend). Otherwise, the runtime behavior of the entire live system might be significantly impaired.

▶ Reorganizing the fact tables involves copying all data records, restructuring indexes, and calculating database statistics. Additional disk space is required for this purpose, and if it does not exist, this will lead to terminations.

▶ During the reorganization, the affected InfoCubes are always locked against all modifying actions (loading data, deleting data, aggregating data, rolling up data into aggregates, setting up aggregates, change runs, and so on) because this is the only way to ensure data consistency. You should schedule these times; they should not occur accidentally through transports.

▶ A partitioning change could be unintentionally imported into the live system through a transport request. For example, person A changes the partitioning of the CUBE InfoCube in the development system but does not write this change on a transport request because he knows the consequences for the live system. Person B adds another key figure to the same CUBE InfoCube and writes the InfoCube on a transport request to activate the change in subsequent systems. This transport request would then also cause the partitioning change to enter the live system without person B, who initiated the transport, being aware of the consequences.

Changes to the partitioning of InfoCubes through a transport are only accepted if InfoCubes in the target system do not contain any data. Although this behavior goes against the concept of properties for partitionings on a local system, it is meant to support SAP NetWeaver BW administrators in distributing all settings for an InfoCube across the system landscape if an InfoCube is created again. If there is already an InfoCube in the target system and this InfoCube does not contain any data, both fact tables for the InfoCube are deleted during importing and created again according to the new description — including the changed partitioning.

Accepting changes

8.9.2 Repartitioning

If data has already been uploaded, you can no longer change partitioning properties of an InfoCube in the maintenance interface. However, you may need, or it may be useful, to change the properties for the following reasons:

▶ The partitioning is offered again for the database used. Already existing InfoCubes should therefore be subsequently partitioned to enable you to benefit from the advantages of partitioning for the existing dataset too (complete repartitioning).

Reasons for making changes

▶ Partitioning is already being used and you want to change it because the current partitioning schema no longer corresponds to requirements. For instance, too much data may be compiled in a partition because the data has grown bigger over time (complete repartitioning).

▶ The time period for the partitioning is too small. For example, when you activated an InfoCube, partitions were created for the period January 2000 to December 2006. To ensure that data for 2007 is not solely collected in the overflow partition, you want to extend the partitioning schema to December 2007 (adding partitions).

▶ Several partitions do not contain any data records, or still only contain a few of them. For example, when you activated an InfoCube, partitions were created for the period January 2000 to December 2008. At the end of 2006 the data from 2000 and 2001 is archived. To ensure that the now empty partitions for 2000 and 2001 do not inflate the database system catalog unnecessarily, you want to merge these partitions in an underflow partition (merging partitions).

Types of repartitioning

To meet these requirements, SAP NetWeaver BW 7.0 provides a tool you can use for repartitioning InfoCubes (see Figure 8.22). We can differentiate between three types of repartitioning:

▸ Complete repartitioning

▸ Adding partitions to an already partitioned E fact table

▸ Merging empty or almost empty partitions of an already partitioned E fact table

Unlike Complete Repartitioning, for which you must completely copy and implement the data of E and F fact tables, the Adding Partitions and Merging Partitions actions are only a sequence of database catalog operations if there is still no data in the overflow partition or the partitions to be merged are empty. The database catalog operations only take a few minutes to run.

Complete repartitioning always requires additional disk space in the size of the InfoCube to be repartitioned. Because you have to physically copy the data, create new indexes, and recalculate table statistics, this action may take several hours depending on the size of the InfoCube. Complete repartitioning is universally useful and can be used for partitioning for the first time and for adding and merging partitions.

Merging and Adding Partitions

You call InfoCube repartitioning from the context menu for the relevant object under MORE FUNCTIONS • REPARTITIONING in Transaction RSA1 (Figure 8.22).

Merge/split

When you add partitions and merge partitions, you can merge Info-Cube partitions at the bottom end of the partitioning schema (*merge*) or add them at the top (*split*). This is ideally only an operation on the database catalog. This is the case if all of the partitions you want to merge are empty and data has not yet been loaded outside the time period you initially defined. The action subsequently only takes a few minutes to run. If there is still data in the partitions that you want to merge or if data was already loaded outside the initially defined time period, the system saves the data in a shadow table and then copies it back into the original table. The runtime will then depend on the volume of data to be copied.

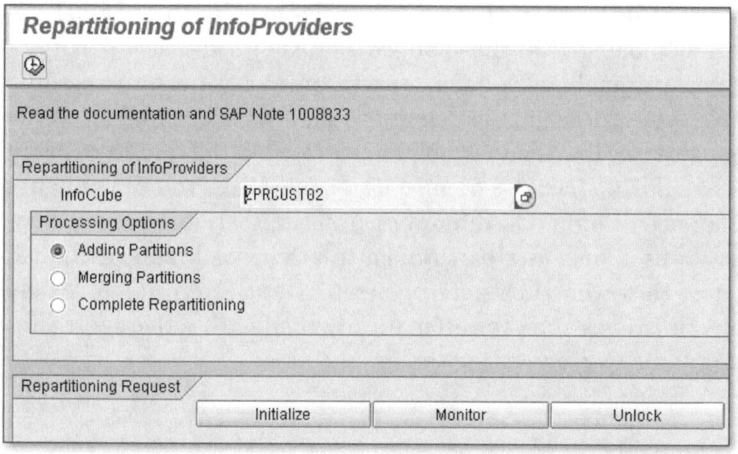

Figure 8.22 Repartitioning InfoProviders

All InfoCube markers for noncumulative InfoCubes are in either the very bottom partition or very top partition of the E fact table. Depending on the processing option, you may therefore also have to copy mass data. Therefore, you are not allowed to merge partitions for noncumulative InfoCubes if all markers are in the very bottom partition. If every marker is in the very top partition, you are not permitted to add partitions. In these cases, use the Complete Repartitioning processing option.

Markers

You can merge and add partitions on InfoCubes and on aggregates. Alternatively, you can reactivate all of the aggregates after you have changed the InfoCube. Because this function only changes the database memory parameters of fact tables, you can also continue using the existing aggregates without having to modify them. We recommend that you perform a complete database backup before you execute this function, to ensure that the system can quickly be restored if an error occurs (for example, during database catalog operations).

Complete Repartitioning

Complete repartitioning implements the fact tables of the InfoCube. The system creates shadow tables with the new partitioning schema and copies all data from the original tables into the shadow tables. As soon as the data is copied, the system creates indexes, and the original table replaces the shadow table. After a partitioning request has

Shadow tables

been successfully completed, both fact tables exist in the original status (shadow table) and in the changed status with the new partitioning schema (original table). After repartitioning has been successfully completed, you can manually delete the shadow tables to free up the used disk space again. Shadow tables are located in the */BIC/4F<name of InfoCube>* and */BIC/4E<name of InfoCube>* namespace. You can only use complete repartitioning on InfoCubes. You can therefore have heterogeneous statuses such as a partitioned InfoCube with nonpartitioned aggregates. However, such heterogeneous statuses do not adversely affect any functions. You can automatically change all active aggregates of the InfoCube by reactivating them.

Monitor

You can monitor repartitioning requests using a monitor (clicking the Monitor button; see Figure 8.22). The monitor shows you the current statuses of the processing steps. When you double-click a request, the relevant logs appear. You can access the following functions from the context menu on a request or a processing step:

▶ **Delete**
You delete the repartitioning request, it no longer appears in the monitor, and you cannot restart the repartitioning request any more. All tables remain in the current status, meaning the InfoCube may be inconsistent.

▶ **Reset request**
You reset the repartitioning request. This deletes all locks on the InfoCube and all of its shadow tables.

▶ **Reset step**
You reset canceled processing steps to their original status.

▶ **Restart**
You restart the repartitioning request in the background. You cannot restart a repartitioning request if it is still highlighted as active (yellow) in the monitor. Check in this case whether the request is still actually active (Transaction SM37) and, if necessary, reset the current processing step before you restart.

Background Information about Copying Data

By default, data is copied with a maximum of six processes in parallel. This involves the main process splitting dialog processes in the background, which each copy smaller data packages and finish with a COM-MIT. If a timeout causes one of these dialog processes to terminate, you can restart the affected copy processes using the Restart Repartitioning Request after you have adjusted the timeout time.

Background Information about Troubleshooting

Even if you can restart the individual processing steps, you should not reset repartitioning requests or individual processing steps without first analyzing the error. During repartitioning, the relevant InfoCube and its aggregates are locked against modifying operations (loading data, aggregation, rollup, and so on) to prevent data inconsistencies. You can unlock objects manually in the initial dialog. This option is only intended for error situations and for use after logs and datasets have been analyzed.

Transport

You cannot transport repartitioning up to and including SAP NetWeaver BW 7.0 SP 12 because this can lead to inconsistencies in the target system. The activation of changed partitioning properties for already filled InfoCubes in the target system is only automatically prevented as of SAP NetWeaver BW 7.0 SP 13.

Only as of SP 13

Always perform repartitioning individually in each system of the system landscape with identical parameters. You have to set the live system temporarily to Modifiable for this purpose. This procedure does not comply with the concept that only consolidated changes are allowed to be imported into the live system via a transport, but owing to the problems mentioned above, which might occur if changed partitioning properties are automatically activated in the live system, handling partitioning properties locally is currently the best option.

8.9.3 Clustering

Clustering enables you to save data records in sorted order in InfoCube fact tables. Data records with the same dimension keys are saved in the same extents (related database storage unit). This prevents the same data records from being spread across a large storage area and thereby reduces the number of extents to be read when a table is accessed. This greatly accelerates read, write, and delete access to a fact table.

Saving data records in sorted order

The function is currently only supported by database platform DB2 for Linux, UNIX, and Windows. You can use partitioning to improve the performance of other databases (see Section 8.9.1, Partitioning). Two types of clustering are available: index clustering and multidimensional clustering (MDC).

Index Clustering

Index clustering organizes the data records of a fact table according to the sort sequence of an index. This results in a linear organization based on the values of index fields. If a data record cannot be added in accordance with the sort sequence because the relevant extent is already full, the data record is inserted into an empty extent at the end of the table. Therefore, the sort sequence is not guaranteed and can degenerate if there are many insert and delete operations. Reorganizing the table restores the sort sequence and releases storage space that is no longer required.

The clustering index of an F fact table is the secondary index on the time dimension by default. The clustering index of an E fact table is the acting primary index (P index) by default. As of SAP NetWeaver BW 2.0, index clustering is already the standard clustering for all InfoCubes and aggregates.

Multidimensional Clustering

Multidimensional clustering (MDC) organizes data records of a fact table according to one or several freely selectable characteristics. The selected fields are also referred to as MDC dimensions. Only data records with the same values in MDC dimensions are saved in an extent. In the context of MDC, an extent is also known as a block. This means the sort sequence is always guaranteed, and tables do not need to be reorganized if there are many insert and delete operations.

Block indexes   Database-internal block indexes instead of default secondary indexes are created on the selected fields. Block indexes reference extents rather than data record numbers and are therefore much smaller. They save storage space, and the system can search through them more quickly. In particular, this speeds up table queries restricted to these fields.

You can select the key fields of the time dimension or all customer-defined dimensions of an InfoCube as an MDC dimension. You cannot select the key field of the package dimension. It is automatically only added to the MDC dimensions in the F fact table.

You can also select a time characteristic instead of the time dimension. In this case, an additional field with SID values of the time characteristic is added to the fact table. Only the Calendar Month (0CALMONTH) and Fiscal Year/Period (0FISCPER) time characteristics are currently supported. The InfoCube must contain the time characteristic. If you select the Fiscal Year/Period (0FISCPER) characteristic, you must set a constant for the Fiscal Year Variant (0FISCVARNT) characteristic.

Clustering for an InfoCube is applied for all of its aggregates. If an aggregate does not contain an MDC dimension of the InfoCube, or if all InfoObjects of an MDC dimension were created in the aggregate as line item dimensions, the clustering for the aggregate is created using the remaining MDC dimensions. If an aggregate does not contain any MDC dimensions for the InfoCube or only contains MDC dimensions, index clustering is used for the aggregate. Multidimensional clustering was introduced for SAP NetWeaver 7.0 and can be set up separately for each InfoCube.

8.9.4 Reclustering

Reclustering enables you to change the clustering of InfoCubes and DataStore objects that already contain data. You may need to make a correction if there are only a few data records for each of the value combinations of the selected MDC dimension and the table consequently uses an unnecessarily large amount of storage space. To improve the performance of database queries, you may subsequently want to introduce multidimensional clustering for InfoCubes or DataStore objects.

Reclustering always involves completely implementing the associated fact tables for the InfoCube. The system creates shadow tables with a new clustering schema and copies all data from the original tables into the shadow tables. As soon as the data is copied, the system creates indexes, and the shadow table is replaced with the original table. After a reclustering request has been successfully completed, both fact tables exist in the original status (name of shadow table) and changed status with the new clustering schema (name of original table). You can only use reclustering on InfoCubes. Reclustering deactivates affected active

Reclustering for InfoCubes

aggregates of InfoCubes and reactivates them after the implementation process.

Reclustering for DataStore objects Reclustering completely implements the active table of the DataStore object. Like the reclustering of InfoCubes, the system creates a shadow table with a new clustering schema and copies all data from the original table into the shadow table. You can only use reclustering on standard DataStore objects and DataStore objects for direct writing operations. You cannot use it for write-optimized DataStore objects. User-defined multidimensional clustering is not available for write-optimized DataStore objects.

Monitor You can monitor clustering requests using a monitor. The monitor shows you the current statuses of the processing steps. When you double-click a clustering request, the relevant logs appear. You can access the following functions from the context menu of a request or processing step:

▶ **Delete**
You delete the clustering request, it no longer appears in the monitor, and you cannot restart the clustering request any more. All tables remain in the current status, meaning the InfoCube or DataStore object may be inconsistent.

▶ **Reset request**
You reset the clustering request. This deletes all locks on the InfoCube and all of its shadow tables.

▶ **Reset step**
You reset canceled processing steps to their original status.

▶ **Restart**
You restart the clustering request in the background.

You access reclustering in the Data Warehousing Workbench (Transaction RSA1) under Administration or from the context menu of the relevant InfoCube or DataStore object.

8.10   Master Data Cleansing

A deletion or an archiving concept within an ILM strategy is much more difficult in the context of master data than transaction data. Transaction data in a DataStore object or InfoCube can often be considered in isolation, whereas master data always refers to transaction data or is an attribute for other master data.

You can delete master data, but the SAP NetWeaver BW system will only allow you to do this if there are no references. The DATAFL flag of the relevant SID table (for example, /BIO/SCOSTCENTER for the cost centers of the 0COSTCENTER characteristic) provides information about whether there are or have been references in transaction data, other master data, or hierarchies. This flag is set when you create a reference, but it is not deleted at a later stage if you remove all references.

References

8.10.1 Deleting Individual Master Data Records

In addition to being able to create and change master data in master data maintenance, which you can call in Transaction RSD1 by selecting DISPLAY • MAINTAIN MASTER DATA (F6) or directly from the context menu for a characteristic, a deletion mode at the single record level is also available. A selection screen appears for limiting master data you want to process. Select the required data using the input help options. This takes you to the list overview of your selection. In the list select the master data records to be deleted and select Delete.

The records you have selected for deletion are first written into the deletion buffer. If you select Save, a where-used list of the records to be deleted will be generated depending on whether the SID table points to references. Master data not being used in other objects is deleted. Note that a complete where-used list can be very time consuming.

Deletion buffer

8.10.2 Deleting All Master Data and Texts

The full deletion of master data is another function (Figure 8.23). Unlike deleting at the single record level, you can use this function to delete all existing master data and texts for a characteristic in one action. For this action too, of course, the restrictions are that the SAP NetWeaver BW system does not contain any transaction data for the master data in question, this data is not being used as attributes for InfoObjects, and there are no hierarchies for this master data. You can access the Delete Master Data function from the InfoObject context menu and in the InfoObject tree and InfoSource tree.

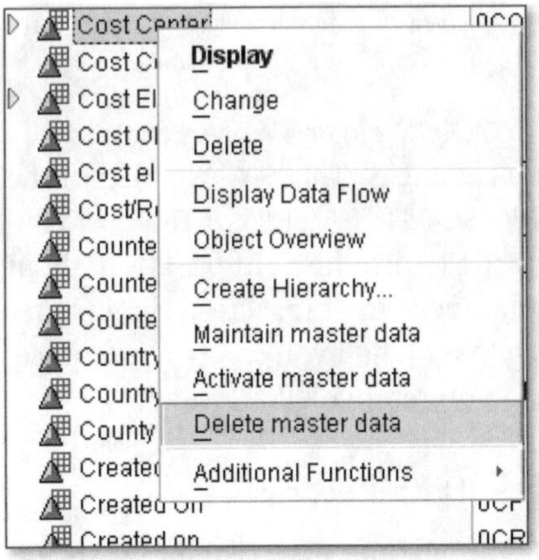

Figure 8.23 Deleting All Master Data and Texts

When you perform this action, the program consecutively checks the entries in the affected master data table to see whether they are being used in other objects.

Deleting SID entries

When deleting SID entries, you can choose whether to keep or delete entries from the SID table for the characteristic. If you delete the SID table entry for a specific characteristic value, the SID value assigned to the characteristic value disappears. So, if you load attributes for this characteristic value again at a later stage, you will have to create a new SID value for the characteristic value. This generally has a negative effect on the runtime required for loading the attributes. In rare cases, deleting entries from the SID table can also cause serious data inconsistencies if the list of used SID values determined by the where-used list is incomplete.

Owing to the consequences mentioned above, as a rule you should select the Delete Retaining SIDs option. For example, if you want to ensure that individual attributes of the characteristic that are no longer required are deleted before you load master data attributes or texts, the option for deleting master data but retaining the SID table entries is completely adequate.

Note that you only need, or may find it useful, to delete SID table entries in exceptional cases if the configuration of the characteristic key has changed fundamentally and you want to swap a larger record of attributes with a different record with new key values.

As part of the unified lifecycle management, software lifecycle management is one of the IT scenarios in SAP NetWeaver and supports administrators in importing corrections and software optimizations. This chapter provides information about the patches of the individual SAP NetWeaver BW components.

9   Maintenance

Software lifecycle management (SLM) consists of the management of SAP products and solutions in real, customer-specific system landscapes and contains focal points of both implementation support and software maintenance. The implementation support focus is made up of the following variants:

▶ Implementing new functions

▶ Implementing and configuring business content

▶ Copying and migrating systems

▶ Creating and propagating customer-specific changes in an existing landscape

Software maintenance consists of these variants:

▶ Updating your system landscape

▶ Upgrading the scenarios implemented in your landscape to new releases

Owing to the complexity of today's landscapes and the interdependencies between individual software components, tool support for landscape-relevant planning, monitoring, maintenance, implementation, and upgrade tasks is a must. The System Landscape Directory (SLD) in SAP NetWeaver provides you with the foundation for tool support to plan any changes in your system landscape. It offers both a directory of installable components that are available from SAP and automatically updated data about systems, components, and business scenarios implemented in your system landscape. Using SLD, you can easily plan and validate the implementation, maintenance, or upgrade of one or more business scenarios. Software lifecycle management is aligned both with SAP Solution Manager scenarios and the de facto standard ITIL (*IT Infrastructure Library*) of the OGC (*Office of Government Commerce*, UK).

9.1 Support Package Stacks, Support Packages, and Patches

SPS   A support package stack (SPS) consists of any corrections in Java, ABAP, and .NET (frontend SAP Business Explorer tools). An SPS can contain functional enhancements. In particular, changes and corrections that require adjustments in Java and ABAP can only be delivered as part of a support package stack.

SP   A support package (SP) contains any corrections in ABAP. Any notes with correction instructions are also contained. A support package can also contain more comprehensive changes and adjustments that cannot be delivered using a note with correction instructions, such as table content changes. Functional enhancements are only possible in the support package. Separate support packages are delivered for Java. The support packages for Java are always delivered as part of a support package stack.

A note with correction instructions contains smaller changes and corrections that can be easily imported using Transaction SNOTE.

Patch   A patch encompasses corrections and smaller changes in Java that are imported using the Software Deployment Manager (SDM). A patch cannot contain any functional enhancements because only corrections with limited scope are possible. New parameters, for example, normally require adjustments in ABAP. A delivery of functional enhancements is therefore only possible within a support package stack.

A frontend patch corresponds to a support package for the SAP Business Explorer tools such as BEx Query Designer or the Web application designer tool. A frontend patch must be installed in the client.

BI ABAP patch   If you look at the current support package stacks for SAP NetWeaver, you will notice that BI ABAP already has a higher level in the sequence of actually adjusted SP levels. BI ABAP SP 18, for example, is part of SAP NetWeaver SPS 16. Using BI ABAP SP 11 and SP 14, corrections for BI ABAP were available between the actual support package stacks. After SAP NetWeaver SPS 10, the strategy was changed so that an intermediate BI ABAP support package was to be released between each SPS to increase the flexibility for corrections. Because the availability of SAP NetWeaver SPS 11 was delayed, this procedure was set aside at that time and then reinstated after SPS 13.

Sap NetWeaver BW/SAP BI frontend software can generally be used with older SAP NetWeaver BW backend releases.

SAP NetWeaver BW frontend patch

Finding Support Packages in the SAP Support Portal

The simplest was to find the necessary support packages and patches for SAP NetWeaver in the Service Marketplace is in the SAP Support Portal via DOWNLOADS • SAP SUPPORT PACKAGES • ENTRY BY APPLICATION GROUP • SAP NETWEAVER • SAP NETWEAVER (Figure 9.1). You can also call the download area (SAP Software Distribution Center) quickly without navigation by using the alias */swdc*.

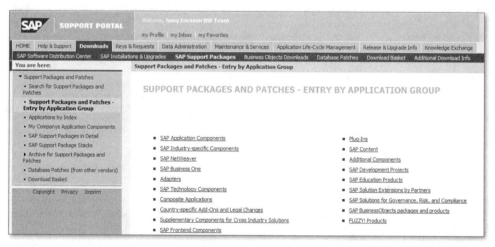

Figure 9.1 Downloads in the Support Portal

Support packages for the components SAP_BW, BI_CONT, and SAP_BASIS, for example, can be found in this area for SAP NetWeaver 7.0 EhP 1 under SAP EHP1 FOR SAP NETWEAVER 7.0 • ENTRY BY COMPONENT • BUSINESS INTELLIGENCE (Figure 9.2).

Under the BI Java components you will also find the patches for the J2EE-based components such as BI Base Service and BI Web Applications.

293

Dateityp	Download Objekt	Titel	Patchlevel	Infodatei	Dateigröße [kb]	Geändert am
☐ ⓘ SCA	BIBASES00_0-10005888.SCA	SP00 for BI BASE SERVICES 7.01	0	Info	24054	05.08.2008
☐ ⓘ SCA	BIBASES02_0-10005888.SCA	SP02 for BI BASE SERVICES 7.01	0	Info	24025	28.10.2008
☐ ⓘ SCA	BIBASES02P_1-10005888.SCA	SP02 for BI BASE SERVICES 7.01	1	Info	24036	16.12.2008
☐ ⓘ SCA	BIBASES03_0-10005888.SCA	SP03 for BI BASE SERVICES 7.01	0	Info	24007	10.12.2008
☐ ⓘ SCA	BIBASES03P_2-10005888.SCA	Patch for BI BASE SERVICES 7.01 SP03	2	Info	23675	30.03.2009

Die folgenden Objekte können heruntergeladen werden:

[Zum Download Basket hinzufügen] [Download Basket verwalten] [Alle auswählen] [Auswahl zurücknehmen]

Figure 9.2 Example of Available Support Packages

9.2   ABAP Support Packages

Depending on the functions in the system, SAP requires the most varied of support packages for enhancements and corrections (Figure 9.3). The ABAP Support Package Manager (SPAM) supports the importing of support packages into a system. The SPAM can be called in the following ways:

- Using the menu path TOOLS • ABAP WORKBENCH • UTILITIES • MAINTENANCE • SPAM.

- Via Transaction SPAM

For the complete functions of the Support Package Manager, authorizations are required for the S_TRANSPORT and S_CTS_ADMIN authorization objects, for example via the S_A.SYSTEM profile.

9.2.1   Functions

SPAM offers the following functions for supporting the importing of support packages:

- Loading support packages to the system from the SAP Service Marketplace or from the delivered CDs

- Restarting after the termination of import processes

- Displaying the current system status

- Minimizing the downtime by using an (optional) import procedure

- Control of the individual phases such as the start time

- Scheduling specific phases as background processes

OCS packages available for this system	Description	Stat	Import Status
▷ ⊘ SAP_OCS	SPAM/SAINT Update		
▷ 🔠 SAP_ABA	Cross-Application Component		
▷ 🔠 SAP_BASIS	SAP Basis Component		
▷ 🔠 ST-PI	SAP Solution Tools Plug-In		
▷ 🔠 PI_BASIS	Basis Plug-In (PI_BASIS) 2006_1_700		
▽ 🔠 SAP_BW	SAP NetWeaver BI 7.0		
⬡ SAPKW70001	BW Support Package 01 for 7.00	☐☐☐	Imported on 2005-05-19 at 14:30:38
⬡ SAPKW70002	BW Support Package 02 for 7.00	☐☐☐	Imported on 2005-11-18 at 10:52:10
⬡ SAPKW70003	BW Support Package 03 for 7.00	☐☐☐	Imported on 2005-11-18 at 11:03:51
⬡ SAPKW70004	BW Support Package 04 for 7.00	☐☐☐	Imported on 2005-11-18 at 11:13:16
⬡ SAPKW70005	BW Support Package 05 for 7.00	☐☐☐	Imported on 2005-11-28 at 11:11:51
⬡ SAPKW70006	BW Support Package 06 for 7.00	☐☐☐	Imported on 2006-01-25 at 16:00:54
▷ ⬡ SAPKW70007	BW Support Package 07 for 7.00	☐☐☐	Imported on 2006-11-11 at 12:24:34
▷ ⬡ SAPKW70008	BW Support Package 08 for 7.00	☐☐☐	Imported on 2006-11-11 at 12:24:38
▷ ⬡ SAPKW70009	BW Support Package 09 for 7.00	☐☐☐	Imported on 2006-11-11 at 12:24:42
▷ ⬡ SAPKW70010	BW Support Package 10 for 7.00	☐☐☐	Imported on 2007-02-10 at 01:00:33
▷ ⬡ SAPKW70011	BW Support Package 11 for 7.00	☐☐☐	Imported on 2007-02-10 at 01:00:34
▷ ⬡ SAPKW70012	BW Support Package 12 for 7.00	☐☐☐	Imported on 2007-07-07 at 20:58:32
▷ ⬡ SAPKW70013	BW Support Package 13 for 7.00	☐☐☐	Imported on 2008-01-19 at 01:18:27
▷ ⬡ SAPKW70014	BW Support Package 14 for 7.00	☐☐☐	Imported on 2008-01-19 at 01:18:28
▽ ⬡ SAPKW70015	BW Support Package 15 for 7.00	☐☐☐	Imported on 2008-01-19 at 01:18:29
▽ 🗋 Prerequisite set 01			
🔠 PI_BASIS,2005_1_70C		✔	
⬡ SAPKIPYJ7D		✖	
🔠 SAP_ABA,700		✔	
⬡ SAPKA70013		✔	
🔠 SAP_BW,700		✔	
⬡ SAPKW70014		✔	
▽ 🗋 Prerequisite set 02			
🔠 PI_BASIS,2006_1_70C		✔	
🔠 SAP_ABA,700		✔	
⬡ SAPKA70013		✔	
🔠 SAP_BW,700		✔	
⬡ SAPKW70014		✔	
▷ ⬡ SAPKW70016	BW Support Package 16 for 7.00	☐☐☐	Imported on 2008-09-20 at 12:01:02
▷ ⬡ SAPKW70017	BW Support Package 17 for 7.00	☐☐☐	Imported on 2008-09-20 at 12:01:03
▷ ⬡ SAPKW70018	BW Support Package 18 for 7.00	☐☐☐	Imported on 2008-09-20 at 12:01:04
▷ ⬡ SAPKW70019	BW Support Package 19 for 7.00	☐☐☐	Imported on 2009-06-13 at 02:09:36
▷ ⬡ SAPKW70020	BW Support Package 20 for 7.00	☐☐☐	Imported on 2009-06-13 at 02:09:37

Figure 9.3 Overview of Imported Packages in SPAM

Before importing support packages, you should ensure that the following requirements are fulfilled:

Importing support packages

▸ The required authorizations are assigned for the Support Package Manager.

▸ The transport program is available and properly configured. You can check this using Transaction SPAM with the aid of the menu path UTILITIES • CHECK TRANSPORT TOOL, for example.

▸ Enough memory is available in the transport directory (corresponding to at least double the size of the OCS files).

- You are using the most recent version of SPAM/SAINT (Support Package Manager/SAP Add-On Installation Tool) to avoid known errors.

- There are no completely imported support packages. To check this, you must ensure that no support packages are listed under DIRECTORY • TERMINATED SUPPORT PACKAGES • DISPLAY.

Test run

After you check the requirements, start the importing by loading the packages from the SAP Service Marketplace or from the ordered CDs, which requires defining an import sequence. An optional test import is possible, for example, which may be useful for checking required adjustments of modifications before the actual import or for determining if there are any repaired objects that have not been released. The test run reduces the lead time and the manual effort required for the import. After the test run, you must redefine the import queue and then restart the complete import of all support packages. If errors occur during the import process, they must be removed directly.

Downtime-Minimized Import Mode

As a rule, the process of importing the latest online correction support (OCS) packages such as support packages, add-on installation packages, and add-on upgrades requires a long system downtime due to the size and scope of these packages. Even though the system is not restarted in the import process, it still should not be used for live operations during this process.

Minimizing downtime

The *downtime-minimized* import mode was therefore developed to reduce the downtime required for package imports. This mode enables you to import the majority of import objects (program coding) during live operation. The downtime can be significantly reduced if a package contains a high portion of program coding (this amount is normally up to 80% for SAP_BASIS and SAP_APPL support packages).

In the downtime-minimized import mode, the objects are imported into the database in an inactive state and are therefore mostly invisible to the system. The system can therefore continue to be used for production.

9.2.2 Adjusting Modifications

If the objects delivered by SAP were modified in the system and if they are a component of the support package to be imported, then they must be adjusted to avoid overwriting the modifications. You adjust ABAP Dictionary objects using Transaction SPDD, and repository objects, using Transaction SPAU. The adjustments are generally performed in the development system and transported to the downstream systems along the normal transport route, where it is recommended that you keep the objects separate. Both transactions can also be reached in the SAP menu under TOOLS • ABAP WORKBENCH • UTILITIES • MAINTENANCE • UPGRADE UTILITIES.

ABAP Dictionary Objects (Transaction SPDD)

You perform the adjustment of modified ABAP Dictionary objects such as domains, data elements, or tables in Transaction SPDD. You must perform the following actions for all objects provided for adjustment:

▶ **Retaining Modifications**

The adoption of the modifications is confirmed and the changes are maintained with the corresponding maintenance transactions.   Actions

▶ **Resetting the modification**
The modification is reset to its original status.

If none of the named actions are performed, the new SAP standard will also be active in your SAP system and modifications will thereby be overwritten. For a later upgrade in such a case, however, you will be prompted to adjust these modifications again. To minimize the effort as much as possible for future upgrades, you should therefore perform one of the two actions in every case. For each object to be adjusted, the status and required actions is represented in the form of a traffic light icon (see Table 9.1).

Icon	Description
Green traffic light	There are no overlaps between the delivered SAP objects and customer modifications. You can therefore either reset to the original status or retain the modification.
Yellow traffic light	There are overlaps between the version delivered by SAP and the modified customer version. The adjustment is supported by additional details in a dialog box.
Red traffic light	The object can be manually processed in the corresponding maintenance transaction of the ABAP Dictionary or using the version management.

Table 9.1 Status of SPDD Objects To Be Adjusted

After you have processed all modifications and decided to either retain or reset the individual modifications, the object will be marked green. If you do not perform any of the described actions, the new SAP standard is activated in the system and the modification is overwritten. These objects will then be listed again as modifications to be adjusted in subsequent upgrades.

ABAP Repository Objects (Transaction SPAU)

Object status

You adjust repository objects, meaning programs, function modules, classes, and so on, using Transaction SPAU. For all objects provided for adjustment, you must decide whether you want to retain the modifications you have made or reset the object to the original status. If you do not perform any of the actions described, the new original will remain active in your system. The objects will remain unadjusted and visible in Transaction SPAU. The icons in Table 9.2 describe the status of the objects.

Icon	Description
Green traffic light	Automatic adjustment
	This icon normally only appears in the With modification assistant category. Customer modifications can be automatically adopted with these objects. Clicking the symbol performs the automatic adjustment.
	In the following case, which is rare, a note correction appears with a green traffic light icon. An example of this case would be a note that contains several correction instructions, each of which has a different validity period. This can have the effect that when a support package is imported, one correction instruction may become obsolete, whereas another may still be valid.
	You can mark a subtree or multiple objects or position the cursor on one individual object for adjustment.
	The adjustment log provides information about which modifications were adopted.
Yellow traffic light	Semi-automatic adjustment
	If only semi-automatic adjustment is possible for modifications using the modification assistant, a yellow traffic light appears in front of the object. Semi-automatic means that adjustment support is provided in the individual tools. The split-screen editor is called when you are adjusting programs while, in other tools, entries in corresponding dialog boxes lead to the removal of collisions that occur.
	The system can display note corrections in the modification comparison function (Transaction SPAU) with a yellow traffic light. The correction that was previously implemented via a note was overwritten by a support package that does not contain these corrections. You can restart the note implementation by clicking the yellow traffic light.

Table 9.2 Status of Objects to Be Adjusted in Transaction SPAU

Icon	Description
	During a modification adjustment, a semi-automatic adjustment is only provided by repository objects in Transaction SPAU in the categories Note Corrections and With Modification Assistant.
	The yellow traffic light is also used for the modification adjustment of dictionary objects in Transaction SPDD. Clicking the traffic light symbol executes special reports that support the adoption of the modifications.
	The migration of customer enhancements (customer exits) to BAdIs (Business Add-Ins) also occurs within Transaction SPAU. The relevant enhancement objects are displayed with a yellow traffic light symbol under the Migration Objects rubric.
Red traffic light	Manual adjustment
	Objects in the Without Modification Assistant subtree can only be post processed manually after the adjustment. A manual adjustment means that you must implement your modifications without special system support.
	You can retrieve old versions or use your recordings to process the newly imported objects via the version management.
	In exceptional cases, the red traffic light can also appear in the With Modification Assistant category if the modification assistant tools cannot completely support the adjustment. In such cases, you should absolutely check the adjustment log.
Blank	This icon only appears in the Note Corrections category.
	If a dark traffic light is displayed for note corrections, the superordinate correction instructions are obsolete. The correction is contained in the upgrade or in the imported support package.
	You can reach a dialog box by clicking the traffic light symbol or using the Reset to Original function. Confirm that you want to reset the note correction to the original status. If you have selected multiple note corrections, you can select Reset All. The dialog box will no longer be displayed.
X	This symbol indicates that first developer who processed the object did not complete the modification adjustment . Postprocessing with additional developers may be necessary.
	The Incomplete Adjustment status remains until all developers for an object have set the completion indicator in the User/Status dialog box.
	Only then will the red X be replaced by a green checkmark. Conversely, a developer can also remove the completion indicator in the User/Status dialogue box if the object is to be processed at a later point in time. The red X will take the place of the green checkmark.
Edit	This status is displayed by the For Retesting icon.
	Even if all developers have completed their work for a modification adjustment, the object may still be being edited by one or more testers. After all testers have set the completion indicator, the Retest Completed symbol will be displayed in front of the object.

Table 9.2 Status of Objects to Be Adjusted in Transaction SPAU (Cont.)

Icon	Description
Question	Unknown adjustment mode
	The adjustment mode (manual, semi-automatic, automatic, obsolete note) for this object could not be determined for modification adjustment with the Modification Assistant or for the adjustment of note corrections.
	If the adjustment mode could not be determined for a note correction, you will be prompted to import the note again. Only then can the adjustment mode be determined again.
	The adjustment modes are determined in the SPAUINFO phase during an upgrade and in the RUN_SPAU_? phase during the import of a support package. To do this, the SAPRUPGM report is conducted in a background process. Because the calculation process may last several minutes, you should regularly refresh the tree display in Transaction SPAU and wait until the green question marks are replaced by traffic light symbols.
Okay	Object adjusted/retest completed
	After the adjustment, the traffic light symbols are replaced with either a green checkmark or a stop sign. For objects supported by the Modification Assistant, you can display the adjustment log by clicking the check mark.
	The Completed icon also appears if testers were entered or the relevant object was entered in the User/Status dialog box and they completed the test of the object.
Stop	Adjustment problems
	If objects in the With Modification Assistant category could not be completely adjusted, a dialog box is displayed indicating that there are unresolved problems.
	The stop sign indicates that problems occurred during the adjustment that usually have to be solved manually.
	Click the stop sign to display the log. There you can find out if there were problems during the upgrade and what actions are necessary. Pay special attention to the Open Problems category.

Table 9.2 Status of Objects to Be Adjusted in Transaction SPAU (Cont.)

9.3   Java Support Packages

With the release of SAP NetWeaver 7.0 (2004s at the time), a new platform and technology was suddenly part of the SAP NetWeaver BW system for many experienced SAP NetWeaver BW administrators: BI Java. In addition to system administration and monitoring, there are also a few changes in the area of software logistics. This section will therefore address BI Java patches in further detail.

What is BI Java?   From a technical viewpoint, BI Java consists of the previously mentioned components of the SAP NetWeaver Portal and AS Java (J2EE engine) and software component archives (SCAs), which make Java-based functions in SAP NetWeaver BW available. SAP NetWeaver BW-relevant software components are primarily BIBASES (BI Basis Services), BIWEBAPP (BI Web Runtime for BI Web Applications), BIIBC (BI Information Broadcasting), BIREPPLAN (BI Reporting and Planning), and BIUDI (BI Universal Data Integration [UDI], for example for UDI access in SAP NetWeaver Visual Composer). The BIMMR (Meta-model Repository) and BIWDALV (BI Web Dynpro ALV) components are used in a broader environment without necessarily incorporating SAP NetWeaver BW functions.

A patch for BI Java normally consists of a series of corrections for the SCAs named above, such as BIBASES.SCA. An important distinction from preliminary corrections of an ABAP note is that corrections in J2EE are always cumulative. A patch with the same SPS version and a higher patch level therefore contains all of the corrections in the patches with a lower patch level. When you are upgrading to a higher support package stack, situations can therefore arise where a certain correction released in a patch is not yet contained in the new support package stack. It is therefore important to keep the new support package stack at the newest available patch level for BI Java.

What is a BI Java patch?

If an SAP Support customer asks for the import of the newest patches for BI Java, this also has a foundation in software logistics and the type of system access: Usually, a BW-RFC connection is established between the customer's ABAP system and a J2EE installation on the developer's computer. This local J2EE developer connection does not make any changes to the settings in the customer's system, but the deployment of the newest patches for the customer's support package stack is used.

Since the BI Java patching strategy changed with SPS 16 patch level 30, both delivery processes must be looked at. Previously, all corrections from a lower support package stack were also available in the higher support package stacks and delivered as a component of the BI Java patch. This was done to prevent regressions from occurring after an upgrade from a lower support package stack (but a current patch level) to a higher support package stack if the errors are not corrected until the first release of the higher support package stack. Accordingly, Support Package Stack 14 (from a certain patch level) contains the same source text as Support Package Stack 15 (with a different patch level) and Support Package 16 (also with a different patch level).

What corrections are in which patches?

New strategy

This strategy was changed in that patches are now only made available for the most recent support package stack. If you use support package stacks that are lower than the most recent ones, you can import these patches without problems. This is for the support package stack with no additional risk associated. This change leads to the following conclusions:

▶ It is no longer necessary to make patches available specifically for the source text lines of a support package stack. Instead, you can simply import them for all support package stacks from SPS 14.

▶ Only patches for the most recent support package stack will be made available to you. If you use lower support package stacks, you can import the same patch without problems occurring.

▶ The strict dependency is no longer present between ABAP support package stacks and Java support package stacks for which an upgrade must always occur in parallel. It is recommended that you keep the ABAP components and the Java components of the server at the same support package stack level or at least close to each other.

▶ Upgrades for ABAP and Java are designed independently and flexibly. This helps reduce the overall costs for the operations, particularly for the testing of upgrades and patches.

Patch numbering

Patch numbering is easily changed to enable the delivery of preliminary corrections (correction for a shutdown in the production system). Previously, Patch 5 was marked with 5. The technical name is now multiplied by 10. Patch 5 therefore is called "Patch 50." Patch 15 is called Patch 150. This is necessary so that the description of the preliminary corrections can occur in sequence with the patches. Accordingly, the first preliminary correction for Patch 50 is called 51, the second, 52, and so on. This begins with the delivery of Support Package Stack 16, Patch 30.

New features are no longer implemented via support package stacks (SPS), but rather, exclusively via enhancement packages (EhPs). Consequently, Java support package stacks and Java patches now only contain corrections for problems that were reported by customers or internal tests. The last feature development in SAP NetWeaver BW 7.0 is delivered with Support Package Stack 14.

Hotfix

SAP only initiates the delivery of a hotfix (correction for serious errors that usually have to be targeted and corrected quickly) if a particularly difficult problem exists in the customer's productive system with regard to damages caused by a shutdown in the production system. All problems that are not related to a shutdown in the production system are solved via the delivery of the standard Java patch. A hotfix is always based on the most recently delivered Java patch. In contrast to the standard Java patches, it only contains the hotfix source text changes. This means, however, that it may contain additional hotfix changes (such as corrections for a shutdown in the production system) that have been created since the delivery of the latest patch. The subsequent regular BI Java patch then contains the hotfix corrections as well, of course.

The Java Support Package Manager (JSPM) is the SAP NetWeaver 7.0 tool used to implement support package stacks and Java support packages and to install additional components such as business packages for the SAP Business Suite applications (ERP, CRM, and SRM). The Software Deployment Manager (SDM) is no longer used for these tasks. JSPM provides the following new functions:

Java Support Package Manager

▶ It enables the deployment of new SAP software components (both components of the SAP usage types and ones that are independent of them) to which support packages can then be applied.

New functions

▶ It is integrated into the SAP NetWeaver Development Infrastructure (NWDI). JSPM recognizes SAP software components that were modified and enables the use of support packages for them.

The following section provides an overview of the management of changes using the Change and Transport System (CTS) and fundamental information about the structure of your transport landscape and transport strategy.

9.4 Transport System

The system provides utilities for you to organize development projects in Customizing and in the ABAP workbench and to transport the changes between the SAP system and its clients in the system landscape. In addition to ABAP objects, you can also transport non-ABAP technologies (such as Web Dynpro Java or SAP NetWeaver Portal) in the system landscape.

9.4.1 Transport Landscape

A typical system landscape consists of a development system, a consolidation (or test) system, and a production system, both on the side of the SAP NetWeaver BW system and on the side of the source system (Figure 9.4). Changes and developments are performed in the development system and then transported to the consolidation or QA system. The transports are checked for correctness and completeness, and an integrated test (thereby incorporating the source systems) is performed for the entire development. After performing all of the tests and, possibly, after changing some objects, the created solution is finally transported to the production system and made available to the users.

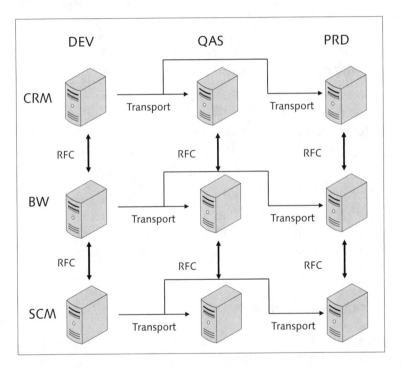

Figure 9.4 Transport Landscape with Source Systems

On the one hand, you should consider the transport within the SAP NetWeaver BW system landscape of both ABAP-based and Java-based objects. On the other hand, you should also consider the dependencies and the interaction between objects, structures, and processes and consequently transports in the respective source systems.

Transport Management System

You can model and manage your system landscape using the Transport Management System (TMS). It provides you with tools for configuring the system landscape and for the organization, execution, and monitoring of the transports.

All SAP systems that are managed using the TMS in Transaction SE10 form a transport domain. This usually means all SAP systems of the system landscape. Certain system settings are the same for all systems within a transport domain, such as the transport routes, for example. To implement this, one SAP system of the transport domain has the reference configuration, and all other SAP systems of the transport domain receive copies of that reference configuration. The system with the reference configuration is called the transport domain controller, and only there can you perform changes to the reference configuration.

Transport domain

During the installation of an SAP system, a transport directory is set up for the system that is used for storing the transport data. Usually, all SAP systems of a transport domain have a common transport directory. There are only exceptions if, for example, different hardware platforms are used or increased security measures do not allow direct data access.

Transport Routes and Transport Layers

All development projects that are performed in an SAP system and transported on the same transport routes are compiled to one transport layer that is created in the transport route editor of the Transport Management System. In addition to the delivered SAP transport layer, you generally only need additional transport layers if you add new development systems to the system group.

A consolidation route is created as a regular transport route to the consolidation system. The consolidation route is defined by the development class and the transport layer for each object. Delivery routes are created as a continuation of the transport route for developments behind the consolidation route, such as in the production systems or possibly even in training systems and so on.

Consolidation route

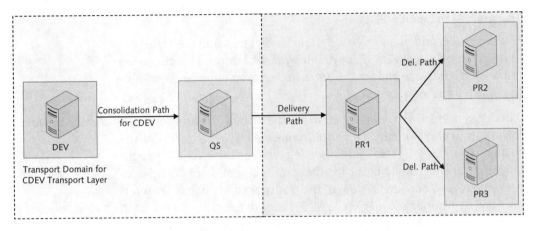

Figure 9.5 Multilevel Delivery

Figure 9.5 shows an example of a more complex system landscape in which a multilevel delivery is necessary. In a group of two or three systems, the multilevel delivery is not necessary, but it can be very useful for distributed production systems or especially for layered development projects that build upon each other.

9.4.2 Change and Transport System

The Transport Management System (TMS) is part of the Change and Transport System (CTS), which also encompasses the Transport Organizer (CTO) and a few other tools for transport support (Figure 9.6). CTS thus provides a series of functions that you can use to compose a transport strategy that is optimally adapted to your situation.

Transport Organizer

The Transport Organizer is available to you for the organized process of development projects. All of the steps are supported, such as recording changes in change requests, processing change orders from creation to release, and monitoring the released transport requests.

Changes that your development team made in the development system are not immediately adopted by the subsequent system (such as your quality assurance and production system) when a change is released. When a change request is released, the order is only placed in the import queue of the target system. Changes can thereby be collected in the development system for a certain period in the import queue and then imported together to the target system (to the quality assurance system, for example) at a later time. Importing the requests allows them to be placed in the import queues of the subsequent systems (such as the production and training systems). Exporting and importing to the different target systems can therefore be performed at completely different times and at different frequencies.

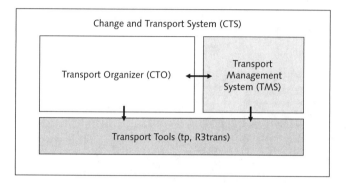

Figure 9.6 Change and Transport System

Import queues are especially well suited for automating transporting in your system landscape. Particularly if you expect a high transport frequency, this can mean a significant workload for the system administration, which is significantly reduced to monitoring and intervening when errors arise.

Transport automation

Import Queue: System Q26

Requests for Q26: 806 / 811   2009.09.28 12:37:31

Number	Request	T	QM	Clt	R/C	I	UMO	Owner	Project	Short Text	Ac	St
305	D26K921070	K	800	800	△	k	I	23055513	D26_P00001	S 13399: AM Fix: 753947-	▯	△
306	D26K920575	K	800	800	△	k	I	23048656	D26_P00014	S 11880: SS - DP/WDSB -	▯	△
307	D26K920788	K	800	800	△	k	I	23048656	D26_P00014	S 12406: SS - DP/WDSB -	▯	△
308	D26K920766	K	800	800	△	k	I	23048656	D26_P00014	S 12338: SS - DP/WDSB -	▯	△
309	D26K921072	K	800	800	▢	k	I	23048656	D26_P00014	S 13414: SM - Sell-Throu	▯	△
310	D26K920864	K	800	800	▢	k	I	23055044	D26_P00014	S 12666: PL_35730_New Lo	▯	△
311	D26K921087	W	800	800	▢	w	I	23054952	D26_P00001	S 13423: Infra656368-Del	▯	△
312	D26K920961	K	800	800	△	k	I	23055044	D26_P00014	S 13090: PL_40320_Automa	▯	△
313	D26K921091	W	800	800	▢	w	I	23054952	D26_P00001	S 13423: Infra656368-Del	▯	△
314	D26K921009	K	800	800	△	k	I	23048656	D26_P00014	S 13240: SS - DP/WDSB -	▯	△
315	D26K920714	K	800	800	▢	k	I	23048656	D26_P00014	S 12191: SS - DP/WDSB -	▯	△
316	D26K920952	K	800	800	△	k	I	23035511	D26_P00014	S 12977: FF_37230_Dataso	▯	△
317	D26K921085	K	800	800	▢	k	I	23051449	D26_P00014	S 12484: SM_R0904 - Dema	▯	△
318	D26K920882	K	800	800	◉	k	I	23048656	D26_P00014	S 12708: SM - Sell-Throu	▯	△
319	D26K920959	K	800	800	◉	k	I	23035511	D26_P00014	S 13057: FF_37230_OHD Tr	▯	△

Figure 9.7 Import Queue

You can easily display and edit import queues using the Transport Management System (Transaction STMS) (Figure 9.7). You can find more information, particularly about the status during a running import, by double-clicking the relevant request as shown in Figure 9.8.

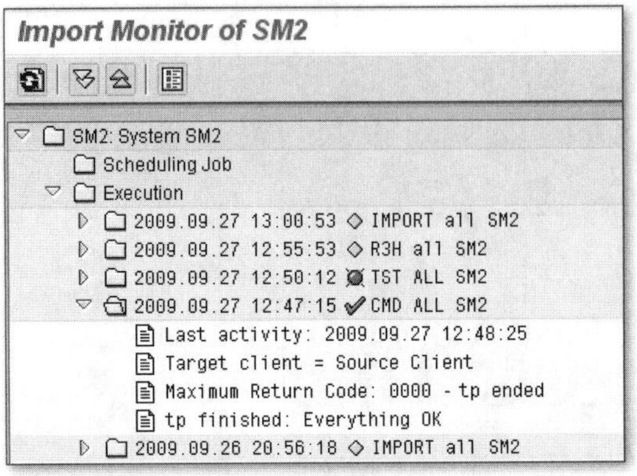

Figure 9.8 Import Status in the Import Monitor

If import queues are edited, two procedures are available for the actual import: mass transports and single imports. With mass transports, all requests pending import are always imported together. The requests are imported into the target systems in the same order in which they were exported from the source system. This minimizes the risk of errors occurring because requests were imported in the wrong order or because objects are missing because they are contained in requests that have not been transported yet.

Single imports   If you use single imports, a portion of the requests are selected from the import queue and imported to the target system. Other requests remain in the import queue and can be imported either later or not at all. Single transports give you a high degree of flexibility but usually require greater administrative effort.

9.4.3   Transporting Roles

Roles are not SAP NetWeaver BW–specific objects and therefore do not follow the version concept (versions A/D). Instead, the indication of the delivery version and the active customer version occurs via namespaces.

BI content roles are identified by the prefix SAP_BW_ and are copied from the content to the namespace SAP_BWC_ when activated. You can transport both roles that are delivered as part of the SAP BI content and customer-specific roles via the BW transport connection. If you want to modify roles that have been delivered by SAP, you must first activate them and thereby adopt them into the namespace SAP_BWC_. When transporting from the role maintenance (Transaction PFCG), you have to pay attention to whether just the authorization profile or possibly also the user assignments should be transported. Proceed as follows:

1. Collect the roles that you want to transport, just as with a standard import.

2. Select the roles and select Transport Objects. You will then reach the Transport Request Prompt dialog box.

3. Write the objects to an available transport request or create a new transport request. Select Continue.

Transport from role maintenance

It is generally recommended that you always transport roles via the Data Warehousing Workbench BW transport connection.

9.4.4 Special Feature When Transporting BW Objects

As in many other areas, when transporting objects in an SAP NetWeaver BW system, you can use some special features. For example, the consistent generation, application, revision, and transport of BW objects is supported by the BW version concept.

BW Version Concept

The BW version and transport concept is significant for customer-specific content developments (customer content). Preconfigured BW objects such as InfoProviders and queries are delivered as part of the BI content. You can use these objects in your system directly or revised. You can also create your own BW objects. The BW version concept enables the delivery and consistent use of BW objects in a system landscape and constitutes an enhancement to the standard transport system. A distinction can be made between multiple object versions (Table 9.3).

Version	Description	Delivery-Relevant	Transport-Relevant
D	Delivery version	Yes	No
A	Active version	No	Yes
M	Revised version	No	Yes
T	Transport version for the import of objects dependent on the source system	No	Yes
Shadow version	Delivery version for objects dependent on the source system	Yes	No
Pseudo D	Delivery version for objects dependent on the source system that is generated in the target system of the delivery	Yes	No

Table 9.3 BW Object Versions

Two object types

An SAP NetWeaver BW system makes a distinction between two kinds of object types: the object type for the active version and the object type for the delivery version. This means there are two logical transport objects (TLOGO) for each deliverable BW object: the transport object for the active version, the A-TLOGO object, and the transport object for the delivery version, the D-TLOGO object. In accordance with the system settings, the system writes the suitable TLOGO object to the transport request when transporting.

Figure 9.9 illustrates working with revised and active versions. In the example, an object is created so that the M (modified) version has the status 1. There is not yet an A (active) version at this point. The two versions correspond when first activated. If the object is then changed, the M version will have status 2, and the A version will still correspond to the old status. After reactivating, the two versions will correspond again — this time with status 2. The Change Back action in the example corresponds to undoing changes (status 3) to return to the current active status of the object.

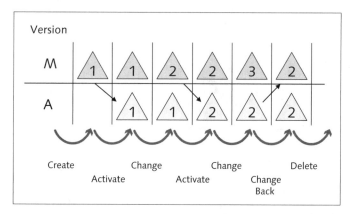

Figure 9.9 Version Concept for Created Objects

If a BW object in an unrevised version (M version) is activated, the dependent objects (DDIC or program objects) are also generated during the activation. An object can only be activated if it is consistent.

In the development system, active objects are exported and then imported to the target system in either the A version or in an M version, depending on the type. Objects that are dependent on the source system are transported in their own version, the transport version (T). InfoCubes or InfoObjects, for example, are transported to the target system in the M version and automatically activated after the import because tables (and other directory objects) are created during the activation. Currency translation types, in contrast, are transported to the target system in the A version because this object type does not require an activation step, and the M version is therefore not supported. After the import, all BW metadata objects are automatically activated via the RS_AFTER_IMPORT after-import method (AIM). The dependent DDIC and program objects are generated in the target system after the import.

Versions during transport

Figure 9.10 illustrates the versions during transport using the example of an object with the after-import method (an InfoCube). The active version that corresponds to processing status 1 in the development system will be exported. The InfoCube that is represented in the figure with status 3 is already present in the target system in an active version and will not be overwritten by the imported version until the AIM step of the import.

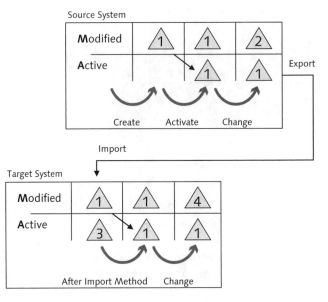

Figure 9.10 Versioning During Transport

Collecting Objects

To determine which objects should be transported with the BW transport connection, the desired objects are collected in the Data Warehousing Workbench in the Transport Connection (Transaction RSOR) functional area (Figure 9.11).

Consistent requests that take object dependencies into account are especially important in the SAP NetWeaver BW system because the metadata objects are activated in the import postprocessing step. If dependent objects are missing in the transport request, this leads to errors during activation that are displayed in the transport request log. Generating a consistent request is more difficult in the SAP NetWeaver BW system than with other program objects for the following reasons:

- The (BW modeler) user group that is addressed does not normally handle delivery questions.
- It should be possible to create objects for testing purposes without having to write a transport request because they are not to be transported.
- There are many object types, and it is difficult to get an overview of the interdependency of the objects.

Consistent requests

▶ In addition to the technical dependencies that lead to inconsistencies, there are other types of dependencies that make it easier to transport a complete scenario.

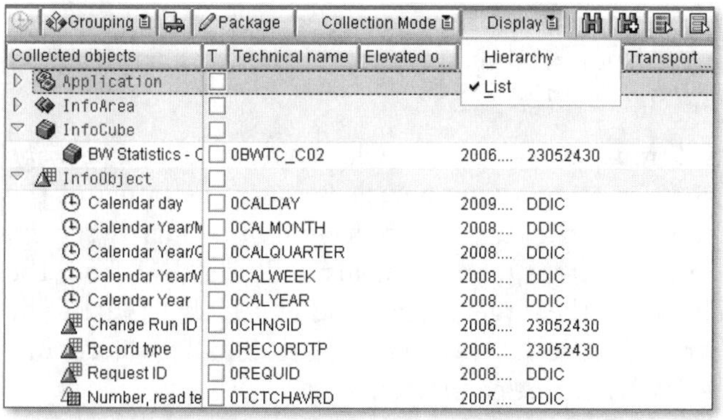

Collected objects	T	Technical name	Elevated o	Hierarchy	Transport
▷ 🌐 Application	☐			✓ List	
▷ ◈ InfoArea	☐				
▽ 🔷 InfoCube	☐				
🔷 BW Statistics - C	☐	0BWTC_C02	2006....	23052430	
▽ 🗂 InfoObject	☐				
🕐 Calendar day	☐	0CALDAY	2009....	DDIC	
🕐 Calendar Year/N	☐	0CALMONTH	2008....	DDIC	
🕐 Calendar Year/Q	☐	0CALQUARTER	2008....	DDIC	
🕐 Calendar Year/V	☐	0CALWEEK	2008....	DDIC	
🕐 Calendar Year	☐	0CALYEAR	2008....	DDIC	
🗂 Change Run ID	☐	0CHNGID	2006....	23052430	
🗂 Record type	☐	0RECORDTP	2006....	23052430	
🗂 Request ID	☐	0REQUID	2008....	DDIC	
🗂 Number, read te	☐	0TCTCHAVRD	2007....	DDIC	

Figure 9.11 Collecting Objects

If you also want to collect source system–dependent objects , select the source systems for which you want to collect objects via Source System Assignment (Figure 9.11). Only the objects assigned to the selected source systems will then be collected.

Collecting source system–dependent objects

In the default setting, only the objects that are essential for activating an object are collected. If you also want to collect objects that are required for activating the other objects you are collecting, select the relevant option: only necessary objects, the data flow before, the data flow afterward, or the data flow before and afterward.

It is recommended that you display the objects as a list if you want to keep an overview of the collected objects. If you want to identify why a specific object was collected or want to work through related objects scenario by scenario, you should choose the tree display.

If objects were collected in the list, objects that are used by multiple other objects are only displayed for editing the first time they occur in the tree display for collected objects. For each subsequent occurrence they are marked gray and not ready for input.

Transport Strategy

You can choose between the following strategies for the transport in an SAP NetWeaver BW system landscape: the standard transport system, where a package is specified when creating an object and the object is written to a transport request, or the BW transport system, where a new object is automatically assigned to a local package and then all objects relevant to the scenario are collected with the BW transport connection at a later time. The standard transport system can be turned on or off in the Transport Connection area of the workbench under EDIT • TRANSPORT (Figure 9.12).

Standard transport system

With the standard transport system , the developer opts for a package and a request when creating a new object. Because the target of the objects is defined via the package, this procedure is primarily recommended if you have different target systems and it is clear from the beginning which will be the target system and which objects are to be transported. There is no special way to deal with the BEx objects like there is with the BW transport connection.

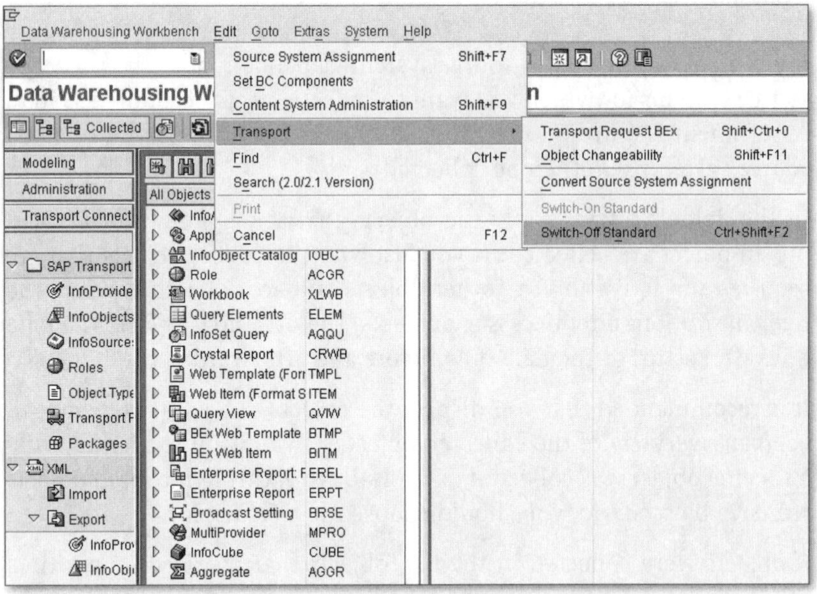

Figure 9.12 Switching Off the Standard Transport System

BW transport connection

When using the BW transport connection, new objects are first automatically created as local objects in the $TMP package. They are therefore not directly written to the transport request. You can develop new scenarios using this procedure without dealing with the transport.

When the scenario is completed, only objects that are necessary in the production system are collected in the transport connection and written to a request. The unnecessary objects remain as local objects and are not transported. Users in the production system can create local queries and workbooks without having to make decisions about the transport in the dialog box.

Each object is assigned to a transportable package only after the point when the objects are to be transported for the first time. Each one must be recorded from this point on.

Transporting BEx objects

BEx objects (queries and workbooks) are dealt with in a special way in the BW transport connection. Because no dialog box can appear during the maintenance of these objects, an administrator must create the requests for these objects in the Data Warehousing Workbench (Transport Connection functional area).

When changes are made, all BEx objects that were already transported and are therefore already assigned to a packet are written to the standard BEx transport request by default (Figure 9.13). The administrator sends this request. All changes to this request are recorded, regardless of the user involved.

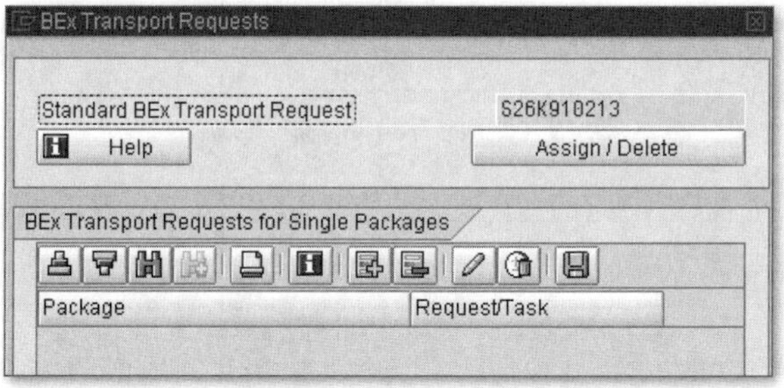

Figure 9.13   BEx Transport Request

If this request is released, the administrator should immediately create a new BEx request. This is because queries and workbooks cannot be edited as long as no request is defined as a BEx request.

Under certain circumstances a request for all BEx objects is insufficient. This can be the case if, for example, you want to transport from one development system to different production systems. In such a case you

Standard BEx transport request

BEx transport requests for individual packages

315

can create a BEx request for each package. The BEx objects are distributed to the different requests via their packages. Because the package specifies the transport target of an object, among other things, you can use this procedure to record those BEx objects in different requests if they are to be transported to different target systems. If there is no special request created for the package of an object, that object will be written to the standard BEx transport request as before. Even with this procedure, it is recommended that you create a new request immediately after a request has been released.

Changeability

Using the settings for BW object changeability, you can set objects of a certain BW object type to Changeable if your system is set to Not Changeable. Production systems are generally set to Not Changeable (Transaction SE06). Queries, workbooks, and InfoPackages, for example, are not changeable, although it may make sense to change these and other objects in a production system. You can set the BW object changeability in Transaction RSA1 in the Transport Connection functional area (Figure 9.14).

Object Type		
AGGR	Aggregate	Everything
ANPR	Analysis Process	Everything
AQQU	InfoSet Query	Everything
BITM	BEx Web Item	Not Chang
BRSE	Broadcast Setting	Everything
BTMP	BEx Web Template	Not Chang
CRWB	Crystal Report	Everything
CTRT	Currency Translation Type	Everything
DEST	Open Hub Destination	Everything
DTPA	Data Transfer Process	Everything
ELEM	Query Element	Everything
EREL	Enterprise Report: Reusable Element	Not Chang
ERPT	Enterprise Report	Not Chang
EVEN	Event Processing Chain	Everything
ISIG	InfoPackage Group	Everything
ISIP	InfoPackage	Everything
ITEM	Web Item (Format SAP BW 3.x)	Everything
PLDS	Data Slices	Not Chang
PLSE	Planning Function	Not Chang
PLSQ	Planning Sequence	Not Chang

Figure 9.14 BW Object Changeability

Change the setting for objects that you want to edit to Original Changeable. It is then possible to edit objects that were created in this system. Note that these objects are no longer linked to the transport system. Only consider switching this off when one of the following situations arises:

▶ The system is set to Not Changeable in the global settings (Transaction SE06).

▶ The Local Developments software components (no automatic transport) or Custom Developments are set to Not Changeable.

▶ The Customer Name Range namespace is set to Not Changeable (Transaction SE06).

▶ The Changes to Cross-Client Objects for the SAP NetWeaver BW clients is set in Transaction SCC4 in such a way that changes are not permitted for repository objects. The selection list is either set to No Changes to Repository Objects or to No Changes to Repository Objects or Cross-Client Customizing Objects.

It is not possible to change objects that were transported to this system either because it is to be expected that these changes will be overwritten again during another transport. If you still want to change all objects of the object type despite this danger, change the settings to Everything Changeable via the context menu.

The Everything Changeable option

Source System–Dependent Objects

Whereas the collection of the dependent objects on the same transport request is sufficient for the consistent transport of objects that are dependent on other BW objects, the dependency of nontransportable objects represents a special challenge that can be used to explain the complexity of dealing with these objects.

Objects are not transported in an SAP NetWeaver BW system, but rather, the meta information that is required for generating an object in the target system is transported. Source system–dependant objects are notably dependant on circumstances in the target system. They can even be distributed physically to an SAP NetWeaver BW system and a source system. As a result, special requirements often exist with regard to source system–dependant objects, such as the following:

▶ An object that was created in the original system for source system A should be created in the target system for one or more source systems (B, C, D, and so on).

▶ Because the definition of a connection to a source system always depends on both sides, namely, the source system and the SAP NetWeaver BW system, an object that was created in both the source and target systems for the same source system physically has two different connections to this system.

Therefore, with source system–dependant objects, a logic runs that defines the name of the source system and the connection to it for which the import and activation of the content is to be executed Source system–dependent objects include, for example, the DataSource and InfoPackage objects and transformation and DTP.

Defining the target source system for imports

To be able to transport source system–dependent BW objects, you have to maintain the RSLOGSYSMAP assignment table in the target system of the transport. You can find this function in Transaction RSA1 in the Modeling functional area under TOOLS • CONVERT LOGICAL SYSTEM NAMES (Figure 9.15).

Conversion of source system names after the transport				
OriginalSourceSystem	Target source system	7.0	+	
D26CLNT800	S26CLNT800	☐	S26 Client 800	
D37CLNT100	S37CLNT100	☐	S37 Client 100	
D38CLNT100	Q38CLNT100	☐	Q38 Client 100	
D47CLNT100	S47CLNT100	☐	S47 Client 100	
D48CLNT100	S48CLNT100	☐	S48 Client 100	

Figure 9.15 Conversion of Source System Names

One or more target source systems are assigned to the original source system in the table. An original source system is generally the OLTP development system. A corresponding target source system is the OLTP system that is linked to the SAP NetWeaver BW target system. The source system–dependent BW objects are converted using the mapping table during the Import Post-Processing step of the transport. Defining the target source system ensures that only the objects that are assigned to the selected source systems will be collected for content adoption into the active version. Objects that are not assigned to the selected source systems are not taken into consideration.

Client-Dependent Objects

In SAP NetWeaver BW there are several object types whose execution is client-dependent. Examples of this are Web service DataSources and process chains. The prerequisite for the import postprocessing of such objects is that a user has been defined for the execution in the background in the Implementation Guide under SAP NETWEAVER • BUSINESS INTELLIGENCE • AUTOMATED PROCESSES • CREATE USER FOR BACKGROUND PROCESSES. This user is also used for data extraction, among other things, and is generally called BWREMOTE. If Web services are being used, you must make sure that the background user is authorized to edit Web service DataSources (authorization object S_RS_WDS).

In addition, the target client that is to be used during import postprocessing for the logon from the 000 client to the specified target clients must be created in the Implementation Guide under SAP NETWEAVER • BUSINESS INTELLIGENCE • TRANSPORT SETTINGS • CREATE DESTINATION FOR IMPORT POST-PROCESSING (Transaction RSTPRFC).

Hierarchy InfoPackages

To ensure that the selection of hierarchies is transferred when you transport an InfoPackage into the target BW system, you have to take into account the special considerations for transporting hierarchy InfoPackages. When you import a hierarchy InfoPackage into the target system, the system checks whether the selected hierarchy is in tables RSOSOHIE and RSOSOHIET. If the entries in the target SAP NetWeaver BW system do not match the source SAP NetWeaver BW system, the target SAP NetWeaver BW system deletes the hierarchy selection for the InfoPackage. Proceed as follows:

1. Transport a hierarchy InfoPackage for the relevant DataSource into the target SAP NetWeaver BW system. The selections are not transferred because entries for this DataSource do not exist in tables RSOSOHIE and RSOSOHIET.

   Transport of a hierarchy InfoPackage

2. Go to the scheduler in the target SAP NetWeaver BW system and refresh the table containing the selected hierarchies under Available Hierarchies from OLTP.

3. Select the Relevant for BW option for each hierarchy that you want to load later using the InfoPackage.

4. Now transport the hierarchy InfoPackage (Figure 9.16). The selections are retained if the hierarchies have exactly the same name in the target SAP NetWeaver BW system as in the source SAP NetWeaver BW system.

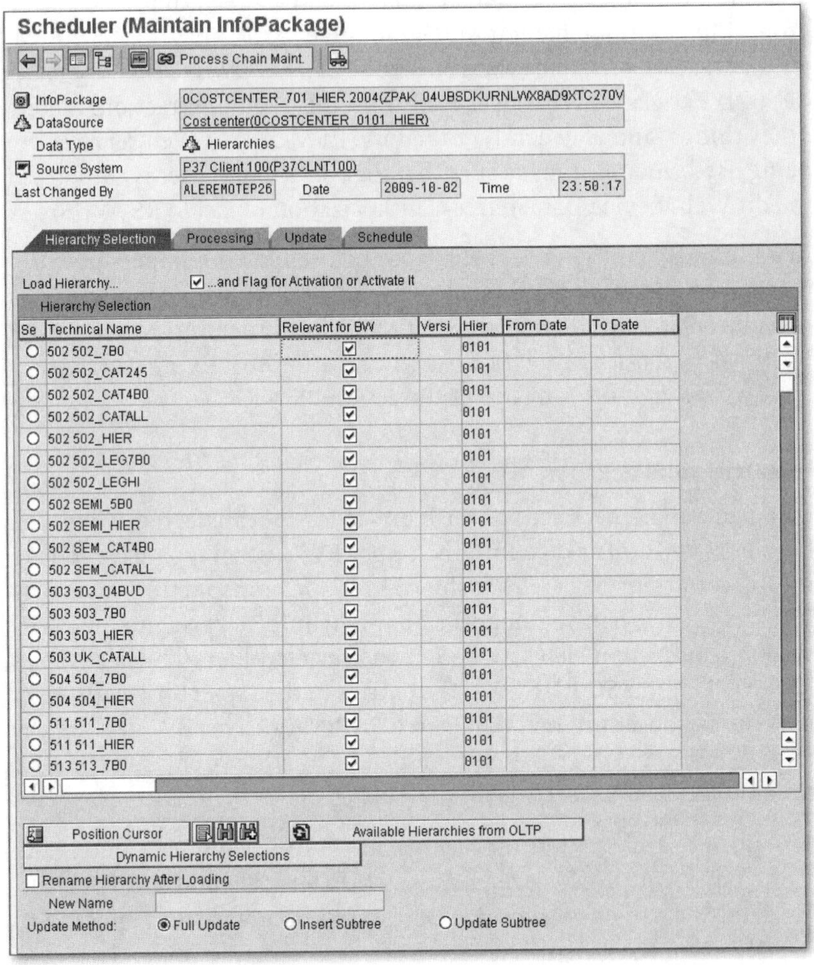

Figure 9.16 Transport of a Hierarchy InfoPackage

9.4.5   SAP Solution Manager

SAP Solution Manager is the central SAP application management solution for system landscapes. The different options that the SAP Solution Manager provides an enterprise cover the entire lifecycle of the applications, beginning with the implementation and spanning the entire operation until the upgrade to a new SAP release.

The larger the range of functions a system landscape has, the more difficult it is to get an overview of the changes to the software applications. The traceability of such changes plays a decisive role, however, when dealing with the revision security and functional security of the individual processes. SAP Solution Manager offers a tool that accompanies the complete lifecycle of a change request, from the request to the transport of a new or changed function to the production system.

Retraceability of changes

Change Request Management

The lifecycle management application requires a change request management (ChaRM) that documents any changes from the request to the approval procedure to the final decision and prepares for the IT project team in the latest condition.

Change request management enables you to process your maintenance and implementation projects extensively: from change management and project planning to resource management and cost control to the physical transport of the changes from the development environment to the production environment.

Permanent changes to the software and configuration, and large implementation projects, are constant challenges faced in the realization of data consistency and secure project control. As part of SAP Solution Manager, change management integrates the functions of the service desk for managing change requests and enhances project control by integrating project planning with the cProjects application for control of the transport workflow.

As part of SAP Solution Manager, ChaRM supports processes such as urgent corrections in the implementation of fast and direct changes in the production environment and activities in the maintenance cycles, for example, regular releases such as maintenance, upgrade, and template projects. It also supports cross-system and cross-component changes. Change request management offers the following benefits:

Advantages

▶ Increased maintenance and project efficiency

▶ Minimization of costs for project management and IT

▶ Reduced risk of corrections or project failure

- Shorter phases for correction, implementation, and going live
- Efficient maintenance of customer developments and implementations

With ChaRM, SAP is geared toward the ITIL processes and simultaneously adheres to the Sarbanes–Oxley Act. ChaRM can be linked to an existing service desk solution in SAP Solution Manager.

Enhanced Change and Transport System (CTS+)

In recent years, SAP has implemented more and more components that are not supported by the classic ABAP transport system. This includes the Enterprise Portal (iViews and so on), parts of SAP NetWeaver Process Integration (PI), and all of the objects developed on the Java stack such as Web Dynpros, Enterprise JavaBeans, servlets, und Java Server Pages (JSPs). SAP provided stand-alone solutions through the years for the deployment of these components such as the Software Deployment Manager and later the Change Management Service (CMS). The decisive weak point of these solutions, however, is the lack of coupling to the ABAP world. For dual-stack systems, for example, synchronous distribution of Java changes and the associated changes in the ABAP environment can only be ensured organizationally.

Cross-system synchronization   An additional challenge is posed by cross-system synchronization, such as the coordinated distribution of portal changes and associated (ABAP) changes within SAP ERP Central Component (SAP ECC). Previously, particularly in an SAP NetWeaver BW system with the intent to coordinate ABAP and Java transports, the following were missing:

- Synchronization of both landscapes
- A solution for the automatable transport of portal content
- A consistent user interface for mixed system landscapes
- Tracking of non-ABAP transports using the Change Request Manager

The logical consequence of the new SAP customer requirements for a technical solution for the synchronization of ABAP and Java objects is the creation of an option to integrate both object types into one transport request. Precisely this option is realized within the SAP CTS+ concept.

With the implementation of this concept, the option now exists in the SAP NetWeaver environment to integrate archive files from Java and Web elements into ABAP transport requests. This includes epa files of the Portal Development Studios and sca archives of the SAP NetWeaver Development Infrastructure (NWDI), for example. In this way, ABAP and Java objects can be packed in a shared transport request in dual-stack environments such as SAP NetWeaver PI. This achieves a maximum level of synchronization for these environments.

The enhanced CTS functions are available with Support Package Stack 15 in SAP NetWeaver 7.0 and require an SAP Application Server Java with the same patch level. Even if none of the SAP Solution Manager functions are directly needed, using SAP Solution Manager is recommended because it can be implemented as a central system for the transport management of the entire system landscape.

Objects such as Java-based or J2EE-based components, non-ABAP objects within SAP NetWeaver PI, or even System Landscape Directory (SLD) objects can be transported with ABAP objects in a shared transport request. During the import, the relevant deployment from the system is automatically performed. The Change and Transport System (CTS), which has been known in the ABAP world for many years, is used as the infrastructure. Both the export and the import of these requests is performed technically using the tp.exe SAP tool just as before. The diagram in Figure 9.17 shows a central dual-stack system that is implemented as a TMS system.

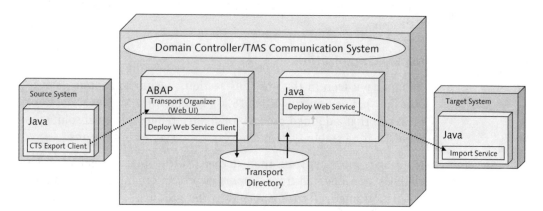

Figure 9.17   CTS+

Third-party
enhancements

If the SAP CTS+ concept now guarantees the optimum synchronicity of ABAP and Java object transport to the same (dual-stack) system, it still does not make any means available to ensure this synchronicity between different components of an SAP environment as well. That is generally ensured organizationally using corresponding processes or solutions from partners such as the TransportManager from Realtech, which has successfully mapped the ABAP world for several years.

TransportManager
5.1

With version 5.1 of the TransportManager, the ABAP world is now extended to include the Java world. The ABAP and/or Java request property, or ABAP and/or Java stack system property, is thereby fully encapsulated. Both are dealt with in absolutely the same way, both visually and administratively. TransportManager 5.1 of course also offers all of the advantages of previous versions, including:

▶ Flexibly configurable workflow scenarios

▶ Expert and technical approval steps for ABAP and Java transports

▶ Automated QA tests

▶ Scheduling of all approved requests

▶ Granular authorization concept

▶ Collision and overtaker checks

▶ Revision-proof tracking and reporting

▶ Support for system copies

Another solution for synchronized transports for ABAP-based and Java-based objects is the Rev-Trac product from Revelation Software Concepts.

9.4.6 Organization

As you have seen in the previous sections, technical support is available for Change Control with CTS, CTS+, and ChaRM. Never overlook, however, that a defined process for change requests is an absolute prerequisite for a stable system landscape and stable applications.

SAP Change
Control

Nothing is more constant than change. At least once a week countless changes are imported from support or project organizations and more or less automatically transported to the product servers. As soon as you are dealing with more complex system landscapes, there is a high risk that something will go wrong. Consistent SAP Change Control supported by tools helps enforce, conduct, and automate the SAP change process to a large extent. A secure auto-deployment for SAP transports for both ABAP and non-ABAP changes throughout system landscapes is within reach for every SAP customer but it is rarely implemented consistently.

This may be because the SAP system, in comparison to some other packaged software systems, is unique in that it offers good options for importing changes throughout system landscapes. In system landscapes and organizations (support, projects) that are not very complex, the SAP utilities for the transport of changes are completely sufficient. SAP allows you to define transport routes throughout systems, submit transport requests for distribution, and install them throughout the system, including certain validation steps.

This sophisticated system has its limits, however. Many things can go wrong when rolling out changes. The fulfillment of compliance regulations cannot be ensured 100% either. Inconsistencies in the system can easily arise. Risks when rolling out changes include the following: **Risks**

▶ Changes are distributed in different transport requests almost in parallel throughout the system's runtime differences in distribution steps, and verification can lead to time-dependent changes being installed in the wrong order.

▶ Changes from different projects can be fundamentally contradictory.

▶ Changes can be carried out manually at the wrong time.

▶ No version or locks are created for customizing changes. An undesired overwrite of customizing can easily occur.

▶ Changes and change sequences, once carried out, cannot be carried out again without additional steps.

You can proactively create remedies for these types of problems with reasonable effort. SAP Change Control with suitable tools and techniques means: **SAP Change Control remedies**

▶ There is always one change request and one approval for all changes to be imported to the system landscape. There are no transports (technical changes) without a change request (organizational change). All changes are documented accordingly.

▶ Packages of changes are compiled into projects and usage areas accordingly so that conflicts can rarely arise during individual transport. The projects thereby have more autonomy when transporting.

▶ Transports and routine tasks are conducted in the proper sequence automatically, including extensive measures to ensure consistency.

▶ Potential errors caused by the overtaking of individual changes during transport or incorrect overwriting are recognized before the distribution and proactively avoided. This also applies to packages with the most varied changes from the most varied SAP and non-SAP systems, such as changed SAP Collaborative Replenishment Planning (CRP) objects, SAP ERP objects, SAP NetWeaver BW objects, customizing settings, Java-based objects, portal configurations, and even many dependencies between changed components.

▶ Entries in the change control documentation are automatically carried out.

▶ Change processes are kept clean.

▶ All changes are carried out securely, and rollback functions are available wherever possible. Changes can be imported again at any time.

▶ A complete audit trail for all changes is available.

Even SAP Change Management does not scale with the system landscape by itself. Experience shows that the consistent implementation of SAP Change Control techniques and tools when distributing changes alone or primarily in the most complex system landscapes can drastically reduce risks and eliminate unnecessary effort and a lot of trouble.

9.5   Maintenance Optimizer

The flexibility of SAP applications results in a considerable increase of included software components that can be user-defined and installed both centrally on a server and in a distributed way on several servers. SAP ERP 2005, for instance, contains more than 50 software components. Professional support is necessary for efficiently managing the resulting combinatorics.

Overview of maintenance activities

Previously, customers selected the maintenance updates that were relevant for them from an unfiltered list of software packages in the SAP

Service Marketplace and started the download. The patches were then imported to the development and quality assurance systems, tested, and finally released for production. These steps are now controlled and managed by SAP Solution Manager, allowing customers to always keep an overview of the maintenance activities of all systems and solutions.

All software packages with corrections for SAP NetWeaver 7.0 and subsequent versions released after April 2, 2007 (including support packages and support package stacks), and all applications based on them (including SAP Business Suite 2005) are now only available via the Maintenance Optimizer in SAP Solution Manager.

The Maintenance Optimizer does not support patches for the operating systems and databases. The support of SAP kernel patches will be available during the course of 2009. Figure 9.18 shows the Maintenance Optimizer options in a system landscape with development systems, test systems, and productive systems.

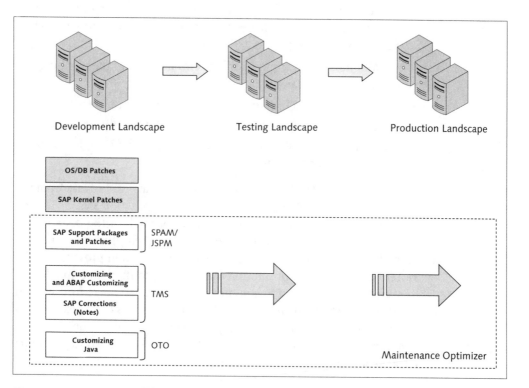

Figure 9.18 Maintenance Optimizer

Optimized Maintenance Process

The Maintenance Optimizer offers a complete and thorough process for software maintenance within SAP Solution Manager:

1. The Maintenance Optimizer shows the relevant maintenance updates for the customer solution.
2. The customer selects the desired packages and approves the download of the updates.
3. The customer downloads the software.
4. The customer imports the software (this is done using the SPAM, SAINT, and other tools just as before).
5. The customer completes the maintenance transaction.

Advantages The Maintenance Optimizer offers you the following advantages:

▶ The uninterrupted software maintenance process increases transparency and enables better traceability of software changes.

▶ The standardization of the support processes is a prerequisite for the preparation for future challenges for support organizations, such as the support of service-oriented architectures.

▶ The Maintenance Optimizer offers central access to the planning and download of software updates.

▶ The Maintenance Optimizer leads to a simplification of software maintenance for your support team and therefore also reduces costs.

▶ SAP Solution Manager enables monitoring of the complete maintenance process of the entire SAP solution.

The Maintenance Optimizer draws its system data exclusively from the system landscape of SAP Solution Manager (Transaction SMSY). During maintenance transactions, it takes into account all of the instances of the product version assigned to the waiting system that are marked as relevant. The data sources for the system information provided in the system landscape by SAP Solution Manager are configurable and dependent upon the system type, among other things. To make information about Java systems available in SAP Solution Manager, for example, a connection to the System Landscape Directory (SLD) is required. Each component of an instance of a product version is assigned to a support package level.

9.6   SAP NetWeaver BW Accelerator Revisions

Whereas SAP NetWeaver BW follows the NetWeaver support package stack (SPS) strategy, independent revisions with coding enhancements and corrections are issued for the SAP NetWeaver BW Accelerator. The support packages and the revisions are normally made available at the same time. There may be deviations, however. SAP guarantees compatibility between a specific support package (SP) and a specific revision of SAP NetWeaver BW Accelerator.

SAP NetWeaver BW Accelerator possesses upward compatibility. This means that the revision of SAP NetWeaver BW Accelerator can be higher than the one specified for the current SAP NetWeaver BW support package. There is no downward compatibility, however. If the revision is lower, it can lead to problems. This problem primarily occurs after importing a new support package for SAP NetWeaver BW if a revision has not yet been updated.

A check is provided to see whether the SP available on the system and the revision of SAP NetWeaver BW Accelerator are compatible. If this is not the case, the system generates a warning. This check is built into both the indexing process for SAP NetWeaver BW Accelerator as well as the SAP NetWeaver BW Accelerator monitor.

Compatibility check

9.7   System Copies

An administrator activity that does not occur every day but is typical is setting up the SAP NetWeaver BW systems. We will not discuss the actual system installation at this point, however. First, it would go beyond the scope of this book (and, from our viewpoint, does not fit with the subject of administration and monitoring), and second, this activity is described in detail in the installation guides on the basis of the most recent information and dependencies.

The activities involved in a system copy behave differently. It is regularly necessary to either test a nonproduction system landscape, to create one for quality assurance or other purposes (meaning copying production systems to nonproduction systems), or to copy a production landscape to a new production landscape to change some properties of the systems such as the hardware, the operating system, or the database (meaning copying production systems to production systems).

This section will therefore discuss the particularities of a system copy of an SAP NetWeaver BW system using the example of a nonproduction copy (such as setting up a test system) and explain the final measures in the target system.

Preparations and copy process No SAP NetWeaver BW–specific preparations or special tasks are necessary in the copy process of the example scenario of a system copy to a nonproduction system. The customary procedure for a system copy is described in the "SAP System Landscape Copy for SAP NetWeaver and mySAP Solutions" SAP Best Practices document that is available in the SAP Service Marketplace.

Final measures To prevent an unintended start of the processes in the target system, set the number of background process to 0 in the SAP profile of the target SAP NetWeaver BW system before restarting the system, so that none of the scheduled processes can be carried out in the copied system.

9.7.1 Deleting Source System Assignments in the Target SAP NetWeaver BW System after Copying

Right after the copy process, a connection exists between the target SAP NetWeaver BW system and the source systems of the original SAP NetWeaver BW system. Delete the source system connections of the target SAP NetWeaver BW system without changing the source system connections in the original SAP source system.

In the target SAP NetWeaver BW system, change the content of the field for the target host in all RFC destinations for the SAP source systems to a nonexistent address (Transaction SM59). This step is very important because otherwise the original source system will be changed.

Delete all SAP source systems of the SAP NetWeaver BW system in the tree for the source systems in Transaction RSA1. This step deletes all transfer rules and PSA tables of these source systems, and the data is lost. Because the host of the RFC connection was deleted, the system generates a message stating that no access to the source system is possible, but you can ignore this message. Delete all (now obsolete) RFC destinations that refer to the original environment.

9.7.2 Renaming the Target SAP NetWeaver BW System and Conversion of Logical System Names

If you want to rename the copied system, start Transaction BDLS to carry out the change of the logical system name in all application tables (Figure 9.19). You can perform further activities (such as executing the Data Warehousing Workbench in Transaction RSA1) during the conversion.

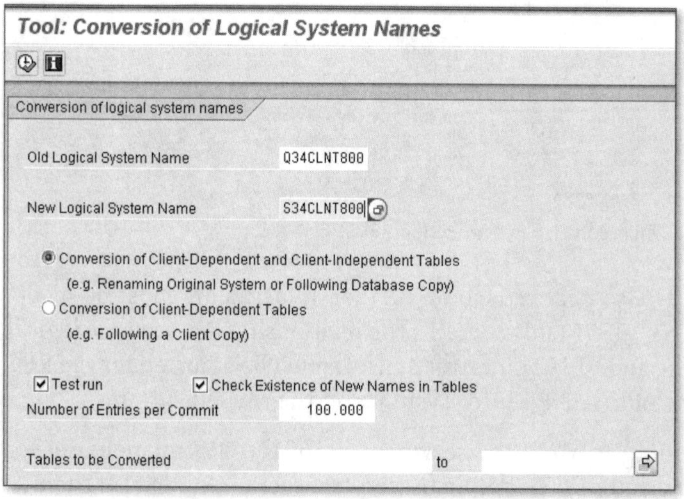

Figure 9.19 Conversion of Logical System Names

Typical applications for a Conversion of Client-Independent and Client-Independent Tables are renaming the logical system or creating a new system by database copy. A conversion of client-dependent tables is typically carried out for a Conversion of the logical System Name Following a Client Copy.

Types of conversion

It is recommended that you start the conversion in test mode first. If you select the Test Run checkbox, first, all relevant tables are analyzed and the number of entries to be converted is determined. These are then output as a list. If the Check Existence of New Names in Tables checkbox is selected, a check will be conducted to see if the new logical system name is already present in application tables. If it is, a warning is output in the results list. Tables in which the logical system name was found must be checked (to see if a conversion is desirable for these entries), and the conversion may have to be terminated.

9.7.3 Executing SAP NetWeaver BW–Specific Adjustments

When you set up the system copy, the logical system name is also generally changed. Therefore, reset the generation flag for the RSDRO_ACTIVATE, RSDRO_EXTRACT, and RSDRO_UPDATE DSO activation programs in Transaction RSSGPCLA (Figure 9.20).

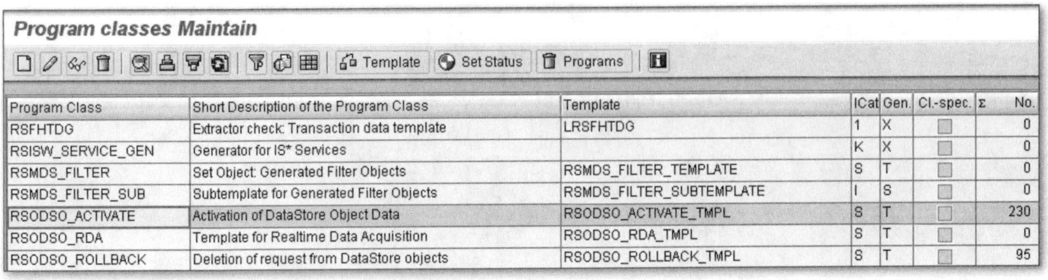

Program classes Maintain

Program Class	Short Description of the Program Class	Template	ICat	Gen.	Cl.-spec.	Σ	No.
RSFHTDG	Extractor check: Transaction data template	LRSFHTDG	1	X	☐		0
RSISW_SERVICE_GEN	Generator for IS* Services		K	X	☐		0
RSMDS_FILTER	Set Object: Generated Filter Objects	RSMDS_FILTER_TEMPLATE	S	T	☐		0
RSMDS_FILTER_SUB	Subtemplate for Generated Filter Objects	RSMDS_FILTER_SUBTEMPLATE	I	S	☐		0
RSODSO_ACTIVATE	Activation of DataStore Object Data	RSODSO_ACTIVATE_TMPL	S	T	☐		230
RSODSO_RDA	Template for Realtime Data Acquisition	RSODSO_RDA_TMPL	S	T	☐		0
RSODSO_ROLLBACK	Deletion of request from DataStore objects	RSODSO_ROLLBACK_TMPL	S	T	☐		95

Figure 9.20 Generation Flag in Transaction RSSGPCLA

Further adjustments

If the host is also changed, some further adjustments must be made. The RSLOGSYSDEST table contains the relationship between the logical system name and the RFC destinations. It must be adjusted for the RFC destinations of the SAP source system and the MySelf system.

If BW planning is used, the server name of the BW enqueue server must be adjusted in the administration transaction RSPLSE. If the BW enqueue server is not adjusted, a termination with the message "RFC connection error" may occur when calling the ready-for-input queries or planning functions because local tables are also copied during the system copy, such as the RSPLS_LOCK_METHS table that contains the host names for storing the lock table of the BW lock server.

The RFC destination must then be reset for the postprocessing of the process chain transport as well. Correct the host using Transaction RSTPRFC.

The BI Administration Cockpit provides a central point of entry for monitoring an SAP NetWeaver BW system landscape and offers cockpits and dashboards that deliver monitors and runtime statistics, for example, for loading processes and reporting. This chapter describes the installation of the technical content and the options provided by the BI Administration Cockpit.

10 Technical Content and BI Administration Cockpit

The BI Administration Cockpit that is based on technical content is an enhancement of SAP NetWeaver BW 7.0 that is definitely useful for administrators. They can use it to monitor the performance of not just one SAP NetWeaver BW system, but all SAP NetWeaver BW systems in a system landscape (Figure 10.1).

The technical content is used for analyzing the system load caused by load and reporting processes. Data is provided with the objects of the technical content in queries and Web templates based on the SAP NetWeaver BW statistics that they use can set depending on the required level. Moreover, users are provided with a business package for defining the cockpit in the portal.

Analyzing the system load

Because the cockpit itself is only a combination of delivered queries and Web templates, you can enhance this portal application according to your own requirements. Depending on the requirements and the system landscape, it can be useful to define your own combination of reports and forego the access via the portal despite the benefits.

The technical content consists of the extractors and DataSources to extract data from the statistics tables and of the SAP NetWeaver BW objects, such as InfoCubes and queries.

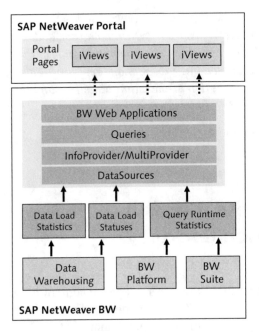

Figure 10.1 Architecture of the BI Administration Cockpit

Unfortunately, all data flows and the reporting objects were implemented using SAP NetWeaver BW 3.x means and tools—understandable only for reporting to avoid the necessity of a BI Java installation.

You use MultiProviders to analyze statistics data. These MultiProviders are based on a basic InfoCube for the analysis of historic data and a virtual InfoCube for direct access to the RSDDSTAT_OLAP and RSDDSTAT_DM views, for instance.

10.1 Updating Statistics Data

Settings for updating statistics are made and checked in Transaction RSDDSTAT (Figure 10.2). In this transaction you can determine objects in the system for which runtime statistics are to be recorded. Queries, InfoProviders, Web templates, and workbooks are available for selection.

| Query | InfoProvider | Web Template | Workbook |

Replace Values | Settings: | X On | 2 All

Query Name	InfoProvider	Author	Last Changed	Statis	OLA	Chan
0TCT_MON_03	0BWTC_C07	23010997	2000.01.18 13:54:1	X	2	☐
0BWTC_C08_Q105	0BWTC_C08	23010997	2000.06.06 10:57:4	X	2	☐
0BWTC_C08_Q106	0BWTC_C08	23010997	2000.06.06 10:58:2	X	2	☐
0BWTC_C08_Q107	0BWTC_C08	23010997	2000.06.06 10:58:5	X	2	☐
0BWTC_C08_Q108	0BWTC_C08	23055213	2000.06.06 10:59:3	X	2	☐
0BWTC_C08_Q109	0BWTC_C08	23010997	2000.06.06 11:00:1	X	2	☐
0BWTC_C08_Q100	0BWTC_C08	23010997	2000.06.06 10:45:2	X	2	☐
0BWTC_C08_Q110	0BWTC_C08	23010997	2000.06.06 11:05:2	X	2	☐
0BWTC_C08_Q101	0BWTC_C08	23010997	2000.06.06 10:53:4	X	2	☐
0BWTC_C08_Q102	0BWTC_C08	23010997	2000.06.06 10:55:3	X	2	☐
0BWTC_C08_Q103	0BWTC_C08	23010997	2000.06.06 10:56:0	X	2	☐
0BWTC_C08_Q104	0BWTC_C08	23054257	2000.06.06 10:56:5	X	2	☐
Z_STATISTICS_0BWTCC10	0BWTC_C10	23010997	2006.01.27 13:17:1	X	2	☐
0BWTC_C10_Q012	0BWTC_C10	23010997	2000.05.11 13:35:0	X	2	☐
0BWTC_C10_Q023	0BWTC_C10	23010997	2002.02.20 13:01:0	X	2	☐
0BWTC_C10_Q017	0BWTC_C10	23010997	2002.02.20 13:01:0	X	2	☐
0BWTC_C10_Q313	0BWTC_C10	23010997	2000.05.11 16:44:4	X	2	☐
0BWTC_C10_Q013	0BWTC_C10	23010997	2000.05.12 14:19:1	X	2	☐
0BWTC_C10_Q018	0BWTC_C10	23010997	2000.05.11 13:44:2	X	2	☐
0BWTC_C10_Q020	0BWTC_C10	23010997	2000.05.11 13:45:4	X	2	☐
0BWTC_C10_Q402	0BWTC_C10	23010997	2001.06.29 08:54:3	X	2	☐
0BWTC_C10_Q507	0BWTC_C10	23010997	2000.11.23 14:53:0	X	2	☐

Figure 10.2 Configuring the Statistics Data in Transaction RSDDSTAT

Note that by default the statistics setting is set to X (statistics on) and the detail level to 2 (all). If logging of performance statistic is not required for certain objects, deactivate them in the transaction to prevent an unnecessary data load during analyses and when you save the statistics data.

Depending on the (user-defined) detail statistics level, the system writes between 20 and 80 data records per navigation step to the SAP NetWeaver BW statistics tables. Therefore, it is mandatory to load the statistical query data to the technical content (InfoCube 0TCT_C01 to 0TCT_C03) and to delete the original data from the SAP NetWeaver BW statistics tables.

10.2 Installing the Technical Content

The objects of the technical content that are required for the analysis of runtime and status information are not provided in active mode.

Activating the new technical content in SAP NetWeaver BW

A corresponding program for an automatic installation is available in the Implementation Guide under SPRO • SAP NETWEAVER • BUSINESS INTELLIGENCE • SETTINGS FOR BI CONTENT • BUSINESS INTELLIGENCE • BI ADMINISTRATION COCKPIT • ACTIVATE TECHNICAL CONTENT IN SAP NETWEAVER BI. With this activity, you call Transaction RSTCC_INST_BIAC or Report RSTCC_ACTIVATE_ADMIN_COCKPIT, which perform the following steps, among other things:

▶ Activate the mySelf source system

▶ Activate and replicate DataSources of the technical content in the mySelf source system

▶ Activate the technical content in the SAP NetWeaver BW system (role SAP_BW_BI_ADMINISTRATOREN and all associated objects)

Because objects of the technical content have been changed in many projects, the retransfer of these objects results in various conflicts that necessitate a reconciliation with the active versions — particularly because objects like the 0TCTUSERNM InfoObject are also used in other areas of business content. Here, you must decide for the various properties whether you want to use the provided content version or the active version of the changed object.

Also note that the technical content involves hundreds of objects whose automatic activation can be very difficult in a grown system environment, so you might prefer a manual activation. Initially transfer the necessary objects for the individual InfoProviders of the technical content. Only after a successful activation should you transfer the previous and subsequent objects in the data flow. If all objects are available in the system, the system assigns the SAP_BW_BI_ADMINISTRATOR role to the SAP NetWeaver BW administrators (users) for the access authorization in Transaction SU01.

10.2.1 Scheduling Process Chains

Process chains of the technical content (0TCT*) must be scheduled in Transaction RSPC: init process chains once, delta process chains regularly, for instance, daily. Table 10.1 lists the process chains that are relevant for the technical content and thus for the BI Administration Cockpit.

Process Chain	Content
0TCT_MD_C_FULL_P01	Content master data such as texts and attributes for Web templates, process types, and open hub destinations
0TCT_MD_S_FULL_P01	System master data such as BW object types
0TCT_C2_DELTA_P01 and 0TCT_C2_INIT_P01	Statistics on data transfer processes (DTPs), InfoPackages, and processes
0TCT_C0_DELTA_P01 and 0TCT_C0_INIT_P01	Statistics on the frontend/OLAP and Data Manager

Table 10.1 Process Chains

The extractors for the master data of the SAP content, for instance, for the attributes of Web templates, and for the system master data are not delta-capable; therefore, you only require one process chain with the load processes in full mode.

10.2.2 Activating the Direct Access for Virtual Providers

The source system must be assigned to all virtual InfoProviders (0TCT_VC*). This is done using the Activate Direct Access command in the context menu of the target structure, in this case the virtual InfoProvider (Figure 10.3).

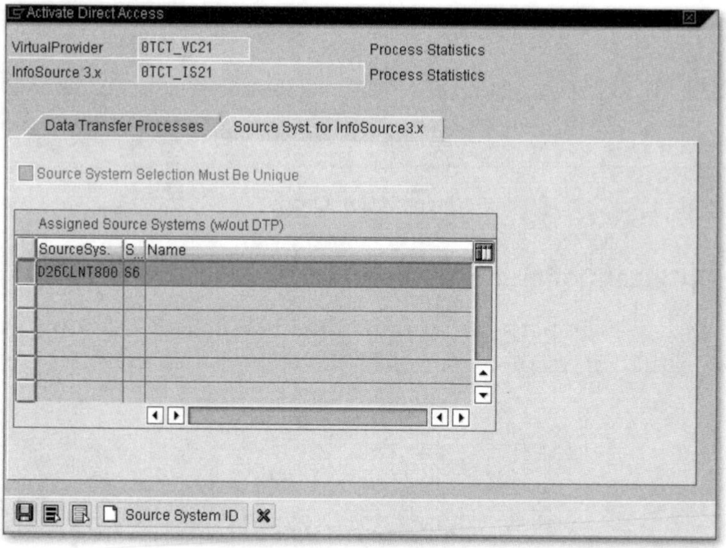

Figure 10.3 Direct Access for Virtual InfoProviders

Here, you specify whether only data of the mySelf system is supposed to be read or whether additional SAP NetWeaver BW systems are supposed to be connected.

10.2.3 BI Administration Business Package

In the SAP Service Marketplace under *http://service.sap.com/swdc* you can download the Business Package BI Administration 1.0 and import it to SAP NetWeaver Portal 7.0. You must assign the portal roles, system administrator and BW administrator, to the administrators. Another prerequisite is that the portal was assigned in the customizing of the BI Administration Cockpit.

Setting up the call from SAP GUI | Moreover, you should set up the call of the BI Administration Cockpit from SAP GUI, for instance, from the Data Warehousing Workbench (Figure 10.4). You can make the corresponding configuration in the Implementation Guide under SPRO • SAP NetWeaver • Business Intelligence • General BI Settings • Settings for BI Administration Cockpit.

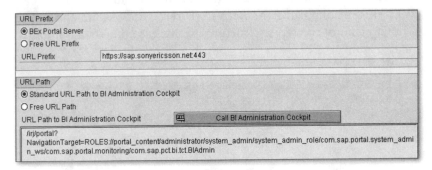

Figure 10.4 URL For Calling the BI Administration Cockpit

10.2.4 Optional Definition of Importance

You can assign an importance to individual BW objects that can be included in the analysis for queries of the technical content (Figure 10.5).

Figure 10.6 shows that you can assign an importance to various objects, for instance, to InfoProviders or process chains, to display a ranking in evaluations or to exclude specific objects with low importance in a report display. Based on this setting, the 0TCTIMPRTNC attribute for the 0TCTBWOBJCT InfoObject is filled when the statistics data records are loaded.

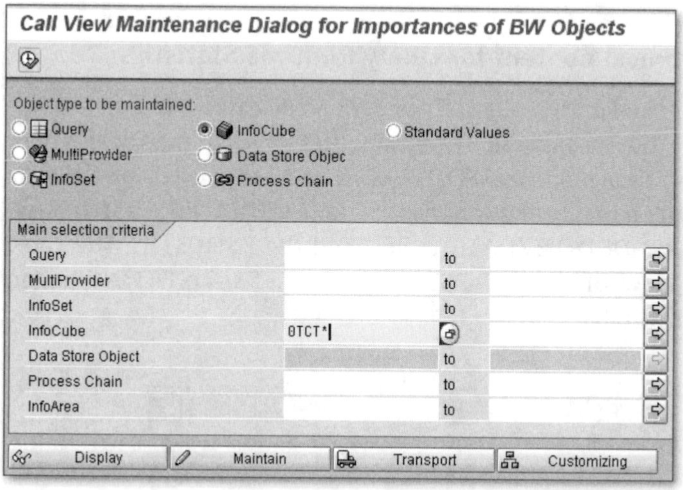

Ranking

Call View Maintenance Dialog for Importances of BW Objects

Object type to be maintained:
- Query
- MultiProvider
- InfoSet
- InfoCube
- Data Store Objec
- Process Chain
- Standard Values

Main selection criteria

Query		to	
MultiProvider		to	
InfoSet		to	
InfoCube	0TCT*		
Data Store Object		to	
Process Chain		to	
InfoArea		to	

Display   Maintain   Transport   Customizing

Figure 10.5 Object Selection for Setting the Importance

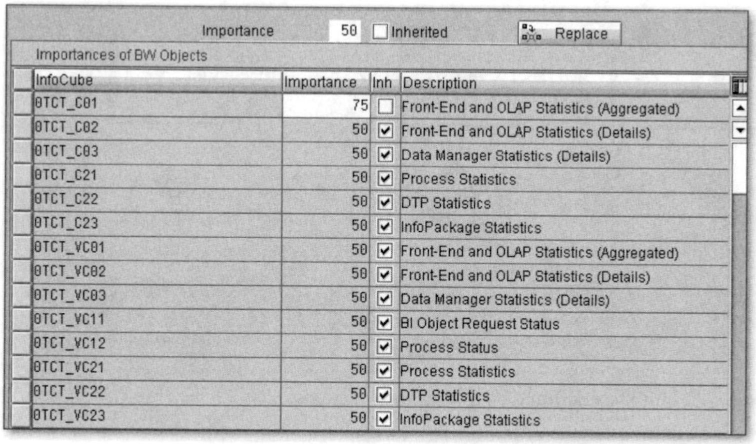

Importance 50 ☐ Inherited   Replace
Importances of BW Objects

InfoCube	Importance	Inh	Description
0TCT_C01	75	☐	Front-End and OLAP Statistics (Aggregated)
0TCT_C02	50	☑	Front-End and OLAP Statistics (Details)
0TCT_C03	50	☑	Data Manager Statistics (Details)
0TCT_C21	50	☑	Process Statistics
0TCT_C22	50	☑	DTP Statistics
0TCT_C23	50	☑	InfoPackage Statistics
0TCT_VC01	50	☑	Front-End and OLAP Statistics (Aggregated)
0TCT_VC02	50	☑	Front-End and OLAP Statistics (Details)
0TCT_VC03	50	☑	Data Manager Statistics (Details)
0TCT_VC11	50	☑	BI Object Request Status
0TCT_VC12	50	☑	Process Status
0TCT_VC21	50	☑	Process Statistics
0TCT_VC22	50	☑	DTP Statistics
0TCT_VC23	50	☑	InfoPackage Statistics

Figure 10.6 Importance of Objects

339

10.3   Runtimes of Queries

The reports of the BI Administration Cockpit provide detailed information about runtimes of executed SAP NetWeaver BW applications (including web templates and workbooks) and the SAP NetWeaver BW application objects used (including primarily queries, but also Web items, query views, and planning functions).

10.3.1   Technical Content for Query Runtime Statistics

The data for the runtime analysis of SAP NetWeaver BW applications (for example, queries) is read by the statistics tables of the OLAP server or the Data Manager. The RSDDSTAT_OLAP table used for the data extraction presents a view of the RSDDSTATHEADER, RSDDSTATINFO, and RSDDSTATEVDATA tables, and the RSDDSTAT_DM table presents a view of the RSDDSTATHEADER, RSDDSTATINFO, and RSDDSTATDM tables.

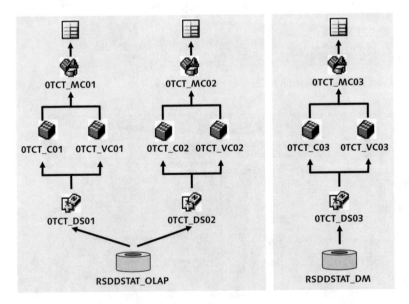

Figure 10.7   Data Flow of the Query Runtime Statistics

Figure 10.7 shows the appropriate data flow via the DataSources, 0TCT_DS01, 0TCT_DS02, and 0TCT_DS03. MultiProviders combine one basic InfoCube for already extracted data and one virtual InfoCube for the direct access to data that has not been extracted yet; for example, you can use the 0TCT_MC01 MultiProvider to evaluate data of the Info-Cubes 0TCT_C01 and 0TCT_VC01 (direct access).

Because the statistics on query runtimes are updated in more detailed tables in SAP NetWeaver BW 7.0, some InfoCubes of the old technical content are now obsolete and cannot be used for the evaluations of new statistics data:

Technical Content in the old SAP NetWeaver BW 3.x model

- ▶ **InfoCube 0BWTC_C03 (details on navigations)**
  The data is still updated, but you should use the new InfoCube 0TCT_C02 for full analysis options.

- ▶ **InfoCube 0BWTC_C02 (WHM)**
  The data is still updated, but you should use the new InfoCube 0TCT_C23 for full analysis options.

- ▶ **InfoCube 0BWTC_C02 (OLAP)**
  The data is no longer updated, because the InfoCubes 0TCT_C01, 0TCT_C02, and 0TCT_C03 are not available.

You cannot migrate old statistics to the new InfoCubes, but you can still evaluate statistics that have been created before the upgrade with these InfoCubes.

10.3.2 Query Execution

To analyze query runtimes, you need to understand the data and object accesses: Which objects are accessed? How do you parallelize? You can use multiple application objects (queries) in an application (Web template). A query, in turn, generally reads the data from a MultiProvider that combines data from multiple InfoProviders (for instance, InfoCubes). Moreover, the system may access aggregates or an SAP NetWeaver BW Accelerator index in case of InfoCubes.

The system can also subdivide a query for an individual InfoCube into subqueries. If a subdivision results in multiple subqueries, for instance, owing to cells with constant selection or in case of complex selections with hierarchy conditions, the read operation is executed in parallel by default. The maximum level of parallelism determines the maximum number of work processes for each query. By default, this value is 6; however, you can change this maximum value by entering a value between 1 and 100 in the QUERY_MAX_WP_DIAG entry in the RSAD-

Subqueries

MIN table. The actual level of parallel execution depends on the current system load and is between 1 (sequential execution) and the maximum value.

Example The results of all subqueries are collected at a synchronization point and combined in an overall result. In the example shown in Figure 10.8, the system executes a Web template to query data via two queries. Query 1 uses the definition of a MultiProvider to read data from an aggregate, a DataStore object, and an SAP NetWeaver BW Accelerator index in parallel.

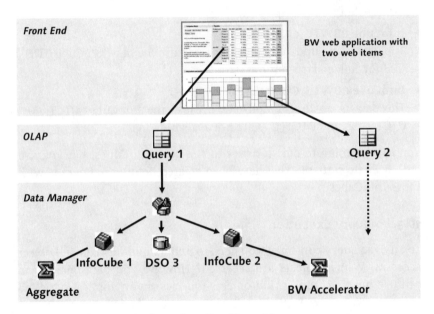

Figure 10.8 Objects in the Query Execution (Example)

Figure 10.9 shows the execution time of query 1 (more precisely, of step 1, for instance, the first call of the query) within a user session.

As shown in the diagram, the two queries are executed in parallel in the first execution step. The execution of query 1 mostly includes runtimes within the Data Manager (reading of data) and times for the OLAP processor, cache, and master data. The access to the actual data in InfoCube 1 (an aggregate is read), InfoCube 2 (SAP NetWeaver BW Accelerator is accessed), and DSO 3 is implemented in parallel in the Data Manager.

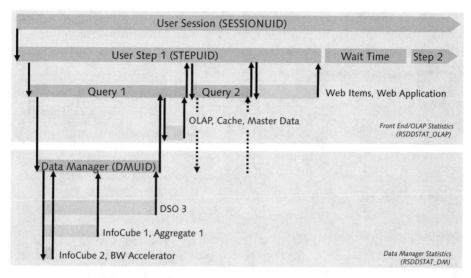

Figure 10.9 Parallelized Query Execution (Example)

10.3.3 Details of Statistics Information

If a query is processed, statistics on the individual events are written as the basis of a complete runtime analysis. Table 10.2 shows some selected statistics events. The complete list of all events used is available in the RSDDSTATEVENTS table.

Event	Description
1	Wait time of the user
2525	Counts the read accesses to the cache
3130	Customer exit for virtual key figures and characteristics
3200	OLAP: data transfer to the frontend
3500	OLAP initialization
4600	Filling the authorization buffer
9000	Data Manager event
9010	Total number of transported records (DBTRANS)
9011	Total number of read records (DBSEL)

Statistics events

Table 10.2 Event IDs for Query Statistics

The concept of these events can be briefly described based on a simple example. You can directly display the runtime statistics in test Trans-

Example

343

action RSRT, for example. Figure 10.10 shows the execution of a query that reads data of multiple InfoCubes via a MultiProvider.

Ste	Ste	User Name	Start Time	Handle ID	Handle T	InfoProvider	Object Name	D	Eve	Event Text	Duration	Counter	Eve
BEX3	1	23010997	2009-09-28 13:59:		DFLT			2		Not Assigned	0,000000	0	1
BEX3	1	23010997	2009-09-28 13:59:	1	BRFC		RRX_SESSIC	2	1000	RFC call	0,000000	0	1
BEX3	1	23010997	2009-09-28 13:59:	2	BRFC		RRX_REPOF	2	1000	RFC call	0,000000	0	1
BEX3	1	23010997	2009-09-28 13:59:	1	OLAP	ZSO_MC004	ZSO_MC004.	2	3010	OLAP: Query	0,515000	0	1
BEX3	1	23010997	2009-09-28 13:59:	1	OLAP	ZSO_MC004	ZSO_MC004.	2	3999	OLAP Other T	0,485000	0	15
BEX3	1	23010997	2009-09-28 13:59:	1	OLAP	ZSO_MC004	ZSO_MC004.	2	1995	3.x Query Viev	0,016000	0	2
BEX3	1	23010997	2009-09-28 13:59:	1	OLAP	ZSO_MC004	ZSO_MC004.	2	1990	3.x Analyzer S	0,015000	120	2
BEX3	1	23010997	2009-09-28 13:59:	1	OLAP	ZSO_MC004	ZSO_MC004.	2	4600	Authorization	0,110000	0	5
BEX3	1	23010997	2009-09-28 13:59:	1	OLAP	ZSO_MC004	ZSO_MC004.	2	4300	Value Authori:	0,000000	0	13
BEX3	1	23010997	2009-09-28 13:59:	1	OLAP	ZSO_MC004	ZSO_MC004.	2	3510	OLAP: EXIT V	0,000000	0	3
BEX3	1	23010997	2009-09-28 13:59:	1	OLAP	ZSO_MC004	ZSO_MC004.	2	4400	Node Authori:	0,000000	0	1
BEX3	1	23010997	2009-09-28 13:59:	1	OLAP	ZSO_MC004	ZSO_MC004.	2	3500	OLAP Initializ	0,485000	0	20
BEX3	1	23010997	2009-09-28 13:59:	1	OLAP	ZSO_MC004	ZSO_MC004.	2	3000	OLAP: Setting	0,327000	0	11
BEX3	1	23010997	2009-09-28 13:59:	1	OLAP	ZSO_MC004	ZSO_MC004.	2	2500	Cache Gener	0,000000	0	6
BEX3	1	23010997	2009-09-28 13:59:	1	OLAP	ZSO_MC004	ZSO_MC004.	2	9000	Data Manage	1,938000	0	9
BEX3	1	23010997	2009-09-28 13:59:	1	OLAP	ZSO_MC004	ZSO_MC004.	2	9010	Total DBTRAI	0,000000	79	1
BEX3	1	23010997	2009-09-28 13:59:	1	OLAP	ZSO_MC004	ZSO_MC004.	2	9011	Total DBSEL	0,000000	400.955	1
BEX3	1	23010997	2009-09-28 13:59:	1	OLAP	ZSO_MC004	ZSO_MC004.	2	3110	OLAP: Data S	0,015000	0	1

Figure 10.10 Example of a Query Execution in Transaction RSRT

Frontend/Calculation Layer

In the Frontend/Calculation Layer tab, the system displays all statistics details for the selected query. The query is executed after some preparatory steps, for example, initialization of the OLAP server and filling the authorization buffer for the current user. You don't need to take the indicated user wait time of 2.7 seconds into account because this is a selection screen for the ready-for-input variables of the query. The Data Manager time is interesting and is only 0.84 seconds thanks to the available SAP NetWeaver BW Accelerator index even though more than 500,000 data records were read. The specifications DBTRANS and DBSEL, respectively, indicate how many data records were relevant for determining the result and were therefore read by the database and how many data records were actually transferred as a result.

Aggregation layer

Information on the Aggregation Layer tab can help you understand the behavior when MultiProviders are used. In this example, nine basis providers are addressed via a MultiProvider for which the system displays information, such as the number of data records that are read. The aggregates and SAP NetWeaver BW Accelerator indexes (in this example for two InfoProviders) are also available in this view. To describe the updated information that is then available for analysis, Table 10.3

contains the most essential information in the InfoProviders (characteristics and key figures).

InfoObject	Description
0TCTSYSID	SAP NetWeaver BW system
0TCTUSERNM	User
0TCTSESUID	Frontend session
0TCTBIOBJCT	BI application
0TCTBIOTYPE	Type of the BI application
0TCTBISBOBJ	BI application object
0TCTBISOTYP	Type of the BI application object
0TCTSTEPUID	Query (navigation) step
0TCTIFPROV	InfoProvider used
0TCTHANDLID	Handle ID, OLAP statistics
0TCTSTEPTP	Step type, OLAP statistics
0TCTSTEPCNT	Number of steps in the query execution
0TCTWTCOUNT	Counter for BI applications
0TCTSTATLEV	Detail level, OLAP statistics
0TCTSTATEVT	Event ID, for example, Data Manager
0TCTQUCOUNT	Counter for BI application objects
0TCTRTIMEC	Runtime category
0TCTDBSEL	Selected database records
0TCTDBTRANS	Number of transferred data records
0TCTTIMEALL	Total time
0TCTTIMSTMP	UTC time stamp

Table 10.3 InfoObjects of the Query Statistics

10.4 Data Load Status

In the area of statistics on the data load status, you can display execution and request statuses of processes, process chains, InfoProviders, and BW objects for a selected SAP NetWeaver BW system.

Figure 10.11 shows a real-life example of the evaluation of process chain runtimes. An initial overview shows the historic view of the runtimes and the number of executions of the selected process chains. Via the context menu, you can obtain additional information, for instance, status values of process chains in specific calendar weeks.

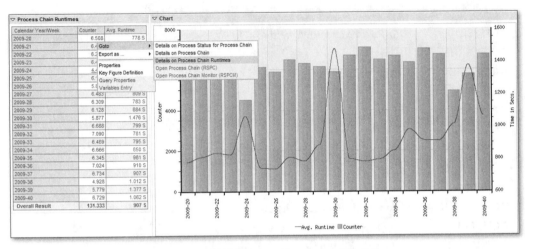

Figure 10.11 Example of Customer-Specific Load Statistics

The following diagrams show the data flow from the status and statistics tables of the technical content to the MultiProviders that are available for reporting. As you can see in Figure 10.12, both direct access to current data and access to data that has already been extracted from the statistics tables is enabled for process statistics. For these analyses, queries are generally defined for comprehensive MultiProviders. In principle, you should implement filtering for the basic InfoCube when you analyze historic developments, to prevent a direct access putting unnecessary load on the performance.

Evaluations of the status of objects and processes are always performed with direct access to the current data; therefore, no basic InfoCubes are provided in the appropriate load flows for saving historic data (see Figure 10.13).

For example, you can use the statistics for determining the status of processes and process chains or the number of erroneous requests and data records.

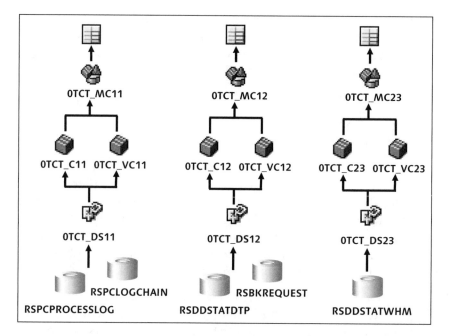

Figure 10.12 Data Flow for Process Statistics

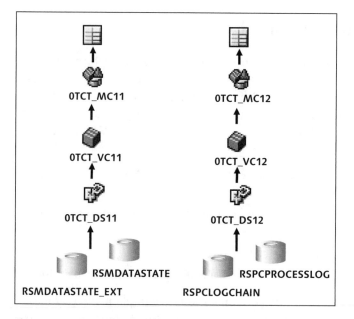

Figure 10.13 Data Flow for Object and Process Status

SAP NetWeaver
BW processes

You can monitor the execution status, the start date, and the start time of SAP NetWeaver BW processes and process chains for a selected process type. The status is highlighted in color. The meaning of the colors is as follows:

- Green: completed successfully
- Yellow: active
- Red: terminated with errors

BW objects

The status of requests and entries for InfoCubes, DataStore objects, and master data can be monitored for selected BW systems. Here, the goal can be to determine objects that have a negative impact on the system performance. You can have the system display the number of requests or data records that are not compressed, aggregated, or activated. Moreover, you are provided with the technical name of the object, the number of erroneous requests or records, and so on.

InfoProvider

You can monitor the statuses of requests and entries for InfoProviders. The system displays detailed information on the correctness of Info-Cubes, on filling aggregates, on the correctness of DataStore objects, and on activating DataStore objects.

10.5 Data Load Statistics

To support the analysis and optimization of system performance, you can compare runtime details of various operations and display deviations of average times. In this context operations include process chains, processes, InfoPackages, and data transfer processes. If you use the BI Administration Cockpit in the portal, several iViews are available for the data load statistics:

- Short-term trends in the total runtimes of SAP NetWeaver BW operations
- Long-term trends in the total runtimes of SAP NetWeaver BW operations
- Total runtimes of SAP NetWeaver BW operations
- Deviations in the total runtimes of SAP NetWeaver BW operations

Detailed analyses of individual operations are implemented by means of the report-report interfaces (RRIs). In addition to more information, such as the average last duration or the deviation, you can use the RRI functions to directly navigate to transactions in the SAP NetWeaver BW system.

Statistics information is determined using the DataSources 0TCT_DS21 (Process Chain Statistics), 0TCT_DS22 (DTP Statistics), and 0TCT_DS23 (InfoPackage Statistics). The Statistics of Process Chain Transaction Data DataSource (0TCT_DS21) provides details on all process chains that have been executed successfully in the system. This process chains have the status green or completed. The data is provided for the analysis in the 0TCT_C21 and 0TCT_V21 InfoProviders. Table 10.4 lists the information available in the InfoProviders.

Process chain statistics

InfoObject	Description
0CALDAY	Calendar day
0CALMONTH	Calendar year/month
0CALQUARTER	Calendar year/quarter
0CALWEEK	Calendar year/week
0CALYEAR	Calendar year
0CHNGID	Change ID
0RECORDTP	Record type
0REQUID	Request ID
0TCTDURTION	Duration
0TCTENDDAT	End date
0TCTENDTIM	End time
0TCTENDTST	End time stamp
0TCTINSTSID	Process instance (SID)
0TCTOBJVERS	Object version
0TCTPCLOGID	Log ID of the process chain
0TCTPRCSCHN	ID of the process chain
0TCTPRCSTYP	Process type
0TCTPRCSVAR	Process variant
0TCTSTAUIK	Frequency
0TCTSTIMEK	Start time
0TCTSTRTDAT	Start date
0TCTSTRTTIM	Start time

Table 10.4 InfoObjects of the Load Statistics

InfoObject	Description
0TCTSTRTTST	Start time stamp
0TCTSYSID	SAP NetWeaver BW system
0TCTTARGET	Target object
0TCTTIMSTMP	UTC time stamp
0WEEKDAY1	Week days

Table 10.4   InfoObjects of the Load Statistics (Cont.)

The DataSource contains the function module extractor, RSDDK_ BIW_GET_DATA. This function module processes deltas internally. The RSDDSTATEXTRACT DB table saves the delta pointer for each executed DataSource. During the next delta extraction, the delta pointer is extracted from this table, and the corresponding delta data is extracted from the RSPCLOGCHAIN and RSPCPROCESSLOG tables.

All of the fields specified in the previous list are directly extracted from the RSPCLOGCHAIN and RSPCPROCESSLOG tables except for SYSID, DURATION, STAUIK, and TIMEK. SYSID is derived in the function module via an object; DURATION is calculated via the fields ENDTIMESTAMP and STARTTIMESTAMP. STAUIK is constantly set to 1 — except for the summary rows where this value is calculated using another formula. TIMEK is the start time that is calculated using the STARTTIMESTAMP field. Only successfully executed process chains are selected.

DTP statistics   The Transaction Data of the DTP Statistics DataSource (0TCT_DS22) provides details on the data transfer processes that have been executed individually as separate processes and as part of the process chain. The fields of the DataSource are listed in the extract structure. If the data transfer process is executed in a process chain, the CHAIN_ID and LOG_ID fields either contain data or they are initial. The summary record is an important function of the DataSource. The DataSource provides two different types of summary records for every DTP for a specific instance:

▶ Summary record for a DTP for every specific data package ID for a specific instance

▶ Summary record for a DTP for a specific instance

The data is provided for the analysis in the 0TCT_C22 and 0TCT_V22 InfoProviders. Table 10.5 lists the information available in the InfoProviders.

InfoObject	Description
0CALDAY	Calendar day
0CALMONTH	Calendar year/month
0CALQUARTER	Calendar year/quarter
0CALWEEK	Calendar year/week
0CALYEAR	Calendar year
0CHNGID	Change ID
0RECORDTP	Record type
0REQUID	Request ID
0TCTDPAKID	Data package ID
0TCTDTPCMD	DTP command
0TCTDTPID	Data transfer process
0TCTDURTION	Duration
0TCTENDDAT	End date
0TCTENDRECS	Number of records at the end
0TCTENDSIZE	Size at the end
0TCTENDTIM	End time
0TCTENDTST	End time stamp
0TCTOBJVERS	Object version
0TCTPCLOGID	Log ID of the process chain
0TCTPRCSCHN	ID of the process chain
0TCTPRCSTYP	Process type
0TCTPRSMODE	Import mode
0TCTREQSID	Data request (SID)
0TCTSOURCE	Source object
0TCTSOURSYS	Source system
0TCTSRCTYP	Source object type
0TCTSRCTYPE	Type of the source system
0TCTSTAUIK	Frequency
0TCTSTIMEK	Start time
0TCTSTRRECS	Number of records at the start

Table 10.5 InfoObjects of the DTP Statistics

351

InfoObject	Description
0TCTSTRSIZE	Size at the start
0TCTSTRTDAT	Start date
0TCTSTRTTIM	Start time
0TCTSTRTTST	Start time stamp
0TCTSUBSTEP	DTP substep
0TCTSYSID	SAP NetWeaver BW system
0TCTTARGET	Target object
0TCTTIMSTMP	UTC time stamp
0TCTTRGTYPE	Target object type
0TCTUSERNM	User
0TCTWHMMAN	Automatic/manual posting
0TCTWHMTFM	Transfer type
0TIME	Time
0WEEKDAY1	Week days

Table 10.5 InfoObjects of the DTP Statistics (Cont.)

For this data as well, the DataSource contains the function module extractor, RSDDK_BIW_GET_DATA. This function module processes the delta internally. The RSDDSTATEXTRACT DB table saves the delta pointer for each executed DataSource. During the next delta extraction, the delta pointer is extracted from this table, and the corresponding delta data is extracted from various database tables.

All of the fields are directly extracted from the RSDDSTATDTP, RSBKREQUEST, RSBSOURCEPROP, and RSBTARGETPROP tables except for SYSID, DURATION, STAUIK, and TIMEK fields of the previous list. If a DTP is executed in a process chain, CHAIN_ID (name of the process chain) and LOG_ID (log ID) from the RSPCLOGCHAIN table are used for the corresponding DTP. SYSID is derived in the function module via an object, DURATION is calculated via the fields ENDTIMESTAMP and STARTTIMESTAMP. STAUIK is constantly set to 1 — except for the summary rows where this value is calculated using another formula. TIMEK is the start time that is calculated using the STARTTIMESTAMP field.

InfoPackage Statistics

The Transaction Data InfoPackages DataSource (0TCT_DS23) provides detailed information on InfoPackages that have been executed either independently or in a process chain. The data is provided for the analysis in the 0TCT_C23 and 0TCT_V23 InfoProviders. Table 10.6 lists the information available in the InfoProviders.

InfoObject	Description
0CALDAY	Calendar day
0CALMONTH	Calendar year/month
0CALQUARTER	Calendar year/quarter
0CALWEEK	Calendar year/week
0CALYEAR	Calendar year
0CHNGID	Change ID
0RECORDTP	Record type
0REQUID	Request ID
0TCTDURTION	Duration
0TCTENDDAT	End date
0TCTENDTIM	End time
0TCTENDTST	End time stamp
0TCTIFPAKID	InfoPackage
0TCTISOURC	InfoSource
0TCTOBJVERS	Object version
0TCTPCLOGID	Log ID of the process chain
0TCTPRCSCHN	ID of the process chain
0TCTPRCSTYP	Process type
0TCTRECORDS	Number of records
0TCTREQSID	Data request (SID)
0TCTSOURCE	Source object
0TCTSRCTYP	Source object type
0TCTSTAUIK	Frequency
0TCTSTRTDAT	Start date
0TCTSTRTTIM	Start time
0TCTSTRTTST	Start time stamp
0TCTSYSID	SAP NetWeaver BW system
0TCTTARGET	Target object
0TCTTIMSTMP	UTC time stamp
0TCTTRGTYPE	Target object type

Table 10.6 InfoObjects of the InfoPackage Statistics

InfoObject	Description
0TCTUSERNM	User
0TCTWHMACT	Process type (WHM)
0TCTWHMMAN	Automatic/manual posting
0TCTWHMTFM	Transfer type (WHM)
0TIME	Time
0WEEKDAY1	Week days

Table 10.6 InfoObjects of the InfoPackage Statistics (Cont.)

This DataSource also contains the function module extractor, RSDDK_ BIW_GET_DATA, which processes the deltas internally.

The function module extractor extracts all InfoPackages that are executed independently or as part of a process chain. The CHAIN_ID field is returned by the DataSource for InfoPackages that are executed in a process chain. RSDDSTATWHM and RSPCLOGCHAIN are connected to extract the required data.

10.6   Evaluation of CPH Data

The monitoring architecture is part of SAP's technology platform and is used to monitor the SAP system landscapes from a central monitoring system (CEN). In this process, performance data of the monitored objects is determined and saved. Thanks to the open concept of the monitoring architecture, you can monitor virtually any objects. Typical examples for such performance values include the following: availabilities of systems and servers, response times in the dialog system, efficiency of buffers, and utilizations of CPUs.

Central Performance History

The *Central Performance History* (CPH) is available to save selected performance data for a period of time or permanently or for a longer period of time. After you have configured the CPH in Transaction RZ23N, it collects, aggregates, and reorganizes the CCMS data automatically. The benefit of the CPH is the central view of all data in the system landscape and the data conversion according to time zones.

As of Release BI Content 7.03 with Plug-in Release 2005, the statistics records are available in an SAP NetWeaver BW system — both the statistics files themselves and the aggregates. This way, the benefits of the SAP NetWeaver BW system also apply to the analysis of CPH data: optimal handling of large data quantities, merging of different (independent) data, evaluation by means of powerful analysis tools, and flexible and customizable reports.

To be able to use CPH data in an SAP NetWeaver BW system, the CPH must be configured and activated in the CPH source system within the monitoring architecture, and the data transfer must be configured in Transaction CCMSBISETUP. Specifically, a configuration requires:

Configuration

▶ Systems whose performance data is supposed to be collected in the CPH must be entered as monitored systems in the monitoring architecture of the CPH source system.

▶ The configuration of the CPH must be completed; a valid collection and reorganization schema must be assigned to the MTE classes (monitoring tree elements) of the desired nodes.

▶ The CPH must be active; that is, the jobs that are responsible for collecting and reorganizing performance data within the CPH must be scheduled.

When you transfer data from the CPH to an SAP NetWeaver BW system, very large quantities of data may have to be processed, depending on the settings. In practice it has emerged that performance problems or instabilities can occur in individual cases, in particular when the delta queue and an ODS object are used. Therefore, additional Data-Sources and InfoSources have been created, which do not use the delta queue and ODS objects. Because it is technically not possible to create a DataSource that supports a delta update but does not use the delta queue, a separate new concept was chosen to do this.

Data flow

Whereas with normal DataSources, the corresponding settings in the InfoPackages determine whether, for example, a delta upload or a delta init is performed, the new DataSources allow only full updates. Whether a delta upload, a delta init, or a delta repeat is performed is determined by the choice of the DataSource itself, that is, the new Data-Sources have the characteristic to extract (in full mode) only a delta upload, a delta init, or a delta repeat. Table 10.7 lists the InfoSources that are available for the CPH data.

If a query is executed on the central MultiProvider 0CPH_ALL, and depending on where the required performance values are already available, the system automatically performs the following steps: If the requested data is already available in SAP NetWeaver BW, the request is filled with this data. However, if the data is not yet available in SAP NetWeaver BW (SAP recommends running the job for transferring this data once a day), the request is directly forwarded to the CPH. If the requested data is already available in the CPH, the request is filled with this data. If the data is not yet available in the CPH (there are jobs for the transfer whose default periods are between 13 minutes and 10 hours depending on the required breakdown), the data is directly taken from the monitored satellite systems.

CPH InfoSources	Description
0CCMS_CPH_DATA — CPH Data	This is the traditional InfoSource for transferring the CPH data from the source systems to SAP NetWeaver BW. It uses the delta queue to do this. The DataStore Object 0CPH_PODS (ODS object for CPH data) is filled by this InfoSource.
0CCMS_CPH_DATA_DELTA—CPH Data (Deltas)	Use this InfoSource to transfer only new data that has not yet been read. To use this InfoSource, it is technically not absolutely necessary to perform a delta initialization using the InfoSource 0CCMS_CPH_DATA_DELTAINIT (see next entry). Nevertheless SAP recommends an initialization of this type if there is already a large data set in the CPH, because the update in InfoCubes is faster during an initialization than during a delta upload.
0CCMS_CPH_DATA_DELTAINIT—CPH-Data (Delta Init)	Use this InfoSource to fill the InfoCubes with the initial set of the CPH data. This means that the system initializes the delta management within the extractor, so only newer data is delivered to the InfoSource 0CCMS_CPH_DATA_DELTA.
0CCMS_CPH_DATA_DELTAREPEAT—CPH Data (Delta Repeat)	Use this InfoSource to repeat a delta extraction. This is useful, for example, if the update in the InfoCubes failed during the previous delta upload.
0CCMS_CPH_DATA_ALTERNATIV—CPH Data (Alternative)	Use this InfoSource to continue to use the delta queue, as with the InfoSource 0CCMS_CPH_DATA. However, as with the other new InfoSources, the collected data is written directly to the InfoCubes, bypassing the ODS objects.

Table 10.7 Overview of the CPH InfoSources

10.7 Workload Monitor (Transaction ST03)

Because all SAP NetWeaver BW statistics have been fully revised, and information is now written to several database tables on an event basis rather than to the RSDDSTAT table only, as of SAP NetWeaver BW 7.0

SPS 09 the workload monitor (Transaction ST03) now accesses the statistics data of the technical content.

InfoCube	No.Queries	No.of Nav.	Total time	Ø Total	MED: Total	OLAP Time	Ø OLAP	DB Time	Ø DB	Frontend	Ø Fronten	Planning	Avg.Plan.	Unass.Time	Avg.Unass.	Selected	Select. / Transf.
TOTAL	78	2.664	4.839,7	1,8	0,2	1.459,2	0,5	2.882,7	1,1	497,9	0,2	0,0	0,0	0,0	0,0	1.835.516	0,1
ZZPRCUSMP	15	139	2.128,3	15,3	2,9	300,8	2,2	1.755,6	12,6	71,9	0,5	0,0	0,0	0,0	0,0	239.551	0,0
ZSS_R057	3	58	838,9	14,5	7,5	342,9	5,9	364,9	6,3	131,1	2,3	0,0	0,0	0,0	0,0	1.119.058	26,5
0CUSTOMER	4	2.117	538,4	0,3	0,2	512,2	0,2	10,7	0,0	15,5	0,0	0,0	0,0	0,0	0,0	99.154	0,8
ZCUP_MC01	1	1	385,7	385,7	385,7	0,5	0,5	385,3	385,3	0,0	0,0	0,0	0,0	0,0	0,0	0	0,0
ZSM_R0003	9	60	183,4	3,1	1,7	97,8	1,6	61,1	1,0	24,5	0,4	0,0	0,0	0,0	0,0	118.979	0,2
ZMDA_MC01	4	43	145,2	3,4	2,1	18,8	0,4	109,5	2,5	16,9	0,4	0,0	0,0	0,0	0,0	1.848	0,0
ZBFA_MC01	1	6	134,3	22,4	27,2	2,5	0,4	131,5	21,9	0,2	0,0	0,0	0,0	0,0	0,0	13.094	0,0
ZSM_R0010	1	19	54,9	2,9	3,3	41,9	2,2	12,9	0,7	0,0	0,0	0,0	0,0	0,0	0,0	0	0,0
ZSM_R0013	1	15	30,6	2,0	1,8	30,6	2,0	0,0	0,0	0,0	0,0	0,0	0,0	0,0	0,0	77	0,4
ZSM_R0014	4	10	29,3	2,9	12,1	12,6	1,3	6,0	0,6	10,7	1,1	0,0	0,0	0,0	0,0	0	0,0
ZSO_MC004	3	4	21,7	5,4	2,2	10,6	2,7	10,3	2,6	0,9	0,2	0,0	0,0	0,0	0,0	47	0,0
ZSS_R130	4	32	21,3	0,7	0,4	9,9	0,3	4,3	0,1	7,1	0,2	0,0	0,0	0,0	0,0	1.733	0,0
ZSS_R119	1	4	17,5	4,4	1,4	15,9	4,0	1,2	0,3	0,4	0,1	0,0	0,0	0,0	0,0	72	0,6
ZFI_R0023	1	2	13,4	6,7	6,7	3,4	1,7	10,0	5,0	0,1	0,1	0,0	0,0	0,0	0,0	88.694	1,0
0MATERIAL	1	32	12,7	0,4	0,2	8,2	0,3	1,8	0,1	2,6	0,1	0,0	0,0	0,0	0,0	53.583	0,5
ZFI_R0008	2	45	10,5	0,2	0,1	5,7	0,1	3,3	0,1	1,5	0,0	0,0	0,0	0,0	0,0	1.322	0,3
ZSS_R048	1	1	9,8	9,8	9,8	9,2	9,2	0,1	0,1	0,5	0,5	0,0	0,0	0,0	0,0	0	0,0
ZSO_MC003	1	1	9,4	9,4	9,4	6,9	6,9	0,0	0,0	2,5	2,5	0,0	0,0	0,0	0,0	0	0,0
ZFIAR_C02	6	8	8,2	1,0	1,1	3,5	0,4	4,6	0,6	0,2	0,0	0,0	0,0	0,0	0,0	96.128	1,0

Figure 10.14 SAP NetWeaver BW Analysis in Transaction ST03

In addition to the reporting statistics, you can also directly analyze process chains in this transaction as of SPS 09.

10.8 Loading and Deleting Statistics Data

Note that the query runtime statistics generate a large quantity of statistics data in the SAP NetWeaver BW statistics tables. Depending on the (user-defined) detail statistics level, the system writes between 20 and 80 data records per navigation step to the SAP NetWeaver BW statistics tables. Therefore, it is mandatory to load the statistical query data to the technical content (InfoCube 0TCT_C01 to 0TCT_C03) and to delete the original data from the SAP NetWeaver BW statistics tables.

By default, in each delta load for every query runtime statistics (DataSource 0TCT_DS01 to 0TCT_DS03), the data of the last 14 days is automatically deleted from the SAP NetWeaver BW statistics tables. This time interval can be modified in the RSADMIN table using the TCT_ KEEP_OLAP_DM_DATA_N_DAYS parameter.

Automatic deletion

357

Additionally, for a manual deletion in Transaction RSDDSTAT, you can specify a date to select data for deletion. For this purpose, you can also call the RSDDSTAT_DATA_DELETE program directly.

10.9 Enhancements

Of course, you can change and enhance the delivered evaluations within the BI Administration Cockpit as required. In principle, you should avoid changes to the objects of the technical content such as the InfoProviders. In the frontend, however, it is not problematic to copy existing objects (queries, web templates), transfer them to your own namespace, and enhance them.

A possible customer-specific enhancement would be, for example, the implementation of a grouping for the analysis applications, with the goal of evaluating different technical and application areas more easily and separating them from one another. Various adaptations using navigation attributes for the 0TCTUSERNM InfoObject (the user) would also be possible, for example, the use of reporting grouped by employee groups, personnel areas, or countries.

Alert Framework The Alert Framework is suitable for supporting the monitor process. You can use simple alerts, for example, owing to too high response times in reporting or terminated load processes. Complex scenarios, for example, with proactive alerts are also possible.

10.9.1 Example: BI Administration Cockpit with SAP NetWeaver BW 7.0 Objects

The elements of the BI Administration Cockpit that SAP provides have been created completely in SAP NetWeaver BW 3.5, which is understandable if you consider the delivery date, especially because the functionality and usability are sufficient for most analyses. The many new options for both the development and handling of reports with the new frontend tools in SAP NetWeaver BW 7.0 suggest use for enhancements, as shown in the example in Figure 10.15.

In the development of Web reports for statistics evaluation, you will quickly appreciate the easy definition of commands for buttons, selection lists, and so on. The drag-and-drop functionality in particular is an invaluable benefit for the actual analysis.

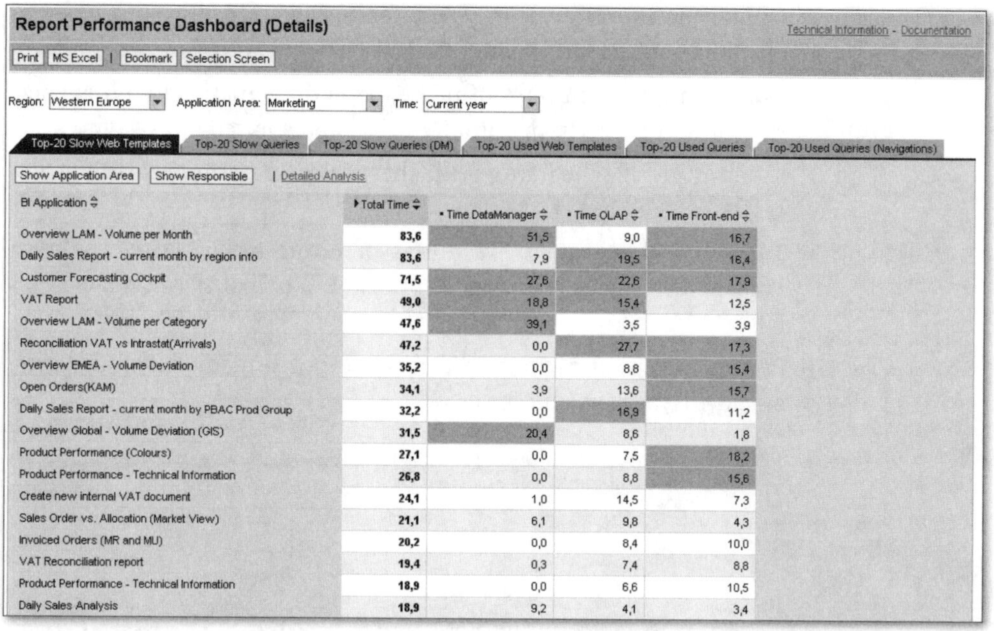

BI Application	Total Time	Time DataManager	Time OLAP	Time Front-end
Overview LAM - Volume per Month	83,6	51,5	9,0	16,7
Daily Sales Report - current month by region info	83,6	7,9	19,5	16,4
Customer Forecasting Cockpit	71,5	27,6	22,6	17,9
VAT Report	49,0	18,8	15,4	12,5
Overview LAM - Volume per Category	47,6	39,1	3,5	3,9
Reconciliation VAT vs Intrastat(Arrivals)	47,2	0,0	27,7	17,3
Overview EMEA - Volume Deviation	35,2	0,0	8,8	15,4
Open Orders(KAM)	34,1	3,9	13,6	15,7
Daily Sales Report - current month by PBAC Prod Group	32,2	0,0	16,9	11,2
Overview Global - Volume Deviation (GIS)	31,5	20,4	8,6	1,8
Product Performance (Colours)	27,1	0,0	7,5	18,2
Product Performance - Technical Information	26,8	0,0	8,8	15,6
Create new internal VAT document	24,1	1,0	14,5	7,3
Sales Order vs. Allocation (Market View)	21,1	6,1	9,8	4,3
Invoiced Orders (MR and MU)	20,2	0,0	8,4	10,0
VAT Reconciliation report	19,4	0,3	7,4	8,8
Product Performance - Technical Information	18,9	0,0	6,6	10,5
Daily Sales Analysis	18,9	9,2	4,1	3,4

Figure 10.15 SAP NetWeaver BW 7.0 Dashboard (Report Performance)

10.9.2 Example: Proactive Alerts

The following section presents an enhancement as a practical example. You can use this enhancement to proactively identify possible errors in the loading processes. Owing to the ever increasing complexity of system landscapes and the continuously rising number of daily loading processes, it becomes more and more difficult for the administration department to keep an overview. On the one hand, the BI Administration Cockpit helps monitor both historic evaluations and the current status, but on the other hand, it provides few options to identify problems at an early stage and remedy errors in time.

Warnings

It would be preferable for the system to issue warnings based on the existing information about old loading processes or based on predefined planning data in control tables before an error actually occurs. For example, in distributed teams the SAP NetWeaver BW administration team sometimes simply forgets to schedule the process chains, and consequently no actual error occurs or alert scenarios take effect. For the users this can mean that business-critical data is not available in the morning. Different functions are possible for proactive alerts:

Possible functions
of proactive alerts

- Online monitoring of processes, for instance, loading processes or attribute change runs (Figure 10.16)

- Monitoring the runtimes of processes and comparison with average runtimes in the past; definition of acceptable exceedings

- Monitoring of scheduling with the goal to determine loading processes that did not start

- Triggering alerts when exceptions or errors occur, using the Alert Framework and the Universal Worklist (UWL) in SAP NetWeaver Portal

- Escalation scenarios in case errors are not remedied, for instance, emails to the next support level

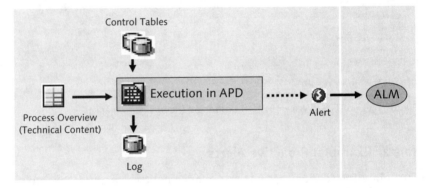

Figure 10.16 Online Monitoring of Processes

The sample application shown in Figure 10.16 consists of the following components:

Overview of the
individual
components

- The execution of the query is scheduled in the Analysis Process Designer (APD), for example, to receive the current status of all loading processes every 10 minutes.

- In the APD, the query result is evaluated in an ABAP process. On the one hand, the system can directly identify recent errors (for example, termination of a data activation of a DSO), and on the other hand, it can compare executed processes with historic information and with specifications in control tables to identify missed or delayed processes.

- Possible specifications in control tables could be the start times of critical process chains with the respective tolerance limits.

*If you use process chains, you can automate the complex pro-
cedures in the SAP NetWeaver BW system using event-driven
processing, visualize the procedures using network graphics, and
centrally control and monitor the processing of the processes. This
chapter describes important processes and the monitoring options
of process chains.*

11 Process Chains

To automate the processes in SAP NetWeaver BW, processes are compiled into process chains. The processes are thereby scheduled in the
background and are linked via events that are triggered by a previous
process to start the follow-up processes.

A process chain consists of a start process, the individual application
processes, and the so-called collection processes, which compile several
chain strands to one strand in the process chain maintenance and can
thereby make multiple scheduling of the actual application processes
unnecessary, among other things. A process is characterized by:

▶ **Process type**

Processes

The process type is the kind of process, for example a loading process.
It defines which tasks and which properties the process has in the
maintenance. The process type is defined in the RSPROCESSTYPES
view.

▶ **Process variant**

The process variant is the name of the process. In the context of the
process chains, it is the configuration of a process defined at the definition time. A variant is only uniquely defined with regard to the
process type. A process can have various variants. During the loading
process, for example, an InfoPackage is a process variant. The process
variant is normally defined by the user during the scheduling of the
process. For certain process types, the variants are internally defined
and saved as GUIDs.

▶ **Process instance**
The process instance is the characteristic value of the process. It contains the most important information that the process wants to communicate to any possible subsequent processes, such as the name of the request during a loading process, for example. If the process is ended, the instance is transferred to the process chain management and saved. The logs for the process are stored under the process instance. The instance is determined by the process itself at runtime and is normally determined uniquely, independent of time or system.

Automatisms
If you use process chains, the automatisms of the integrated processes (update PSA data in the data target or activate data in the DataStore object, for example) are ignored, and you must implement them using the process chain. If you schedule a specific process in a chain, you support the automatic insertion of additional relevant standard processes taking such automatisms into account.

11.1 Processes Relevant for the Operation

Numerous processes are available for defining process chains, which fall into the following categories:

▶ General services (such as the start process or ABAP program)

▶ Loading processes and follow-up actions (such as InfoPackage or DTPs)

▶ Data target administration (such as DSO activation or indexes)

▶ Reporting agent (such as precalculations)

▶ Other SAP NetWeaver BW processes (such as an attribute change run)

▶ Retail (transferring point-of-sales data to SAP NetWeaver PI)

▶ Global spend analyses (such as classifications)

▶ Other such as jobs in SAP Central Process Scheduling

The next section will describe the flow of process types supporting process chains in further detail.

11.1.1   Interrupt Process

If a process chain is only to be processed in its entirety or in parts, and if more than one start condition is met, use this process type to specify the additional conditions. The chain starts if the start process condition is met, but the interrupt process interrupts the processing of the chain (while it retains the active status) until the interrupt process condition is met. If the start process condition is met again before the interrupt process condition is fulfilled, the chain starts again and runs until the interrupt, just as before. As soon as the condition for the interrupt process is met, only the last run of the chain is continued. The previous runs remain unchanged.

The interrupt process schedules an additional background job that starts with the respective condition. The interrupt process is therefore not actually active during the interruption phase, and no resources are used during it. If the interrupt process condition is met before the start process condition, the chain starts as soon as the start condition is met, but the interrupt process no longer interrupts the chain because its conditions was already previously met. If the interrupt process condition is met once again before the start condition of the chain is met, it has no influence on the processing of the chain, the interrupt process does not stop it. Note that the chain retains the active status until the interrupt process is completed. This process type is therefore unsuitable for excluding specific branches of the chain from processing. To do so, use the Condition *process type*.

No usage of resources

The interrupt process enables the AND link of start conditions in a process chain according to the design described. If you need OR links (such as "Chain starts Mondays or when another process ends"), you can model this via meta chains (see the following section), one of which is scheduled for each of the conditions and which starts the actual chain.

11.1.2   Start Process

The options in the background control are available to you for direct scheduling of the start process. You can, for example, start the process chains immediately (meaning when the process chain is activated), at a certain time, or after a certain event. The start process schedules your processes in the background accordingly when you activate the process chain. A start process has the following particularities:

▸ Only the start process can be scheduled without a previous process.

▸ The start process cannot be the successor to another process.

▸ Only one start process is permitted per process chain.

▸ A start process can only be used in one process chain.

Triggering a
process via API
If the options available here are insufficient, you can also trigger the start of the process chain via an API. The SAP NetWeaver Scheduling Framework can start the chain in this way and has more extensive scheduling options.

Meta chains
You can also trigger the start of a process chain via a meta chain. If the process chain for which you define this start condition is integrated in another chain, which is then referred to as a meta chain, this meta chain starts it directly. If you start the start process via a meta chain, it is not scheduled after you have activated the corresponding process chain. The process chain is not started until all of the meta chains into which it is integrated run. The other processes of a chain, such as the application processes and the collection processes, are scheduled waiting for an event.

11.1.3 AND (Last), OR (Every), and EXOR (First)

Collection
processes
The process chain management handles the collection processes AND, OR, and EXOR in a special way. The system uniquely defines the names of the variants, and it is guaranteed that multiply scheduled processes of the same name will all trigger the same event. This enables you to combine several process strands into a single strand, which makes multiple scheduling of the actual application process unnecessary.

▸ **AND**
Does not trigger a follow-up event until the last of the events that it was waiting for has been triggered. This process is useful if you want to combine processes, and the postprocessing is dependent on all of these previous processes.

▸ **OR**
Triggers a follow-up event every time an event it was waiting for has been triggered. This process is useful for avoiding multiple scheduling of the actual work processes.

▶ **EXOR**

Triggers a follow-up event when the first of the events that it was waiting for has been triggered. This process is useful if you run the processes parallel to each other and you want to schedule additional independent processes after these processes.

Note that no distinction can be made whether a 0 entry (no event received) means that the entry was never received or simply not yet received, because the tests do not occur constantly but rather only when an event is received. Owing to the time components, the collection processes do not display logical gates in the normal sense.

11.1.4 ABAP Program

If you want to use a simple independent program in a chain or a program that is scheduled in the background by another program or a user, then use the ABAP Program process type. You then have the option to schedule any program (ABAP report) in a process chain with or without program variants.

You can schedule a program either synchronously or asynchronously. In synchronous scheduling, the program is executed in the background on the same server on which the process chain is scheduled. The process chain waits for the program to be completed before it continues with any successors.

Synchronous and asynchronous scheduling

With the asynchronous scheduling option, a program is scheduled as an asynchronous process (distributed process). Distributed processes are characterized by the fact that various work processes are involved in a specific task. If a program is asynchronous, it does not complete the task that it began itself. If a process is asynchronous, the process chain maintenance does not equate the end of the process with the end of the background process. The status of the process remains active. In asynchronous processes, the successor events are not automatically triggered. You need to call the remote-enabled RSPC_ABAP_FINISH function module at the end of your program to signify the real end of your process. The process is then highlighted as completed, and the successor events are triggered.

It is generally recommended that you map more complex processes that are not covered by the SAP NetWeaver BW process types by implementing your own process type.

11.1.5 Operating System Command

You can use this process type to place an external command in an application server's operating system. Define the following in the Operating System Command process maintenance:

▶ The logical name of the operating system command that you want to place. This is a command defined in Transaction SM49. You can also adjust this command via the Change button.

▶ The operating system of the application server on which you want to execute the command.

▶ Additional parameters, providing these are allowed by the defined command.

▶ The application server on which the command is to be executed. If you want to always use the current host, select the corresponding indicator. If you enter a different host from the current one in the Target Machine field, the system automatically removes the selection of current hosts.

You have the option to rate the process as failed or successful if the output of the command contains the character string you specified. If the system does not find a certain character string, for example, the process will be ended with the opposite status or will be repeated. If you have defined that the process is to be repeated, you can specify after how many seconds and how often it should be repeated. In this way you can check whether a certain file exists in a directory before loading that file. If the file is not present in the directory, the check is repeated in the previously defined intervals before the process ends and the loading starts.

11.1.6 Local Process Chain and Remote Process Chain

Process chains can be scheduled in other process chains called meta chains. If the process chain to be executed is located in the same system as the meta chain, use the local process chain process type. The local process chain consists of processes that are scheduled in the same system as the meta chain.

If the process chain to be executed is located in a different remote system, use the remote process chain process type. A remote process chain is a local process in the calling system that calls a process chain that needs to be run there by using a destination in another system. The remote process chain therefore takes over communication with the remote system and starts the process chain to be executed there synchronously. After terminating the process chain in the remote system, the system reports this to the meta chain in the calling system.

11.1.7 Deciding Between Multiple Alternatives

The Decision process type allows you to define any amount of conditions that form the basis of a decision in accordance with the following logic: If condition A is filled, option X applies; if condition B is filled, option Y applies. . .otherwise, option Z applies. The conditions have a description and are formulated as logical expressions using the formula builder.

In the formula builder, only syntax fields that enable decisions on the basis of date and time in particular are directly available as fields. To incorporate this, SAP has enhanced the function library in the formula builder with the DATE_WEEKDAY1 formula function. The DATE_WEEKDAY1 formula function calculates the day of the week as a technical specification (1. . .7) based on the date. For example, you can check the form DATE_WEEKDAY1(date of the weekday) = "6" OR DATE_WEEKDAY1(date of the weekday) = "7", which allows you to change the way the chain runs at the weekend in comparison to the other days of the week

Formula builder

The function library of the formula builder has also been enhanced by the Process Chain category, enabling you to access additional information within the formula. The process chain category contains the following formula functions:

Formula functions in process chains

▶ **PREDECESSOR_PARAMETER**
Runtime parameter of the direct predecessor

▶ **PROCESS_PARAMETER**
Runtime parameter of a process in the current chain

▶ **PROCESS_VALUE_EXISTS**
The process in the chain has a parameter value

These functions allow you to access values from predecessor (and successor) processes of the current process chain. If the process is a predecessor process, the system requests the instance values; otherwise, it requests the maintained variant values.

367

11.2 Administration of Process Chains

The administration of process chains encompasses some settings in addition to monitoring process chain runs, such as defining the user for execution and handling of terminated processes.

11.2.1 User for Execution

In the standard setting, an SAP NetWeaver BW background user executes the process chain (BWREMOTE). You have the option to change the standard setting (Figure 11.1) so that you can see which user is executing the process chain and thereby the processes in the job overview (Transaction SM37). You can select the current dialog user who schedules the process chain job or specify a different user.

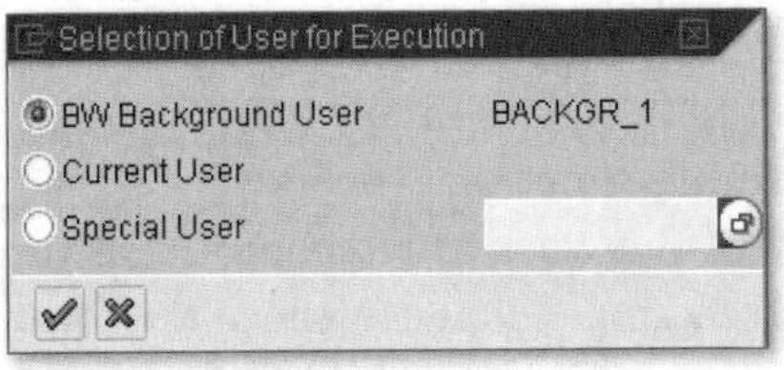

Figure 11.1 User for Execution

The SAP NetWeaver BW background user has the required authorizations to execute all SAP NetWeaver BW process types. You have to assign these authorizations to other users yourself so that authorization errors do not occur during the processing.

11.2.2 Starting Terminated Processes

If a process (instance) in the chain is terminated, you have the option to restart the process and thereby end the chain run via GO TO • LOG VIEW in the log view. There are two options, depending on the process type:

Options for restarting

▸ **A process can be repaired.**
In this case, the terminated instance is executed again. This enables you to restart processes that cannot be repeated with a new instance because the data to be edited is attached to the instance (such as during a data transfer process). A data transfer process cannot be repeated with a new request number, for example, because the data itself is attached to the request.

▶ **A process can be repaired.**
In such a case, a new instance is generated.

You can restart a terminated process in the log view of process chain maintenance if it is possible for the process type. In the plan view of process chain maintenance you can set whether a process can be repaired or repeated when terminated, under SETTINGS • MAINTAIN PROCESS TYPES (RSPROCESSTYPES table).

In the log view of the affected process chain, select Repeat or Repair from the context menu of the terminated process. If the process cannot be repaired or repeated after termination, the corresponding entry is missing from the context menu in the log view of process chain maintenance. In this case, you are able to start the subsequent processes. A corresponding entry can be found in the context menu for these subsequent processes.

11.2.3   Process Status Valuation

Using the settings for process status valuation, you can specify that processes that have scheduled an event Upon Error will be valuated as successful for the calculation of the overall status of the chain run despite having errors (Figure 11.2).

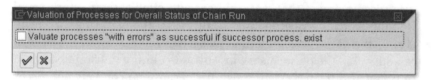

Figure 11.2   Status Valuation for a Process Chain

If you set the indicator under PROCESS CHAIN • ATTRIBUTES • PROCESS CHAIN VALUATION, the system classifies all of the incorrect processes of the chain as successful with regard to the overall status of the run if you have scheduled a subsequent process Upon Error or Always. You can use this indicator to valuate a subchain run in meta chains as successful despite errors in noncritical processes. The successors to these processes are scheduled for Always, whereas the successors only schedule important processes Upon Success. Accordingly, the successor can only be scheduled to the subchain within the meta chain Upon Success; it will be continued despite that fact, however, if errors only occur in noncritical processes of the subchain.

11.2.4 Executing Process Chains Synchronously

Serial processing   You can execute a process chain in the dialog using synchronous execution instead of scheduling and executing it in the background. The processes in the chain are thereby processed serially using a dialog process (see runtime in Figure 11.3). Even the distributed processes themselves are serially processed where possible. If this is not the case (depending on the process type), the synchronous processing is terminated at this point and not continued until the distributed process has reported its termination to the process chain.

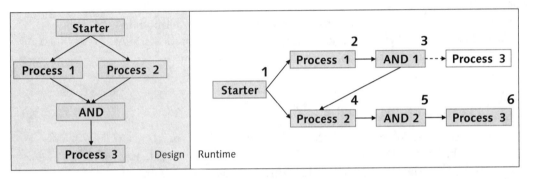

Figure 11.3 Synchronous Execution (Runtime) of a Process Chain (Design)

Recommendations   It is recommended that you only execute simple chains with small amounts of data synchronously. In this case, the performance advantage of the dialog execution (no background jobs must be scheduled) can outweigh the performance loss by not running in parallel. Several runs can also be processed in parallel because no conflicts will occur with regard to the required background jobs.

11.2.5 Alerting

You can send alerts if errors occur while processing processes or in the background processing for a process chain. Process chain maintenance uses alert management for this purpose. The alert is sent to the user who scheduled the process chain. You can assign additional recipients by assigning roles or specifying individual users in alert category maintenance (Transaction ALRTCATDEF).

The recipient's display program displays the alerts. The display program can be the Universal Worklist (UWL) in the portal, the alert inbox

(Transaction ALRTINBOX,) or an application that calls alerts using API. Depending on the configuration, you can also send alerts by email, fax, or SMS. If you have set the indicator in attribute maintenance for the process chain, an alert is sent by default for each process that has errors.

Before the system can trigger and send alerts, alert categories have to be assigned to the process types. You can define the recipient, texts, priorities, escalation options, and so on in an alert category. The system determines the alert category as follows:

Alert categories

▶ **Errors in background processing**
Alert category BWAC_PROCESS_CHAIN_FRAMEWORK is used for errors in background processing. For this category, fixed alert texts are delivered that can be sent to the recipients if an alert occurs.

▶ **Errors in the process**
The system searches table RSPC_ALERT_CAT for an entry for the process type (PROCESS CHAIN MAINTENANCE • SETTINGS • MAINTAIN ALERT CATEGORIES). You can change the entries in this table without modifications. It is protected against changes via SAP deliveries, meaning that additional entries that are delivered can be transferred, but the existing entries are not overwritten.

If you do not enter a customer-specific alert category in the table, the system uses the alert category delivered for this process type. You can exclude a process type from alerting by selecting No Alert for the process type in the RCPC_ALERT_CAT table.

No Alert process type

11.2.6 Batch Process Requirements

If a process chain is checked, one of the things calculated is the number of parallel processes during an optimum execution run. The goal of this check, which also takes all local process chains into account, is to make a comparison with the available batch processes. If the number of batch processes is overwritten on the server defined for scheduling, a corresponding error message is output.

If no more batch processes are available in a subsequent execution at a certain time, for example, this can lead to a deadlock in the job processing if the process chain starts many parallel subchains. Note that an additional batch process is required for a short time when starting a subchain. You must ensure that enough batch processes are available in the system. If the minimum requirement is not available, it is recommended that you restructure the chain accordingly to decrease the number of parallel subchains. You should take both the minimum and the optimum case into consideration during the calculations for your chain processes:

▸ **Minimum (chain runs more or less serially)**
The minimum case is the number of parallel subchains at the widest point in the chain + 1. Chains that start other subchains must be broken down accordingly for the calculation.

▸ **Optimum (higher parallelism)**
The optimum case is the number of parallel process at the widest point of the chain +1. Each subchain counts in this formula with the number of its parallel processes at its widest point.

In the example chain shown in Figure 11.4, some loading processes are running in parallel in another subchain.

In this example you need a minimum of two batch processes (one process for the subchain and one process for the start process). Assuming that the subchain has three loading processes at its widest point, the optimum number of batch processes would be six (two loading processes + three loading processes for the subchain + the start process). Please note that higher parallelism and therefore also more batch processes is only useful if the system has the corresponding capacities (CPUs). Approximately one CPU is required for each batch process.

11.2.7 Monitoring Process Chains

Various work environments are available for monitoring process chain runs. In addition to monitoring logs directly in the log view in Transaction RSPC or in the view for a specific process chain in Transaction RSPC1, technical content, the monitoring transaction RSPCM, and the CCMS as a central tool are also available.

Use Transaction RSPCM to regularly check the status of current runs for selected process chains. You can navigate from there to the detailed log view for a process chain run. Figure 11.5 illustrates an example of process chain runtime statistics based on technical content.

Chapter 10, Technical Content and BI Administration Cockpit, deals with technical content using the BW Administration Cockpit, among other things.

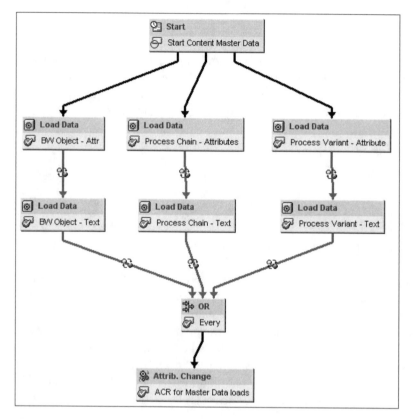

Figure 11.4 Parallelism in Process Chains

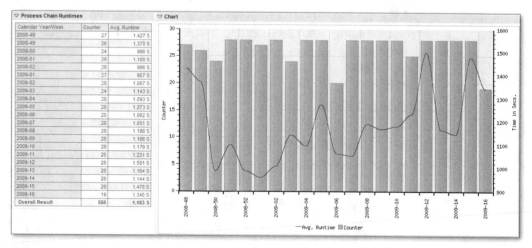

Figure 11.5 Process Chains Runtimes

373

Monitoring in the CCMS

You can use the BI Monitor in the Computing Center Management System (CCMS) to monitor your system landscape centrally and comprehensively and, if necessary, implement external monitoring tools as well. To call it, start the overview of all CCMS monitors via Transaction RZ20 or start the monitor directly using Transaction BWCCMS.

```
Process Chains
   ZCPL_COMP_FORE
   ZMETA_SM_ST1125

       DESCRIPTION                              Sell Through Data for APO DP [META]
       D6MQUV8HNUW4RMS6OUCRNUAWE 10/06 15:00:18  Entire chain now has status '6'    , Green 2009-10-06 , 16:38:57
       D6MS9PQ59A4NCAQ1B12DU6TN6 10/06 19:00:11  Entire chain now has status '6'    , Green 2009-10-06 , 20:39:10
       D6N3KSE5JNJR3VAY5UTTZM10U 10/08 03:00:40  Entire chain now has status '6'    , Green 2009-10-08 , 08:09:20
```

Figure 11.6 Process Chain in Transaction BWCCMS

Method definition   The Process Chains monitor tree contains all process chains that have run since the last start of the system (Figure 11.6). By setting the DAYS_TO_KEEP_LOGS transfer parameter for method execution in the RSPC_CCMS_STARTUP method definition, you can specify the process chain runs that you want to display from those that ended before the BI system was last started. By default, this parameter is set at seven days, meaning that the process chain runs from the last seven days are displayed. You can find the method definition in Transaction RZ21 via METHODS • DEFINITIONS.

In addition to the status, the log ID and the time are also displayed for the process chain runs. The agent for the data collection runs at a maximum of every 10 minutes and monitors all displayed runs. The corresponding batch job is called SAP_CCMS_MONI_BATCH_DP and is scheduled once per hour by default, but you can change this in Transaction SM37.

Process Chain Run Logs

You can call the logs via Display Messages in the context menu of a process. The logs are displayed in the subsequent dialog box in the Chain, Batch, and Process tabs.

▸ The Chain tab contains information about the start and end of the process and the generated instance.

▸ In the Batch tab in the SAP List Viewer Grid Control, the logs are displayed for the job in which the process itself was run. You can reach the job overview for your job via the Batch Monitor button.

▶ The Process tab contains the process-related messages. This tab is displayed if the process type writes its own log or implements the `IF_RSPC_GET_LOG` and/or `IF_RSPC_CALL_MONITOR` interfaces for the process type. In processes for which a special monitor is linked, for example, when loading data with InfoPackages or during data transfer processes, you have the option to jump to this monitor via the process monitor.

You can display the processes that have not yet run in gray via VIEW • MERGE ACTIVE VERSION if the chain has been changed since the run to be checked. This is particularly helpful if the chain is to be continued after an error even though it was reactivated and/or scheduled in the meantime.

Continuing chains after an error

Automated Monitoring

Process chains can be excluded from automatic monitoring by the CCMS (RSPC_WATCHDOG program). If terminations occur in processes of this chain, they are not automatically recognized. Change the automatic monitoring settings in the process chain maintenance under PROCESS CHAIN • ATTRIBUTES • MONITORING.

11.3 Jobs in Process Chains

The names of all jobs created by process chains have the format BI_PROCESS_<Type>, where the type is the technical name of the process type. You can find a quick overview of all process types and their corresponding technical names in the RSPROCESSTYPEST table (Figure 11.7).

All process types are executed as background processes started by events. Exceptions to this are the directly scheduled start process types (TRIGGERS) for which all job control options are available, if it is not driven by the SAP NetWeaver BW service API. If all relevant jobs are listed in the SM37 standard job display, you must not forget to also select event-driven jobs. To do this, set the Or upon Event parameter for the job start conditions. A better overview with automatic selection of corresponding jobs is available from the RSPC_DISPLAY_JOBS report, which you can start directly from the process chain maintenance in Transaction RSPC.

Start process types

```
Table:          RSPROCESSTYPEST
Displayed Fields:   4 of   4  Fixed Columns:              |2  List Width 0250

  LANGU TYPE         ICON_TEXT              DESCRIPTION
  D     ABAP         Programm              ABAP Programm
  D     AGGRFILL     initial füllen        Initiales Füllen neuer Aggregate
  D     AND          AND                   AND (Letzter)
  D     ARCHIVE      Archivierungsprozeß   Daten aus einem InfoProvider archivieren
  D     ATTRIBCHAN   Attributsänderung     Attributsänderungslauf
  D     AUTOCLASS    Automatische Klass.   Automatische Klassifizierung
  D     BIAINDEX     BIA-Indizes füllen    Initiales Aktivieren und Füllen von BIA-Indizes
  D     CHAIN        lokal                 Prozesskette lokal
  D     CHGLOGDEL    ChangeLog  löschen    Löschen von Requests aus dem ChangeLog
  D     CLEARTODS    Leere trans. ODS      Lösche gesamten Inhalt des gekoppelten transaktionalen ODS
  D     COMMAND      Systemkommando        Betriebssystemkommando
  D     COMPRESS     Komprimieren          Komprimieren des InfoCubes
  D     CPS_EVENT    CPS Ereignis          Ereignis in SAP CPS
  D     CPS_JOB      CPS Job               Job in SAP CPS
  D     DATACHANGE   Event Datenänderung   Event Datenänderung  auslösen (für Broadcaster)
  D     DBSTAT       DB-Statistik          Datenbankstatistik aufbauen
  D     DECISION     Entscheidung          Entscheidung zwischen mehreren Alternativen
  D     DROPCUBE     Inhalt Datenziel      Vollständiges Löschen des Datenziel-Inhalts
  D     DROPINDEX    Indizes               Index löschen
  D     DSOREPLIC    DataStore Obj.-Repl.  DataStore Object-Replikation
  D     DTP_LOAD     Datentransferprozess  Datentransferprozess
```

Figure 11.7 Process Types

Background Job Name	Job no.	User	I	Status	Del	Selection	Selection value	Selection	Value	Selection	Selection value	Selection	Value
BI_PROCESS_TRIGGER	12232400	23010997		Released	0	CHAIN	0TCT_C2_INIT_P01	TYPE	TRIGGER	VARIANT	ZTCT_C2_INIT_START	WAIT	0
BI_PROCESS_LOADING	12232400	23010997		Released	0	CHAIN	0TCT_C2_INIT_P01	TYPE	LOADING	VARIANT	0PAK_1S5EQH9LSZWi0WN5571AOYXiW	WAIT	0
BI_PROCESS_LOADING	12232401	23010997		Released	0	CHAIN	0TCT_C2_INIT_P01	TYPE		VARIANT	0PAK_9P1JQB7X15HYNCWCW6X145RAT	WAIT	0
BI_PROCESS_LOADING	12232402	23010997		Released	0	CHAIN	0TCT_C2_INIT_P01	TYPE		VARIANT	0PAK_C5RG7AMNRIENDKOQYCR0J8R64	WAIT	0
BI_PROCESS_INDEX	12232300	23010997		Released	0	CHAIN	0TCT_C2_INIT_P01	TYPE	INDEX	VARIANT	GENERATE_INDEX_C21_INIT	WAIT	0
BI_PROCESS_INDEX	12232300	23010997		Released	0	CHAIN	0TCT_C2_INIT_P01	TYPE		VARIANT	GENERATE_INDEX_C22_INIT	WAIT	0
BI_PROCESS_INDEX	12232301	23010997		Released	0	CHAIN	0TCT_C2_INIT_P01	TYPE		VARIANT	GENERATE_INDEX_C23_INIT	WAIT	0
BI_PROCESS_DROPINDEX	12232300	23010997		Released	0	CHAIN	0TCT_C2_INIT_P01	TYPE	DROPINDEX	VARIANT	DELETE_INDEX_INIT	WAIT	0

Figure 11.8 Job View for a Process Chain

As you can see in the example in Figure 11.8, the event-driven jobs do not have a start time. If you start the start process via a meta chain, it is be scheduled after you have activated the corresponding process chain. The process chain will not be started until all of the meta chains into which it is integrated run. The other processes of a chain, such as the application processes and the collection processes, are scheduled waiting for an event. To find out which process chains belong to a particular job in the standard job view, you can proceed as follows:

1. Open the step overview for the job and copy the parameter for the RSPROCESS program, for example "&0000000006489".

2. Open the variant screen for the RSPROCESS program in Transaction SE38.

3. The Chain field in the values for the selected variants shows the technical names of the process chains.

Building on the technical foundations of processes and objects in an SAP NetWeaver BW system, this chapter will explain the administration and monitoring of SAP NetWeaver BW processes in more detail.

12 Administration of SAP NetWeaver BW Processes in Detail

The following sections will deal with administration of the most important SAP NetWeaver BW processes. They will focus on topics dealing primarily with modeling in SAP NetWeaver BW systems, which are of great importance for system operations but unfortunately are not often discussed in enough detail in information sources. In addition to loading processes, the sequence of changes, and the administration of Info-Cubes and DataStore objects, we will also explain the monitoring and administration of analysis projects. Chapter 13, Reporting Monitoring and Administration, will deal with the administration of objects and processes in reporting.

12.1 Extraction and Load Processes

Application-specific extractors are available that are each hard-coded for a specific DataSource provided with the SAP NetWeaver BW system and fill the extract structure of that DataSource. In addition, there are also generic extractors you can use to extract additional data from the SAP source system and transfer it to the SAP NetWeaver BW system. Only when a generic extractor is executed does it know from which tables and into which structure it should extract the data from the name of the DataSource to which the data should be extracted. In this way, it can fill various extract structures and DataSources.

Generic data extraction exists in various application areas of the SAP source system, such as the Logistics Information System (LO-LIS), Profitability Analysis (CO-PA), Special Purpose Ledger (FI-SL), and

SAP ERP Human Capital Management (HCM). LO-LIS, for example, uses a generic extractor to read information structures. DataSources are generated on the basis of these (individually) defined information structures. Generic data extraction from applications are called custom DataSources.

Generic DataSources

Regardless of the application, you can also execute a generic extraction of master data attributes, texts, or transaction data from any transparent tables, database views, or functional areas of the SAP Query application or via a function module. You can generate specific DataSources for this. These are referred to as generic DataSources. To transfer the data into the inbound layer of the SAP NetWeaver BW system, the persistent staging area (PSA), define the loading process in the scheduler with an InfoPackage. The data loading process is triggered by a request IDoc to the source system when the InfoPackage is executed. The following sections will deal with the monitoring settings and options for the loading process.

Runtime measurements of individual loading steps

The runtime measurement of individual loading steps in the RSDSRUN-TIMETRACE table can be helpful for a comprehensive analysis of loading processes. Activating the `RSDSRUNTIMETRACE` RSADMIN parameter with the aid of the RSSM_TRACE_SWITCH report, for example, causes selected loading steps to be logged and the runtimes valuated with the `RSDS_RUNTIME_RESULT` function module while being loaded into the PSA.

12.1.1 Delta Queue

The delta queue constitutes data storage in the source system into which data records can be automatically written either via a posting procedure in the source system (such as with FI documents) or via the extraction using a function module after a data request from the SAP NetWeaver BW system.

Logical unit of work

Data in the delta queue is compressed and saved in an RFC cluster table in a logical unit of work (LUW). With applications that write their data directly to the delta queue as transactions, in particular, multiple data records can be compressed and compiled in an LUW. Regardless of the maximum size setting and the system-internal conditions, the extractor first reads a specific number of LUWs as blocks into internal tables, which then always have to be processed and sent to the SAP NetWeaver

BW system. As a part of the processing, first, the compressed data of the LUWs read as blocks is unpacked. A single LUW is always viewed as a unit during this process, meaning it is never divided into multiple data packages. If an LUW already contains so many data records that it has reached the size of a data package, however, subsequent LUWs are sent in additional packages. The check of whether the setting for the maximum number of data packages was reached or even exceeded is not run until the block of read LUWs is completely unpacked and sent. If the number has been reached, no new block of LUWs is read for further processing, but rather the request is completed.

Monitoring the Delta Queue

The individual queues and the data written to them can be monitored in the queue monitor (Transaction RSA7) (Figure 12.1). The status symbol of a DataSource indicates whether a delta queue is activated for the update. If the status symbol is green, then the delta queue is activated, meaning it will be filled with data records during the next posting transaction or data request from the SAP NetWeaver BW system. The prerequisite for the delta update is the successful completion of the initialization of the delta procedure in the scheduler of the SAP NetWeaver BW system.

BW Delta Queue Maintenance

Stat.	DataSource	BW System	Total	Stat.	
○○○	6AZLOG_DS02	D26CLNT800	19		
○○○	6AZLOG_DS01	D26CLNT800	4		
○○○	0TCT_DS23	D26CLNT800	1		
○○○	0TCT_DS21	D26CLNT800	1		
○○○	0TCT_DS03	D26CLNT800	1	P	
○○○	0TCT_DS02	D26CLNT800	1	P	
○○○	0BWTC_C09	D26CLNT800	1		
○○○	ZCPL_FORECAST	D26CLNT800	0	P	
○○○	6AZ_XML_PSI_DATA	D26CLNT800	0		
○○○	6AZ_PSI_XML_VENDOR	D26CLNT800	0		
○○○	6AZTAT_SHIPMENT2	D26CLNT800	0		
○○○	6AZTAT_SHIPMENT	D26CLNT800	0		
○○○	6AZTAT_IS01	D26CLNT800	0		
○○○	6AZSM_TAT_IS02	D26CLNT800	0		
○○○	6AZPOS_01	D26CLNT800	0		
○○○	0BWTC_C03	D26CLNT800	0		
○○○	0BWTC_C04	D26CLNT800	0		

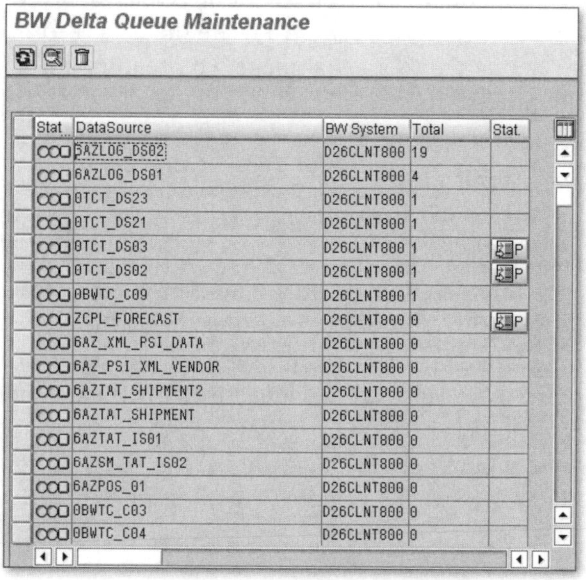

Figure 12.1 Administration of the Delta Queue

Displaying delta
queue data records

To check if, how much, and which data is contained in a delta queue, mark the delta queue and select Display Data Records. You will reach a dialog window where you can specify which data records are to be shown. You can select data packages whose data records you want to see or select specific data records from the data packages. In addition, you can carry out a simulation of the extraction parameters to display the data records.

Displaying the
current status of
the delta-relevant
field

For DataSources that support a generic delta, you can display the current value of the delta-relevant field in the delta queue by clicking the Detail button in the Status column. The value displayed contains the greatest value of the last extraction with regard to the delta-relevant field. It serves as a lower limit for the next extraction. If you select Refresh, newly activated delta queues are displayed, data records newly written to the delta queue are taken into consideration, and data records that have been deleted because of the last reading are no longer displayed.

Deleting the data
of a queue

To delete the data of a delta queue for a DataSource, mark the delta queue and select Delete Data via the context menu. Deleting the data of a delta queue does not require a new installation of the delta procedure to write the data records of the DataSource to the delta queue. Please note that even data that has not yet been read from the delta queue is also deleted. An existing delta update is therefore invalidated. Therefore, only use this function if you are aware of this. You can delete the entire queue via QUEUE • DELETE QUEUE. To write the data records of the corresponding DataSource to a delta queue, you require a new installation of the delta procedure.

Red Lights in the Queue Monitor

Red lights in the queue monitor generally mean that no information about the transfer structure exists for the DataSource in the ROOSGEN table (generated objects for the OLTP source). These problems often occur if the source system copy was deleted but not the RFC connection after a system copy, for example. In such cases, the transfer structures and any existing transfer rules are newly activated with the aid of the program. Executing this program restores the information for the (new) source system, where possible, and the light in the monitor is set to green again. Please note that it is merely the transfer structures

for SAP NetWeaver BW 3.x DataSources that are activated with the RS_
TRANSTRU_ACTIVATE_ALL program. To activate SAP NetWeaver BW
7.x DataSources as quickly as possible, you can use the RSDS_DATA-
SOURCE_ACTIVATE_ALL program. In general, only the DataSources
that are already known to be active in the system are activated so that
an A version exists in the database.

Delta Master Data Using Change Pointers

For many master data files, changes are logged for delta management
using ALE change pointers. In such cases when changes have been
made, the application writes a change document whose content is
transferred to the SMD (Shared Master Data Tool). Whenever a change
is made that is relevant for a DataSource, a change pointer of a specific
message type is written to the repository (BDCPV table) (Figure 12.2).

ALE change pointer

The message type of the DataSource (such as RS0027) is shown in the
ROOSGEN table in the MSGTYP field. Table fields are linked to message types in the TDB62 table, which can be maintained in Transaction
BD52 so that change pointers are only generated for the listed fields in
this table exclusively (even if additional fields are supposed to be a part
of the DataSource). Figure 12.3 illustrates this point using the example
of message type RS0027.

```
Table:        BDCPV
Displayed Fields:  8 of  8  Fixed Columns:          |3  List Width 0999
```

CPIDENT	MESTYPE	FLDNAME	CRETIME	CDOBJCL	CDOBJID
0054176768	RS0010	KEY	20080414202100	MATERIAL	1210-0256.1B
0054176780	RS0010	KEY	20080414202515	MATERIAL	1210-0885.1B
0054176797	RS0010	KEY	20080414202616	MATERIAL	1210-0889.1B
0054176809	RS0010	KEY	20080414203024	MATERIAL	1211-7715
0054176821	RS0010	KEY	20080414203025	MATERIAL	1211-7715.1
0054176833	RS0010	KEY	20080414204327	MATERIAL	1211-7721
0054176845	RS0010	KEY	20080414204327	MATERIAL	1211-7721.1
0054176857	RS0010	KEY	20080414204522	MATERIAL	1211-7715.1A
0054177339	RS0010	PRDHA	20080415013525	MATERIAL	1211-7303
0054177392	RS0010	LVORM	20080415014357	MATERIAL	BELLAKRHIA
0054177489	RS0010	PRDHA	20080415013525	MATERIAL	1211-7315
0054177490	RS0010	PRDHA	20080415013553	MATERIAL	1211-6968
0054177579	RS0010	MAGRV	20080415014148	MATERIAL	BELLADPYA

Figure 12.2 Change Pointer for MARA Table in BDCPV Table

Change document items for message type		
Object	Table Name	Field Name
MATERIAL	MARA	AEKLK
MATERIAL	MARA	AENAM
MATERIAL	MARA	AESZN
MATERIAL	MARA	ATTYP
MATERIAL	MARA	BEGRU
MATERIAL	MARA	BEHVO

Figure 12.3 Message Type for 0MATERIAL_ATTR

The assignment of a DataSource to a table, and therefore also to a change pointer, is carried out in the ROMDELTA table (Figure 12.4); this table is generally filled with the activation of a DataSource in Transaction RSA5.

Data Browser: Table ROMDDELTA Select Entries   2

Check Table...

Table: ROMDDELTA
Displayed Fields: 4 of 4 Fixed Columns: |2 List Width 0250

DataSource	OLPTSrc Version	Change doc. object	Table Name
0MATERIAL_ATTR	A	MATERIAL	MARA
0MATERIAL_ATTR	D	MATERIAL	MARA

Figure 12.4 Assignment of a Table to a DataSource

12.1.2 Number of Packages and Request Size

When loading very large amounts of data, you may often notice that the loading performance drops with an increasing number of loaded data packages for the same request or that the loading performance drops as more data targets are simultaneously updated. The following specifications are average empirical values that can vary greatly depending on the fundamental hardware, the system configuration, and the operating load.

Empirical values When loading data in SAP NetWeaver BW, you should ensure that no more than about 1,000 data packages are generated per request and no more than 10 million sentences are loaded per request. These numbers are not fixed upper limits for technical reasons, but rather amounts below which there should be few, if any, performance problems. If you have selected several data targets, you should divide the 1,000 data packages by the number of data targets. For five simultaneously updated data targets, therefore, no more than 200 data packages should be generated or loaded for a request.

Experience shows that, for requests with fewer than 1,500 data packages, all data packages are processed at the same speed, and no decrease in the runtime occurs even with an increase in the number of packages. From 1,500 packages and up, however, the runtime increases exponentially. This is caused by the functionality of the monitor log module, which selects all of the messages sent to the monitor for the request with each new message and adds the new message to the log. This log is used to determine whether the request will be yellow (in process), red (concluded with an error), or green (successfully concluded). If two data targets are simultaneously filled by a request instead of one data target, then twice as many messages occur. The upper limit of data packages should therefore be divided by the number of data targets.

If it is impossible to generate smaller requests or fewer than 1,000 data packages, then you should only load into the PSA and then fill each data target separately with this request. Each PSA process or rebuild is given its own log ID for the monitor so that not all data targets are logged in the same request log (in the loading log of the request). The first data target built by a PSA process or rebuild is logged under the request number itself (REQU_...), whereas all others are logged under their own REBU_... log number. These logs are then displayed in the monitor under the subnode Rebuild in the detail tree.

12.1.3 Common Loading Processes

If you have data that has to be loaded very often, you should use real-time data acquisition (RDA). If you are not able to do so, for instance, because the DataSource does not support RDA, then you must watch the increase in the number of requests carefully because there is an upper limit to the number of requests a system can process. The increase in the number of requests has two effects on the system:

▶ A new partition is created in an Oracle database on the basis of each   **Effects**
loading of data. The increase in the number of uncompressed requests leads to a great number of partitions in the system and causes over-

head for the administration of the database catalog. Therefore, regular compression of the InfoCube is necessary. Even if the compression does not reduce the number of entries in the InfoCube (compression rate = 1), it is nevertheless recommended from the viewpoint of database administration that you regularly compress the requests.

▶ The size of the status tables for the processing of requests also increases. Based on extensive logs in SAP NetWeaver BW, the number of requests per data target should not exceed 30,000 (10,000 in SAP NetWeaver BW 3.x).

Archiving status tables

As of Release 7.0, you can archive the administration information on the load times of the requests so that the size of the status tables for the requests (such as RSMONMES or RSSELDONE) can be controlled. If you execute the following operation, the administration information on the requests in the targets must be checked and changed for all of the requests for which data is present in the InfoCube. This includes the compressed InfoCubes and is necessary for the subsequent processing. Deactivate the delta administration and the reinitialization; delete the aggregate or SAP NetWeaver BW Accelerator indexes of an InfoCube and reactivate it. The reactivation of the aggregate and the SAP NetWeaver BW Accelerator index is necessary because, as of Release 7.0, fast access tables are available for the status controls, which behave as follows: If you initialize a delta or aggregate, or if you build SAP NetWeaver BW Accelerator indexes, change the markers for all transferred requests in the fast access tables (DM field, rollup field, and so on) and thereby show that they have been transferred to another data target.

The status fields of all requests must be checked for the first delta or rollup. Therefore, the first execution takes a bit longer. The subsequent deltas or rollups are then faster because only the new or changed requests have to be checked instead of all of them. This is a new feature in Release 7.x, and it has improved the performance of normal deltas and rollups. Nevertheless, note that the system must read, prepare, and edit all of the status table entries of the compressed and uncompressed requests from the database during the first delta or rollup, so too many requests in the first delta or rollup can lead to noticeable performance problems.

If the subsequent deltas or rollups lead to performance problems after you have initialized a delta or built an aggregate or SAP NetWeaver BW Accelerator index, and if the cause is that the check phase for the status control table takes a long time because of the large number of requests, then the only solution is to lower the number of requests in the InfoCube.

12.1.4 InfoPackage in Process Chains

If an InfoPackage is loaded in a process chain, then all automatic functions are inactive, and no postprocessing is carried out. Only processes that follow the loading process in the process chain are carried out. The following automatic functions are not carried out:

Automatic functions and postprocessing

- ▶ Automatic rollup
- ▶ Automatic compression
- ▶ Automatic activation (for ODS objects)
- ▶ Automatic updates (for ODS)
- ▶ Automatic deletion of overlapping requests
- ▶ Automatic deletion of the data target content
- ▶ Automatic index statistic rebuild
- ▶ Automatic deletion of indexes
- ▶ Automatic updates from the PSA

No postprocessing for the triggering of events or calling of BAdIs or function modules is carried out in the old InfoPackage either. The only automatic function that is still carried out is the automatic setting of the QM status (quality status of the request) because there is no process type in the process chain that can set this indicator. For all other automatic functions (such as rollup or compression), on the other hand, there are process chain processes that can carry out these actions. The user can replace or reproduce BAdIs, events, and so on with the aid of a simple customer report and the ABAP process type.

12.1.5 Number of Dialog Processes

With SAP NetWeaver BW Service API 7.0, the transfer of data in combination with a BW system from SAP NetWeaver 7.0 has been set to

New methods for data transfer

the standard tRFC scheduler. Up to and including SAP NetWeaver BW Service API 3.0C, the transfer of the data packages is carried out by the expansions of the outbound scheduling (QOUT Scheduler) that are now available. Settings in the corresponding SMQS control transaction were irrelevant. In certain cases it was necessary to explicitly deregister the SAP NetWeaver BW destination, however. The old method dealt with the transfer per DataSource controlled by the service API (S-API), which can be configured via entries in the ROIDOCPRMS or ROOSPRMS table.

As of the SAP NetWeaver BW Service API status in SAP NetWeaver 7.0 (plug-in basis 2005.1), the control of the transfer is (optionally) set to the standardized outbound scheduling of the queued RFC (qRFC). The use of the standard RFC scheduler for SAP NetWeaver BW data transfers between SAP systems is a logical progression toward the use of the same internal procedures for various applications. The new functionality of the data loading in SAP NetWeaver BW 7.0 via new DataSources, DTPs, and transformations is adapted to the data transfer in the PSA as an inbound layer of the SAP NetWeaver BW system. The differences are as follows:

▸ **If the release of the connected SAP NetWeaver BW system ≤ SAP BW 3.5**
The default remains unchanged. You can change the setting manually with the RSA1_TRFC_OPTION_SET program. Alternatively, you can automate the deregistration of the SAP NetWeaver BW destination.

▸ **If the release of the connected SAP NetWeaver BW system ≥ SAP NetWeaver 7.0**
The default is changed, but you can undo the change using the program mentioned above.

If the standardized outbound scheduling is used, the number of processes used to transfer the data packages to the SAP NetWeaver BW system must be maintained in Transaction SMQS for the SAP NetWeaver BW destination.

Global settings The global settings for data transfer (see SAP CUSTOMIZING IMPLEMENTATION GUIDE (Transaction SPRO) • INTEGRATION WITH OTHER SAP COMPONENTS • DATA TRANSFER TO THE SAP BUSINESS INFORMATION WAREHOUSE • GENERAL SETTINGS • MAINTAIN CONTROL PARAMETERS FOR

DATA TRANSFER) only influence the number of processes with which the data packages are transferred to the tRFC by the extraction process for transfer.

Using the RSA1_TRFC_OPTION_SET program (called in Transaction SA38), you define how the data transfer is triggered in the SAP source system.

Performance Problems

Because the data is normally transferred to the PSA very quickly, transfer in the standard RFC is not problematic for scenarios in SAP NetWeaver BW 7.0. The same is true for old 3.5 loading scenarios, where data was merely loaded into the PSA and then subsequently loaded into the data target. The RFC scheduler then frees the connection again right after the confirmation that the posting to the PSA was successfully completed.

There are often performance problems with old loading scenarios that already fill one or more InfoProviders as an input data target. The RFC connection is not freed again until the data of a package has also been updated to the last InfoProvider of the request.

However, because all requests, even of different DataSources, are processed in a queue of the RFC scheduler, subsequent packages must wait for these long-running requests. It is not unusual for an update of the SAP NetWeaver BW system to terminate with a TIME_OUT short dump. In the monitor, the error message usually indicates an error with "caller 70." The methods were therefore expanded with SAP NetWeaver BW 7.0 Support Package 18:

▶ Requests that do not end in the PSA are now automatically controlled by S-API and sent according to the old procedure.

▶ Requests according to the new procedure (via DTP) or the old procedure using a PSA use the RFC scheduler by default.

The following section explains how you can prevent activities from being terminated because of authorization errors.

12.1.6 Defining the Server or Host and User

The termination of activities such as data extraction, update, and other process steps because the wrong user is used is a common problem. There are several places in the SAP NetWeaver BW system where the host or server and/or the user to be used for an activity can be set.

Process chains During an execution, the user for which the job is carried out and the server can be selected in the background for all main processes of the process chain (therefore, all BI_PROCESS_* jobs). You select the user for execution in the menu under PROCESS CHAIN • ATTRIBUTES • USER FOR EXECUTION and the background server under PROCESS CHAIN • ATTRIBUTES • BACKGROUND SERVER.

Loading process via InfoPackage The data request (collection and check) is always executed by the user who starts the InfoPackage. As long as it is part of a process chain, this is the user and server that are set there.

Sending the request As long as the source system is the MySelf system, the request is processed in the source system under the same user and server that compiled the data request. This user must therefore have the profile S_BI-WX_RFC and, as long as you extract from BW objects (InfoCubes and so on), the user must also have the profile S_BI-WHM_RFC to be authorized to access SAP NetWeaver BW data.

If the source system is a remote system (or another client), the request is sent via RFC. In doing so, the server and user are normally switched to the destination settings. The entered user must have the profile S_BI-WX_RFC. You can find the destination via the Connection Parameters menu entry in the context menu of the source system in the Data Warehousing Workbench.

Data extraction The extraction in the source system occurs in a background job that is planned on a random server by default. You can explicitly select a server via the IMG function Maintain Control Parameters for Data Transfer in Transaction SBIW (ROIDOCPRMS table).

Data dispatch The extracted data is sent back to the SAP NetWeaver BW system via qRFC. When this occurs, the server and user are normally switched to the destination settings. The entered user must have the profile S_BI-WHM_RFC. The destination used has the same name as the logical name of the SAP NetWeaver BW system.

If you are dealing with the MySelf system, there are a few peculiarities to note. If a destination of the type ERP does not have a host or a system number entered, a logon is executed in the current system during an RFC. If neither server nor user is indicated, no actual logon is executed. If you still want to maintain the data because a special server is to be used, you must note the following:

▶ When copying or moving the SAP NetWeaver BW system, the destination must be adjusted or else errors will occur during the extraction or activation of ODS objects because the corresponding functions are executed on the old server.

▶ You are required to enter the client if you enter a user, because otherwise errors will occur during the import postprocessing.

▶ The user entered must have the profiles S_BI-WX_RFC and S_BI-WHM_RFC because the destination is used for both access to the source system and access to the SAP NetWeaver BW system. There must also be a dialog user, or else no remote dialog functions such as the display of logs can be executed.

The processing of a DTP request is divided into two parts. The creation part takes place with the user and the server that are set for the process chain. For the processing part, you can specify the server for the processing in the DTP maintenance in the menu GOTO • BATCH MANAGER SETTINGS. The degree of parallelism can also be set there.

Loading process via data transfer process

For the activities listed in Table 12.1, subactivities are executed in parallel batch processes that are controlled by the batch manager.

Parallelism using a batch manager

Process	Activity
InfoPackage (DataSource 7.x)	Updating the data to the PSA
Data transfer process (DTP)	Transformation and updating
DataStore data activation	SID verification and writing to the A table
DataStore data deletion	Rolling back change log data
Initial filling of aggregates	Writing to empty aggregates
Rollup of data	Filling aggregates further
DataStore data archiving	Archiving of DataStore data
Attribute change run	Adjusting aggregates and hierarchies

Table 12.1 Subactivities in Batch Processes

Process	Activity
Building a BIA index	Building one or more indexes
PSA process	Updating data from the PSA with SAP NetWeaver BW 3.x logic
Remodeling	Remodeling data in InfoCubes
Master data	Where-used list and activation of master data

Table 12.1 Subactivities in Batch Processes (Cont.)

The batch manager allows you to select the server (or host or server group) on which the parent process generates its child processes. These generally run with the same user as the parent process. The settings for the individual processes must initially be carried out on the process itself, meaning in the variant maintenance of the process chain. After this has been done once, however, all existing variants and their settings in Transaction RSBATCH can be maintained with the Mass Maintenance of Settings for Parallel Processing function.

Import postprocessing   A special destination is used in the import postprocessing (after import) for the planning of the process chains and for the activation of Web service DataSources. You maintained these via Transaction RSTPRFC. This generally does not involve the MySelf destination mentioned above, because you must enter all of the parameters (client, user, and password) for the destination used here. The user must have the profile S_BI-WHM_RFC in the target client.

Real-time data acquisition   As of SAP NetWeaver 7.1, with real-time data acquisition you can configure a user for execution similarly to the process chains (in the RDA monitor, Transaction RSRDA, under DAEMON • SETTINGS • USER FOR EXECUTION). The SAP NetWeaver BW background user is used as the default setting. In SAP NetWeaver 7.0, the user who starts the daemon is always used for executing the background job. Executing the background job includes the loading process in the SAP NetWeaver BW system (not the part in the source system), the data transfer process, and the activation of the data in the InfoProvider. The user for execution requires the appropriate authorizations for these activities. You will find more information about the RDA in Section 12.1.10, Real-Time Data Acquisition.

12.1.7   Direct Loading of Master Data

In the maintenance of the data transfer process (DTP) you can specify that the data is not extracted from the PSA of the DataSource, but rather is requested directly from the data source during the runtime of the DTPs. The Don't extract from PSA, but access data source (for small data amounts) flag is shown for the full-extraction mode if the source of the DTP is a DataSource. It is recommended that you only use that flag for small amounts of data, particularly for small amounts of master data.

If you set this flag, no InfoPackage is necessary to extract the data from the source. When extracting from data source systems, ensure that the file is present on the application server. The extraction via the direct access mode has the following implications, particularly for SAP source systems (extraction via the service API):

Interdependencies

▶ The data is extracted synchronously, which means special demands on the main memory, primarily in the source system.

▶ The SAPI extractors may behave differently than with asynchronous loading because they are informed via direct access.

▶ No SAPI customer enhancements are processed. Fields that were added to the DataSource with append technology remain empty. The customer exits RSAP0001, EXIT_SAPLRSAP_001, EXIT_SAPLRSAP_002, and EXIT_SAPLRSAP_004 do not run.

▶ If there are errors in the processing in the SAP NetWeaver BW system, you have to extract the data again because the PSA is not available as a buffer. For the same reason, no delta is possible.

▶ The filters in the DTP only contain the fields that the DataSource permits as selection fields. With an intermediate PSA you can use all of the fields for filtering in the DTP.

The extraction is based on the technology of synchronous direct access to the DataSource where the data is not shown as it usually is with a direct access, but rather is updated in a data target without saving in the PSA.

12.1.8 Extractor Checker

You can text the extraction from DataSources independently of a SAP NetWeaver BW system by using the extractor checker in Transaction RSA3 (Figure 12.5). After the test extraction, you can display the extracted data and the corresponding logs.

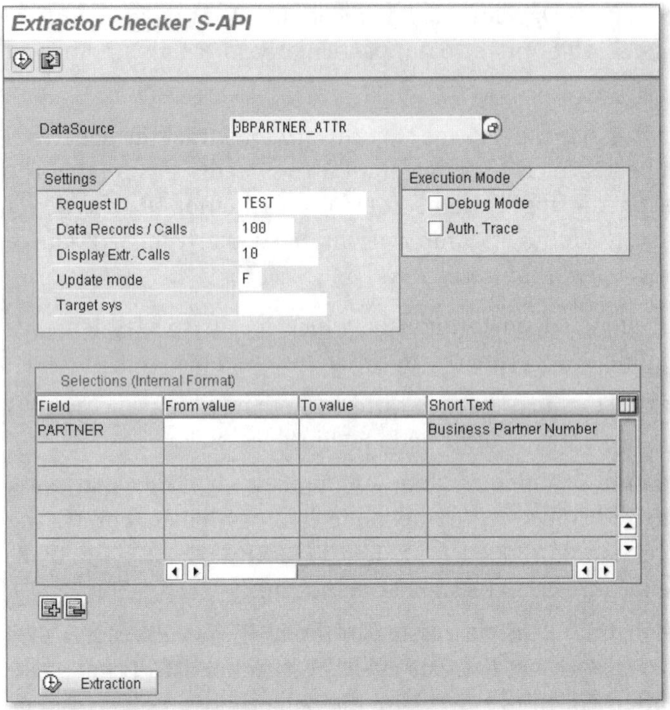

Figure 12.5 Extractor Checker (Transaction RSA3)

When an extraction has been successfully completed, you receive a message indicating the number of extracted records. The Display list (displays the data packages), Display log (calls the use logs), and Display trace buttons appear on the screen. To run a test of the extraction, proceed as follows:

Test of the extraction

1. Enter the technical name of the DataSource.

2. Specify how many data records should be read per call of the extractor.

3. The service API calls the extractor until no more data is present. In the Number of Extractor Calls field you can specify how often the extractor should be called at most. You can therefore restrict the number of data packages while testing the extraction of a DataSource. In a real extraction, data packages would be transferred for as long as it takes until no more data is found.

4. Depending on the definition of the DataSource, you can test the extraction in various update modes. For DataSources that support delta procedures, you can also test deltas and reports in addition to the full update. The delta and repeat modes are only available for testing if the extractor supports a mode in which data is read but the status tables of the delta administration are not modified. To avoid inconsistencies with the SAP NetWeaver BW system, you cannot change the pointers and time stamp stored in the delta administration during the testing. Before you can test the extraction in a delta mode in the source system, in SAP NetWeaver BW you must run an initialization of the delta procedure or a simulation of the initialization for this DataSource. For noncumulative values, you can test the transfer of an opening stock.

5. Enter the selection for the test extraction. Only the fields of the extract structure that you have marked accordingly in the DataSource maintenance are available for selection. To be able to enter several selections for a field, add new rows to this field in the selection table.

6. Select whether you want to execute the test extraction in debug mode or with a recording of an authorization trace. When you test the extraction in debug mode, a breakpoint is set shortly before the initialization call of the extractor. If you record an authorization trace, you can call it after the test via Display trace.

7. Start the extraction.

Up to and including Service API Release 3.0, all fields of a DataSource were used in the extractor checker (Transaction RSA3). The transfer structure on a DataSource in the SAP NetWeaver BW system, in contrast, can only contain a lower amount of the fields of a DataSource. If the transfer structure contains a reduced number of fields, only these fields are extracted from the source system by a BW request. This can lead to the extraction result of Transaction RSA and that of the BW request being different from one another, particularly when using the

Differences between extraction and extraction checker

S-API customer exit. One of the reasons for this can be that fields are used in the customer exit that are not contained in the transfer structure of the DataSource in the SAP NetWeaver BW system.

Another cause of differing results can be the package size, which you can manually set in the extractor checker. In the BW request, the package size is calculated from the specifications in the ROIDOCPRMS table, which you can maintain via the SAP NetWeaver BW customizing (Transaction SBIW). Some extractors and customer exits provide different data depending on what size of packages were requested. For a realistic test, set the package size in Transaction RSA3 to be the same as that used by SAP NetWeaver BW. The following causes are also conceivable for differing results:

► Instead of DATETO/DATEFROM fields, the extract structure contains the BEGDA/ENDDA or DATAB/DATBI fields. Transaction RSA3 does not react to them, but the SAP NetWeaver BW system cannot work with these fields. The background of this behavior is the fact that the extract structure of the DataSource must contain the DATETO and DATEFROM fields to properly extract time-dependent master data. The fields of the extract structure, in turn, must correspond exactly to those in the view from which the extraction occurs. The date fields must therefore already have the names DATETO and DATEFROM in the view. If the table that the view is based on has other field names, these table fields must be assigned to the DATETO and DATEFROM view fields within the view maintenance.

► Authorizations for the ALEREMOTE user are different than for the RSA3 user. Authorizations are often requested during the extraction from SAP ERP HCM DataSources and the generic extraction on the basis of SAP queries or InfoSet queries. The extraction can therefore output different key figures with the same selection conditions. For testing, the extraction should be carried out in the extractor checker with a user who has the same authorizations as the remote user.

► A dialog user is always used in the extractor checker. The SAP NetWeaver BW extraction user can be a system user under certain conditions, however.

► The customer exit of the service API is only called if at least one data record is found. If nothing is found in the SAP NetWeaver BW system via selection (in the case of time-dependent DataSources, for example), then the customer exit is not executed. The extractor checker does find data records, however, because selections via the DATETO/ DATEFROM fields are not explicitly expressed, for example. As a result, the customer exit runs, which means data can be added or existing data can be changed.

▶ The transfer structure in the source system is inactive. The name of the transfer structure is found in the ROOSGEN table in the TFSTRUC field. The field list that is actually used for extraction is that of the active transfer structure.

▶ For a delta extraction using the generic delta determination, keep in mind that the extractor must always call the right selection on the delta-relevant field for a delta or delta init to achieve a comparable result in the extractor checker. To test the delta init of a DataSource with a calendar day as a delta-relevant field, for instance, a full update must be carried out in the extractor checker with the selection 01.01.1000 to the current date minus 1 (yesterday's date).

▶ In a test extraction, the SAP NetWeaver system completes selection criteria in the language field according to the `zcsa/ installed_lan- guages` (language vector) system parameter. These selection criteria are not visible in the InfoPackage, but they can be displayed in the request IDoc, for example. To select a comparable amount of data in the extractor checker, you must also filter the language field there accordingly.

The following section will show you how to avoid errors caused by IDocs that are not transferred.

12.1.9 IDoc Errors

A common problem in the extraction process is that requests with a yellow status get stuck in the load monitor and, after a time out, finally switch to red status. Info IDocs with the status 64 can be seen in the Details tab. IDoc types for SAP NetWeaver BW (RSINFO, RSRQST, RSSEND) are processed immediately. If no free dialog process is available, however, they remain where they are and must be started again to transfer the request information. With the asynchronous processing selected, it can often occur that no dialog processes for tRFCs are available for short periods of time. IDocs with the status 64 can also occur

Pending requests with IDocs in status 64

for other reasons, for example, because of a rollback in the application that updates the IDocs.

So how can these problems be solved? For SAP NetWeaver BW systems, the basic recommendation is asynchronous processing. To avoid bottlenecks in the dialog processing and checking of the IDocs for SAP NetWeaver BW, the following basic recommendations also apply:

- You should ensure that there are always enough dialog processes (DIA) available, meaning one DIA more than all of the other work processes together. With 15 available work processes, for example, at least eight dialog processes should be defined. Also take note that, in SAP NetWeaver BW systems, two UPD processes are sufficient, and no UP2 processes are necessary.

- You should manually process unprocessed Info IDocs within the request in the SAP NetWeaver BW system; each IDoc can be started again in the Detail tab with Update manually (right-click the context menu).

- You should check the system for unprocessed IDocs with Transaction BD87 every day or when needed if a problem arises, and restart them if necessary. Before doing that, however, you must first ensure that these IDocs can actually be assigned to the current status of requests. You should also use Transaction SM58 to check for problematic tRFC entries.

Missing Info IDocs is another common problem. If a request is loaded via a data mart update, the extracted requests are only marked as retrieved in the data administration of the source after the extraction has been successfully completed. That means that if even just one Info IDoc was sent incorrectly, the sent data is not marked as retrieved in the data administration of the source.

12.1.10 Real-Time Data Acquisition

When using real-time data acquisition (RDA), problems can occur during the data transfer to the PSA and the updating of the data from the PSA to an InfoProvider. If the data transfer for a DataSource terminates and only this DataSource is assigned to the daemon, the daemon also terminates. If additional DataSources are assigned to the daemon, however, only the data transfer with the error terminates. In this case the daemon remains active as long as the data transfer for one of the DataSources assigned to it runs correctly.

The daemon records every successfully completed step in a control table. It is therefore in the position to restart after a termination in an extraction or update and then continue the process from the step where it terminated. In doing so, it repeats the complete step to the level of detail of one data package. If the execution of the DTP is terminated, for example, the daemon draws the new data from the source and loads it into the InfoProvider along with the data packages that were previously terminated. In the InfoPackage you can define the maximum number of such failed attempts during the loading or closing of requests by the daemon before the final termination.

In the monitor for real-time data acquisition (Transaction RSRDA), the daemons present in the system are displayed in a tree structure along with the objects assigned to them (Figure 12.6). The monitor displays the status of the daemons and their assigned objects and thereby provides the option to monitor both the daemon itself and the update of the data to the PSA and to an InfoProvider.

RDA monitor

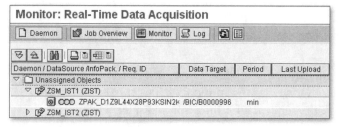

Figure 12.6 RDA Monitor (Transaction RSRDA)

The system displays all DataSources that are assigned to a daemon underneath that daemon. Under a DataSource, the associated InfoPackage for real-time data acquisition that contains the parameters for the data transfer is displayed. DataSources with InfoPackages that you have not yet assigned to any daemon are listed in the system under Unassigned Objects. If you have assigned a data transfer process (DTP) to the DataSource, the system displays it at the same rank as the InfoPackage. Under an InfoPackage or data transfer process, the open request that updates the data to the PSA table or to the DataStore object is displayed. The system only shows the DTP request if data is present in the PSA. If

397

you have assigned a subsequent process chain to a daemon via a data transfer process, the process chain is displayed under the data transfer process. At any level of the overview, you can access the display of the daemon job via GOTO • JOB OVERVIEW or via the corresponding context menu entry.

Daemon log

For an analysis of any errors, the log can be called via the context menu of a daemon or via GOTO • LOG. You can restrict the log display to the relevant period via the application log (Transaction SLG1). To do this, select RSAP as the object in the application log and REALTIME as the subobject. Enter the InfoPackage ID as the external identification and specify the time period for which the log should be displayed. On the basis of the messages, you can usually quickly determine whether the error occurred in the extraction or in the transformation.

Correcting extraction errors

If the PSA request is marked red because an error occurred during the extraction, for example, if the RFC connection was interrupted, the background job was deleted, or the system terminated, proceed as follows:

1. Check the data in the PSA. To do this, select the Monitor PSA request in the context menu. In the monitor you can display the data in the PSA via PSA Maintenance. If the technical status of the request is red and you have corrected the error in the extraction, proceed as with the next step.

2. Delete the request from the PSA. To do this, call the list of requests in the PSA by double-clicking in the Data Target column for the PSA request. Mark the request with the error and select Delete.

3. To repeat the last delta update (Repeat), create a (standard) InfoPackage for the DataSource in the Data Warehousing Workbench, select Delta Update in the Update tab, and execute the InfoPackage.

4. Check the status of the PSA request in the extraction monitor and then return to the monitor for real-time data acquisition.

Repair process chain

5. Select Generate Repair Process Chain in the context menu of the data transfer processes that are assigned to the DataSource. The system generates a process chain for a data transfer process in the Repair Process Chain for Real-Time Data Acquisition (RDA) display component. In addition to the start process, the chain also contains the data transfer process and, if necessary, the activation of the data in the Data-

Store object and subsequent process chains, to the extent to which they can be defined for the data transfer process.

6. Select Execute Repair Process Chain in the context menu for the data transfer process. The relevant process chain starts immediately and conducts the repair as follows: The standard DTP is executed. When this occurs, all data from the PSA that is not yet present in the DataStore object is transferred to the DataStore object. For standard DataStore objects, when the data is successfully updated in the DataStore object, the activation of the data is executed. If subsequent process chains are present for the data transfer process, these are executed.

7. Activate the data transfer with real-time data acquisition once more. If the daemon was previously terminated, restart it via Restart Batch Job in the context menu of the daemon. If you have previously deleted the assignment of the DataSource to the daemon because the daemon is still processing other DataSources, and if the daemon is already running, then reassign the DataSource to the daemon via Assign to Daemon in the context menu of the DataSource. The daemon then adopts the DataSource into the processing with a few minutes of delay.

12.1.11 Replication of DataSources

In the SAP source system, the DataSource is the SAP NetWeaver BW–relevant metaobject that makes the source data available in a flat structure for data transfer to the SAP NetWeaver BW system. A DataSource can be present in the source system in the SAP delivery version (D version: object type R3TR OSOD) and the active version (A version: object type R3TR OSOA).

The metadata from SAP source systems is independent of the metadata of the SAP NetWeaver BW system. There is no implicit assignment of the objects via name similarities. The relevant metadata in SAP NetWeaver BW is made known via the replication to accelerate the rereading. The assignment of source system objects to BW objects is carried out exclusively and centrally in the SAP NetWeaver BW system.

There are two types of DataSources in the SAP NetWeaver BW system. A DataSource can be present as either a DataSource (R3TR RSDS) or as a DataSource 3.x (R3TR ISFS). Figure 12.7 shows the emulated display of a DataSource in SAP NetWeaver BW 3.x format. Because it is not possible for a specific DataSource in a specific source system to be pres-

DataSource and DataSource 3.x

ent in both objects in the system at the same time, and because these objects are not differentiated in the source system, you must decide which object the metadata should be replicated to when executing the replication.

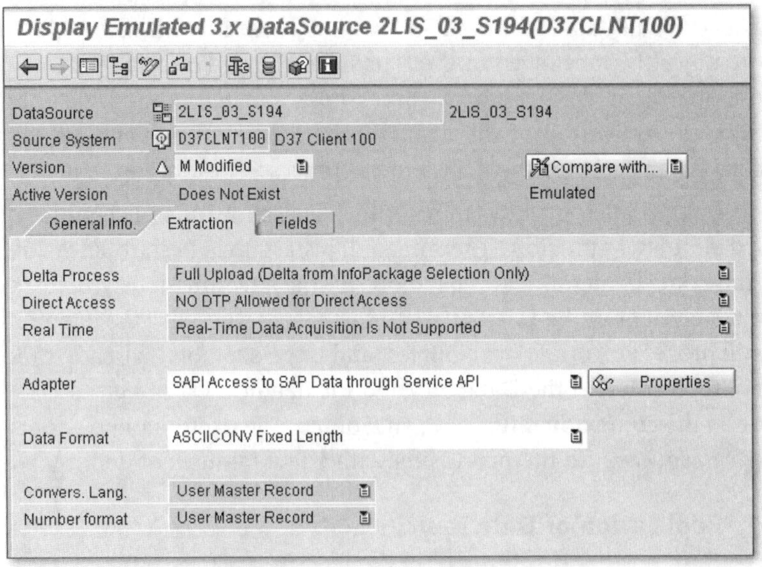

Display Emulated 3.x DataSource 2LIS_03_S194(D37CLNT100)

DataSource	2LIS_03_S194		2LIS_03_S194	
Source System	D37CLNT100	D37 Client 100		
Version	△ M Modified			Compare with...
Active Version	Does Not Exist			Emulated

General Info.	Extraction	Fields

Delta Process	Full Upload (Delta from InfoPackage Selection Only)
Direct Access	NO DTP Allowed for Direct Access
Real Time	Real-Time Data Acquisition Is Not Supported
Adapter	SAPI Access to SAP Data through Service API Properties
Data Format	ASCIICONV Fixed Length
Convers. Lang.	User Master Record
Number format	User Master Record

Figure 12.7 Emulated Display of a 3.x DataSource

Depending on your needs, you can replicate the entire metadata of an SAP source system (application component hierarchy and DataSources), the DataSources of an application component of a source system, or individual DataSources of a source system in the SAP NetWeaver BW system. When you create an SAP source system, an automatic replication of the metadata occurs. During a data request, an automatic replication of the DataSource occurs if the DataSource in the source system has changed.

Replication Procedure

Replication of D versions In the first step, only the DataSource header tables of Business Content DataSources are saved as a D version in SAP NetWeaver BW. The replication of the header tables is a prerequisite for collecting and activating the BI Content.

- If SHDS is available for the SHDS D-TLOGO object in the SAP NetWeaver BW system shadow content, the relevant metadata is replicated to the DataSource (R3TR RSDS). The replication is only performed if no A (or M) version of the other object type R3TR ISFS exists for the DataSource.

- If SHMP (mapping of the 3.x DataSource) is available for the D-TLOGO object in the BI shadow content, the relevant metadata is replicated in the 3.x DataSource (R3TR ISFS). The replication is only performed if no A (or M) version of the other object type R3TR RSDS exists for the DataSource.

- If no BI content exists in the D version for a DataSource (R3TR OSOD) in the SAP NetWeaver BW system, the D version cannot be replicated because this version is only used in SAP NetWeaver BW for the activation of BI Content.

In the second step, DataSources (R3TR RSDS) are saved in the M version in SAP NetWeaver BW with all relevant metadata. This avoids generating an unnecessary amount of DDIC objects as long as the DataSource is not yet being used, meaning as long as there is not yet any transformation for the DataSource. 3.x DataSources (R3TR ISFS) are saved in the SAP NetWeaver BW system in the A version with all of the relevant metadata.

Replication of A versions

- As a basic principle, the object type of the A version follows the object type of the D version. If the DataSource already exists in the SAP NetWeaver BW system in the A or D version, the DataSource is replicated to the existing object

- If the DataSource does not yet exist in the SAP NetWeaver BW system, the system conducts the replication according to the following logic:

  - If it is a hierarchy or export DataSource, the object type is specified for the replication. Hierarchy DataSources and export DataSources (8*) are replicated to 3.x DataSources.

  - If there is a D version in the SAP NetWeaver BW system for a mapping object (R3TR ISMP), the system performs replication to the 3.x DataSource (R3TR ISFS).

  - Otherwise, the system asks the user to which object type the DataSource is to be replicated. Ensure that you replicate the DataSource correctly: For example, if you have modeled the data flow with 3.x objects from BI Content and are therefore using update and transfer rules, ensure that you replicate the DataSource to a 3.x DataSource. If you have replicated the DataSource incorrectly, you can no longer use the BI Content data model.

Keep in mind that, even in the Business Content delivered by SAP, many data flows are still based on objects from SAP NetWeaver BW 3.x, yet some were already migrated to the new technology. As a result, some objects exist in both versions, which you must take into account when activating content.

Deleting Data Sources During Replication

DataSources are only deleted during replication if you perform replication for an entire source system or for a particular DataSource. The system does not delete any DataSources during the replication of DataSources for a particular application component because they may have been assigned to another application component in the meantime. If, during replication, the system determines that the D version of a DataSource in the source system or the associated BI Content (shadow objects of DataSource R3TR SHDS or shadow objects of mapping R3TR SHMP) is not available in the SAP NetWeaver BW system (anymore), the system automatically deletes the D version in the SAP NetWeaver BW system.

If, during replication, the system determines that the A version of a DataSource in the source system is not or is no longer available, the SAP NetWeaver BW system asks whether you want to delete the DataSource in the SAP NetWeaver BW system. If you confirm that you want to delete the DataSource, the system also deletes all dependent objects, the PSA, InfoPackage, transformation, data transfer process (where applicable), and in the case of 3.x DataSource, the mapping and transfer structure, if they exist. Before confirming that you want to delete the DataSource and related objects, ensure that you are no longer using the objects that will be deleted. If it is only temporarily not possible to replicate the DataSource, confirming the deletion prompt may cause relevant objects to be deleted.

Automatic Replication During Data Request

You can use a setting in the InfoPackage maintenance under Extras •
Synchronize metadata to define that automatic synchronization of the
metadata in the SAP NetWeaver BW system with the metadata in the
source system is to take place whenever there is a data request. If this
checkbox is selected, the DataSource is automatically replicated from
the SAP NetWeaver BW system upon each data request if the Data-
Source has changed in the source system (Figure 12.8).

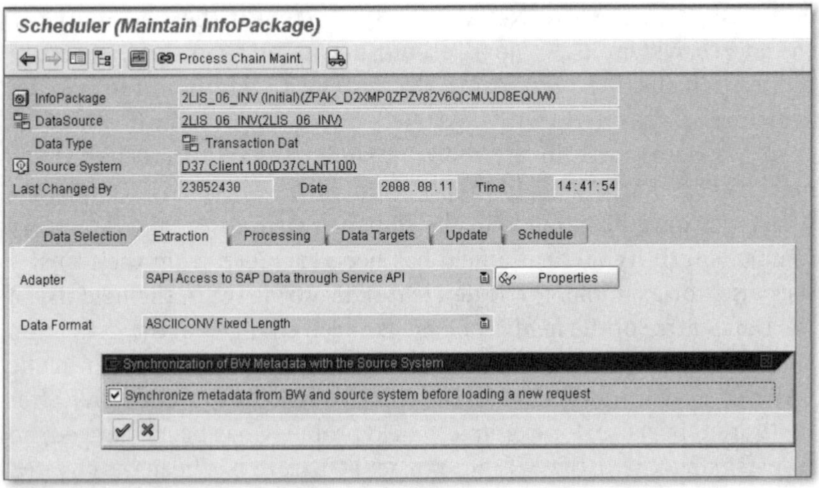

Synchronization of the metadata

Figure 12.8 Automatic Replication

This function ensures that requests are not refused in the source system
because of the default time stamp comparison, even though the Data-
Source has not really changed. With replication, a distinction must be
made between DataSource types and the types of changes in the source
system.

When a request is created in the InfoPackage, the DataSource is
refreshed in the SAP NetWeaver BW system if the DataSource in the
source system has a more recent time stamp than the DataSource in the
SAP NetWeaver BW system. In addition, the DataSource is activated in
the SAP NetWeaver BW system (including the transfer structure generation in the source system) if it is older than the DataSource in the
source system. It is only activated if the object status was active after

DataSource (R3TR RSDS)

replication, however. This is not the case if changes have been made in the source system to the field property (name, length, type) or if a field has been excluded from the transfer (because, for example, the Hide Field indicator is set in the field list of the DataSource or the field property has been changed in the extraction structure). In these cases, the DataSource is deactivated in the SAP NetWeaver BW system. If the DataSource is not active after replication, the system produces an error message, and the DataSource must then be activated manually.

DataSource 3.x
(R3TR ISFS)

When a request is created in the InfoPackage, the DataSource replicate is refreshed in the SAP NetWeaver BW system if the DataSource in the source system has a more recent time stamp than the DataSource replicate in the SAP NetWeaver BW system. In addition, the transfer structure is activated in the SAP NetWeaver BW system if it is older than the DataSource in the source system. It is only activated if the object status was active after replication, however. This is not the case if changes have been made in the source system to the field property (name, length, type) or if a field has been excluded from the transfer (because, for example, the Hide Field indicator is set in the field list of the DataSource or the field property has been changed in the extraction structure). In these cases, the transfer structure is deactivated in the SAP NetWeaver BW system. If the transfer structure is not active after replication because, for example, a field property has been changed, no transfer structure exists; if the transfer structure has been deactivated because of changes to the data flow, the system produces an error message, and you have to activate the transfer structure manually.

12.2 Change Run

If changes have been made to master data (navigation attributes) used in aggregates or to the hierarchies of a characteristic, these objects must be adjusted accordingly. This guarantees consistency between queries that access the InfoCube or assigned aggregates. In contrast to the aggregates, no data referring to navigation attributes or hierarchies is stored in the InfoCube itself. The relevant master data or hierarchy tables are linked to the tables of the InfoCube when a query is executed.

Regardless of whether aggregates exist, changes to master data records are not automatically adopted, but rather must be explicitly activated.

If aggregates are affected, they must be adjusted before the changes to the data records are released using the change run.

12.2.1 Detailed Flow

You can start the change run as a process in a process chain or via the Administrator Workbench (AWB): TRANSACTION RSA1 • TOOLS • HIER-ARCHY/ATTRIBUTE CHANGES (Figure 12.9).

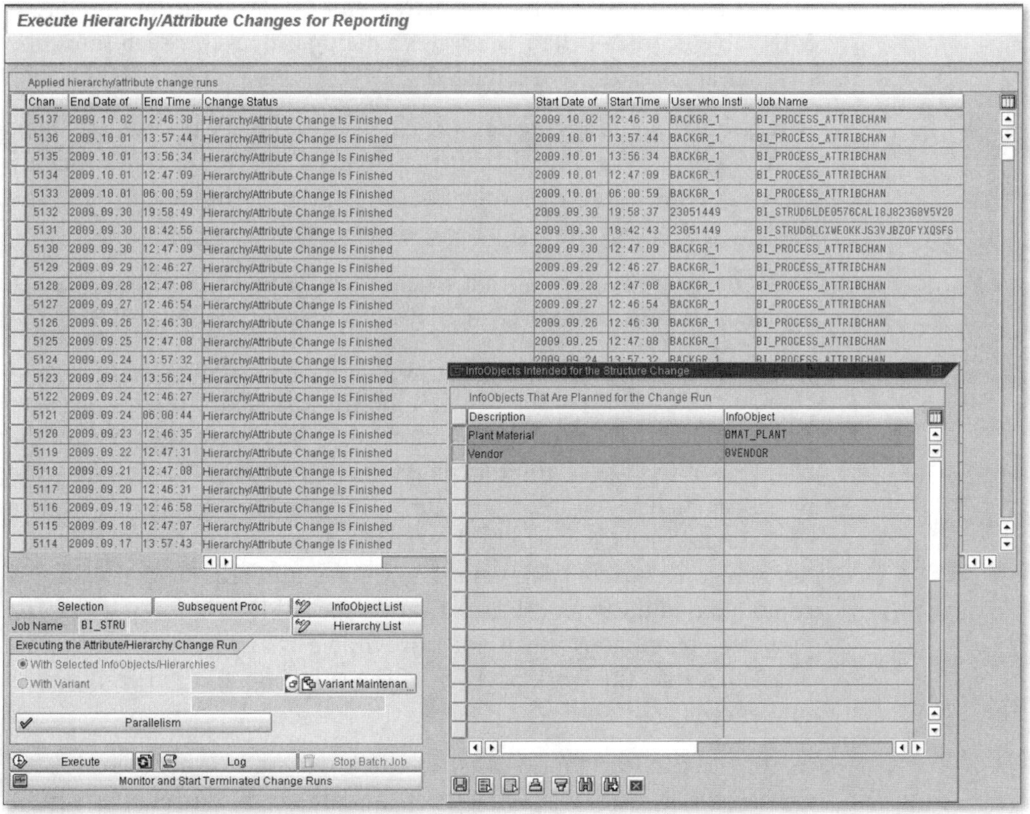

Figure 12.9 Hierarchy and Attribute Changes

The most important steps of the change run are processed in the function module RSDDS_AGGREGATES_MAINTAIN.

During the start phase, the change run checks to see which character- **Start phase** istics and hierarchies had changes made to them since the last change run. The change run specifies which aggregates must be adjusted before they can be activated and upon which InfoCubes these aggregates are built. In other words, the change run defines its work package that will be processed in the next phase. The CHNGRUN_ST lock is set during the start phase.

Work phase | During the work phase, the change run works on its work package and adjusts the aggregates that need work to be done to them. This is done for each InfoCube, during which the central change run, which is running as a background job (if the parameter CR_MAXWPC from the RSAD-MIN table is greater than 1), creates a dialog process for each InfoCube that has aggregates to be adjusted.

After adjusting the aggregates, the changes to the master data and hierarchies are activated, and then the changed aggregates are officially released, concluding the work phase of the current change run. The CHANGERUN lock is set during the work phase.

Locks | Both phases are protected from other processes by SAP locks (enqueues, visible in Transaction SM12): CHNGRUN_ST and CHANGERUN.

The first lock, CHNGRUN_ST, is the start lock that prevents other change runs from starting at the same time. It is also used to prevent processes such as the rollup from starting in the entire system after the change run has begun its start phase. If CHNGRUN_ST is set, no more processes such as rollups, aggregate building, or changes to master data and hierarchies are started. The start lock freezes the current status of aggregates, master data, and hierarchies until the work package is compiled and does not release it until a special lock is configured. The processes listed above may not run while a change run is in its start phase, because the work package of the running change run could be influenced.

As soon as the start phase ends, an attempt is made to set a specialized CHANGERUN work lock. This special lock takes the current work package into account and thereby determines which InfoCubes, InfoObjects, and hierarchies must be adjusted or activated and then only locks those. When the work lock is successfully set, the CHNGRUN_ST start lock is removed. When the work is finally completed, the CHANGERUN work lock is removed and the current change run is concluded.

There can only ever be one change run in its start phase at any particular time. Any other change run immediately fails when it unsuccessfully attempts to set the start lock. There is no queue for this.

Waiting scenarios

Only if the current change run is in its work phase can a second change run enter its start phase and wait there as long as defined in the CR_MAXWAIT RSADMIN parameter. As long as the second change run is in its start phase, all other change runs immediately fail during their start attempt. This is a very critical moment: As long as the second change run is in its start phase waiting for the corresponding time defined in the CR_MAXWAIT parameter, this change run locks the aggregate processes listed above so that they cannot be executed. Therefore, no rollup occurs for the time defined in CR_MAXWAIT; there is no master data or hierarchy upload, no rebuild, and no compression of the aggregates. The intention of the CR_MAXWAIT parameter is the following.

You have regular change runs planned that occur every 15 minutes. These change runs normally require five minutes. For unknown reasons, a change run now requires 15 minutes. Without CR_MAXWAIT, the change run that lies within the 17-minute execution time of the previous change run would fail. If CR_MAXWAIT is set to 5, the change run that lies within the 17-minute execution time waits a maximum of 5 minutes in the start phase and attempt to enter the work phase once every 30 seconds. In doing so, the change run does not fail.

The CR_MAXWAIT parameter is not intended to control the planned execution of change runs that are started from various locations. If you have regular change runs that last N minutes on average, it would be helpful to set CR_MAXWAIT to $N + 5$ minutes. Always keep in mind that while the change run is in the start phase for a maximum of $N + 5$ minutes, some aggregate, master file, and hierarchy processes will fail.

Executing the Changes

All affected InfoCubes are processed in a loop, and each one is processed in succession. Here you have the option to run the process for the InfoCubes in parallel to increase performance.

One aggregate after the other are now changed for a particular InfoCube, proceeding from top to bottom through the so-called aggregate hierarchy (aggregate tree). There are three adjustment modes:

Adjustment modes

▶ **Delta mode (D)**

In this mode the aggregates are adjusted via a delta request containing the changes. You can define a value for this in the customizing, which specifies which percentage of the changes to the master files or hierarchies should be switched from delta procedures to the rebuild. Transaction SPRO: BW CUSTOMIZING • BW • GENERAL BW SETTINGS • PARAMETERS FOR AGGREGATES or Transaction RSCUSTV8 (corresponds to the DELTALIMIT field in the RSADMINC table).

A parameter of 0% would mean that all aggregates are always recreated, which would of course generally lead to poor runtimes.

The delta process is only used for aggregates whose InfoCubes contain summarizable key figures or noncumulative key figures. If key figures with the MINIMUM or MAXIMUM aggregations exist in the InfoCube, a complete rebuild of the aggregate must be executed in every case.

▶ **Rollup (R)**

If the superordinate aggregate was adjusted in delta mode, the corresponding request can be transferred directly to the subordinate aggregate.

▶ **Rebuild (N)**

If the delta limit explained above is exceeded, the aggregate is completely rebuilt. When this occurs, the fact tables of the affected aggregate are copied without content (for example, from /BIC/F100001 and /BIC/E100001 to /BIC/F200001 and /BIC/E200001) and refilled. The original tables are then deleted, and the newly created tables are renamed accordingly.

If all aggregates of all InfoCubes involved are processed, the new data in the aggregates can be released and the new master data (hierarchies) can be activated. This occurs in an LUW (logical unit of work) to guarantee a complete rollback in case of a termination. The aggregates may then be compressed, if necessary.

Parallel Processing

The number of processes to be used can be defined in BI background management for attribute change runs without process change variants (ATTRIBCHAN process type) and is preconfigured with the value of 3. If no value is entered, the system selects the standard setting. If serial processing is defined (number of processes = 1), the background administration is not used, but rather the old program flow as before SAP NetWeaver 7.0 continues to be used.

12.2.2 Important Notes

Please note the following information on terminated change runs, parallelism, time-dependent aggregates, and the BLOCKSIZE parameter.

Terminated Change Runs

If the change run terminates (or is terminated by the administrator), barely any work is repeated when it is restarted. It restarts at the last aggregate that was adjusted. All changes that have already been made to the other aggregates are saved in the /BIC/F* and /BIC/E2* tables or in the unreleased requests (in the R and D modes).

If a change run with specific selections (with regard to InfoObjects or hierarchies) is terminated and another change run (with other selections) is started, a restart of the terminated change run occurs. Consequently, the selections of the terminated process are adopted for the restart. In such cases, this is noted accordingly in the log: "Restarting change run. Original entries are used."

Restart

Parallel Change Runs

It is generally impossible to execute multiple change runs in parallel (not to be confused with the described parallel execution).

Time-Dependent Aggregates

Another process deals with the adjustment of aggregates with time-dependent navigation attributes or hierarchies; it can only be started using a process chain. The process type for this is TIMCHNGRUN (adjustment of time-dependent aggregates).

In this type of change run, no changed master data is activated, but rather the aggregates regarding the key date are adjusted. If you define an aggregate (Transaction RSDDV), a key date (or a key date variable) is requested when using time-dependent objects. The query can only ever use such an aggregate if the key date of the query matches the key date of the aggregate. If you have not executed a time-dependent change run for a long time, the queries may no longer use certain aggregates.

Key date

BLOCKSIZE Parameter

In addition to the previously mentioned DELTALIMIT parameter, the BLOCKSIZE parameter (RSADMINC table) also plays an important role if many aggregates have to be built during a change run. If the value of BLOCKSIZE is too high, the SQL statements that read the data from the source can be slowed down because the amount of results may not fit in the main memory and data is written to temporary tables. Furthermore, large values for BLOCKSIZE can also lead to high memory use for the log.

If the value for the BLOCKSIZE parameter is too low, the SQL statements that read the data from the source can be slowed down because the WHERE condition that is being used may not be using a clustered index. The program first attempts to use a partitioning characteristic (such as the request ID for an F table or a corresponding time characteristic for an E table) as the block characteristic. If not enough blocks can be formed that way, it searches for another appropriate characteristic. If the block characteristic is not the partitioning characteristic, it can have negative effects on the runtime under certain conditions because all partitions have to be read each time a block is read. The SQL statement that is used depending on the value of the BLOCKSIZE parameter can be displayed via the Pre-analysis of the Aggregate Filling in the aggregate maintenance dialog and investigated further in terms of the indexes used in Transaction ST05 (Figure 12.10). As you can see in Figure 12.11, not only can the SQL statement being used be displayed, but the execution plan, for example, the use of indexes, can be analyzed in detail.

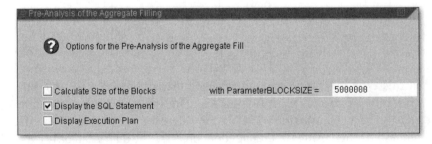

Figure 12.10 Pre-Analysis for the Filling of Aggregates

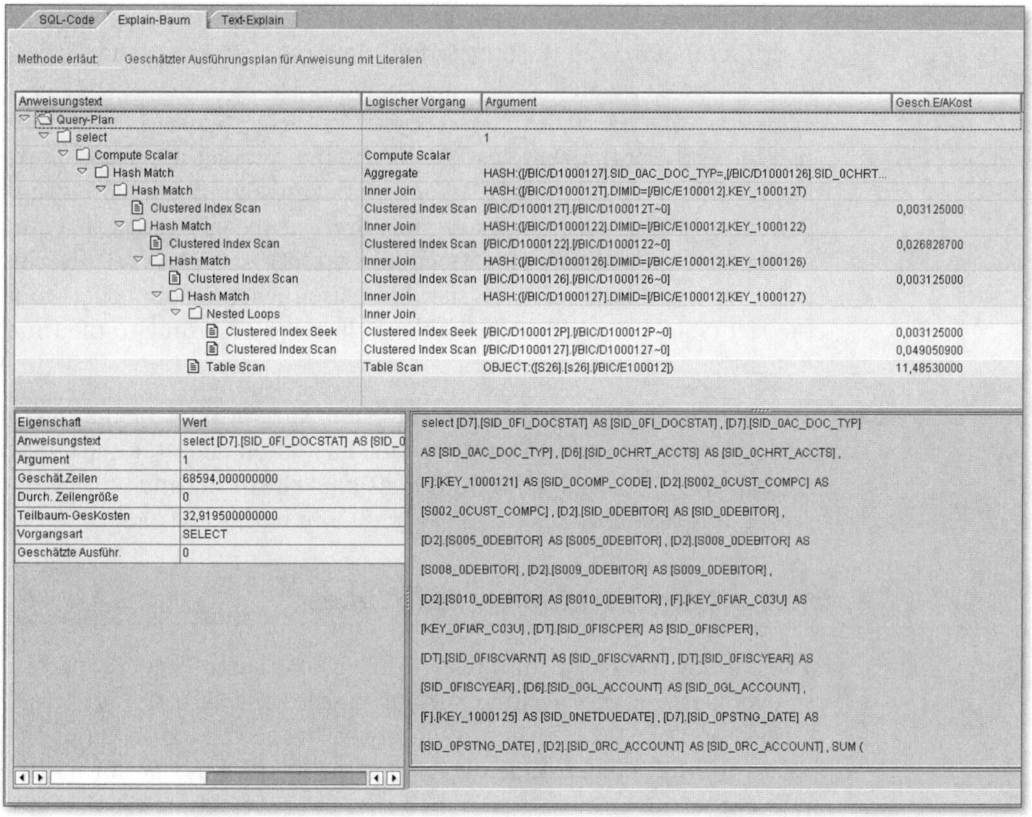

Figure 12.11 Analyzing the Access While Filling

It is also possible to calculate the block size in the pre-analysis, for example. If the aggregate is built in blocks, the system specifies the size of the blocks as follows: The number of records that are present and would be read during filling is recounted in the fact table on the basis of the block definitions. This option can take some time, particularly if many of these counting processes are submitted to large fact tables. It is therefore recommended that you only select this option when you expect that there is a problematic distribution of the data that could cause performance and memory problems.

Calculating Block Sizes

The block size is set to 100,000,000 by default, which generally fits for the use of an Oracle database. As large a `BLOCKSIZE` as possible is generally recommended for an Oracle database.

Oracle

It is recommended that you set BLOCKSIZE to a value between 5,000,000 and 10,000,000, with the target of minimizing the joining and sorting on the hard drive and the log memory use. Do not set BLOCKSIZE to a value less than 5,000,000, because that can lead to a WHERE condition that forces the optimizer to use a different index than the cluster index. For systems with less than 10 GB of physical memory, 5,000,000 is suggested. If you have more physical memory, it is recommended that you set the BLOCKSIZE parameter to a value of up to 10,000,000. Ideally, the index for the time dimension should be used when reading data from the fact table, because the fact table is clustered according to the time dimension.

IBM DB6   SAP Note 980314 provides a new IBM DB6–specific implementation to find a good block factor. This new implementation takes the clustering functions of DB6, such as multidimensional clustering and index clustering, into account to build the aggregate in blocks.

12.3   Administration of InfoCubes

The administration of InfoCubes in terms of content, request status, or even performance settings such as indexes and statistics is carried out in the Data Warehousing Workbench in the context menu of the relevant InfoProvider under Manage. One of the ways performance-relevant settings can be maintained is to use Transaction RSDIPROP.

12.3.1   InfoCube Content

Using this function you can check whether the data that you have loaded into the InfoCube contains errors. You also have the option to access loaded requests that are not yet available for actual reporting. You can execute any number of queries in the InfoCube by selecting navigation attributes, characteristics, and key figures of the InfoCube to be displayed and, if necessary, specifying restrictions to characteristics and navigation attributes (such as only displaying the data for one particular cost center). The InfoCube Content maintenance is divided into three areas.

- ▶ Restrictions to characteristics and navigation attributes
- ▶ Field selection of the characteristics and key figures for the output list
- ▶ Other options

If the InfoCube is too large, you must preselect the characteristics, navigation attributes, and key figures. Only the selected objects can then be selected again or specified in these restrictions. Several functions are available to you:

- ▶ **Field Selection for Output**
  You can select from all characteristics, navigation attributes, and key figures. You specify the characteristics and key figures that should be displayed in the output list. The features that should not appear in the list are used for aggregation.

- ▶ **Do Not Use Conversion**
  Using the Do Not Use Conversion function, you can check how the data is stored in the database. The data is displayed in the format in which it is stored in the database. The date is saved in the database in the format 19991230, whereas in the SAP NetWeaver BW system it is displayed as 30.12.1999 (depending on the settings in the user master record). A key figure with a currency always has two decimal places in the database. Because some currencies have a different number of decimal places, the values are stored in the database with the values shifted accordingly. For example, 1,000 lira would be saved as 10.00 lira, but 1,000 euros would be saved as 1,000.00 euros. Conversion is deactivated by default.

- ▶ **Use Materialized Aggregates**
  You define whether aggregates defined for the InfoCube should be used in the preparation of the list output. If you select the Use Materialized Aggregates entry, the query is executed directly in the fact table, but created aggregate tables are used and the performance improves. This option can therefore be used to check the consistency between fact tables and aggregate tables. If you want to check the fact table data, you should deactivate this option.

- ▶ **Use DB Aggregation**
  With the Use DB Aggregation option you can specify whether all records that match in your key should be aggregated to a record or whether each record should be written separately to the output list. If you want to check the individual records and the exact content of the database, deactivate this option.

► **Maximum Number of Hits**

Using the Maximum Number of Hits option, you can define the maximum amount of data that should be returned. This is important if you have very large InfoCubes and want to avoid millions of records being returned, for example.

► **Output Number of Hits**

If you have activated the DB aggregation option, several records are taken from the database and brought together in one row of the list under certain conditions. If you select the Output number of hits option, an additional key figure is generated in the output list that shows how many records the record is comprised of, that is, how many data records it took to produce the output record. You can also use this option to determine how many records are in a particular selection condition in the InfoCube. Enter a selection condition, but do not select any characteristics or key figures. In the return list you then only receive the Row Count column with the number entries that match this selection condition.

► **Display Modified Structures**

When you upload master data, it is initially stored in the modified version. Only after the master data is activated are these older entries replaced and the new ones are available for reporting in the BEx Analyzer. If you select the Display Modified Structures option, you can check at this point how the data would look in reporting once activated. Using Key Date for Time-Dependent Characteristics, you can determine when you want to read time-dependent master data The current date is entered as the default value. The attribute values for a characteristic can be valid from 01.01.2000 until 06.01.2000, for example, after which time the attributes have new values. If you choose the key date between 01.01.2000 and 06.01.2000, you get a different result in the list output than if you choose a later date.

► **Displaying the SQL Query**

In support of the debugging function, you can display the SQL query, which is generated according to the field selection and restrictions and sent to the database. The SQL query is displayed in an editor.

► **Displaying the Run Schedule**

For each query, the database optimizer can decide how it collects data. To understand exactly what the database optimizer does, you can display the run schedule. You can, for example, determine whether the database uses indexes for procuring data with a particular selection or whether it reads the entire table.

In the following section you will find information on how you can delete specific data from an InfoCube.

12.3.2 Selective Deletion

Besides deleting entire requests, you also have the option of deleting data from the fact table according to business-orientated aspects. You can delete the data for a specific cost center or customer, for example, even if it is spread over several requests. If you delete data selectively from an InfoCube, the data of the aggregates belonging to that Info-Cube is also automatically deleted. In the selection for data deletion you can select the option to restructure and activate all of the aggregates belonging to it.

You should also note the effects that selective deletion has on an SAP NetWeaver BW Accelerator index. Because it is structured differently than a database, an existing index for an InfoCube is always deleted automatically if data is selectively deleted from that InfoCube. It is not possible to remove individual records from an accelerator index.

Effect on the SAP NetWeaver Accelerator index

After selective deletion, the index is normally (depending on the patch level) restructured automatically in the batch. If you start selective deletion from Transaction RSA1 or Transaction DELETE_FACTS and there is already an accelerator index for an InfoCube, the Rebuild BIA Index parameter is available under BIA Options. The application log (Transaction SLG1) was expanded so that both the deletion procedure and the rebuilding of the accelerator is noted there.

12.3.3 Requests in InfoCubes

All of the requests that have run in the InfoCube are displayed, and you can delete requests again, if necessary. In addition, you can see whether the requests are scheduled for aggregation, if they have been aggregated already, or if they are scheduled for deletion. You can use the update date to limit the number of requests that are displayed, and you can control the superordinate monitor status of a request individually for an InfoCube. The majority of the status information available in the InfoCube administration, such as the most recent request available for reporting and the compression status, is contained in the RSMDAT-

ASTATE table, which you can directly evaluate for integrated analyses in certain cases.

The Request is Available for Reporting information is displayed when the request has been successfully updated to the InfoCube.

Status of the InfoCube

You can only aggregate data packages that have the green traffic light status (meaning data quality is ensured). The green traffic light status means that the process is still running A red traffic light means that problems occurred during uploading of the data and these problems are preventing a secure upload. Causes for this could be errors in the definition of the transfer structure, for example. Data packages with red or yellow traffic light status cannot be considered when you execute a query. In this case follow-up data packages with green traffic light status are not used in the query either, because the consistency of the data in the query can no longer be guaranteed.

Setting the status manually In certain cases it makes sense to change the request status from red to green for specific InfoCubes. Let's say you update to two InfoCubes during the initial load. If the load process runs successfully for InfoCube 1, but is unsuccessful for InfoCube 2, the superordinate monitor status for the affected requests is set to red. As a result, you cannot use the requests that were successfully loaded into InfoCube 1 for reporting. You can set the request status for InfoCube 1 to green by clicking the status symbol of the request.

You can reinstate the original monitor request status by clicking the request status symbol and selecting Delete Status, Back to Request Status. If you delete or rebuild a request, an application log is automatically generated. You can display the log by selecting the request and clicking the Application Log button.

Data Mart Status of the Request

If a request is updated to other InfoProviders, the data mart status of the request is displayed. You can use the corresponding button to manage the distribution of a request.

Using Request got from InfoProvider, you can display the InfoProviders into which the request was updated. You can find more information under the Where-Used List for DTP Requests (Figure 12.12). The icon shows you that the request has already been updated into other InfoProviders, but it is still possible to repeat the update of the request. If you think data was not correctly posted, you can reset the monitor status and request a repeat so that the request can be updated again. To do this, select Request Reverse Posting in the monitor.

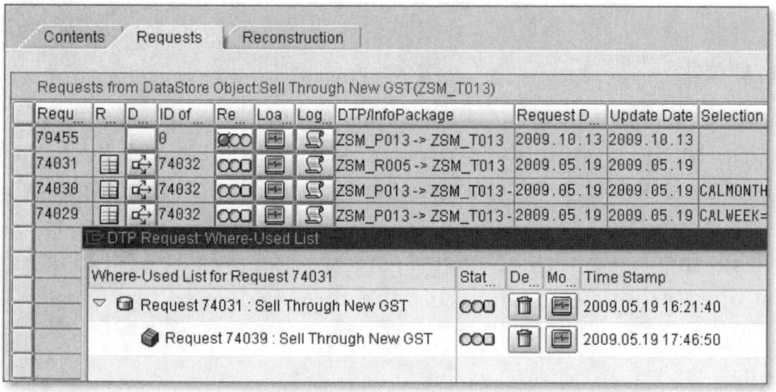

Figure 12.12 Data Mart Status with Where-Used List

Checking Data Consistency of Requests in the InfoCube

You can check the consistency of an InfoCube request for overlaps in the data selections. For individual requests in the InfoCube, the InfoObjects or fields of the source system are displayed in the Selection Conditions column along with the request selection conditions. The data consistency check runs using the information in this column. To start a check, select the requests that you want to check on the Requests tab in the InfoCube.

Click the Check Data Consistency button. A separate session opens where you can enter any other requests you may want to check. On this screen you can also specify whether you want to have only errors (partial overlapping of the data selections) and/or only complete overlaps displayed via the buttons. If you have not chosen any requests from the table, all requests are checked. A report that can be run in the background is started that compares each selected request with every other request in the InfoCube and generates an ABAP list. This list contains information about the status of the update, overlaps with other requests, and information about the options for compressing, aggregating, or deleting InfoCube data.

Scheduling Background Jobs

Select Selection to schedule the update of requests individually or as an event chain in the background. In addition, the Subsequent Processing function allows you to specify the events that you want to execute once the processing is complete. The Delete button triggers the background job or can be used to delete it directly.

Request Check

You can specify if you want to check whether the request IDs are actually present in the InfoCube. To do this, select ENVIRONMENT • COMPLETE CHECK OF REQUEST ID in the main menu. If the check is activated, you can refresh the request display. This checks whether all of the requests that have not been aggregated or compressed still exist in the InfoCube. If they no longer exist, the entry is deleted.

Log Display

You can call application logs for the requests in the InfoCube. To do this, select the request you want to analyze from the Requests tab and select ENVIRONMENT • APPLICATION LOG from the main menu or click the Application Log button. All of the logs that were written for this request are displayed. In the log display, you can analyze and access more detailed information about the logs or their messages. A navigation tree allows you to navigate among the messages; the messages you have selected are displayed in a list.

Short log   In addition, you can display short logs for InfoCube administration actions in the Performance tab. You can analyze the process flow for these actions by checking the status notifications and messages for these logs. The creation and deletion of indexes, rebuilding of statistics, and selective deletion from the InfoCube, as well as aggregation, compression, and rebuilding of the InfoCube are all supported in the log display. In the application log, you can also call logs for the short logs. To do this, select Application Log and enter the date and time for the log entry.

12.3.4 Automatic Further Processing

If you still use a 3.x InfoPackage to load data, you can activate several automatisms to further process the data in the InfoCube. If you use the data transfer process and process chains that SAP recommends, however, you cannot use these automatisms. It is recommended that you always use process chains. During the parallel loading of requests into an InfoCube, these automatic processes can lock each other out if they do not use process chains.

You can specify that the system automatically sets the quality status of the data to OK after it is loaded into the InfoCube. This needs to happen before the requests can be processed further.

Setting the quality status to OK

You can automatically roll up requests with green traffic light status, meaning those with ensured data quality, and transfer them into the aggregate. The process terminates if no active, initially filled aggregates exist in the system.

Rollup

After the rollup, the system automatically compresses the InfoCube content by deleting the request IDs, which improves performance. If aggregates exist, only requests that have already been rolled up are compressed. If no aggregates exist, all requests that have not been compressed yet are aggregated. This function is critical, because you cannot delete compressed data from the InfoCube using its request ID anymore. You must be absolutely certain that the data loaded into the InfoCube is correct.

Compressing InfoCubes

12.3.5 Rebuilding InfoCubes

With the rebuild function, you can fill an InfoCube with requests that have already been loaded into another InfoCube. This function is only necessary for InfoCubes that have received their data via InfoPackages, so only the InfoPackage requests are displayed here for you. For Info-Cubes that were loaded via a data transfer process, additional objects are filled with this information via data transfer processes. This function is especially useful if you have deltas, that is, data that you cannot even request from the source system.

You can select an InfoCube, and InfoSource, and time period or a source system, and all requests that were already loaded to your selection will be displayed. You can select individual requests and use them to rebuild the InfoCube. You can start the loading of the InfoCube immediately in the background, or you can schedule it or have it triggered by an event. If the requests contained in the InfoCube were already rolled up in aggregates or in SAP NetWeaver BW Accelerator indexes, then these requests can no longer be used for a rebuild. Only the last (topmost) request is then available for a rebuild.

12.4 Performance Settings for InfoCubes

In the Performance tab in InfoCube Administration, there are options to influence both the loading performance and the query performance (Figure 12.13). The performance context of an InfoCube is determined by the fact table indexes, the aggregate fact table indexes, and the existence and integrity of the statistic information in the database for the InfoCube tables. The individual traffic light colors have the following meanings:

▶ Green: everything is all right

▶ Yellow: discrepancy; medium-term troubleshooting required

▶ Red: discrepancy; short-term troubleshooting required

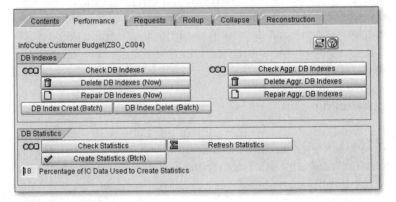

Figure 12.13 InfoCube Performance

Integrating automatic processes If you use process chains to guarantee the serial processing of processes, these settings are not supported in the object. In such a case, you must include the automatic processes as process types in the process chain.

12.4.1 Indexes

Using the Check indexes button, you can check if there are already existing indexes and if the existing indexes are present in the correct type (Bitmap indexes).

Checking indexes

▶ **Yellow Status Display**
Indexes with the wrong type are present.

▶ **Red Status Display**
There are either no indexes or one or more indexes are defective.

Missing indexes can also be listed via Transaction DB02 by clicking the Missing Indexes button. If a very large number of indexes are missing, it can be helpful to run the SAP_UPDATE_DBDIFF and SAP_INFO-CUBE_INDEXES_REPAIR ABAP reports as described in the database portion of this book.

For delta uploads with large amounts of data (more than a million data records), you should not align the database indexes of the InfoCube for every rollup, but rather delete the indexes and then rebuild them completely after the rollup. Using this function you can create missing indexes or regenerate deleted indexes. Faulty indexes are corrected.

You can delete indexes before each data load and then rebuild them. You can also set this automatic index build for delta uploads. If the InfoCube contains more than 50 million records, you should, as a rule, refrain from deleting and rebuilding indexes.

You can maintain the aggregate table indexes the same way as the fact table indexes. The maintenance of the aggregate table indexes affects all aggregate tables of the InfoCube.

Aggregate table indexes

12.4.2 Database Statistics

The system uses database statistics to optimize query performance. Therefore, the database statistics should always be kept up to date. It is recommended that you always update the statistics if you have loaded more than a million new records into the InfoCube since the last update. You can also have the database statistics automatically recalculated after each loading or after each delta upload.

Click the Check Statistics button to check the InfoCube to see if statistics exist. If no statistics exist yet, the status display changes to red.

Using Recalculate Statistics, you can add the missing InfoCube statistics in the background.

You can define the percentage of InfoCube data that is used for creating the statistics. The percentage is set to 10% by default. The larger the InfoCube, the smaller the percentage you should select, because the demand on the system for creating the statistics increases with the change in size. For InfoCubes with up to 10 million entries, you should set the percentage of InfoCube data that is used for creating the statistics to 100%

12.5 Compressing InfoCubes

When data is into the InfoCube, entire requests are inserted at the same time. Each of these requests has its own request ID, which is included in the fact table in the packet dimension. This makes it possible to pay particular attention to individual requests. One advantage of the request ID concept is that you can subsequently delete complete requests from the InfoCube. However, the request ID concept can also cause the same data records (all characteristics agree, with the exception of the request ID) to appear more than once in the fact table. This unnecessarily increases the volume of data and reduces performance in reporting, because the system has to perform aggregation using the request ID every time you execute a query.

You can use compressing to eliminate these disadvantages and compile data from different requests into one request (request ID 0). If you want to prevent the InfoCube from containing entries whose key figures are zero values (in reverse posting, for example) you can run a zero-elimination at the same time as the compression. In this case the entries in which all key figures are equal to 0 are deleted from the fact table. For performance reasons, and to save memory space, summarize a request as soon as you have established that it is correct and is not to be removed from the InfoCube. Please note that you cannot delete compressed data from the InfoCube using its request ID anymore.

Locking during compression

It is important to understand what interdependencies exist with other processes to avoid possible object locks. You are not permitted to execute two compressions for the same InfoCube at the same time. Loading data into an InfoCube for which a compression is running must be possible, however, if you do not attempt to compromise requests that are located in the phase for loading and updating data into the Info-Cube. No compression can be executed while you are deleting selectively from the InfoCube or while a change run is active.

If you are using an Oracle database, you can also execute queries on the relevant InfoCube during a compression run. With other manufacturers' databases, you see a warning if you try to execute a query on an InfoCube while the compression is running.

Because the distribution of the data from the E fact table and F fact table is changed by a compression, the request performance can be noticeably influenced. Normally, the compression leads to a better result, but you must take care that the statistics remain current so that the optimizer can select an appropriate access method. This means that after the first compression of a significant amount of data, the E fact table of the cube must be analyzed, because otherwise the optimizer still assumes that this table is empty. This is the same reason the F fact table may not be analyzed if all queries are compressed, because the optimizer then assumes that the F fact table is empty. You must therefore analyze the F fact table if a normal number of requests that are not compressed exist in the InfoCube.

Performance after compression

The compression factor is determined completely by the data loaded into the InfoCube. Compression merely means that data peaks are compiled in a single record with identical, logical keys in the fact table (the term *logical key* encompasses all dimension identities with the exception of the technical dimension). If you load data on a daily basis, for example, but the InfoCube has Month as its smallest time characteristic, this may result in a compression factor of 1/30.

Compression factor

The other extreme is as follows: If the record you are loading is different from the previously loaded records (because it contains a sequence number, for example), the compression factor is 1, meaning the actual compression does not take place. Even in this case, however, you should compress the data if you have partitioned the E fact table because the data partitioning is only used for compressed data.

The only size restriction for compression is that all rollback data for the compression of a single request must fit in the rollback segments. For each record in the request that should be compressed, either an update of the corresponding record is executed in the E fact table or the record is reinserted. Because DROP PARTITION is normally used for deletion, it is

Optimal data amounts

not critical for the rollback. Because neither operation requires much effort (with regard to memory), they should not be critical.

The performance depends greatly on the hardware. As a rule of thumb, you can expect that around 2 million rows can be compressed per hour if the InfoCube does not contain any noncumulative key figures. If the InfoCube contains such key figures, about 1 million rows can be compressed per hour.

Checking the indexes It is very important that either the P index or the primary index 0 exists in the E fact table during the compression. Before executing a compression, use Transaction DB02 to check whether the P index is present in the E fact table. If this index is missing, a compression is virtually impossible and should be created via a reactivation of the InfoCube. There is one exception to this rule: If only one request is selected for the compression and it is the first request for this InfoCube that is to be compressed, the P index is automatically deleted for performance reasons and then automatically re-created after the compression. If you execute queries at the same time as the compression, the secondary index must be active.

To check the existing indexes, you can use Transaction RSRV and select the elementary database check for the indexes of an InfoCube and its aggregates there. This check is more informative than the traffic light colors in the performance register of InfoCube maintenance.

12.5.1 Compression After a Change Run

In SAP NetWeaver BW 3.x, the compression of aggregates after a change run was not supported and had to be explicitly activated with the CHANGERUN_CONDENSE parameter in the RSADMIN table to prevent the next rollup from taking too long because of the large number of data records.

As of Support Package 17, it is exactly the other way around in SAP NetWeaver BW 7.0. The change run automatically compresses the aggregates up to the necessary request, which can be prevented by setting the CHANGERUN_DOES_NOT_CONDENSE RSADMIN parameter so that the next rollup takes care of this compression as well. You should only set the CHANGERUN_DOES_NOT_CONDENSE parameter in exceptional cases when you have sufficient reason, however.

12.5.2   Compressing All Aggregates

The problem often arises that an aggregate seems to be compressed up to the highest request (in such cases, the COMPR_AGGR field in the RSMDATASTATE table displays the highest request for the compression), but it still contains data from fact table F. The cause for this is normally errors right before the compression. You can use the RSCDS_CONDENSE_CUBE program to compress such aggregates, however not all aggregates of the InfoCube can be compressed with one program run.

If multiple aggregates with the same problem exist in the same InfoCube, then executing the SAP_AGGREGATES_CONDENSE report leads to a compression of all aggregates of the InfoCube.

12.5.3   Noncumulative InfoCubes

A noncumulative key figure is modeled in the SAP NetWeaver BW system using the corresponding field for the noncumulative value change or the corresponding fields for inflows or outflows in the InfoObject maintenance. You can determine the current noncumulative or the noncumulative at a particular time from the current end noncumulative and the noncumulative changes or the inflows and outflows. A noncumulative InfoCube is modeled with at least one noncumulative key figure.

With non-cumulative InfoCubes, compression has an additional effect on query performance because the marker for noncumulatives is updated in them. This means that less data is generally read for a noncumulative query and the reply time is thereby reduced. For noncumulative InfoCubes, you can prevent the update of the noncumulative marker by setting the No Marker Updating indicator. You have to use this option if you are loading historic noncumulative value changes into an InfoCube after an initialization has already taken place with the current noncumulative. Otherwise, the results produced in the query will not be correct. For performance reasons, you should compress subsequent delta requests using marker updating.

Query performance

12.6   Further Processing of Data in a DSO

If you have loaded data into a DataStore object (DSO), you can use this DataStore object as the source for another InfoProvider. For you to do this, the data must be active. Use process chains to ensure that one process has ended before any subsequent processes are triggered. The process flow for updating DataStore object data is as follows:

Activating DSO data

1. **Activate the DataStore object data**
   The data is in the activation queue. When you activate the data, the change log is filled with the data required for a delta update, and the data appears in the table of active data.

2. **Update the data to the connected InfoProviders**
   Using the transformation rules, the change log data (the delta) that has not yet been processed is updated to other InfoProviders. The data is already available in a cleansed and consolidated format.

If you still use a 3.x InfoPackage to load data, you can activate several automatisms to further process the data in the DataStore object. If you use the data transfer process and process chains that SAP recommends, however, you cannot use these automatisms. Switch on automatic activation and automatic update only if you are sure that these processes do not overlap.

12.6.1   Activating Data

Upon activation of the data , the system writes data from the activation queue to the table of active data. The system determines the SIDs before the process of activating the data starts. The process of activating the data only begins after the SIDs have been determined. If the activation process terminates while the SIDs are being determined, the data retains its inactive status and remains in the activation queue.

Sorting When the data is activated, it is written to the table of active data, where it is then available for reporting (Figure 12.14). Requests are sorted by the key of the DataStore object, request ID, data package ID, or data record number. This ensures that the data is updated to the table of active data in the correct request sequence.

Requ	R	D	ID of	Re	Log	DTP/InfoPackage	Request D	Update Date	Selection Conditions	Transferred	Added Rec	Type of Data Update	Source/InfoSource	Name of Source	DataSource
74336			74341			PC: ZSM_001 -> ZSM_T002	2009.05.27	2009.05.27		57	57	Delta update	DTASRC	DataSource	ZSM_001
74278			74281			PC: ZSM_001 -> ZSM_T002	2009.05.25	2009.05.25		2	57	Delta update	DTASRC	DataSource	ZSM_001
74288			74271			PC: ZSM_001 -> ZSM_T002	2009.05.25	2009.05.25		4	4	Delta update	DTASRC	DataSource	ZSM_001
74246			74249			PC: ZSM_001 -> ZSM_T002	2009.05.25	2009.05.25		3	3	Delta update	DTASRC	DataSource	ZSM_001
74103			74106			PC: ZSM_001 -> ZSM_T002	2009.05.20	2009.05.20		1	1	Delta update	DTASRC	DataSource	ZSM_001
74096			74099			PC: ZSM_001 -> ZSM_T002	2009.05.20	2009.05.20		8	8	Delta update	DTASRC	DataSource	ZSM_001
74091			74092			PC: ZSM_001 -> ZSM_T002	2009.05.20	2009.05.20		1801	1801	Delta update	DTASRC	DataSource	ZSM_001
73029			73033			PC: ZSM_001 -> ZSM_T002	2009.05.04	2009.05.04		79	79	Delta update	DTASRC	DataSource	ZSM_001
72736			72741			PC: ZSM_001 -> ZSM_T002	2009.04.14	2009.04.14		24	24	Delta update	DTASRC	DataSource	ZSM_001
72533			72535			PC: ZSM_001 -> ZSM_T002	2009.04.06	2009.04.06		4	4	Delta update	DTASRC	DataSource	ZSM_001
72501			72504			PC: ZSM_001 -> ZSM_T002	2009.04.03	2009.04.03		2	2	Delta update	DTASRC	DataSource	ZSM_001
72494			72497			PC: ZSM_001 -> ZSM_T002	2009.04.03	2009.04.03		1	1	Delta update	DTASRC	DataSource	ZSM_001
72487			72490			PC: ZSM_001 -> ZSM_T002	2009.04.03	2009.04.03		4	4	Delta update	DTASRC	DataSource	ZSM_001
72456			72459			PC: ZSM_001 -> ZSM_T002	2009.04.03	2009.04.03		1	1	Delta update	DTASRC	DataSource	ZSM_001
72449			72452			PC: ZSM_001 -> ZSM_T002	2009.04.03	2009.04.03		8	8	Delta update	DTASRC	DataSource	ZSM_001
72442			72444			PC: ZSM_001 -> ZSM_T002	2009.04.02	2009.04.02		1	1	Delta update	DTASRC	DataSource	ZSM_001

Figure 12.14 DataStore Object Requests

During an activation session, packages (from several DTP requests) are created that can be activated in parallel. Multiple activation sessions cannot run in parallel, however, but rather must be triggered in sequence. This is, however, only relevant when data is activated automatically. When you activate data manually, the corresponding is only available again after the current activation run is complete. If an activation process is canceled, you cannot activate any subsequent requests. You have to keep repeating the activation process that was canceled until it is completed successfully.

If you set the Do Not Compress Requests into a Single Request When Activation Takes Place indicator, a request is generated in the change log for each of the loaded requests after the activation. This enables you to delete requests individually to restore a previous status of the DataStore object. When you update to another InfoProvider, however, all requests that are active but have not yet been updated are combined into a single request. If you want to update requests to connected Info-Providers individually, you have to update the requests immediately after you have activated them. You can do this using process chains.

Do not compress in a request

For determining SIDs and for activating requests, processing is set to be carried out in three parallel processes. You can change this order data. If you change the setting to 1, serial processing occurs. The processing is controlled by BI background management, where you can find more information (Transaction RSBATCH).

Settings for parallel processing

12.6.2 Analysis of Unexpected Data

If unexpected data is displayed when you use a standard DSO in reporting, the reason is often development errors in the data flow. Common causes of inconsistent or unexpected data in DataStore objects include:

▶ Routine errors in the transformation or updating rules so that, for example, inconsistent data records are saved in the DataStore object

▶ Updating from multiple sources without following the loading sequence, resulting in undesired overwriting or initializing of fields

▶ Differing keys for the source and the DataStore object, so that data records are aggregated according to missing key elements during the loading into the DataStore object, for example

Executing the GET_ODS_OSS_INFORMATION report in Transaction SE38 (Figure 12.15) is helpful for an analysis of data in a DataStore object and for various other problems and errors.

```
┌────────────────────────────────────────────────────────────────────────────────────────┐
│ Information About DataStore Object and Request                                           │
├────────────────────────────────────────────────────────────────────────────────────────┤
│                                                                                          │
│ Information About DataStore Object and Request                                           │
│                                                                                          │
│ ODS object:          ZSM_T013           Used Database:  MSSQL                            │
│                                                                                          │
│ Tables associated to the ODS object                                                      │
│ Active table:             /BIC/AZSM_T01300                                               │
│ Activation queue table: /BIC/AZSM_T01340                                                 │
│ Change log table:                                                                        │
│ Technical name:           /BIC/B0002036000                                               │
│ Logical name:             8ZSM_T013_0A                                                   │
│                                                                                          │
│ Information concerning PSA request(s)                                                     │
│    DTP SID         DTP GUID                       PSA SID     PSA GUID                     │
│    2.009.115       DTPR_D6NJVE2K0CTVM5SZQF0E2W5U8                                          │
│                                                                                          │
│ Load - PSA table:                                                                        │
│ Technical name:                                                                          │
│ Logical name:                                                                            │
│ Generated activation program:                    6PD6EIOEHE5A9302RXRLMXU051U             │
│ Generated rollback program:                      6PD5VUZQ6K72HBK470F3CXKSLV2             │
│                                                                                          │
│ Statusinformation derived from table RSODSACTREQ:                                        │
│                                                                                          │
│ Loadrequest                    LoadSID    Datapackage  Operation  Status  Activationrequest                ActSID      Logically deleted │
│ DTPR_D6NJVE2K0CTVM5SZQF0E2W5U8  2.009.115  000000       0          A       ODSR_D6NJWRMLU6AX6AY75KDYH4MUM  2.009.121                     │
└────────────────────────────────────────────────────────────────────────────────────────┘
```

Figure 12.15 GET_ODS_OSS_INFORMATION Report

The report provides all of the technical information for a DataStore object or, optionally, for a concrete request such as the technical names of the tables or the names of the corresponding PSA table. A complete analysis of the data consistency is normally only possible if all requests involved are present in the PSA tables. For an analysis drawing on the history of affected data records, proceed as follows:

Analysis of affected
data records

1. Identify the (complete) key of the data providing unexpected results in reporting. You can find the key fields in the modeling view of the DataStore object.

2. In the administration view of the DataStore object, go to the Content tab and select Change Log. Ensure that the key fields of the DataStore object are available for selection and then select all data records for the key values noted in the previous step.

You then see all changes that have been made to that key. They must then be put into the correct order. Use the REQUEST-SID, DATAPAKID, and RECORD fields as sorting criteria. Because the request GUID is saved in the change log, it must be "translated" into the request SID accordingly. To do this, proceed as follows:

1. Open the /BIO/SREQUID table in Transaction SE16.

2. For the REQUID column, select the Request GUIDs of the change log as the selection criteria.

3. You then receive the Request SIDs corresponding to the Request GUIDs.

4. Order the result of the change log selection according to the REQUEST SID, DATAPAKID, and RECORD search criteria and note the result.

Be sure to incorporate the RECORDMODE field in your analyses. It provides information about the type of change to a data record in the active data table. The following attributes can be saved:

▶ **N**
The record was newly added to the active data table.

▶ **R**
The record was deleted from the active data table.

▶ **X**
The record remains how it was saved in the active data table before the modification. Depending on the aggregation behavior, key figures are saved in inverted format.

▶ **" " (blank)**
The record is how it was saved in the active data table after the modification.

To find out which source requests for the basis for the activation requests, the data in the RSODSACTREQ table is evaluated. Select the corresponding DataStore object as the selection criteria. For the ACTREQ column, enter the change log requests. As a result of the selection you receive the load requests corresponding to the activation requests in the REQUEST column.

Analysis of source requests

Analysis of the load request
If the individual values saved in the change log are not plausible, check whether the values were correctly transferred from the source to the DataStore object. To do this, you can simulate the update and analyze the results without having to execute the loading process again. This step is especially relevant when you are using routines in the transformation.

When using DTP technology, select the debugging option in the load request monitor. You now have the option to display the data after the various extraction steps. Take particular note of the values after the execution of the start, end, or expert routines.

If you are still using SAP NetWeaver BW 3.x technology for the extraction, select a data package in the detail view of the request monitor under the Extraction node and start the simulation via the context menu by selecting Simulate Update.

12.6.3 Troubleshooting

Starting point
The starting point of any troubleshooting should be the monitor for the data transfer process request that displays the detail information for processing the request, in addition to the header information. On the first level of the detail tree, the system displays the status of the requests at various points during the processing such as the generation, the processing of the steps in the DTP program run, and the setting of the technical status and the entire status of the request. The processing status display is divided further according to the data transfer process program flow and displays the status and messages for the individual processing steps and data packages in the processing steps.

Processing steps
On the level of a processing step you can also jump to the temporary storage display if you have specified in the DTP maintenance that it should be filled for this step. You can jump to the PSA maintenance for the error stack via the Error Stack button if data has been written but not yet updated to the error stack.

You can jump to the where-used list for the request from the monitor (Figure 12.16). You therefore have the option to display dependent target requests and consistent requests. You can also jump to the administration of the source and the target (DataSource or InfoProvider) and the job and process overview.

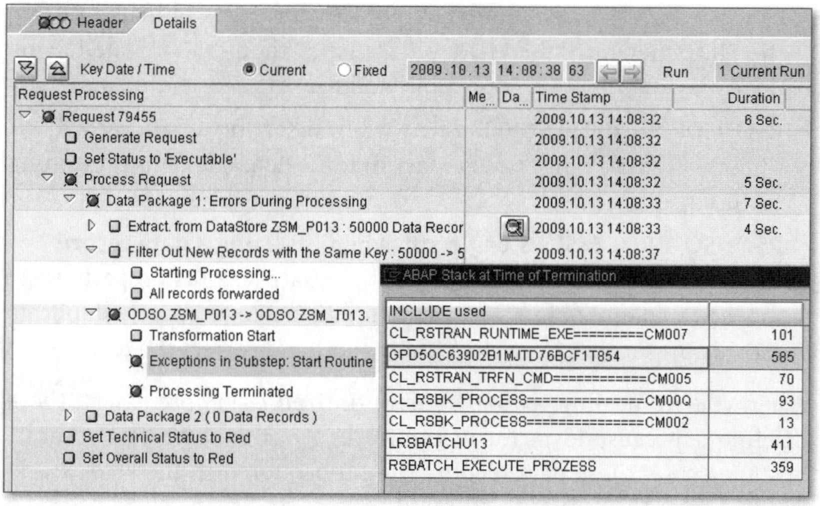

Figure 12.16 Troubleshooting in the DTP Monitor

In the detail view open the red node for the data package and display all of the corresponding error messages. The cause of the error is normally quickly identifiable from these messages. For further analysis of program terminations, you also have the option to display the ABAP stack at the point of termination and jump directly to the point of termination.

If errors occur when you are generating master data SID values, it is usually related to characters that are not permitted. Detailed information about this is displayed in the DTP monitor. Characters that are not permitted are displayed under the SID generation nodes with additional information such as the corresponding InfoObject. To correct the error, the data must be corrected in the PSA or in the source system and then reloaded. Some frequent errors that are displayed in the monitor under the nodes for a data package include:

Errors in SID generation

▶ **No batch process available**

Ensure that enough processes are available on the relevant application server. Also check whether the process ran both on the server and at the time that you planned. Monitor the settings for the parallel processes in Transaction RSODSO_SETTINGS.

Frequent errors

▶ **Termination after runtime that is too long**

Use Transaction RSODSO_SETTINGS to set a higher value for the

Maximum wait time parameter. If an activation is terminated during the SID generation, the SID table statistics should be updated using the RSDU_ANALYZE_TABLE function module.

▸ **RSODSO_PROCESSING 002 error when inserting a data record**
Check whether a unique secondary index is defined that is preventing the insertion.

▸ **RSODSO_PROCESSING 049 error when inserting a data record**
This error normally occurs if the Unique Data Records property is set for the DataStore object, but an attempt is made to activate duplicate records. In such a case, delete the request and correct the data.

Errors in a write-optimized DSO
When you are dealing with a write-optimized DataStore object, there is a frequent cause for error in the loading of duplicate data records. In such a case, these data records should be stored in the error stack, and you have the option to correct the stack and then reload using an error DTP.

12.6.4 Simulating and Debugging a DTP Request

Simulating the data update and debugging a data transfer process request (DTP request) help you analyze an incorrect DTP request. In this way you can also simulate a transformation prior to the actual data transfer if you want to check whether it provides the desired results.

Simple Simulation and Debugging
If you want to execute a standard DTP in debug mode, select Serially in the Dialog Process (for Debugging) as the processing mode on the Execute tab in the DTP maintenance. In the overview for program execution, define breakpoints for debugging and start the simulation. The simulation request is started according to your settings and processed synchronously in a dialog process. If you defined breakpoints, you go to the ABAP Debugger. The result of the simulation is displayed in the DTP monitor.

Expert mode
In addition to setting breakpoints, expert mode enables you to specify selections for simulating the request and for defining the substep after which you want to write to temporary storage during the simulation. In the DTP maintenance, select the Serially in the Dialog Process (for Debugging) processing mode on the Execute tab and set the Expert Mode indicator.

Select the Debugging area in the monitor and make the adjustments to the filter settings. When you call the simulation from the DTP monitor, the filter settings that are initially displayed are copied from the request that is displayed in the monitor. When you call it from the DTP maintenance, the filter settings initially displayed are copied from the next request of the DTP. In addition to the selection with the fields of the source, you can also restrict the request ID (REQUID), data package ID (DATAPKID), and data record number (RECORD) with the technical fields. You should restrict the data to prevent the simulation from running for a long time, for example, if you loaded a large amount of data. Selections are also recommended if the fields refer to certain data records in the source or to a certain selection of data in the source.

Filter settings

Likewise, make the adjustments to the settings for temporary storage and breakpoints. You can define if and when to write data to temporary storage during processing and set breakpoints at different times.

When that is done, start the simulation request. The request is processed synchronously in a dialog process. If you defined breakpoints, you go to the ABAP Debugger, from where you can jump directly to the corresponding data. The result of the simulation is displayed in the monitor and you can analyze it further.

12.7   Deleting Data from a DSO

The deletion of individual requests primarily serves to remove requests that have errors in them from the DataStore object. Just as with Info-Cubes, you can delete all data from a DataStore object or even delete the entire DataStore object itself.

When deleting data, you must make a distinction between the deletion of already activated data and data that is not yet activated. If the data is not yet activated, the requests are simply deleted from the activation queue during the deletion process. Because it was not yet activated, no adjustments have to be made to the table with the active data or to the change logs. Deleting already active data can also mean activities for connected InfoProviders, among other things.

Active and inactive data

12.7.1   Delete by Request

This function allows you to delete both inactive and active requests from DataStore objects. It enables you to delete incorrect requests because the system usually only recognizes errors in the data or update rules after the request has been activated. The request is deleted from both the table for active data and the change log. An error message appears if the request has already been updated into additional Info-Providers. In this case you first have to delete the request to be deleted from the data targets.

Resetting the data mart status

Afterward, you have to manually reset the data mart status in the DataStore object. Then you can delete the request. You can load more deltas after this. If you do not reset the data mart status, the delta update is deactivated in the connected InfoProvider when deletion is performed. You can only directly delete requests that have not yet been activated. The system uses rollback for requests that have already been activated.

If deletion by request is started, the individual requests are processed in a loop in descending order according to the SID of the activation requests. The active table data is rolled back according to the RECORD-MODE field and deleted from the change log table in descending order according to the data package and data record number. The corresponding information is then still be removed from the activation queue and the tables used in the monitor, such as RSICCONT, RSMONICDP, RSODSACTREQ, and RSODSACTUPDTYPE.

Rollback

With rollback, the system reverts back to the status in the DataStore object before you updated the incorrect requests, meaning that all requests that were updated after the incorrect request are also deleted. You can repost requests that are available in the PSA afterward.

You can perform processing upon deletion in parallel on a package-by-package basis. In this case the packages in a request are processed in parallel. This is possible because the package has a unique key. Processing upon deletion is only ever performed in serial for requests that have been loaded and activated using a DTP for real-time data acquisition.

12.7.2 Selective Deletion

Selective deletion allows you to delete on the characteristic level in addition to deleting by request. With selective deletion, you are only deleting from the table with active data. The activation queue and the change log remain unchanged. Before you delete selectively, all data needs to have been activated. The deletion is recorded in the application log so that you can follow the individual activities.

Figure 12.17 shows how deletion criteria can be specified. Data is deleted according to the criteria Distribution Channel = 02 and Fiscal Year = 2009 in data target 0RMP_DS01.

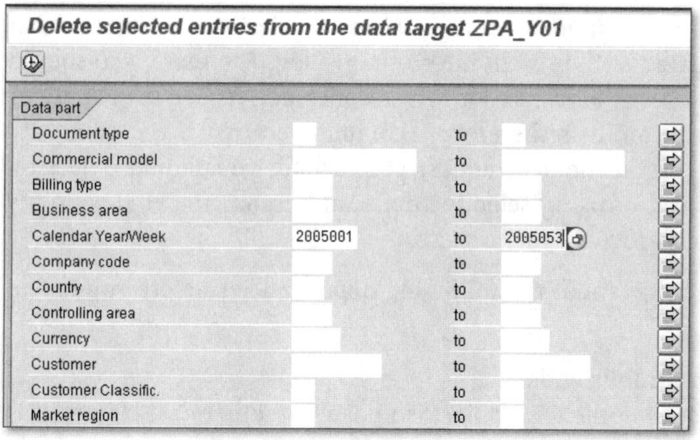

Figure 12.17 Deletion Selections

The planned deletion action in the example is represented in Figure 12.18 by the started job name BI_INDX*.

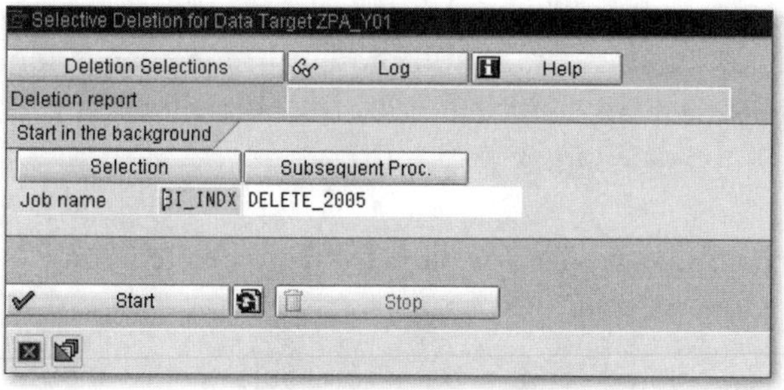

Figure 12.18 Selective Deletion

435

Obsolete data

Selection deletion can be used to delete records with keys into which no more data will be loaded from the ODS object. This would be the case, for example, if a product was taken from the product range and no more data would be loaded to its product number or, for example, if you want to delete data that is no longer needed because it is more than three years old. Both cases are also typical application scenarios for data archiving where selective deletion is also used after successful archiving.

Data with errors

You can also selectively delete data that has errors due to processing in the SAP NetWeaver BW system. Data that was created with errors in the source system, on the other hand, should not be selectively deleted but should be corrected with reverse postings. Note that no changes are made in the change log during selective deletion. This means that erroneous data is still present in the change log. Therefore, you should take into account the restrictions for reconstruction (see list below) or selective deletion. It is therefore recommended that if the data only contains errors in the last request you loaded, you should delete by request instead of using selective deletion because the change log is adjusted accordingly in the process.

Interdependencies

You should be aware of the following dependencies before you delete selectively:

▶ **Connected InfoProviders**
If the data from the ODS object is updated to other data targets, it is not automatically adjusted during selective deletion. You can only adjust it manually by selectively deleting from the connected data target.

▶ **Reconstruction**
During reconstruction (Reconstruct tab in the administration of the ODS object), the data from the change log is used. If you have selectively deleted previously, this data is still present in the change log and is loaded into the data target during reconstruction, although you no longer want it in the data target.

▶ **Delete by request**
Requests from which records have been selectively deleted can no longer be deleted by request.

If you have selectively deleted from a DataStore object, you should choose to update to an InfoProvider via the context menu in the Data-

Store object instead of reconstruction. Then update the data with init or full updating, which fills the connected data target with the active data.

12.7.3 Deleting from the Change Log

It is recommended that you delete data from the change log of a Data-Store object if several requests that are no longer needed for the delta update and are no longer used for an initialization from the change log have already been loaded into the DataStore object. If a delta initialization is available for updates to connected InfoProviders, requests have to be updated before the corresponding data can be deleted from the change log. A temporary, limited history is retained. In some cases the change log becomes so large that is advisable to reduce the volume of data and delete data from a specific time period. In the Deletion of Requests from the Change Log process variant, you can create selection patters and thereby flexibly delete requests.

12.7.4 Deleting Already Updated Data

If you want to delete requests that have already been updated in connected InfoProviders, you have to adjust the connected InfoProviders manually:

1. Start the data mart status administration of the data target for your request to be deleted. The dialog box that appears displays the request that was updated in additional data targets.

2. Open the monitor for this request.

3. Start the administration of the connected InfoProvider and delete the corresponding request there.

4. Now reset the delta administration. To do this, select the Data Mart status of the InfoProvider and select Reset Delta Administration from the subsequent dialog box.

5. Now you can also delete the request from the source DataStore object. You can now load data as full or delta again.

Manual adjustments

12.8 Monitoring Analysis Processes

The monitor for analyses can be reached from both the analysis process designer (Transaction RSANWB) and from the Data Mining Workbench (Transaction RSDMWB) (Figure 12.19).

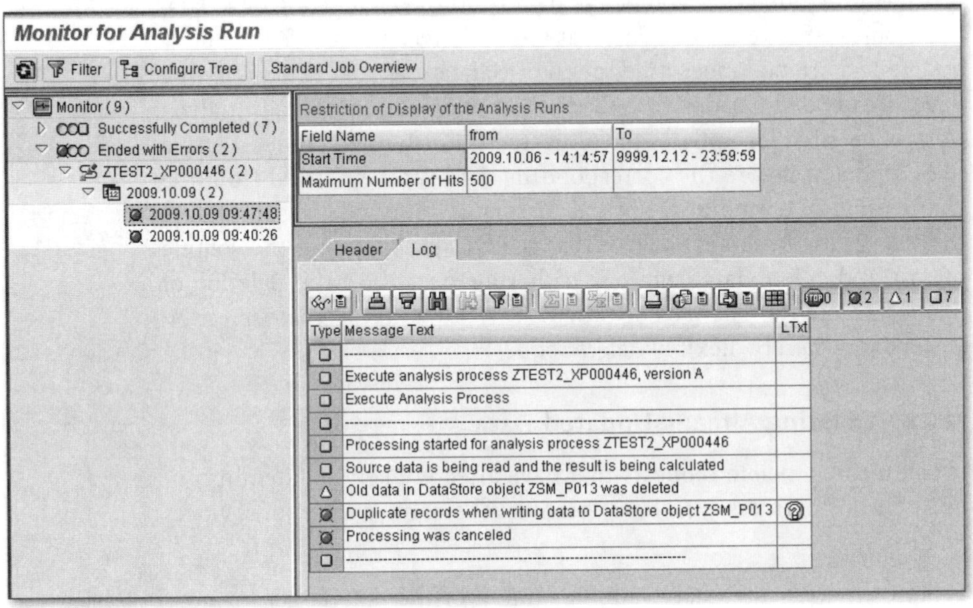

Figure 12.19 Monitor for Analysis Runs

The tree for the overview of all analysis runs can be configured and filtered just as in other monitors. You can, for example, display only the runs ended with errors in the past two days. In addition to the status, detailed information is available for each run so that errors can be easily analyzed. The following sections deal with typical problems and errors in analysis runs.

12.8.1 Exceeding the Maximum Allowed Runtime

Simulation   The analysis process is aimed at modeling transformations for mass data. The simulation function is provided so that you can easily understand transformation steps during the modeling phase with low data volumes. During a simulation, the part of the analysis process that has already been modeled is executed with all of the data. Depending on the concept, this can lead to a dump because the maximum allowed runtime has been exceeded. The following measures can help in such cases:

▶ Execute the analysis process in the background maintenance.

▶ Use filters for the simulation to reduce the data volume. The restriction in the filter must be deleted before the actual execution, of course.

▶ Generate an interim result at any transformation node and calculate the interim results in the background maintenance. This result is saved in a table in the database so that this data can then be read when the simulation function is used instead of having to completely recalculate it every time.

In the customizing you can specify a server, a server group, or a host for the execution of analysis processes in the background under SAP NETWEAVER • BUSINESS INTELLIGENCE • PERFORMANCE SETTINGS. You can use this to control the load distribution during the background execution of analysis processes (including the calculation of interim results in the background) by specifying an application server or server group for it.

Customizing for load distribution

12.8.2 Memory Overflow During Executions and Simulations

The data is processed in packages during the runtime of an analysis process, though most transformations require a sorting of the entire dataset that is executed completely in the main memory by default. This behavior can lead to a memory overflow with larger data volumes. If this occurs, deactivate the Process Data in the Memory option in the performance properties so that the data is stored in temporary database tables during sorting processes.

If a memory overflow occurs when you are using an InfoObject data source, a dump normally occurs in the RSD_CHA_GET_VALUES function modules of the SAPLRSDM_F4 function group.

InfoObject as data source

An InfoObject data source for reading master data is currently based on a function module that loads all data to the main memory in an inefficient data structure, and the data source is therefore only suitable for reading master data with few data records. For master data tables with many records, such as in the tables for the Business Partner (InfoObject

0BPPARTNER) or Product (InfoObject 0MATERIAL) characteristics, a memory overflow can occur regardless of the Process Data in Memory flag. If this occurs, set the InfoObject to be available as an InfoProvider. Then use the InfoProvider data source in the analysis process instead of the InfoObject data source.

InfoProvider as data source

Data is read from an InfoProvider in packets, so only a small portion of the entire amount of data is in the main memory at any time. During the reading of corresponding master data, however, all data is still loaded to the main memory, though in a more efficient data structure than with an InfoObject data source. If a memory overflow still occurs anyway, the following workaround should help: Create an InfoSet that only contains the affected InfoObject. Then use that InfoSet instead of the InfoProvider. You can also process large master data tables using this approach.

Transformation using filters

The conditions stored in the filter are optimized during the execution and transferred to the previous data source where possible. If filter conditions cannot be transferred during execution (as is sometimes the case with conditions for key figures), all data is read, and then all irrelevant data records are discarded. Always use the filter transformations in the dataflow to reduce the data volumes as early as possible.

Transformation using routines

If grouping fields are selected in the transformation parameterization, the routine is called exactly one time, and the entire dataset is transferred. This can lead to memory overflow depending on the number or length of the data records.

Check whether it is necessary to transfer all of the data to the routine at one time. If the processing can be executed record by record in the routine, for example, then use strongly selective fields such as the product field as the grouping fields. This causes the routine to be called per product, meaning only the data of one product is transferred. When using grouping fields, the data is presorted according to the grouping fields. The sorting is also carried out in the database (for more information, see the previous comments about the Process Data in Memory performance property). If the routine absolutely has to receive all data records with one call, reduce the number of fields in the input and output structure to the bare minimum. The less complex the data structures are, the less memory is needed.

A join modeled in the analysis process is currently always executed on the application server and not in the database. The join transformation is implemented as a *sort merge join*, meaning all data from both data sources is read first, and then each is sorted and finally linked to each other via merging.

Transformations using links

If the runtime of the analysis process is too long and only contains one join from master data, DataStore objects, and InfoSets, you can define an InfoSet that already maps the join in the database. Then replace the entire branch by reading from this InfoSet.

12.8.3 Using Queries

The execution of analysis process runs through the following software layers for calculating query results in the call sequence:

1. Analysis process
2. OLAP BAPI
3. OLE DB for OLAP
4. OLAP processor

The technical limitations of the intermediate layers have an effect on the query results accordingly. Because nothing can be determined about the size of a query result in advance, the analysis process also attempts to execute giant queries. Such queries can then terminate because of insufficient memory or lead to a long runtime, which generally cannot be prevented.

There are also some special cases which are possible using the query with normal execution but which are not supported when using the analysis process designer (APD). Pay special attention to the restrictions from SAP Note 605208.

The OLAP processor is basically optimized to calculate and then display small result sets based on large amounts of data. Queries with very large results (mass data) often lead to unacceptable runtimes or bottlenecks in the main memory. When possible, always use an InfoProvider as the data source for mass data in the analysis process, particularly because simple queries that only aggregate the InfoProvider data can usually be replaced by reading directly from the InfoProvider, for example. For more complex queries such as those with calculated

How can long runtimes be prevented?

key figures, check whether the calculations in the query can be mapped by transformations in the analysis process.

As long as it does not lead to a termination because of insufficient main memory, the query runtime cannot be improved by making changes to the analysis process. Check whether you can do without individual query components such as conditions or key figures. You should deactivate the OLAP cache in the query properties (Transaction RSRT) because caching in conjunction with analysis processes does not gain any performance advantage because the data is only is only being read.

Main memory problems

If you have main memory problems, you should use partitioning. The query is basically reorganized into subqueries to calculate the large overall result in steps and then compile it at the end. To do this, select a partitioning characteristic and a package size in the advanced settings. To find effective settings it is important to understand the way the partitioning functions. The system reads all instances (values) of the partitioning characteristic in the InfoProvider. These instances are sorted and distributed to packages corresponding to the specified package size. Each package represents a filter for the query execution, meaning the characteristic values from the package are used for filtering the query.

The distribution in the query result is decisive in the choice of partitioning characteristic. A characteristic with a compressed property such as the Customer Group characteristic is better to use than a characteristic with many instances such as Customer, because fewer values are involved.

It is often difficult to choose the package size because large packages cause heavy main memory usage, and small packages increase the number of query calls. Because a significant portion of the query runtime cannot be reduced through filtering, this causes the runtime of the analysis process to be much longer. A package size that is too small therefore leads to unacceptable runtimes. An optimal package size is one that makes best use of the main memory of your system. To do this, analyze the main memory usage with the aid of representative data. You do not necessarily need the same amount of data as in the productive system, but it is important to determine the scale of the query result, at least for certain values of the partitioning characteristic.

This chapter details all aspects of reporting that are relevant for the administrator. It discusses topics such as administration and monitoring of aggregates and SAP NetWeaver BW Accelerator, and of ICF and Information Broadcasting, as well as the procedure for problems with the portal integration and erroneous reporting results.

13 Reporting Monitoring and Administration

The topic of monitoring and administration of reporting includes both reporting objects, such as queries and Web templates the user knows, and processes and functions in the backend (BI ABAP), in BI Java, and in the portal.

13.1 Administration of the BEx Analyzer

Problems in reporting using the BEx Analyzer are usually associated with incorrect installations or performance problems with inappropriately structured workbooks. The next sections detail how you can check the installation of the SAP BEx tools and log the execution of SAP BEx workbooks.

13.1.1 SAP NetWeaver Check Workstation Wizard

It is always possible that performance problems occur owing to an error of the SAP NetWeaver frontend installation. In principle, it is recommended that you start an analysis of existing performance problems with a check of the frontend installation using the SAP NetWeaver Check Workstation Wizard to ensure that the problems are not caused by an inconsistency of the frontend software.

To execute the SAP NetWeaver Check Workstation Wizard, you simply call it via the start menu (Figure 13.1). Enter "NwCheckWorkstation.

exe" under START MENU • EXECUTE.... Then the system displays occurring errors in a log that is stored in a compressed file together with further information for the SAP support.

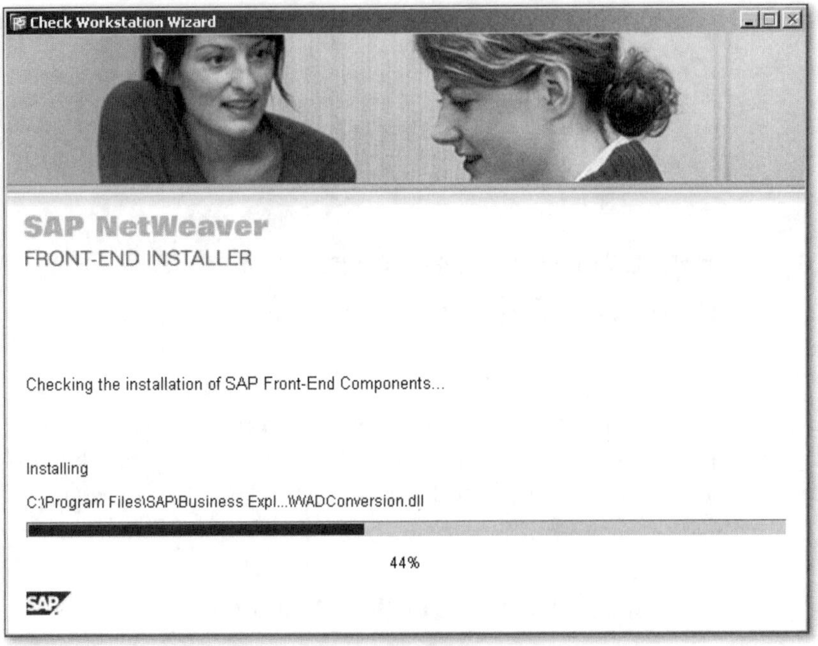

Figure 13.1 SAP NetWeaver Check Workstation Wizard

13.1.2 SAP BEx Installation Check

SAP BEx frontend check tool

The *sapbexc.xla* SAP BEx frontend check tool is an Excel file with macros that carry out a version check of all BW frontend files (Figure 13.2). Erroneous or problematic files are highlighted, and an Excel comment is attached. This way, you can indicate possible sources of errors during the installation of the frontend and options to remedy them. You can check the SAP NetWeaver BW frontend installation both on a PC and directory on a server. A new *sapbexc.xla* file is provided with each patch. Ensure that you have opened the current *sapbexc.xla* file for your patch level.

	A	B	C	D	E	F	G
1	**Check Installation on PC**						
2		Computer Name:	DEWDFM0030				
3		File Location:	C:\DOCUME~1\C5124003\LOCALS~1\Temp\9\sapBEX_PC_0424_091413.xls				
4		Check done on:	24.04.2009 09:14:13				
5		Excel Version:	Excel 2003 11.0 8237 (001)				
6		Windows Version:	Windows Server 2003 Service Pack 2 (3790)				
7							
8		SAP GUI	710 Patch 12				
9							
10	Filename	File Version on PC	File Version delivered	Path	Date/Time	Size	CompName
139							
140	**SAP GUI core components**						
141	chart.ocx	3.80.6.91	3.80.6.15	Version of file icdataflow.ocx on the PC is higher than on the Installation CD.	21.08.2008 12:26	2.232.320 Bytes	
142	icdataflow.ocx	2.0.0.27	This might be a problem but in general there is no problem.		26.02.2009 14:39	888.832 Bytes	
143	icjoin.ocx	1.0.1.35	1.		29.12.2006 16:15	786.432 Bytes	
144							
145	sapgradp.ocx	7100.3.12.481	71		26.02.2009 14:39	294.912 Bytes	
146	sapcalen.ocx	7100.3.12.137	7100.1.0.106	c:\PROGRA~1\sap\frontend\sapgui	26.02.2009 14:39	339.968 Bytes	SAP.CalendarControl.1
147	sapchart.ocx	7100.3.12.1018	7100.1.0.302	c:\PROGRA~1\COMMON~1\SAPSHA~1	26.02.2009 14:39	4.681.728 Bytes	SAPGraphics.Chart.1
148							
149	sapbtmp.dll	7100.3.12.1309	7100.1.0.1309	C:\WINDOWS\system32	26.02.2009 14:39	1.654.784 Bytes	
150	librfc32.dll	7100.3.141.6078	7100.1.0.4883	C:\WINDOWS\system32	26.02.2009 14:39	3.842.048 Bytes	
151							
152	wdtlog.ocx	7100.3.12.80	7100.1.0.66	c:\PROGRA~1\COMMON~1\SAPSHA~1	26.02.2009 14:39	495.616 Bytes	SAP.LogonControl.1
153	wdttree.ocx	7100.3.12.300	7100.1.0.286	c:\PROGRA~1\sap\frontend\sapgui	26.02.2009 14:39	720.896 Bytes	SAP.TableTreeControl.1
154	wdtaocx.ocx	7100.3.12.62	7100.1.0.61	c:\PROGRA~1\sap\frontend\sapgui	26.02.2009 14:39	2.781.184 Bytes	SAP.TableFactory.1
155	sapdatap.ocx	7100.3.12.266	7100.1.0.244	c:\program files\sap\frontend\sapgui	26.02.2009 14:39	495.616 Bytes	SAP.DataProvider.1

Figure 13.2 BEx Frontend Check Tool "sapbexc.xla"

In addition to the SAP NetWeaver BW components, you also check the SAP GUI components, files for OLE DB for OLAP, and others. Test results are highlighted in red, yellow, green, and blue. The meaning of the colors is as follows:

Test results

▶ Green indicates that everything is okay.

▶ Yellow indicates that the version on the PC or in the installation directory is higher than expected. However, this doesn't necessarily pose a problem.

▶ Red indicates that a version is lower than required. This problem should be remedied before entering a problem message or prior to installation.

▶ Blue indicates that the version of files is higher than required. Files that are highlighted in blue are not part of SAP NetWeaver BW directly, but are used by the that system. This may be a problem, but not necessarily.

The XLA file (the tool) is available in SAP Note 1229206. SAP Note 197460 provides information on executing the check tool and understanding the results.

13.1.3   Statistics Workbook

The method that is possibly the easiest to solve a problem in the area of BEx Analyzer performance is the function of automatic creation of a statistics workbook, which is available with SAP NetWeaver BW 7.0 BEx Analyzer. The statistics workbook displays all statistics events that occurred in a frontend session together with further information, for instance, the duration of the individual events or the occurrence frequency of events (Figure 13.3). In addition to information of the SAP NetWeaver BW statistics, such as OLAP times and the number of transferred cell data, the statistics workbook also provides details on the creation of all design elements in the workbook.

Statistic for Session:D6X1ST07QFBGDS1I44DTIXJ8U		
	Author	Status of Data 2009-11-19 09:02:35

| Chart | Filter | Information |

Information			
Author		Last Refreshed	2009-11-19 09:02:35
Current User	²3010997	Key Date	2009-11-19
Last Changed By		Changed At	
InfoProvider	@2D6X1T1CBP2D6EFYQQZ3N5GJ	Status of Data	2009-11-19 09:02:35
Query Technical Name	@2D6X1T1CBP2D6EFYQQZ3N5GJ	Relevance of Data (Date)	2009-11-19
Query Description	Statistic for Session:D6X1ST07QFBGDS1I44	Relevance of Data (Time)	09:02:35

Filter
(Nav.) Step Counter
Detail Level
Event
HANDLETP
InfoProvider
Internal ID of a Query R
Key Figures
Statistic Objekt Name ((

Table				
(Nav.) Step Counter	Event	Validity Period	Number	Counter for Statistic Event Calls
1	3.x Query View Open	,0.000000	,0	1,0
1	Authorization Buffer	,188.000000	,0	4,0
1	Bytes Transferred	,0.000000	124628,0	12,0
1	Derserialize Metadat	,015.623000	,0	1,0
1	Generate Workbook	,203.000000	,0	1,0
1	Load Local Workbook	2,093.504000	,0	1,0
1	Node Authorizations	,016.000000	,0	1,0
1	Not Assigned	2,939.371000	,0	1,0
1	OLAP Initialization	,233.000000	,0	18,0
1	OLAP Other Time	,297.000000	,0	2,0
1	OLAP: EXIT Variables	,016.000000	,0	3,0
1	OLAP: Query Gen.	,359.000000	,0	1,0
1	Persist MIME	,062.502000	,0	1,0
1	Process Command	,204.000000	,0	5,0
1	Process Dialog	24,079.000000	,0	2,0
1	RFC call	,483.000000	,0	10,0
1	Read Data	,0.000000	,0	1,0
1	Read System Info.	,062.000000	,0	1,0
1	Read Themes	,109.000000	,0	1,0
1	Serialize Data	,047.000000	,0	1,0
1	Serialize Navigation	,0.000000	,0	1,0
1	User Interaction	,0.000000	,0	1,0
1	Value Authorizations	,0.000000	,0	10,0
1	Result	31,407.000000	124628,0	80,0

Figure 13.3 Statistics Workbooks

Creating a statistics workbook

Proceed as follows to create a statistics workbook of the current frontend session:

1. Open SAP NetWeaver BW 7.0 BEx Analyzer, and log on to the SAP NetWeaver BW system (or start the analyzer from SAP GUI using Transaction RRMX).

2. In Microsoft Excel, click the icon of global settings in the SAP BEx add-in, or start it via the menu under BEx Analyzer • Global Settings.

3. Ensure that the collection of statistics is enabled (flag in the Statistics tab).

4. After a new logon, you need to execute all actions for which statistics information is supposed to be written.

5. Then create the statistics overview using the Show Statistics button in the global settings.

6. In the created workbook, expand the object characteristic in the rows.

Statistics workbooks support an analysis of workbook compression, for example. This function in the workbook settings enables you to compress the data that is contained in your workbook upon saving. Use this option if your workbook contains a lot of information and metadata so that your workbook consumes less space. To compare bytes transferred and the overall processing time, create a statistic for which compression is not enabled and a statistic for which compression is enabled.

13.1.4 BEx Analyzer Trace

The use of the BEx Analyzer Trace tool is recommended if you want to examine performance problems in general and require a better understanding of the activities and the process of BEx Analyzer or if you want to analyze the stack trace of an error that occurred. The following steps describe in detail how the system records a trace and how you need to analyze it:

1. You must ensure that the tracing is activated in the BEx Analyzer. For this purpose, open the global settings in the BEx Analyzer and check whether the flag for updating statistics is set.

Recording and analyzing a trace

2. Now implement the actions in the BEx Analyzer that are supposed to be analyzed or that result in an error.

The recorded trace is available in the global settings under Display Statistics. The results are opened as a text file. Note that you must close Microsoft Excel and open it again if a new file is supposed to be created because otherwise the new statistics are attached to the existing data. If, for example, Microsoft Excel is closed due to an error and you are therefore not able to view the statistics, you can directly open the file in the TEMP directory under *%temp%\bw\analyzer\traces*.

13.2   Query Administration

In the area of query administration, the focus is on the settings for caching and the read mode. Additional topics include the backup version of query elements and the parallel execution of queries. The descriptions and information on query statistics in Chapter 10, Technical Content and BI Administration Cockpit, are interesting and may help you understand the process of a query execution.

13.2.1   Processing Queries

The system can subdivide a query into subqueries. There are several reasons for subdividing queries, for instance, the use of constant selections, the execution via a MultiProvider, or in case of an execution in an InfoCube, the reading from both the E fact table and the F fact table (if the database view via both fact tables is not used). If this subdivision results in more than one subquery, the read process is executed in parallel by default.

Parallel execution Multiple dialog work processes are required for parallel execution of queries. The maximum level of parallelism determines how many work processes are used at most for each query. By default, this value is limited to 6. You can change this maximum value by entering a value between 1 and 100 in the QUERY_MAX_WP_DIAG entry in Table RSADMIN. The actual level of parallel execution depends on the current system load and is between 1 (sequential execution) and the maximum value. If the number of subqueries is larger than the maximum parallelism, all existing subqueries are distributed across the work processes that are specified by the level of parallelism. The results of all subqueries are collected at a synchronization point and combined in an overall result.

As of SAP NetWeaver 7.0, the system can easily manage large interim results of parallel processing. The system no longer cancels like in previous releases if a certain size of interim results is reached, and it reads sequentially again. Therefore, the RSADMIN parameter that was used in previous releases for nonparallel reading of a MultiProvider is no longer used.

Disabling parallel If you set the Not Using Parallel Processing flag in the query proper-
processing ties, the selected query is processed sequentially. Disabling the par-

allel processing can be beneficial because the query consumes fewer system resources in nonparallel processing. For queries with very fast response times, the effort for parallel processing can be higher than the possible gain of time. In this case it can also make sense to disable parallel processing.

13.2.2   Query Read Mode

The read mode determines how the OLAP processor gets data during navigation. You can set the mode in Customizing for an InfoProvider and in the Query Monitor for a query. The following types are supported:

▶ **Query To Be Read When You Navigate or Expand Hierarchies**
The amount of data transferred from the database to the OLAP processor is the smallest in this mode. However, it has the highest number of read processes. In the Query to Read Data During Navigation mode, the data for the fully expanded hierarchy is requested for a hierarchy drilldown. In the Query To Be Read When you Navigate or Expand Hierarchies mode, the data across the hierarchy is aggregated and transferred to the OLAP processor on the hierarchy level that is the lowest in the start list. When you expand a hierarchy node, the children of this node are then read. You can improve the performance of queries with large presentation hierarchies by creating aggregates on a middle hierarchy level that is greater than or the same as the hierarchy start level.

▶ **Query To Start During Navigation**
The OLAP processor only requests data that is needed for each navigational status of the query in SAP Business Explorer. The data that is needed is read for each step in the navigation. In contrast to the Query To Be Read When You Navigate or Expand Hierarchies mode, presentation hierarchies are always imported completely on a leaf level here. The OLAP processor can read data from the main memory when the nodes are expanded. When accessing the database, the best aggregate table is used and, if possible, data is aggregated in the database.

▶ **Query To Read All Data At Once**
There is only one read process in this mode. When you execute the query in SAP Business Explorer, all data in the main memory area of the OLAP processor that is needed for all possible navigational steps

of this query is read. During navigation, all new navigational states are aggregated and calculated from the data from the main memory.

The read mode Query To Be Read When you Navigate or Expand Hierarchies significantly improves performance in almost all cases compared to the other two modes. The reason for this is that only the data the user wants to see is requested in this mode. Compared to the Query To Be Read When You Navigate or Expand Hierarchies mode, the setting Query To Read Data During Navigation only effects performance for queries with presentation hierarchies.

Unlike the other two modes, the Query To Read All Data At Once setting also affects performance for queries with free characteristics. The OLAP processor aggregates on the corresponding query view. Therefore, the aggregation concept, that is, working with preaggregated data, is least supported in the Query To Read All Data At Once mode.

It is recommended that you select the Query To Be Read When You Navigate or Expand Hierarchies mode. Only select a different read mode in exceptional circumstances. The read mode Query To Read All Data At Once may be of use, for example, if the InfoProvider does not support selection (the OLAP processor reads significantly more data than the query needs anyway) or if a customer exit is active in a query for virtual key figures that prevents data from being aggregated in the database.

13.2.3 Cache Mode

The cache mode defines whether and how the query results and navigational states calculated by the OLAP processor should be saved as highly compressed data in a cache. You can define the mode for an InfoProvider as the standard value in Customizing (for instance, using Transaction RSDIPROP) and for a query in the Query Monitor (Transaction RSRT) (Figure 13.4).

Caching is a means for improving the query performance. However, you should ensure a balance between benefit (improved response times) and costs (effort for setting up and retaining data in the cache). Section 13.4, OLAP Caching, includes general information on the cache. If you decide on caching, you can choose from the following cache modes:

▸ **Cache Is Inactive**

The cross-transactional cache is deactivated in a targeted manner.

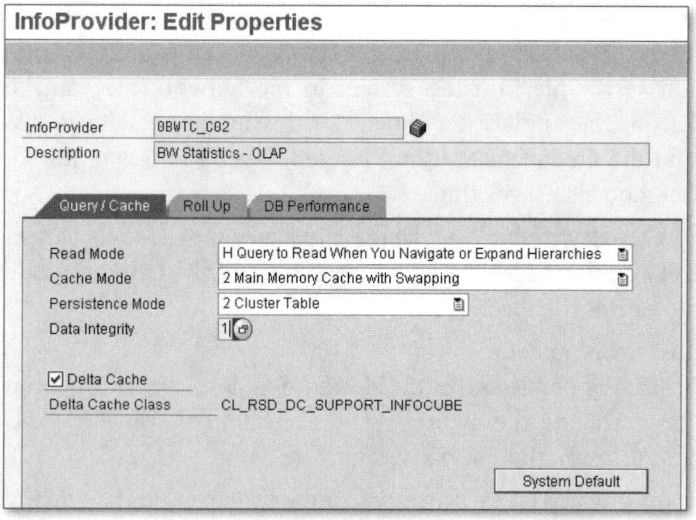

Figure 13.4 Settings in Transaction RSDIPROP

▶ **Main Memory Cache Without Swapping**
The cache data is stored in the main memory. When the cache memory is exhausted, excess data is displaced according to the last recently used (LRU) algorithm, that is, deleted from memory. If the query is then requested again, the result must be read from the InfoProvider once again.

▶ **Main Memory Cache With Swapping**
The cache data is stored in the main memory. When the cache memory is exhausted, the data to be displaced is written to a background store and can be loaded back into the cache memory if there is another request.

▶ **Persistent Cache per Application Server**
The cache data is stored persistently as a database table or as a file in a directory that can be accessed from the application server. It is recommended that you select a directory that is near the application server.

If you save the cache data in a database table, this puts a heavy load on the database, but accessing cached data in the database is also significantly faster. In comparison to storing data in, for example, a star schema, fewer tables are read and fewer indexes are accessed.

▶ **Cross-Application Server Persistent Cache**

The cache data is stored persistently as a database table or as a cross-application server file in a file system in the network that can be accessed from the application server. In this mode no data is displaced, and the memory size is not limited. More space is required, but this method also saves time.

If you use a database table, the database instance for the table carries the load. If you use a file, the operating system of the network node for the file carries the load.

▶ **BLOB/Cluster Enhanced**

The cache data is persistent in the database tables. In this mode no data is displaced, and the memory size is not limited. More space is required, but this method also saves time.

The way in which data is processed and saved has fundamentally changed in this cache mode compared to the cache modes specified previously. No lock concept is used, and there is no central directory of cache elements.

The BLOB/Cluster Enhanced cache mode is not available by default. To be able to use this cache mode, you must activate the RSADMIN parameter, `RSR_CACHE_ACTIVATE_NEW` (`VALUE=x`).

Persistence mode For some of the mentioned modes (Main Memory Cache with Swapping, Persistent Cache per Application Server, or Cross-Application Server Persistent Cache) you can specify how the displaced or cached data is supposed to be stored. You can select the following persistence modes:

▶ **Inactive**

If you select this option, the system resets the cache mode to Main Memory Cache without Swapping (1).

▶ **Flat File**

Storage in a file.

▶ **Cluster Table**

Storage in a nontransparent database table of the CLUSTER type.

▶ **Transparent Table (BLOB)**

Storage in a transparent database table with BLOB (binary large object). Compared to the Cluster Table, the Transparent Table (BLOB) leads to better system performance if you have large result sets because fewer database operations need to be executed. With smaller result sets, the Cluster Table can be advantageous because the BLOB fields require more administrative effort with regard to the database.

Usually, the settings should be made in such a way that you use main memory cache with swapping for cluster tables for displayed data.

13.2.4   Delta Caching

The delta cache process enables you to add specific data for a request to the cache. This means that when the data basis changes, you do not have to read all data for the request from the database. Whether the data is read directly from the database or from the cache doesn't have any impact on the query results. InfoCubes are suited to the delta cache process because their request ID can be used to identify which entries have been added. Assuming the InfoProvider is suited for the process, you can activate or deactivate the delta cache process for the selected query by selecting the Update Cache Objects in Delta Cache Process option in the query properties.

You can optimize the delta cache process by using the grouping setting. If a query is based on a MultiProvider, you can specify that the data that each of the InfoProviders for the MultiProvider supplies is to be treated separately and stored separately in the cache.

Grouping for delta caching

The benefit of this grouping is that when data for just one InfoProvider in the MultiProvider changes, you do not have to read all data for all InfoProviders again. The disadvantage of this grouping, however, is that it requires more memory space because the data cannot be aggregated using the various InfoProviders. The data is not aggregated until the query is run. The grouping is only considered if the delta cache process is activated for the query.

If you use the delta process and the query is based on a MultiProvider, select the required setting for the option Grouping. The following modes are supported:

▶ **No Grouping**
Partitioning does not take place; all results of the InfoProviders are merged into one result and cached. If the data for an InfoProvider changes, the cache has to be rebuilt.

▸ **Grouping Depending on InfoProvider Types**
With grouping based on the InfoProvider types, all InfoCubes are saved in a group. The remaining InfoProviders are either stored in one group or stored in multiple groups according to their properties. For example, VirtualProviders, DataStore objects, or InfoProviders that can supply hierarchy nodes are grouped. Open requests for a real-time InfoCube are also stored separately from standard Info-Cubes.

▸ **Grouping Depending on InfoProvider Types, InfoCubes Separately**
The difference from the Grouping Depending on InfoProvider Types is that with this option, the InfoCubes are also stored separately.

▸ **Every Provider Separate**
With this setting, all InfoProviders are stored separately.

Usually, a delta cache provides significant benefits and should therefore be used. With regard to the grouping, a separate use for each InfoProvider is recommended.

13.2.5 Caching for Virtual Characteristics and Key Figures

By default, the use of the cache is deactivated if virtual characteristics or key figures are used in the query because these InfoObjects are filled user-specifically via a customer exit (SAP Enhancement RSR00002 or the RSR_OLAP_BADI BAdI) and are only written to the queue afterwards. Using the Using Cache Despite Virtual Characteristics/Key Figures option in the query properties, you can explicitly determine that this data is supposed be written to the cache after it has been read by the database and has run through the customer exit.

Note that a change to the data via the customer exit does not lead to invalidation of the cache. If the data coming out of the customer exit depends not only on the inbound data, but for example, also on the user, on the time, or on other tables, the cached data can deviate from the data that is determined at that moment. The Using Cache Despite Virtual Characteristics/Key Figures option should therefore only be activated in exceptional cases and after precise analysis of SAP Enhancement RSR00002 or the RSR_OLAP_BADI BAdI.

13.2.6 Backup Versions

An automatic backup process was implemented with Support Package 09 for SAP NetWeaver BI 2004s (as it was formerly called). The intention of this process is to save a backup version of queries or other reusable components that you have created using BEx Query Designer Version 3.x. The backup process minimizes the possible risk of data loss for the occasional migration of queries and query components from SAP NetWeaver BW 3.x to SAP NetWeaver BW 7.x.

When you save a 3.x query, a variable, or a key figure in a 7.x version, a backup version is written to the database so that these objects are available not only in the common versions, such as A (Active) or M (Modified), but also as B version (Figure 13.5).

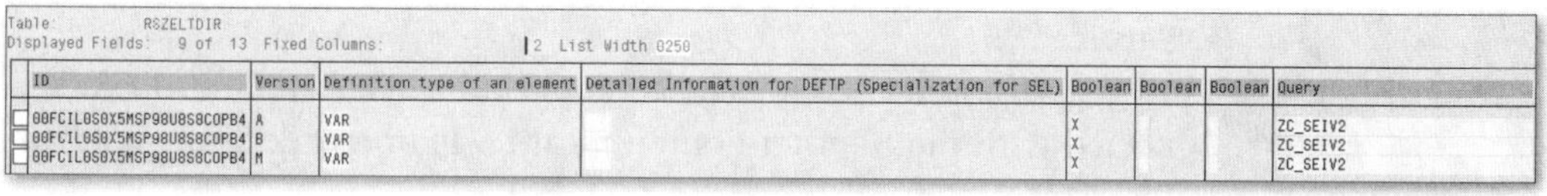

ID	Version	Definition type of an element	Detailed Information for DEFTP (Specialization for SEL)	Boolean	Boolean	Boolean	Query
00FCILOSOX5MSP98U8S8COPB4	A	VAR		X			ZC_SEIV2
00FCILOSOX5MSP98U8S8COPB4	B	VAR		X			ZC_SEIV2
00FCILOSOX5MSP98U8S8COPB4	M	VAR		X			ZC_SEIV2

Table: RSZELTDIR
Displayed Fields: 9 of 13 Fixed Columns: |2 List Width 0250

Figure 13.5 Version of Reporting Elements

In urgent cases, you can restore the existing backup version using Report COMPONENT_RESTORE (called with Transaction SA38) for an occasional migration of a query or query component of Version 3.x. The report overwrites the existing, active version by using the backup version as the source and hence enables the further processing of a query using the BEx Query Designer Version 3.x.

Restore

You can delete query components in a backup version via Transaction RSZDELETE and using the object version B (Backup) in the selection screen. This also ensures that no reference to a query is deleted from the roles or favorites when a backup version is deleted.

13.3 Internet Communication Frameworks Administration

Once you have set up the services required for reporting, the administration and monitoring is usually limited to the configuration and monitoring of the Internet Communication Manager (ICM). The following sections discuss the Internet Communication Framework (ICF) and in particular, describe the relevant ICM parameters and the caching.

13.3.1 ICF Services

You configure and test services via the service maintenance in Transaction SICF (Report RSICFTREE) (Figure 13.6). This transaction is used to maintain HTTP services for the HTTP communication of the SAP system via the Internet Communication Manager and the Internet Communication Framework. The following services or objects are differentiated:

▶ **Virtual host (HTTP and SMTP)**
Via a virtual host you can address a server in different ways through different combinations of host and port.

▶ **Service**
You can use a service to start an application. This application is connected with the Internet Communication Framework through a handler.

▶ **Internal aliases**
An internal alias is a pointer to a service. This enables you to configure certain settings (user, security procedure, and so on) differently for a service.

HTTP request handler
Each service includes a list of HTTP request handlers that are implemented as ABAP Object classes. If it is determined that the URL of an inbound request contains a string that was defined as a service or alias for a service, the HTTP request handler is called that is defined for this service.

A service in the HTTP service tree can be active (black font) or inactive (gray font). A client can only call active services. If you call an inactive service, you will see a message that access to this page is locked.

Security risk
Activated ICF services pose a security risk insofar that they can be accessed directly over the Internet via HTTP protocol. You must therefore ensure that access is restricted using appropriate methods, such as ensuring that the ICF service can be accessed only by users with appropriate authorization. The services provided by SAP are stored in the ICF service hierarchy under the virtual host, default_host, and the service node, SAP.

Virtuelle Hosts / Services	Documentation
▽ 🖥 default_host	VIRTUAL DEFAULT HOST
▽ 🌐 sap	SAP NAMESPACE; SAP IS OBLIGED NOT T...
▷ ⦿ option	RESERVED SERVICES AVAILABLE GLOBA...
▷ ⦿ public	PUBLIC SERVICES
🌐 ap	Application Platform
▷ 🌐 bc	BASIS TREE (BASIS FUNCTIONS)
🌐 bic	SERVICE FOR BIC DOCUMENT
▽ 🌐 bw	BW
▷ 🌐 bct	Business Content
🌐 BEx	Business Explorer
🌐 ce_url	CALL URL
▷ 🌐 doc	BW DOKUMENTE
🌐 dr	DRAG & RELATE
🌐 Mime	MIME IN WEB REPORTING
▷ 🌐 xml	XML SERVER

Figure 13.6 Services in Transaction SICF

13.3.2 Internet Communication Manager

You can monitor and manage the Internet Communication Manager (ICM), which receives and sends requests to and from the Internet (in the server role, for example, incoming HTTP requests). You can call the Internet Communication Manager (ICM) under ADMINISTRATION • SYSTEM ADMINISTRATION • MONITOR • SYSTEM MONITORING • INTERNET COMMUNICATION MANAGER or via Transaction SMICM. The ICM Monitor provides you with different functions to check the functioning and the status of the ICM and to detect possible errors.

To display or reset the *dev_icm* trace file and to set the trace level, select GOTO • TRACE FILE or GOTO • TRACE (values between 0 and 3 are possible; the default value is 1). You can also display just the start or the end of the file (the first or last 1,000 lines). This is a very useful function for large files.

Trace files

Select GOTO • PARAMETER to display or change the ICM profile parameters (Figure 13.7). In addition, Transaction RZ11 provides the documentation for each parameter executed. The value field is ready for input for parameters that can be changed dynamically. Note that with dynamic changes, these are lost the next time the instance is started.

Parameter

By selecting GOTO • HTTP SERVER you can display information on the HTTP application server, that is, information about the active AS ABAP or AS Java and the URL prefix table. If no AS Java has been configured (J2EE Server configured = FALSE), then all HTTP requests are passed to the AS ABAP.

HTTP server

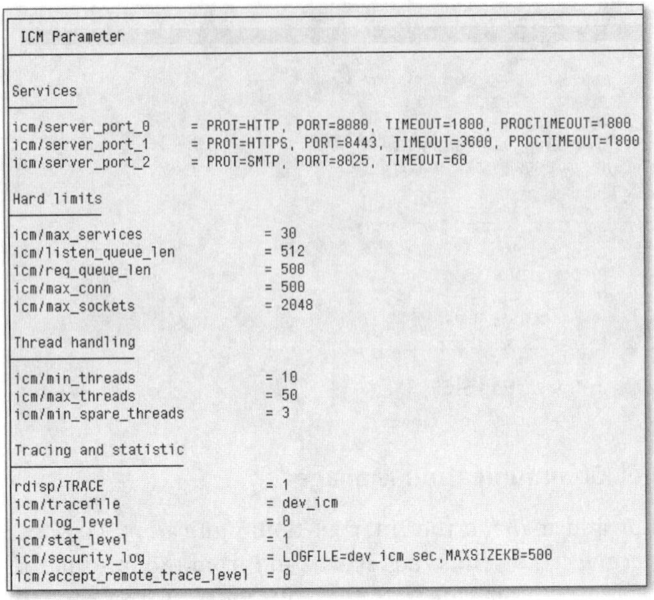

```
 ICM Parameter

 Services

 icm/server_port_0    = PROT=HTTP, PORT=8080, TIMEOUT=1800, PROCTIMEOUT=1800
 icm/server_port_1    = PROT=HTTPS, PORT=8443, TIMEOUT=3600, PROCTIMEOUT=1800
 icm/server_port_2    = PROT=SMTP, PORT=8025, TIMEOUT=60

 Hard limits

 icm/max_services          = 30
 icm/listen_queue_len      = 512
 icm/req_queue_len         = 500
 icm/max_conn              = 500
 icm/max_sockets           = 2048

 Thread handling

 icm/min_threads           = 10
 icm/max_threads           = 50
 icm/min_spare_threads     = 3

 Tracing and statistic

 rdisp/TRACE               = 1
 icm/tracefile             = dev_icm
 icm/log_level             = 0
 icm/stat_level            = 1
 icm/security_log          = LOGFILE=dev_icm_sec,MAXSIZEKB=500
 icm/accept_remote_trace_level = 0
```

Figure 13.7 ICM Parameter

If AS Java is active, the ICM decides whether the request is forwarded to AS ABAP or AS Java based on the URL prefix table. All URL prefixes contained in the list go to AS ABAP, and all others to AS Java. The table is determined from the possible prefixes (HTTP service tree and external aliases) of the Internet Communication Framework.

Administration of the ICM Server Cache

You can monitor the server cache in the ICM Monitor under GOTO • HTTP SERVER CACHE. For all objects retained in the cache, you can view the file size, the time of generation, and the validity period that is specified using the ICM profile parameter, `icm/HTTP/server_cache_<xx>/ expiration`.

Invalidating the cache
You can browse the list, sort the list, view objects by double-clicking them in the lower window, and invalidate individual cache entries. An invalidation of the cache is possible both for the local server and globally for the entire system. For this purpose, select EDIT • INVALIDATE CACHE. Here, you can then choose from ONLY LOCAL and GLOBAL IN the

SYSTEM. Local means that the entry in the ICM's cache of the current instance is invalidated. Global means that the invalidation of the entry is made for all instances of the SAP system.

Troubleshooting

The initial screen of Transaction SMICM provides an initial overview of possible problems of the ICM. This initial screen displays the ICM status, among other things. You should, in particular, include the ICM trace (GOTO • TRACE FILE) and services (GOTO • SERVICES) in an analysis.

If you cannot create a new network connection to the ICM, you should first compare the values for the used connections in the initial screen. In case of problems with new connections, you can usually determine that the peak and maximum values are identical. This means that all connections were used up at a point in time. For such problems, increase the `icm/max_conn` parameter, which is set to 500 by default.

Number of connections

Before a request is accepted, it is written to the queue, and the ICM control then assigns a thread to the request. If the ICM queue for requests overflows, the ICM monitor indicates for the used queue entries that the peak and maximum values are identical. You have either configured too few threads or the threads are blocked. In the first case, increase the number of threads (`icm/max_threads` parameter). In the second case, double-click the hanging threads to determine why they are hanging.

Number of threads

The data transfer between the ICM and the SAP work processes in AS ABAP is carried out via *memory pipes* (MPIs), which are structures based on shared memory (Figure 13.8). The MPI interface is also used for the communication of the ICM with AS Java (Java Dispatcher) and between the Web dispatcher and the ICM.

Buffer size

If no MPI buffer is left in the ICM, the client receives an error message. Select GOTO • MEMORY PIPES • DISPLAY DATA to check whether all MPIs or buffers are used or have been used. The value of #MPI Pipes Used should not exceed the limit of 2,000, and the value of Peak Buffer Usage should not reach Total #MPI Buffer.

```
MPI Status Information

Global settings

Total MPI size (Byte)      = 83886080
MPI buffer size (Byte)     = 65584
MPI header size (Byte)     = 32
MPI body size (Byte)       = 65536
Total #Mpi Buffer          = 1279

Current usage

#MPI Buffers used          = 2
#MPI Pipes used            = 2

Misc information

Peak buffer usage          = 3
Transaction count          = 1
```

Figure 13.8 Information on Memory Pipes

13.4 OLAP Caching

To improve the query performance, SAP NetWeaver BW provides three options for preprocessing: aggregates or an SAP NetWeaver BW Accelerator index, the OLAP cache, and the precalculation within broadcasting. Also note the caching-relevant query properties, which are detailed in Section 13.2, Query Administration.

OLAP cache An object in the OLAP cache (see the example in Figure 13.9) can only be used by the corresponding query, but it still depends on many settings, such as different sortings, number or characteristics display, filterings, or navigations. The OLAP cache persists the data in a special format that depends on the query (query cube).

In this complex ABAP table SP, a majority of the processing and calculation tasks are carried out. These are implemented by the OLAP processor to display the data of the structure and detailing of the InfoProvider in the list.

Parts of the OLAP processing are therefore performed when this storage table SP is filled; the remaining processing operations are always carried out when the list is generated at the different OLAP levels (backend and frontend).

The usage of the OLAP cache should always be transparent; that is, the displayed list may not indicate whether it was generated using the cache or not. Therefore, a cache object must always be invalidated or adjusted if something changes that effects its calculation.

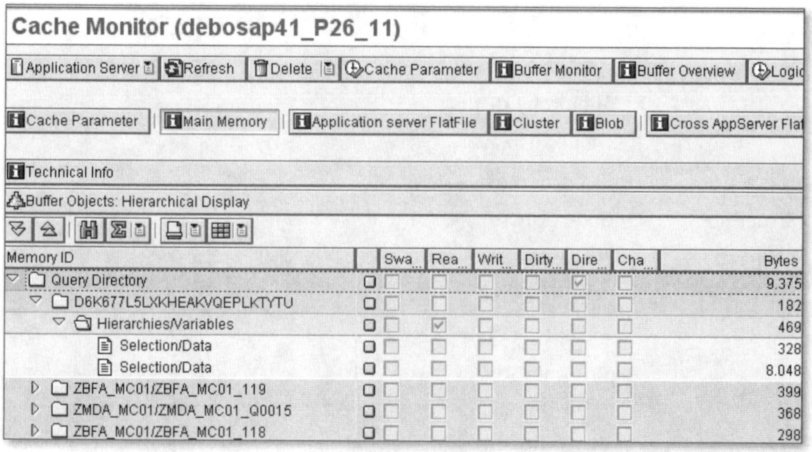

Cache Monitor (debosap41_P26_11)

| Application Server 🗒 | 🔄Refresh | 🗑Delete 🗒 | ⊕Cache Parameter | ℹBuffer Monitor | ℹBuffer Overview | ⊕Logic |

| ℹCache Parameter | ℹMain Memory | ℹApplication server FlatFile | ℹCluster | ℹBlob | ℹCross AppServer Flat |

ℹTechnical Info

⚠Buffer Objects: Hierarchical Display

Memory ID		Swa	Rea	Writ	Dirty	Dire	Cha		Bytes
▽ 🗂 Query Directory	☐	☐	☐	☐	☐	☑	☐		9.375
▽ 🗂 D6K677L5LXKHEAKVQEPLKTYTU	☐	☐	☐	☐	☐	☐	☐		182
▽ 🗂 Hierarchies/Variables	☐	☐	☑	☐	☐	☐	☐		469
📄 Selection/Data	☐	☐	☐	☐	☐	☐	☐		328
📄 Selection/Data	☐	☐	☐	☐	☐	☐	☐		8.048
▷ 🗂 ZBFA_MC01/ZBFA_MC01_119	☐	☐	☐	☐	☐	☐	☐		399
▷ 🗂 ZMDA_MC01/ZMDA_MC01_Q0015	☐	☐	☐	☐	☐	☐	☐		368
▷ 🗂 ZBFA_MC01/ZBFA_MC01_118	☐	☐	☐	☐	☐	☐	☐		298

Figure 13.9 OLAP Cache

Such effects include changes to the metadata (InfoProvider and InfoObjects), all changes in the query definition, and all changes to the data (InfoProvider, master data, hierarchies). The system recognizes these changes based on time stamps, but checks very precisely whether they affect the first part of the processing, that is, whether they really affect the content of the cache object.

Table 13.1 shows the behavior of the OLAP cache regarding cached data. After the table, you can find a description of the characters.

Effects of changes

Area	Change To	Cache	Delta
Metadata	InfoProvider	X	X
	InfoObject of the provider	X	X
Query definition	Characteristic restrictions	X	X
	Default values	–	–
	Free characteristics	X	X
	Conditions/exceptions	–	–
	Characteristics display	–	–
	Sorting	–	–
	Result rows	–	–
	Result position	–	–

Table 13.1 Effects on the OLAP Cache

461

Area	Change To	Cache	Delta
	Zero suppression	–	–
	Hierarchy display	–	–
	Value display	–	–
	Texts/names	–	–
Structure element	Selections	X	X
	Formulas	X	X
	Aggregation	X	X
	Exception cells	X	X
	Presentation	–	–
	Constant selection	X	X
	Quantity/currency translation	X	X
	Input readiness	X	X
	Calculations (result/single value)	–	–
Variables	Selections	F	F
	Formulas	X	X
	Text	–	–
InfoProvider	New values (requests)	X	U
	Deletion of data	X	R
	Selective deletion	X	X
Master data	New values	I	I
	Activation run	Y	Y
	Navigation attribute	T	T
	Display attribute	–	–
	Long, medium, and short text	–	–
Rates/factors	Exchange rates	C	C
	Quantity factors	X	X
Hierarchy	New values	I	I
	Activation	X	X
	Time dependency	T	T
Generation	RSRT ® generate	X	X
	RSRDUMMY (SNOTE or SP)	X	X

Table 13.1 Effects on the OLAP Cache (Cont.)

The following list describes the characters in Table 13.1:

▶ **X**

The cache entry for this query is completely invalidated. No precise analysis is implemented for metadata changes.

▶ **F**

Changes to selection variables that are only used in default values (state) are harmless.

▶ **U**

This is the actual delta procedure in which new requests are read and the cache object is rewritten with changed data.

▶ **R**

It only needs to be invalidated if the request is less than or equal to the ROLLUP request.

▶ **C**

For a time-dependent currency conversion, the system checks whether one of the currencies that were used for the creation of the cache object has been changed. However, there are exceptional cases (for instance, "calculate before aggregation") in which every change to the table of exchange rates (TCUR) leads to invalidation.

▶ **I**

If new values are posted for a characteristic ABC, you need to invalidate the cache objects for the InfoProvider ABC (of the InfoObject type).

▶ **Y**

If changes of a characteristic C are activated, the system checks whether the query contains an attribute of C as a navigation attribute. If so, the cache object is invalidated.

▶ **T**

If the query contains a time-dependent attribute, the system checks whether a factual assignment change exists in the time interval between the generation of the cache object and the current time. If so, the cache object is invalidated.

If you understand the (persistent) OLAP cache as a query-specific aggregate, the delta cache process corresponds to the aggregate rollup. In every cache object, the fill level is kept for each part InfoProvider analogous to table RSMDATASTATE. It is recorded up to which request ID

Delta cache process

data has been imported into the cache object. To use the cache object, you only need to read the newly added requests. They are added to the cache object via Collect, and the cache object is then rewritten. A process for adjusting the cache object in case of changes to the master data or hierarchy like the change run does not exist for the OLAP cache.

To read missing requests for a cache object, it is necessary that the request information (InfoObject 0REQUID) is still visible in the Info-Cube. If an InfoCube is automatically compressed upon loading, the delta process has no effect because you can no longer access the delta. If the aggregates are compressed immediately after rollup, the delta process is not very effective here either. The system still has the option to decide whether it reads the delta requests from the fact table or completely from the aggregate.

An InfoProvider can participate in a delta process if a class was specified for it for which the IF_RSD_DELTACACHE_SUPPORT interface is implemented. Currently, this is only possible for the regular basic InfoCubes and for the virtual InfoCubes of SAP SEM-BCS (Business Consolidation) with the CL_RSSEM_DC_SUPPORT_VP_BCS class. For all other InfoProviders or for queries with the setting DELTACACHE = false, the OLAP cache behaves like in SAP NetWeaver BW 3.x. The cache object must be rejected as soon as new data has been added. However, the determination of the time stamp has been improved so that even InfoSets are cache-capable in principle.

Cache partitions One of the most critical enhancements of the OLAP cache in SAP NetWeaver BW 7.0 was the implementation of query partitions in the OLAP cache. With this change, a separate cache object is managed for each query partition. Among other things, this happens because:

▸ The functions for constant selections have been implemented completely anew with SAP NetWeaver BW 7.0.

▸ MultiProviders can use this new function to store cache entries for sub-InfoProviders separately, and you therefore do not need to reread the data of all InfoProviders from the database if you need to update the data of only one sub-InfoProvider.

For example, if you considered the cache behavior of a MultiProvider that consists of a basic InfoCube and a virtual InfoProvider, in SAP NetWeaver BW 3.x no cache object would be created by default.

Virtual Characteristics and Key Figures

Any influencing values, for example, time-dependent influencing values in Customer Exit RSR00002 or in the RSR_OLAB_BADI BAdI (virtual characteristics and key figures), result in the cache being invalidated. If you can ensure that no further changes affect the cache validity from the routines (customer exit or BAdI), you can make this setting for the corresponding query in Transaction RSRT under PROPERTIES • CACHE USE DESPITE VIRTUAL CHARACTERISTICS/KEY FIGURES.

Remote-InfoProvider

For basic InfoCubes, nontransactional DataStore objects, and master data InfoProviders, the system automatically sets a time stamp in Table RSDINFOPROVDATA when the data is changed (insert, update, delete). For the implementation, this time stamp is compared with a time stamp in the cache package and is ignored if the RSDINFOPROVDATA time stamp is newer than the time stamp of the package. For MultiProviders or InfoSets, the maximum number of time stamps of the sub-InfoProviders involved is used.

Because the system has no information on the changes to the data storage that are made by a remote-InfoProvider, queries on a remote-InfoCube, a MultiProvider with remote sub-InfoProvider, and an InfoSet that uses a transactional DataStore object cannot use data from the OLAP cache.

13.5   Aggregates

If you want the system to propose aggregates, you must meet some prerequisites. You must have created at least one query for the selected InfoCube (or for a MultiProvider that uses the InfoCube). When you start the queries and navigate in them, the system can propose the required aggregates. Ensure that the collection of SAP NetWeaver BW statistics is activated for the selected InfoCube in the OLAP area. To define aggregates, proceed as follows:

1. In the context menu for the InfoCube, select Maintain Aggregate.

2. Determine that the system is to propose aggregates. A dialog window opens in which you specify the statistics data. Another window opens for the maintenance of the aggregates. The aggregates proposed by

Defining
aggregates

the system are listed on the right side of the screen, and you can change them by adding and removing dimensions, characteristics, or attributes via drag-and-drop.

3. If you want to check the definition of the aggregates for inconsistencies, select Check Definition.

4. Save the aggregates.

Editing aggregates manually

You can start the manual maintenance of aggregates both via the Data Warehousing Workbench (Transaction RSA1) and directly via Transaction RSDDV. In the Modeling functional area of the Data Warehousing Workbench, select the Maintain Aggregate function in the context menu of the InfoCube that you selected in the InfoProvider tree. If you have already created aggregates for the InfoCube, you can start the aggregate maintenance with a double-click. On the left side of the screen, the system displays the dimensions, characteristics, and navigation attributes of the selected InfoCube in a tree structure as a template for aggregates. Select one or more objects to be copied to the aggregate. Define the granularity you need for the data in the aggregate.

You should also add all characteristics that can be derived from the selected characteristics. For example, if you define an aggregate for the month, you should also include the quarter and the year in the aggregate. This enhancement does not increase the data set, but permits a year aggregate to be built from this aggregate, and those who need the annual values can also use queries of this aggregate.

Including attributes

You can only include a characteristic and one of its attributes in an aggregate in expert mode (EXTRAS • SWITCH EXPERT MODE ON/OFF). Such an aggregate has the same granularity and size as an aggregate that was built only with the characteristic but is affected by the hierarchy/attribute change run. Compared with the aggregate for the characteristic in which the attribute information is defined by a join with the master data table, the aggregate for the characteristic and the attribute only saves the database join. It is therefore recommended that you either build an aggregate using the characteristic or define a (much smaller) aggregate using the attribute.

Creating the aggregate

To create an aggregate, you either transfer the selected objects to the Aggregates column on the right side of the screen using drag-and-drop or select Create New Aggregate. In the following steps you enter a short and a long description (which can be changed later via the context menu of the aggregate). The system then displays the actual screen for the aggregate maintenance in which the aggregate is shown in the upper area and the logging the lower area.

If an aggregate contains a time-dependent component, you must assign a key date to the aggregate. When you fill the aggregate, the key date behaves like the key date of a query. The time-dependent attributes and hierarchies are evaluated on this key date. Therefore, aggregates with a time-dependent component can only be used in a query if the key date of the query is the same as the key date of the aggregate.

Time-dependent components

In the dialog window, you select either a variable or a fixed date as the key date. In this case, variables are normal reporting variables that can be used in queries for the key date and can be calculated automatically (typically in the SAP Exit or Customer Exit processing types):

▶ **0CWD**
Current workday

▶ **0DAT**
Current calendar day

▶ **0P_KEYDT**
Key date of due date

▶ **0P_KEYD2**
Key date of posting (from key date of due date)

▶ **0P_KEYD3**
Key date of clearing (from key date of due date)

▶ **0P_KEYD4**
Key date of posting (posting date)

▶ **0P_KEYD5**
Key date of clearing (from key date of posting)

Aggregates with a variable key date must be updated regularly. This process must be included in a process chain (FURTHER BI PROCESSES • ADJUST TIME-DEPENDENT AGGREGATES). To enter a fixed calendar day, you can select the date from a calendar. After the aggregate has been activated and filled, the system copies the key date when the aggregate was filled and that was calculated from the variable into the Key Date LINE.

Partitioning By default, the aggregate fact tables are partitioned when the associated InfoCube is partitioned, and the partitioning characteristic exists in the aggregate. Select PROPERTIES • CHANGE PARTITIONING to suppress the partitioning of individual aggregates. If aggregates contain only a small amount of data, this can result in many small partitions. This affects the read performance, and you should therefore not partition aggregates with small amounts of data. If this property is changed to Not Partitioned for an existing aggregate, you must activate and fill it again.

Adapting existing aggregates You can change the structure of the aggregate by adding components or deleting existing ones. You can also change the key date. Components are inserted in an aggregate, and one or more objects are selected in the template for aggregates and copied to the aggregate to be changed on the right side of the screen via drag-and-drop. You can change the selection type (All Characteristic Values, Hierarchy Level, Fixed Value) via the corresponding entry in the context menu. Because aggregates that contain fewer than 14 components are stored in an optimized from in the database, you should take into account that characteristics defined in the InfoCube are also included in the aggregate, and the number of components increases even though these are not visible in the screen display.

You can delete components from an aggregate by selecting the component in the aggregate tree and selecting Remove Component in the context menu or by moving the component to the left area of the screen using drag-and-drop. To delete a dimension from an aggregate, you have to delete all of the characteristics and navigation attributes of this dimension. If you change the key date of an aggregate via the context menu, the key date calculated from a changed variable is not copied to the Key Date line until the Adjust Time-Dependent Aggregates process has been performed.

Check and save You can select Check Definition to check the aggregate definition for inconsistencies. You can then save the new or changed aggregate.

13.5.1 Displaying Aggregates and Their Components

In the Displaying Aggregates and their Components screen area of the Maintenance for Aggregates screen, the system displays aggregates and their components in a logical tree. You can use this screen area to define aggregates and to obtain information about the status of individual aggregates.

In principle, you can define any number of aggregates for an InfoCube. However, ensure that a balance exists between the aggregate's advantages and disadvantages. On the one hand, aggregates improve the performance of queries; on the other hand, you must keep an eye on the disadvantages: increased load times through data package uploads, through the hierarchy/attribute change run after loading master data, and through adjusting time-dependent aggregates.

To optimize an InfoCube, you should repeatedly check whether additional aggregates are required or whether created aggregates are no longer used. The aggregates display in the Maintenance for Aggregates screen helps you evaluate aggregates. Table 13.2 provides a detailed description.

Column	Description
Aggregates	Aggregates with all transferred components in a tree display.
Technical name	Technical name of the aggregate.
Save	Indicates new or changed aggregates.
Proposed action	The system proposes actions if necessary.
Details on the respective components	Every component of an aggregate (characteristics and navigation attributes) must be assigned to a selection type that indicates the degree of detail to which the data of an InfoCube is compressed in an aggregate. ▶ All characteristic values (*): Data is grouped by all values of the characteristic or the navigation attribute. ▶ Hierarchy level (H): The data is grouped according to the nodes of a hierarchy level. ▶ Fixed value (F): Data is filtered according to a single value. The details displayed match the selected hierarchy, the selected hierarchy level, or the selected fixed value.
Status	The status is displayed using traffic light colors: ▶ Red: created, not active

Table 13.2 Information in the Aggregate Overview

Column	Description
	▸ Yellow: Changed (The modified aggregate definition is no longer the same as the active aggregate definition.) ▸ Green: active, saved
Filled/switched off	The flag is displayed using traffic light colors: ▸ Red: not filled with data ▸ Green: filled with data
Evaluation	The evaluation is based on various criteria. At the moment the compression of the data compared with the InfoCube (How much smaller is the aggregate compared to the InfoCube?) and the last use (When was the aggregate last used?) is used in the evaluation. The representation is in a bar chart: The larger the number of minus signs, the worse is the evaluation of the aggregate (----- means the aggregate can possibly be deleted). The larger the number of plus signs, the better is the evaluation of the aggregate (+++++ means the aggregate could make a lot of sense).
Records	Number of records in the filled aggregate.
Records (compressed)	Average number of records read from the source to create a record in the aggregate This number provides information about the quality of the aggregate. The larger the value, the greater is the compression and the better the quality of aggregate. Because an aggregate should be 1/10 the size of its source, the number should be larger than 10. If the value is 1, the aggregate is a copy of the InfoCube and can be deleted if required.
Use	Number of uses (in queries), that is, how often the aggregate has been used for reporting.
Last used	Date on which the aggregate was last used for reporting. If an aggregate has not been used for a long time, you should deactivate or delete it. Note, however, that certain aggregates cannot be used at certain times (for example, during vacation). Do not delete basic aggregates that you created to accelerate the hierarchy/attribute change run.

Table 13.2 Information in the Aggregate Overview (Cont.)

Column	Description
Last rollup	Date on which the aggregate was last provided with data.
Last rollup by	User name of the person who scheduled the last upload.
Last changed on	Date on which the aggregate definition was last changed.
Last change by	User name of the person who made the last change.

Table 13.2 Information in the Aggregate Overview (Cont.)

You can find a status display for all of the aggregates in the SAP NetWeaver BW system in the Administration functional area of the Data Warehousing Workbench. In the navigation window under Monitors select Aggregates. The Status of the Aggregates screen area lists all InfoCubes and all existing aggregates under each InfoCube. Compared to the aggregate maintenance transaction, you can view the status of the aggregates but not their components. If you double-click a specific aggregate, the system takes you to a detailed screen of the aggregate including the components.

Status overview of the aggregates

13.5.2 Further Processing Functions for Aggregates

To be able to efficiently work with aggregates, it is essential to check the structure of the aggregates and their use. This enables you, for example, to save time during upload if you deactivate or delete aggregates that are no longer used for reporting.

In the Aggregate tree dialog window, the system shows the relationships of aggregates of an InfoCube, that is, which aggregate can be built from which other aggregate. With the help of the aggregate tree, you can identify similar aggregates and manually optimize the specific aggregates on this basis.

Aggregate tree

You can temporarily switch off an aggregate to check if its use makes sense. An aggregate that is switched off is not used when a query is executed. For this purpose, select the relevant aggregate and select Switch On/Off from the context menu. An aggregate that is switched off is marked accordingly in the Filled/Switched Off column. Because aggregates that are switched off must also be consistent, you do not

Switch on/off

have to activate the aggregate again or to fill it when you switch it back on. To test whether the switched-off aggregate makes sense for the performance optimization in reporting, execute a query or trace that would use it. Compare the time the database needs without the use of the aggregate with the time the query needs when using the aggregate. This comparison then indicates whether you can deactivate or delete the aggregate.

Deactivate

When you deactivate an aggregate, the system deletes all of its data and database tables. However, the definition of the aggregate is not deleted, so you can activate and fill it again if required. To deactivate an aggregate, select the Deactivate entry from the context menu.

Delete

With the deletion function in the context menu of an aggregate, you not only deactivate the aggregate, but also delete it completely. You also remove the definition of the aggregate.

13.5.3 Activating Aggregates and Providing Them with Data

Activating and filling aggregates

After you define a new aggregate or change the structure of an existing aggregate, the next activity is to activate and then fill the new aggregate with data. When you start the activation and (initial) filling, the system creates the tables that are required according to the definition of the aggregate in the database. Aggregates are created based on the same schema as InfoCubes: An aggregate contains two fact tables (E and F) and multiple dimension tables, whereas you derive the table names from technical names of the aggregate.

If the aggregate is active (indicated, for example, in the Status column, in which the color changes to green), you can start the filling immediately or schedule it for an execution at a later time. Because it can take a long time to build an aggregate from an InfoCube, all of the aggregates are always filled in the background. However, an aggregate can also read data from a larger aggregate that is already filled, and you can therefore assign data to compressed aggregates quickly. Logs for filling are written to the application log (Transaction SLG1) with the following information: object RSSM, subobject MON, external identification as specified in Table 13.3.

Log	External Identification
All	*<InfoCube>*
Filling new aggregates	MON:PROTOCOLL_ACTION-AGGR2-<InfoCube>
Rolling up already existing aggregates	MON:PROTOCOLL_ACTION-AGGR1-<InfoCube>

Table 13.3 Identifiers in the Application Log

If new data packages (requests) are loaded into the InfoCube, they are not immediately available for reporting via an aggregate. To provide the aggregate with the new data from the InfoCube, you must first load the data into the aggregate tables at a time that you can set. This process is known as a *rollup* and requires that new data packages (requests with data packages) were loaded into an InfoCube and aggregates for this InfoCube were already activated and filled with data. Rolling up data into an aggregate

Use the manual procedure if the data of multiple data packages forms one logical unit and should therefore only be released together. An example is requests for data from individual departments that is not available at time but is supposed to be available only collectively (consistently) for reporting. A check in process chains is often not possible in such cases. The steps of a manual rollup are as follows: Manual rollup

1. Select the Rollup tab in the aggregate maintenance.
2. Choose Selection. The Start Time dialog box opens.
3. Select the start time (Immediate Start, Date/Time, After Job, After Event, At Operation Mode).
4. Set the appropriate flag if you want to run the job periodically.
5. Save your entries.

In principle, it is recommended that you include the rollup as a process in the process chain, particularly for complex flows, for difficulties with automations and event collectors, and for all new developments. Rollup as a process in a process chain

Procedure in Case of Master Data and Hierarchy Changes

If hierarchies and attributes for characteristics of an InfoCube have been changed, you have to make structural changes to the aggregates to modify the data accordingly. With a structural change, all of the aggregates of all InfoCubes are modified if they are affected by the changes to the hierarchies and InfoObjects. Understandably, this may take some time. You can still report on the old hierarchies and attributes during the change run.

If the changes affect an amount of data that exceeds a certain threshold value, modifying the aggregate is more time-consuming than rebuilding it. You can change this threshold value. In the Implementation Guide (IMG), select SAP NETWEAVER • BUSINESS INTELLIGENCE • PERFORMANCE SETTINGS• PARAMETERS FOR AGGREGATES IN THE Percentage Change of Delta Process section. In the Limit with Delta field, enter the required percentage (a number between 0 and 99). 0 means the aggregate is always rebuilt. If an aggregate is affected by changes to the data, it is either modified (in a delta process) or — depending on the threshold value — rebuilt. When you modify an aggregate, the obsolete data records are posted negatively, and the new data records are posted positively.

You can modify aggregates manually or automatically using a program, and you can start multiple change runs simultaneously. A prerequisite for a simultaneous run is that the lists of master data and hierarchies to be activated are different and that the changes affect different Info-Cubes. If a change run terminates, you have to start it again. You do this by starting the change run again with the same parameters (same list of characteristics and hierarchies).

Loading Data into Aggregates Efficiently

Automatic compression
In the administration of an InfoCube, you specify in the Rollup tab whether the aggregates of an InfoCube are compressed automatically when it is filled with data or after the rollup of data packages. If possible, you should always compress because otherwise the aggregates can become rather large, which affects performance. If you switch on the automatic compression, the aggregates of an InfoCube are automatically compressed when it is filled with data or after the rollup of data packages. If you want to delete a data package (request) from the Info-Cube and the InfoCube has already been rolled up to the aggregate, you must deactivate the aggregates and rebuild them.

If the automatic compression is not switched on, the aggregates are first compressed together with the InfoCube, which makes sense if requests need to be deleted frequently from the InfoCube. When a request is deleted from the InfoCube, it can also be deleted from the aggregates.

If the amount of data is very large when you fill the InfoCube, the system reads the data in blocks and not all at one time. This avoids problems with the temporary table space on the database that may occur if you have very large sources (InfoCubes or aggregates). You can find more information about the block size settings under SAP CUSTOMIZING Implementation Guide (IMG) • SAP NETWEAVER • BUSINESS INTELLIGENCE • PERFORMANCE SETTINGS• PARAMETERS FOR AGGREGATES (Figure 13.10). The block size specified here indicates the approximate size of the individual blocks, and it should be selected depending on the size of the temporary table space on the database. If the parameter is too small, there are too many read processes, which increases the runtime. If the parameter is too large, the temporary table space on the database overflows.

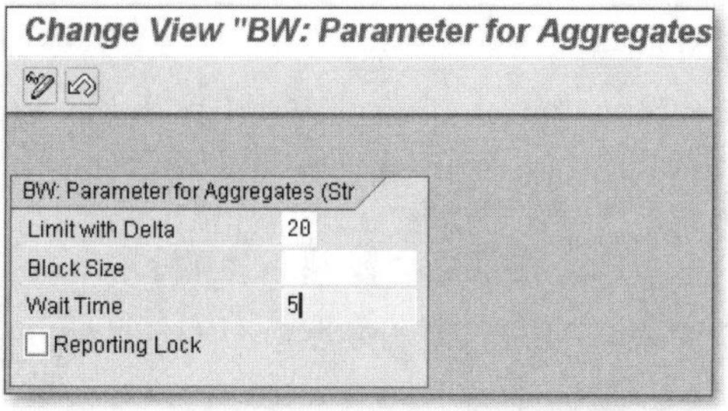

Reading data in blocks

Figure 13.10 Performance Settings for Aggregates

Additional parameters in the customizing for aggregates include Limit with Delta (percentage to switch from delta method to rebuild), Wait Time in minutes (before the process is terminated owing to a block), and Reporting Lock (relevant for Oracle databases to protect against overflow of rollback segments).

Aggregates with fewer than 14 characteristics are created for all databases in such a way that each characteristic is in a separate (artificial) dimension, and these dimensions are created as line item dimensions. Aggregates that consist only of line item dimensions are filled with data from the database only. This improves the performance when filling and rolling up. This is not evident in the presentation of the aggregate in the maintenance transaction: The logical tree display is copied from the left area (Selection Options for Aggregates) but does not reflect this special form of storage on the database.

Optimizing the performance

To optimize data load performance, you can specify that you want to automatically delete indexes before the load operation and recreate them when the data load is complete. Building indexes in this way accelerates the data load process, although it has a negative impact on read performance (for reporting or also for an internal update in other InfoProviders, for example). Therefore, you should only use this method if no read processes take place during the data load. If you want to switch on index building during rollup anyway, you have the following options:

- In the Modeling area of the Data Warehousing Workbench, select Display or Change from the context menu of the required InfoCube. Then select ENVIRONMENT • INFOPROVIDER PROPERTIES • DISPLAY or CHANGE. In the Database Performance tab, select the option Delete Index Before Each Data Load and Then Recreate or Delete Index Before Each Delta Load and Then Recreate.

- In the Modeling area of the Data Warehousing Workbench, select Manage from the context menu of the required InfoCube. In the Performance tab, select the Create Index (batch) option and select the required option: Delete InfoCubes Indexes Before each Data Load and Then Refresh or Also Delete and then Refresh Indexes with Each Delta Upload.

Parallel execution of processes for multiple aggregates
In the BI background management transaction (Transaction code RSBATCH), you can specify the settings for parallel processing to ensure that the individual processes of aggregate processing are carried out in parallel. Parallel processing is applied to the aggregates in any number of InfoCubes. Processes of aggregate processing include the initial filling of aggregates, the attribute change run, the check of aggregates during rollup, the compression of aggregates, and the rollup of data.

13.5.4 Checking Aggregates

To check aggregates for the correctness of their data records, you can implement aggregate checks. You can define any number of aggregate checks for each InfoCube. You have the option to check the required aggregates at any time in different check modes.

You can also perform a daily aggregate check after the rollup using check aggregates or high characteristic restrictions, and you can schedule a complete check on the weekend for critical aggregates or implement a weekly change run.

The results of the check are available in the application log. When the system finds erroneous records, the incorrect records are stored in a new database table (/BIO/01xxxxxx). The log messages indicate the name of the table and its size.

Aggregate checks cannot be transported because the number, type, and size of the aggregates usually differ in test and live systems. Therefore, create your own aggregate checks in the appropriate system. You can create corresponding checks with identical check IDs in the different systems.

The technical information on aggregate checks is stored in the tables RSDDAGGRCHECKDIR, RSDDAGGRCHECKSEL, and RSDDAGGRCHECKT. The CL_RSDDK_AGGR_AUTOCHECK class and the RSDDK2_CHECK function group contain the program source text. The following programs are available for the aggregate check:

Technical details

▶ **RSDDK_CHECK_AGGREGATE**
Checks any number of aggregates; also aggregates from different InfoCubes in the modes A (all), Q (aggregated), and C (check aggregate).

▶ **RSDDK_CHECK_AGGREGATE_SELOPT**
Used to enter characteristic restrictions and the subsequent aggregate check.

▶ **RSDDK_CHECK_AGGREGATE_CHECKID**
Performs a specific check that has already been defined in Transaction RSDDAGGRCHECK.

You can find the maintenance of the aggregate check either via the aggregate maintenance (Transaction code RSDDV) in EXTRAS • AUTOMATIC CHECK (ON/OFF/CHANGE) or via Transaction RSDDAGGRCHECK. Every check is specified by the InfoCube name and an ID. Enter the name of the InfoCube and a valid check ID. If you want to display, edit, execute, or delete an already existing check, enter the corresponding check ID. Input helps are available both for the InfoCube name and for the check ID. If you want to create a new check, you can specify a check ID (unused) or have the system select a new check ID. The following sections describe the possible functions.

Maintenance of aggregate checks

Display

The system displays the screen Display Check Time of Aggregates. The system shows the aggregate tree of the selected aggregates with the check modes and the check times.

If you have defined characteristic restrictions for the check for one or more aggregates, they are displayed in a dialog window.

Edit

The system takes you to the Selection of Check Time of Individual Aggregates screen. Here, you can view and change the description of the check and the settings of the check mode, the check time, and the characteristic restrictions. The old settings are overwritten when you save the check.

Create

The system takes you to the Selection of Check Time of Individual Aggregates screen. The system shows the aggregate tree with all aggregates of the InfoCube. Proceed as follows:

1. Select the aggregates to be checked.
2. Specify the check time by setting the corresponding flag.
3. Select the check mode from the context menu of the aggregate to be checked. If you select the Selection Options check mode, the system displays the Characteristic Restrictions for Checking Aggregates screen. Enter the appropriate restrictions in this screen.
4. In the next step, the system checks whether new check aggregates need to be created or whether check aggregates exist that are no longer required, for example, because the aggregates have been deleted. The Confirmation of the Aggregate Checks screen opens, in which you can view the corresponding information in the Check Overview area.
5. Enter the following general check parameter:
   ▸ Description and texts (short description, long description) for the check.
   ▸ Block size for check: This value is not the block size you must consider when you build the aggregates; however, the mechanism behaves accordingly and ensures that you can also check large

aggregates without encountering problems with the temporary table space.

6. Save the check.

If you need to create check aggregates for this purpose, you first create and activate the corresponding aggregates and tables. You navigate to the dialog window for filling the check aggregates (see Section 13.5.3, Activating Aggregates and Providing Them with Data). If you have aggregates with the Schedule check time in the check, the system takes you to the dialog window for scheduling in background processing. If the check aggregates are not filled before you start a check that requires these check aggregates, the aggregate concerned is not checked. If you selected aggregates with Now as the check time, the system performs this part of the check in the dialog and then shows the results in the application log. The settings for aggregates with the Now check time are not transferred to the definition of the aggregate check.

Delete

The check is deleted when you confirm the confirmation prompt.

Execute

The selected check is executed the in dialog. The system displays the results in the application log.

Ad-hoc

The system takes you to the Selection of Check Time of Individual Aggregates screen. Select the aggregates to be checked, and set Now as the check time. Select the check mode from the context menu of the aggregate to be checked. You can select the Check Aggregate check mode only if a corresponding check aggregate already exists. The selected check is executed in dialog after another confirmation.

Logs

If the check is executed After Change Run, After Rollup, or After Deletion, the logs of the aggregate checks are available in the logs of the main process. If you selected Check Now or executed an ad-hoc check, the system automatically displays the application log when the check is completed.

If the check is scheduled for the background processing and executed in the background, the logs are available in the application log under the RSRV object AGGRCHECK subobject; the InfoCube name and the check ID are recorded in the identifier.

Check Time

The check time is the use-specified time at which an aggregate is to be checked. Table 13.4 summarizes the possible times.

Time	Description
After Change Run	The aggregates are checked immediately after the change run. The system only checks aggregates if they have been modified in a previous change run for which the check is switched on.
After Rollup	The aggregates are checked immediately after the data from the InfoCube has been rolled up. The system only checks aggregates for which the check is switched on.
After Deletion	See After Rollup.
Schedule	You can specify that you want to execute the check at a particular time or periodically in background processing.

If you want to execute a particular check frequently but not on a regular basis, create this check with the corresponding check time. If you cancel the scheduling after saving the parameters, you can execute this check at any time in the dialog or in the background processing using the RSDDK_CHECK_ AGGREGATE_CHECKID ABAP program. |
| Now | The check is started immediately as a dialog process. Aggregates that are checked with check time Now are not included in the definition of an aggregate check and are not saved. |

Table 13.4 Check Times for Aggregates

Check Mode

The check mode determines how an aggregate is supposed to be checked. There are options to check aggregates of an InfoCube. The following list provides an overview:

▶ **Full**

For the full check, the system rebuilds the aggregate from the Info-Cube as an internal table and compares it with the data of the aggregate in the database, record by record. This check can take a lot of time, but it offers the highest level of security.

▶ **Selection Options**

For the restricted check, you can set restrictions for characteristics on the Characteristic Restrictions screen for checking aggregates. You can select only characteristics that exist in the aggregate and do not have hierarchies or fixed value restrictions defined for them. The system runs the check in the same way as it runs the full check, but only for InfoCube or aggregate data that meets the defined restrictions. Depending on how strict the restrictions are, this check can be considerably faster than the full check. This type of check is particularly useful if the data in the aggregate only changes in a particular time frame. In this case you can restrict the dataset considerably by restricting the check to this time frame.

▶ **Aggregated**

For the aggregated check, the system aggregates all of the characteristics in the InfoCube and aggregate and compares the result of each key figure. This check is three t0 four times faster than the full check but does not provide the same level of security. You cannot perform this check for the following aggregates: aggregates of noncumulative InfoCubes, aggregates with fixed values, and aggregates with a nonunique hierarchy or a hierarchy that does not have nonassigned nodes.

▶ **Check Aggregate**

For the check with check aggregates, the system creates a check aggregate that is aggregated using all characteristics. A check aggregate of this type is created for each fixed value combination that occurs in the aggregates you have selected. The check aggregates are filled from the InfoCube and are always modified during rollup or deletion. The check checks the consistency of the key figure totals. This check is very fast, but it cannot find every potential inconsistency in the aggregates. You cannot create check aggregates for the following aggregates: aggregates of noncumulative InfoCubes, aggregates with fixed values for a navigation attribute, and aggregates with a nonunique hierarchy or a hierarchy that does not have nonassigned nodes.

If the check is executed After Change Run, After Rollup, or After Deletion, the logs of the aggregate checks are available in the logs of the main process. If you execute with the Check Now time or an ad-hoc check, the system automatically displays the application log when the check is completed.

Background processing

If the check is scheduled for the background processing and executed in the background, the logs are available in the application log under the RSRV object AGGRCHECK subobject; the InfoCube name and the check ID are recorded in the identifier. These logs are also displayed if you select the Maintain Aggregate Check: Select InfoCube screen.

13.6 SAP NetWeaver BW Accelerator

Part I of this book discussed the functions of SAP NetWeaver BW Accelerator (formerly referred to as SAP NetWeaver BI Accelerator). This section discusses the procedure for the optimal execution and use of SAP NetWeaver BW Accelerator in more detail. The following subsections contain information on different administration tasks and list tools that can be used to perform the tasks. Table 13.5 lists the relevant transactions to provide an overview of this topic.

Overview of relevant transactions

Tasks	Transaction
Management of RFC connection between SAP NetWeaver BW Accelerator and SAP NetWeaver BW system	SM59, RSCUSTA
Central point of access for monitoring and maintenance	RSDDBIAMON, RSDDBIAMON2
Index maintenance	RSDDV
Analysis and repair	RSRV
Query monitor	RSRT
TREX monitoring and administration	TREXADMIN

Table 13.5 Transactions of SAP NetWeaver BW Accelerator Administration

13.6.1 Connection to SAP NetWeaver BW Accelerator

The following section describes administration tasks that must be performed once after the installation of SAP NetWeaver BW Accelerator. They are also available for checking the connection between the SAP NetWeaver BW system and SAP NetWeaver BW Accelerator.

You can use Transaction SM59 to create and maintain an RFC destination in the SAP system (Figure 13.11). Maintain the connection to SAP NetWeaver BW Accelerator in this transaction or perform a connection test for the existing settings. The standard name for the RFC destination to SAP NetWeaver BW Accelerator is TREX_HPA (derived from the fact that SAP NetWeaver BW Accelerator is based on the TREX technology and was initially referred to as High Performance Analytics).

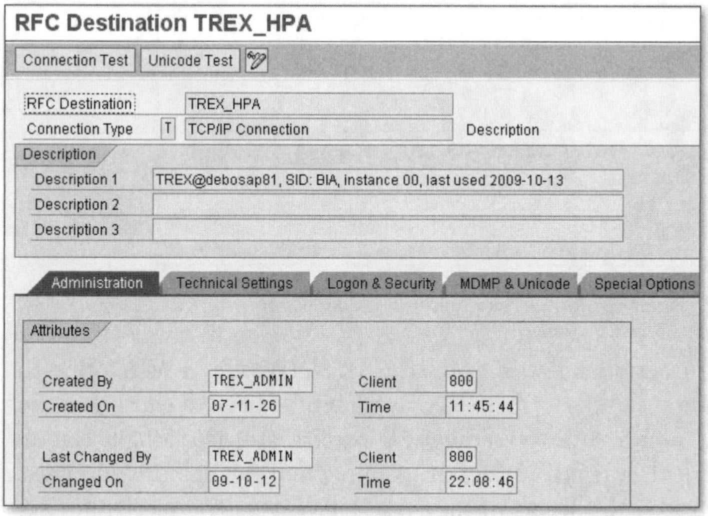

RFC connection

Figure 13.11 RFC Connection TREX_HPA

To determine which RFC connection is supposed to be used for the communication between the SAP NetWeaver BW system and SAP NetWeaver BW Accelerator, you must maintain a corresponding RSADMIN parameter (Figure 13.12). Start Transaction RSCUSTA to maintain the parameter (maintenance view for RSADMINA). Here, you can check and, if required, change the RFC BI Accelerator parameter.

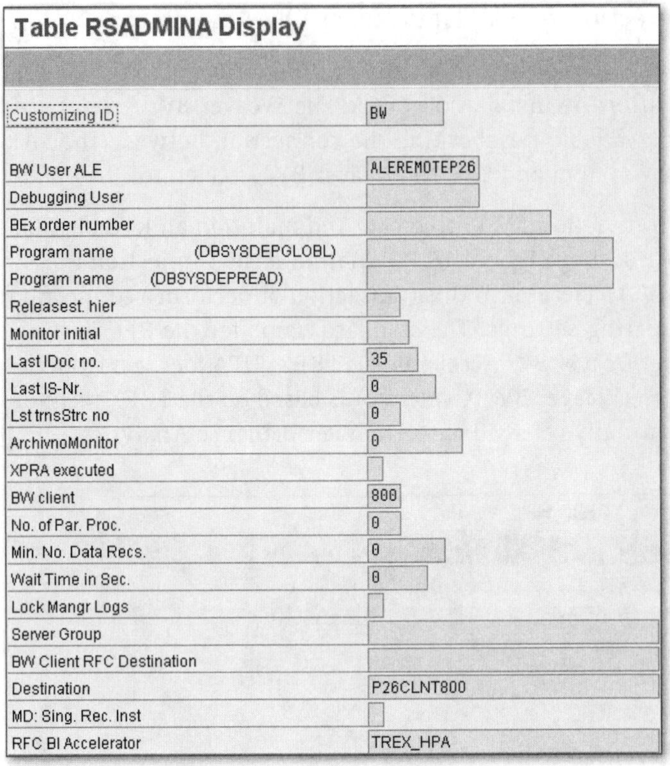

Table RSADMINA Display

Customizing ID	BW
BW User ALE	ALEREMOTEP26
Debugging User	
BEx order number	
Program name (DBSYSDEPGLOBL)	
Program name (DBSYSDEPREAD)	
Releasest. hier	
Monitor initial	
Last IDoc no.	35
Last IS-Nr.	0
Lst trnsStrc no	0
ArchivnoMonitor	0
XPRA executed	
BW client	800
No. of Par. Proc.	0
Min. No. Data Recs.	0
Wait Time in Sec.	0
Lock Mangr Logs	
Server Group	
BW Client RFC Destination	
Destination	P26CLNT800
MD: Sing. Rec. Inst	
RFC BI Accelerator	TREX_HPA

Figure 13.12 Parameter for the Accelerator RFC Connection

Testing the connection availability

Using Transaction RSDDBIAMON (SAP NetWeaver BW Accelerator Monitor), you can perform an RFC availability check to check whether the connection to SAP NetWeaver BW Accelerator is available (Figure 13.13). For this purpose, select BIA Connection Availability and check the message on the status of the SAP NetWeaver BW Accelerator service. A percentage indicates how many connections are available. In the monitor, you are provided with additional checks, for instance, whether a reorganization is required or and the memory consumption.

Connection test

You can also check the RFC connection using Transaction TREXADMIN (Figure 13.14). If you perform the connection test in the RFC Management tab, the system displays a summary of the test results in which all flags must be set to green.

SAP NetWeaver BI Accelerator Monitor

| | 🔾 BIA Connection Availability | 🔾 System Check | 🔾 BIA Load Monitor Activate |

BIA Check Results

Summary | Current Results | History

Status	Check Description	LTxt	Details	Action	Execute	Act
△	Index checks returned at least one warning as	ⓐ	🔲			

Check Details

BIA Actions

Execute Actions

☐ Restart Host
☐ Restart BIA Server
☐ Restart BIA Index Server
☐ Reorganize BIA Landscape

☐ Rebuild BIA Indexes

⊕ Execute

BIA Action Messages

Ty.	Message Text	Le	LTxt
☐	BI Accelerator services are fully available	1	ⓐ
ⓘ	Status information read from BI Accelerator	1	
△	At least one of the checks (type Current Results) i	1	ⓐ
ⓘ	Status information read from BI Accelerator	1	
△	At least one of the checks (type Current Results) i	1	ⓐ

Figure 13.13 Checks in the SAP NetWeaver BW Accelerator Monitor

TREX Administration Tool (RFC Destination TREX_HPA)

| Advanced Mode | TREX ABAP Customizing |

Services | Summary | Trace | Ini Files | Alert | RFC Monitor | Search | Index Landscape | Index Admin

🔲 🔲 🔲 🔲 | 🔲 🔲 Test Connection

RFC - Connection test TREX_HPA

Application Server	Stat	Error text	Gateway Ho	Gateway	Program ID
debosap171_P26_11	⦿⦿	No Error	*debosap171	sapgw11	Trex_P26_2007112
debosap170_P26_11	⦿⦿	No Error	*debosap17C	sapgw11	Trex_P26_2007112
debosap41_P26_11	⦿⦿	No Error	*debosap41	sapgw11	Trex_P26_2007112
debosap40_P26_11	⦿⦿	No Error	*debosap40	sapgw11	Trex_P26_2007112
debosap30_P26_11	⦿⦿	No Error	*debosap30	sapgw11	Trex_P26_2007112
debosap31_P26_11	⦿⦿	No Error	*debosap31	sapgw11	Trex_P26_2007112

Figure 13.14 RFC Monitor

13.6.2 Which InfoCubes Should Be Indexed?

One of the first steps of an accelerator implementation is to develop a concept for indexing. Which InfoCube data should be available as an index in SAP NetWeaver BW Accelerator, and for which InfoCubes do aggregates and database indexes suffice for a high-performance query execution?

Of course, it would be possible to index the data of all InfoCubes and to benefit from a simplified administration (for instance, avoiding rollup activities for aggregates) and from the very good and, in particular, the continuous performance of SAP NetWeaver BW Accelerator. On the other hand, the immense costs of such a concept are only acceptable in exceptional scenarios owing to the high number of blades required.

The statistics of the technical content (for instance, in a BI Administration Cockpit) form the basis for the initial consideration with regard to the indexing strategy because you can use the query runtime statistics to find those InfoCubes for which a lot of time must be consumed for the database access. The statistics for the individual events are also available directly in the execution of a query in Transaction RSRT (Figure 13.15).

Statistics Data for Query Runtime

Session UID	Step UID	Ste	Ste	User Name	Start Time	Ha	Han	InfoProvider	Object Name	D	Eve	Event Text	Duration	Co	Eve
D6N6895JDP9SCUNBFR4AFCYGW		1	23010997		2009-10-08 11:31:I			DIAL		2	1	Wait Time, U	5,079000	0	1
D6N6895JDF	D6N6895JDF	BEX3	1	23010997	2009-10-08 11:31:I		1	OLAP	ZZPRCUSMP	Y_SM_ZZPR(	2	3500	OLAP Initializ	0,453000	0	20
D6N6895JDF	D6N6895JDF	BEX3	1	23010997	2009-10-08 11:31:I			DIAL		2	1990	3.x Analyzer V	0,406000	0	1
D6N6895JDF	D6N6895JDF	BEX3	1	23010997	2009-10-08 11:31:I		1	OLAP	ZZPRCUSMP	Y_SM_ZZPR(	2	9000	Data Manage	0,265000	0	3
D6N6895JDF	D6N6895JDF	BEX3	1	23010997	2009-10-08 11:31:I		1	OLAP	ZZPRCUSMP	Y_SM_ZZPR(	2	3000	OLAP: Setting	0,187000	0	10
D6N6895JDF	D6N6895JDF	BEX3	1	23010997	2009-10-08 11:31:I		1	OLAP	ZZPRCUSMP	Y_SM_ZZPR(	2	3900	OLAP: Read⁻	0,157000	0	2
D6N6895JDF	D6N6895JDF	BEX3	1	23010997	2009-10-08 11:31:I		1	OLAP	ZZPRCUSMP	Y_SM_ZZPR(	2	3200	OLAP: Data T	0,093000	1.608	1
D6N6895JDF	D6N6895JDF	BEX3	1	23010997	2009-10-08 11:31:I		1	OLAP	ZZPRCUSMP	Y_SM_ZZPR(	2	3999	OLAP Other T	0,078000	0	14
D6N6895JDF	D6N6895JDF	BEX3	1	23010997	2009-10-08 11:31:I		1	OLAP	ZZPRCUSMP	Y_SM_ZZPR(	2	4600	Authorization	0,078000	0	4
D6N6895JDF	D6N6895JDF	BEX3	1	23010997	2009-10-08 11:31:I		1	OLAP	ZZPRCUSMP	Y_SM_ZZPR(	2	2510	Write Cache	0,047000	0	5
D6N6895JDF	D6N6895JDF	BEX3	1	23010997	2009-10-08 11:31:I		1	OLAP	ZZPRCUSMP	Y_SM_ZZPR(	2	1995	3.x Query Viev	0,032000	0	2
D6N6895JDF	D6N6895JDF	BEX3	1	23010997	2009-10-08 11:31:I		1	OLAP	ZZPRCUSMP	Y_SM_ZZPR(	2	3110	OLAP: Data S	0,032000	0	1
D6N6895JDF	D6N6895JDF	BEX3	1	23010997	2009-10-08 11:31:I			DFLT		2		Not Assigned	0,016000	0	1
D6N6895JDF	D6N6895JDF	BEX3	1	23010997	2009-10-08 11:31:I		1	OLAP	ZZPRCUSMP	Y_SM_ZZPR(	2	3010	OLAP: Query	0,016000	0	1
D6N6895JDF	D6N6895JDF	BEX3	1	23010997	2009-10-08 11:31:I		1	OLAP	ZZPRCUSMP	Y_SM_ZZPR(	2	2515	Delete Cache	0,016000	0	1
D6N6895JDF	D6N6895JDF	BEX3	1	23010997	2009-10-08 11:31:I		3	BRFC		RRX_GRID_(	2	1000	RFC call	0,016000	0	1
D6N6895JDF	D6N6895JDF	BEX3	1	23010997	2009-10-08 11:31:I		2	BRFC		RRX_REPOR	2	1000	RFC call	0,015000	0	1
D6N6895JDF	D6N6895JDF	BEX3	1	23010997	2009-10-08 11:31:I		1	OLAP	ZZPRCUSMP	Y_SM_ZZPR(	2	1990	3.x Analyzer S	0,015000	1.454	2
D6N6895JDF	D6N6895JDF	BEX3	1	23010997	2009-10-08 11:31:I		1	OLAP	ZZPRCUSMP	Y_SM_ZZPR(	2	2500	Cache Gener	0,015000	0	6
D6N6895JDF	D6N6895JDF	BEX3	1	23010997	2009-10-08 11:31:I		1	BRFC		RRX_SESSIC	2	1000	RFC call	0,000000	0	1
D6N6895JDF	D6N6895JDF	BEX3	1	23010997	2009-10-08 11:31:I		1	OLAP	ZZPRCUSMP	Y_SM_ZZPR(	2	4300	Value Authori	0,000000	0	7
D6N6895JDF	D6N6895JDF	BEX3	1	23010997	2009-10-08 11:31:I		1	OLAP	ZZPRCUSMP	Y_SM_ZZPR(	2	3510	OLAP: EXIT V	0,000000	0	3
D6N6895JDF	D6N6895JDF	BEX3	1	23010997	2009-10-08 11:31:I		1	OLAP	ZZPRCUSMP	Y_SM_ZZPR(	2	2505	Read Cache	0,000000	0	4

Figure 13.15 Statistics Data in Transaction RSRT

Data Manager event

The statistics overview includes the time for the Data Manager event, among other things. This event indicates the time that was required for reading the data from the database. Because queries usually use MultiProviders to access individual InfoCubes and DataStore objects, the more detailed view in the Aggregation Layer tab is particularly helpful because the appropriate database time is indicated for each InfoProvider (or aggregate) here.

13.6.3 SAP NetWeaver BW Accelerator Index Maintenance Wizard

You can use the SAP NetWeaver BW Accelerator index maintenance wizard to activate an SAP NetWeaver BW Accelerator index in separate steps and then fill or, if required, delete it. To call the wizard, either use the context menu of the InfoCube, Maintain BI Accelerator Index, or select the InfoCube in Transaction RSDDV.

Creating SAP NetWeaver BW Accelerator Indexes

You can only create one SAP NetWeaver BW Accelerator index per InfoCube that contains all data of the InfoCube. Unlike the aggregates, it is not necessary to make certain selections and restrictions for the definition of the SAP NetWeaver BW Accelerator index.

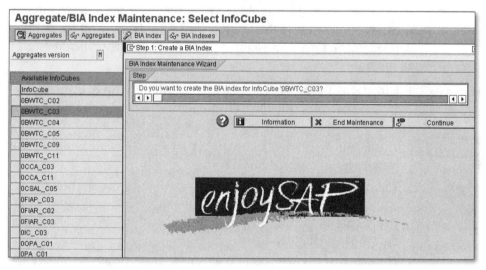

Figure 13.16 Creating an Index

When you execute this step, the system creates the indexes on the SAP NetWeaver BW Accelerator server for the tables of the InfoCube star schema, provided that they have not been created by other accelerator indexes yet. These tables include the fact and dimension tables of the

487

InfoCube and the required SID-bearing master data tables, that is, the S, X, and Y tables of the InfoObjects. Additionally, the system creates a logical index that includes the metadata of the SAP NetWeaver BW Accelerator index.

To be able to use the SAP NetWeaver BW Accelerator index in reporting, you must fill it with data. To be able to schedule the filling of the SAP NetWeaver BW Accelerator index in the background processing, click Next in the dialog for creating the index.

Filling and Activating Indexes

In the Determine the Start Date dialog window, you determine when the job for filling (RSDDTREX_AGGREGATES_FILL) is to be scheduled in the background processing. When you execute this step, the system starts a process in the background processing in which it reads the data from the tables of the InfoCube star schema from the database and writes to the corresponding indexes on the SAP NetWeaver BW Accelerator server. If the index of a master data table (S, X, and Y tables) has already been created by another SAP NetWeaver BW Accelerator index, you only need to index the newly added records (read/fill mode D for indexing). The system implements the following steps when it creates an index:

Creating an index
1. For a table, the index is created on the SAP NetWeaver BW Accelerator server according to the table properties. Depending on the current size of the table, you specify into how many parts the index is split.

2. The data is transferred and written into a temporary file on the SAP NetWeaver BW Accelerator server.

3. The data from the temporary file is processed (that is, compressed, encrypted, and so on) as required for the search and aggregation. Depending on the distribution of the index, this step can take longer than the indexing step itself.

4. The data that has been optimized is now made visible. A rollback for an index rolls the data back to the last Commit Optimize.

The name of the index results from the system ID and the table name: *<system ID>_<table name>*. In the table name, the system deletes the first slash and replaces the second slash with a colon. In the example shown in Figure 13.17 you can see that the index name of the S table /BIO/ STCTQUERY in system P26 is now P26_BIO:STCTQUERY.

All BIA Indexes (Display Only), Maintenance with Wizard

InfoCubes for the BIA Ind	Technical name		Name	Technical name	O	O	Number of	M	Delta I	L
▽ ☐ InfoCubes			▽ CCA: Costs and Alloc	0CCA_C11						
▷ Product/Custom ZZPRCUST			▷ BIA Index	0CCA_C11$X	☐	☐				2
▷ PSI - Plan data ZSS_R043			▽ BW Statistics - OLAP	0BWTC_C02						
▷ Forecast Water ZSS_R035			▽ BIA Index	0BWTC_C02$X	☐	◙				2
▷ Sell Through Ne ZSM_R13			▽ ▦ Tables/Indexes							
▷ Sell Through GS ZSM_R005			/BIO/D0BWTC_C02T	P26_BIO:D0BWTC_C02T	◇		1767			
▷ Sales Orders - A ZSM_R0008			/BIO/D0BWTC_C024	P26_BIO:D0BWTC_C024	◇		3666643			
▷ Sales Orders - F ZSM_R0007			/BIO/D0BWTC_C02P	P26_BIO:D0BWTC_C02P	◇		405			
▷ PSI - Inventory d ZPSI_C03			/BIO/D0BWTC_C021	P26_BIO:D0BWTC_C021	◇		596463			
▷ PSI - Actual Date ZPSI_C01			Fact Table (E-/F Table)	P26_BIO:F0BWTC_C02	◇		17489997			
▷ Product/Custom ZPRCUST08			/BIO/STCTQUERY	P26_BIO:STCTQUERY	◇		34107			
▷ Product/Custom ZPRCUST07			/BIO/STCTELEMTYP	P26_BIO:STCTELEMTYP	◇		8			
▷ Sales Orders ZLOG01			/BIO/STCTSYSID	P26_BIO:STCTSYSID	☐		974	☑		
▷ Material stock/m ZIC_C03_M			/BIO/STCTSESUID	P26_BIO:STCTSESUID	◇		3364197			
▷ CCA: Previous Y ZFI_R0025			/BIO/STCTSTAUID	P26_BIO:STCTSTAUID	◇		22249183			
▷ Matching ZFI_R0016			/BIO/SCOMP_CODE	P26_BIO:SCOMP_CODE	☐		92	☑		
▷ VAT (Actual) ZFI_R0012			/BIO/SCOUNTRY_ID	P26_BIO:SCOUNTRY_ID	◇		59			
▷ CPFR Forecast ZCPFR_FOR			/BIO/SCO_AREA	P26_BIO:SCO_AREA	☐		41	☑		
▷ CCA: Costs and 0CCA_C11			/BIO/SCOSTCENTER	P26_BIO:SCOSTCENTER	☐		8850	☑		
▽ BW Statistics - C 0BWTC_C02			/BIO/SORG_KEY	P26_BIO:SORG_KEY	◇		1			
▷ Time			/BIO/SPERS_AREA	P26_BIO:SPERS_AREA	◇		68			
▷ Frontend Se			/BIO/SPERS_SAREA	P26_BIO:SPERS_SAREA	◇		192			
▷ Start Time			/BIO/STCTIFCUBE	P26_BIO:STCTIFCUBE	◇		2692			
▷ Statistics UII			/BIO/STCTIFAREA	P26_BIO:STCTIFAREA	◇		688			
▷ General Dat			/BIO/STCTTIMSTMP	P26_BIO:STCTTIMSTMP	◇		16033705			

Figure 13.17 Overview of Index Tables

Usually, it is possible to activate and fill indexes for different InfoCubes at the same time. Because there can only be one accelerator index per InfoCube, this does not pose any problems with regard to the tables of the InfoCube. However, overlaps may occur if several indexing jobs try to index the same master data tables simultaneously. In this case, the first job locks the table and performs indexing. The other jobs see the lock and schedule the indexing run to take place later. If no new data is loaded in the meantime, the system simply checks that indexing was performed successfully by the competing job. This step is necessary to avoid the system setting an SAP NetWeaver BW Accelerator index to active when the index is not actually available on the accelerator server because the job was terminated.

Competing processes

The subsequent jobs try five times to start the indexing process or determine the status of the index. If this is not possible owing to a long-running process or termination, the system terminates the entire indexing process for the index and notes the InfoCube of the locking process. You have to wait until the current program has finished or the error has been fixed before restarting the indexing process.

Deleting Indexes

By deleting an index, the system deletes the definition and the settings of the SAP NetWeaver BW Accelerator index in the SAP NetWeaver BW system and the logical index (metadata) and all indexes for the tables of the enhanced star schema of the InfoCubes on the accelerator server. The only exception is indexes for master data tables that are still used by other SAP NetWeaver BW Accelerator indexes.

Deactivation   A temporary deactivation can make sense if you want to ensure that the system uses no SAP NetWeaver BW Accelerator index for performance measurements or analyses of data consistency. Select BIA Index Properties to deactivate an SAP NetWeaver BW Accelerator index only temporarily. The system takes you to the Maintain BI Accelerator Index Properties dialog window in which you can set the status of the index to inactive.

An SAP NetWeaver BW Accelerator index that is switched off is not used when a query is executed. Because SAP NetWeaver BW Accelerator indexes that are switched off must also be consistent, you do not have to activate the accelerator index again or to fill it when you switch it back on.

13.6.4 Effects of Data Changes

If an InfoCube that forms the basis of an SAP NetWeaver BW Accelerator index is compressed later or data is deleted from it, it is recommended that you rebuild the accelerator index. Because the data of the master data table (X and Y tables) is stored as indexes on the SAP NetWeaver BW Accelerator server, accelerator indexes, like aggregates, are affected by master data changes. In contrast to aggregates, however, the current data of the master data is not materialized in the facts. Therefore, you do not have to run the potentially time-consuming delta calculations that you have to run for aggregates. Instead, you only transfer the changed records of the master data tables and change them in the indexes on the SAP NetWeaver BW Accelerator server. In most cases, this procedure is considerably faster than the aggregate adjustment.

Because the hierarchy tables are not in the SAP NetWeaver BW Accelerator index either, there are no preaggregations at certain hierarchy levels as is the case with aggregates. Here as well, the calculation and adjustment is unnecessary. However, as with the SAP NetWeaver BW hierarchy buffer, some views of hierarchies that occur in queries are stored on the accelerator server as temporary indexes so they can be reused. If the hierarchy changes, you must delete these temporary indexes.

The system changes both the master data and the temporary hierarchy indexes during the hierarchy/attribute change run. In this process, you specify the objects, aggregates, and SAP NetWeaver BW Accelerator indexes for selected InfoObjects that have been changed previously. First, the system modifies the aggregates in accordance with the changes. Then the system performs the two very fast processes that have been previously described for the relevant SAP NetWeaver BW Accelerator indexes.

Hierarchy/attribute change run

▸ The X and Y indexes are filled with the changed records.

▸ The hierarchy buffer is deleted from the accelerator index.

Then the system activates the master data and displays the changed aggregates and SAP NetWeaver BW Accelerator indexes with the new data for reporting.

With SAP NetWeaver BW Accelerator indexes you do not have to compress after rolling up data packages. The data on the SAP NetWeaver BW Accelerator server already exists in a read-optimized format. However, in the following cases it may be useful to rebuild the accelerator index, although this is not strictly necessary.

Compression

For example, an SAP NetWeaver BW accelerator index was created for an InfoCube that is not compressed, or a large number of data packages was later loaded to this InfoCube. If you compress this InfoCube only, more data is contained in the accelerator index than in the InfoCube itself, and the data in the accelerator index has a higher level of detail. If compression results in a large aggregation factor (>1.5), it may be useful to rebuild the SAP NetWeaver BW Accelerator index. This ensures that the dataset is reduced in the accelerator index, too. Noncumulative InfoCubes, that is, InfoCubes with at least one noncumulative key figure, should be rebuilt in large intervals after compression. This is especially recommended if the time to calculate the markers at query runtime is long.

Deleting data   If you delete data from the InfoCube selectively, the SAP NetWeaver BW Accelerator index has to be rebuilt. When you execute selective deletion, the system automatically deletes the affected accelerator index. When you delete a data package (that is not compressed) from an Info-Cube, the index for the package dimension table is deleted and rebuilt. The facts in the fact index remain but are "hidden" because they are no longer referenced by an entry in the package dimension table. Therefore, more entries exist in the index than in the table of the InfoCube. If you regularly delete data packages, the number of unused records grows and the memory consumption increases. This can have a negative effect on performance. In this case you should consider rebuilding the SAP NetWeaver BW Accelerator index regularly.

13.6.5 SAP NetWeaver BW Accelerator Delta Indexes

You can create a delta index for an SAP NetWeaver BW Accelerator index. If a delta index exists, the system does not write to the main index during each delta indexing or each indexing activity (except the initial filling and indexing), and the main index is not optimized. Instead, the system writes data to a second index that has the same structure as the main index but is usually smaller. The smaller the delta index, the faster the subsequent optimizing procedure and therefore the whole process of rolling up data or making modifications after a hierarchy or attribute change run.

Recommendation   Because read performance deteriorates the larger the delta index gets, it is recommended that you switch on the delta index only for essential indexes such as fact indexes and X/Y indexes. This improves performance when you modify data after a hierarchy or attribute change run. To set the delta index for an SAP NetWeaver BW Accelerator index, on the SAP NetWeaver BW Accelerator monitor select BI ACCELERATOR • INDEX INFORMATION • SET DELTA INDEX. The Change Property of Delta Index dialog window appears (Figure 13.18).

In the Delta Index column, select the corresponding checkbox if you want the table to use a delta index. The new setting takes effect with the next delta indexing operation.

Table Name	Table Size	Delta In
/BIC/FZPSI_C03	72.295.139	☐
/BIC/FZSS_R043	60.893.389	☐
/BIC/FZPSI_C01	20.407.277	☑
/BIC/FZLOG01	15.685.662	☐
/BIC/DZLOG013	10.658.124	☐
/BI0/SAC_DOC_NO	9.557.193	☐
/BIC/FZSS_R035	7.942.083	☐
/BIC/FZIC_C03_M	6.780.151	☐
/BI0/SREF_DOC_N	4.301.478	☐
/BIC/FZPRCUST08	3.654.768	☐
/BI0/F0CCA_C11	3.545.227	☐
/BIC/FZFI_R0016	3.349.031	☐
/BI0/SDOC_NUMBE	3.034.821	☐
/BIC/FZZPRCUST	2.915.745	☐
/BIC/DZSM_R0007	2.829.025	☐
/BIC/FZPRCUST07	2.767.813	☐
/BIC/DZLOG01B	2.552.453	☐
/BIC/FZSM_R0007	2.421.133	☐
/BIC/FZFI_R0025	2.189.034	☐
/BI0/SBILL_NUM	1.884.225	☐
/BIC/DZLOG011	1.783.939	☐
/BIC/FZSM_R13	1.721.818	☐
/BIC/DZLOG01A	1.446.955	☐
/BIC/SZSHIPDOC	1.272.616	☐
/BIC/SZFI_DOC	1.248.313	☐
/BI0/SDELIV_NUMB	1.215.030	☐

Figure 13.18 Delta Index Property

With a delta index, you optimize the rollup of data. It is recommended that you regularly merge the delta indexes with your main index so that read performance is not negatively affected. You can do this in several ways:

Merging of delta and main index

▶ On the Analysis and Repair of BI Objects screen (Transaction RSRV) in the BI Accelerator • BI Accelerator Performance area, you can select the Size of Delta Index elementary test. Using the troubleshooting option of Transaction RSRV, you can execute a MERGE action for the indexes.

▶ You can schedule the RSDDTREX_DELTAINDEX_MERGE program.

The index maintenance provides details on the index, as described in the following.

13.6.6 Information about Existing Indexes

The design of an SAP NetWeaver BW Accelerator index is meant to provide information on the structure, properties, and status of the SAP

NetWeaver BW Accelerator index and its tables and indexes. Tables that are part of the enhanced star schema of the selected InfoCube and are required in the corresponding SAP NetWeaver BW Accelerator index form part of the description of the accelerator index.

In the index maintenance, you can view some detail data on the index. For a more detailed view of the information on indexes, you should use the SAP NetWeaver BW Accelerator Monitor BW Accelerator monitor (Transaction RSDDBIAMON2) because this view displays the relevant object version and the object status, for example. Select BI ACCELERATOR • INDEX INFORMATION • DISPLAY ALL BIA INDEXES to display the dialog window with the index information. The system displays all of the SAP NetWeaver BW Accelerator indexes that exist in the system. Table 13.6 shows the information that is available in the monitor for indexes.

Column	Description
InfoCube	Technical name of the indexed InfoCube
Version	Active or not active
Status	Filled or not filled
Table Name	Technical name of the indexed tables (for instance, SID tables)
Table Size	Approximate size of the index in the number of data records that are derived from the database statistics
Individual Status	Status of the table index
Delta Index	Flag that indicates that it is a delta index
Multiple Usage	Flag that indicates that the table is also used by other indexed InfoCubes and is already indexed (particularly S, X, or Y tables)
Changed By	Name of user who made the last change
Time Stamp	Date and time of the last change

Table 13.6 Monitor Information on the SAP NetWeaver BW Accelerator Indexes

As you can see in Figure 13.19, the version and status information is indicated as traffic lights (object version, object status, single status).

InfoCube	V	S	Table Name	Table Size	Ind	Bo	Bo	Changed	Time Stamp
0CCA_C11	☐	☐	/BI0/D0CCA_C111	3.051	☐	☐	☐	ALEREMO⁻	20.091.009.202.704
			/BI0/D0CCA_C112	2.511	☐	☐	☐	ALEREMO⁻	20.091.001.023.422
			/BI0/D0CCA_C113	8	☐	☐	☐	23010997	20.090.614.064.709
			/BI0/D0CCA_C114	90.028	☐	☐	☐	ALEREMO⁻	20.091.013.082.721
			/BI0/D0CCA_C115	3	☐	☐	☐	23010997	20.090.614.064.709
			/BI0/D0CCA_C117	1	☐	☐	☐	23010997	20.090.614.064.708
			/BI0/D0CCA_C11P	1.349	☐	☐	☐	ALEREMO⁻	20.091.013.082.721
			/BI0/D0CCA_C11T	25	☐	☐	☐	ALEREMO⁻	20.090.930.142.825
			/BI0/D0CCA_C11U	63	☐	☐	☐	ALEREMO⁻	20.090.731.142.501
			/BI0/F0CCA_C11	3.545.227	☐	☐	☐	ALEREMO⁻	20.091.013.082.721
			/BI0/SABCPROCESS	18	☐	☐	☑	23010997	20.090.614.064.553
			/BI0/SACTTYPE	55	☐	☐	☑	23010997	20.090.614.064.553
			/BI0/SCALMONTH	26.544	☐	☐	☑	23010997	20.081.028.064.318
			/BI0/SCALMONTH2	15	☐	☐	☑	23010997	20.090.614.064.531
			/BI0/SCALQUARTER	4.106	☐	☐	☑	23010997	20.081.028.064.317
			/BI0/SCALYEAR	321	☐	☐	☑	23010997	20.081.028.064.316
			/BI0/SCHRT_ACCTS	3	☐	☐	☑	23052430	20.090.614.053.237
			/BI0/SCOORDER	44.886	☐	☐	☑	ALEREMO⁻	20.091.013.022.948
			/BI0/SCOSTCENTER	8.850	☐	☐	☑	ALEREMO⁻	20.091.013.022.949
			/BI0/SCOSTELMNT	9.505	☐	☐	☑	ALEREMO⁻	20.091.009.082.719
			/BI0/SCO_AREA	41	☐	☐	☑	ALEREMO⁻	20.090.819.142.432
			/BI0/SCURRENCY	210	☐	☐	☑	23052430	20.090.614.052.410
			/BI0/SCURTYPE	16	☐	☐	☑	23010997	20.090.614.064.549
			/BI0/SCUSTOMER	33.474	☐	☐	☑	ALEREMO⁻	20.091.013.131.359
			/BI0/SCUST_GROUP	35	☐	☐	☑	ALEREMO⁻	20.090.713.201.306
			/BI0/SDATE	9.189	☐	☐	☑	23010997	20.081.028.064.318
			/BI0/SDB_CR_IND	3	☐	☐	☑	23010997	20.090.614.064.550
			/BI0/SFISCPER	654.080	☐	☐	☑	23052430	20.090.614.052.006
			/BI0/SFISCPER3	35	☐	☐	☑	23052430	20.090.614.051.844
			/BI0/SFISCVARNT	14	☐	☐	☑	23052430	20.090.614.052.006
			/BI0/SFISCYEAR	87	☐	☐	☑	ALEREMO⁻	20.090.830.094.550
			/BI0/SGL_ACCOUNT	2.472	☐	☐	☑	ALEREMO⁻	20.091.001.112.329

Figure 13.19 Information About an Existing Index

All of the dimension tables of the InfoCube are required for the star schema of the SAP NetWeaver BW Accelerator index. The E and F fact tables of the InfoCube form one fact index. From the master data tables, only the X and Y tables (which contain the SIDs) are required; the P and Q tables (which contain the key values) are not required. The SID tables (S tables) are required if the InfoObject has a nonnumeric key.

Tables

13.6.7 Analysis and Repair of Indexes

In the analysis and repair environment (Transaction RSRV), you can implement consistency checks of the data and metadata that is stored in an SAP NetWeaver BW system. Therefore, many functions are available for checking and repairing accelerator indexes (Figure 13.20), which are presented in the following sections.

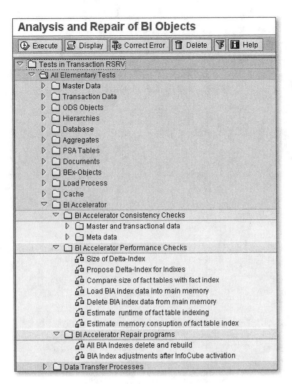

Figure 13.20 Analyses and Repairs in Transaction RSRV

Compare Data in the SAP NetWeaver BW Tables and the Accelerator Indexes

The system compares the content of each table with the content of the corresponding index on a record-by-record basis. This check is only suitable for tables or indexes that do not contain a large data volume (dimension tables, some SID, X, and Y tables), but usually not for fact tables. A table is not checked if it contains 10,000 records or more.

Check Sums of Key Figures of SAP NetWeaver BW Accelerator Queries

First, the system executes a query on the accelerator index, which is aggregated using all key figures. Next, all of the characteristics and navigation attributes that exist in the InfoCube are included in the drill-down individually, and the totals are calculated. The system compares the result with the result of the first query. This test checks the completeness of the join paths from the SID table to the dimension table to the fact tables. The runtime of the test depends on the number of characteristics and navigation attributes and on the number of records in the fact table.

Compare Sums of Key Figures of Accelerator Queries with Database

First, the system executes a query on the SAP NetWeaver BW Accelerator index and the database, which is aggregated using all key figures. Next, all of the characteristics and navigation attributes that exist in the InfoCube are included in the drill-down individually, and the totals are calculated. The system compares the result on the database with the result of the SAP NetWeaver BW Accelerator query. For large Info-Cubes the runtime may already be considerable, because queries to the database take longer.

Existence of Indexes for Database Tables

An index is created for (almost) every table of the SAP NetWeaver BW InfoCube enhanced star schema: fact (F) tables, dimension (D) tables, and attribute tables (X and Y); the only exception is SID tables with numeric characteristic values. This test checks whether the named indexes have been created on the SAP NetWeaver BW Accelerator server.

Consistency Check with Random Queries

The system executes random queries and reads the data once from the database and once from the accelerator. It then compares the results. If the results differ, an error message is output.

Note that there can be different results if the data of the InfoCube is changed between execution of the query on the database and the SAP NetWeaver BW Accelerator (for example by a change run or by rolling up new requests). You can verify the results by executing the RSDRT_INFOPROV_RANDOM_QUERIES program with the following parameters:

Verifying results

▸ InfoProvider: Name of the InfoCube

▸ Number of queries: 10

▸ Trace comparison: X

You can leave all other values unchanged. You can also execute the program in the background and view the results in the spool list.

Verification of the Entries in the Accelerator Hierarchy Buffer

When queries in hierarchies are executed, the relevant hierarchy nodes are expanded to the relevant leaves. This leaf-node relation is saved in a temporary index in the SAP NetWeaver BW Accelerator. The hierarchy buffer manages expanded hierarchies according to an LRU algorithm. The check verifies whether all temporary indexes in the hierarchy buffer contain the correct data.

Check for Negative or Larger DIMIDs or SIDs

This test checks whether the SAP NetWeaver BW Accelerator indexes of one or all InfoCubes have negative IDs or larger IDs than on the database exists. The system checks the DIMIDs of the fact table, the dimension tables, and the SIDs of the dimensions and the S, X, and Y indexes. In the SAP NetWeaver BW system the interval is checked in which a DIMID or SID of a certain table must be. Then the relevant SAP NetWeaver BW Accelerator indexes are checked for whether the DIMIDs and SIDs are within this interval.

Thanks to the fast execution, you can use this test as an initial plausibility check to find out which index possibly contains invalid DIMIDs or SIDs. You can specify an InfoCube as the input parameter. If you do not specify an InfoCube, all InfoCubes are checked for which accelerator indexes are active.

Check the Definition of Logical Indexes

In this test, the system compares the definitions of the indexes for an accelerator index with the current versions of the database tables. It checks whether the number, name, and type of the table fields in the database match the definition for the index on the accelerator server.

Repairing the accelerator index
An index may have changed if, for example, the InfoCube was changed. If this is the case, you must repair the accelerator index (BIA Index Adjustments After InfoCube Activation). Note that if you do not specify an InfoCube, the system executes the test for all InfoCubes that have an accelerator index.

Compare the Index Definition with Tables on Database

In this test, the system checks the logical index of an SAP NetWeaver BW Accelerator index. The logical index contains the metadata of the accelerator index, such as the join conditions and the names of the fields. The logical index may have changed if, for example, the InfoCube was changed. Then you must repair the accelerator index (BIA Index Adjustments After InfoCube Activation). Note that if you do not specify an InfoCube, the system executes the test for all InfoCubes that have an accelerator index.

Size of the Delta Index

If you have chosen delta mode for an index of a table, new data is written not to the main index, but to the delta index. This can significantly improve performance during indexing. If the delta index is very large, this can have a negative impact on performance when you execute queries. When the delta index reaches 10% of the main index, the system displays a warning.

Propose Delta Index for Indexes

It is useful to create a delta index for large indexes that are often updated with new data. New data is written not to the main index, but to the delta index. This significantly improves the performance of indexing, because the system only performs the OPTIMIZE step on the smaller set of data from the delta index. The data from the delta index is considered at query runtime.

The system determines proposals from the statistics data: Proposals are indexes that received new data more than ten times during the last ten days. A prerequisite for these proposals is that the statistics for the InfoCube are switched on. You should perform a MERGE action for data in the main index and delta index at regular intervals (see Size of the Delta Index test above).

Proposals

Compare Size of Fact Tables with Fact Index

The system calculates the number of records in both fact tables (E and F tables) for the InfoCube and compares them with the number of records in the fact index of the SAP NetWeaver BW Accelerator index. If the number of records in the accelerator index is significantly greater than the number in the InfoCube (more than 10%), you can improve query performance by rebuilding the accelerator index. The following circumstances can result in differences in the numbers of records:

▶ The InfoCube was compressed after the accelerator index was built. Because the accelerator index is not compressed, it may contain more records than the InfoCube.

▶ Requests were deleted from the InfoCube after the accelerator index was built. The requests are deleted from the accelerator index in the package dimension only. The records in the fact index are therefore no longer referenced and no longer taken into account when the query is executed; however, they are not deleted.

Note that the database statistics for calculating the size of the fact table must be up to date, because the test does not recount; it uses the database statistics from the tables.

Load Accelerator Index Data into Main Memory

You use this test to load all of the data for an SAP NetWeaver BW Accelerator from the file server into the main memory if the data is not already in the main memory. This action is useful if you want to ensure that queries executed in the corresponding InfoCube achieve optimal performance the first time they are executed and do not have to read data anew from the file server.

Data for an index is deleted from the main memory, for example, when new data is added to this index (during rollup or a change run). You can also adjust the settings for the SAP NetWeaver BW Accelerator index (BIA Index Properties button) so that data is loaded automatically to the main memory every time changes are made. Note that if you do not specify an InfoCube, the system executes the test for all accelerator indexes that are active and filled.

Delete Accelerator Index Data from Main Memory

You use this test to delete all data for an SAP NetWeaver BW Accelerator index from the main memory. Master data indexes that are still required by other InfoCubes are not deleted from the main memory. The accelerator index is still active after its deletion from the main memory because the data is not deleted from the file server.

This action is useful if there is little space in the main memory on the accelerator server and you have data in the main memory that is no longer used or is rarely used or for which the performance of the initial query execution is not significant (and when the file server is read in the main memory). Note that if you do not specify an InfoCube, the system runs the test for all accelerator indexes that are active and filled.

Estimate Runtime of Fact Table Indexing

The system estimates the time required to fill the fact index. It uses the current parameter values for background and dialog parallel processing. The time taken is calculated from the processes available and the estimated maximal throughput of data records in the database, the application server, and the SAP NetWeaver BW Accelerator server. The calculated duration is an estimate; the load on the system (database, application server, accelerator server), the distribution of data across block criteria, and deviations during processing can all affect the actual time taken.

Estimate Memory Consumption of Fact Table Index

The system estimates the size of the fact index of an accelerator index. In doing so, the system analyzes the data in the fact table and provides a projection. Note that if data distribution is poor, the actual memory consumption can deviate from the projected value. A more exact analysis would consume more time than that required to rebuild the index, because the number of different values in the fact table needs to be determined for each column (COUNT DISTINCT SQL statement).

Delete and Rebuild All Accelerator Indexes

All accelerator indexes in the system are deleted, and if you selected this option, the indexes are then directly rebuilt and filled. You sometimes required this for a successful restart with consistent data if a critical error occurs.

Accelerator Index Changes after InfoCube Activation

If an InfoCube is changed as a result of the addition of key figures, for example, the system does not automatically adjust the SAP NetWeaver BW Accelerator index. If this process should not have been executed or been terminated, this check displays a warning or an error.

Rebuild All Master Data Indexes of the Accelerator Index

All indexes for master data tables in an accelerator index are rebuilt. This includes indexes of the SID, X, and Y tables. When an entire accelerator index is rebuilt, these tables are not always rebuilt because they are also used by other accelerator indexes. If this results in data consistency problems, it may be necessary to rebuild the indexes for the master data tables.

13.6.8 Analysis of SAP NetWeaver BW Accelerator Data

If an SAP NetWeaver BW Accelerator index provides incorrect data or if the data differs from the results that are returned by the database when reading, and if you want to analyze this data, there are some special prerequisites and checks with regard to the accelerator in addition to the general procedures for analyzing query results and the tests and corrections in Transaction RSRV:

Additional checks

- ▶ Check whether you have imported the most current patches for SAP NetWeaver BW Accelerator, because you can often resolve problems caused by incorrect data using a more recent patch.

- ▶ For examining the configuration of the SAP NetWeaver BW Accelerator or the data in the accelerator, the SAP support requires a technical connection to SAP NetWeaver BW Accelerator in addition to the regular connection to the SAP ERP system (see Section 14.5.4, Connection to SAP NetWeaver BW Accelerator, in Chapter 14).

- ▶ Check the data using shadow indexes and the RSDDTREX_INDEX-DATA_DISPLAY program (or provide this data to the SAP support).

- ▶ For MultiProvider queries with incorrect data you can identify the SAP NetWeaver BW Accelerator index causing the problem by temporarily switching off all accelerator indexes involved consecutively until the query result changes. The accelerator index that was switched off last is then responsible for the incorrect result. All accelerator indexes that are not responsible for the incorrect result can be activated again.

- ▶ If the incorrect result is caused by expanding a characteristic or a navigation attribute, it is likely that the data saved in SAP NetWeaver BW Accelerator is incorrect.

▶ You can use the consistency check center to check the correctness of data in the individual SAP NetWeaver BW Accelerator indexes or in the whole accelerator index compound. This center is available in the SAP NetWeaver BW Accelerator monitor (Transaction RSDDBIA-MON2) via the menu path GOTO • CONSISTENCY CHECKS. Alternatively, you can execute SAP NetWeaver BW Accelerator checks using Transaction RSRV.

The next section describes how you can create an additional accelerator index for an InfoCube.

Shadow Indexes

You can use the RSDDTREX_SHADOWINDEX_CREATE program to create a second accelerator index (shadow index) for an InfoCube that generates new (shadow) indexes for selected tables. For example, you can create an accelerator shadow index that uses all indexes of the original except for the fact index. The fact index is then newly created as a shadow index without having to change the original fact index.

These shadow indexes are particularly helpful for the SAP support, but experienced administrators can also use this function to analyze the accelerator data. You can create a shadow index for a query in Transaction RSRT using the debug option Default Breakpoint: BIA Server Interface. At the first breakpoint, the system changes the value of the L_INDEX variable to the name of the accelerator shadow index and compares the data. The name derives from the name of the original index (*<SystemID>_<InfoCube>*) plus the "_SSS" postfix. The shadow indexes for individual tables also have the same name as the original index with the "_SSS" postfix. You should delete the SAP NetWeaver BW Accelerator shadow index after the final analysis, using the RSDDTREX_SHAD-OWINDEX_DELETE program.

SE16-Like Data Display

If you want to view the data of an index on the accelerator server for analysis purposes, the RSDDTREX_INDEXDATA_DISPLAY program provides a simple option with the following parameters:

▶ **Name**
Name of a table or index

▶ **Table name or index ID**
Is the previous name a table name or an index ID on the SAP NetWeaver BW Accelerator server?

▶ **Maximum number of selections**
The maximum number of restrictions to be provided in the next screen

▶ **Maximum number of records**
The maximum number of records that are supposed to be read and displayed

After you have executed the program, you navigate to the selection input. The number of rows displayed here depends on your specifications in the previous dialog window. All attributes of the SAP NetWeaver BW Accelerator index are listed so that you can now define restrictions in the form of RANGE conditions (use the usual operators: BT, LT, LE, GE, GT, and EQ).

13.6.9 Tracing of SAP NetWeaver BW Accelerator

In case of errors in the query execution or problems with the SAP NetWeaver BW Accelerator performance, you can create a trace file to analyze these errors yourself or send them to the SAP support. For errors, it can be useful to record the system responses as traces. The SAP support has special tools for evaluating these traces. Traces can be helpful if query results based on accelerator data differ from the data without using SAP NetWeaver BW Accelerator. To record traces for the query execution, you can use the query monitor (Transaction RSRT); to record performance traces, you can use the SAP NetWeaver BW Accelerator Monitor (Transaction RSDDBIAMON2).

Tracing in the Query Monitor

In the query monitor you can execute BW queries and debugging. For this purpose, start the monitor (Transaction RSRT) and select the query for which you want to record a trace.

Select Execute + Debug and BIA SERVER • BIA DEFAULT TRACE in the dialog window for debugging options. If you set the BIA Default Trace flag, the system automatically activates all traces that are listed in this option. They record information on the query that is currently executed. However, you can also select only one trace type. Table 13.7 lists the trace types that are available for SAP NetWeaver BW Accelerator.

Trace Type	Description
BIA Python Trace	Trace of the index server of SAP NetWeaver BW Accelerator; the system generates a Python program that can be executed. The SAP support can reproduce a query (without recording the ABAP read interface), for example, to find the selection for a query.
BIA Plan Trace	A trace is recorded for the executing component of SAP NetWeaver BW Accelerator; the system generates a Python program that can be executed. The SAP support can reproduce a query (without recording the ABAP read interface), for example, to analyze the steps performed by SAP NetWeaver BW Accelerator.
BIA ABAP Trace	The system records the parameterization of the read interface. The SAP support can reproduce a query based on the accelerator indexes (without InfoCubes) to analyze problems with the RFC server.
BIA Standard Trace	The system records a trace with specific internal settings (trace level). The result is returned as a text file and is linked with the query so that it is only valid for this query. This trace records error messages. If, for example, a query throws an exception, you can replay the trace to receive more detailed error messages.

Trace types

Table 13.7 Trace Types for SAP NetWeaver BW Accelerator

If you have activated one of the four trace types, the system displays the trace after the query has been executed. You can change the trace file and save it locally. Runtime problems may arise for large trace files. Therefore, you can also save the trace file without displaying it.

Tracing in SAP NetWeaver BW Accelerator Monitor

The results of a performance trace in the SAP NetWeaver BW Accelerator Monitor is written in save-optimized format (*.tpt*). This information can be evaluated by the SAP support using special tools. To log the system response time in the monitor, you can start the trace in

Transaction RSDDBIAMON2 in the PERFORMANCE TRACE • START TRACE RECORDING menu. You must specify whether you want to start the trace for a specific user and when the trace is supposed to be stopped. For performance reasons, it is recommended that you do not choose a time that is too far in the future. In the status bar, the system shows how long trace recording has left to run (for instance, "BI Accelerator Monitor (Trace Recording Still Active 00:10:30)").

If a trace recording is already running, you cannot start a new one. To stop a trace that is running, select PERFORMANCE TRACE • STOP TRACE RECORDING from the menu. If you do not stop a trace this way, the system stops recording automatically at the time you defined.

Statistics on Maintenance Processes

To obtain an overview of the runtimes of specific subprocesses in the index maintenance of SAP NetWeaver BW Accelerator, you can view the RSDDSTATTREX table. The system writes the runtimes of specific subprocesses to this statistics table for the following processes: initial indexing, rollup, and adjustments after a change run. A prerequisite is that the statistics are switched on for the corresponding InfoProvider. You can make this setting in the maintenance of the statistics properties (in the Data Warehousing Workbench via the menu path TOOLS • BI STATISTICS SETTINGS). The system records information such as the fill mode (for instance, delta), the activation time, and the number of data records in the statistics table.

13.7 Information Broadcasting

To use information broadcasting, various settings are required in the system administration. There are also several broadcasting functions that are executed by business experts and in the system administration. Ensure that you have the administration authorizations for broadcasting. For this purpose, you require the S_RS_ADMWB authorization object with the RSADMWBOBJ = BR_SETTING field. In the running operation, you manage not only the broadcasting settings, but also their scheduling and objects (bookmark IDs and view IDs) that are created during broadcasting.

Settings for broadcasting
Broadcasting settings and their scheduling are browsed by different criteria and edited in the broadcasting administration (Transaction code

RSRD_ADMIN). You can delete settings that are no longer required. Additionally, you can browse log entries and display them for error analysis.

13.7.1 Sending Email

SAPconnect provides a standard interface for external communication that supports using telecommunication services such as fax, text messages (pager/SMS), Internet mail, and X.400, as well as sending to printers and between different SAP systems. SAPconnect provides a direct connection to the Internet via the SMTP plug-in of SAP NetWeaver Application Server. Moreover, you can directly send and receive Internet mail, faxes, and text messages (pager/SMS) without using additional external communication systems. A prerequisite is that the email addresses are maintained in the user master data and that the mail server was set up in Customizing under SAP NETWEAVER • BUSINESS INTELLIGENCE • SETTINGS FOR REPORTING AND ANALYSIS • SETTINGS FOR INFORMATION BROADCASTING • SET UP MAIL SERVER.

You can monitor and test the distribution of SAP NetWeaver BW content via email in the SAPconnect administration (Transaction SCOT). Select UTILITIES • ROUTING TEST FROM the menu and enter the user names for the SAP NetWeaver BW system as the sender (Figure 13.21). You must also enter the recipient address type INT (Internet mail address) and the email address of the SAP NetWeaver BW user as the recipient address. To test the routing and to get descriptions, select ROUTES • EXPLAIN from the menu.

Routing test

You can view and monitor send requests and the status of sent emails in Transaction SCOT in the UTILITIES • OVERVIEW OF SEND REQUESTS menu. If you receive the message 672: Waiting for Communication Service, the system is unable to output the send status as transmitted.

Monitoring send requests

In this case check the selected settings in the menu under SETTINGS • CONFIRMATION OF RECEIPT. Ensure that the SAPconnect Does Not Expect Receipt Confirmation for Internet Mail option is selected. If you have selected the SAPconnect Expects Receipt Confirmations for Internet Mail option, it is possible that the recipient of the emails does not return a receipt confirmation and that the system outputs message number 672.

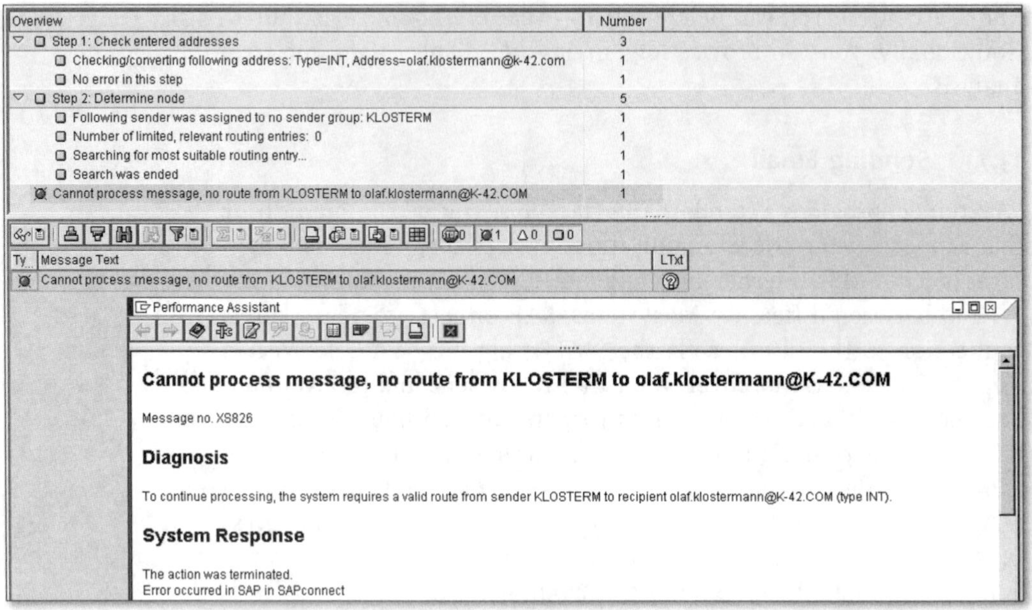

Overview	Number	
▽ ▢ Step 1: Check entered addresses	3	
▢ Checking/converting following address: Type=INT, Address=olaf.klostermann@k-42.com	1	
▢ No error in this step	1	
▽ ▢ Step 2: Determine node	5	
▢ Following sender was assigned to no sender group: KLOSTERM	1	
▢ Number of limited, relevant routing entries: 0	1	
▢ Searching for most suitable routing entry...	1	
▢ Search was ended	1	
▧ Cannot process message, no route from KLOSTERM to olaf.klostermann@K-42.COM	1	

Ty	Message Text	LTxt
▧	Cannot process message, no route from KLOSTERM to olaf.klostermann@K-42.COM	⑦

Performance Assistant

Cannot process message, no route from KLOSTERM to olaf.klostermann@K-42.COM

Message no. XS826

Diagnosis

To continue processing, the system requires a valid route from sender KLOSTERM to recipient olaf.klostermann@K-42.COM (type INT).

System Response

The action was terminated.
Error occurred in SAP in SAPconnect

Figure 13.21 Routing Test in Transaction SCOT

13.7.2 Reorganization

A bookmark ID is the identification number (ID) of a saved navigational state for a Web application; a view ID is the identification number of a saved navigational state for a query. These IDs result from the creation of online links for information broadcasting and can be viewed in the RSZWBOOKMARK header table.

Using the RSRD_BOOKMARK_REORGANISATION report (or Transaction RSRD_ADMIN), you have the option to reorganize and delete bookmark IDs and view IDs that the system generated for information broadcasting and that are no longer required (Figure 13.22).

Temporary bookmark IDs/ view IDs — You can use the function for temporary bookmark IDs and view IDs to delete IDs that the system generated to create online links. The bookmark IDs and view IDs are no longer used in broadcast settings and are not part of URLs in sent online links. You can select them for deletion and specify a time (for instance, automatic deletion of bookmark IDs or view IDs that are older than eight days).

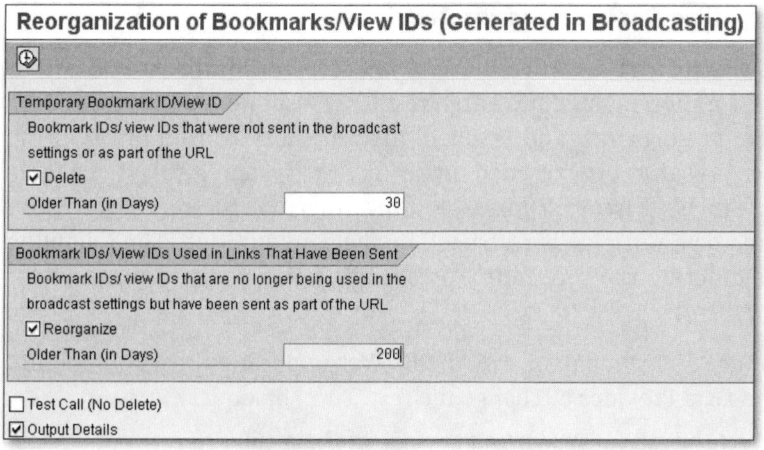

Figure 13.22 Reorganization of Bookmarks

Under Bookmark IDs/View IDs Used in Links That Have Been Sent, you can reorganize bookmark IDs and view IDs that are no longer being used in broadcast settings but have been sent as part of URLs in sent online links. This means the bookmark IDs and view IDs can only be deleted when they are no longer being used in a broadcast setting. You can select these IDs for the reorganization and specify the time.

Bookmark IDs/ view IDs used in sent links

If you first want to view which bookmark IDs and view IDs are available for deletion according to your specifications without actually deleting them, select Test Call (No Delete). To get the bookmark IDs and view IDs in a detailed list, select Output Details. In the results list, Referenced means the IDs are used in a broadcast setting. Sent means the IDs have been sent as part of the URLs.

13.8   Results in Reporting

Often, a report result is not transparent for users and is therefore questioned, and the tracing of calculations and aggregations in reports is either very time-consuming or cannot be carried out at all. The following sections describe the restrictions for the result sets and the analysis of unexpected query results.

13.8.1 Size Restrictions for Result Sets

Via a size restriction for result sets, you can prevent the end user from requesting too much data. Large result sets can negatively impact the system performance and result in high memory consumption. If the allowed result set is exceeded, instead of the system displaying a table with values, it issues a message indicating that the result set is too big and data retrieval is restricted by the configuration. The following steps describe the procedure for changing this security measure for query views:

1. In the context menu of an SAP BEx Web application, select Properties and Data Provider to change the restriction of a query view.

2. Select the tab for restricting the size of the result sets.

3. To set the maximum number of cells for the result set, select an entry from the dropdown box: Maximum Number, Standard Number, or User-Defined Number. Under maximum number and standard number, you can find the numbers that are currently defined in the RSAD-MIN customizing table.

4. Save the query view and use it in another Web template.

The maximum number (BICS_DA_RESULT_SET_LIMIT_MAX) and the standard number (BICS_DA_RESULT_SET_LIMIT_DEF) are defined in the RSADMIN customizing table. The maximum number defines the maximum number of cells a user can manually enter for a specific query view (see above). The standard number contains the number of cells used for all queries (and query views) without a user-defined number.

Data cells versus table cells
The number of cells refers to the number of data cells and differs in the number of table cells, that is, from cells that are visible in the HTML table. The number of table cells is higher than the number of data cells because for table cells you also require the column and row headers (texts and keys for characteristic members, attributes, and so on). The maximum number of cells is checked when the data cells are transferred from ABAP to Java via an RFC. Before this data transmission is started, the system checks the maximum number of cells. In the BW query runtime statistics, you can have the system display the number of transferred cells using the event ID 3200.

13.8.2 Analysis of Report Results

In particular, the combination of the functions Exception Aggregation, Constant Selection, Conditions, Exception Cells; priority rules for queries with two structures; and numeric values with replacement path or other complex formulas and Calculate as... can lead to unexpected (but not necessarily incorrect) results. Incomprehensible results can also occur for virtual key figures and certain remote InfoProviders, in which numbers are generated by a program.

It is possible that an error exists in the programs or that the query uses one or more special functions or properties that each have a clearly defined behavior, but when they are used in combination, this can lead to results that can be understood only with difficulty or not at all.

So which basic knowledge do you need here, and how can you analyze the report results? The query results can be analyzed with a high level of detail in Transaction RSRT. If you execute a query and select Execute + Debug, the system outputs all possibly suppressed warnings. These warnings with additionally available long texts indicate situations that you should be certain to consider. Moreover, in this mode all numbers, which were calculated not only by means of addition operations, are highlighted in color and put in parentheses.

Another option is Key Figure Definition in the extended context menu for each numeric cell. The system uses the definition and all properties that are deployed in this cell to generate and execute a query that is as simple as possible. In doing so, the characteristics 0REQUEST, 0INFOPROV, and 1CUDIM are automatically incorporated from the free characteristics if required. With this result you can analyze the key figure value to be examined by sub-InfoProvider and request, or you can have the system display the different incoming units or currencies. Moreover, the formula components are exploded in a hierarchical view so that you can retrace the individual steps in detail.

Defining key figures

If the Calculate as... function is active on a structure element, the values displayed in the Key Figure Definition field may vary. In this case the displayed value is being recalculated based on the values of the list. However, the key figure definition always shows a context-free original value, and the system indicates this situation with information message

Brain 110. If the key figure definition displays the same value as the original list, it is very likely that no program error exists.

Initially, a value is always calculated independently of its context (in the sense of being mathematically well defined). This means, for example, that a value in a result cell is independent of the values of the subordinate detail cells (this value must not change if another characteristic is added to the drill-down or if a hierarchy node is expanded). Virtual key figures and specific remote InfoProviders form an exception here for which numbers are generated in routines defined by the user and which the system cannot control. Complex formulas that use numeric variables with replacement paths are generally not well defined.

If the values vary, you must first check that Calculate as... is inactive (message Brain 110). If the key figure definition displays the same value, you can assume that the query displays values that are correct according to the definition. If this data is still incomprehensible or does not meet the expectations, experience has shown that the query is defined incorrectly. Often, the application problem can only be solved by changing the data model, and in rare cases there is no proper solution at all.

13.8.3 Query Execution in Safe Mode

If you suspect that errors exist on the OLAP server, as of SP 18 in SAP NetWeaver BW you can temporarily switch off all optimizations, such as the use of OLAP caches, aggregates, or SAP NetWeaver BW Accelerator, in a single step using Transaction RSRT (query monitor) when you execute a query. This option is available under EXECUTE + DEBUG • EXECUTE IN SAFE MODE (Figure 13.23).

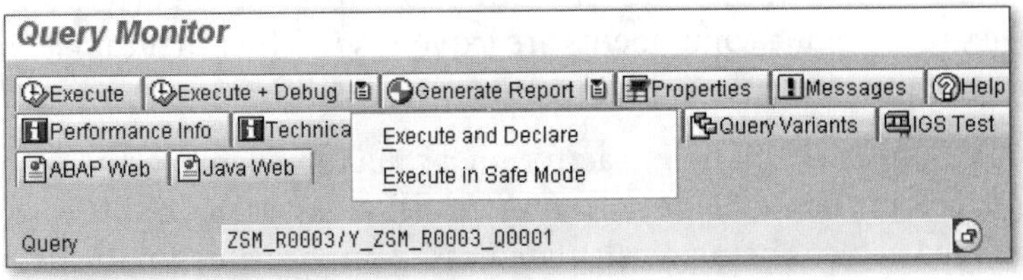

Query Monitor

⊕ Execute	⊕ Execute + Debug	📄	🔄 Generate Report	📄	🖥 Properties	🛈 Messages	❓ Help
🛈 Performance Info	🛈 Technica	Execute and Declare			🗒 Query Variants	📑 IGS Test
📄 ABAP Web	📄 Java Web	Execute in Safe Mode				

| Query | ZSM_R0003/Y_ZSM_R0003_Q0001 | ⏎ |

Figure 13.23 Safe Mode in Transaction RSRT

If the query displays correct numbers in safe mode, it is very likely that the error is not in the OLAP, but in another location. The following settings are made in the safe mode:

Settings in safe mode

- ▶ Do not use aggregates
- ▶ Do not use BIA index
- ▶ Do not use cache
- ▶ No parallel processing
- ▶ Switch off extended DB Optimizer functions
- ▶ Check data of virtual provider
- ▶ Messages/warnings are not suppressed
- ▶ Display empty query result

If the execution in safe mode delivers correct data, you execute the query multiple times in Transaction RSRT using the Execute + Debug button. Then you can gradually determine which optimizations cause the error by switching the individual switches on and off manually. Therefore, a customer message can be opened in the appropriate software component, which usually results in faster processing.

13.8.4 Different Data in ABAP and Java

If a query exhibits a differing system behavior when it is executed in different environments (for instance, in Transaction RSRT and in the portal), you must take into account that the new Java runtime layer is used in the portal. The results in Transaction RSRT, in BEx Analyzer (workbooks), and in ABAP Web are usually identical because all three frontend tools use the ABAP runtime layer.

After the OLAP layer has calculated the basic result set, the result is transferred to the runtime layer so that it is formatted for the output. Exceptions and local calculations are processed in the runtime layer. In SAP NetWeaver BW 7.0 there are two versions of the runtime layer: The ABAP version is used for output via Transaction RSRT, BEx Analyzer, and the Web, and the Java version is used for portal applications. Owing to revised guidelines, the two runtime layers exhibit a different system behavior in certain situations in which various options are possible.

Formatting in the runtime layer

Local exception aggregation of a hierarchy node

In the Java system a local exception aggregation is used on a hierarchy node. For example, if a local exception aggregation MAX exists for the single values 1,000, 2,000, and 3,000, the node displays 3,000.

In the ABAP system the node always displays the total of its leaves and accordingly the value 6,000 for the previous example. This system behavior is not an error because there is no definite rule in this special situation. The ABAP source text follows the general concept that a hierarchy node always indicates the total of its leaves by definition. Java follows the more intuitive concept that the exception aggregation is to apply whenever values are aggregated. This is supposed to apply also for hierarchy nodes.

Zero suppression of a hierarchy node

In the Java system a hierarchy node is suppressed (not displayed) if the zero suppression is active for the results and the leaves of the node aggregate to zero. In the ABAP system, however, a hierarchy node is always displayed even if its value is zero and zero suppression is active.

The considerations mentioned previously also apply here: The Java runtime considers a node only as a case of an aggregated value. All aggregation rules apply including the zero suppression. In the ABAP system, a node is not just considered as an aggregation.

When a node in the Java system disappears in the navigation (compression of a node), it possibly does not reappear if you expand this node again. The expansion of a node is only a delta operation. You must rebuild the entire hierarchy tree (for example, using the Expand A Hierarchy To... operation) so that the system displays the suppressed zero nodes and its leaves that are unequal to zero.

Displaying an exception for another column

In the BEx Query Designer you can define an exception in such a way that one structure element is used for the calculation and another structure element is used to display the result (colored cells). This new feature is not implemented in the ABAP runtime and is only available in the Java runtime.

13.8.5 Incorrect Data When Using Aggregates

Problems that are caused by incorrect data in aggregates are difficult to analyze and consume a lot of time. If a query displays incorrect data when aggregates are used, but these errors do not occur if no aggregates are used, the following steps can help you analyze the problem more closely and find the cause:

1. Use Transaction RSRT (Execute + Debug) to browse for inconsistent aggregates: For this purpose, execute the query using the Show Found Aggregate option. Use the Select Aggregate option to deselect all aggregates except for one until you find the aggregate that provides incorrect results.

   Causes for incorrect data

2. Switch this aggregate off in Transaction RSDDV (without deactivating it) to prevent the query from using it. Then copy the aggregate, fill it using the RSDDK_AGGREGATE_DIRECT_FILL report (source = cube), and check whether the data is still incorrect when you use this aggregate. If this is the case, the SAP support can easily reproduce the problem.

3. Check the inconsistent aggregate. You can view it with the RSDDK_CHECK_AGGREGATE report or with Transaction RSDDAGGRCHECK (enter the temporary table /BI0/01... from the log). SAP Notes 537422 and 646402 provide further information on this topic.

4. Check the RSDDAGGR_V view in Transaction SE16 and search for the navigation attributes or hierarchies that are used in the aggregate. On the one hand, check whether the problem also exists if no navigation attributes are used, and on the other hand, whether the master data of the characteristic is consistent (composite master data test in Transaction RSRV). Also check whether the use of hierarchies is the cause for the error and delete them through reactivation from the buffer if required.

If possible, you can also check whether the use of blocks has any effect on the problem. The BLOCK_SIZE RSADMIN parameter specifies whether the builds of aggregates are carried out in blocks (see SAP Note 653469).

13.9 Integrating SAP NetWeaver BW Contents into SAP NetWeaver Portal

Integrating SAP NetWeaver BW contents into the portal requires knowledge of both SAP NetWeaver BW and SAP NetWeaver Portal.

Close cooperation of the administrators of the SAP NetWeaver BW system and the portal is essential for making the necessary settings.

SAP NetWeaver BW contents can be mapped in different ways in the portal. BEx Web applications can be included as iViews, precalculated documents, or links in the portal. In addition, you can display BEx Analyzer workbooks and SAP NetWeaver BW documents in the portal.

SAP BEx Web application or BEx query as iView in the portal

Web-based SAP NetWeaver BW applications, that is, BEx Web applications or queries, can be displayed as iViews in the portal (for instance, the BEx Web analyzer tool). BEx Web applications are Web templates that are executed on the Web and are created using the BEx web application designer tool. Queries that are Web-based SAP NetWeaver BW applications and are displayed in a standard view as an iView in the portal are a special form of BEx Web applications. iViews are of the BEx Web Application iView type and have the code link *com.sap.portal.appintegrator.sap.BWReport*. You must select the desired version of BEx web: BEx web application iView (SAP BW 3.x format) or BEx web application iView (SAP NetWeaver BW 7.0 format). The two most critical properties, System and BEx Web Application Query String, are set automatically in the BEx Web application designer tool and BEx Query Designer, so the details are not discussed here.

Contents as document or link in knowledge management

BEx Web applications or queries can be stored as a document or a link with historic data in knowledge management . Links to current data require the Repository Manager for SAP NetWeaver BW metadata.

BEx Analyzer workbook

Microsoft Excel workbooks with one or more embedded queries can be provided in a portal. The workbooks are displayed in a separate Microsoft Excel window because opening workbooks with the web browser window is not possible for technical reasons. You require a local installation of the BEx Analyzer. The iViews that are created using the Portal Content Studio or the role upload are of the SAP Transaction iView type and have the code link *com.sap.portal.appintegrator.sap*. The transaction code (RRMXP for all workbooks) and the application (WBID=<WORKBOOK_ID>) must be maintained as parameters.

Microsoft Excel workbooks containing one or more embedded queries can be stored in a knowledge management folder as precalculated documents with historic data.

13.10   Analysis and Monitoring in the Portal

SAP NetWeaver Portal, which is used in an SAP NetWeaver BW system as part of BI Java, does not make as high demands on the administration as a portal that is used as an enterprise portal.

Besides some administration tasks, such as the administration of roles and groups, you must also consider the monitoring and the analysis in case of problems. Therefore, the following sections briefly discuss possible availability checks, the monitoring of log files, and the administration of the portal cache.

13.10.1   Availability Checks

SAP provides various availability check mechanisms. All of these mechanisms have the following in common:

▸ The availability information is usually of a technical nature.

▸ The availability check — once it has been set up — is carried out periodically and without user interaction.

▸ The result of the check is sent to the central Computing Center Management System (CCMS) and thus to SAP Solution Manager. In this respect, you can centrally set up an availability monitor that displays the status of the individual components. In addition, autoreactions enable you to implement automations and notifications.

▸ At application level, the availability is checked with the *Generic Request and Message Generator* (GRMG).

When you use the GRMG, the central system periodically calls a GRMG application via a URL. The GRMG application performs component-specific checks and returns the check results to the central system. If a GRMG check is not possible or is not useful for a component, you can at least verify the existence of the corresponding process at the operating system level. Such a check determines the necessary (but not adequate) prerequisite for the component availability. The check is carried out by the SAPOSCOL program and the SAPCCMSR agent.

GRMG

As described previously, you can also use GRMG to monitor the availability of BI Java components. A prerequisite is the registration and start of the CCMS agent, SAPCCMSR. This way, you can monitor the following components:

Availability checks for BI Java

▶ Universal Data Connect (UDC) Enterprise Beans

▶ BI Java connectors

▶ Metamodel Repository

▶ RFC destination for the SAP NetWeaver BW system

For the monitoring process that uses Universal Data Connect, you must configure the settings that are relevant for the installation in question. You can configure the *grmg-customizing.xml* file required for this purpose using SAP J2EE Visual Administrator or via Transaction GRMG. SAP Note 706290 provides more detailed information on the configuration.

13.10.2 Monitoring of Log Files

Java-based applications write notifications to log files. In complex applications, important notifications can be distributed across more than 100 log files that you should regularly check for error messages to ensure a consistent operation.

SAP provides a mechanism for the automatic analysis of log files. The CCMS agent SAPCCMSR checks the log files every minute according to predefined search patterns. If the agent finds the pattern, it sends an alert to the central monitoring system so that the administrator can be informed.

Alert monitor   You as the administrator can view all checked log files in the alert monitor (Transaction RZ20) of the central monitoring system. In case of an error, you can expand the corresponding subtree in the Logfile Monitoring monitor and take the name and the path of the log file in which an error was logged from the Complete Name node.

The benefits of the central log file monitoring and alerting are:

▶ The regular check of the many log files is automatic.

▶ The administrator can be notified automatically in case of a problem.

▶ The Standalone Log Viewer provides central access to all log files of your SAP NetWeaver landscape (even if the corresponding J2EE Engine no longer runs).

▶ The Standalone Log Viewer can also display ASCII-based logs of other applications, such as the database.

The monitor creates a subtree for each monitored file. The name of the subtree consists of a prefix and the name of the file. With this prefix, which you set in the monitoring configuration file, you can differentiate different files with identical names that you want the system to monitor. Each subtree in turn consists of several Monitoring Tree Elements (MTEs), for instance, the already mentioned node, Complete Name.

13.10.3 Usage of the Portal Cache (BW iViews)

To use the portal cache, you need the properties, cache level, cache validity period, and isolation method. The usage of the portal cache has the following benefits:

▸ Significant improvement of the interface response time

▸ Prevention of unnecessary rerendering of the page when the portal page is called again

▸ Web browser–like caching for server-based, dynamic pages on the Web (such as SAP BEx Web applications)

You can make the following settings for the cache level:

▸ **No Caching**
With the None option, the SAP BEx Web application is called again in the SAP NetWeaver BW system with every call.

▸ **Session Related**
With the Session option, the cache is filled specific to the user. After finishing the current session by closing all web browser windows, the cache is invalidated.

▸ **Common for All Users**
With the Shared option, the cache is not filled specific to the user; instead, it is filled the same for all users. Personalization is not taken into account.

▸ **Own User**
With the User option, the cache is filled specific to the user. The cache is updated or invalidated automatically by the cache validity period process. SAP NetWeaver BW personalization and iView personalization are taken into account.

The cache validity period is specified in milliseconds. The isolation method has to be set to URL. The administrator should manually perform the settings for the use of the portal cache for every iView with SAP BEx Web applications.

The use of the portal cache enables a full proxy mode of the portal. Full proxy mode means that only the portal server communicates directly with the SAP NetWeaver BW server. All requests (HTTP requests) from the user's web browser (client) are answered by the portal server. The user's web browser does not have direct access to the SAP NetWeaver BW server. The SAP NetWeaver BW server can thus be protected from external access and is located in the internal network zone. For external access, the portal server can be located in the demilitarized zone (DMZ) of the network . The protocol for communication between the web browser of the user and the portal server, and between the portal server and the SAP NetWeaver BW server, is either HTTP or HTTPS. The port number can be configured in both cases.

13.11   Communication Problems with BEx Web Java

If problems occur in the communication between SAP NetWeaver Application Server Java and SAP NetWeaver Application Server ABAP when you test the configuration or execute an application (information broadcasting or BEx Web Application Java), you should first categorize the problem. Information broadcasting and BEx Web Application Java have different methods for the communication between Java and ABAP. Initially, you must differentiate between two protocols:

▶ **RFC communication**

Different protocols

RFC-based communication is always used if SAP NetWeaver Application Server Java and ABAP communicate in the background; that is, they communicate on the server side. Examples include reading query results for displaying them in BEx Web Application Java or generating precalculated HTML pages in a batch job and the subsequent distribution of pages to a knowledge management folder using information broadcasting.

▶ **HTTP(S)-based communication**

This type of communication uses the web browser as an interim step. For example, it is used if you call the BEx Broadcaster that is implemented as BEx Web Application ABAP from a BEx Web Application Java. Another application case in BEx Broadcaster is the call of the folder selection dialog for export to the portal that is implemented as a Java iView. Technically, these two actions are executed via the client-side start of a URL.

Additionally, it is important to consider the communication direction. A communication from Java to ABAP is present if the initiator of the action is on the Java side and the data receiver is on the ABAP side. A communication from ABAP to Java is present if the initiator of the action is on the ABAP side and the data receiver on the Java side.

There are two problem areas. On the one hand, errors can occur in the communication structure. No technical connection between the two systems can be established in these cases. On the other hand, errors occur with the authentication. The technical connection is established in these cases, but a problem exists in the identification of the user on the receiver side that is assigned to the user on the caller side. Because both Java and ABAP require authenticated users and not service users, a correct logon of the user to the called system is mandatory for the functioning of the scenario.

Problem areas

Note that logon tickets are used in the area of information broadcasting and BEx Web Application Java. In these scenarios, you are not required to log on twice to the web browser or SAP GUI. Double logon indicates an error in the configuration. Exceptions to this rule that require a new logon only exist when an SAP BEx Web application or the BEx Broadcaster is called from an SAP BEx tool, such as the SAP BEx web application designer tool, or in case of certain export formats that refer to content (for instance, MIME objects) on the SAP NetWeaver Application Server or other servers.

13.11.1 Usage of RFC

To obtain more details on the error cause in RFC communication, you should check the last entries in the *dev_jrfc.trc* file of the following directory:

/usr/sap/<SID>/JC<SYSNR>/j2ee/cluster/server<#>/

In this file, the system logs all RFC errors irrespective of the communication direction. Often, the error cause can be narrowed down here. Additionally, you can find log entries of the individual components involved in the *defaultTrace.trc* file in the following directory:

/usr/sap/<SID>/JC<SYSNR>/j2ee/cluster/server<#>/log/

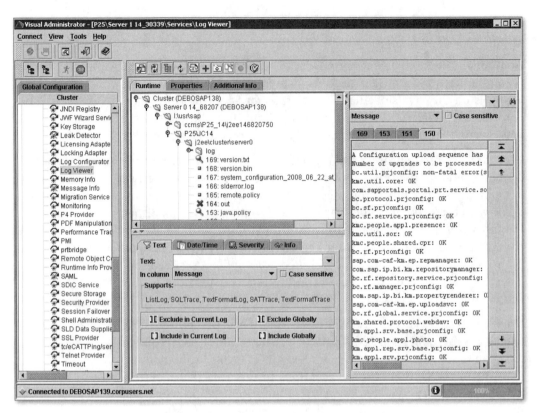

Figure 13.24 Log Viewer in Visual Administrator

Log Viewer   You can view the log entries using the Log Viewer in the SAP J2EE
Visual Administrator (Figure 13.24). In contrast to the *dev_jrfc.trc* file,
the most recent entries are displayed at the top in the Log Viewer.
The settings for the individual tracing locations are prerequisites for a
comprehensive logging. Should problems occur when you use RFC as
a communication protocol; in SAP J2EE Visual Administrator under
<J2EE _ SID> • SERVER • SERVICES • LOG CONFIGURATOR in the Locations
tab you must set Severity "ALL" for the following tracing locations to
obtain more detailed information:

Tracing locations   ▶ com.sap.ip.bi.webapplications

▶ com.sap.portal.connectors.BW

▶ com.sap.portal.ivs.semantic.systemLandscape

▶ com.sap.portal.ivs.systemConnectionTests

- com.sap.security.api.saml
- com.sap.security.core.server.jaas
- com.sap.security.core.server.saml
- com.sap.security.core.session
- com.sap.security.core.ticket
- com.sap.security.core.umap
- com.sap.security.core.util

Remember to reset them to their standard values as soon as you have found the cause. This avoids unnecessary log entries and a negative effect on the system performance.

To determine the appropriate ABAP system, the system tries to determine the correct logon parameter for an RFC logon in the portal system landscape via the alias. Once that has been done, the parameters are transferred to the JRFC interface that carries out the actual communication.

Java-to-ABAP communication

A typical problem is a missing read authorization for the system alias in the portal system landscape. In the portal system landscape maintenance, select the User checkbox under Authorizations for the everyone user group, for another role or user group to which the user is assigned, or for a list of individual users.

In an ABAP-to-Java communication, the SAP J2EE Engine functions as an RFC server. When you start up the J2EE Engine, the JCo RFC Provider registers in the RFC gateway with a unique name. After successful registration, an RFC call is possible from ABAP. This call is directed to the RFC gateway that forwards it to the JCo RFC Provider of the SAP J2EE Engine. If a system parameter is specified incorrectly under <J2EE _ SID> • SERVER • SERVICES • JCO RFC PROVIDER, the system fails to establish a connection.

ABAP-to-Java communication

After the physical connection has been established, SAP NetWeaver Application Server ABAP tries to log on the users based on the available information. For information broadcasting and the IT scenario Enterprise Reporting, Query, and Analysis, the logon is typically made using logon tickets.

Authentication

To authenticate a user on the J2EE side, Java Authentication and Authorization Service (JAAS) login modules are run. The *com.sap.security.*

core.server.jaas.EvaluateAssertionTicketLoginModule login module is used for the RFC-based ABAP-to-Java communication. This login module accepts only logon tickets from systems whose certificate is known to the J2EE Engine and that are specified in the configuration of the login module. If the J2EE user ID differs from the ABAP user ID, an inverse user mapping is performed to determine the J2EE user ID. For this purpose, the user mapping is interpreted in reverse for the UME master system.

13.11.2 Usage of HTTP(S)

If you use HTTP(S) as the communication protocol, it is important to know the URL from which the erroneous page is called. Additionally, you must determine the URL that is called. You can determine both URLs from the properties of their respective pages in the browser. The two URLs determined should be inserted in a customer message.

Java-to-ABAP communication | In the Java-to-ABAP communication, the URL is generated based on information that is defined for the SAP NetWeaver Application Server ABAP under Web Application Server (WAS) in the portal's System Landscape Editor.

ABAP-to-Java communication | In the ABAP-to-Java communication, the URL is generated based on information that is defined in SAP NetWeaver Application Server ABAP in the RSPOR_T_PORTAL view. You can view this information using Transaction SM30 and modify it if required.

Authentication | SAP NetWeaver Application Server ABAP only accepts requests via HTTP(S) that come from a system whose certificate is known to the system. Generally, the same problems as in the RFC-based Java-to-ABAP communication can occur. Additionally, problems in the format of the URL can prevent cookies being exchanged between Java and ABAP, and consequently the single sign-on behavior (SSO) is incorrect.

Here as well, the JAAS login modules are run for the authentication of a user on the J2EE side. The *EvaluateTicketLoginModule* is used for the HTTP(S)-based ABAP-to-Java communication. This login module accepts only logon tickets from systems whose certificate is known to the J2EE Engine and that are specified in the configuration of the login module. If the J2EE user ID differs from the ABAP user ID, an inverse user mapping is also performed for this communication to determine the J2EE user ID.

13.12 Performance of Web Applications

If performance problems occur during the execution of Web applications that were created using the SAP BEx Web application designer tool, you must primarily determine which type of application it is and how the problems are caused. In particular, it must be clear whether it is a Web application for SAP NetWeaver BW 3.x (BI ABAP) or SAP NetWeaver BW 7.0 (BI Java).

13.12.1 Runtime Measurements in BI Java

In case of wait times that are unexpectedly long when you execute a BI Java Web application or navigate in one, it can be helpful to record statistics to narrow down the performance problem. These statistics contain both the data of the OLAP statistics and the information about the runtimes on the Java side.

Start the Web application with the *&PROFILING=X* addition by executing the Web template via the BEx web application designer tool on the Web and attaching the addition to the URL in the address area of the web browser. Carry out these steps until the performance problem occurs.

Owing to the *&PROFILING=X* addition, the system writes detailed statistics information about the runtimes on the Java and the ABAP sides (OLAP statistics) that can be called via an automatically generated link at the beginning of the Web page (SAP NetWeaver BW statistics).

13.12.2 Guidelines for Performance Improvements

The following sections provide options for solving performance problems in the execution of Web applications. In principle, you should first ensure that no performance problems exist with underlying queries and views. Also note that performance measurements from Transaction RSRT in HTML mode have no informative value about the actual system behavior because a lot of additional coding must be run through for the emulation of a browser in the backend. You can only use requests for the analysis that were actually executed in a web browser.

▸ Check whether the Web template contains multiple data providers or Web items. To compare the runtime of the data providers, you can call the queries or query views using the standard Web template

Number of data providers and Web items

0QUERY_TEMPLATE or the BEx Analyzer to find out which data provider is causing the long runtime of the Web application. This query should then be further limited using variables or filter values to decrease the result set.

Read mode ▶ If the Web template contains one or more Web items of the Dropdown Box *type*, you should check whether a different read mode improves the runtime of the Web application. The read mode is defined using the BOOKED_VALUES parameter and has the following parameter values:

▶ **M**
All values from the master data table. In some circumstances values might also be displayed that do not appear in the data provider under the current filter conditions and that have the result "No suitable data found" when filtered. However, this process is fastest under certain conditions.

▶ **D**
Values that are basically posted, whereby the current drilldown status is not fully taken into consideration.

▶ **Q**
Only values are displayed that are also posted in the data provider under the currently valid filter conditions. This can take a long time under certain circumstances.

The best read mode depends on the data model (basic InfoCube, MultiProvider, and so on). In general, however, read mode Q should be slower than read modes M and D because the filter values that are defined at runtime must be taken into account. An exception can be the Dropdown Box web item in which the MAXVALUES parameter contains a high value and therefore requires a longer period of time to generate the HTML coding of the Web item.

The standard read mode depends on the Web item. A Navigation Block Web item, for example, has the standard read mode Q; the Dropdown Box Web item the standard read mode D. The BOOKED_VALUES parameter of the Web item overrides the read mode that was set in the InfoObject maintenance.

In the Web reporting, the read mode, BOOKED_VALUES=Q, is often used if no other template was specified.

▶ If you want to find out which Web item of a Web application causes a long runtime, a detailed trace may provide help:

    ▶ 1. Call Transaction RSRTRACE and activate the user, which then executes the Web application in the web browser.

    ▶ 2. Select the user and call the dialog for more detailed traces using the Configure User button.

    ▶ 3. In the topic areas, select the WEB (Web Reporting) entry and save the setting.

    ▶ 4. A trace is available in Transaction RSRTRACE in the subsequent call of the Web application with the user for which the trace was activated. It contains information at the Web item level. This way, you can determine the Web item that causes the long runtime of the Web application.

Trace

▶ If the call of the Web application consumes a lot of time, but the navigation is then limited to the selection of filter values to restrict the result, you should consider using a precalculation of the Web application via the reporting agent. You must take into account that a precalculated Web application does not contain any navigation links, but that you can set filter values via the dropdown boxes that were filled with possible characteristic combinations during the precalculation.

Precalculation

▶ If you use command sequences within a Web application, for instance, in the form of a link, you should ensure that you use relative URLs and not absolute URLs. An absolute URL generates another session that requires additional resources; a relative URL, however, uses the same session. You can check the additional generation of sessions using Transaction SM04. Here you must observe that Transaction SM04 is called on the same application server that is used in the URL of the Web application that was called in the web browser.

Relative URLs

If the check in Transaction SM04 should reveal that many sessions of the Plug-in HTTP type are displayed although the users have already closed the web browser and therefore no longer access the Web application, you can use the USE_PAGE_WRAPPER parameter to release a session that is no longer required. If you do not use this parameter in the Web application, the session is not terminated until timeout, even though the web browser has already been closed.

Unused data provider

▶ When you create a Web template, you should note that data providers contained in the Web template affect the runtime of the Web application whose data is not used by a Web item. In Table RSDDSTAT, entries are generated in the QTIMEOLAPINIT field for this data provider even if the corresponding query is not executed subsequently. It is therefore recommended that you remove unneeded data providers from the Web template.

Collapsed Web items

▶ If a Web application contains Web items that are initially collapsed, these must also be processed when the Web application is called, and they therefore impact the initial runtime of the Web application. The data providers of collapsed Web items are executed in the initial call; only the HTML rendering is implemented when the Web item is shown or hidden. To decrease the initial runtime, you should consider whether the data providers of existing Web items can be exchanged at runtime using a command sequence.

Variable screen

▶ If a Web application only contains data providers with optional variables, the system does not display a variable screen if the VARIABLE_SCREEN=X parameter was not set. When the Web application is executed, no variable value is transferred to the data providers if no default value or previous value exists that is stored in a query view. This can also result in a long runtime of the Web application. Check whether a variable screen is displayed in which no variable values are defined by attaching the &VARIABLE_SCREEN=X parameter to the URL of the Web application.

Part III
Management and Support

This chapter discusses how the SAP support helps you in case of problems, which technical or organizational prerequisites must be met on the customer side, and how the SAP Solution Manager and SAP Support Portal functions support administration in the best possible way.

14   SAP Support

The SAP service and support infrastructure is a prerequisite for an efficient SAP support. It consists of the SAP Service Marketplace, which is operated by SAP, and the SAP Solution Manager, which is integrated with the customer's system landscape. This infrastructure enables an optimized cooperation between SAP, its service partners, and the customers.

14.1   Tools for the Support

Despite the provision of the SAP Solution Manager, the ST-A/PI and ST-PI solution tools (previous: TCC Basis Tools) are still useful and not obsolete. However, neither tool is available in the standard version, and they must therefore be integrated retroactively. They are available as add-ons.

The *Support Tool* plug-in (ST-PI) contains general support tools. The *Service Tools for Applications* plug-in (ST-A/PI) includes application-specific tools for the SAP support and provides the following transactions and reports in addition to other functions:

- Transaction ST14 (Application Analysis)
- Report RTCCTOOL (Service Tools)
- Transaction ST12 (ABAP Trace for EarlyWatch/GoingLive)
- Transaction ST13 (Launch Pad for Further Analysis Tools)

The RTCCTOOL report (SAP Service Tools Update) checks the availability of the required tools for SAP service sessions (Figure 14.1). The

Service Tools for Applications

SAP Service Tools Update

report connects to the SAP Service Marketplace and determines a list of necessary add-ons, notes, and transports for your system configuration. It checks whether these are maintained and displays missing add-ons, notes, and transports. This list provides all information required, such as SAP Notes, implementation statuses, short descriptions, and implementation texts. The tool contains useful procedures regarding service tools and upgrades so that the implementation of transports can be supported in the best possible way.

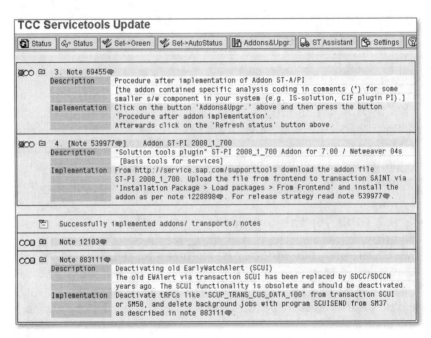

Figure 14.1 Checking the Service Tools in the RTCCTOOL Report

The ST14 application monitor is primarily used during the SAP GoingLive Optimization Session. In the background, analysis jobs collect performance-relevant key figures about document statistics or customizing settings. You can display the analysis results as a tree or download them to a service session.

With Transaction ST13 (Analysis & Service Tools Launch Pad), you can start the ITS Trace Viewer tool or analysis reports for the SAP NetWeaver BW system.

Similar to Transaction SE30, Transaction ST12 (ABAP Trace for Early-Watch/GoingLive) enables you to record ABAP traces; however, it provides additional options to activate the trace (activate trace for other users, for incoming RFCs) or evaluate the ABAP trace (bottom-up/top-down call hierarchies, internal table names, and so on).

14.2 SAP Solution Manager

SAP Solution Manager supports you throughout the entire lifecycle of your solutions, from Business Blueprint, to configuration, to production processing. It provides central access to tools, methods, and pre-configured contents that you can use during evaluation, implementation, and operational processing of your systems (Figure 14.2).

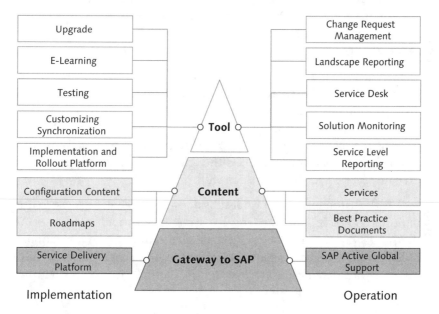

Figure 14.2 Overview of SAP Solution Manager

SAP Solution Manager provides functions for implementations with integrated project management, for the synchronization of the customizing (for example, Customizing Scout), for testing, and for global rollouts, for instance. This book, however, focuses particularly on Solution Monitoring with central system administration and monitoring and service-level reporting, SAP services especially for perfor-

Functions of SAP Solution Manager

533

mance and availability monitoring, and the Service Desk and change management.

SAP Solution Manager provides a platform for the SAP support services. On the basis of the information on the system landscape, it proposes suitable services for the handling of technical risks and ensures the technical stability of SAP solutions. These services include SAP GoingLive Functional Upgrade Check, SAP Interface Management, and SAP Operations Competence Empowering. It is very easy to order and execute these services via SAP Solution Manager; you can even implement some services as self-services independently of the SAP support. This leads to improved IT services and less downtime for the solution.

System landscape of SAP Solution Manager

A one-system landscape is sufficient to execute SAP Solution Manager for minimum processing (for example, Maintenance Optimizer, EarlyWatch Alert). For business-critical processes (managing change requests, system monitoring), you should execute SAP Solution Manager on a three-system landscape (DEV, QAS, PROD).

You can operate multiple SAP Solution Manager live systems. However, to optimally utilize the advantage of a close functional integration, SAP recommends implementing all scenarios on the same SAP Solution Manager. You should implement all SAP Solution Manager scenarios (such as the management of change requests, root cause analysis, and so on) in only one live system, although it is technically possible to execute several SAP Solution Managers in parallel.

For major customers with several subsidiaries, it may make sense to use multiple SAP Solution Manager live systems with multiple live solutions. This depends on the requirements regarding the organizational independence and the use of specific SAP Solution Manager tools. You can exchange data between various SAP Solution Manager systems to a limited extent only.

14.3 SAP Active Global Support

SAP Active Global Support provides comprehensive support services, which enable you to continuously enhance operation and administration and optimally use the SAP NetWeaver BW systems. The goal is to generally reduce the total cost of ownership (TOC) for your SAP

NetWeaver BW landscape and your IT infrastructure and achieve a faster and more comprehensive return on investment (ROI).

End-to-end solution operations include an overall concept that allows for an optimization of the operation of your SAP solutions. SAP provides tools, useful courses, services, and further training to enable your support employees to ensure that your SAP solutions are deployed in the best possible way.

End-to-end solution operations

14.3.1　SAP Enterprise Support

Using the cooperation options in the global SAP support network as a part of SAP Enterprise Support, you can ensure that causes are analyzed precisely and problems solved quickly. Among other things, this support also includes global incident management provided by SAP Active Global Support. Here, service-level agreements define short initial response times and fast corrective measures. With SAP Enterprise Support, you benefit from the following advantages:

▶ Flexible adjustment to changing requirements through the provision of SAP enhancement packages and support packages

Benefits of SAP Enterprise Support

▶ Faster reaction to problems owing to retrievable expert knowledge

▶ Efficient change management and quality tests

▶ Fewer risks owing to industry-leading standards that minimize the complexity of your SAP IT system landscape and partner applications

▶ Reduced downtimes owing to an integrated provision and standardization of diagnosis tools, integration tests, and business process monitoring

▶ Cost reduction owing to consistent tools and methods in heterogeneous system landscapes and competitive service-level agreements that minimize problem solution times

With SAP Enterprise Support, SAP not only supports the code in the software by means of a support model, but also provides platform support, SOA support, and application support.

14.3.2 Run SAP

Run SAP is a proven method that enables you to implement and ensure an end-to-end and smooth operation of applications, such as SAP NetWeaver BW systems, in organizations in the long run. The Run SAP method includes standards for the operation of SAP solutions, a roadmap for setting up a reliable operation of SAP solutions, training and certification programs, SAP Solution Manager for application management and services and support (Figure 14.3).

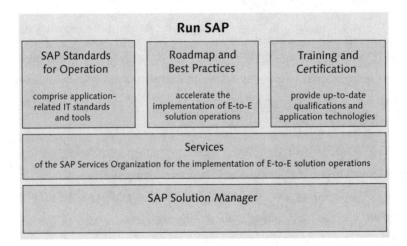

Figure 14.3 Run SAP Method

Support for administration The standards developed by SAP and the roadmap included in SAP Solution Manager, in particular, provide major support for administration. The SAP standards for the operation of SAP solutions are led by the idea of a clear IT governance that controls technical and personnel resources and complexity, risks, and costs in the overall context of the operation of the SAP solutions. These standards define, for example, guidelines on the technical operation (system administration and monitoring) and on the process flow (job scheduling management, management of the data volume, and so on).

Roadmap The Run SAP roadmap enables you to specify the operational planning framework, plan the details, and configure your operation in such a way that all processes are reliably supported. In addition, the roadmap helps you find the appropriate strategy and tools and provides information on what is to be implemented and on how it is to be implemented.

In this context, successful best practices indicate how you can get the best out of your SAP applications.

14.3.3 SAP MaxAttention

With SAP MaxAttention, SAP customers gain the highest level of support. This is a holistic support offer that includes expert services and continuous monitoring by the management and covers all phases of the lifecycle of your SAP solution (Figure 14.4) — from the implementation to running operation to upgrade projects. The technical support within SAP MaxAttention mainly focuses on the following aspects:

▶ Reduction of the TCO

▶ Technical quality management to minimize the technical risks of your implementation or upgrade projects

▶ Protection of investment

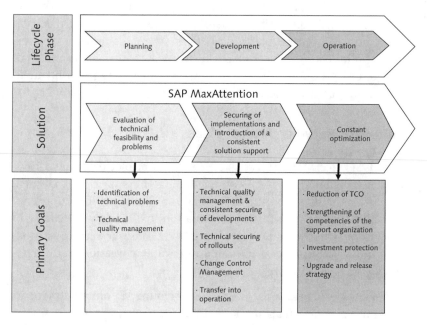

Figure 14.4 SAP MaxAttention

The tailored expert services and the involvement of the management ensure that the customers are provided with the necessary support and that the service quality is monitored. A *balanced scorecard* assesses the success of the project. For this purpose, SAP and the customer agree upon specific main areas and key performance indicators (KPIs). The customer and an executive sponsor from SAP then measure and evaluate these KPIs during the progress of the project.

Safeguarding

Safeguarding for implementation projects is based on the service portfolio of SAP Safeguarding. Within SAP MaxAttention, the technical SAP Quality Manager is responsible for the definition and coordination of the safeguarding services. SAP Safeguarding for Implementation ensures that core business processes meet requirements regarding performance, availability, data consistency, and maintainability. It also ensures that SAP solutions and the configuration of the SAP system landscape have the desired stability and that all applications and systems are prepared for a smooth operation.

During the *continuous improvement* phase, customers improve the performance, business processes, availability, and maintainability of their SAP solutions. This way they can reduce their TCO and increase the ROI for their SAP applications. Customers who use SAP MaxAttention for upgrade and release planning benefit from a comprehensive service portfolio. These services meet the business requirements and challenges of complex upgrades and ensure a seamless and smooth transition to an updated solution or a new release.

14.4 SAP Service Marketplace

The SAP Service Marketplace is SAP's extranet platform that allows for a true collaboration of customers and partners with SAP. Divided into portals that focus on the individual requirements, it provides not only central access to exclusive information, but also a wide choice of services, software, and support (Figure 14.5). The SAP Service Marketplace guides you through the evaluation, implementation, and operation of your SAP solution.

SAP Support Portal

The SAP Support Portal aims at supporting your SAP solution during its entire lifecycle and ensuring that your SAP systems and SAP BusinessObjects systems run without problems and with an optimized performance during the entire lifecycle. The support ranges from backing up your implementation project to solving your customer request or providing support services for an optimization of your SAP solution.

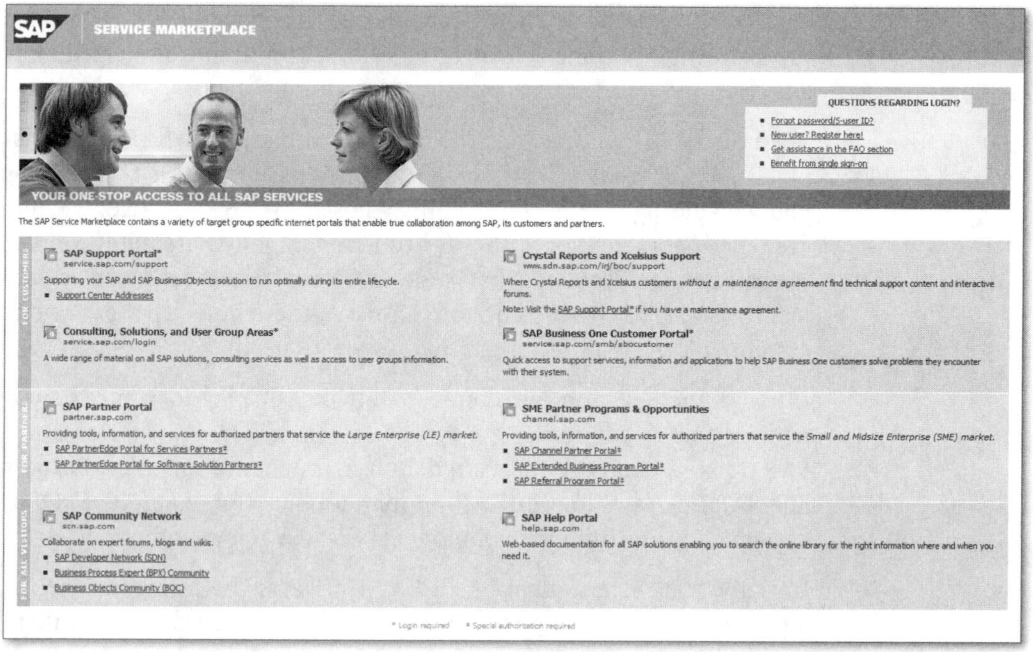

Figure 14.5 Service Marketplace

The SAP Help Portal provides documentation for all SAP solutions. This way you can browse the online library for appropriate information when required. You can find the documentation for SAP NetWeaver BW 7.0 EhP 1 in the SAP Help Portal under DOCUMENTATION • SAP NETWEAVER • SAP NETWEAVER 7.0 INCLUDING ENHANCEMENT PACKAGE 1 • GERMAN.

SAP Help Portal

This documentation includes content on the Data Warehousing IT scenario under the following path: SAP NETWEAVER LIBRARY • KEY AREAS OF SAP NETWEAVER • KEY AREAS OF INFORMATION INTEGRATION • BUSINESS INTELLIGENCE • DATA WAREHOUSING.

The users that can access the services in the SAP Service Marketplace must be configured specifically. One SAP Service Marketplace user with full administration rights is defined per customer number. This user can then create additional users for the customer number and assign the required rights. You can find this function in the SAP Service Marketplace using the */user-admin* quick link. By entering the customer number, you can directly request users on the start page. The users are then created without authorizations; that is, the administrator must

Configuring users

customize the users on the customer side. The created IDs always have the S<10-digit_number> format; therefore, they are also referred to as S users.

SAP HotNews and SAP TopNotes

With the SAP HotNews and SAP TopNotes applications, SAP offers display functions that display solely the information that is relevant for you, depending on the components you selected. SAP HotNews items are SAP customer notes with priority 1 (very high). These notes contain the solutions to problems that could cause a system breakdown or data loss in the SAP system. Therefore, if one of these notes applies to your system, it is very important that you take it seriously.

Initially, the SAP TopNotes or SAP HotNews display for your components is empty. You can create appropriate filters for SAP TopNotes and SAP HotNews and use the shared filter maintenance for SAP TopNotes and SAP HotNews to create a filter for a product (for example, APO) or system and thus limit the components that are relevant for you.

Initially, the system displays all SAP HotNews that are available for your selected components (Figure 14.6). You can select and confirm notes that you have already read and implemented in your system if necessary. The system then hides the confirmed notes so that you are solely provided with recent, not yet confirmed notes.

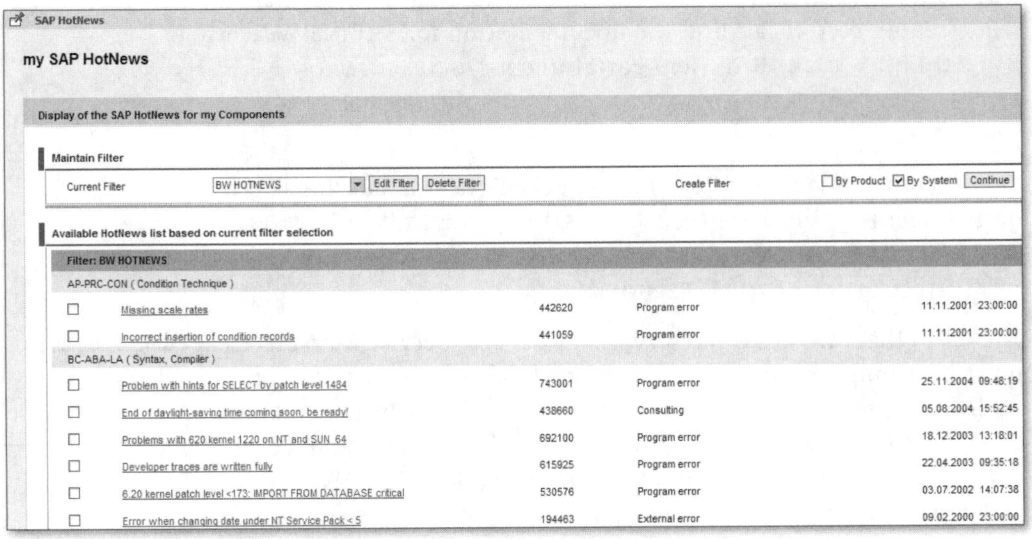

Figure 14.6 HotNews Display in the SAP Support Portal

You can also comfortably receive the SAP HotNews and SAP TopNotes that are relevant for you via email. To enable this, you must select the HotNews and SAP TopNotes areas under My Profile • Maintain Newsletter Subscription in the SAP Service Marketplace.

Information via email

14.5 Service Connections

If you need the support of SAP and its partners, it is usually necessary that the employees log on to your systems via remote connections. You should implement the prerequisites at an early stage before incidents occur to set up the connections without problems in emergency situations.

14.5.1 Basic Setup

You can only maintain service connection data in the SAP Support Portal (SAP Service Marketplace) under */serviceconnection*.

A prerequisite for opening a service connection is an existing physical network connection — via Integrated Services Digital Network (ISDN)), Virtual Private Network (VPN), Secure Network Communication (SNC), X.25, and so on — to SAP's support backend (between SAProuter on the customer side and SAProuter of SAP). The network connection needs to be initiated via SAProuter on the customer side to prevent unauthorized access to the customer system.

SAProuter

SAProuter is software that can monitor the access between your SAP ERP server and the corresponding frontend computers. Connections that are set up with SAProuter provide the additional benefit that no end-to-end communication between systems is required at the network level. For example, if a frontend computer accesses an SAP ERP server through an intermediate router, it is not necessary to define the entire way between the two systems at the TCP/IP level. It is sufficient that both sides reach SAProuter. From the perspective of the SAP communication, this is a central point in your network, which serves as a basis for any subconnection. Each subnetwork that is logically stored behind SAProuter is consequently reduced to the network address of SAProuter.

SAP operates SAProuter servers that are used to create connections from the customer to SAP. The SAProuters listed in Table 14.1 are currently used at SAP.

Server	Location
sapserv1	Connection via the Internet (VPN)
sapserv2	Connection via the Internet (SNC)
sapserv3	Walldorf (Germany)
sapserv4	Philadelphia (USA)
sapserv5	Tokyo (Japan)
sapserv6	Sydney (Australia)
sapserv7	Singapore (Singapore)

Table 14.1 SAProuter Servers

Owing to the benefits mentioned above, SAP Active Global Support merely supports SAProuter connections. Because SAP forwards all accesses to customer systems via an SAProuter, the connection between SAP and the customer is reduced to a plain SAProuter-SAProuter connection. In colloquial language, SAProuter also refers to the computer on which SAProuter runs, although it is usually only one of the many functions of this computer.

System Data

To enable SAP employees to access your systems, the system data must be completely maintained in the SAP Support Portal under the */systemdata* quick link. Here you can also find a description of the system data maintenance. Please note that SAP employees can only log on to systems or servers that are maintained in the system data. SAP employees cannot manually select the target system or server, for example, by manually entering one of your IP addresses. If you use SAP Solution Manager, you can also have the system transfer your system data periodically to the SAP Support Portal via a background job.

Automatic updates

After you have integrated the automatic data determination for a system landscape in SAP Solution Manager, SAP Solution Manager updates the system data in the system landscape automatically. EarlyWatch Alert automatically updates only system data of live systems in the SAP Support Portal monthly. SAP Solution Manager, however, enables you to update system data of all systems periodically (daily, for instance) and when required in the SAP Support Portal.

Steps for Opening a Service Connection

The process of establishing service connections is divided into the following substeps: configuration in SAProuter, maintenance of the system data in the SAP Support Portal of the SAP Service Marketplace, and configuration of the service and opening the service connection.

You create the services in the SAP Service Marketplace with the */service-connection* alias. If you use SAP Solution Manager, you can also establish service connections using Transaction SOLMAN_CONNECT. It is also possible to migrate already existing connections in the SAP Support Portal to SAP Solution Manager.

Creating services

You can access your connections in the service portal via HELP & SUPPORT • YOUR CONNECTIONS TO SAP • MANAGE CONNECTIONS. First, select the system for which you want to open a connection. You can either view the selection of recently used systems or search for systems. If you search for systems, you can enter a system ID or select a customer number. In addition, you can display all systems for which you have an authorization to open a service connection and then make your selection.

Managing connections

In addition to system IDs, the list of available systems also includes system types, connection statuses, and installation numbers. The connection status can assume one of the following status levels:

Connection status

▶ **Green**
At least one service connection and the network connection are open.

▶ **Red**
The service connections and the network connection are closed.

▶ **Yellow**
The host did not respond.

▶ **Gray**
At least one service connection is open, but the network connection is interrupted. This status is assumed when the service connection is generally open, but your SAProuter host does not respond to nine

subsequent pings, which leads to the assumption that the network connection is currently interrupted.

Setting up a connection

To set up a connection, select the system and then the desired connection type (for example, HTTPconnect) and maintain the relevant data in the subsequent input screens.

The Open/Close Connections area displays the list of active services (Figure 14.7). If the service is not shown here, you have to activate it. By clicking the service, you open the corresponding service connection (Figure 14.8). Select the required opening time (default value: 8 hours) and specify a contact person, either manually or by selecting a person from the list of registered contact persons.

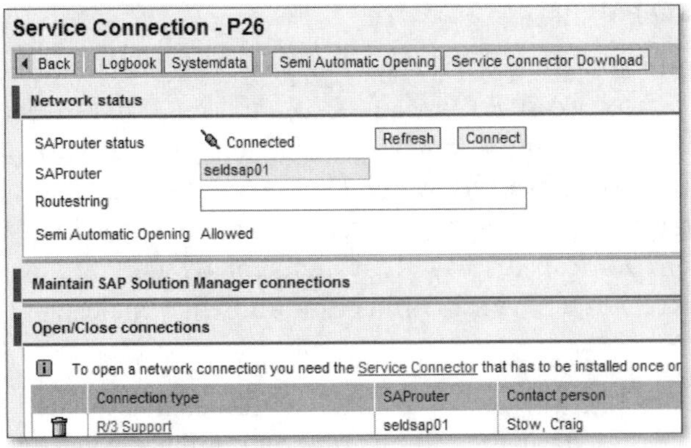

Figure 14.7 Service Overview with an Open Connection

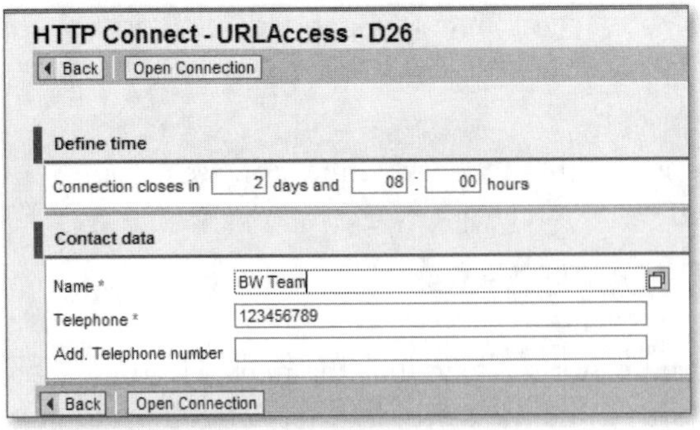

Figure 14.8 Opening a Connection

By confirming the time frame and contact data, you open the connection (the status of SAProuter switches from Connection... to Connected), which SAP employees can now be use to log on to your system.

14.5.2 BW RFC and BW GUI Service Types

If problems with the frontend of SAP NetWeaver BW occur, the two following connection types must be open in addition to the SAP ERP service type:

▶ BW RFC connection

▶ BW GUI connection

Because the Business Explorer Analyzer is implemented as an RFC client and — at least in the current version — some SAP GUI-based dialogs are used simultaneously, the firewall of the SAP-specific router must be overcome with valid passwords in case of remote connections. By opening the BW RFC and BW GUI connection types, you can obtain passwords for the RFC and GUI connections.

Passwords

The creation of the two SAP NetWeaver BW services is identical to the creation of the SAP ERP service type. In the service selection, you must select BW GUI Connection (or BW RFC Connection). Regarding the configuration file, bear in mind that the 32xx or 33xx TCP/IP port is used and that you have to release these ports explicitly. The configuration file (*saprouttab*) defines which connections are allowed for the respective ports. For example, if the SAP NetWeaver BW system has instance number 02, the following entries must be available (P = permit):

▶ P <sapservX> <saprouter> 3299

▶ P <sapservX> <target BW system> 3202

▶ P <sapservX> <saprouter> 3399

▶ P <sapservX> <target BW system> 3302

If you want to allow for a connection from any computer to any other computer, you do not have to further define the computers but can specify them with meta characters (*).

14.5.3 HTTPconnect Service Type

If you want to allow GUI access not only to a system but also to Web-based reports for the SAP support, for example, you need the HTTPconnect service. Please note that only the current SAProuter software version supports all services. That means you may have to update your software. After you have created the services as described above, you must define an additional URL for HTTPconnect in the Open/Close Connections area before you open the connection by specifying the contact data and time frame.

For this purpose, expand the URL area, enter a description, for example, "portal access," and select the HTTP Connect – URLAccess service type from the list. Finally, enter the actual URL for your portal or the SAP BEx Web application designer tool report in the *http://<server>.<domain>:<port>/* format (Figure 14.9).

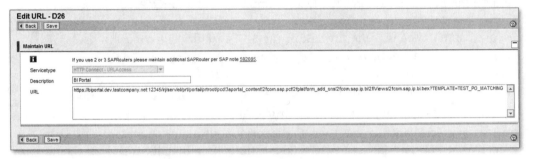

Figure 14.9 URL of an HTTPconnect Connection

Bookmarks If problems occur with Web reports, you should define a direct link to the report as a URL to facilitate the access for the SAP support. You can generate the appropriate link (bookmark) in the SAP BEx Web application designer tool without any problems or copy it from the URL field of the browser after the report has been executed.

14.5.4 Connection to SAP NetWeaver BW Accelerator

SAP provides a new service type, TREX/BIA, to enable the SAP support to access all blades of a distributed SAP NetWeaver BW Accelerator landscape for problem analysis. As a prerequisite for its use, ensure that the saprouttab table contains the correct entry for the SAP NetWeaver BW Accelerator instance. The format of the entry is *P <SAP-SR IP address> < IP server> 3XX09, where XX* in the port number corresponds to the SAP NetWeaver BW Accelerator instance number. The instance number is assigned during the installation process and can be viewed in the TREX administration (Python) under LANDSCAPE • HOSTS • INSTANCE. Generic entries in the "P * * *" format are not valid, because the wildcard (*) only releases ports 3200 and 3299. To set up the service type for the first time, you must also create it in the SAP Service Marketplace. Proceed as follows:

1. Select the TREX/BIA connection and enter the 3XX09 port number for your server.

2. Save the data and then enter the server data by selecting TREX Server: host name, IP address, operating system, and version of the operating system.

Setting up the service type

You open connections with this new service type as described above.

14.6 Customer Messages

The form for entering messages in the support portal under HELP & SUPPORT • PRODUCT ERRORS is divided into the following eight areas:

▶ Status of the message including the message number, the person who sent the message, the person who changed it last, the creation date, and the last change date

▶ Selected system with defined system data and software details

▶ Classification of the message

▶ Specification of the message

▶ Performed troubleshooting

▶ Contact person for the message

▶ Notification settings

▶ Message attachments

The messages entered this way are forwarded to the SAP customer service system, where they are then processed by SAP service employees. Figure 14.10 shows an example of a customer message. It is a message with medium priority regarding the BW-BCT-AP-BP application component, which is intended for messages for the business partner object in Business Content.

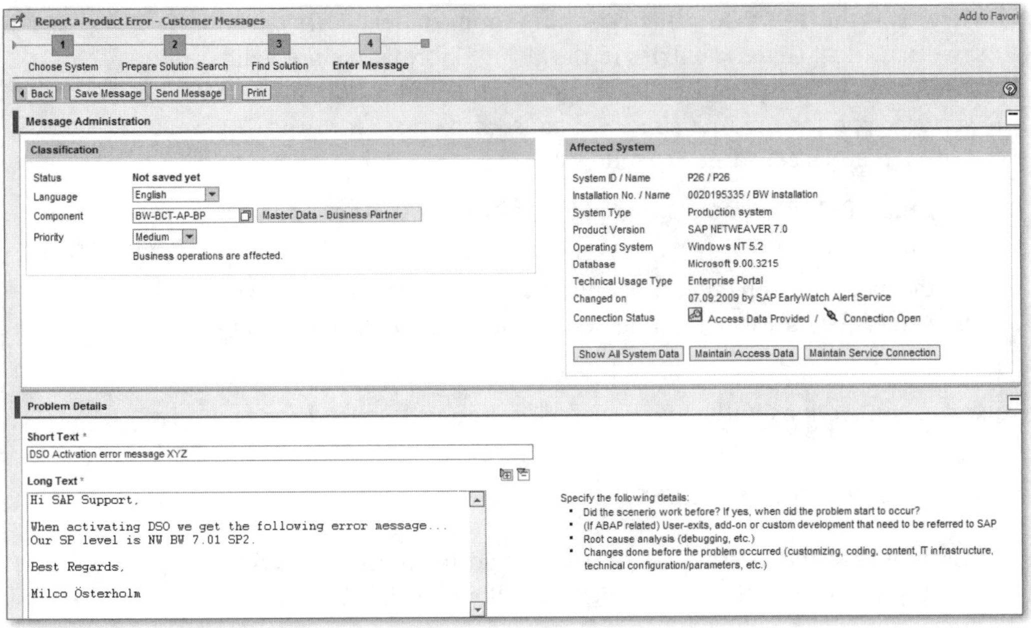

Figure 14.10 Creating a Customer Message

14.6.1 Procedure for SAP NetWeaver BW-Specific Messages

Business Content messages

Before you create a customer message that refers to problems with Business Content, you should again copy objects from Business Content and check whether all affected objects are active.

In a message that refers to problems with this component, specify the following information if possible:

▸ In which systems does the problem occur (SAP NetWeaver BW or OLTP)?

▸ Which SAP NetWeaver BW release and patch status do you have?

▸ Which system release, plug-in release, plug-in patch, and support package statuses do you have?

▸ Enter the logon data and provide access to the system until the problem is solved.

▸ Have notes already been included in the error context? Which notes?

▸ Assign the appropriate authorizations in the system to the SAP support.

- What kind of system is involved here (test or live system)? What is allowed in the system (loading data, installing content, creating documents in OLTP)?

- Enter a step-by-step description with a concrete example so that the problem can be reproduced.

- Which DataSource or InfoSource is affected?

- Which transaction and program is called?

- In which context does the error occur?

- Which data can be used to reproduce the error?

SAP NetWeaver BW warehouse management errors usually occur when the Administrator Workbench (Transaction RSA1) is used. You have to differentiate between two areas here: the data basis that includes the technical objects for the data administration and data staging that affects the administration of the data itself. The following prerequisites and details are inevitable within a message for targeted troubleshooting:

Warehouse management messages

- General:

  - SAP NetWeaver BW release and support package level of the affected system

  - Access data for the system and an open SAP ERP support connection

  - Sufficient authorization for the support user (particularly debugging authorization; authorization for Transactions SM51 and SM50; if process chains are involved, the S_BTCH_ALL authorization; if transports are affected, authorizations at the operating system level are required to implement transport requests)

  - Step-by-step instructions for a reproducible example

  - Long text and error number of the error

  - Specification of already checked notes (for example, regarding the error number)

  - The short dump included as an attachment in the event of runtime errors

- In the data basis area:

  - Specification of the technical names of the objects involved (for example, InfoObject, InfoCube, database tables)

- In case of hierarchies: InfoObject, request, DataSource, hierarchy name, hierarchy ID (if possible), loading method (PSA or IDoc), error messages from the consistency check (error log from the monitor)

  - Specification of the request ID involved (if possible)

- In the data staging area:

  - Specification of the technical names of the objects involved (for example, InfoSource, DataSource, database tables)

  - Specification of the request number (for example, REQU_ E69L5KQJJH8XMT BED11PV2OLR) of an erroneous data request

  - Error analysis in the monitor detail screen including specification of the corresponding messages

  - When process chains are loaded: specification of the log ID of the affected run

  - In case of other errors with source system connections: check the source system and define the error number if possible

- In the MetaData Repository area:

  - In case of transport errors: specification of the transport request and the objects involved

  - Specification of all relevant messages from the activation logs

SAP Business Explorer messages

If errors occur in the SAP Business Explorer area, open the BW GUI and BW RFC service types in addition to the SAP ERP service type and enter concrete information, for example, the technical name of the query and the InfoProvider, so that the error can be reproduced.

If the problem does not occur when the query is simply executed (with Transaction RSRT, for instance), you need an OLAP trace that has been created with Transaction RSRTRACE. Because the SAP NetWeaver BW system stores this trace, you merely have to specify the trace number or recording key data, that is, the time and date of the recording and user ID, to enable the system to determine the corresponding OLAP trace for the remote login.

Basis and installation messages

In case of error messages that refer to the basis or an installation, you should at least specify the support package release and level for the SAP_BW, SAP_ABA, SAP_BASIS, kernel, database, SAP NetWeaver BW frontend, and SAP GUI software components.

14.6.2 Priority

The priority of your message is categorized into low, medium, high, and very high. The corresponding justifications and use cases and the resulting prerequisites, such as the contact availability, are clearly defined.

▶ A message with low priority is justified if normal business processes are not or are only slightly affected. This is caused by a faulty or failed function of the SAP system that is not needed daily or rarely used.

▶ A message with medium priority is justified if normal business processes are affected. This is caused by a faulty or failed function of the SAP system.

▶ A message with high priority is justified if normal business processes are affected to a large extent. Necessary tasks cannot be carried out. This is caused by a faulty or failed function of the SAP system that is urgently needed in the current situation. The message requires fast processing, because a continuous malfunction can result in a serious failure of the entire production business process.

▶ A message with very high priority is justified if normal business processes are seriously affected. Tasks that cannot be delayed cannot be performed in such a case. This occurs, for example, in case of a complete breakdown of a live system or if a pending go-live or upgrade is jeopardized for which no workaround is available.

Always take into account the necessary prerequisites on the customer side for fast processing of messages with very high priority. Immediate remote access to the system affected must be ensured, and a contact person for queries regarding the problem must be available. To ensure 24/7 processing and global SAP support, the problem must be described in English.

14.6.3 Secure Area for Access Data

Never specify access data directly in a customer message. You should use only the secure area to safely specify system logon data in customer messages for remote access to an SAP system (Figure 14.11). The secure area has the following advantages:

▶ As of early 2007, logon data refers to a system and no longer to a message.   Advantages

▸ Logon data is only to be created once for each system and can be used for any message with regard to this system.

▸ You can explicitly assign logon data to a specific message to limit the user view for SAP.

▸ You can change the logon data any time.

▸ A history log stores all data changes and accesses to the secure area.

▸ Customer messages indicate whether logon data has been defined for the system.

You can access and maintain logon data either directly via a customer message by clicking Change User Data or centrally via the system data application by clicking Access Data of the Selected System.

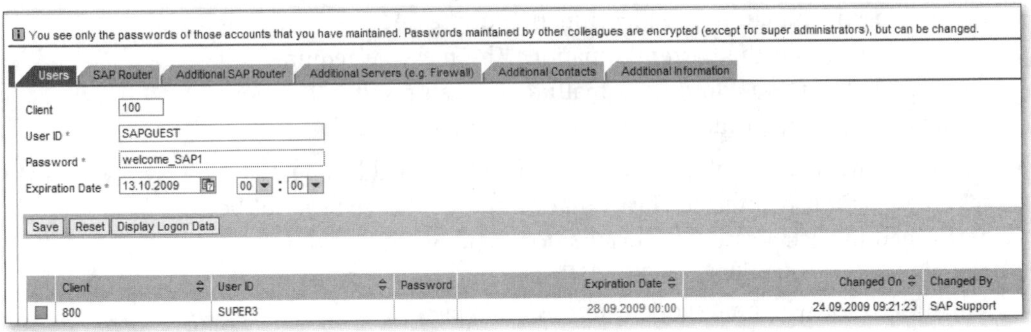

Figure 14.11 Secure Area for Access Data

Click Display Logon Data after you have entered all data. All data specified is displayed in an overview. Only users who entered this data or users with the Maintain All Customer Logon Data authorization can view the stored passwords. Users with the Maintain My Customer Logon Data authorization cannot view the stored passwords of their colleagues. However, they can overwrite the passwords so that the passwords are newly set.

Limited user view   When you create a customer message or process a customer message, you can restrict the usage of the SAP system users for this message by limiting the number of users available for the SAP message processors for this message. To do so, assign one or several users to a specific customer message.

This limitation refers only to SAP system users and does not affect any other users, such as SAProuter users or users of other servers. Users of other systems or installations can also be selected in the limited user view. If users have been explicitly assigned to a message, the process mode of the message displays only these users. No other users are shown. If no user has been explicitly assigned, there is no limitation regarding the visibility of logon data. SAP can view all defined users and passwords for the system.

14.6.4 Faster Processing

Any experienced administrator who frequently creates customer messages has probably been annoyed at least once by first support responses in which issues are queried that are — from the customer perspective — natural or not related to the problem and therefore unnecessary or that recommend procedures that have already been implemented.

In such moments, you should keep in mind that you as the administrator know all conditions and circumstances, of course. You know the system landscape with the exact support package levels and the processes, the technical implementation, and the user behavior for the customer solution and maybe also the history of the problem and previous solution attempts. The SAP support employee has only the information that is provided in the message.

You should generally provide as many pieces of information for the SAP support as possible and lay the technical foundation for best possible support. Although the requirements of the support may heavily depend on the systems involved and the reported problems, you should consider the following factors to ensure fast processing:

▶ Provide detailed description of the scenario with clear technical specifications, such as transactions, programs, dumps, error codes, and error and table names. Attach screenshots to the message if they are useful for reproducing and restricting the problems.

Providing critical information

▶ Give step-by-step instructions to allow for a reproduction of the problem.

▶ Provide an example that is kept as simple as possible and that restricts the problem so that the error can be reproduced (for example, a plain Web report without JavaScript).

▶ Ensure that access via the service connections is possible and, ideally, open all relevant connection types immediately when creating the message.

- ▶ Provide access data with sufficient authorizations in the development or live system.
- ▶ Maintain contact data with a telephone number to enable the SAP support employee to directly contact the person responsible.
- ▶ Ensure that the requirements for patches, plug-ins, add-ons, or specific notes are met.
- ▶ The current version of the BI Diagnostics & Support Desktop Tool must be installed.
- ▶ For best possible support, SAP Solution Manager should be installed.
- ▶ EarlyWatch Alert should be set up and processed respectively, particularly for performance issues.
- ▶ Solution Manager Diagnostics should be available for J2EE-based solutions.

If the processing time of a customer message does not meet the expectations even though all prerequisites have been met and if the project or live operation requires a faster solution of the problem reported, you can still use the escalation option.

14.6.5 Message Escalation

If you want to receive a solution for a customer message that you sent to the SAP support more quickly, you can escalate the message by following an official procedure. In this case, the Customer Interaction Center (CIC) is responsible. You trigger the message escalation process by calling the CIC. The SAP Support Portal merely provides the option to increase or decrease the urgency of a message, but you cannot escalate a customer message. You can find all telephone numbers for the CIC worldwide in SAP Note 560499.

Assessing effects

If you want to escalate a message, you must be prepared for some questions from the SAP escalation group, because the group has to assess the effects of the problems for the enterprise correctly:

- ▶ Live system:
  - ▶ Is the core business affected (financial loss)?
  - ▶ Are comprehensive manual workarounds required?
  - ▶ How many users are involved?
  - ▶ For how long has the problem existed?

- Test/development system:
  - What kind of project are you planning?
  - Go-live date, product, and release? Showstopper: yes or no?
  - Does the problem affect the go-live date?

In addition, you always have to specify a contact person for the message. Have all contact information on hand, for example, office telephone number, mobile phone number, and email address. Also, assign priorities if there is more than one message.

The escalation group then uses the answers to the escalation questions above to determine if the severity of your problem justifies a message escalation. If so, the message is assigned highest priority, and the support employees process it first. In addition, the progress is monitored more precisely. If the message escalation is not justified, the SAP support provides feedback to your message with as much information as possible.

14.7   Additional Functions in the SAP Service Marketplace

The SAP Service Marketplace provides numerous additional functions and information that not only make the daily work of administrators easier, but are critical for ensuring stable system operation.

Very important SAP Notes and the registration of object changes and namespaces are used as examples here. For tasks within a software lifecycle management (SLM) strategy, the Product Availability Matrix (PAM) provides critical information, such as the maintenance end of a specific SAP software release.

14.7.1   SAP Notes Search

SAP Notes are used to avoid and solve errors. For better handling, they are either classified and assigned to software components when they are created or release-independent. The /notes quick link provides direct access to this topic. The input screen has the following functionality:

- Clear search screen with simple input options for search criteria
- Automatic import of the defined system data when you select an SAP system

▶ Display of the SAP Notes that are relevant for your SAP system only

▶ Limit by release-dependent or release-independent notes

▶ Search with linguistic (unclear) or exact search behavior

▶ Default setting specifying the desired results per page, the display, and the sorting of the result page

▶ Template function for storing and reusing popular search queries

Search term You can enter short text, key words, transactions, or a part of the code as search terms, for instance. Wildcards (*) enable you to search for search terms with different endings. Avoid searches with informative terms, such as articles, prepositions, and the like. You can enter the desired search terms into the input field, separated by blanks.

In the Component field, select the component for which you want to search for notes. If you do not know the exact description, you can call a list of all components using the possible entries button. If you also want to browse subordinate components of a specific component, use a wildcard (for example, BC*). Each note is assigned to a primary component and to one, no, or various secondary components. If you enter or select a component, all (primary and secondary) components of a note are browsed.

System-based SAP Notes search You obtain the best search results if you use a system-based SAP Notes search. In this case, the SAP Notes search is linked to the system data application so that only the SAP Notes that are relevant for your system are displayed. SAP Notes of lower support package levels are not displayed, which considerably minimizes the time required to find the appropriate solution. If you use SAP EarlyWatch Alert, the software components, support package levels, and release levels of your system data are updated automatically. The result page has the following functionality:

▶ Result page that can be customized individually: display, number of columns, sorting, and results per page

▶ Searching within the search: refinement of the search by adding search terms

▶ Guided navigation: starting a new search with related search terms

▶ Search for similar SAP Notes

▶ Download and printing of result lists: local storage of the lists as a CSV or HTML file

▶ Download and printing of note texts: local storage and printing of previously selected SAP Notes

▶ Display of relevant SAP TopNotes and search in SDN discussion forums

14.7.2 SAP Software Change Registration

If you want to modify objects in your system that are not contained in the customer namespace, you have to generate a key for the developer or object in the SAP Service Marketplace. Developers have to request a key once and are then registered. The key is queried when the developer changes an SAP object (SAP Source or SAP Dictionary object) for the first time.

The registration of an object (SAP Software Change Registration, SAP SCR) is necessary when the object is changed by a registered development user in your SAP ERP system for the first time. If the object is changed later by a registered user, the key is not queried again.

14.7.3 Namespaces

Traditionally, SAP NetWeaver BW mainly contains two namespaces: The SAP namespace is provided for the development at SAP, and the customer namespace is available to all customers for their custom developments. You have to distinguish between the following cases where naming conflicts may occur:

1. **Distributed development in a group of systems**
   An SAP customer or partner develops various projects in multiple development systems. These projects are transported into a shared consolidation system and forwarded to a shared live system. You have to avoid naming conflicts in the consolidation system here.

2. **Delivery of developments**
   An SAP customer or partner develops enhancements for the standard SAP objects and delivers them to third parties that may implement their own developments. If the vendor and the recipient work with customer namespaces, you can always expect naming conflicts. These naming conflicts must be avoided for the installation (import) of enhancements.

Naming conflicts

In the SAP NetWeaver BW system, the use of namespaces has been possible since Release 3.x. A reserved namespace, such as /ABC/, therefore enables you to separate special developments from developments in the usual customer namespace, A* to Z*, and ensure a distributed development. A typical scenario is the development of a group template that is delivered to other systems in the group organization.

In this case, you have to request both a development namespace and a generation namespace in the SAP Service Marketplace, which are then released in the customer development system after approval by SAP.

Creating namespaces
You use Transaction SE03 to create namespaces with a specification of the developer license and repair license (Figure 14.12).

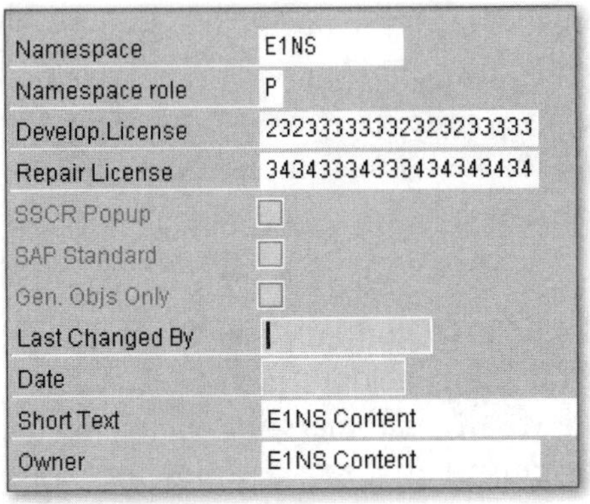

Namespace	E1NS
Namespace role	P
Develop.License	2323333332323233333
Repair License	34343334333434343434
SSCR Popup	☐
SAP Standard	☐
Gen. Objs Only	☐
Last Changed By	
Date	
Short Text	E1NS Content
Owner	E1NS Content

Figure 14.12 Creating a New Namespace

The SAP NetWeaver BW–specific maintenance of namespaces, for example, the assignment of a generation namespace, is implemented in Transaction RSNSPACE (Figure 14.13). This transaction has a transport connection; that is, the entries made are recorded in a request and can thus be transported to a target system. Partner and customer namespaces, such as /ABC/, are written to the RSPSPACE table. The RSNSPACE table is used for standard SAP NetWeaver BW namespaces only, such as /BIO/ and /BIC/.

BW Partner Namespaces					
Namespace	Gen NS	BW appl.	System type	Active	Long descriptio
/E1NS/	/B12/	BW	PAR	X	

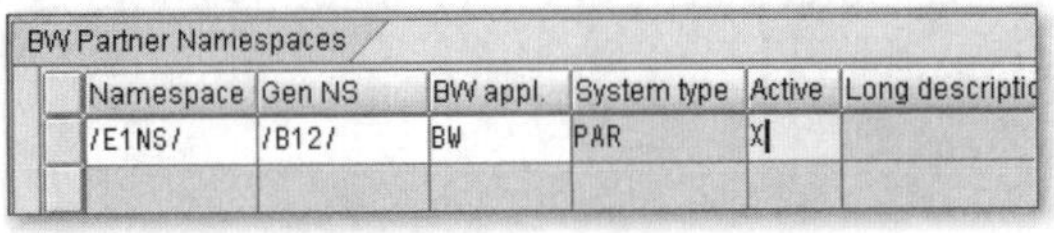

Figure 14.13 Namespace Maintenance in Transaction RSNSPACE

14.7.4 Product Availability Matrix

The Product Availability Matrix (PAM) summarizes technical and general release planning information for all SAP product versions in a clear overview (Figure 14.14). In addition to technical information, such as information on database platforms and operating systems, this overview also contains information on availabilities, maintenance cycles (maintenance end dates and so on), and upgrade options.

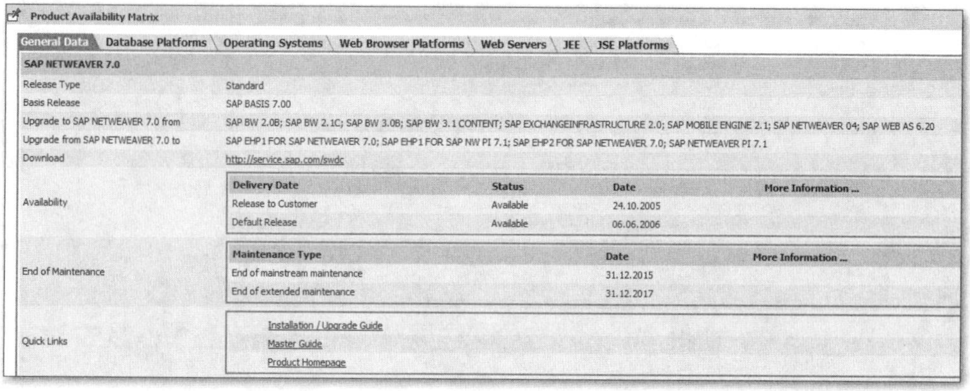

Figure 14.14 Product Availability Matrix

This information for SAP product versions is structured in instances, which are bundles of technically dependent component versions that are installed on a system. For the SAP NetWeaver 7.0 example this means the product version consists of the Application Server ABAP, Application Server Java, Enterprise Portal, Frontend instances, and so on. Application Server ABAP, in turn, mainly consists of the SAP BW 7.00, SAP ABA 7.00 software component versions, and so on. You can access the PAM in the support portal via the */PAM* quick link or the menu path RELEASE & UPGRADE INFO • PRODUCT AVAILABILITY MATRIX.

Instances

14.8 BI Diagnostics & Support Desktop Tool

To process a customer message quickly, the SAP support requires some settings that need to be implemented manually at various points, such as in the SAP J2EE Visual Administrator or UIs of the portal administration. The SAP NetWeaver BI Diagnostics & Support Desktop Tool automates the information gathering process (Figure 14.15). In addition, the tool contains a complete set of all general configuration checks that are necessary for the configuration of BI Java. It also provides information on the causes of configuration problems and instructions for correcting the configuration. As the administrator, you can call the SAP NetWeaver BI Diagnostics & Support Desktop Tool via *<http|https>://<Server>:<Port>/irj/servlet/prt/portal/prtroot/com.sap.ip.bi. supportdesk.default.*

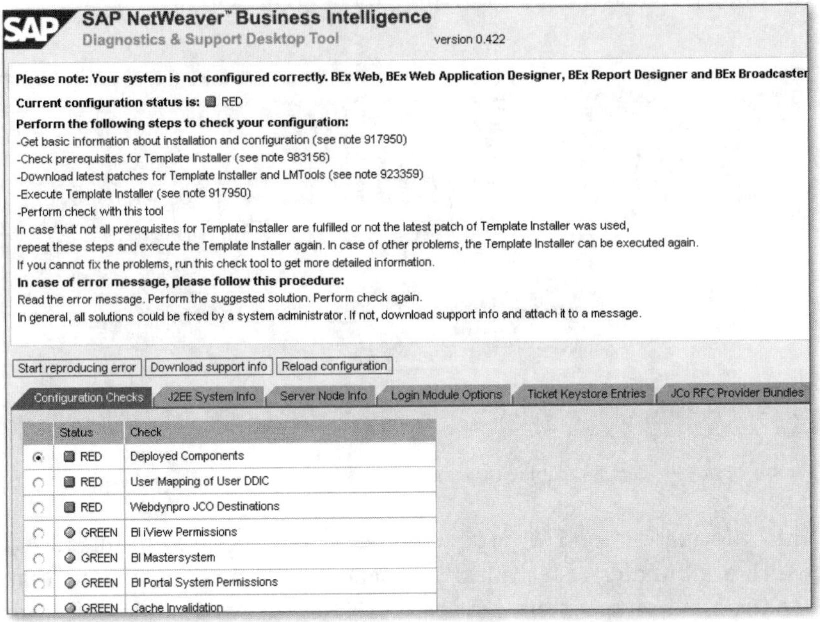

Figure 14.15 SAP NetWeaver BI Diagnostics & Support Desktop Tool

If the initial screen of the tool displays a red traffic light (which indicates a configuration problem), the system provides more information on the configuration problems via a link.

Error reproduction

If a specific error situation is identified that occurs, for example, during the navigation step in BEx Web Application Java, you can start the reproduction of the error. Even if a specific problem that has been reported via a customer message may not be configuration-relevant at first glance, the dependency between a wrong configuration and an error in BEx Web Application Java can hardly be localized if detailed information on technical aspects is missing. For example, Java-based BEx Web Applications can already be called with an incomplete configuration. However, problems may occur if you only call the BEx Broadcaster, because BEx broadcasting is implemented as an ABAP-based BEx Web Application only, and the AS ABAP configuration in the portal system landscape is incorrect. To add all configuration information and the error reproduction information in a customer message, you can download the data to a ZIP file.

14.9   SAP EarlyWatch Alert and other Solutions

It is critical to identify and analyze all factors that affect the performance and stability of a live SAP NetWeaver BW system to manage the system or system landscape proactively and not wait to respond when the system is not available for users. To ensure a good performance and a stable, failsafe system after the going live, you should use the SAP support services, for example, GoingLive Check or SAP EarlyWatch Alert (Figure 14.16).

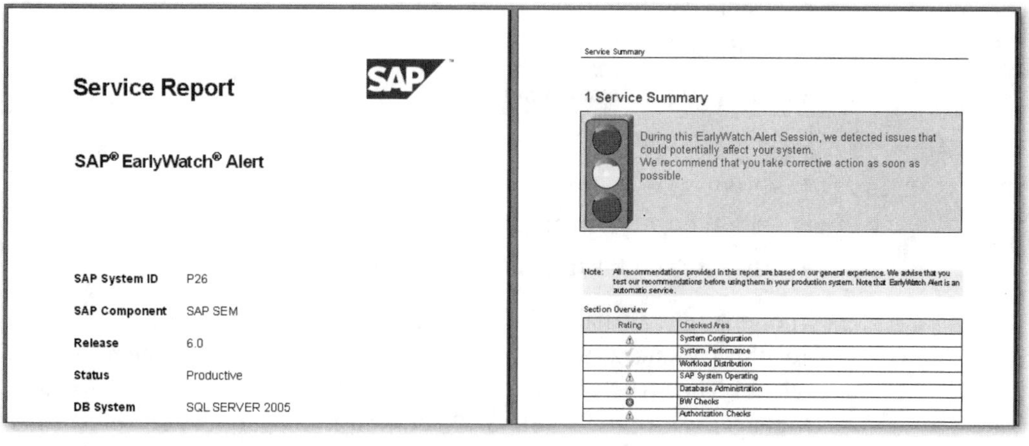

Figure 14.16   SAP EarlyWatch Alert

SAP EarlyWatch Alert periodically monitors the individual components of an overall solution, such as the database or OLAP server. This enables you to identify potential problems early on and avoid impacts on the business processes as a result of fast processing. The following goals are pursued:

Periodical monitoring

- ▶ Avoidance of bottlenecks (disk space, memory, processes, and so on)
- ▶ Early detection of potential problems
- ▶ Automatic and regular monitoring of the performance

561

- Automatic and regular monitoring of critical administrative areas
- Creation of a regular report

In a live system, SAP EarlyWatch Alert should be set up for all components to allow for holistic monitoring of all components and their effects on the performance and stability. You can also implement the service for nonproduction systems (development or test system, for instance); however, note that some events are not relevant here. This includes the results for database backups, for instance.

For reporting, SAP EarlyWatch Alert analyzes the system data and compares it with threshold values. Depending on the analysis, the deviations are indicated with traffic lights in the report in XML format and in the monitoring of SAP Solution Manager. SAP EarlyWatch Alert monitors and analyzes the following component and system areas:

- General status of various components
- System configuration
- Hardware
- Performance development
- Average response times
- Current system load
- Critical error messages and process terminations
- Database administration

The service is available for products that are based on SAP NetWeaver. For the Java stack, SAP J2EE Engine 6.40 is required as the minimum release. The SAP EarlyWatch Alert content is provided in SAP Solution Manager with the ST-SER (SAP Solution Manager Service Tools) component and in ABAP-based source systems with the ST-PI (SAP Solution Tools Plug-In) and ST/A-PI (Application Service Tools) components in the SAP NetWeaver BW system, for instance.

Activation in the Service Data Control Center The Service Data Control Center (SDCC) by SAP manages processes as tasks (Figure 14.17). It manages and logs all performed tasks and enables you to monitor the progress of the individual tasks.

Before you create the tasks via SAP EarlyWatch Alert, you have to define the interval for the service in the customizing. You should send EWA data to SAP every seven days.

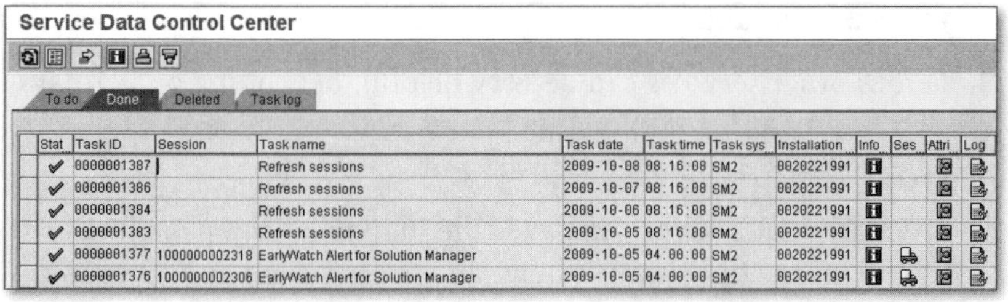

Stat	Task ID	Session	Task name	Task date	Task time	Task sys	Installation	Info	Ses	Attri	Log
✔	0000001387		Refresh sessions	2009-10-08	08:16:08	SM2	0020221991				
✔	0000001386		Refresh sessions	2009-10-07	08:16:08	SM2	0020221991				
✔	0000001384		Refresh sessions	2009-10-06	08:16:08	SM2	0020221991				
✔	0000001383		Refresh sessions	2009-10-05	08:16:08	SM2	0020221991				
✔	0000001377	1000000002318	EarlyWatch Alert for Solution Manager	2009-10-05	04:00:00	SM2	0020221991				
✔	0000001376	1000000002306	EarlyWatch Alert for Solution Manager	2009-10-05	04:00:00	SM2	0020221991				

Figure 14.17 SAP Service Data Control Center (Transaction SDCC)

14.9.1 SAP EarlyWatch Alert in SAP Solution Manager

You should execute SAP EarlyWatch Alert should be executed in SAP Solution Manager. A major advantage of the use of the SAP Solution Manager as a central administration system of all SAP solutions is the central activation and execution of the service for all components, for example, to provide an overview of how often the individual components are evaluated and to be able to compare previous reports with current data. If SAP EarlyWatch Alert detects significant deviations (red alerts), SAP Solution Manager sends a copy of the result report to SAP to determine if an SAP EarlyWatch Check is required to solve the problem. In addition to providing an overview of the system performance, SAP EarlyWatch Alert also serves as a data source for additional SAP support services, such as SAP Solution Manager Assessment and SAP SQL Statement Optimization.

14.9.2 SAP EarlyWatch Alert Processed at SAP

If you cannot process SAP EarlyWatch Alert in your local SAP Solution Manager system, you can configure a restricted SAP EarlyWatch Alert version for ABAP-based systems so that the data is processed at SAP instead. SAP then provides you with the SAP EarlyWatch Alert report via the SAP Service Marketplace. Previously, this procedure was the standard method for SAP EarlyWatch Alert, and it is still available during the transition phase. Because both sessions (in SAP Solution Manager or at SAP) analyze the same data, scheduling both sessions does not provide additional advantages.

Access to EarlyWatch Alert reports

The system creates a service message, which is called a session report, after every service session. This report contains a link to the corresponding service report in the SAP Service Marketplace. Please note that the SAP Service Channel provides only the 12 most recent SAP EarlyWatch Alert reports.

14.9.3 Additional Services

Numerous other services can be very helpful, depending on your system types and project or operation phases. Some of the services that are relevant for the system operation are presented below.

SAP EarlyWatch Check

An SAP EarlyWatch Check analyzes the individual components of the SAP solution, the operating system, and the database and formats the results for the customer with the goal of improving the performance and minimizing the TCO. The checks usually start automatically based on the SAP EarlyWatch Alert result.

SAP GoingLive Check

An SAP GoingLive Check consists of the three service phases, *analysis*, *optimization*, and *verification*, which SAP consultants remotely implement. Its goal is to prepare your SAP solution for go-live in the best possible way and ensure that the solution operates with optimum performance, availability, and maintainability.

SAP Technical Performance Optimization

SAP Technical Performance Optimization focuses on the elimination of performance problems on the platform and hardware side, for example, regarding CPU, storage, database, and storage solutions and the set up of continuous capacity and availability management.

SAP system administration

A review of the SAP system administration analyzes the main aspects of the system operation, such as interface configurations, database administration, backup and recovery, or the administration of SAP liveCache. To meet the requirements of the system administration of the various systems, the service is available as a standard version and as special versions tailored to SAP APO and SAP CRM.

SAP Data Volume Management

SAP provides SAP Data Volume Management (SAP DVM) to support customers in the development of a data volume management strategy and in the monitoring of customer-specific strategies. Using data prevention, data aggregation, data elimination, and data archiving, concepts are defined to organize and monitor the data growth and reduce existing datasets.

SAP Continuity Management Optimization

The SAP Continuity Management Optimization service helps customers perform the challenging task of ensuring a reliable operation of their systems and system landscapes in accordance with the requirements for data and system availability and the organization in case of system failures.

A well-organized administration team is essential for good daily operations and, in particular, for optimal fault handling. In this chapter, we deal with two main issues: ITIL processes and regular tasks in SAP NetWeaver BW systems.

15 Organizing SAP NetWeaver BW Administration Teams

It goes without saying that team members with a good knowledge of all of the topics of relevance to the team are a desirable resource. However, it is also important to use the competencies in a team to the team's best advantage and to ensure that responsibilities and tasks are clearly defined. Because of the stability requirements of SAP NetWeaver BW systems, team administration should be organized in the most efficient way possible — using best practices, for example.

15.1 Teams and Responsibilities

Administration, monitoring, operations, and maintenance tasks can be carried out by a range of entities, from a single-person team to a highly collaborative process in which different tasks are the responsibility of different teams and service providers. Which model is used depends on the complexity of the solution and the technical environment. The operations concept defines participants, roles (such as first-level and second-level support), lines of communication, and communication paths. This concept applies to faults, escalations, and new requirements as well as to daily operations. Clearly defined roles and communication paths are the basis of effective fault management and an efficient change management system.

Usually, administrators (or, as the case may be, general operations and repairs staff) are not involved in development processes, such as those of a new SAP NetWeaver BW solution. It is all the more important then to plan and schedule the resources required for orientation and train-

Know-how transfer and documentation

ing and, if necessary, to hire new employees for the maintenance and operations phase. An orientation process can consist of the following steps:

▸ Work through example scenarios and typical processes.

▸ Fix controlled errors.

▸ Make coaching available — in the form of contact persons in the development department, for example.

It is very important in the initial operations phase of a new solution that the central subject matter experts be available when required. Developers, for example, should be assigned sufficient time to be available to advise and support the system administrators after a project is completed. Also, communication with and support from contact persons in external service provider companies should be arranged and defined in advance (as part of a maintenance contract, for example).

Besides the documentation of the development phases in design and implementation, there should also be technical documentation of the topics of architecture, interfaces, system resources, and system environment, among others. Because not every problem can be solved using documentation alone, it is also important to define which contact people can support which components of the solution.

15.2 Best Practices (ITIL)

The realization that companies and public administration bodies are highly dependent on the availability of information systems led to the establishment of the *Central Computer and Telecommunications Agency (CCTA)* by the British government at the end of the 1980s, with the aim of designing and developing the *IT Infrastructure Library* (ITIL). The main aim of the development process was to define shared best practices for all of the data centers operated by the British government to ensure consistency of operations. The core ITIL publications are as follows.

▸ **Service Strategy**

Core ITIL publications

This is a guide to how services are positioned and defined as strategic values. The principles described here lay the groundwork of the service lifecycle by providing useful guidelines and tips, as well as context-oriented processes on the following lifecycle phases: service design, service transition, service operation, and continual service improvement.

▶ **Service Design**
This is a guide to the design and development of services and service management processes. It consists of design principles and methods for implementing strategic goals in service portfolios and service assets and describes the changes and improvements required to maintain or increase the added value of services across the individual lifecycles to ensure the continuity of these, to achieve the required service level, and to fulfill regulatory requirements.

▶ **Service Transition**
This guide provides support in transferring new or modified services to operations, gives advice on how to effectively implement the requirements of the service strategy in service operation, and makes recommendations on how to avoid the risks of system failure and downtime.

▶ **Service Operation**
This guide describes best practices in the management of service operation. It also contains advice on maintaining service stability and shows you how to make changes in the design, scaling, scope, and service level areas.

▶ **Continual Service Improvement**
This guide combines principles, practices, and methods in quality management and change management and describes process improvements that you can use to optimize service quality. The recommendations in this guide are directly linked in to the service strategy, design, and transition phases.

The Service Operation guide is of most interest to us for the purposes of this book.

15.2.1 Service Desk

The service desk is the single point of contact (SPOC) for all operational inquiries coming from the main body of the company to the IT department. The service desk function is therefore a central one, and as such is a reflection of the overall capacity and capability of the IT department. Typical user inquiries include service requests, such as requests for documentation or internal training; change requests, such as installation requests, moves, and support queries in the case of faults; and requests for user support.

Proactive
information A proactive service desk can also perform operational tasks such as data backups, service monitoring, and training coordination. The user enjoys first-class service and can rely on the service desk to solve his problem satisfactorily and within an acceptable time frame. Proactive information on the status of queries is expected, because the service desk is also the single point of responsibility.

15.2.2 Technical Management

The goal of technical management is to optimally design powerful, cost-efficient technology infrastructures. Being able to provide appropriate mechanisms for maintaining components and making diagnoses when errors occur is an important prerequisite for planning, implementing, and repairing stable infrastructures and thus for supporting business processes.

The technical management function applies to the teams that provide technical expertise and the superordinate IT infrastructure management. These teams fulfill a double role. One is to store and maintain the specialist technical knowledge that is necessary to design, test, operate, and optimize IT services. The other is to provide the appropriate resources for supporting the IT service management lifecycle (ITSM) and to ensure that the required knowledge is transferred in the design, build, transition, and technology operation phases.

15.2.3 Application Management

Regardless of whether the software in question is developed in-house or purchased from a third party, application management has the technical knowledge required to control and monitor the applications. Application management also provides the resources required to support the ITSM lifecycle and thus ensures that knowledge transfer takes place in the proper way, that is, from design to the transition phase to operations.

The application management function is responsible for managing applications during their entire lifecycles. This function is fulfilled by all of the teams that are involved in controlling and supporting operational applications. Application management also plays a central role in designing, testing, and improving the applications that form the functional part of an IT service. Correspondingly, these teams are also involved in development projects.

15.2.4 Operations Management

IT operations is a self-contained function with clearly defined tasks and authorizations within the IT department. Often, however, technical management and application management also fulfill some of the tasks of daily operations and thus form an integrated, cross-team operations function. There is no centralized method of delineating the tasks of operations and engineering, because these tasks depend largely on the maturity and stability of the IT infrastructure.

In companies, the term *operations management* refers to that part of the organization that controls and monitors on the operational level the daily business of the company. This is the case in IT: There is a whole range of activities to do with the provision of IT services, such as those that ensure that systems are started, data backed up, reports printed, and batch jobs run.

The goal of the IT operations management role is to execute ongoing activities and to control and maintain the IT infrastructure so that the services in question can be delivered in accordance with the relevant service-level agreement (SLA) and that support can always be provided.

This role can be summarized as follows. It is comprised of operations control, that is, running console management, job scheduling, backup and restore procedures, print and output management, and maintenance of the various technologies. It also includes facility management, which simply means the management of the physical IT environment. Usually, this environment consists of the data center facilities, recovery sites, and network rooms. Facility management also involves maintaining the air conditioning and electricity supply.

15.3 Operating Documentation

To be able to monitor the operation of the system landscape and ensure that the total cost of ownership is kept low in accordance with the planning details, and to be able to react to all possible emergencies with clearly defined activities and responsibilities, the operating documentation has to specify the appropriate concepts. The following documentation is the minimum that is required:

Concepts
- Operating concept
- Support concept
- Emergency concept
- Transport concept
- Security concept

Before it goes into production use, the operation of an application (on the basis of an SAP NetWeaver BW system, for example) has to be planned and designed, just like the process of application development.

The operating concept provides a comprehensive description of the operation of the application in accordance with specified quality criteria. Parts of the operating concept can and must be partially defined in the early phases of the software lifecycle. In many cases these parts are planning components that are defined in the design phase, such as hardware selection, infrastructure planning, SLA definition, operational organization, and staff costs. The design phase, in particular, results in important tasks and framework conditions that have to be taken into account in the operating concept. The operating concept has the following goals:

- To define the processes, responsibilities, tasks (functional specification), and quality level
- To define the technical and organizational activities in production operations
- To check the costs and cost-effectiveness of the solution

Results of the operating concept
The operating concept also has to deliver the following results:

- Defining the processes, participants, and responsibilities:
  - Define service level management.
  - Clarify the communication paths for reporting errors and faults; define escalation levels.
  - Define roles and responsibilities, including those of external service providers.

- ▶ Define change management tasks.
- ▶ Define the technical and organization activities:
  - ▶ Define the procedure for data backups and restoration (emergency concept).
  - ▶ Design the procedure for automatic system monitoring and application monitoring.
  - ▶ Define the system support concept, including resource planning.
- ▶ Check costs and cost-effectiveness:
  - ▶ Determine and verify all costs involved in providing staff, hardware, licenses, network services, and so on.
  - ▶ Ensure that all costs can be invoiced to the benefit of the (internal) customer.
  - ▶ Create a forecast to establish future cost-effectiveness.
- ▶ Agree on maintenance contracts (with the [internal] customer and any external service providers).

If the system landscape in question is a very complex one, ensure that the system operation is as smooth and homogeneous as possible. If this homogeneity exists even in distributed, independent systems, it will be easier for administrators in the different teams to take on new tasks, which in turn helps to prevent errors.

15.4 Regular Tasks

There is no generic list of tasks to be completed and their frequency, because the tasks depend on individual requirements. Here are some parameters for creating a task list that suits your particular system:

- ▶ How business-critical is availability?
- ▶ What is the data volume, and at what rate does it grow?
- ▶ What is defined in the SLA?
- ▶ How much time and how many staff members are available?
- ▶ How important is good performance?
- ▶ What functionalities (such as planning) are used?
- ▶ How stable is the system historically?

Regular tasks The most important thing is that the tasks are defined and responsibilities assigned. You can use Table 15.1 as an initial template for dividing up daily, weekly, and monthly tasks into separate areas. Both the tasks and their frequency can be adapted to requirements on a rolling basis and expanded and corrected in accordance with any problems that may arise. Thus, it is much more important (that is, more business-critical) to check the load processes at the end of the year, for example, because critical business planning and data consolidation may be carried out on the basis of the loaded data.

Area	Task	Frequency
General remarks	EarlyWatch Alert	Weekly
Basis	Jobs	Weekly
	Monitoring	Daily
Applications	Load processes	Daily
	Query performance	Weekly
Performance	Compression	Daily
	Statistics	Daily
	Indexes	Weekly
	Status of InfoCube data with report SAP_INFOCUBE_DESIGNS	Monthly
	OLAP cache	Daily
	Aggregate/SAP NetWeaver BW Accelerator	Daily
	Delete aggregate	Quarterly
Information Lifecycle management (ILM)	Archiving	Monthly
	PSA data	Weekly
	DTP temporary storage	Weekly
	Admin tables	Weekly
	SAP NetWeaver BW statistics	Quarterly
	tRFC queues	Weekly
	Reporting objects	Quarterly
	Temporary objects	Monthly
Data quality	RSRV tests	Weekly

Table 15.1 Table 15.1 Sample List of Regular Tasks

In addition to a list, it is also useful to teams such as the administration team to have a central calendar in which all tasks are entered (Figure 15.1). Also, the completion of individual activities should be logged (at least in abbreviated form), so that resources and results can be tracked.

Central calendar

Figure 15.1 BW Administration Calendar

A   Transactions, Reports, and Function Modules

Transaction	Description
BWCCMS	SAP NetWeaver BW Monitors in CCMS
CCMSBISETUP	Setup for extraction from CCMS/CPH
RSBATCH	BI background banagement
RSDODADMIN_DOC	Maintenance of SAP NetWeaver BW eocuments
RSM37	BI view for jobs
RSRV	Analysis and repair of SAP NetWeaver BW Objects
RZ20	CCMS
RZ21	Settings for monitoring
RZ23N	Central performance history
SE30	Runtime analysis
SICF	ICF services management
SIGS	IGS management
SLG0, SLG1, SLG2	Management of application logs
SM12	Lock management
SM21	System log
SM37	Job overview
SM49	Operating system commands
SM59	RFC destinations
SMICM	ICM monitor
SOAMANAGER	Administration of Web services (new)
SPRO	Customizing
ST01	System trace
ST03G	Global System Load Monitor
ST05	Performance analysis
ST07	Application monitor
WSADMIN, WSCONFIG	Administration of Web services (old)

Table A.1 Basic Transactions

Report/Function Module	Description
GRAPHICS_IGS_ADMIN	IGS management
RSSM_TRACE_SWITCH	Settings for the system log
RSPARAM, RSPFPAR	Profile parameter
RSA1_TRFC_OPTION_SET	Settings for tRFC outbound scheduling of S-API
SBAL_DELETE	Deletion of application logs

Table A.2 Basic Reports and Function Modules

Transaction	Description
BDLS	Conversion of logical system names
RSTPRFC	Destination for postimport processing
RSOR	Transport connection in Transaction RSA1
RSSGPCLA	Maintenance of program classes (for instance, Generation flag)
SCC4	Client maintenance (changeability, among others)
SE06	System change option
SE10	Transport organizer
SNOTE	SAP Notes
SPAM	Support Package Manager
SPAU	Adjustment of modified repository objects
SPDD	Adjustment of modified dictionary objects
STMS	Transport management system

Table A.3 Software Lifecycle Management – Transactions

Transaction	Description
AS_AFB	Archive file browser
DB02	Display missing indexes
DB15	Table and archiving objects
DBACOCKPIT	Central database monitor
RSDANLCON	Nearline storage connections
SAR_SHOW_MONITOR	Data Archiving Monitor
SARA	Archiving
SARI	Archive Information System

Table A.4 Databases, Indexes, and Archiving – Transactions

Transaction	Description
SE11	Creating indexes
ST04	Analyzing quality of indexes
TAANA	Table analysis

Table A.4 Databases, Indexes, and Archiving – Transactions (Cont.)

Report/Function Module	Description
RSDU_ANALYZE_TABLE	Creating statistics

Table A.5 Databases, Indexes, and Archiving – Reports and Function Modules

Transaction	Description
RSA3	Extractor checker
RSA5	Install DataSources from BCT (Business Content)
RSA7	Delta queue
RSMO	Extraction monitor
RSPC	Maintenance of process chains
RSPCM	Process chain monitor
RSRDA	RDA monitor
SBIW	Customizing of extraction
SMQS	qRFC monitor

Table A.6 Source System, Extraction, and Loading Processes – Transactions

Report/Function Module	Description
RSPC_DISPLAY_JOBS	Jobs in process chains
RSSTATMAN_CHECK_CONVERT_DTA	InfoProvider status management
RSSTATMAN_CHECK_CONVERT_PSA	PSA status management

Table A.7 Source System, Extraction, and Loading Processes – Reports and Function Modules

Transaction	Description
RSD1	Maintenance of InfoObjects
RSDMD_CHECKPRG_ALL	Checking characteristics

Table A.8 Master Data – Transactions

Report/Function Module	Description
RSD_IOBJ_GET	Information on InfoObjects

Table A.9 Master Data – Reports and Function Modules

Transaction	Description
DELETE_FACTS	Selective deletion
LISTSCHEMA	Display InfoCube structure
LISTCUBE	Direct access to InfoCube data
RSDCUBEM	Processing of InfoCubes
RSDDAGGRCHECK	Aggregate check
RSDDBIAMON, RSDDBIAMON2	SAP NetWeaver BW Accelerator Monitor
RSDDV	Maintenance of aggregates
RSDIPROP	InfoProvider properties
RSDMPRO	Editing MultiProviders
RSDODS	Editing DSOs
RSODSO_BRKPNT	DSO breakpoints
RSODSO_RUNTIME	DSO runtime measurement
RSODSO_SETTINGS	DSO settings
RSODSO_SHOWLOG	DSO logs
TREXADMIN	TREX monitoring and administration

Table A.10 InfoProviders, Aggregates, and SAP NetWeaver BW Accelerator – Transactions

Report/Function Module	Description
GET_ODS_OSS_INFORMATION	Information on requests in DSOs
RSDDK_AGGREGATE_DIRECT_FILL	Filling an aggregate
RSDDS_AGGREGATES_MAINTAIN	Hierarchy and attribute change run
RSDDK_CHECK_AGGREGATE	Aggregate check
RSD_CUBE_GET	Information on InfoCubes
SAP_AGGREGATES_CONDENSE	Compressing all aggregates of an InfoCubes
SAP_INFOCUBE_DESIGNS	List of InfoCubes

Table A.11 InfoProviders, Aggregates, and SAP NetWeaver BW Accelerator – Reports and Function Modules

Transaction	Description
GRAPHICS_IGS_ADMIN	IGS administration
MDXTEST	Testing MDX statements
RRMX	BEx Analyzer
RRMXP	Executing workbooks
RSBB_URL_PREFIX_GET	URL display
RSRD_ADMIN	Broadcasting Administration (bookmarks)
RSRT, RSRT2	Query Monitor
RSRTRACE	Trace tool
RSTT	Trace tool for SAP NetWeaver BW reporting
RSZDELETE	Deletion of queries
RSZT	Testing of function modules of reporting
SCOT	SAPconnect Administration (for instance, for emails)
SMICM	Internet Communication Manager (ICM)
SICF	Services (Internet Communication Framework, ICF)

Table A.12 Reporting – Transactions

Report/Function Module	Description
COMPONENT_RESTORE	Recovery of SAP NetWeaver BW 3.x versions
RSRD_BOOKMARK_ REORGANISATION	Managing bookmarks
RSWR_CACHE_INVALIDATE	Invalidation of the portal cache
RSZ_X_COMPONENT_GET	Display of a component with all dependent elements
RSZ_X_INFO_OBJECTS_GET	List of all InfoObjects of an InfoCube
RSZ_X_INFOCUBES_GET	List of InfoCubes by InfoAreas
RSZ_X_QUERY_GET	Display of query properties

Table A.13 Reporting – Reports and Function Modules

Transaction	Description
PFCG	Role maintenance
RSECADMIN	Analysis authorizations
RSECPROT	Protocols for analysis authorizations
RSRAM	Reporting agent monitor
RSUDO	Run report as another user
SU01	User administration
SUIM	User Information System
SUPC	Generation of profiles

Table A.14 Authorizations – Transactions

Report/Function Module	Description
RSEC_GET_USERNAME	Determining the user name in customer exits
PFCG_ORGFIELD_CREATE	Creating organizational levels
PFCG_TIME_DEPENDENCY	Reconciling User Master Data

Table A.15 Authorizations – Reports and Function Modules

Transaction	Description
ALRTCATDEF	Alert categories
ALRTINBOX	Alert Inbox
BD52	Maintenance of message types
RSANWB	Analysis processes
RSDDSTAT	Settings of updating statistics
RSDMWB	Data Mining Workbench
RSNSPACE	SAP NetWeaver BW–specific namespaces
RSTCC_INST_BIAC	Activating the BI Administration Cockpit

Table A.16 Other Transactions

Report/Function Module	Description
RSTCC_ACTIVATE_ADMIN_COCKPIT	Activating the BI Administration Cockpit
RTCCTOOL	Service tool

Table A.17 Other Reports and Function Modules

B   Glossary

ABAP   Advanced Business Application Programming. Programming language of the SAP system to develop applications programs.

Activation queue (initial table of DataStore objects)   New data is stored in this table before it is activated. Its structure is similar to that of a PSA table: The key is built from the request, data package, and data record number. After all of the requests in the activation queue have been successfully activated, they are deleted from the activation queue.

ADK   See Archive Development Kit.

Aggregate   Stores the dataset of a BasicCube redundantly and persistently in a summarized form in the database. Because aggregates use the same form of storage (fact and dimension tables) as BasicCubes, they are often called aggregate cubes. Aggregates enable you to access BasicCubes quickly for reporting. Thus, aggregates help improve performance. Because a BasicCube can possess several aggregates, the optimizer of the OLAP processor automatically accesses the most appropriate aggregate during execution of a query. The decision to use a BasicCube or an aggregate for reporting is not transparent to the end user. Information on aggregates, such as technical, content, and status properties, are stored in table RSDDAGGRDIR.

ALE   See Application Link Enabling.

Alert Monitor   A monitoring tool for displaying exceptions whose threshold values have been exceeded or have not been reached. The exceptions that occur are found in background processing with the help of the reporting agent. They are then displayed in the alert monitor as a follow-up action. Exceptions are displayed in the BEx Analyzer and in the reporting agent scheduler of the Administrator Workbench. Exceptions can be displayed as an alert monitor in a Web application.

Application Link Enabling (ALE)   ALE supports the configuration and operation of distributed application systems — between SAP systems themselves and between SAP systems and external systems. For communication (data exchange) among distributed application systems, ALE provides tolls and services such as consistency checks, monitoring of data transfer, error handling, and synchronous and asynchronous connections. It thus guarantees controlled data exchange among the distributed application systems and consistent data storage.

Application process   A process that is automated in process chain maintenance. Example: a data loading process or an attribute change run.

Application server   A computer on which at least one SAP instance runs.

Archive Development Kit (ADK)   The ADK of mySAP Technology – Basis is used for archiving. The ADK provides the runtime environment for archiving. You mainly use it to read and write data to and from archive files. The ADK guarantees platform and release independence for archived data.

Archiving   Data archiving enables you to archive data from basic InfoCubes and DataStore objects (tables with active data). In other words, you can store the data as a flat structure in a file system and delete it from the basic InfoCube or DataStore object.

Archiving object All archiving requires archiving objects that describe related business data with a data structure and that are used to define and execute reading, writing, and deleting in the context of the archiving process. They are the link between the ADK and SAP NetWeaver BW objects.

Background See Background processing.

Background processing Processing that does not take place on the screen. Data is processed in the background while other functions can be executed in parallel on the screen. Background processes have the same priority as online processes, although they are not visible to users and run without immediate user interactions (that is, there is no dialog).

BAPI See Business Application Programming Interface.

BCT. See Business Content.

Business Application Programming Interface (BAPI) BAPIs are open, standard interfaces defined at the application layer (Transaction BAPI). These interfaces provided by SAP enable communication between SAP systems and applications developed by third parties. From a technical viewpoint, calling a BAPI calls a function module with RFC or tRFC.

Business Content (BCT) An important advantage of SAP NetWeaver BW over other data warehouse solutions is Business Content (BCT) that SAP delivers and continues to develop. BCT involves a comprehensive, predefined information model for the analysis of business processes. It contains the entire definition of all required SAP NetWeaver BW objects, including InfoAreas, InfoObject catalogs, roles, workbooks, query elements, InfoCubes, InfoObjects, DataStore objects, transformations, currency translation types, extractors, DataSources, and so on.

BCT for SAP source systems is imported with plug-ins. If SAP NetWeaver BW systems are connected to other SAP NetWeaver BW systems as source systems, the import of plug-ins is not required. Before you can use elements of BCT, you must adopt or activate them explicitly. You do so with Transaction SBIW in the source system and with Transaction RSORBCT in the SAP NetWeaver BW system.

CCMS See Computing Center Management System.

Change and Transport System (CTS) The Change and Transport System provides the tools to organize development projects in Customizing and in the ABAP Workbench and transport the changes between SAP systems and their clients. The CTS consists of the following blocks: Transport Organizer, Transport Management System, and Transport Tools.

Change log (output table of a Data-Store object) During an activation run, the modifications are stored in the change log. The change log thus contains all of the complete (activation) history of the modifications because the contents of the change log are not automatically deleted. If the connected data targets are supplied from the DataStore object in a delta process, the data targets are updated from the change log. The change log is a PSA table and can be maintained in the PSA tree of the AWB. Accordingly, the change log has a technical key derived from the request, data package, and data record number.

Common Programming Interface Communication (CPI-C) Programming interface — the basis for synchronous, system-to-system, program-to-program communication.

Compress Every basic InfoCube possesses a data package dimension table (set by the system) that stores the SID for the OREQUID (request ID) technical characteristic. Every load process fills this dimension table. As a result, the fact table stores data with a higher level of detail than required from a business viewpoint. Depending on the modeling of the basic InfoCubes, the frequency of load processes, and the composition of loaded data, the level of detail can significantly affect the volume of data in the basic InfoCubes. After the disappearance of the request ID, the data volume can be reduced considerably without having any disadvantages from the business perspective. The Compress function fills the E table with data from the F table. The entire F table or only an older portion of the requests can be compressed. New requests are written to the F table and can then be compressed. The compression of aggregates behaves similarly. The disadvantage of compression is that it cannot be reversed.

Computing Center Management System (CCMS) Tool to monitor, control, and configure the SAP system. The CCMS supports 24/7 system administration functions. You can use it to analyze the system load and monitor the distributed resource requirements of the system components.

CPI-C See Common Programming Interface Communication.

CTS See Change and Transport System.

Database server Computer on which (at least) one database instance is located.

Data Dictionary (DDIC) The (ABAP) Data Dictionary enables central description and management of all the data definitions used in the system. The DDIC is completely integrated into the ABAP Workbench. It supports the definition of user-defined types (for example, data elements, structures, and table types). You can also define the structure of database objects (tables, indexes, and views) in the DDIC. You can use this definition

for automatic creation of the objects in the database.

Data granularity Data granularity describes the level of detail of data. Very detailed data has low granularity; increasing aggregation produces higher granularity. Granularity affects disk space, the quantity of information, and read performance. In SAP NetWeaver BW, detailed data for reporting is usually stored in DataStore objects; aggregated data is stored in InfoCubes or aggregates.

Data Manager Part of the OLAP processor: It executes the database accesses that result from the definition of a query. Part of warehouse management: It writes data to the database.

Data Mart Interface The Data Mart Interface enables updating data from one InfoProvider into another InfoProvider. If you exchange data between SAP NetWeaver BW systems, the system that delivers the data is called the source BW; the receiving system is called the target BW. Individual SAP NetWeaver BW systems in such a landscape are called data marts.

An export DataSource is required for transferring data from a source BW to a target BW (or within an SAP NetWeaver BW system in which the source BW is identical to the target BW). Export DataSources for InfoCubes and DataStore objects contain all characteristics and key figures of the InfoProvider. Export DataSources for master data contain the metadata for all attributes, texts, and hierarchies of an InfoObject.

DataSource Comprise of a quantity of fields in the SAP NetWeaver BW system offered in a flat structure, the extract structure, to transfer data. The Data-Source also describes the properties of the corresponding extractor in terms of transferring data into the SAP NetWeaver BW system. A DataSource describes a business unit of master data (material master data, for example) and transaction data (sales data, for example). From the viewpoint of the source system, meta-information (fields and field descriptions of the master and transaction data and programs) belongs to each DataSource; the meta-information describes how the extraction is executed. This information is specific to the source system; that is, a DataSource depends on the source system.

Data staging   Formatting process for retrieving data in SAP NetWeaver BW.

Data transfer process (DTP)   DTPs serve to update data into data targets. They have been available since SAP NetWeaver BI Release 7.0. DTPs always connect persistent objects and are thus involved in each transformation. Compared to the InfoPackage used in SAP NetWeaver BW 3.x, the error handling feature of data transfer processes has been improved.

Data warehouse (DWH)   A system that stores decision-relevant data in a subject-oriented, nonvolatile, and time-related manner. The functions of a data warehouse are to combine data from sources within an enterprise and outside of it, to cleanse the data, to consolidate the data, and to make it available consistently with analysis, reporting, and evaluation tools. The knowledge gained in this manner creates the foundation for decision-making that applies to the control of a company. A data warehouse is thus a system primarily used to support enterprise control. The integration of OLAP tools in a DWH system is not mandatory. Nevertheless, manufacturers currently offer more and more DWH systems with integrated OLAP tools. Such DWH systems are often called OLAP systems or DWH solutions. Accordingly, SAP NetWeaver BW is a DWH solution.

DDIC   See Data Dictionary.

Deadlock   Several transactions keep locking themselves while each waits for the other to release blocked objects.

Delta process   Extractor feature. It specifies how the data is to be transferred. As a DataSource attribute, the delta process specifies how the DataSource data is to be transmitted to the data target. The user can determine, for example, with which data targets a DataSource is compatible, how the data can be updated, and how serialization is to take place.

Delta queue   Data storage in the SAP NetWeaver BW source system. Data records are automatically written to the delta queue in the source system with a posting procedure or are written after a data request from SAP NetWeaver BW via extraction with a function module. The data is transferred to SAP NetWeaver BW during a delta requirement of the SAP NetWeaver BW scheduler.

Delta update   A delta update requests only data that has been created since the last update. It fills the corresponding data targets with the (new) data. Before you can request a delta update, you must first initialize the data process. A delta update is independent of the DataSource. In SAP source systems, the DataSource properties are stored in the ROOSOURCE and RODELTAM tables; in SAP NetWeaver BW systems, it is stored in the RSOLTPSOURCE table.

DIAG   See Dynamic information and action gateway.

Dialog work process   An SAP work process used to process user requests that run in dialog mode.

Dimension   The grouping of logically related characteristics into one generic term. A total of 248 characteristics can be combined within one dimension. From a technical viewpoint, a dimension consists of a basic InfoCube from a dimension table (if it is not a line item dimension), SID tables, and master data tables. During definition of an InfoCube, characteristics are summarized into dimensions to store them in a table of the star schema (dimension table). See also Line item dimension.

Dimension identification (DIMID) The relationship between a fact table and its dimension tables to a basic InfoCube is created with a system-generated INT4 key, also called DIMIDs. During loading of transaction data into the basic InfoCube, DIMID values are assigned nonambiguously: Each DIMID value is assigned unambiguously to a combination of SID values of the various characteristics.

DIMID See Dimension identification.

Dispatcher Coordinating process of the work processes of an instance.

DTP See Data transfer process.

DWH See Data warehouse.

Dynamic Information and Action Gateway (DIAG) Communication protocol between SAP GUI and dialog work processes on the SAP application level.

ETL process Extraction transformation loading; the loading process from a source system through to the multidimensional structures (InfoCubes) of a data warehouse. The extraction process involves the actual data request; the transformation process cleanses and consolidates the incoming data. Loading refers to the final process of updating the data in the multidimensional data containers.

Event A signal to background control that a specific state in the SAP system has been reached. Background control then starts all of the processes waiting for the event.

Export DataSource See Data mart interface.

Fact table A basic InfoCube consists of two fact tables, each of which stores the key figures: the F table that is partitioned with regard to the request ID and the compressed E table without the request ID.

Full update A full update requests all of the data that corresponds to the selection criteria specified in the selection criteria. Unlike with a delta update, every DataSource supports a full update.

Generation template A template from which a program is generated. A generation template is used when the desired program cannot be written generically and therefore must be generated anew and appropriately for each new situation.

Granularity See Data granularity.

High availability Property of a service or a system to remain in live operation for a large proportion of the time. High availability for an SAP system means that unplanned and planned downtimes are reduced to a minimum. Good system administration is decisive here. You can reduce unplanned downtime by using preventive hardware and software solutions that are designed to reduce single points of failure in the services that support the SAP system. You can reduce the planned downtime by optimizing the scheduling of necessary maintenance activities.

Hot package See Support package.

HTTP See Hypertext Transfer Protocol.

Hypertext Transfer Protocol (HTTP) Protocol to transfer data between a Seb server and the Web client.

IDoc See Intermediate document.

InfoPackage In SAP NetWeaver BW 3.x, InfoPackages are used to request data from a source system and to update this data in data targets. As of SAP NetWeaver BI 7.0, however, InfoPackages are only responsible for requesting data, whereas the data update is carried out by a data transfer process.

Instance SAP instance. An administrative unit combines processes of an SAP system that offer one or more services. An SAP instance consists of a dispatcher and one or more SAP work processes for each of the services, as well as a common set of SAP buffers in the shared memory. The dispatcher manages processing requests, and work processes execute these requests. Each instance provides at least one dialog service and a gateway. Optionally, the dispatcher can provide additional services. However, there must be only one instance that provides the SAP lock management service.

Intermediate document (IDoc) Data contained for the exchange of data among SAP systems, non-SAP systems, and external systems. It uses ALE technology. IDocs are used to load data into the SAP NetWeaver BW system if the PSA transfer method was selected in the maintenance of the transfer method.

Internet Transaction Server (ITS) The interface between the SAP system and a Web server for generating dynamic HTML pages.

ITS See Internet Transaction Server.

Line item dimension Characteristics can be defined as line items; that is, no additional characteristics can be assigned to a dimension along with this characteristic. Such a dimension is called a line item dimension (i.e., degenerated dimension). Unlike a typical dimension, a line item dimension does not receive a dimension table. The SID table of the line item is linked directly with the fact table over a foreign-primary key relationship. This option is used if a characteristic, such as an order number, has a large quantity of values. Using this option can improve the performance of queries.

Logical Unit of Work (LUW) From the viewpoint of business logic, an LUW is an indivisible sequence of database operations that conform to the ACID principle (according to which transactions must be Atomic, Consistent, Isolated, and Durable). From the viewpoint of a database system, this sequence represents a unit that plays a decisive role in securing data integrity.

LUW See Logical Unit of Work.

MDX See Multidimensional expressions.

Metadata Metadata includes data and information about data that describes the origin, history, and other aspects of the data. Metadata enables effective use of the information stored in SAP NetWeaver BW for reporting and analysis.

Metadata repository Contains the various classes of metadata. This type of data storage and presentation results in a consistent and homogeneous data model across all source systems. The metadata repository is comprised of all metaobjects (InfoCubes, InfoObjects, queries, and so on) in the SAP NetWeaver BW system and their relationships to each other.

MOLAP See Multidimensional online analytical processing.

Multidimensional expressions (MDX) Query language for queries on data stored in multidimensional cubes.

Multidimensional Online Analytical Processing (MOLAP) Multidimensional OLAP. Multidimensional data storage in special data structures based on arrays or cubes. MOLAP is mostly used in comparison with or as an alternative to ROLAP. See also OLAP.

Myself System A system connected to itself for data extraction over the data mart interface. Such a connection means that data from data targets can be updated to additional data targets. See also Data mart interface.

OLAP See Online analytical processing.

OLTP See Online transaction processing.

Online analytical processing (OLAP) The core of this software technology is multidimensional retrieval of data. Multidimensionality allows creation of very flexible query and analysis tools that enable rapid, interactive, and flexible access to the relevant information.

Online Service System (OSS) One of SAP's central service and support systems. All SAP customers and partners can use it; however, new service offers are provided exclusively via the SAP Service Marketplace.

Online Transaction Processing (OLTP) The core of this software technology is the relational retrieval of data for processing and the documentation of business processes (billing and inventory management, for example). However, the required standardization makes the queries more and more complex because many tables must be read.

OSS See Online Service System.

Persistent staging area (PSA) The PSA represents the initial view into SAP NetWeaver BW architecture. It consists of transparent database tables (PSA tables) that can be used for (temporary) storage of unmodified data from the source system. One PSA is created for each DataSource and source system. The key fields of the PSA consist of the request, data package, and data record number.

Profile generator Tool for generating profiles in role maintenance. The authorization profiles are generated automatically based on the activities in a role.

PSA. See Persistent staging area.

P Table Master data table for time-independent master data.

Relational online analytical processing (ROLAP) The storage of multidimensional data in a relational database: in tables organized in a star schema. MOLAP is the opposite model. See also: Online analytical processing.

Remote function call (RFC) You can use RFC to transfer data reliably between SAP systems and programs you have developed yourself. RFCs call a function module in another SAP system, an SAP NetWeaver BW system, or a program you have developed or within an SAP system. The data is transmitted with TCP/IP or X.400 as a byte stream. If the call is asynchronous, this is referred to as transactional RFC (tRFC).

RFC. See Remote function call.

ROLAP. See Relational online analytical processing.

Shared memory Main memory area that can be accessed by several operating system processes, for example, by all work processes of an instance. Also used in the area of relational database management systems (RDBMS). In this context, it also refers to the main memory area shared by the RDBMS processes.

SID See Surrogate identification.

Support package Set of corrections for errors provided by SAP for a defined release status of an SAP component (previously: hot package).

Surrogate identification (SID) System-generated INT4 keys. An SID key is generated for each characteristic. This assignment is implemented in an SID table for each characteristic: The characteristic is the primary key of the SID table. The SID table is linked to the related master data tables (if present) via the characteristic key. If a characteristic is assigned to a basic InfoCube when it is created, the SID table of the characteristic is linked to the corresponding dimension table after the activation of the basic InfoCube.

SID values are generated during loading of master data or transaction data and written to the appropriate SID tables. They are also written to the dimension tables for InfoCubes. The use of INT4 keys (SID and DIMID key) enables faster access to the data than long alphanumeric keys do. The SID technique in the SAP NetWeaver BW star schema also enables use of master data across basic InfoCubes.

Surrogate index A special SAP NetWeaver BW index of all key figures of a fact table. The surrogate index is created on a fact table in place of the primary index. Unlike the primary index, the surrogate index does not have a `UNIQUE` limitation. Reporting is based on one-dimensional tables; that is, analysis is limited to one dimension with its attributes. In contrast to OLAP reporting, you can arrange columns as required during the design of a query in tabular editing mode of the BEx Query Designer. For example, you can place a characteristics column between two key figure columns. The column presentation is fixed and is set at the time of design.

TCT See Technical content.

Technical Content (TCT) TCT makes the required SAP NetWeaver BW objects and tools available for the use of the BI Administration Cockpit. The BI Administration Cockpit is a tool for the analysis and optimization of processes such as access time to data with queries and loading times. The data of the SAP NetWeaver BW statistics is stored in SAP NetWeaver BW via a MultiProvider that is based on several SAP NetWeaver BW basic InfoCubes. TCT is transferred in the same manner as Business Content.

TemSe Temporary sequential objects. Data storage for output management.

T-logo object Logical transport object. A T-logo object consists of the total of several table entries that are transported together. Example: The InfoObject T-logo object consists of table entries of the InfoObject table, the characteristics

table, the text table, and the basic characteristics table.

Transformation In SAP NetWeaver BI 7.0, the transformation replaces the transfer and update rules that are used in earlier releases. It is used to transform source fields into target fields and provides a higher degree of flexibility in the update process.

Transport domain Logical group of SAP systems to which defined rules apply for transport. The Transport Domain Controller exercises control over the transport domain.

UD Connect SAP NetWeaver BW component that enables you to access all relational multidimensional data sources via SAP NetWeaver AS J2EE connectivity. To connect to the data sources, UD Connect (Universal Data Connect) uses the Bi Java connectors as a resource adapter. The data can either be transferred to SAP NetWeaver BW or read directly via a RemoteCube.

Work process The application services of the SAP system process-specific processes, for example, for dialog management, updating of change documents, background processing, spooling, or lock management. Work processes are assigned to dedicated application servers.

XML for Analysis A protocol specified by Microsoft to exchange analytical data between client applications and servers via HTTP and SOAP as a service on the web. XML for Analysis is not limited to a specific platform, application, or development language.

X Table Attribute SID table for time-independent master data.

Y Table Attribute SID table for time-dependent master data.

C   Bibliography

Banner, Marcus; Latka, Berthold; Schroth, Roland; Spee, Michael: *Praxishandbuch SAP NetWeaver Portal*. SAP PRESS 2008.

Föse, Frank; Hagemann, Sigrid; Will, Liane: *SAP NetWeaver AS ABAP – Systemadministration*. SAP PRESS 2008 (3rd, updated and extended edition).

SAP AG: installation guides on various topics (*http://service.sap.com/instguides*).

SAP AG: SDN blogs/articles/forums/wiki (*http://www.sdn.sap.com/ irj/ sdn/nw-informationmanagement*).

Schröder, Thomas: *SAP NetWeaver BW-Performanceoptimierung*. SAP PRESS 2009 (2nd, updated and extended edition).

Staade, Michael; Schüler, Bernd: *SAP BI-Projektmanagement*. SAP PRESS 2007.

Weidmann, Corina; Teuber, Lars: *Konzeption und Einrichtung des Systemmonitorings mit dem SAP Solution Manager*. SAP PRESS 2009 (2nd, updated and extended edition).

D   The Authors

Olaf Klostermann is an SAP BI solution architect at K-42 eG (*www.k-42.com*), where he is a cofounder and board member. His consulting specializations are technical issues in SAP NetWeaver BW, particularly architecture and performance. He has many years of international project experience in the design and implementation of SAP NetWeaver BW, including several years at SAP in Germany. Previously, he worked for a long period as a developer and technical consultant for database systems and BI solutions.

Milco Österholm is an SAP BI solution architect and cofounder of the Swedish consulting company E1NS (*www.eins.se*). As a project leader, he has managed large SAP implementation projects for many years. Currently, alongside his work in BI architecture teams, he manages the operation of SAP NetWeaver BW systems for various clients. Milco Österholm has been active in technical consulting and project management in the BI area of SAP for several years. He also has many years of experience of FI-CO and SD development.

Index

A

ABAP
authorization concept, 207
dump, 151
runtime error, 151
runtime layer, 513
ABAP Dictionary, 85
ABAP Support Package Manager, 294, 296
Access control list, 216
Access data, 551
ACL, 216, 218
Activation, 429
ADK, 253, 255, 261
Advanced Planner and Optimizer, 65
After-import method, 311
Aggregate, 189, 465
check, 476
fill, 472
materialized, 413
Aggregate check, 51, 477
Aggregated value, 234
Aggregate tree, 407, 471
Aggregation, 198
exception, 199
AIM, 311
ALE, 48, 109, 111, 113, 381
Alert category, 370
Alerting, 370
Analysis, 166
authorization, 219
process, 438
tool, 166
Analysis Process Designer, 29, 360
Analytical engine, 196
API, 64
Application log, 128
Application monitor, 150
Application Programming Interface, 64
Application server, 133
ARC, 263

Archive administration, 259
Archive Explorer, 263
Archive File Browser, 263
Archive Information System, 262
Archive Retrieval Configurator, 263
Archiving
ADK-based, 253
concept, 249
AS ABAP, 31, 200, 217
AS Java, 33, 200, 216
Authorization
check, 140, 218
concept, 227
dimension, 228
field, 225
log, 243
standard, 219
trace, 139

B

Background
job, 159, 160, 418
process, 155
processing, 159
user, 104
work process, 159
Background management, 155
Backup, 101, 455
BAdI, 299
Balanced scorecard, 537
BAPI, 111
Base parameter, 41
Batch manager, 155, 389
Batch process, 155, 371
BCT, 577
Best Practice, 566
BEx Analyzer, 25, 165, 443, 516
BEx Analyzer Trace, 447
BEx frontend check tool, 444
BEx Installation Check, 444
BEx transport request, 315
BEx Web Application, 516, 560
BEx Web Java, 520

BI Administration Business Package, 338
BI Administration Cockpit, 333
BI Consumer Services, 197
BICS, 197
Binary search, 77
Binary tree, 77
Bitmap index, 75, 79
BIWEBAPP, 301
Blade, 193
Bookmark, 508, 546
BOR, 120
Breakdown
vertical, 191
BSP, 126
B tree, 75, 77, 78
Buffer, 143
Buffer monitor, 143
Business Add-In, 299
Business Application Programming Interface, 111
Business Consolidation, 464
Business Content, 577
Business Object Repository, 120
Business planning and analytical services, 28
Business planning and simulation, 112
Business Server Pages, 126
BW Accelerator, 190
tracing, 504
BW integrated planning, 28
BW-IP, 28

C

Cache
main memory, 453
mode, 450
monitor, 165
Calculation, 198
Cardinality, 77, 80
CATT, 183
CCMS, 154, 374, 517
CCTA, 566

Central Computer and
Telecommunications Agency, 566
Central instance, 36
Central monitoring system, 354
Central Performance History, 125
Central Process Scheduling, 125
Central service, 33
Central User Administration, 209
Change log, 429, 437
Change Management Service,
322
Change pointer, 112, 381
Change request management,
321
Change run, 404, 409, 424
ChaRM, 321
Check
    mode, 480
    time, 480
CIC, 554
Client-dependent object, 319
Cluster
    index, 76
    table, 453
Clustering, 285
CMS, 322
Collaboration, 38
Comma-separated values, 57
Common Programming Interface
for Communication, 46
Compression, 422, 424
    automatic, 474
    factor, 423
Computer Aided Test Tool, 183
Connection
    availability, 484
    parameters, 388
    set up, 544
    test, 484
    type, 544
Connection request handler, 34
Consistency check, 166
Consolidation route, 305
Content
    technical, 333
Continuous improvement, 538
Control parameters, 388
Conversion, 318
CO-PA, 377

CPH, 354
CPI-C, 46
CPS, 125
CPU, 150
CSV, 57
CTS, 303, 306
CTS+, 322
CUA, 209
Customer exit, 391
Customer message, 547

D

Daemon, 390, 398
DAP, 252, 267
Data
    activation, 426
    aggregate, 252
    buffer, 147, 148
    compression, 265
    consistency, 417
    delete, 252
    deletion, 433
    load statistics, 348
    load status, 345
    prevention, 252
    type, 90
Data archiving, 251
    monitor, 260
Database
    monitor, 147
    performance analysis, 147
    statistic, 421
Database management system,
76
Database shared library, 94
Data Dictionary, 92
Data extraction
    generic, 377
Data Manager, 255, 344
Data marts, 103, 255, 416
DataSource, 378, 399
Data transfer process, 397, 432
    RSANWB, 438
    RSDMWB, 438
Data Warehousing Workbench,
84, 104
DB02, 96
DB4, 96

DB6, 96
DBMS, 76
DBSEL, 344
DBSL, 94
DBSL library, 95
DBTRANS, 344
DDIC, 92
Debugging, 165, 432
Delete
    by request, 434
Deletion
    selective, 415, 435
Delta administration, 195
Delta cache, 453, 463
Delta queue, 378, 379
Demilitarized zone, 520
DIA, 385, 396
DIMID, 71, 81, 177
Display attribute, 238
Distributed statistics records, 147
DMZ, 520
Document, 202
Documentation, 570
Document Relationship Browser,
263
DSO, 84, 185, 240, 426
    for direct update, 186
    standard, 185
    write-optimized, 186, 265
DSR, 147
DTP, 432
Dump, 151

E

EarlyWatch Alert, 542
EDI, 108
EDW, 27, 272
Electronic data interchange, 108
Email, 507, 541
End-to-end solution operations,
535
Enqueue, 61
    server, 33, 68
    work process, 68
Enterprise reporting, query, and
analysis, 28
EP Core, 37
Exception, 152

Exception aggregation, 199
Exclusive lock, 67
Extended memory, 44
Extent, 90
Extraction
 error, 398
 monitor, 161
Extractor, 378
Extractor checker, 392

F

Facility management, 569
Fact index, 499
Federated portal network, 37
File server, 193
FI-SL, 377
FPN, 37
Frontend patch, 292
Full proxy mode, 520
Function module
 *CONVERSION_EXIT_ALPHA_*
 INPUT, 174
 *CONVERSION_EXIT_ALPHA_*
 OUTPUT, 174
 *RRSV_VALUE_CHECK_*
 PLAUSIBILITY, 173
 RSBB_URL_PREFIX_GET, 119
 RSD_CHA_GET_VALUES, 439
 RSD_CUBE_GET, 71
 RSDDK_BIW_GET_DATA, 350,
 354
 *RSDDS_AGGREGATES_*
 MAINTAIN, 405
 RSD_IOBJ_GET, 73
 RSDS_RUNTIME_RESULT,
 135, 378
 RSDU_ANALYZE_TABLE, 432
 RSDU_ANALYZE_TABLE_DB2,
 97
 RSEC_GET_USERNAME, 243
 RSPC_ABAP_FINISH, 365
 RSZ_X_INFO_OBJECTS_GET,
 184

G

Garbage collection, 47
Generation, 239

Generic Request and Message
Generator, 517
Governance, risk, and
compliance, 215
GRC, 215
GRMG, 517, 518
Guided procedure, 38

H

Hierarchy
 authorization, 235
 InfoPackage, 319
 node, 514
High Performance Analytics, 483
Hint, 76
Hit ratio, 148
Hotfix, 302
HotNews, 540
HTTP, 200, 457
HTTPconnect, 544, 545
HTTP request, 456
HTTPS, 200
Human Capital Management, 378
Hypertext Transfer Protocol
Secure, 200

I

ICF, 35, 199, 456
ICM, 35, 455, 457
 monitor, 201
 server cache, 201
 trace, 459
Identity management, 214
IDoc, 108, 109
 error, 395
 Info, 112
 interface, 108
IFRS, 216
IGS, 164, 203
ILM, 250, 266, 267
Importance, 338
Import mode, 296
Inconsistency, 167
Index, 75
 clustering, 83, 286
InfoCube, 188, 419
 compression, 422
 content, 412

delete, 189
performance, 420
real-time, 188
Info IDoc, 112
InfoPackage, 385
Information broadcasting, 506
InfoSpoke, 194
Initial value, 170
Instance, 35
Integrated Services Digital
Network, 541
International Financial Reporting
Standards, 216
Internet Transaction Server, 147
Interrupt process, 363
ISDN, 541
ITIL, 292, 566
ITS, 147
IT service management, 568
ITSM, 568
iViews, 516

J

J2EE, 31
J2EE Engine, 33
J2EE Visual Administrator, 518
JAAS, 523
 login module, 523
Java
 Java Virtual Machine, 47
 runtime layer, 513
 support package, 300
Java 2 Enterprise Edition, 31
Java Connector, 33
Java Support Package Manager,
303
JCo, 33
JCo RFC Provider, 523
Job, 155, 375
 overview, 135
 status, 136, 144
JSP, 322
JSPM, 303

K

Key date, 409
Knowledge management, 202,
516

L

LAN, 150
Last recently used, 451
LDAP, 217
Least privilege, 215
Lightweight Directory Access
Protocol, 217
Line item dimension, 475
List calculation, 198
Loading performance, 382
Loading process, 383
Load request, 430
Local area network, 150
Lock
    optimistic, 68
Lock management, 67
Lock table, 68
Log, 130, 134
Logical system, 106, 318
Logistics Information System,
377
Log Viewer, 522
LO-LIS, 377
LRU, 451
LRU algorithm, 451
LUW, 69, 108, 378

M

Main memory cache, 453
Maintenance Optimizer, 326
Master data
    cleansing, 288
    delta, 381
    maintenance, 289
    record, 289
MaxWare, 215
MDC, 180, 286
MDX, 118, 119, 120
Memory
    extended, 44
    management, 142
    shared, 44
Memory pipe, 459
Merge, 282
Message
    escalation, 554
    priority, 551

Message server, 32
Meta chain, 364
Metadata, 403, 490
Microsoft SQL Server, 99
Migration, 247
MIME, 202
Modification, 296
Modification assistant, 299
Monitor
    BI monitor, 154
    buffer, 143
    cache, 165
    data archiving, 260
    database, 147
    extraction, 161
    ICM, 201
    open hub, 196
    operating system, 150
    process chain, 160
    query, 163
    queue, 379
    RDA, 390
    SAP NetWeaver BW
    Accelerator Monitor BW
    Accelerator, 494
    workload, 146, 147, 356
Monitoring tree element, 355
Monitoring Tree Element, 519
MPI, 459
MTE, 355, 519
Multiple Virtual Storage, 96
Multipurpose Internet Mail
Extensions, 202
MVS, 96

N

Namespace, 557
Navigation attribute, 170
NLS, 252, 266, 268
Noncumulative InfoCube, 425
Noncumulative lock
    exclusive, 68
Note
    with correction instructions,
    292
Number range, 70
    buffer, 70
    inconsistency, 74

object, 70, 71
NWDI, 323

O

Object
    changeability, 316
    client-dependent, 319
    source systemñdependent, 313,
    317
    S_RS_ADMWB, 220
Object class
    RS, 220
    RSAN, 220
OCS, 296
ODS, 51
Office of Government
Commerce, 292
OGC, 292
OLAP
    BAPI, 120
    caching, 460
    server, 196
OLE DB for OLAP, 118
OLTP, 75
Online correction support, 296
Online transaction processing, 75
Open hub
    destination, 194
    monitor, 196
    service, 194
Operating documentation, 569
Operating system, 150
    command, 366
    monitor, 150
Operational Data Store, 51
Operations control, 569
Operations management, 569
Optimistic lock, 68
Optimizer, 75
Organizational level, 225
Organization level, 225
OS, 150
OS monitor, 150

P

Package, 382
PAM, 555, 559

Parallelism, 389
Parallel processing, 408, 448
Parameter
   BLOCKSIZE, 410
   DB6_COMPRESS_PARALLEL,
   98
   DB6_DELETE_PIECEWISE, 98
   DB6_PINDEX_ON_FTABLE,
   98
   DBMS_MAX_DELETE, 98
   INTRA_PARALLEL, 98
   RSDSRUNTIMETRACE, 135
   SAPPARAM, 134
Partitioning, 192, 277
Patch, 292, 301
PDK for .Net, 39
Performance, 127, 149, 190, 420,
475, 525
Persistence mode, 452
Portal, 37
Portal cache, 519
Portal Content Directory, 218
Portal Development Kit for .Net,
39
Portal runtime, 37
Portal services, 37
Pre-analysis, 410
Primary index, 76
Priority, 551
Process, 361
   overview, 137
   status valuation, 369
   type, 361
   variant, 361
Process chain, 160, 273, 361,
366, 385
   monitor, 160
Process instance, 362
Product error, 547
Profile
   parameter, 41
   S_A_SYSTEM, 209
Program
   MSSPROCS, 93
   RSA1_TRFC_OPTION_SET, 386
   RSCDS_CONDENSE_CUBE,
   425
   RSDDK_CHECK_AGGREGATE,
   477

RSDDK_CHECK_AGGREGATE_
CHECKID, 477
RSDDK_CHECK_AGGREGATE_
SELOPT, 477
RSDDSTAT_DATA_DELETE,
358
RSDDTREX_DELTAINDEX_
MERGE, 493
RSDDTREX_INDEXDATA_
DISPLAY, 502, 503
RSDDTREX_SHADOWINDEX_
CREATE, 503
RSDDTREX_SHADOWINDEX_
DELETE, 503
RSDRO_ACTIVATE, 332
RSDRT_INFOPROV_
RANDOM_QUERIES, 497
RSDS_DATASOURCE_
ACTIVATE_ALL, 381
RSEC_GENERATE_
AUTHORIZATIONS, 242
RSEC_MIGRATION, 228
RSPC_WATCHDOG, 375
RSPROCESS, 376
RSRV_JOB_RUNNER, 168
RS_TRANSTRU_ACTIVATE_
ALL, 380
SAP_INFOCUBE_INDEXES_
REPAIR, 87
SAPOSCOL, 150, 517
SAPPFPAR, 42
SAP_RSADMIN_MAINTAIN,
50
SAP_RSDB6_PINDEX_ON_
FTABLE, 83
SAP_UPDATE_DBDIFF, 87
SAPXPG, 137
PSA, 90, 117, 272, 378, 396
Pull mechanism, 112
Push package, 118
Python trace, 505

Q

QM, 162, 385
QOUT Scheduler, 386
qRFC, 108, 386
Query, 448
   execution, 341

monitor, 504
monitor, 163
trace, 165
Queue monitor, 379

R

RDA, 117, 272, 383, 396
RDA monitor, 390
RDL, 37
Read mode, 449, 526
Read performance, 190
Reclustering, 287
Red alert, 563
Redwood, 125
Remote delta links, 37
Remote role assignment, 37
Reorganization, 508
Repair, 167
Repartitioning, 281
   request, 284
Replication, 399
   automatic, 403
Report
   COMPONENT_RESTORE, 455
   generate, 163
   GET_ODS_OSS_
   INFORMATION, 428
   GRAPHICS_IGS_ADMIN, 204
   PFCG_ORGFIELD_CREATE,
   225
   PFCG_TIME_DEPENDENCY,
   224
   RSA1_TRFC_OPTION_SET, 64
   RSDDK_CHECK_AGGREGATE,
   515
   RSDD_MSSQL_PROG_01, 99
   RSDMD_CHECKPRG_ALL, 169
   RSICFTREE, 456
   RSPARAM, 42
   RSPC_DISPLAY_JOBS, 375
   RSPFPAR, 42
   RSRD_BOOKMARK_
   REORGANISATION, 508
   RSSTATMAN_CHECK_
   CONVERT_DTA, 157
   RSSTATMAN_CHECK_
   CONVERT_PSA, 157

*RSTCC_ACTIVATE_ADMIN_*
COCKPIT, 336
RSUSR002, 213
RTCCTOOL, 531
*SAP_AGGREGATES_*
CONDENSE, 425
SAPRUPGM, 300
SBAL_DELETE, 131
Report-report interface, 348
Report result, 511
Request, 162
  check, 418
  deletion, 433
  for activation, 429
  ID, 422
  IDoc, 112
  management data, 270
  number, 114
  size, 382
Result set, 510
Reverse key index, 75
Revision, 329
RFC, 46, 107, 388
  transactional, 108
RFC scheduler, 386
Roadmap, 536
ROI, 535, 538
Role administration, 208
Rollup, 473
Routing test, 507
RRA, 37
RRI, 348
RS Trace Tool, 183
Run SAP, 536
Run schedule, 414
RUNSTATS, 96
Runtime, 340
  analysis, 125
  measurement, 187

S

Safeguarding, 538
Safe mode, 512
SAINT, 296
SAP Add-On Installation Tool, 296
SAP APO, 65
SAP ArchiveLink, 255

SAP BusinessObjects, 538
SAPconnect, 507
SAP Continuity Management Optimization, 564
SAP Data Volume Management, 564
SAP DVM, 564
SAP EarlyWatch Alert, 556, 561
SAP EarlyWatch Check, 564
SAP EcoHub, 273
SAP Enterprise Support, 535
SAP ERP Central Component, 322
SAP ERP HCM, 378
SAP GoingLive Check, 564
SAP GRC, 215
SAP Help Portal, 539
SAP HotNews, 540
S-API, 386
SAP ILM, 249, 266
SAP Java Connector, 33
SAP List Viewer Grid Control, 374
SAP MaxAttention, 537
SAP Memory, 145
SAP Microsoft Management Console, 42
SAP MMC, 42
SAP NetWeaver Administrator, 123
SAP NetWeaver Application Server, 31
SAP NetWeaver BI Diagnostics & Support Desktop Tool, 559
SAP NetWeaver BW, 314
  Transport connection, 314
  version concept, 309
SAP NetWeaver BW Accelerator, 482
  revision, 329
SAP NetWeaver Check Workstation Wizard, 443
SAP NetWeaver Development Infrastructure, 323
SAP NetWeaver Portal, 515
SAP NetWeaver Visual Composer, 39
SAP Note
  search, 153, 555

SAProuter, 541
SAP Safeguarding for Implementation, 538
SAP SCR, 557
SAP SEM, 65
SAP SEM-BCS, 464
SAP Service Marketplace, 538
SAP SLM, 555
SAP Solution Manager, 320, 533, 563
SAP Support Portal, 538
SAP Systems Manager, 43
SAP Technical Performance Optimization, 564
SAP TopNotes, 540, 557
SAP Transaction iView, 516
SAP Web dispatcher, 32, 200
SCA, 39, 301
Scheduler, 162
Scheduling calendar, 94
SDCC, 562
SDM, 292, 303
Search
  binary, 77
Secondary index, 76
Secure area, 551
Secure Network Communication, 541
Server blade, 193
Service
  API, 386
  connection, 541
  create, 543
Service API, 386
Service Data Control Center, 562
Service-oriented architecture, 125
Service Tools for Applications, 531
Service type
  BW GUI, 545
  BW RFC, 545
SGA, 147
Shared lock, 67
Shared memory, 44
SID, 63, 71, 81
Simple Mail Transfer Protocol, 200
Simulation, 432